# Being Together, Working Apart

Working mothers and fathers are now splitting three jobs between two people as they divide responsibilities for the family in addition to managing their own professional careers or jobs. Yet despite the fact that most parents are employed, how work affects the lives and well-being of parents and their children remains relatively unexplored. A recent study of 500 families, which focuses on middle-class dual-career families in eight communities across the US provides a holistic view of the complexities of work and family life experienced by parents and their children. This unique study has resulted in an unusually rich data set due to the variety of methods used. Drawing on the study, this book explores how dual-earner families cope with the stresses and demands of balancing work and family life, whether the time parents spend working is negatively affecting their children, how mothers feel managing both work and household responsibilities, and what role fathers are taking in family life. In answering these questions the authors argue for a new balance between work and family life. The book with its rich data, findings, and commentary from an interdisciplinary group of scholars provides a valuable resource for academics, policy makers, and working parents.

BARBARA SCHNEIDER is a Professor of Sociology at the University of Chicago, Principal Investigator for the new Data Research and Development Center at NORC and the University of Chicago, and Co-Director of the Alfred P. Sloan Center on Parents, Children, and Work. She is also a Senior Social Scientist at NORC and the University of Chicago and a Research Associate at the Ogburn-Stouffer Center for the Study of Population and Social Organization.

LINDA J. WAITE is the Lucy Flower Professor of Sociology at the University of Chicago and Co-Director of the Alfred P. Sloan Center on Parents, Children, and Work. She is also a Senior Social Scientist at NORC and the University of Chicago.

# Being Together, Working Apart

*Dual-Career Families and
the Work-Life Balance*

*Edited by*

Barbara Schneider and Linda J. Waite

CAMBRIDGE
UNIVERSITY PRESS

PUBLISHED BY THE PRESS SYNDICATE OF THE UNIVERSITY OF CAMBRIDGE
The Pitt Building, Trumpington Street, Cambridge, United Kingdom

CAMBRIDGE UNIVERSITY PRESS
The Edinburgh Building, Cambridge, CB2 2RU, UK
40 West 20th Street, New York, NY 10011–4211, USA
477 Williamstown Road, Port Melbourne, VIC 3207, Australia
Ruiz de Alarcón 13, 28014 Madrid, Spain
Dock House, The Waterfront, Cape Town 8001, South Africa

http://www.cambridge.org

© Cambridge University Press 2005

First published 2005

Printed in the United Kingdom at the University Press, Cambridge

*Typeface* Plantin 10/12 pt.    *System* LaTeX 2ε   [TB]

*A catalogue record for this book is available from the British Library*

*Library of Congress Cataloging in Publication Data*
Being together, working apart: dual-career families and the work–life balance /
edited by Barbara Schneider and Linda J. Waite.
   p.   cm.
Includes bibliographical references and index.
ISBN 0 521 84571 8 (alk. paper) – ISBN 0 521 60789 2 (pbk: alk. paper)
1. Dual-career families – United States.   2. Middle-class families – United
States.    3. Work and family – United States.    I. Schneider, Barbara L.
II. Waite, Linda J.
HQ536.B432   2005
306.872 – dc22       2004056818

ISBN 0 521 84571 8 hardback
ISBN 0 521 60789 2 paperback

# Contents

## Part VI  Lessons to be learned

## Technical appendices

# Figures

# Tables

# Contributors

## Authors

EMMA K. ADAM, Assistant Professor, Program on Human Development and Social Policy, School of Education and Social Policy, Northwestern University

KATHLEEN E. CHRISTENSEN, Ph.D., Director, Program on Workplace, Workforce, and Working Families, Alfred P. Sloan Foundation

NICHOLAS P. DEMPSEY, Ph.D. candidate, Department of Sociology, University of Chicago

AMY F. FELDMAN, Ph.D., Research Associate, Public/Private Ventures

LISA HOOGSTRA, Ph.D., Director of Research Services, Alfred P. Sloan Center on Parents, Children, and Work, University of Chicago

JAE-GEA JEONG, Ph.D. candidate, Department of Sociology, University of Chicago

ARIEL KALIL, Assistant Professor, Harris School of Public Policy Studies, University of Chicago

CHI-YOUNG KOH, Ph.D. candidate, Department of Sociology, University of Chicago

YUN-SUK LEE, Assistant Professor, Department of Urban Sociology, University of Seoul

JUDITH A. LEVINE, Assistant Professor, School of Social Service Administration, University of Chicago

KIMBERLY S. MAIER, Assistant Professor, Measurement and Quantitative Methods, College of Education, Michigan State University

ELAINE MARCHENA, Postdoctoral Fellow, Emory Center for Myth and Ritual in American Life, A. Sloan Center on Working Families

SYLVIA MARTINEZ, Ph.D. candidate, Department of Sociology, University of Chicago

JENNIFER L. MATJASKO, Assistant Professor, Department of Human Ecology, Division of Human Development and Family Sciences, The University of Texas at Austin

CASEY B. MULLIGAN, Professor, Department of Economics, University of Chicago

THE REVEREND MARK R. NIELSEN, Ph.D., Research Affiliate, Alfred P. Sloan Center on Parents, Children, and Work, University of Chicago

YONA RUBINSTEIN, Assistant Professor, The Eitan Berglas School of Economics, Tel Aviv University

JENNIFER A. SCHMIDT, Assistant Professor of Educational Psychology, Northern Illinois University

BARBARA SCHNEIDER, Professor of Sociology and Human Development, Co-Director, Alfred P. Sloan Center on Parents, Children, and Work, University of Chicago

HOLLY R. SEXTON, MA, Data Administrator/Research Analyst, Alfred P. Sloan Center on Parents, Children, and Work, University of Chicago

CAROLYN P. STUENKEL, Ph.D, Research Affiliate, Alfred P. Sloan Center on Parents, Children, and Work, University of Chicago

LINDA J. WAITE, Lucy Flower Professor of Sociology, Co-Director, Alfred P. Sloan Center on Parents, Children, and Work, University of Chicago

MATTHEW N. WEINSHENKER, Ph.D. candidate, Department of Sociology, University of Chicago

KATHLEEN M. ZIOL-GUEST, Ph.D. candidate, Harris School of Public Policy Studies, University of Chicago

### Commentators

SUZANNE M. BIANCHI, Professor of Sociology, University of Maryland

DON S. BROWNING, Alexander Campbell Professor of Religious Ethics and the Social Sciences, Emeritus, Divinity School, and Director of the Religion, Culture, and Family Project, University of Chicago

MIHALY CSIKSZENTMIHALYI, Director, Quality of Life Research Center, Drucker School of Management, Claremont Graduate University

MICK CUNNINGHAM, Assistant Professor of Sociology, Western Washington University

WILLIAM J. DOHERTY, Professor and Director of the Marriage and Family Therapy Program, Department of Family Social Science, University of Minnesota

TOM FRICKE, Professor of Anthropology, Director, Center for the Ethnography of Everyday Life, University of Michigan

NANCY L. GALAMBOS, Professor of Psychology, University of Alberta

JENNIFER GLASS, Professor of Sociology, University of Iowa

NORVAL D. GLENN, Ashbel Smith Professor, Stiles Professor in American, Studies, Department of Sociology, Population Research Center, University of Texas at Austin

RALPH E. GOMORY, President, Alfred P. Sloan Foundation

DOUGLAS A. GRANGER, Associate Professor, Department of Biobehavioral Health, Pennsylvania State University

PHILLIP L. HAMMACK, Ph.D. candidate, Committee on Human Development, University of Chicago

JENNIFER HANIS-MARTIN, Ph.D. candidate, Department of Sociology, University of Chicago

JOEL M. HEKTNER, Assistant Professor, Child Development and Family Science, North Dakota State University

JERRY A. JACOBS, Merriam Term Professor of Sociology, University of Pennsylvania

TALI KLIMA, MA, Department of Psychology, University of California, Los Angeles

TAMAR KREMER-SADLIK, Ph.D., Director of Research, UCLA Center on Everyday Lives of Families, A. Sloan Center on Working Families

ROBERT KUBEY, Director, Center for Media Studies, SCILS, Rutgers University

REED LARSON, Pampered Chef Endowed Chair in Family Resiliency, Department of Human and Community Development, University of Illinois, Urbana-Champaign

LARS LEFGREN, Assistant Professor of Economics, Brigham Young University

ALISA C. LEWIN, Postdoctoral Fellow, Alfred P. Sloan Center on Parents, Children, and Work, University of Chicago, Lecturer, University of Haifa

PHYLLIS MOEN, McKnight Presidential Chair, Sociology, University of Minnesota

JEYLAN T. MORTIMER, Professor of Sociology, University of Minnesota

SHIRA OFFER, Ph.D. candidate, Department of Sociology, University of Chicago

PATRICIA M. RASKIN, Associate Professor, Program in Social-Organizational Psychology, Department of Education and Leadership, Teachers College, Columbia University

RENA L. REPETTI, Professor, UCLA Department of Psychology, Core Faculty Member, UCLA Center on Everyday Lives of Families, A. Sloan Center on Working Families

ELIZABETH A. SHIRTCLIFF, Ph.D. candidate, Biobehavioral Health, Pennsylvania State University

GLENNA SPITZE, Distinguished Service Professor, Department of Sociology, University at Albany, SUNY

SCOTT M. STANLEY, Ph.D., Co-Director, Center for Marital and Family Studies, University of Denver

ROSS M. STOLZENBERG, Professor, Department of Sociology, University of Chicago

ELAINE WETHINGTON, Associate Professor and Co-Director, Cornell Institute for Translational Research on Aging, Department of Human Development and Department of Sociology, Cornell University

KAZUO YAMAGUCHI, Professor, Department of Sociology, University of Chicago

JIRI ZUZANEK, Distinguished Professor Emeritus, Department of Recreation and Leisure Studies, University of Waterloo

# Preface

Over the past thirty years, the life of the American family has experienced profound changes. Rather than the traditional arrangement of two adults with two jobs for them to do, one the breadwinner and one the homemaker, most families today have three jobs, two breadwinner jobs and one homemaker job, to distribute among its two adults. It is not surprising that in today's world people often feel there is too much to do.

Recognizing that we are living through a historic change in middle-class family life, the Alfred P. Sloan Foundation established the *Workforce, Workplace and Working Families Program* in 1994. The goal of the program is to produce much-needed scholarship focused on working families; and to educate the next generation of scholars on issues of working families.

At the heart of the program have been our six Centers on Working Families. The Centers function as both regional and national laboratories for the rigorous examination of the issues faced by families in which both parents work. Housed within leading research universities across the country, the Centers focus on issues ranging from employment options for older workers and retirees, to the role of myth and ritual in family life, to the changing nature of the ordinary activities of everyday life.

The research efforts and policy recommendations of the Centers contribute to national discussion through conferences, publications, and media dialogue. The graduate and undergraduate students at the Centers receive important training that will help them to contribute to society's ability to integrate work and family life.

Founded in 1997 at the University of Chicago, the Center on Parents, Children, and Work is headed by Barbara Schneider and Linda Waite. Under their direction, the Center undertook a major research effort: the 500 Family Study. Using innovative research methods and in-depth analyses they and the scholars who wrote the chapters in this book paint a rich and detailed picture of what life is like today for middle-class families in which both parents work. Through their research, they provide a compelling description both of the challenges that Americans face in trying to handle the dual demands of work and family, and of the ways in which work and family nurture them and engage them.

*President, Alfred P. Sloan Foundation*                    RALPH E. GOMORY

# Acknowledgments

Many individuals helped to make this book a reality. First and foremost are the 500 families who participated in our study. Despite their busy lives, they let us into the privacy of their homes, answered our many questions, and responded every day for a week to a watch that beeped at the most inopportune moments. We owe them our deepest thanks and appreciation. We are also indebted to the Alfred P. Sloan Foundation, and particularly Kathleen Christensen, our Program Director, for their generous support in establishing the Sloan Center on Parents, Children, and Work, which made it possible for us to conduct the 500 Family Study. A decade ago, the Foundation, under the direction of Ralph Gomory, embarked on a bold initiative to create a vital research community throughout the US and abroad committed to the study of working families. Our work has greatly benefited from the Foundation's efforts, which included networking and collaborating with other Sloan Center directors and researchers.

The interdisciplinary community at the University of Chicago facilitated our research. A special thanks to Craig Coelen, President of NORC, who generously housed and administratively supported our Center. Richard Saller, Provost, and Mark Hansen, Dean of the Social Sciences Division, provided us with support for graduate students, workshops, and conferences. We would especially like to thank Kathleen Parks, Director of the Academic Research Centers at NORC, who assisted in numerous ways with staffing, office space, and Institutional Review Board issues; Isabel Garcia, Grants and Contracts Administrator, who provided budget oversight and reimbursements; Brian Whitely, who supplied editorial assistance; and Gail Spann and Adelle Hinojosa who made the little everyday problems disappear.

The 500 Family Study relied on the scholarly contributions of many researchers, including those who designed the study, the graduate and undergraduate assistants who collected, coded, and analyzed the data, and the staff members who supervised them. In designing the study and instruments we owe special thanks to several Center Research Associates: Charles Bidwell, William Claude Reavis Professor Emeritus of Sociology and Education at the University of Chicago; Mihaly Csikszentmihalyi, C. S. and D. J. Davidson Professor of Management at Claremont Graduate University and Professor Emeritus of Psychology, Human Development, and Education at the University of Chicago; Janet Shibley Hyde, Helen Thompson Woolley Professor of Psychology and Women's Studies at the University of Wisconsin; Lindsay Chase-Lansdale, Professor of Social Policy at Northwestern University; Rita Gorawara-Bhat, Research Associate, Department of Medicine at the University of Chicago; Reed Larson, Professor of Human and Community Development, Psychology, Leisure Studies, and Kinesiology, University of Illinois, Urbana-Champaign; Kevin Rathunde, Associate Professor, Department of Family and Community Studies, University of Utah; and Ariel Kalil, Susan Lambert, Judith Levine, Casey Mulligan, Damon Phillips, Ross M. Stolzenberg, and Kazuo Yamaguchi, all professors at the University of Chicago. We would also like to thank Emma Adam, Richard Bernard, Regina Bures, Qin Chen, Rachel Gordon, Lisa Hoogstra, Lianne Kurina, Kim Maier, Jennifer Schmidt, and Maud Schaafsma, former postdoctoral fellows with the Center who are now pursuing careers in teaching and research. Each chapter in this volume was critiqued by senior scholars: Their reviews of earlier versions of the chapters were invaluable in helping authors refine their arguments and analyses. We gratefully appreciate the careful, thoughtful reviews of these scholars, who also contributed the chapter commentaries that appear in this volume.

Fielding the 500 Family Study involved the efforts of countless graduate and undergraduate assistants who helped with phone calls, scheduled interviews, visited families and conducted interviews at various sites across the country, and followed up and retrieved data from study participants. Space does not allow us to thank every person, but we have singled out a few who deserve special thanks for their hard work and dedication. We particularly thank Jennifer Schmidt, former Director of Research for the Center, who oversaw training, data collection, and coding for the 500 Family Study and without whose hard work, experience, and calm direction the study could not have been completed. Special thanks to Colleen Spence, Jennifer Hanis, Gloria Williams-McCowen, Ali Swanson, and Christine Li for their coordination of fieldwork efforts. Thanks also to the graduate and undergraduate students who helped with various phases of data collection, transcription, coding, and data analysis, including Alisa Ainbinder, Nora Broege, Nicholas Dempsey, Allison Deschamps, Chi-Young Koh, Jennifer Kottler-Smith, Page Lessy, Laura Lewellyn, Elaine Marchena, Maureen Marshall, Sylvia Martinez, Mark Nielsen, Carolyn Stuenkel, Cheryl Sutherland, Matthew Weinshenker, Emily Bernstein, Sarah Crane, Sunny Chang, Joelle Gruber, Sara Ann Jachym, Lars Jarkko,

Mary Elizabeth Jowers, Dana Kolom, Jennifer Lohmann, Melinda Luo, Annie Maxfield, Nick Papageorge, and Clara Park. We also thank Tom Howe for preparing the data files for the 500 Family Study.

Several undergraduates need to be acknowledged for their contributions to the preparations of this volume, including Allison Atteberry, Paul Hanselman, Jessica Lester, Ann Owens, Jacob Rogers, and Emily Rook-Koepsel. We appreciate their hard work in formatting chapters and tables, entering editorial corrections, proofreading, checking references, and indexing. Thanks also to Ye Luo, Senior Research Analyst with the Center, who helped with data analysis in chapter 2, and Surella Seelig, former Project Administrator for the Center, who was involved with the early stages of the book's preparation.

Three individuals helped transform early manuscripts into chapters. Jason Labate, the Administrative Director of the Center, was command central; his organizational skills helped to keep us on schedule, track changes, and coordinate the efforts of a rocking and rolling staff. Holly Sexton, our Data Administrator, checked every analysis, oversaw all editorial changes, and could be depended on to catch every wrong number in the text and tables. And then there is Lisa Hoogstra, Director of Research Services, whose careful, meticulous, helpful critiques created a book. Thank you all.

*Part I*

# Studying working families: an experiential approach

# 1    Why study working families?

*Barbara Schneider and Linda J. Waite*

*Nanette Foley, sales representative for a telecommunications company and mother of two teenagers, rushes in the door of her suburban home frantically worrying if her husband, an accountant, remembered to pick up their daughter at basketball practice and whether she can get dinner ready in time to take their son to his math tutor. Opening the mail while turning on the oven and talking on the cell phone to her daughter, who impatiently waits outside the high school for her ride, Nanette reflects on the pace and demands of her life and how it differs from that of her mother. Was life this hectic and stressful? Were her parents better communicators about their feelings toward each other and their children? How did her parents negotiate the sharing of family and household responsibilities? Did her father regret not being more involved in the lives of his children? Did she have a more satisfying life than her mother who stayed at home? Would the lives of her family be happier and more satisfying if Nanette worked part time?*

Today, one experience of family life shared by most children under the age of eighteen is that their fathers and mothers are both working. This is not only the situation for families with limited resources struggling to make ends meet; rather it is the predominant pattern for middle-class families (US Bureau of the Census 2000). Working mothers and fathers are now splitting three jobs between two people as they divide responsibilities for the family in addition to managing their own professional careers or jobs (Christensen and Gomory 1999).[1] Yet despite the fact that most middle-class parents are employed, how work affects the lives and well-being of parents and their children remains relatively unexplored. To understand how marital relationships, child development, and family life are being influenced by the dramatic movement of married women with children from home to the workplace, the Alfred P. Sloan Center on Parents, Children, and Work has undertaken a major research initiative: the 500 Family Study. This study of middle-class dual-earner families across the US includes 300 families with adolescents and 200 families with kindergarten children. Surveys, time diaries, and personal interviews were used to gain a holistic view of the complexities of work and family life experienced by middle-class parents and their children. Nanette's experiences during the "arsenic dinner hours," where the burdens of household tasks overwhelm the already tired worker, highlight the challenges working families face in achieving a feasible balance between work and family demands. How families negotiate the conflicts between home and work is the cornerstone of the 500 Family Study.

The intersection between family and career demands has been the topic of several recent books written by US scholars who initiated the field of working families. *It's About Time* (2003) by Phyllis Moen is based on the Cornell Couples and Career Study, a rich database of over a thousand middle-class dual-earner households. Focusing on how work influences decisions in the life course, Moen finds that work demands often conflict with worker preferences, resulting in delays in child bearing, career choices, and time spent in leisure activities. When families make decisions about their employment, these decisions are not strictly determined by economic needs but by other factors, such as the availability of good schools or adequate childcare.

*Working Families: the Transformation of the American Home*, edited by Rosanna Hertz and Nancy Marshall (2001), emerged from a 1998 conference on working families. Multiple data sets and various analytical tools inform the chapters in this book, which present a broad range of issues confronting working families. Lynn Casper and Suzanne Bianchi (2001), Jennifer Glass (2000), Arlie Hochschild (1997), Jerry Jacobs and Katherine Gerson (2004), and Harriet Presser (2003), leading figures in work and family research, have recently published or are in the process of releasing new studies that offer strong critiques on how working families are coping and modifying their life styles to meet the demands of an uncompromising workplace traditionally organized for fathers who were the single earners in their families. This is not just a US phenomenon; internationally, scholars such as Catherine Hakim, an economist, have been studying women's work issues, and assessing how work policies affect women's employment decisions. Taking a global perspective, Hochschild and Ehrenreich (2003) draw the connection between the international labor market and US working mothers, arguing that middle-class families are importing childcare providers from other countries to act as surrogate mothers for their children.[2]

This book differs in several important ways from previous publications and offers a unique and comprehensive assessment of the lives of working families. First, it is a study of working parents and their children, so the unit of analysis is the family, not just the working couple. Second, because of its innovative methodology, the study brings the lives of the families under the social scientist's microscope to reveal the intricate complexities of work and family life, including aspects of family life that bear the brunt of work–family conflict. Third, all the chapters in the book are based on the 500 Family Study, which provides an intellectual and methodological coherence achieved by multiple authors who shared ideas, arguments, methods, and interpretations with each other over the course of several years.

Charting the types of activities working families engage in, including how they allocate their time and how these allocations affect their feelings about themselves and others, the chapters in this volume coalesce around four overriding themes: Experiences at Work and at Home; Marriage and Family; Making it Work at Home; and Parenting and Adolescent Development. Often addressed through overlapping methodological approaches, these themes form the conceptual nexus of the volume. Consequently, this is not an edited volume, but rather the integrated product of a team of graduate students, postdoctoral fellows, and faculty from multiple disciplines taking different perspectives on problems that confront working families. To place each of the chapters in a broader framework, commentaries were sought from leading experts in the field represented within each chapter. The book includes contributions by twenty-four individuals affiliated with the Center on Parents, Children, and Work as well as critiques by twenty-seven distinguished scholars from a variety of disciplines.

The design of the 500 Family Study, described in chapter 2 by Lisa Hoogstra, draws its families from eight sites across the US varying in their degree of urbanization, labor force composition, and socioeconomic characteristics. To obtain a detailed picture of work and family life, mothers, fathers, and their children were asked to complete a series of instruments, including surveys, in-depth interviews, and time diaries. These instruments were designed to be complementary and provide information about work, marriage, childcare and parent supervision, management of household tasks, time allocations, coping strategies, and psychological well-being. Several items from national studies were included in the parent and adolescent surveys, allowing for comparisons between the study and nationally representative samples.

One instrument used in this study is the Experience Sampling Method (ESM), a ground-breaking method for examining how individuals spend their time, who they spend it with, and what activities they are engaged in over the course of a typical week. Developed by Mihaly Csikszentmihalyi and his colleagues (Csikszentmihalyi and Larson 1984; Csikszentmihalyi 1997), the ESM provides detailed information regarding participants' subjective interpretations of their daily life experiences. The ability to capture individuals' subjective evaluations of events at specific moments during a week is particularly valuable for studying emotions such as stress, since it is possible to determine a person's overall feelings of stress as well as identify instances when it occurs. Unique to the 500 Family Study, members of the same family, at nearly the same moments, report on their own activities and feelings.

Even though the ESM has certain advantages over other methods for understanding emotions and time use, it is not without its own set of methodological issues, including individuals' failure to respond to signals when beeped. The authors have taken this non-response issue into account in their analyses. One innovative solution to this problem is described by Jae-Gea Jeong in appendix A. Another technical limitation of the 500 Family Study, which occurs both in national and small-scale studies of families, is the coding of household income. When annual income is reported in surveys, the response categories tend to be broad, since many individuals are reluctant to report their exact income and other assets. Consequently, reported income data are often imprecise. Appendix B describes a method developed by Yona Rubinstein and Casey Mulligan for obtaining more accurate estimates of income.

## Experiences at Work and at Home

*Jane, a psychiatrist, places her patient files in her briefcase; there hadn't been enough time during the day to fill out the newest forms requested by the insurance company. Reflecting back on her day she wonders "Where did the hours go?" Now it is time to start the hour commute home and plan her evening: dinner, homework, and patient calls – the extension of the eight hour day to fourteen. Despite the flurry of activity in the office and the vanishing hours, it was a successful day and she looks forward to seeing her husband and hearing about her daughter's presentation on Harriet Tubman. Pulling into the driveway, she meets her daughter, whose enthusiasm over her report envelops Jane; the patient files remain locked in the trunk. Why is it that some parents feel positive both at work and at home? What do women find satisfying about their jobs? Are there conditions at the workplace that increase a busy parent's ability to manage stress? Does a good or bad day at the office influence the emotions of other family members?*

Work plays a significant role in the lives of working families, not only in terms of time spent in work-related pursuits, but also with respect to parents' attitudes toward work and how these experiences and emotions spill over into the home. The majority of the parents in the 500 Family Study are employed or looking for work and 75 percent of them work full-time (93 percent of fathers and 61 percent of mothers). Many of these couples are working more hours per week than the national average, with 16 percent working more than 50 hours per week (31 percent of fathers and 7 percent of mothers). These additional work hours often intrude on family life. Nearly all mothers and fathers report conflicts between work and family, and when these conflicts occur, the family is more likely to suffer than work. For most working parents, trade-offs and compromises between family and work obligations appear to be unavoidable.

Overworking is pervasive among the families in the study. Approximately 40 percent of the parents report arriving early to work or staying late for three or more hours in a given week; nearly 60 percent report working at home, with 54 percent indicating that they feel pressured to bring work home in order to keep up. Among the parents in the 500 Family Study, long work hours appear to contribute to higher levels of stress. High-stress mothers and fathers are twice as likely as low-stress mothers and fathers to work three or more hours at home on weekends; these high-stress parents are also more likely to work three or more hours at home during the week. With both parents working a longer work week, and many of them taking their work home, working families confront multiple constraints in trying to balance their busy lives.

Long work hours do not necessarily represent a desire to devote large amounts of time to work, particularly on the part of mothers. Among mothers in the sample, 64 percent express an interest in working part time.[3] Most fathers who are currently working feel that they do not have the choice to work part time. Given the long hours and the stress of work, why do parents work in such demanding jobs? If mothers would rather be at home at least part time and fathers are working full time because they feel they have no choice, how do they feel about their jobs? How do both positive and negative experiences at work cross over into family life?

Focusing on the kinds of tasks parents are engaged in at work, chapter 3 by Holly Sexton describes what tasks people do, how much time they spend engaged in various activities, and how they feel about these activities. Sexton finds that people employed in management jobs and professional careers spend, on average, only one-fourth of their workday engaged in primary tasks – a surgeon, for example, repairing a blocked artery. Being involved in primary work tasks is associated with higher levels of positive affect; individuals are significantly more engaged and have a higher sense of self-esteem than when performing work tasks perceived as less central to their professions.

Sexton suggests that one reason people may want to work in demanding jobs is that they feel significantly more cognitively engaged and have higher self-esteem when at work than at home. For many parents, work provides an environment of challenge and interest that does not occur elsewhere. One reason mothers work is not because they are unhappy at home, but because they gain intellectual satisfaction from working. Job autonomy also appears to contribute to more positive feelings about work.

Individuals who perceive that they have high degrees of self-direction in their jobs have higher levels of positive affect, engagement, and self-esteem compared with those who perceive themselves as having jobs with less self-direction. When work experiences involve greater self-direction, mothers and fathers also tend to have higher levels of positive affect, engagement, and self-esteem at home.

The emotional effects of being at work and at home thus appear to be more complex than suggested by Hochschild (1997). Overall, individuals have higher positive affect at home, yet they are more engaged and experience higher self-esteem while at work. Perhaps engagement in work tasks is necessary to increase positive affect both at work and at home. However, there appear to be distinct benefits of spending time at home that are not found at work. Sexton finds that while parents feel more intellectually engaged at work, they feel more relaxed at home. These findings suggest that sources of dissatisfaction among some employed parents may be associated with the type of work they perform, the control they can exercise in their jobs, and their general outlook on work.

In chapter 4, Sylvia Martinez also provides a potential explanation for why parents work in demanding jobs. Drawing on the psychological literature on intrinsic and extrinsic task motivation, Martinez identifies mothers as having primarily an intrinsic or extrinsic work orientation. Mothers with an intrinsic orientation are more likely to report that they work because they like the challenge and enjoy their tasks, whereas those with an extrinsic orientation work primarily for financial security and job benefits such as health insurance. Martinez finds that mothers who are intrinsically motivated have higher levels of job prestige and autonomy, and lower levels of boredom at work. Her work supports that of Sexton in that enjoyment and challenge in one's job or career is associated with autonomy and self-direction at work. On the other hand, women who are extrinsically motivated tend to work longer hours, which diminishes enjoyment of work and intrinsic motivation. For mothers, just as for fathers, the challenge is finding a balance between financial security and job satisfaction.

In contrast to studies that examine general workplace characteristics (e.g., hours worked, type of work, occupational prestige) and how they affect individual well-being, our work focuses on what parents actually do at their jobs, how they feel about their work, their motivations for working, and what happens when there is emotional spillover from work to home or home to work. In chapter 5, Emma Adam takes a cutting-edge biobehavioral approach to analyzing the relationship among engagement in activities at work, at home, and in public, emotional well-being, and levels of stress. A subsample of the 500 Family Study participated in this innovative study which determined stress from time-diary reports in conjunction with samples of saliva that were used to measure cortisol, a stress-sensitive hormone. It is important to underscore that social scientists are becoming increasingly aware that the experiences of family and work extend beyond cognitive and emotional responses to physiological functioning. Essentially Adam, along with other social scientists such as Cacioppo et al. (2000) and Booth, Carver, and Granger (2000), argues that the behavior of individuals cannot be understood without taking into account their physiological and emotional states; conversely, physiological functioning cannot be understood without reference to emotions and the social contexts in which they occur.

Adam confirms the expected pattern of cortisol levels, which are highest in the morning, decline throughout the day, and approach zero at bedtime. Negative emotional states are associated with higher levels of cortisol, and this is more the case for fathers than mothers. For parents, feeling positive, cheerful, friendly, and caring is associated with lower levels of cortisol than would be expected at a given time of day. Similar effects are found when individuals feel hardworking and productive: their cortisol levels are lower than expected. When taking environment into account, Adam's results are consistent with those of Sexton. Parents experience greater feelings of productivity and higher levels of involvement when they are at work, and cortisol levels are correspondingly lower when in work settings independent of time of day. A positive work environment, including tasks that are challenging and rewarding, reduces stress. These results do not indicate that being at home, on average, elevates stress for working mothers and fathers. Rather, experiences at home, like those at work, produce lower stress levels than expected when they are positive and engaging; such experiences may help to maintain good physical health in the long term.

In chapter 6, Jennifer Matjasko and Amy Feldman examine not only the carryover of emotions from work to home, but how these emotions affect the transfer of feelings between parents and adolescents. In other words, if a parent is happy or angry at work, is he or she more likely to be happy or angry when returning home and, if so, does his or her teenager react similarly by becoming happy or angry? The authors find evidence of emotional crossover between parents and adolescents. In general, fathers who have positive relationships with their sons and daughters are more likely to shield their children from negative experiences they encounter at work. Even if they work long hours, fathers seem to be able to leave work at the office. Mothers, on the other hand, tend not to separate emotions at work from those at home. When happy or angry at work, mothers are more likely to transfer their happiness or anger to their adolescents.

Surprisingly, for mothers, taking more time for oneself does not positively affect their adolescents' happiness, suggesting that an afternoon of exercise or other forms of recreation does not reduce negative or increase positive work–family emotional crossover. These analyses suggest that transitions from work to home are more emotionally challenging for mothers, who have greater difficulty compartmentalizing emotions at work from emotions at home.

## Marriage and Family

*George and Angela, parents of twin sixteen-year-old sons, have been married for nineteen years. George is a software consultant for several major companies and Angela is a second grade teacher at the local elementary school. Every night before they go to bed, they have a daily routine that starts, "How was your day? Tell me all about it." It is during this time that the stresses and demands of the day are intimately reviewed, and new strategies for dealing with the pressures of the next day are discussed. One topic that always comes up is how they will celebrate their twentieth anniversary. What makes for a satisfying marriage, particularly among dual-earner couples with children? Do conditions at work influence how couples relate to one another? Do couples feel the same when they spend time with each other and when they spend time with their children?*

Work–family conflict appears to affect two important dimensions of family life: parent–child relationships and husband–wife relationships. Research has clearly demonstrated that marriage provides positive emotional, health, and economic benefits for spouses and their children (Waite and Gallagher 2000). However, one might expect that when both partners in a marriage are working, feeling pressure and stress at work could create tension and dissatisfaction between spouses and in their relationships with their children. Turning attention to couples, we begin by examining how working parents experience their everyday lives, their perceptions of each other, and the core of the relationship, their marriage. Using couples rather than individuals as the unit of analysis, the authors explore what factors are associated with marital satisfaction, how the emotions of wives and husbands vary from work to home when they are alone, with each other, and with their children, and what activities at home are associated with emotional well-being for husbands and wives.

Chapter 7, by Chi-Young Koh, is an in-depth analysis of couples' day-to-day emotions as they move through different locations and activities in their daily lives. Koh asks if spouses feel the same way when they are together, if they feel similar levels of responsibility toward their children, and whether the well-being of their children is of equal importance to each of them. When describing the emotional landscape of couples over the course of a week, spouses tend to look similar with respect to how positive and in control they feel, how responsible they feel about a given situation and how important it is to them, and how much they enjoy and willingly participate in the activities they are engaged in. It appears that the emotions experienced at work and at home are not gender specific.

There are consistent differences, however, in husbands' and wives' emotions that occur when they interact with their children. Compared with work or chores at home, spending time with their children is one of the most positive experiences for husbands. On the other hand, while spending time in family activities is a positive experience for wives, they experience higher positive affect, self-esteem, and intrinsic motivation when engaged in social activities. The complexity of working mothers' emotional lives is further complicated by their interest, participation in, and satisfaction from multiple domains, including work, home, and public arenas. These findings suggest that women enjoy both time with their families and time away from home, whereas working fathers feel most comfortable at home.

In chapter 8, Mark Nielsen finds that highly satisfied couples are those in which both spouses tend to agree on the positive and negative aspects of their relationship. Highly satisfied couples feel that they perform their roles well, make decisions and resolve disagreements amicably, communicate effectively, and are comfortable with each other. In contrast, less satisfied couples focus their energy on external aspects of their relationship such as parenting, but tend not to agree on emotional aspects of their relationship with each other. Couples who feel less satisfied with their relationship may focus their emotional energy on their children rather than themselves.

Probing deeper into the lives of both satisfied and dissatisfied couples, Nielsen finds that husbands with lower levels of marital satisfaction experience a higher number of depressive symptoms than husbands with higher levels of marital satisfaction. On the other hand, dissatisfied wives are more likely to report lower levels of self-esteem than wives who have high levels of marital satisfaction. However, these psychological characteristics are mediated by the couples' relationship, particularly role management, spouse's personality and traits, communication, and affection and sexual relations. These results suggest that marital satisfaction involves not only role clarity but intimacy and communication.

## Making it Work at Home

*The dishes are piled high on the sink. Gloria knows it was Richard's turn to scrape and load: What happened? The garage is still not clean, the laundry is not folded, and Roger needs someone to help with his bar mitzvah speech. Gloria thinks, "What I need is a housework technician – that or more hours in the day." Turning off the television program he and Roger have been watching, Richard declares, "Let's get started on that speech." Roger wishes his father wanted to see the next show as much as he does, leaving the speech for another day. Father and son walk into the kitchen and sheepishly smile at the vanishing pile of dishes, remembering it was their turn to clean. Richard knows he can count on Gloria to get things done; even after spending a full day successfully managing her staff, she still is able to manage the house. Has the division of household labor changed? Are husbands more involved in housework than they once were? What types of help and services do working couples purchase? What activities do parents and their adolescents typically do together? How does religion affect the quality of experience of working parents and their children?*

Time is often a scarce commodity for working families as they struggle to balance work and home life. Parents find themselves multi-tasking in order to meet job demands and ensure quality time at home. With its multiple data sources, the 500 Family Study allows for intensive study of daily life at work and home, including time demands, time allocations, and tensions between work and family. This section investigates how working families share household tasks, what and how they outsource in order to save time, the effects of television on daily life, and the role of religion in working families.

In this new era of working families where housework is frequently negotiated among parents and children, having precise measures of who does what helps researchers understand family conflict and time pressures. The ESM is particularly useful for obtaining accurate information on time allocation, including both primary and secondary tasks. Consistent with past research, Yun-Suk Lee in chapter 9 finds that women perform approximately 60 percent of household tasks. In general, women devote more time to housework than men, especially when household management is included in the measurement of housework. Husbands and wives agree that wives are primarily responsible for the majority of household tasks. However, when comparing experience sampling results to survey estimates, Lee finds that wives make accurate estimates of the amount of time husbands spend on housework, whereas husbands overestimate the amount of time wives spend on housework. These biases lead men and women to have different perceptions about the size of the gender gap in household labor. Part of this discrepancy may be due to differences in definitions of housework, which often tend to underestimate the amount of time women are spending.

Several factors contribute to miscalculations of household labor. First, the amount of time spent on the mental labor of housework – time spent thinking about, planning, coordinating, and managing household tasks – is often hidden and therefore unmeasured, and these tasks are usually performed by women. Second, women are more likely to multi-task, and researchers tend to undercount the time women spend on housework as a secondary activity, thus biasing the estimates of housework downward. Women continue to work more in the home than their husbands; perhaps that is why they have more positive feelings when in public and when engaged in social activities: they are free from the burdens of home care.

Doing housework together as a family activity helps to reduce the negative feelings commonly experienced when engaged in tasks seen as routine. Despite the positive lift from being together, nobody enjoys housework or looks forward to doing it. Chapter 10, by Carolyn Stuenkel, describes one way families cope with housework and other household tasks – outsourcing. Relying on intensive interviews with a subset of participants in the 500 Family Study, Stuenkel investigates why families purchase household services, which services are most popular among families of different income levels, and the costs associated with what are commonly assumed to be labor-saving services.

Stuenkel begins by describing the services many families purchase, including several newer ones such as household organizing and Internet-based services. She finds that purchasing household services is a learned behavior that takes place within a cultural context. Three routes lead to high levels of commodification: having a high income, having high-commodifying friends, and growing up in a high-commodifying household. Even among high-commodifying families, however, there are some household tasks that are viewed as traditional family activities and are immutable to neighborhood pressure, such as gardening instead of using a landscaping service. When families' resources are limited and purchasing services is not an option, some families participate in an exchange of services: "I will drop off the children at school on my way to work every morning if you take the girls to basketball after school," or "I can babysit for your son on Tuesday and Wednesday mornings, but could you watch my daughter when I attend night school on Monday and Wednesday evenings?"

Like most learned behaviors, buying household services is a self-reinforcing strategy. Positive experiences tend to lead to higher levels of outsourcing. Although potentially time- and labor-saving, outsourcing involves a certain amount of work (including locating service providers, setting up the transaction, and evaluating the service) which commonly falls on the shoulders of mothers.

An activity that families still do together and that accounts for a considerable amount of time spent at home is watching television. In chapter 11, Nicholas Dempsey finds that television viewing habits are strongly linked within families; parents who watch more television have children who watch more television. Time spent watching television appears to have different effects on parents and adolescents. Whereas television viewing significantly affects the frequency of family interactions for adolescents, it affects the *quality* of these interactions for adults. Adolescents who watch no television report talking with their families 50 percent more often than adolescents who watch television eighteen or more hours per week. Parents feel less happy and have a lower sense of self-worth when they both watch television and are involved in activities with their children and spouse such as eating dinner. This is not the case when parents are engaged with their adolescents in other leisure activities. These findings suggest that working parents would probably derive a more positive sense of self from engaging in activities other than television viewing with their children.

While working families struggle to squeeze quality time with their children into their busy schedules, activities such as volunteering and organized religious involvement may be given short shrift, as Putnam (2000) has argued. In chapter 12, Jennifer Schmidt finds evidence that despite time constraints, many working families make an effort to include religion in their lives. Nearly half of the 500 Family Study participants report regularly attending formal religious services, an attendance rate considerably higher than that found in national studies. Religious participation may be higher among families in the 500 Family Study because families with school-aged children are more likely to participate in religious activities (Hadaway et al. 1993).

Participation in religion seems to have a positive emotional effect on study participants. Very religious mothers and adolescents are generally happier and have higher levels of self-esteem than those who are non-religious. Religious mothers also feel more caring towards family and friends, spend more time with their children, and are more likely to discuss values, rules, and beliefs with them than non-religious mothers. Results show that the time religious mothers gain with their children is equivalent to the time lost when both parents are working full time, suggesting that the inclusion of personal faith in family life may create a greater balance between work and family.

## Parenting and Adolescent Development

*Jennifer pulls up the virtual tour of her father's alma mater from the University's website; it doesn't have a strong physics program, but she thought she would give it a look. Her younger brother Michael strolls into her bedroom and sees the college brochures strewn across her bed. "Wow," he says, picking up one glossy pamphlet, "I bet Mom and Dad would love for you to go here – they have a great pre-law program, you could join Dad's firm." Jennifer glares at her brother, "I'm going to be an astrophysicist." Michael scoffs, "Oh yeah, a pocket protector? I thought you wanted to get married and have a job like mom so you could be home more and make your children miserable, like you make me." What impact do parents' careers and life choices have on the educational and occupational aspirations of their children? How do adolescents learn career management and household roles, and what influence do these experiences have on their expectations for their futures?*

Children are affected by the work experiences of both their mothers and fathers. A particular weakness of previous research is that it has examined mothers' employment decisions and experiences in isolation rather than looking at such experiences within the context of the family. This focus is problematic, especially when examining dual-earner families. First, couples may make employment decisions jointly, and the problems associated with mothers' work may be masking issues surrounding fathers' employment. Second, although mothers may be managing their work and family life successfully, this may not be the case for their spouses. When fathers' attitudes and experiences are examined along with those of mothers, there are unexpected differences in parenting styles, and the effects on their children are not necessarily similar.

In chapter 13, Elaine Marchena shows the complex relationships between adolescents' perceptions of their parents' ability to successfully manage work and family demands and parents' perceptions of work–family conflict. Although parents report experiencing moderate to high levels of conflict between work and family, adolescents make fairly positive assessments of their parents' role management, especially their mothers. Adolescents, however, make less favorable assessments of mothers and fathers when parents' jobs frequently interrupt routines of daily life.

Since the "breadwinner" role is now being shared by both parents in dual-earner families, we might expect adolescents to think in relatively egalitarian terms as they begin to form ideas about how they will organize their own lives, particularly with respect to who will have major responsibility for earning an income, taking care of the children, and doing household chores. The strength of children's egalitarian orientations might be expected to vary depending on whether parents are equal partners, or whether the husband remains the primary earner while the wife retains most of the responsibility for the home and children. In chapter 14, Matthew Weinshenker shows this to be the case. When a father participates more equally in "female" housework tasks such as cooking and cleaning, his children are more likely to expect equal sharing of household responsibilities in their own marriages. This is especially true for daughters.

Weinshenker also finds that expectations appear to vary by parenting style. Parents who have supportive parenting styles have teenagers who are more likely to expect an equal division of responsibility for childcare.

In contrast, parents who have challenging parenting styles – those who hold high expectations for their children – have children with less egalitarian attitudes. Furthermore, sons who have high educational and occupational aspirations are not likely to have egalitarian expectations about paid work, suggesting that some of the seeds for work–family conflict are being nurtured in the process of adolescent career development.

In chapter 15, Kim Maier investigates how parents in different occupations, specifically those in math and science professions, transmit educational values to their children. Maier finds that mothers in math/science occupations provide their daughters and sons with comparable levels of challenge and support and seem especially able to boost their adolescents' mood and self-esteem at school. Parents in math/science professions (both mothers and fathers) enhance their adolescents' feelings of well-being and provide encouragement by discussing current courses, plans for college, and future careers with them. These parents also employ stricter monitoring of adolescents of both genders, and thereby concretely communicate their high standards. However, parents in non-math/science occupations tend to treat their daughters and sons differently, providing their daughters with more support than their sons. These results suggest that everyday parenting practices are related to parents' professions and that parents who are not employed in math/science professions tend to reinforce traditional gender roles despite high levels of education, social status, and household income.

Many studies have found that parent educational attainment and occupational status are associated with their children's educational and occupational aspirations, although the processes by which these linkages occur have not been fully explored. In chapter 16, Ariel Kalil, Judith Levine, and Kathleen Ziol-Guest examine these linkages by investigating the effects of parents' work characteristics and parent–child discussions about parents' work on children's aspirations to hold jobs like their parents. When fathers have jobs that are high in autonomy and are substantively complex, adolescents express greater interest in having jobs like their fathers'. However, these characteristics of mothers' jobs have no effect on teenagers' interest in having jobs like their mothers'. Results suggest that intergenerational links exist between fathers' jobs and adolescents' aspirations, but this is not the case for mothers, leading one to cautiously conclude that working mothers are less likely than working fathers to serve as career role models for their sons and daughters. The authors discuss potential differences in how and what parents communicate to children about each parent's work life as a possible explanation for the relative attractiveness to adolescents of fathers' jobs.

## Lessons to be Learned

Working parents, contrary to conventional wisdom, enjoy their work when it is engaging, involves a high level of autonomy, and provides a sense of security. Moreover, these positive emotions carry over into the home. However, the types of jobs that produce these benefits often require long hours and involve high levels of pressure and stress, forcing parents to make compromises that often shortchange their families. The problems faced by working families begin at the workplace not in the home, although the consequences of an unforgiving workplace play out in the home. The last chapter, written by Kathleen Christensen, links the findings of the 500 Family Study with actions that can be taken by businesses, communities, and policy makers to educate the public about the needs of working families. The approach taken here recognizes that the structuring of current labor conditions is unlikely to change radically in the coming years. Institutional change comes slowly and only with the support of many different people. Christensen thus articulates a public awareness agenda that highlights the problems faced by working families, and the values and attitudes that parents, their employers, and the general public need to embrace for practical change to occur.

## NOTES

1. The evidence as to whether individuals are working longer hours has been inconclusive. In most families, there was once one spouse at home taking care of household responsibilities while the other worked full time for pay; now with both parents working, the household worker has disappeared (Jacobs and Gerson, 2001). Among professionals, there does seem to be some evidence that they are indeed working longer hours (Jacobs and Gerson, 1998).
2. One major theme examined by European scholars is that employment opportunities for working women are often concentrated in domestic work, which is now the largest employment sector for immigrant women workers in the European Union. Anderson (2000) argues that the presence of these domestic workers has allowed middle-class mothers to remain in or re-enter the workforce.
3. Preference for part-time work was also expressed by mothers who are not currently working and among those looking for work.

# 2   The design of the 500 Family Study

*Lisa Hoogstra*

The 500 Family Study was designed to obtain in-depth information on middle-class dual-career families across the US. To understand the complex dynamics of today's families and the strategies they use to balance the demands of work and family, over 500 families from eight cities across the US were studied. To address different issues facing parents with older and younger children, both families with adolescents and those with kindergarteners were included in the sample. Multiple methods were used to learn about family and work experiences. The study's unusually rich data set allows investigators to explore a broad range of questions: How does work influence parents' investments of time and resources at home and with children? What is the quality of relationships among family members? What stresses and conflicts do parents experience in trying to balance demands of work and family? How do parents transmit values and norms to their children?

## Selecting the Sample

### Choosing the sites

The initial sample was selected from the Alfred P. Sloan Study of Youth and Social Development, a five-year national longitudinal study of middle-school and high-school students conducted between 1992 and 1997. This study produced a wealth of information on young people, their families, schools, and communities. Thirteen communities from across the US were included in the adolescent study; seven of these communities are included in the current study. An eighth community was added to increase access to families with kindergarteners; this community was the only site not included in the adolescent study.

The sites selected for this study retain much of the diversity of the earlier sample. Five of the sites are located in the Midwest (Maple, Forest Bluff, Kingston, Metawa, and Cedar), one is located in the Southeast (Feldnor), one in the Northeast (Middle Brook), and one on the West

Coast (Del Mar).[1] The communities vary in their levels of urbanization, labor-force composition, and socioeconomic characteristics. Four of the communities are predominantly upper middle class. The majority (60 to 70 percent) of parents in these communities are college-educated professionals with family incomes above the national median of $50,000 per year. The four remaining communities are middle or lower middle class. Approximately 20 to 30 percent of adults in these communities have earned college or advanced degrees; a similar percentage is employed in managerial or professional jobs; and median family income ranges from $40,000 to $44,000 per year (US Bureau of the Census 2002).

### Choosing the families

Families in the study were recruited through solicitation by phone, mail, and newspaper advertisements.[2] At each of the sites, permission to send out informational packets about the study was obtained from local high schools and elementary schools. Two sites included letters in school newsletters inviting families to participate. Advertisements were also run in local newspapers asking families to contact the Sloan Center if they were interested in participating in the study. In addition, families were referred to the Center by parents already participating in the study, and these families were contacted by phone. Of the 512 families who participated in the study, 327 were families with teenagers, 157 had kindergarteners, and 28 had both teenagers and kindergartners.[3]

## Study Approach

Several methods were used to examine the family and work experiences of the parents and children in the study, including surveys, a time diary study, and in-depth interviews. By triangulating data obtained through these different methods, a fairly comprehensive picture of work and family life can be constructed. Surveys, interviews, and time diaries were designed to be complementary, and together provide detailed information about work, marriage, childcare and parental supervision, management of household tasks, time allocation, coping strategies, and psychological well-being. Several items from national studies were also included in surveys, making it possible to compare findings from the study to those of larger, nationally representative samples.

### The Experience Sampling Method

Developed by Mihaly Csikszentmihalyi and his colleagues (Csikszentmihalyi 1997; Csikszentmihalyi and Larson 1984), the Experience Sampling

Method (ESM) is a unique method for examining how individuals spend their time, who they spend it with, and what activities they are engaged in over the course of a typical week. The ESM also provides detailed information about participants' subjective interpretations of their experiences. The ability to capture individuals' evaluations of events at particular moments over the course of a day and week is particularly valuable for studying emotions such as stress, since it is possible to determine a person's stress level as well as to identify specific instances when stress increases or decreases.

The ESM is a week-long data-collection process during which participants are asked to wear wristwatches that are pre-programmed to emit several signals each day. Watches are set to beep randomly in two-hour blocks during participants' waking hours, with the restriction that no two signals are less than 30 minutes apart. When beeped, an individual describes his or her feelings at that moment, overcoming the problem of time-elapsed recall. The emotion is recorded as it is experienced naturally rather than being experimentally induced as in a laboratory.

To the extent possible, members of the same family were placed on identical signaling schedules. In response to the signals, participants were asked to complete a self-report form in which they answered a number of open-ended and scaled questions about their location, activities, companions, and psychological states at the moment signaled. A number of Likert and semantic-differential scales were used to assess participants' psychological states. Trained coders, using detailed schemes, coded the open-ended responses. Inter-rater reliabilities for ESM coding, based on person agreement, range from .79 to .95.

Research examining the quality of the ESM data concludes that these data are reliable and valid when compared with data obtained from other instruments (Csikszentmihalyi and Larson 1987; Mulligan, Schneider, and Wolfe 2003; Robinson 1999). Findings indicate that respondents are generally truthful in reporting their immediate subjective experiences (Hedges, Janorf, and Stone 1985), thus confirming the validity of the ESM. Rates of response to individual beeps are typically high and stable at around 80 percent; in turn, respondents show relatively short differentials between signal and answering times, suggesting that participants are willing to comply with ESM procedures (Hormuth 1986). Studies comparing various means of obtaining information on psychological states find strong correlations between immediate psychological states, obtained via telephone survey or the ESM, and general subjective states obtained in questionnaires; these immediate subjective experiences have also been shown to be stable and consistent over time (Csikszentmihalyi and Larson 1987).

Respondents provided more than 45,000 ESM responses during the week of experience sampling. Participants were typically signaled 8 times each day for 7 consecutive days, for a total of 56 signals per person for the entire week. Signaling schedules were modified slightly in cases where participants were typically awake for substantially fewer or greater than 16 hours each day. Although participants were asked to respond as often as possible, there were times when it was difficult or inconvenient to respond (e.g., while driving or talking with a client). In such instances, participants were asked to complete the ESM form as soon as possible after being signaled. (Participants were asked to write down both the time they were signaled and the time they responded when filling out the response form.) On average, mothers responded to 44 signals over the course of a week (a 78 percent response rate), and fathers responded to 41 signals (a 73 percent response rate). Response rates were lowest among adolescents. Teenagers responded to an average of 30 out of 56 beeps over the course of the week, with girls having higher response rates than boys (girls responded to 34 signals on average, while boys responded to 27).[4]

In most statistical analyses of ESM data, mean values are calculated for each person's responses to a given item, and these means, rather than specific responses, are used in analysis. Thus the unit of analysis is the *person*, not the *response*. For example, in examining whether fathers or mothers report greater stress, the appropriate comparison is between the mean stress scores of fathers and mothers. However, because ESM data consist of responses nested within individuals, it is possible to analyze the data at two levels – the beep level and person level – using nested techniques such as hierarchical linear modeling. Several of the chapters in this volume make use of these techniques to analyze variations in responses at both levels (see, e.g., chapters by Sexton, Adam, Matjasko and Feldman, and Maier).

### Surveys

*Parent surveys* The parent survey was specifically designed to obtain information on parents' family and work lives. Versions of the survey were developed for mothers and fathers and both parents were asked to complete a survey. To reduce respondent burden, only mothers were asked to complete questions about household composition (number, age, gender, and relationship to focal child of each member of the household).[5] To assure comparability with national data sets, several items were drawn from a variety of sources, including the 1990 US Census, the Current Population Survey, the National Survey of Families and Households, the General Social Survey, the Quality of Employment Survey, and the National Education Longitudinal Study of 1988–2000 (NELS:1988–2000).

In addition to standard background questions about the respondent's race/ethnicity, religious affiliation, and educational attainment, the survey contains detailed questions about the parent's occupation, job duties, income, work schedule, work benefits (e.g., flexible work hours, health benefits, and family leave) and drawbacks (e.g., long hours, job stress). Mothers and fathers were also asked the extent to which they experienced work–family conflict, and what changes might help them better balance the demands of work and family (e.g., more flexible work hours, more help from spouses with household and childcare responsibilities, improved childcare and afterschool care arrangements). To examine changing gender roles within families, parents were asked to indicate their attitudes toward traditional arrangements (e.g., the extent to which they agreed or disagreed with statements such as "If his wife works full time, a husband should share equally in household chores"), how household tasks are actually divided among family members, and how often the family paid for services such as cleaning, yard work, and meal preparation.

A second focus of the study is on how children are socialized in families with two working parents. One section of the survey thus asks about the frequency with which parents engage in various activities with their children (e.g., talking, eating meals together, attending religious services). Parents of teenagers were also asked how frequently they monitored their teenager's activities and how often they talked with their teenager about school activities, plans for college, career plans, and friendships and peer pressure. In addition, parents were asked to indicate how well their children were doing in school (e.g., grades and awards received, and frequency of behavioral problems such as skipping class or getting into fights). To investigate how well parents were coping with the demands of work and family, several survey items were designed to measure psychological well-being, including established scales of depression and marital satisfaction: the 20-item Center for Epidemiologic Studies Depression (CES-D) scale, which measures the frequency of depressive symptoms experienced by respondents over the course of the previous week (Radloff 1977), and the 15-item ENRICH Marital Satisfaction Scale (Olson, Fournier, and Druckman 1987), which asks couples to assess their satisfaction with key aspects of their marriage, such as communication, financial management, and parenting (see Fowers and Olson 1993 for a discussion of the reliability and validity of this scale). Additional items measuring anxiety, anger, self-esteem, and stress were drawn from Rosenberg's Self-Esteem Scale (Rosenberg 1979), Taylor's Anxiety and Anger Inventories (Taylor and Tomasic 1996), and Cohen's

Perceived Stress Scale (Cohen and Williamson 1988). Parents were also asked to complete an inventory of stressful life events, which was based on a modification of items originally included in NELS:1988–2000. In addition, mothers and fathers of kindergartners were asked to complete a 20-item Parenting Hassles Scale, developed by Crnic and Greenberg (1990), which assesses the degree of stress or difficulty parents experience in dealing with conflicts that routinely occur in families with young children (e.g., difficulties in getting children ready for outings, sibling arguments or fights).

*Adolescent survey*  The adolescent survey focuses on family relationships and experiences, school experiences (academic coursework, grades, and participation in extracurricular activities), paid work, psychological well-being and behavioral problems, and plans for the future (e.g., college, career, and marriage – including expectations regarding spouses' sharing of responsibility for childcare, cooking, chores, and paid work). To ensure comparability with national surveys of adolescents, survey items were drawn from several previous studies, including NELS:1988–2000, the Sloan Study of Youth and Social Development, the General Social Survey, and the Families in Communities Study. A modification of items from the Inventory of Parent and Peer Attachment (Armsden and Greenberg 1987) was also included as a measure of adolescent attachment. To allow for comparison of parents' and adolescents' responses to similar questions, several items appear in both the adolescent and parent surveys, including those assessing the frequency with which parents and adolescents discuss school events, college and career plans, and participate together in religious and other activities; gender role attitudes and the division of household tasks within the family; and items measuring depression, stress, and anxiety.

*Interviews*

Interviews with parents and adolescents explored many of the survey topics in greater detail. Parent interviews were specifically designed to examine how dual-earner parents with children cope with the demands of work and family life, including the parent's career history; changes in career or work life made in response to family responsibilities; when parents made the decision to start a family and factors that influenced that decision; time allocated to work and family responsibilities and how parents achieve or fail to achieve balance in meeting those responsibilities; how parents cope with time pressures and stress; parents' definitions of "quality time" with children and spouse; how parents monitor their children's activities; and specific values and beliefs that children are learning from their parents and others.

Interviews with adolescents addressed similar themes, but asked about adolescents' perceptions of their mother's and father's family and work lives: what parents did on a typical work day; what adolescents found interesting or disliked about their parents' jobs; whether parents had difficulty balancing work and family responsibilities and how this affected family members. Additional questions addressed adolescents' educational expectations, career aspirations, and plans to marry and have children; how adolescents cope with school, peer, and family pressures; communicating with family members and spending time with them; and beliefs and values learned from parents and others.

Interviews were also conducted with kindergarteners. By necessity these interviews were brief and focused on children's afterschool arrangements (who picked them up from school, where they went after school, and what they did); childcare arrangements (who they usually stay with when they are away from their parents); spending time with their parents (what they like best about spending time with their mother and with their father); and perceptions of their parents' jobs (what their mother and father do at work and whether they have ever visited their mother's or father's workplace).

### Standardized child assessments

Three sets of standardized assessments were used to assess young children's cognitive and social competence, school readiness, and behavioral problems: the Peabody Picture Vocabulary Test (PPVT), the Harter Pictorial Scale of Perceived Competence and Social Acceptance for Young Children, and the Child Behavior Checklist. The PPVT is a widely used test of receptive vocabulary that was first published in 1959 (Dunn 1959) and is now in its third edition (PPVT-III, Dunn and Dunn 1997). The test is nationally normed and is relatively easy to administer to young children in a short time period. The Harter Pictorial Scale, developed by Harter and Pike (1984), assesses young children's perceived cognitive competence, physical competence, maternal acceptance, and peer acceptance. The scale is a downward extension of the Perceived Competence Scale for Young Children (Harter 1982) that employs a pictorial format rather than a written questionnaire. Like the PPVT-III, the Pictorial Scale is relatively easy to administer to young children and is an age-appropriate form of assessment.

To assess behavioral difficulties that kindergartners might be experiencing, mothers of young children were asked to complete the Child

Behavior Checklist for Ages 4 to 18, a nationally normed instrument developed by Achenbach (1991) that obtains parents' reports of children's competencies and behavioral problems. The competence items ask the parent to assess the amount and quality of the child's participation in sports, non-sports activities, organizations, jobs and chores, friendships and relationships with significant others, and school performance. The problem behaviors checklist includes descriptions of common behavioral/emotional problems such as *sad, nervous, cries a lot*, and *runs away*.

### Collecting the Data

Data were collected from 1999 to 2000. Teams of two to three researchers met with all participating family members in their homes for a period of $2\frac{1}{2}$ to 3 hours.[6] Team members held a brief orientation meeting during which participants were given surveys and materials necessary to complete the ESM. To ensure confidentiality, all materials were identified by an individually assigned ID number; names did not appear on any study materials. After the orientation, one-to-one interviews were conducted with participating family members. Interviews were conducted, when possible, with both mothers and fathers in each family; adolescents also completed interviews. Due to their age, kindergarteners were not given surveys or the ESM; they were interviewed, and during this interview were assessed using the PPVT-III and the Harter Pictorial Scale. All interviews were tape-recorded after obtaining permission from participants (for adolescents and young children, permission was obtained from parents). Interviews are currently being transcribed and coded using qualitative software. To ensure confidentiality, individually assigned pseudonyms appear in the transcripts rather than actual names or locations.

The period of ESM signaling began the day after the orientation meeting, and participants were instructed to fill out their surveys during the week of ESM signaling. To prevent family members from influencing each other's responses to the survey, researchers asked that participants not share their responses with other family members. After the week of ESM signaling, participants sent their materials back to the Sloan Center via Federal Express.

The quality of the data was carefully monitored by the Center's Fieldwork Coordinator. Surveys were examined upon their return to the Center and, if necessary, mothers, fathers, and adolescents were contacted by phone to retrieve missing or uninterpretable information. Field workers returning from a site visit were required to report on the outcome of the visit and any necessary follow-up. Weekly reports were prepared indicating the numbers of families completed, scheduled, and waiting to be scheduled.

### Supplementary data collection

*Adolescents and parents*    In response to a request by the school system in one of the Midwestern communities included in the study, abridged versions of the adolescent and parent surveys were administered to a cohort of ninth graders and their parents. Surveys were completed by 527 ninth graders; 182 of these students' parents also completed surveys.

*Physiological stress study*    A study of physiological stress was also conducted with a subsample of parents and children from the larger study. Parents and teenagers who agreed to participate in the physiological study completed an additional two days of ESM data collection during which they responded to six ESM signals per day and provided samples of salivary cortisol 20 minutes after each ESM signal.[7] In addition, parents and adolescents completed a brief health questionnaire that included questions about dietary and health factors that may affect cortisol levels. Parents also reported on the health of the children (teenagers and kindergartners) participating in the study. An abbreviated cortisol study was conducted with kindergartners who supplied saliva samples immediately at waking and at bedtime over two days. Overall, 70 families participated in the study (69 mothers, 43 fathers, 39 adolescents, and 37 kindergartners). (See Adam, this volume, for an analysis of parent data from the physiological stress study.)

*Purchase of household services study*    Follow-up interviews were conducted in the summer of 2001 with a subsample of 31 mothers to obtain detailed information on household services purchased by dual-earner families. Interviews focused on the types of services purchased, the process of selecting and hiring a service provider, and the influence of values, work-related demands, and social networks on purchasing decisions. (See Stuenkel, this volume, for the criteria used in selecting this subsample and an analysis of the follow-up interviews.)

## Characteristics of the Sample

### Parents' educational and work characteristics

While the intent of the study was to examine dual-career couples with children, changes in the status of participating families inevitably occurred during the course of the data collection; some parents lost their jobs, others divorced or separated. In the majority of families in the study (80 percent) the parents are married and living together. However, several other types of families are represented within the sample. In 4 percent of the families, parents live together in a marriage-like relationship, including 6 same-sex couples with children (see Deschamps 2002 for an analysis of parent involvement in 500 Family Study families headed by same-sex couples); 11 percent of parents are divorced; 4 percent are headed by single mothers who are not living with their child's father; and less than 1 percent are widowed.

As shown in table 2.1, the parents in the study are highly educated: in over 90 percent of the families, at least one parent has completed a four-year college degree or higher; 50 percent of the mothers and 65 percent of the fathers hold a master's degree or higher. These parents work in a variety of professions, with the highest proportion (over 30 percent of mothers and fathers) being employed as executives or managers. Consistent with their high levels of educational and occupational attainment, parents in the study earn relatively high incomes. Over 50 percent of the fathers earn more than $75,000 per year. Although mothers are less likely than fathers to report such high earnings, 14 percent of mothers report annual incomes of more than $75,000. Like most full-time professionals, parents in the 500 Family Study tend to have relatively long work weeks. More than 50 percent of fathers report working 46 or more hours per week. Compared with fathers, mothers are more likely to be employed part time and work fewer hours per week. However, more than 20 percent of mothers report workweeks of 46 hours or more.

### Comparing the 500 Family Study with the Current Population Survey

To provide a national comparison group of middle-class parents with children, college-educated parents with children under the age of 18 were selected from the March 2000 Current Population Survey (CPS) and compared with parents with similar levels of education from the 500 Family Study.[8] The Sloan college-educated sample is quite similar to the full Sloan sample with respect to occupation, income, work status, and work hours. However, in comparing parents in the Sloan and CPS college-educated samples, several differences are apparent. As shown in table 2.2, parents in the Sloan sample are clearly more highly educated than those in the CPS sample: 70 percent of fathers and 55 percent of mothers in the Sloan sample hold a master's degree or higher compared with 29 percent of fathers and 21 percent of mothers in the CPS sample.

Table 2.1 *Background and work characteristics of sampled parents*

|  | percent | |
|---|---|---|
|  | Mothers (n = 508) | Fathers (n = 376) |
| Race/Ethnicity | | |
| Asian/Pacific Islander | 2 | 1 |
| Hispanic | 3 | 2 |
| African American | 7 | 6 |
| White | 82 | 89 |
| Identifies with two or more categories | 3 | 1 |
| Missing | 3 | 1 |
| Education | | |
| High School or less | 6 | 2 |
| Some College | 14 | 8 |
| Bachelor's Degree | 29 | 24 |
| Master's Degree | 33 | 34 |
| Ph.D., M.D., J.D., or other professional degree | 17 | 31 |
| Missing | 2 | 0 |
| Occupation | | |
| Executive/Managerial | 31 | 32 |
| Physician | 3 | 7 |
| Nurse/Therapist/Counselor | 6 | 1 |
| Engineer/Architect | 2 | 9 |
| Professor/Scientist/Social Scientist (PhD) | 5 | 7 |
| Scientist/Social Scientist/Technician (non PhD) | 6 | 5 |
| Lawyer/Judge | 3 | 10 |
| Teacher/Librarian/Religious Worker | 11 | 5 |
| Writer/Artist | 5 | 4 |
| Sales/Public Relations | 5 | 10 |
| Service/Clerical/Manual | 14 | 9 |
| Not in the Labor Force | 9 | 2 |
| Missing | 1 | 1 |
| Annual earnings | | |
| $0–20,000 | 21 | 3 |
| $20,001–35,000 | 18 | 6 |
| $35,001–50,000 | 19 | 13 |
| $50,001–75,000 | 17 | 19 |
| $75,001–100,000 | 7 | 19 |
| More than $100,000 | 7 | 36 |
| NA/not working | 4 | 1 |
| Missing | 8 | 5 |
| Work status | | |
| Full-time | 54 | 88 |
| Part-time | 31 | 6 |
| Unemployed/looking for work | 2 | 1 |
| Not in Labor Force/not looking for work | 9 | 2 |
| Missing | 4 | 4 |

Table 2.1 (*cont.*)

| | percent | |
|---|---|---|
| | Mothers (n = 508) | Fathers (n = 376) |
| Work hours (main job) (hours per week) | | |
| 1–15 | 8 | 1 |
| 16–25 | 14 | 1 |
| 26–37 | 16 | 6 |
| 38–45 | 30 | 28 |
| 46–50 | 16 | 26 |
| 51–60 | 5 | 20 |
| More than 60 | 1 | 7 |
| Not applicable/not working | 11 | 3 |
| Missing | 1 | 7 |

Parents in the 500 Family Study are also more likely to hold professional jobs. Only 6 percent of fathers and 12 percent of mothers in the Sloan sample are employed in manual, service, or clerical jobs compared with 20 percent of fathers and mothers in the CPS sample; a larger proportion of 500 Family Study respondents are employed as business executives, physicians, professors, and lawyers.

The average earnings of parents in the 500 Family Study are also substantially higher than those of parents in the CPS. While 58 percent of fathers in the Sloan college-educated sample report earnings of more than $75,000 per year, only 26 percent of fathers in the CPS sample report annual incomes this high. Similarly, 14 percent of mothers in the Sloan sample reported earnings of more than $75,000 per year compared with only 4 percent of mothers in the CPS sample. With respect to work status, mothers in the 500 Family Study are more likely to be employed than those in the CPS; however, a higher proportion of both mothers and fathers in the Sloan sample are employed in part-time jobs. Nonetheless, Sloan respondents are much more likely to work long hours: 55 percent of fathers and 22 percent of mothers in the Sloan sample reported working more than 45 hours per week compared with 36 percent of fathers and 8 percent of mothers in the CPS sample.

### Participation by both mothers and fathers

In many national studies, information about the family is obtained from only one family member, usually the mother. A strength of the 500 Family

Table 2.2 *Comparison of the March 2000 CPS and 500 Family Study college-educated subsamples*

| | percent | | | |
|---|---|---|---|---|
| | CPS married with children 0–18[a] | | 500 Family parents[a] | |
| | | | Mothers (n = 463) | Fathers (n = 353) |
| | Mothers | Fathers | | |
| Race/Ethnicity | | | | |
| Asian/Pacific Islander | 7 | 6 | 2 | 1 |
| Hispanic | 6 | 5 | 3 | 2 |
| African American | 6 | 6 | 7 | 5 |
| White | 81 | 82 | 82 | 90 |
| Identifies with two or more categories | –[b] | – | 2 | 1 |
| Missing | – | – | 3 | 1 |
| Education | | | | |
| High School or less | 10 | 8 | 2 | 0 |
| Some College | 19 | 13 | 10 | 5 |
| Bachelor's Degree | 51 | 50 | 31 | 26 |
| Master's Degree | 16 | 18 | 36 | 37 |
| Ph.D., M.D., J.D., or other professional degree | 5 | 11 | 19 | 33 |
| Missing | – | – | 2 | 0 |
| Occupation | | | | |
| Executive/Managerial | 14 | 29 | 31 | 33 |
| Physician | 1 | 3 | 3 | 7 |
| Nurse/Therapist/Counselor | 7 | 1 | 6 | 1 |
| Engineer/Architect | 2 | 12 | 2 | 9 |
| Professor/Scientist/Social Scientist (PhD) | 1 | 1 | 6 | 7 |
| Scientist/Social Scientist/Technician (non PhD) | 5 | 5 | 6 | 5 |
| Lawyer/Judge | 1 | 3 | 3 | 10 |
| Teacher/Librarian/ Religious Worker | 15 | 6 | 12 | 5 |
| Writer/Artist | 2 | 2 | 5 | 4 |
| Sales/Public Relations | 7 | 14 | 5 | 10 |
| Service/Clerical/Manual | 19 | 21 | 12 | 6 |
| Not in labor force | 26 | 3 | 8 | 1 |
| Missing | – | – | 1 | 1 |
| Annual earnings | | | | |
| $0–20,000 | 53 | 10 | 21 | 3 |
| $20,001–35,000 | 21 | 16 | 16 | 5 |
| $35,001–50,000 | 14 | 21 | 20 | 10 |
| $50,001–75,000 | 8 | 26 | 18 | 18 |
| $75,001–100,000 | 2 | 12 | 7 | 20 |

Table 2.2 (*cont.*)

| | percent | | | |
|---|---|---|---|---|
| | CPS married with children 0–18[a] | | 500 Family parents[a] | |
| | | | Mothers (n = 463) | Fathers (n = 353) |
| | Mothers | Fathers | | |
| More than $100,000 | 2 | 14 | 7 | 38 |
| Not applicable/not working | – | – | 4 | 1 |
| Missing | – | – | 7 | 5 |
| Work status | | | | |
| Full-time | 49 | 94 | 55 | 88 |
| Part-time | 22 | 2 | 32 | 5 |
| Unemployed/looking for work | 1 | 1 | 2 | 1 |
| Not in labor force/not looking for work | 28 | 3 | 8 | 1 |
| Missing | – | – | 4 | 4 |
| Work hours (main job) (hours per week) | | | | |
| 01–15 | 6 | 0 | 8 | 1 |
| 16–25 | 10 | 1 | 14 | 1 |
| 26–27 | 9 | 3 | 15 | 6 |
| 38–45 | 35 | 50 | 29 | 26 |
| 46–50 | 5 | 18 | 16 | 27 |
| 51–60 | 2 | 14 | 5 | 21 |
| More than 60 | 1 | 4 | 1 | 7 |
| Hours vary | 4 | 6 | – | – |
| Not applicable/not working | 28 | 4 | 10 | 3 |
| Missing | – | – | 1 | 7 |

Source for CPS data: US Department of Commerce, Bureau of the Census. Current Population Survey: Annual Demographic File, 2000 [Computer file].

*Notes:* This table compares CPS respondents who were married and had children between 0 and 18 where at least one parent had a 4-year college degree or higher with parents in the 500 Family Study with comparable levels of education. CPS distributions have been weighted to represent the US civilian population. Numbers do not add to 100 percent due to rounding.

[a] At least 1 parent ≥ 4-yr college degree.

[b] This category is not available in the CPS. The results from CPS were based on imputed variables, and thus there are no missing categories.

Study is the high participation rates of fathers. In 71 percent of families in the study (n = 365) both husbands and wives participated; for the remaining families only one spouse/partner participated. With respect to background and work characteristics (race/ethnicity, education, occupation, income, and work hours), the distribution of the couples sample is almost identical to the larger parent sample described in table 2.1, indicating that the two samples do not differ significantly in composition.[9]

Because information was obtained from both husbands and wives, their responses to questions about gender role attitudes, the division of household labor, and marital satisfaction can be compared (see Lee, this volume, for a comparison of couples' reports of time spent on housework; see Nielsen, this volume, for a comparison of spouses' reports of marital satisfaction). Among couples in the sample, over 80 percent of husbands and wives indicate that they are satisfied with their marriage. (Only 8 percent of husbands and wives report being dissatisfied with their marriage.) For most couples (approximately 80 percent), this is their first marriage; 69 percent have been together for more than 10 years.

### Psychological characteristics of mothers and fathers

In contrast to many large-scale national studies such as the CPS, the 500 Family Study includes several measures of psychological and emotional well-being. In addition to standard survey questions that measure marital satisfaction, depression, and self-esteem, the ESM contains detailed measures of participants' emotional states as well as the activities they were engaged in when signaled. Table 2.3 presents a summary of mothers' and fathers' responses to several of these measures.

With respect to emotional states, mothers and fathers report relatively low levels of stress, anger, worry, frustration, and irritation over the week of ESM participation. In contrast, they report feeling moderately cheerful, cooperative, caring, relaxed, and friendly. While the general patterns of response are similar for mothers and fathers, some significant gender differences emerge. Mothers score significantly higher than fathers on measures of caring, but report feeling significantly more worried and significantly less cooperative, friendly, and relaxed ($p < .05$; see Koh, this volume, for a detailed comparison of mothers and fathers' emotional states over the week of ESM signaling).

With regard to depressive symptoms, measured by the CES-D scale, the proportions of parents in the sample who exhibit moderate to high levels of depression are similar to the proportions in the general population. The possible range of scores on the 20-item CES-D is 0 to 60. A score of 16 or higher is indicative of depression, while a score of 28 or higher indicates severe depression. Within the general population, approximately 20 percent of respondents score 16 or above on the CES-D, and approximately 5 percent score 28 or above on the scale (Radloff 1977).

Table 2.3 *Emotional states and personal well-being of sampled parents*

| | Mean | |
|---|---|---|
| Emotions (from the ESM) | (n = 461) Mothers | (n = 323) Fathers |
| Cheerful (Range 0 to 3) | 1.66 | 1.60 |
| Cooperative (Range 0 to 3) | 1.40 | 1.50 |
| Caring (Range 0 to 3) | 1.67 | 1.55 |
| Relaxed (Range 0 to 3) | 1.49 | 1.65 |
| Friendly (Range 0 to 3) | 1.52 | 1.61 |
| Stressed (Range 0 to 3) | .62 | .56 |
| Angry (Range 0 to 2) | .15 | .18 |
| Worried (Range 0 to 3) | .49 | .42 |
| Irritated (Range 0 to 3) | .38 | .39 |
| Frustrated (Range 0 to 3) | .48 | .50 |

| | percent | |
|---|---|---|
| Depressive Symptoms Scale (from the Parent Survey)[a] | (n = 508) | (n = 376) |
| Not Depressed | 81 | 81 |
| Depressed | 11 | 11 |
| Severely Depressed | 3 | 3 |
| Missing | 5 | 5 |

*Note*: [a] Based on the CES-D Scale. A cutoff of 16 (those at and above a score of 16 on the scale) distinguishes those with depressive symptoms. This was the approximate 80th percentile in the original Community Mental Health Assessment (CMHA) study which used the CES-D scale. A higher cutoff score of 28 (those at and above 28 on the scale) was used to identify more severe cases, which selected about 5 percent of the original CMHA adult sample.

Within the Sloan sample these proportions are lower: 14 percent of mothers and fathers scored 16 or higher on the CES-D scale and 3 percent scored 28 or higher.[10]

*Adolescents in the study*

Table 2.4 presents characteristics of the 465 adolescents who participated in the study.[11] The sample is fairly evenly divided by gender (52 percent female; 48 percent male). 75 percent of adolescents were in high school (grades 9 through 12) and 22 percent were in middle school (grades 6 through 8); the remaining students had either recently graduated from

Table 2.4 *Characteristics of sampled adolescents*

|  | percent | |
| --- | --- | --- |
|  | Female (n = 242) | Male (n = 223) |
| Race/Ethnicity | | |
| Asian/Pacific Islander | 1 | 0 |
| Hispanic | 5 | 4 |
| African American | 8 | 9 |
| White | 77 | 83 |
| Identifies with two or more categories | 5 | 4 |
| Missing | 4 | 1 |
| Grade in School | | |
| Sixth | 5 | 5 |
| Seventh | 7 | 9 |
| Eighth | 7 | 9 |
| Ninth | 32 | 25 |
| Tenth | 17 | 15 |
| Eleventh | 11 | 14 |
| Twelfth | 17 | 19 |
| Other | 2 | 2 |
| Missing | 1 | 0 |
| Grades on last report card | | |
| Mostly As | 43 | 27 |
| As & Bs | 25 | 22 |
| Mostly Bs | 15 | 17 |
| Bs & Cs | 6 | 10 |
| Cs or below | 3 | 10 |
| Missing | 9 | 13 |
| Educational Aspirations | | |
| High School or less | 0 | 3 |
| Some College | 2 | 4 |
| Bachelor's Degree | 38 | 46 |
| Advanced Degree | 52 | 39 |
| Don't Know | 5 | 8 |
| Missing | 1 | 0 |
| Occupational Aspirations | | |
| Executive/Managerial | 7 | 4 |
| Physician/Veterinarian | 12 | 5 |
| Nurse/Therapist/Counselor | 2 | 1 |
| Engineer/Architect | 2 | 4 |
| Scientist/Social Scientist | 5 | 4 |
| Technician/Technologist | 1 | 5 |
| Lawyer/Judge | 8 | 2 |
| Teacher | 8 | 4 |
| Writer/Artist/Athlete | 17 | 13 |
| Sales/Public Relations | 1 | 1 |
| Service/Clerical/Manual | 4 | 10 |
| Don't Know | 24 | 39 |
| Missing | 9 | 8 |

high school or were missing grade information. Most adolescents in the sample reported grades of B or higher on their last report card. Consistent with studies documenting gender differences in academic achievement, girls typically reported higher grades than boys (83 percent of girls reported grades of B or higher compared with 66 percent of boys). While most adolescents in the sample expected to earn a college degree or higher (90 percent of girls and 85 percent of boys), a large proportion were undecided about the occupation they expected to pursue as adults. Almost 40 percent of boys and 25 percent of girls indicated that they did not know what occupation they expected to have at age 30. The most prevalent occupational categories named by the remaining students were writer/artist/athlete, followed by physician/veterinarian.[12]

### Young children in the study

The young children who participated in the study were typically 5 or 6 years of age and were enrolled in kindergarten. Like the adolescent sample, this sample is fairly evenly divided by gender (52 percent boys and 48 percent girls). Table 2.5 presents background characteristics for these children, together with their summary scores on the Child Behavior Checklist (CBCL), the PPVT-III, and the Harter Pictorial Scale of Perceived Competence and Social Acceptance for Young Children.

As shown in table 2.5, a higher proportion of children in the Sloan sample fall within the borderline and clinical ranges of the CBCL than in normative samples (4 percent of children in the Sloan sample have scores in the clinical range compared with 2 percent of children in normative samples; 8 percent of girls and 4 percent of boys in the Sloan sample have scores in the borderline range compared to 3 percent of children in normative samples). With respect to scores on the PPVT-III, children in the Sloan sample tend to score higher than those in normative samples. 50 percent of girls and 56 percent of boys in the Sloan sample score above the 80th percentile on this assessment. Given the composition of the families in the sample and the educational resources that are typically available to children in these families, these scores are not surprising. Scores on the Harter Pictorial Scale are also skewed toward the high end of the scale. These scores are consistent with those reported by Harter and Pike, who observe that "[children's] use of the upper ranges of the scales is not thought to reflect social desirability response tendencies so much as the young child's blurring of the boundaries between reality and the wish to be competent or accepted" (1984: 1974).

Table 2.5 *Characteristics of sampled kindergarteners*

| | percent | |
|---|---|---|
| | Female (n = 95) | Male (n = 103) |
| Age | | |
| Five | 56 | 55 |
| Six | 43 | 45 |
| Seven | 1 | 0 |
| Race/Ethnicity | | |
| Asian/Pacific Islander | 0 | 2 |
| Hispanic | 2 | 3 |
| African American | 6 | 8 |
| White | 77 | 72 |
| Identified as Mixed/Biracial | 8 | 11 |
| Missing | 6 | 5 |
| Child Behavior Checklist | | |
| Normal | 77 | 77 |
| Borderline Problem Behavior | 8 | 4 |
| Serious Problem Behavior (Clinical Range) | 4 | 4 |
| Parent did not complete instrument | 11 | 16 |
| Peabody Picture Vocabulary Test-III | | |
| 1st–10th percentile | 1 | 2 |
| 11th–20th percentile | 0 | 1 |
| 21st–30th percentile | 0 | 1 |
| 31st–40th percentile | 1 | 2 |
| 41st–50th percentile | 5 | 5 |
| 51st–60th percentile | 5 | 5 |
| 61st–70th percentile | 11 | 14 |
| 71st–80th percentile | 23 | 12 |
| 81st–90th percentile | 24 | 22 |
| 91st–100th percentile | 26 | 34 |
| Child did not complete instrument | 3 | 3 |
| Harter Scale of Competence and Acceptance | Mean | |
| Cognitive Competence (Range 2.33 to 4) | 3.60 | 3.66 |
| Physical Competence (Range 2 to 4) | 3.47 | 3.27 |
| Maternal Acceptance (Range 1.67 to 4) | 2.89 | 2.93 |
| Peer Acceptance (Range 1.33 to 4) | 2.80 | 2.84 |

## Summary

The 500 Family Study provides unusually rich data on middle- and upper-middle-class dual-earner families. For the most part, these are families where women work by choice rather than necessity and have greater flexibility in arranging their work schedules and hours. Because these women are typically well-educated and hold professional jobs, they often contribute substantially to the family's income and may be more likely to renegotiate traditional gender roles and responsibilities, in some cases by purchasing services such as childcare, and in others by reallocating responsibilities within the household. It is thus possible to investigate how these dual-earner couples and their children are coping with changes in the organization of work and family life. The data also allow investigators to examine multiple dimensions of work and family life from the perspectives of both parents and children.

Despite the richness of the data set, there are still methodological issues that must be considered when analyzing these data. For example, because the ESM is burdensome for respondents, many participants fail to respond to all of the signals. This issue of non-response is examined by Jeong (technical appendix A), and a method is proposed for correcting it. Drawing on data from the CPS, Rubinstein and Mulligan (technical appendix B) address another limitation of the Sloan data: the categorical coding of annual earnings for husbands and wives. Employing a subsample from the CPS that replicates the characteristics of the Sloan sample, they estimate mean earnings within each of the Sloan earnings categories, conditional upon personal, spouse, and family characteristics, to provide more accurate earnings estimates for Sloan mothers and fathers.

NOTES

1. All communities have been assigned pseudonyms. For the seven communities that were included in both the Sloan Study of Youth and Social Development and the current study, the pseudonyms are the same as those previously assigned. See Csikszentmihalyi and Schneider (2000) for a detailed description of these communities and the criteria used in their selection.
2. Fifty families from the earlier adolescent study participated in the 500 Family Study. These were families whose children had reached adolescence (the older siblings of these children had been adolescents when the earlier study was conducted). The inclusion of these families makes it possible to link five years of data from the adolescent study with data from the current study. Linking these two data sets provides an unusual opportunity to see how working families socialize their children through middle school and adolescence.

3. Because of the difficulties of scheduling visits with young children and their families, data collection for families with kindergartners was restricted to the Chicago area.

4. These results are based on all parents and adolescents who participated in the ESM, even those who responded to only a few signals. To ensure adequate sampling of experiences, analysts typically exclude participants who respond to fewer than 15 signals during the week of ESM participation. See Jeong (technical appendix A) for an analysis of ESM response rates and a method for adjusting for non-response in these data.

5. Because survey response rates tend to be higher among women, which was also the case in this study, mothers were asked to complete questions about their spouse's employment status and occupation; questions about spouse's employment were not asked of fathers.

6. Families were not compensated for their participation in the study. As a token of appreciation for participating, each family was given a Blockbuster gift certificate and a Sloan Center mug and t-shirt. Families were also sent periodic updates of study findings after data collection was completed.

7. Cortisol is a stress hormone that tends to increase when a person is challenged or stressed. Because accurate estimates of cortisol levels can be easily made from saliva samples, researchers have become interested in using cortisol as a biomarker for stress. In addition to this physiological measure of stress, several items in the ESM and the parent and adolescent surveys also measured stress, making it possible to examine the relationship between self-reported stress and physiological responses to stress.

8. This analysis was undertaken to determine how the 500 Family sample differs from a nationally representative sample of middle-class parents with children under the age of 18. Such comparisons allow analysts to develop sample weights to correct for sampling bias (see Jeong, technical appendix A, for a description of the procedures used in developing such weights).

9. Descriptive characteristics of couples in the study are available from the author.

10. In the current analysis, the scale was considered unusable if 4 or more items were missing; 5 percent of mothers and fathers in the sample had 4 or more missing items for the scale.

11. In many cases, more than one adolescent in each family participated. Of the 465 adolescents who completed surveys, 350 were from different families.

12. Adolescents were asked, "What job do you expect to have at age 30?" Responses were open ended and were coded into 70 specific categories (e.g., history teacher, mechanical engineer, musician, author) based on verbatim responses. Using the *Classified Index of Industries and Occupations* (US Department of Commerce 1992), which groups occupations into categories based on similarities in job content, these specific occupations were recoded into 12 summary categories, using education and training as additional criteria in defining categories.

# Commentary

*Joel M. Hektner*

*The 500 Family Study is difficult to categorize because it transcends all the traditional labels. The research is both theoretically grounded and applied, both quantitative and qualitative, both sociological and psychological. It is simultaneously a study of young children, adolescents, workers, parents, and families. At a time when researchers in the social sciences are becoming increasingly specialized, Schneider and Waite have resisted the trend to narrow in on an arcane slice of life disconnected from meaningful context. As noted in the chapter, the design of the study allows them to explore an extensive array of topics directly relevant to the daily lives of millions of Americans. Other studies have also attempted to achieve this degree of breadth, but they are like a pool one mile wide and an inch deep. The methodology for these kinds of studies has been to survey a nationally representative sample at a single point in time with a standard set of questions yielding quantitative responses. Information collected from such studies has been useful, but it leaves us with a sketchy profile of "an average family" drained of the richness and color that can come only from asking families about the idiosyncrasies of their daily lives. In the 500 Family Study, depth is not sacrificed; intensiveness was just as much a goal of the design as extensiveness.*

*Hoogstra aptly describes their methodological strategy as "triangulation," and the descriptors "multi-construct, multi-method, multi-informant" would also apply. This approach is taught as the gold standard for social science research. Its application in the 500 Family Study is particularly strong, involving several interlocking components. First, the researchers gathered information on both the internal and external dimensions of experience: thoughts and actions, feelings and daily events, family dynamics and family routines. Second, this information was collected via three complementary methods. Used together, the survey, the Experience Sampling Method, and the interview generate information that is more valuable than would be derived from a simple sum of the three. The advantage is more than just the ability to cross-validate and corroborate. Each method can tell us something related to, but different from, what we learn from the others. The result is a more complete representation of family life. The third "triangle" involves the three or four individuals in each family from whom data were collected. By asking different family members the same questions at the same time, the researchers treat the family as the system that it is – a whole made up of individuals who have both unique and collective experiences. Thus we may see how the mother's experience of family is different from the father's, and how the parents' experience affects and is affected by their teenager's experience. Given the traditional reliance on the mother as an informant on the family, it is particularly important that this study included fathers.*

*At each of these three levels, diverse pieces of information are collected and then integrated. Achieving all three of these levels with a sample involving over 1,500 individuals is a monumental accomplishment, but the 500 Family Study researchers also added a fourth degree of integration. Many of the questions they asked were also asked of many thousands of other individuals across many years and several studies. This overlap allows for the direct comparison and integration of their findings with those from a large body of prior research.*

*The process of making these comparisons has already started with this chapter. One of the conclusions clearly evident from these comparisons is that the 500 families do not constitute a nationally representative sample. The focus of the study was on dual-career families, so representation of all types of families was not a goal. However, the sample is also not representative of dual-earner families in the US. This is a limitation, a tradeoff made in order to fulfill the study's other priorities. However, it would have been extremely difficult to collect the depth of information obtained in this study from a nationally representative sample. Fortunately, the same comparisons that illuminate the upward socio-economic skew in the sample also allow the researchers to specify exactly how the sample differs from the population and to compute statistical weights to correct for those differences. Even without any weighting, we may use the sample as is to learn about upper-middle-class dual-earner families and to generate questions about how the lives of families who have fewer resources would compare.*

*As noted, the families included in this study have above average socioeconomic status, as indicated by all three traditional measures – income, occupation, and education. The information included in the chapter then gives us a glimpse of some of the issues these families are experiencing. One of the most striking details in this profile concerns the large number of hours both mothers and fathers work in a typical week. Americans spend more time at work than workers in other industrialized countries, and these data suggest that the professional, well-paid sector of the labor force experiences some of the longest work days. Although fathers typically work longer hours than mothers, mothers seem to be carrying the greater emotional burden, as evidenced by their higher levels of worry and lower relaxation. Of course, results such as these only scratch the surface of what the data could reveal and we should not rush to conclusions before reading further analyses in the rest of this book.*

*The relationship between socioeconomic status and academic preparedness is also clearly evident in these data. Over 30 percent of the kindergartners in the sample have developed a more extensive vocabulary than 90 percent of their peers nationwide. Their parents have no doubt been able to provide them with a developmentally rich environment, including shelves of books, experiences in preschool, and time spent reading together. Behaviorally, however, these children appear to fare no better, and possibly even worse, than children from less advantaged families. Given the long work hours of the parents, it may be tempting to infer that the above average incidence of "clinical" and "borderline" behavior problems in this sample resulted from too much time spent in childcare, not enough time spent with parents in the home, or indulgent parenting. Yet all of these conclusions are merely speculations. Without more data, particularly from comparison samples of children whose parents have other work patterns, we cannot draw firm conclusions.*

*The chapter also provides us with a glimpse into the aspirations of upper-middle-class teenagers. These adolescents usually do not want to replicate their parents' careers, but they do want to replicate their level of education. Less than 5 percent say they are aiming for anything less than a bachelor's degree. Anticipating at least four years to spend in college, many apparently do not feel the need at this age to narrow their career aspirations. The largest proportion of them do not yet know what they expect to do. Those who do have an idea do not tend to list the executive and managerial occupations held by their parents but rather choose more expressive careers that would not necessarily require all the education they plan to pursue. Their short-term goals for education reflect a realistic assessment of what it will take to reach or surpass their parents' standard of living, but their long-term aspirations for careers reveal an idealistic wish for occupations with more obvious intrinsic rewards. Although their parents may indeed derive great satisfaction from their careers, many adolescents are drawn to careers they think will be more fun. For this particular group of teens, the mix we are seeing at this stage of realism in educational goals and idealism in career aspirations could be taken as a sign of a healthy developmental process. Whether the same healthy process occurs for other teens is unclear, since the realism of their goals is more difficult to judge.*

## Jiri Zuzanek

*Not so long ago, the World Health Organization expressed concern that "school-aged children, as a defined population group, have until recently been neglected by national and international public health researchers." This situation may be changing, however. The 500 Family Study, funded by the Alfred P. Sloan*

*Foundation and described in this chapter, represents a comprehensive attempt to examine the dynamics of parent–adolescent interaction in working families and its effects on adolescents' social, emotional, cognitive, and health development.*

*The chapter provides a detailed description of the study's methodology, the type of information collected, and some of the study's preliminary findings. In my commentary, I shall first draw attention to the social and policy concerns currently underlying interest in the study of work–family and parent–child relationships, and then address some methodological and substantive issues raised in the chapter.*

*Contrary to optimistic forecasts that life in modern societies will become more leisure-oriented, recent national time-budget, workforce, and health surveys indicate that employed people in contemporary industrial societies feel more pressed for time than they have in the past. In 1977, 40 percent of Americans surveyed stated that they "never have enough time" to get everything done on the job. By 1997 this figure had risen to 60 percent. In Canada, according to the 1998 General Social Survey, over 66 percent of the population felt more rushed at the end of the 1990s than they did "five years ago." Among employed parents with children under the age of 12 the percentage of those who felt more rushed was even higher, at 87.5 percent. A study recently released by the Conference Board of Canada found that the number of Canadians who reported moderate and high levels of stress as a result of work–family imbalance had increased from 26.7 percent in 1989 to 46.2 percent in 1999.*

*These trends affect the adolescent population as well. In the early 1990s, 66 percent of American adolescents aged 18 to 20 reported experiencing moderate or high levels of stress compared to 65 percent for the total surveyed population. The US General Social Survey data from 1996 show, likewise, that adolescents aged 18 to 20 report higher levels of anxiety, fears, worries, and loneliness, and lower levels of self-assessed health than do adults aged 21 and over. In 1992, 62 percent of Canadian adolescents aged 15 to 19, attending school and living with parents, reported feeling rushed every day or a few times a week. By 1998 this figure had climbed to 68 percent, a higher proportion than for the adult population. By the end of the 1990s, over 49 percent of Canadian adolescents aged 15 to 19 reported experiencing moderate or high levels of stress, which is only 5 percent less than for the rest of the population.*

*These trends have drawn researchers' attention to the study of the determinants of youths' emotional well-being and health. It has become increasingly clear that adolescents' physical and mental health and its manifestations, such as risk behavior, sedentary habits, and obesity, are imbedded in youths' daily behavior and experiences and are influenced, in part, by the growing work and time pressures experienced by working families.*

*In an attempt to examine the dynamics of parent–adolescent relationships, the authors of the Sloan Family study used a "triangulation" strategy. They* collected detailed information about parents' and adolescents' behavior and attitudes by administering standard survey questionnaires as well as collecting detailed Experience Sampling self-reports for one-week periods in the respondents' lives.

These data were further supplemented by in-depth personal interviews focusing on the circumstances and quality of parent–adolescent interactions, as well as by the administration of standardized psychological and behavioral child assessments, and measurements of physiological stress based on the analysis of sampled salivary cortisol. To compare their findings with national trends and averages, the authors of the study incorporated into their survey a number of benchmark questions from national surveys, such as the CPS.

If a new word were to be coined to describe the study's approach, the term "triangulation" could be justifiably replaced by that of "six-" or "septangulation." The author's contention that their study provides a "fairly comprehensive picture of work and family life" is certainly not an overstatement.

In a study of such detail and complexity, sampling typically poses a serious challenge. As the author admits, the 500 Family Study provides rich information about middle- and upper-middle-class families rather than the entire US working population. Although one should be cognizant of this fact when interpreting the findings of the study, the limitations of the sampling may to some extent reflect the study's objectives. The 500 Family Study aimed at explaining the dynamics or mechanisms of parent–child interactions rather than at preparing a "state of the union" report. To use a medical metaphor, this study is diagnostic rather than epidemiological. It is up to practitioners and policy makers to draw from it the "epidemiological" or societal conclusions. This said, the question of whether the determinants of families' health or malaise are universal or class specific deserves separate attention.

This latter point became apparent when comparing some of the findings reported in this chapter with Canadian findings collected as part of a study of work–family interface and parent–child relationships conducted by myself and Professor Mannell in the Kitchener-Waterloo area of Ontario. Such a comparison is particularly interesting because the Canadian study, funded by the Canada's Social Sciences and Humanities Research Council, was informally coordinated with the 500 Family Study and addressed some of the same issues that are at the center of the Sloan project.

While there are considerable design similarities between the two studies, the K-W sample focused on the middle- and lower-middle-class groups of the urban population to a greater extent than did the US study, and this may explain some differences in the findings. For example, there were more full-time and fewer part-time employed mothers in the Canadian sample than there were in the US (61 percent and 22 percent respectively in Canada, compared to 54 percent and 31 percent in the US). As well, fewer than 10 percent of

*Canadian mothers graduated from an MA, Ph.D., or professional program, compared to 50 percent in the US.*

*It is plausible that these differences account for the fact that only 8 percent of US employed mothers expressed dissatisfaction with their marital arrangements compared to 15 percent in Canada. As well, there are other differences that are interesting to explore and that may be caused by cultural as well as social economic factors. Even a superficial comparison of the US and Canadian findings points to the importance of cross-sectional as well as cross-cultural analyses, and testifies to the significance of the 500 Family Study as a benchmark for the study of parent–adolescent interactions in different social and comparative contexts.*

*The major challenge for the use of this extremely rich source of data is to match the human and financial resources allocated to the administration of the survey and collection of the data by an equal amount of support for the analysis and interpretation of its findings. Both methodologically and substantively the Sloan 500 Family Study represents an important contribution to the research of work–family interface, and its findings cannot be ignored in the ongoing policy debate over the future development of our families and youth.*

*Part II*

# Experiences at work and at home

# Overview

*Jennifer Hanis-Martin*

*These chapters paint a very complex picture of the associations between experiences at work and at home. They illustrate the dialectic relationship between the dynamic inner lives of parents and the social environments in which they are embedded. Given these varied contexts, it cannot be taken for granted that being a parent or a worker is the same experience for everyone. The results in this section suggest that people's approaches to their identities as parents and workers are varied, and looking at their day-to-day experiences sheds light on their approaches to these different roles. These rich data provide insights into the connections between experience and identity and challenge accepted conceptions of work–life balance.*

*Contrary to Hochschild (1997), who found some evidence that women find refuge from home and family responsibilities when they are at work, neither Sexton nor Adam find evidence to support this view. Sexton finds that on average men and women both feel more positively at home than they do at work, and Adam finds that women experience more positive affect at home. It seems that many parents find intellectual challenge and develop positive self-esteem at work, but this is not the same as escaping from home. This is not to say that home is an unproblematic sanctuary either. Home certainly has its own challenges, but parents seem to relax a bit more there.*

*In addition, by looking at parents' feelings and motivations it is possible to see that the orientation they have toward work may be associated with their orientation toward home and family. Based on data showing that fathers with high intrinsic motivation are not emotionally in synch with their teens, Matjasko and Feldman suggest that parents who work in jobs that are personally satisfying may invest less in their role as parents. This highlights a potentially important relationship between different identities – as worker, parent, spouse – and the emotional well-being of the family.*

*Similarly, Martinez examines mothers' orientations toward paid work, raising similar questions about worker identity and its relationship to family life. Her findings encourage us to think about how the roles we occupy differ and overlap.*

# 3 Spending time at work and at home: what workers do, how they feel about it, and how these emotions affect family life

*Holly R. Sexton*

Computers, e-mail, and the Internet are integral and common to the workplace, and anecdotal reports suggest that these technologies have become so overused that they may actually distract employees from their primary work tasks and decrease productivity. Workers, for example, often complain that they receive more e-mail – and more junk e-mail – than they would prefer. Technological advances appear to be having even more profound effects on the organization of core tasks in many occupations (Cappelli 1993). In engineering, the use of computer-aided design (CAD) has increased the work capabilities of a single engineer so that one worker can now perform the tasks of as many as ten to twelve engineers, thus freeing up the engineer to do a variety of tasks (Goodman 1996). Engineers are now frequently asked to join the sales force in order to infuse knowledge into sales interactions (Darr 2002). Engineers are not a single example; most highly skilled professionals are now expected to be knowledgeable about a wide range of tasks. As Carnoy notes in his assessment of the current work economy, "The amount and diversity of knowledge demanded in higher-paying jobs are increasing; yet, more important, the knowledge base required just to function effectively in flexible labor markets, no matter what the job, is also becoming more complex" (2000:12–13).

Given recent changes in the organization of work in several professions, this chapter examines two dimensions of work experience: time allocation and the emotional experience of work. With respect to time allocation, how do people spend their time at work? What percent of time do workers spend on the primary or core aspects of their jobs? Does the amount of time spent in various types of tasks vary by occupation or gender? With respect to the emotional experience of work, how do individuals feel when engaged in primary work tasks versus other types of tasks? Do individuals who are more autonomous or self-directed at work feel happier, more engaged, and more successful when they are at work? Does this positive experience of work have spillover effects at home?

### Spending time at work

Occupations that once had clearly defined duties, such as doctors, nurses, and engineers, are now incorporating responsibilities outside of their professional domain. Several recent investigations document changes in the nature and scope of work duties for many occupations. For the most part, however, these studies focus on the impact of technology on specific occupations or work practices (i.e., training, assessment, telecommuting, worker development); few studies examine what professionals in various occupations actually do at work.

A limited number of researchers have looked at the range and variety of work tasks performed by workers, especially with respect to tasks that are considered the primary or core duties of an occupation. One study identified the proportion of time that professors spent on various work tasks (e.g., lecturing, research, administrative duties, etc.). However, this study did not distinguish between core and ancillary work tasks and examined time allocation for only one occupation (Kesic and Previsic 1996). Because the nature and scope of work have changed for many occupations, little is known about the core tasks performed by individuals in these occupations and the time allocated to these tasks. This chapter identifies core (primary) and ancillary (secondary) work tasks for several different occupations and examines the amount of time workers devote to these tasks.

### The influence of work characteristics on job satisfaction and experiences of work

Research has consistently shown that an individual's overall mood at work is an important predictor of job performance and satisfaction (Brief and Weiss 2002; Fisher and Ashkanasy 2000). Certain characteristics of work, such as long work hours and unexpected job demands, have been significantly associated with increasing stress and dissatisfaction with work life (Bond, Galinsky, and Swanberg 1998; Marchena, this volume).[1] The types of tasks performed by workers may also contribute to worker satisfaction or dissatisfaction.

Research conducted by Kohn and Schooler has examined the relationships among the tasks individuals are engaged in at work, their emotional experiences and satisfaction with these tasks, and the impact these emotions have on their lives at home (Kohn 1990; Kohn and Schooler 1982, 1983). Their research focuses on the relationships between work characteristics and personality. Specifically, they analyze various aspects of work tasks, determine the extent to which these tasks exhibit characteristics of intellectual flexibility and substantive complexity, and then relate these measures to an individual's psychological functioning.

Using a large representative sample of workers from varied occupations, Kohn and colleagues inventoried workers' job conditions and differentiated the psychological attributes of various components of their work. They found that variables related to control over the work process (how closely supervised one is at work, the extent to which work tasks are routinized, and the substantive complexity of work tasks) have significant effects on an individual's experience of work. In general, those who are not allowed significant flexibility and direction in work tasks and those who are required to perform with little intellectual challenge or variation have more negative experiences of work. Job satisfaction is determined by how complex a job is, how closely an individual is supervised, the types of pressures the work entails, and whether individuals are self-directed or conforming in their work orientations.

### Work-to-home spillover

Worker dissatisfaction is of particular concern to researchers investigating work–family conflict. Studies indicate that how individuals feel at work often spills over into their interactions with spouses and children (Larson and Almeida 1999; Klute et al. 2001). Several studies have shown that mothers are more likely to protect their children and hide their feelings of dissatisfaction; fathers, on the other hand, are more likely to transmit their feelings of dissatisfaction to their wives (Adams, King, and King 1996; Repetti 1989; Williams and Alliger 1994).

A number of studies have highlighted the negative association between job satisfaction and work–family conflict (Bruck, Allen, and Spector 2002; Martins, Eddleston, and Velga 2002; Perrewe, Hochwarter, and Kiewitz 1999). Most of these studies, however, employ general measures of job satisfaction rather than examining specific components of worker satisfaction, such as work benefits and job autonomy. Although the links between self-directedness at work and job satisfaction (see Kohn and Schooler above) and between job satisfaction and work–family conflict have each been separately identified, the relationship between self-directedness at work and emotions at work and at home has not been directly researched.

### Research focus

This chapter examines the characteristics of specific occupations, the tasks a person engages in at work, the emotional experiences associated with those tasks, including the perceived control over work, and whether these experiences carry over to the home. To some extent, researchers have examined how workers feel about their jobs with retrospective, self-report data (Taber and Alliger 1995). However, recent papers have stressed the need for "real time" or moment-to-moment data, a point articulated most clearly in studies that have used time diaries to capture emotional variations that occur across the workday (Alliger and Williams 1993; Fisher 2000; Williams and Alliger 1994). Few of these studies, however, evaluate the real-time emotions related to primary versus other types of work tasks. Using data from the Experience Sample Method (ESM), this chapter provides a comprehensive description of the tasks individuals perform at work and how they feel when performing these tasks.

## Hypotheses

Kohn and Schooler's research on substantive complexity and job satisfaction suggests several hypotheses:

*Hypothesis 1a and 1b.* When engaged in their primary work tasks, individuals will have more positive and less negative emotional experiences at work than when they are engaged in secondary tasks.

*Hypothesis 2a and 2b.* Individuals will spend as much time in primary work as possible because of the positive rewards associated with work that is more cognitively engaging. In addition, those workers who perceive themselves as having more control over work tasks (i.e., those who are self-directed in their work orientation) will spend higher percentages of their work day engaged in primary work and have more positive emotional experiences at work.

*Hypothesis 3.* The positive emotional experiences that are associated with work will carry over to the home.

## Method

### Sample

Analyses are based on responses to the parent survey and the ESM by a subsample of individuals who participated in the 500 Family Study. Several criteria were used in selecting the subsample: (1) Only those who had completed both the survey and ESM were selected; (2) Since the primary purpose of this study is to examine experiences at work, only those who indicated that they were working full time were included;[2] (3) To ensure that analyses would not be skewed by non-response, individuals who had fewer than three "beeps" occurring at work were excluded;[3] (4) Only those whose jobs could be classified into occupational categories found in the Census Codes were included in the sample. (See table 3.1 for a list of the occupational categories). Applying these four selection criteria, the final sample size was 426, fairly evenly divided by gender (221 males and 205 females).[4] Respondents are primarily white, non-Hispanic, in the middle- to upper-income bracket, with relatively high levels of education, and parents of teenagers. Most work 38 hours or more per week.

## Measures

*Primary and secondary work*    To classify work tasks for each occupation, four main categories were identified: primary work, related work tasks, preparation work, and personal care/social interaction. The first three categories include tasks performed at work that are directly relevant to job duties. The fourth category, personal care/social, includes tasks that are performed at work but are not related to job duties (e.g., meals, socializing with work colleagues, talking with family members).

On the survey, individuals were asked to list some of their primary work tasks: responses were matched with descriptions of work activities that respondents provided on the ESM. Based on survey and ESM responses, these activities were classified and then summarized by occupation. Six raters placed each of the work activities from the ESM into one of the four categories based on the occupational descriptions of primary job duties provided by respondents and summaries in the *Occupational Handbook.* One rater served as the tiebreaker in the case of split decisions among the raters.[5] The identification of tasks for the primary work category for each occupation was thus initially provided by participants in their survey and ESM responses and then finalized by the six raters; tasks for the other three categories were classified by the six independent raters using ESM responses and information from the *Occupational Handbook.*

The tasks in the primary work category for each occupation are presented in table 3.1.[6] The primary work category for each occupation is comprised of a small number of tasks since the raters attempted to isolate the core duties associated with each occupation. In some instances, overlap in primary work tasks occurs between similar occupations; for example, physicians and other health professionals (e.g., nurses, social workers) both have meetings with clients or patients as a primary work task. Occupational groups that are less similar in nature have relatively

Table 3.1 *Primary work tasks by occupation category*

| | Administrative Support | Physician | Financial Analyst/Accountant | Health Professional | Lawyer | Manager (high prestige)[a] | Manager (mid prestige) | Professor | Psychologist | Salesperson | Scientist | Systems Analyst | Teacher | Writer |
|---|---|---|---|---|---|---|---|---|---|---|---|---|---|---|
| Frequency (N = 426) | 19 | 19 | 23 | 21 | 35 | 65 | 93 | 29 | 8 | 33 | 26 | 12 | 30 | 13 |
| Analyzing data/performing calculations | | | X | | | | | | | | X | | | |
| Editing/revising | | | | | | | | | | | X | | | X |
| Filing | X | | | | | | | | | | | | | |
| Financial activity (i.e. writing check for work) | X | | X | | | | | | | | | | | |
| General organizing/planning/scheduling | X | | | | | | | | | | | | | |
| Having a meeting (work) | | | | | | X | X | | | | | | | |
| Inspecting (not just watching) | | X | | X | X | X | | | | | X | | | |
| Meeting with clients/patients | | | X | X | X | | | | X | X | | | | |
| Mentoring/supervision/disciplining | | | | | | | X | | | X | | | X | |
| Miscellaneous computer related activity (work) | | | X | | | | | | | | X | X | | |

| Activity | Group 1 | Group 2 | Group 3 | Group 4 | Group 5 | Group 6 |
|---|---|---|---|---|---|---|
| On the phone (work-related) |  |  | X |  | X |  |
| Reading work-related material/researching | X |  | X | X | X | X |
| Routine paperwork (e.g., filling out forms, report) | X | X |  |  | X |  |
| Substantive writing (i.e., articles, legal briefs) | X |  | X | X | X | X |
| Talking about business matters w/boss |  | X | X |  |  |  |
| Talking about business matters w/co-workers |  | X | X |  |  |  |
| Talking about business matters w/employees |  | X | X |  |  |  |
| Talking to/serving customers | X | X | X |  | X |  |
| Talking w/classmates/teammates/co-workers |  |  |  |  | X |  |
| Talking w/students |  |  |  |  | X | X |
| Teaching/coaching (school seminar) |  |  |  |  | X | X |
| Tutoring |  |  |  |  |  | X |
| Typing/word-processing/faxing | X |  |  |  |  |  |
| Unspecified/Other Reading |  |  |  |  | X |  |
| Unspecified/Other Writing | X |  |  |  |  |  |
| Watching attentively/examining |  | X |  |  |  | X |

Notes: [a] The distinction between high and mid prestige for the two manager groups comes from prestige scores for Census Codes, as explained by Nakao and Treas (1994). For the mid-prestige manager group, prestige scores ranged from 42 to 54, whereas the high-prestige manager group had prestige scores between 59 and 70. Overall prestige scores for the sample ranged from 28 to 86, with an overall mean of 60.

little overlap in primary work tasks. Note that the primary work tasks for the administrative support category include tasks that are considered related work or preparation work for most of the other occupations. Individuals in other occupations may now be performing tasks that in the past were perhaps the sole responsibility of individuals in administrative support fields.

*Demographic, work, and family characteristics*    Measures of family income, educational attainment, and perceived work–family conflict were obtained from parent surveys. Information on hours worked per week was obtained from ESM and the March 2000 Current Population Survey (CPS) as well as parent surveys.

*Emotion measures*    ESM responses were used to assess emotional states at work and at home.[7] *Positive* and *negative* affect variables were constructed using items that asked about the specific emotional experiences associated with an activity. For *positive affect*, these items include: Were you feeling happy? Did you enjoy what you were doing? Were you feeling caring? Were you feeling cheerful? Were you feeling cooperative? Were you feeling relaxed? Were you feeling excited (versus bored)? Were you feeling proud? Items related to *negative affect* focus more on tension or stress related to an activity and ask: Were you feeling worried? Were you feeling frustrated? Were you feeling stressed? Were you feeling lonely? Were you feeling nervous? Were you feeling angry? Were you feeling strained? Were you feeling irritated?

An *engagement* variable was constructed to capture the individual's interest in particular activities. Items for this variable include: Were you feeling productive? How well were you concentrating? Did you feel active (versus passive)? Were you feeling responsible?

A *self-esteem* variable identifies how positively a person is assessing his or her abilities and level of accomplishment. Items used in constructing this variable include: Did the situation allow you to be involved or to act? Did you have the abilities to deal with the situation? Were you succeeding at what you were doing? Was the activity important to you? Were you living up to your own expectations? Were others expecting a lot from you? Did you feel good about yourself? Did you feel strong (versus weak)? Did you feel friendly?

*Self-directed and conforming work orientations*    Based on Kohn and Schooler's (1983) descriptions of self-directed and conforming emotional characteristics, two ESM items – Did you feel in control of the situation? and Was the activity interesting? – were used to create a categorical variable that identifies individuals as self-directed or conforming. To isolate whether an individual was self-directed or conforming at work, only responses to beeps occurring at work were used. Classification as self-directed or conforming comes from work beeps; these categorizations do not refer to personality characteristics but instead describe an individual's orientation toward work. Out of the 426 participants in the sample, 209 were classified as self-directed, and 212 were classified as conforming.[8]

## Results

### Time spent at work in various activities

*Work categories*    Using ESM responses and the March 2000 Current Population Survey (CPS), the number of hours and minutes in an average workday were estimated. The average number of hours worked per week by individuals in the sample was 46.81 (49.41 for males and 44.00 for females).[9] For each individual, the proportion of time spent in the four work categories (primary work, related work, preparation work, and personal care/social) was calculated by dividing the beeps spent in each type of work by the number of beeps spent at work overall. The average proportion was then multiplied by the number of minutes worked in an average workday to find the average time spent each day in each work category. Results of these analyses indicate that individuals spend, on average, nearly half of the workday on related work activities and another quarter of the day in preparation work and personal tasks. Only one-fourth of the workday is actually spent completing those activities that are considered the core duties of their occupation.[10]

*Gender and occupation*    To determine whether the percent of time spent in each work category varies by gender or occupation, two-factor Analyses of Variance (ANOVAs) were conducted for each of the four work categories. The proportion of time spent in primary work varies significantly for only one occupational category, teachers ($F_{(13, 398)} = 2.77$, $p < .01$). Post-hoc analyses with Bonferroni corrections reveal that teachers spend significantly more time in primary work than financial analysts/accountants or mid-level managers. Teachers also spend more time in primary work than scientists, although this difference is only marginally significant ($p = .06$). This finding is not unexpected since teachers have more clearly delineated primary work tasks, and their time in the classroom is more temporally bounded than other occupations. There are no other significant differences among the work categories by

Table 3.2 *Means for the composite variables, positive affect, negative affect, engagement, and self-esteem, for different types of work*

|  | Primary work | Related work | Preparation work | $F^a$ |
|---|---|---|---|---|
| Positive affect | 13.01 | 12.13 | 11.71 | 10.31***[b] |
| Negative affect | 3.46 | 3.56 | 3.51 | .08 |
| Engagement | 9.00 | 8.58 | 8.07 | 21.53***[c] |
| Self-esteem | 20.47 | 19.32 | 18.67 | 20.61***[d] |

*Notes:* [a] F-values for positive affect, engagement, and self-esteem are significant at $p < .001$. Negative affect was not significant.
[b] Post hoc analyses show primary work to be significantly different from related work tasks and preparation work.
[c] Post hoc analyses indicate that primary work is significantly different from related work tasks and preparation work. Related work tasks are also significantly different from preparation work.
[d] Post hoc analyses show that primary work is significantly different from related work tasks and preparation work. Related work tasks are marginally different from preparation work ($p = .06$).

occupation once corrections are made; no significant main effects are found for any of the four categories by gender (all F's < 2.22, n.s.), nor are there significant interactions between gender and occupation for any of the work categories (all F's < .91, n.s.).

### Emotional responses to various types of work

The next set of analyses examines workers' quality of experience when at work. There are four main variables of interest: positive affect, negative affect, engagement, and self-esteem. Analyses were conducted on the mean responses for the composite variables aggregated over beeps for each individual. A one-way ANOVA was performed for each of the four composite variables by work category.[11] Results are presented in table 3.2.

As might be expected, positive affect varies significantly by work category and is significantly higher in primary work than in either related work activities or preparation work. However, this change in positive affect is relatively small, with a 7 percent decrease in positive affect when performing related work tasks compared to primary work. This percentage slightly increases when comparing primary work to preparation work, where there is a decrease of 10 percent in positive affect.[12] There are no significant effects for negative affect by any type of work category.

There is a significant main effect for engagement by work category. When participants are involved in primary work, they are significantly more engaged than when involved in related work activities or preparation work. Again, there are relatively small effects for engagement across different work tasks. There is a 5 percent decrease in engagement when involved in related work activities compared to primary work, and a 10 percent decrease in engagement in work preparation tasks contrasted with primary work.

A significant main effect is also found for self-esteem by work category. Self-esteem is significantly higher during primary work tasks than during related work tasks or preparation work. Self-esteem decreases by 6 percent in related work activities in contrast to primary work; self-esteem during work preparation is 9 percent lower relative to primary work. Although significant differences in emotional states are found across work contexts, actual changes in emotional states are not large, suggesting that while individuals are not as positive about secondary work activities, they are relatively unbothered when engaged in these activities.[13]

### Self-directed and conforming work orientations

One possible explanation for individuals' higher positive responses when they are engaged in primary versus other kinds of work tasks may be related to issues of flexibility and autonomy at work, as described by Kohn and Schooler (1983). It is possible that the ability to spend time in primary work is associated with having greater flexibility and choice in task selection (i.e., self-direction at work). The next set of analyses examines differences in the work experiences of individuals who are classified as self-directed or conforming in work orientation.

*Who is self-directed?*    To determine what variables might be associated with being self-directed at work, a series of chi-square analyses was conducted with basic demographic and work-related variables. Results of these analyses indicate that being self-directed or conforming in work orientation does not vary significantly by gender, occupation, number of hours worked per week, or annual salary (all $\chi^2 \leq 17.75$, n.s., with varying degrees of freedom). There is a marginally significant effect for education level ($\chi^2 (6) = 12.31$, $p = .06$). Individuals who have continued their education beyond college are more likely to be self-directed at work than those who either do not finish the undergraduate degree or do not continue beyond a bachelor's degree. Aside from education level, individuals categorized as being self-directed in work orientation do not look significantly different from those who are conforming with respect to demographic and work characteristics.

*Time spent at work in various activities*    One-way ANOVAs for the proportion of time spent in each of the four work categories by self-directed/conforming work orientation were conducted. Results show no significant main effects of self-direction for any work category (all F's < 2.48, n.s.). As previously hypothesized, one could argue that if individuals are self-directed at work, then they have more control over how they spend time at work and may choose to focus on tasks that are more interesting and enjoyable – that is, primary work. However, as this analysis shows, people spend approximately the same amount of time in each of the four work categories, regardless of work orientation. Therefore, any differences in emotional experiences between individuals who are self-directed and conforming at work are not attributable to variations in time spent in primary work or any of the other work categories.

*Emotions at work by self-directed and conforming work orientation*    If work orientation does not vary by demographic characteristics or by how people spend time at work, then perhaps it varies by emotional charac-teristics. The next analysis examines the ESM composite variables, pos-itive affect, negative affect, engagement, and self-esteem, for individuals who are self-directed or conforming in work orientation using a one-way ANOVA. Results confirm those of Kohn and Schooler (1983), indicating that individuals who are self-directed in work orientation have signifi-cantly higher levels of positive affect, engagement, and self-esteem while at work regardless of the type of work they are performing.[14] Individuals who are conforming at work have significantly higher levels of negative affect when at work regardless of work task (see table 3.3).[15]

### Spillover effects at home

These results suggest that individuals who are self-directed in work orien-tation have significantly different emotional experiences at work. The next set of analyses examines whether these differences carry over to the home. One might expect that individuals who are conforming in work orienta-tion would experience more negative spillover from work to home. What is less clear is whether positive affect spills over from work to home for those who are self-directed at work. Incorporating ESM composite variables at home, these analyses are designed to determine what the emotional spillover effects are for individuals who differ in work orientation. Four two-way ANOVAs for positive affect, negative affect, engagement, and

Table 3.3 *Means for the composite variables, positive affect, negative affect, engagement, and self-esteem, at work for individuals who are self-directed versus conforming in work orientation*

|                 | Self-directed | Conforming | F          |
|-----------------|---------------|------------|------------|
| Positive affect | 14.30         | 10.84      | 162.62***  |
| Negative affect | 2.55          | 4.14       | 42.59***   |
| Engagement      | 9.26          | 7.70       | 160.22***  |
| Self-esteem     | 21.44         | 17.63      | 258.19***  |

*Note:* *** p < .001

self-esteem by place (home or work) and work orientation (self-directed or conforming) were conducted.

For positive affect, there is a significant main effect for self-directed and conforming work orientation (F $(1, 815)$ = 181.92, p < .001). Individuals who are self-directed in work orientation score 24 percent higher on positive affect than those who are conforming regardless of whether they are at home or at work, suggesting that autonomy and control at work are associated with positive spillover effects at home. There is no main effect for place (F $(1, 815)$ = .94, n.s.); mean positive affect is the same at home and at work. There is, however, a significant interaction between place and work orientation (F $(1,815)$ = 15.52, p < .001). To isolate significant effects within the interaction, follow-up one-way ANOVAs for positive affect by home and work were calculated separately for each work orientation. Individuals who are self-directed at work have a slight but significant increase (4 percent) in positive affect in moving from home to work (F $(1, 402)$ = 3.91, p < .05, $\bar{X}$ = 13.71 for home, $\bar{X}$ = 14.30 for work). In contrast, individuals who are conforming at work show a small but significant decrease (8 percent) in positive affect in moving from home to work (F $(1, 413)$ = 13.72, p < .001, $\bar{X}$ = 11.81 for home, $\bar{X}$ = 10.84 for work). Figure 3.1 graphically represents the interaction between work orientation and place for positive affect.

Negative affect varies significantly by both place and work orientation (F $(1, 827)$ = 23.32, p < .001 and F $(1, 827)$ = 44.48, p < .001, respectively). Regardless of whether individuals are self-directed or conforming in work orientation, there is a 32 percent increase in negative affect in moving from home to work, suggesting that being at work is more stressful, frustrating, and anxiety-producing than being at home. Regardless of place (work or home), individuals who have a conforming work orientation are more negative than those who are self-directed; overall, these

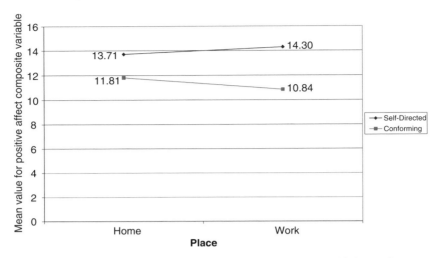

Figure 3.1 Positive affect at home and work by self-directed versus conforming work orientation

individuals score 32 percent higher on negative affect than those who are self-directed.

There is also a significant interaction of place and work orientation (F (1,827) = 8.24, p < .01). One-way ANOVAs for negative affect by place for individuals who are self-directed or conforming in work orientation were performed to determine exactly how negative affect differs at home and at work. As figure 3.2 shows, for individuals who are self-directed in work orientation, there is no effect of place on negative affect (F (1, 410 = 2.94, n.s.); negative affect remains relatively constant between home and work ($\bar{X}$ = 2.23 for home, $\bar{X}$ = 2.55 for work). However, for individuals who are conforming in work orientation, negative affect increases 45 percent in moving from home to work ($\bar{X}$ = 2.86 for home, $\bar{X}$ = 4.14 for work, F (1, 417) = 22.17, p < .001), suggesting that the overall increase in negative affect at work is primarily driven by those individuals who perceive their work as uninteresting and see themselves as having little control over their work tasks.

As shown in figure 3.3, engagement also varies significantly by place (F (1, 829) = 449.02, p < .001). For all individuals regardless of work orientation, there is a 31 percent increase in engagement at work compared to home. There is also a significant main effect for work orientation (F (1,829) = 206.49, p < .001). Individuals who are self-directed in work orientation are 20 percent more engaged than those who are conforming

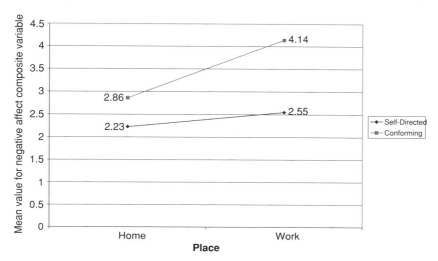

Figure 3.2 Negative affect at home and work by self-directed versus conforming work orientation

regardless of whether they are at home or at work. In turn, there is a significant interaction between place and work orientation (F (1, 829) = 4.66, p < .05). Post-hoc one-way ANOVAs for engagement by place were performed for individuals who were self-directed or conforming in work orientation. Regardless of work orientation, engagement differs significantly by place (F (1, 410) = 270.12, p < .001; F (1, 419) = 182.78, p < .001, for self-directed and conforming, respectively). All individuals are significantly more engaged at work than at home; however, those who are self-directed in work orientation have higher engagement scores overall.

As shown in figure 3.4, the analysis for self-esteem indicates there is a significant main effect for place (F (1, 820) = 119.83, p < .001). Overall, individuals report significantly higher (11 percent) self-esteem at work than at home. There is also a significant main effect for work orientation (F (1, 820) = 305.77, p < .001); individuals who are self-directed at work report significantly higher (19 percent) self-esteem than those who are conforming. In turn, there is a significant interaction of place and work orientation for self-esteem (F (1, 820) = 13.06, p < .001). One-way ANOVAs of self-esteem by place were conducted separately by work orientation. Those who are self-directed in work orientation have a significant main effect of place on self-esteem (F (1, 407) = 110.13, p < .001). These individuals score 14 percent higher on self-esteem at work than at

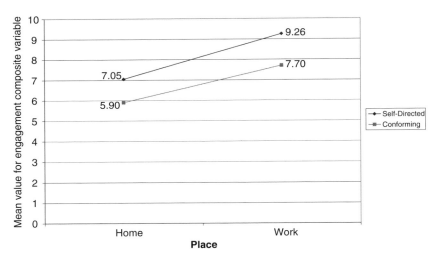

Figure 3.3 Engagement at home and work by self-directed versus conforming work orientation

home. Workers with a conforming work orientation also have a significant main effect of place (F (1, 413) = 25.95, p < .001); they score 8 percent higher on self-esteem at work than at home. Overall, however, individuals who are self-directed at work have higher self-esteem and experience an increase between home and work that is nearly twice that of those who are conforming.

### Nesting emotions within individuals: multi-level models

The univariate two-factor analyses reported above suggest a spillover effect from work to home. One limitation of these analyses is that the ESM composite variables are aggregated at the individual level. Hierarchical linear modeling (HLM) allows for the analysis of both real-time data (ESM beeps) and individual-level characteristics that may predict moment-to-moment emotion outcomes. Multi-level models were therefore constructed to examine the effects of both beep-level and individual-level characteristics on emotion outcomes.[16]

For all models, an ESM composite variable (positive affect, negative affect, engagement, or self-esteem) created at the beep level was the outcome at Level-1. The primary Level-1 predictor of interest is whether individuals were at home or at work.[17] Although multiple predictors were considered at the person level (Level-2), analyses showed that the dichotomous variable identifying individuals who are self-directed

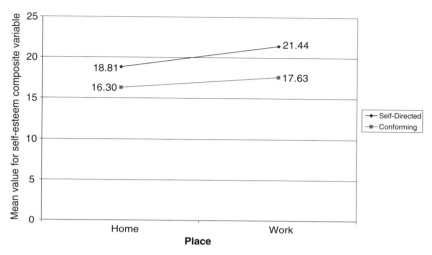

Figure 3.4 Self-esteem at home and work by self-directed versus conforming work orientation

versus conforming in work orientation was the strongest individual predictor with the most explanatory power for between-person variation.[18] Therefore, the final model for all three "positive" ESM variables included place (uncentered) at Level-1 and self-directed/conforming (uncentered) entered on both the intercept and slope at Level-2.[19]

The unconditional model for all four ESM variables (one-way ANOVA with random effects) resulted in significant variance both within and between individuals, which justified the addition of predictors at both the beep and individual levels. To determine the explanatory capacity of both Level-1 and Level-2 predictors, the proportions of variance in the outcome variable that exist within and between people were calculated.[20] The addition of place (home or work) as a predictor at Level-1, explained between 6 and 19 percent of the within-person variance (positive affect = 6%, engagement = 19%, self-esteem = 10%).[21] When work orientation was included as a predictor at the intercept (home) at Level-2, 10 to 18 percent of the variance between individuals at home was explained (positive affect = 10%, engagement = 16%, self-esteem = 18%). For the slope (work) at Level-2, the addition of work orientation explained between 10 and 14 percent of the variation between individuals at work (positive affect = 14%, engagement = 10%, self-esteem = 10%).

The final models for positive affect, engagement, and self-esteem support the results from the two-way ANOVAs. Individuals have higher positive affect when they are at home compared to work. However, those who are self-directed in work orientation have higher values for positive affect both at home and work compared to individuals who are conforming. Engagement is higher overall at work, and those who are self-directed in work orientation find both home and work experiences to be more engaging than individuals who are conforming. The results for self-esteem are similar to those for engagement. Overall, individuals have higher self-esteem when they are at work, but individuals who are self-directed in work orientation report higher self-esteem both at home and work compared to those who are conforming. The similarity in the results for the three positive variables is not surprising. Individuals who are more self-directed in work orientation have greater autonomy and control at work and consequently are more positive, engaged, and have higher self-esteem.[22]

What is most interesting about the three final HLM models is that engagement is the "strongest" model in terms of variance explained by the predictors. The inclusion of place at Level-1 explains 19 percent of the variance in engagement that occurs within persons. Therefore, simply being at work explains nearly one-fifth of the variation that occurs within an individual's moment-to-moment assessments of engagement for beeps occurring at home and work. Similarly, incorporating self-direction at Level-2 explains 16 percent of the variation in engagement that occurs between persons at home, and 10 percent of the between-person variation at work. It appears, then, that self-direction has a strong association with task engagement. These analyses combine to suggest that it is not necessarily the characteristics of the job itself that determine whether someone has a self-directed work orientation or not, but how engaged the individual is with the task. This is supported by the finding that individuals who are self-directed in work orientation do not spend significantly more time in primary work compared to individuals who are conforming. Instead, it appears that self-directed individuals may be more engaged in their work, regardless of whether it is primary or secondary work.

## Discussion

The results presented in this chapter indicate that people spend only 2 to 2.5 hours a day engaged in primary work tasks (i.e., approximately one-fourth of their time at work), and this does not seem to vary by occupational category or gender. Though not surprising, this finding does provide confirmation of people's suspicions that they are spending less time at work doing what they consider their "real job." When individuals are engaged in primary work tasks, they have the most positive emotional experiences at work. They are more positive in their affect, more engaged, and have higher assessments of self-esteem than when involved in secondary tasks. However, the actual differences in emotional states experienced in primary versus secondary work tasks are relatively small, with decreases in positive emotions ranging from 5 to 10 percent when comparing secondary to primary tasks.

Regardless of work orientation, individuals spend similar amounts of time engaged in primary and secondary work tasks. Therefore, it is not the case that self-directed individuals spend a higher proportion of time engaged in primary work, which helps to explain the small effect sizes for primary versus secondary work. Nonetheless, individuals who are self-directed in work orientation do have more positive experiences at work, and report higher positive affect, lower negative affect, and higher engagement and self-esteem than those who are conforming. What seems to be important for job satisfaction, then, is not the type of work individuals are doing, but how self-directed they are in their work. The effect sizes for work orientation are more than twice as large as those for primary versus secondary work, ranging from 20 to 32 percent on positive affect, engagement, and self-esteem. For negative affect, the effect is even greater: conforming individuals are 38 percent higher on negative affect than self-directed individuals.

At both home and work, self-directed individuals are more positive, more engaged, and have higher self-esteem than conforming individuals. For positive affect, self-directed individuals see a small but significant *decrease* from work to home, whereas conforming individuals see a small but significant *increase* from work to home. For engagement, both self-directed and conforming individuals see a significant and fairly large decrease (approximately 31 percent) from work to home, although self-directed individuals are more engaged overall both at home and at work. Results for self-esteem are similar to those for engagement: both self-directed and conforming individuals see a significant decrease from work to home, with self-directed individuals having higher self-esteem overall. These findings thus suggest that individuals who are self-directed in work orientation do experience positive spillover from work to home since they score significantly higher on all measures at home as well as at work.

With respect to negative affect, individuals who are conforming in work orientation see a large increase (45 percent) in negative affect at work, whereas there is no increase in negative affect from home to work for self-directed individuals. Contrary to Hochschild (1997), it is not the case that individuals, particularly women, feel happier at work compared to home; overall, workers experience a decrease in positive affect at work compared to home. Rather, it appears that people are more engaged at work than at home, and that job satisfaction may be more dependent on engagement than on whether the job is stressful or whether someone is generally a happy person. Combining these results with those related to self-direction, it seems that individuals who have the flexibility to direct their own work tasks arrange their workday so that more time is spent in tasks that are engaging and from which they experience higher levels of self-esteem. Additional analyses seem to support this. Individuals who are self-directed at work are more likely to respond that they are performing the current activity because they want to; those who are conforming are more likely to be performing the current activity because they have to.[23] This could help explain why self-directed individuals still have higher values for positive affect, engagement, and self-esteem, even though they do not spend significantly more time in primary work.

Individuals, overall, have higher positive affect at home, and yet they are more engaged and experience higher self-esteem while at work. Perhaps engagement in work tasks is necessary to increasing both positive affect at work and subsequent job satisfaction but is not a requirement for positive affect at home. It is possible that there is an increase in positive affect that is associated simply with being in the home environment. Alternatively, the tasks in which individuals are highly engaged at work may not always be positive, such as losing a case or failing to get an account. An individual could experience high levels of engagement at work compared to home without experiencing high levels of positive affect. When work orientation is taken into account, results suggest that individuals who are self-directed experience a small increase in positive affect at work versus home in contrast to those who are conforming. It may be that having the ability to direct work tasks serves as a mediating variable rather than being directly predictive of emotional states.

The number of hours worked per week has not changed significantly in the last thirty years. However, there have been shifts in the numbers of hours worked per week for various populations (Jacobs and Gerson 1998, 2001). Incorporating part-time employees into future analysis would allow for analyses comparing the emotional states and range of tasks for full-time and part-time workers. Part-time employees may be able to spend more time in primary work because they have more limited work time overall or they may find themselves more stressed because they have to perform complicated tasks within a shorter time frame. Self-direction may be less likely in part-time work because of time constraints. It may be that the opportunities for self-direction are a real benefit of full-time workers.

Self-direction at work (interest and control) has a greater effect on both job satisfaction and overall satisfaction than the amount of time individuals spend in primary work. Allowing individuals to have more opportunities for flexibility and control in decision-making at work is likely to have the greatest effect on engagement and job satisfaction. These findings, however, should be viewed in the context of an in-depth evaluation of emotional experience and job satisfaction over a *limited* period of time. It is difficult to draw conclusions related to long-term job satisfaction. A future direction for research on work satisfaction would be to combine the real-time assessments used in this chapter with more global and retrospective assessments.

## NOTES

1. An increase in female participation in the workforce along with increases in educational attainment have resulted in longer workweeks for certain segments of the population. The subsample analyzed in this chapter includes only men and women who are working full time, most of whom have high levels of education. The sample thus represents the segment of the population experiencing an increase in the number of hours worked per week.
2. An individual was considered working full time using two criteria: self-reported full-time status and the number of hours worked in a week (both from the survey). Those who indicated that they worked part time but worked more than 38 hours per week as well as those who indicated that they worked full time were selected for analysis.
3. The mean number of work beeps in the final sample is 14 with a standard deviation of 6. Respondents with fewer than three beeps at work were two standard deviations below the mean.
4. Comparisons on demographic variables between those included in and excluded from the sample analyzed were not significant.
5. Inter-rater reliability analysis resulted in a Cronbach's alpha of .96 with inter-rater correlations ranging from 0.76 to 0.85.
6. Tables describing the tasks for the three other categories (related work, preparation work, personal care/social interaction) are available from the author.
7. ESM measures used in the analysis use the same 0-to-3 scale. Composite ESM variables were constructed by combining emotional state measures at the beep level. These composite variables were then aggregated as means to the individual level for analyses with survey variables.
8. Responses to these items for beeps occurring at work were aggregated to individual level means; values for feeling in control of the situation (control) range from 0.60 to 3.00 and values for interest in the activity (interest) range from 0.13 to 3.00. Individuals who had an aggregated mean on *both* control and interest over 2 were categorized as self-directed in work orientation, while those who had an aggregated mean below 2 for both control and interest were categorized as conforming in work orientation; 228 participants were categorized with this method. The remaining participants were categorized as follows: a mean was calculated for the two variables, interest and control. Individuals with mean values below 2 were classified as conforming while those with mean

values of 2 and greater were classified as self-directed. Five individuals were excluded from analyses because of missing data.

9. Hours worked per week was measured categorically in grouped hour intervals. To obtain an idea of the average number of hours worked per week using a continuous variable, a representative sample from the March 2000 CPS was used to obtain an estimate of the average hours for each interval (analyses available from author). The average for each interval from the CPS was then assigned to each person who fell into that interval for this sample (based on gender). Based on this data, the average workday is 9.36 hours per day (assuming that most people work five days per week). This value was multiplied by 60 to get 561.72 minutes in the average workday.

10. Respondents spent 45.51 percent of the workday doing work-related activities, 26.43 percent of their day doing primary work, 14.89 percent of their day doing preparation work, and 12.30 percent of their day taking care of personal or social matters.

11. The category of personal care/social is excluded from these analyses since it is not a category of primary interest.

12. In computing effect sizes the following formula was used: $(M_{RW}-M_{PW})/M_{PW}$, where $M_{RW} =$ the mean for work related activities and $M_{PW} =$ the mean for primary work. This formula was used in calculating effect sizes for subsequent analyses, substituting appropriate variable means.

13. The ESM form asks respondents the primary reason for performing a task including options "wanted to" and "had to". The proportion of "wanted to" and "had to" work beeps was calculated by dividing the number of responses for each option by the total number of responses in each work category. Analysis of variance tests for these proportions by work category were not significant for the wanted to or had to categories (all F's < 1.70, n.s.). Individuals equally "wanted to" and "had to" perform primary work, related work, and preparation work tasks.

14. Those self-directed in work orientation score 32 percent higher on positive affect, 20 percent higher on engagement, and 22 percent higher on self-esteem than those who are conforming in work orientation.

15. Those conforming in work orientation score 38 percent higher on negative affect than those who are self-directed in work orientation.

16. For all multi-level analyses, HLM (Raudenbush, Bryk, and Congdon 2000) was used. Model development followed standard protocol by beginning with the unconditional model followed by the addition of predictors at both Level-1 and Level-2.

17. The place variable was created with home equal to 0 and work equal to 1. With this method, the place variable can be entered uncentered and the intercept then represents the value at home.

18. Other individual characteristics were also examined, including gender, hours worked per week, job prestige, occupation and work–family conflict. Gender and self-directed versus conforming work orientation were dummy coded so that when entered uncentered into the model, the intercept value is interpretable. Male is coded as 0 and female as 1. Conforming is coded as 0, self-directed as 1. The fourteen occupations were combined into four groups

based on similarity of job duties and job prestige: (1) administrative support, systems analysts, and salespersons; (2) physicians and lawyers; (3) financial analysts/accountants, mid- and high-level managers; and (4) health professionals (other than physicians), professors, psychologists, scientists, writers, and teachers.

19. The equations for Level-1 and Level-2 outcomes for all models with place at Level-1 and self-directed/conforming at Level-2 are as follows:

$$\text{Level-1: } Y = \beta_0 + \beta_1(\text{PLACE}) + r$$
$$\text{Level-2:} \beta_0 = \gamma_{00} + \gamma_{01}(\text{SELFDIR}) + u_0$$
$$\beta_1 = \gamma_{10} + \gamma_{11}(\text{SELFDIR}) + u_1$$

20. This proportion is represented by the intra-class correlation. The formula for calculating differences within people is $\rho = \sigma^2/(\gamma_{00} + \sigma^2)$ and the formula for between people is: $\rho = \gamma_{00}/(\gamma_{00} + \sigma^2)$.

21. The same series of models was run with negative affect as an outcome variable. However, given that prior research has demonstrated that negative spillover occurs between work and home, the three "positive" variables were the primary focus of the multi-level models. The final model for negative affect added place as a Level-1 predictor, self-directed/conforming as a Level-2 predictor, and work–family conflict (entered grand mean centered) as a Level-2 predictor. At home, individuals who are self-directed in work orientation are less likely to be affected by work–family conflict. Overall, high work–family conflict is associated with higher values for negative affect.

22. Because the results from the multi-level analysis were similar to those of the two-way ANOVAs, a complete write-up of the HLM analyses, including tables, is not included here but is available from the author.

23. Individuals who were self-directed in work orientation had a higher proportion of work beeps in which they wanted to perform the current task ($t(419) = -2.92$, $p < .01$; $\bar{X} = .31$ [self-directed] $\bar{X} = .24$ [conforming]). Individuals who were conforming in their work orientation had a higher proportion of work beeps in which they had to perform the current task ($t(419) = 5.20$, $p < .001$; $\bar{X} = .37$ [self-directed] $\bar{X} = .51$ [conforming]). Respondents who were self-directed in work orientation also had a higher proportion of work beeps in which they were performing the current task because they wanted to, had to, *and* had nothing else to do ($t(419) = -2.82$, $p < .01$; $\bar{X} = .32$ [self-directed] $\bar{X} = .24$ [conforming]).

# Commentary

## *Jerry A. Jacobs*

*The use of the ESM to assess happiness, engagement, and self-esteem at work and at home brings important new data to bear on important questions of long-standing interest. Sexton's chapter shows that both work orientation and job tasks are associated with positive and negative affect on the job. These and a series of other specific findings represent substantial contributions to the literature. Sexton is to be commended for distilling a great deal of complex material into an analysis that is relatively simple and easy to understand. My comments focus on four points: (a) the amount of the workday devoted to primary tasks; (b) the nature of self-direction and conformity; (c) the significance of particular moments in time; and (d) a variety of suggestions for future research.*

### Time on task

*One of Sexton's most dramatic findings is that employees spend only a small fraction of their time at work on their primary work tasks. She estimates that only about one quarter of the workday is spent on primary tasks, while about half is spent on related tasks. The remaining quarter is divided between preparing for work and personal and social activities.*

*While I have a number of concerns about the specifics, I think there is an important kernel of truth in the overall conclusion. The principal reservation I have is that a number of the rules for classifying work into "primary work activities" and "other work" are open to challenge. For example, the time managers spend in meetings is classified as a core activity but the time they spend preparing for a meeting is not. Now, surely in many cases, the preparation time is the real work. Many of us have participated in meetings which were productive because of the excellent preparation work done for those meetings and sat glumly through meetings that wasted everyone's time because the groundwork had not been completed. As a result, I am not willing to accept the particular percentages reported in this chapter as the final word on the subject. Nor am I willing to accept the conclusion that there is no variation across occupations in time spent on core activities, since the sample sizes for many of the occupations are quite small. I would also be most interested to know how respondents described a given activity – as essential, peripheral, busywork, and so on.*

*Nonetheless, the bottom line – that a sizable fraction of the workday is spent on non-core activities – may well be the case in many professional and managerial occupations. The cause may be the reduction in support staff that has occurred over the last generation. Secretaries and other administrative personnel used to perform many tasks that professionals now do for themselves. These data suggest that in some cases there might be opportunities for improvements in efficiency if professionals were provided with more support staff. Second, there may be room to reduce the time spent on some of these non-essential tasks. Those of us interested in promoting a shorter workweek see opportunities in these data. Finally, these data should be of interest to those interested in job redesign, since the evidence suggests that there may well be opportunities to restructure jobs in order to improve both satisfaction and efficiency.*

*The link between core activities and positive affect is an important if not surprising finding. If we had an improved classification of activities, we might find even stronger relationships. I found it surprising that negative affect was not higher when professionals were engaged in non-core activities. The physicians I know complain about the time they spend on paperwork, yet this everyday phenomenon does not appear to hold in these data.*

*One possible direction for future research is that job tasks could be classified more finely with respect to their centrality. At one extreme, a few moments may be considered peak aspects of the job. For example, for a professor, giving a keynote address or accepting an award might qualify. Other core tasks could be distinguished more finely. For example, the time surgeons spend talking with their patients surely is a core aspect of the job, but surgeons probably feel that performing surgery is even more central to their mission and, among surgery procedures, some are more challenging and consequential than others. One might call these hard-core and soft-core aspects of the job, although perhaps other, more suitable terminology might be devised. In any event, Sexton's work leads us to think about the range of tasks, from the most central and most satisfying to the most peripheral and least satisfying. This could be useful for practitioners interested in redesigning work, and for those interested in enhancing productivity on the job.*

## Self-Direction and Conformity

*A second notable finding is that self-direction is associated with greater engage-ment at work and positive affect at home. Sexton interprets the good news on the home front as a positive spillover from work to home. This interpretation is in keeping with the Kohn and Schooler view of work as shaping personality. But another possibility is that self-direction is a point of view rather than a description of the nature of a particular task. In other words, whether respondents indicate they are self-directed or conforming at a given point in time, might be viewed as a structural attribute of the job or alternatively as an attitudinal disposition. Whether one's work is self-directed is often ambiguous, and the same situation may be viewed by some as self-directed and by others as conforming. Most people have a boss, and those who do not have clients or others who are at least partly directing their work. In short, it is possible that those who view their work as self-directed are generally more engaged and have higher positive affect throughout their lives. It might be possible in future research to explore the sense of control and interest in housework and other activities at home. Having the same type of data at home and at work would help future researchers to differentiate between these two interpretations of the self-direction effect.*

## Anticipation, reflection, and the moment

*A third topic I would like to discuss concerns a basic assumption of the paper, indeed the whole project, namely that the best way to assess experience is to get as close to it in time as possible. When I first learned of the Experience Sampling Method, the analogy to the work of the impressionist painter George Seurat came to mind. Seurat attempted to depict a scene, such as a tranquil afternoon in the park, as a series of dots on the canvas. While this was a novel way to display light and color in Seurat's day, the concept has become familiar to us today when photographs are stored as a series of dots in digital cameras. The ESM method borrows this logic and applies it to time and experience rather than pictures. Collecting each of these dots is time consuming and expensive at the moment, but perhaps over time the system will provide ever more detail, just as Seurat's thousands of hand-painted dots were eventually followed by the millions of dots stored in a megapixel digital camera.*

*Surely this is a useful and important new methodology that is generating new insights and raising new questions. Perhaps the most useful feature of this approach is that emotional responses can be linked to particular activities occurring at the same time. But I would like to raise the possibility that there are some important aspects of human experience that are likely to be missed in this approach, even if we were to collect a great deal more data on many more subjects. Among the missing elements are the anticipation of future events and the retrospective reassessment of past events. We are more than the sum of our moods measured at particular instants in time. In other words, if you ask me if I feel proud of my work, I might say "no" in an instantaneous reading because the computer just crashed, the database manager is acting kooky, I am having trouble keeping straight all the papers for the conference I am organizing, etc. But if you ask me about this again after the conference,, I might just say*

*"Yes, I'm proud of how it turned out." This feeling would not be the same as whether I am engaged or bored at any particular moment. The same point could be made for anyone involved in long-term projects, such as lawyers working on a case that stretched out over years or project managers involved in rolling out a new product. Thus, I would submit that job satisfaction for professionals is not solely the sum of instantaneous moments but is really a long-term issue that needs to be assessed partly in terms of their anticipation of the significance of their work, and partly in terms of their assessment of projects, and even their unfolding career. Job satisfaction, and presumably satisfaction with other aspects of life as well, has a long-term as well as a short-term element or dimension.*

## Future directions

*Given the ground-breaking nature of this project, it is inevitable that its entire implications are not fully tapped in the first set of papers. I now sketch out a few topics which I hope would be addressed in future work in this area.*

*This chapter is limited to full-timers. In future research it would be nice to include part-time workers as well. Part-time work is very important for work–family researchers and for women's employment in general. The relationship between satisfaction on the job and at home is particularly interesting for part-timers. Even if any given part-timer did not have enough beeps at work, my guess is that adding this group up would produce more than enough beeps for at least some summary statistics. I was pleased to see that this was among the directions that Sexton mentions for future research.*

*The chapter mentions time and pressures on the job, but this focus is not carried through in the empirical sections. Perhaps in future papers more analysis of job stresses and the issue of time spent on the job could be explored. One way to do this might be to explore the issue of multi-tasking at work.*

*Another key finding in this paper is that engagement and self-esteem are higher at work. But respondents are nonetheless less happy at work than at home. Why is this? This is a paradox that remains to be explored. Sexton reports that the greater negative affect is not because of time spent on non-core tasks. I think the answer may be that there is more pressure and stress at work, which generates a greater sense of engagement but also more negative affect. In any event, I would encourage Sexton and her colleagues to address this issue in the future.*

*Self-selection into job types is another topic that warrants further inquiry. I was surprised to find the weakness of the relationship between job type and job orientation. I assume that, in some jobs, such as being a professor, being self-directed is essential for success. The fact that there is no zero-order relationship between job orientation and job type was quite striking.*

*I hope these comments convey the fact that I enjoyed the opportunity to read and comment on this chapter, and that I look forward to learning more of what the ESM approach to studying daily life can teach us.*

## Patricia M. Raskin

*This highly original, well-thought-out research on workers' feelings about what they do at home and at work is an important contribution, not only to the work–family literature, but to the literature on individual differences and the nature of work.*

*Sexton found that most workers spend only about a quarter of their day doing "primary work," and that this time distribution did not differ across occupation (with the exception of teachers) or gender. She also found that positive affect, engagement, and self-esteem increase slightly when individuals are engaged in primary work and that negative affect does not change. Sexton suggests that one explanation for her findings is the degree of flexibility and autonomy people may have when they are engaged in their primary work, at least in this largely professional sample.*

*Although Sexton did not specifically study autonomy and flexibility, she has considered work orientation (self-directed vs. conforming). Work orientation thus becomes the way that workers "own" their work, creating their own meaning, and experiencing autonomy because of their self-directedness. Once again, no differences are found among occupations or between men and women. Work orientation is not just an attitude. Rather, it is probably a personality trait, or individual difference and it takes the lead in both Sexton's research and her argument about autonomy.*

*She reports (almost as an aside) that more education is associated with greater self-direction, but does not consider it central to her research results. In her conclusions she omits this finding as well. Research suggests that this finding is not trivial – more education has been found to be associated with greater career salience which, in turn, has been associated with greater work–family conflict (Raskin 2002), as well as turnover intentions in a sample of middle-class women (Raskin et al. 2001). Friedman and Greenhaus (2000) report findings in their study of business professionals: the more roles are internalized, the less work– family conflict occurs. Although career salience and job involvement are not quite the same variables as self-direction, they are clearly related constructs, and may have the same deep structure origins.*

*Sexton's findings are all in the expected direction: engagement, self-esteem, and positive affect are associated with self-direction, whereas conformists have higher levels of negative affect. One of the questions these findings raise is about the underlying individual difference between these two groups. If self-direction is more than an attitude about work, perhaps even a deep-seated schema associated with career salience and a sense of self-efficacy, then conforming workers may be indicating much more about their general approach to the world – an absence of self-efficacy, or belief that they have some control over their lives. Judge and his colleagues have suggested that self-esteem, self-efficacy, the absence of neuroticism, and locus of control may be markers of a higher order concept, i.e., the absence of neuroticism (Judge et al. 2002). Indeed, Sexton's findings suggest that this may be the case: self-directed individuals have higher positive affect than conforming workers both at work and at home. Conforming individuals decrease in positive affect when they go from home to work (a place where they feel less in control?), whereas self-directed individuals increase slightly in positive affect. Sexton also found general differences in negative affect: conformers have more negative affect than self-directed individuals, regardless of place, and regardless of the increase in negative affect between home and work for both groups.*

*Work orientation is also associated with levels of engagement: self-directed individuals are more engaged than conformers, both at home and at work, even though both types of individuals report more engagement at work than at home. This finding is similar to that of Friedman and Greenhaus (2000). The same findings hold for self-esteem. Self-directed individuals have greater self-esteem than conforming individuals, even though both groups report more self-esteem at work.*

*In contrast to much of the research on work and family, in this study, individual differences made more of an overall difference than place or task. Perhaps this is in part attributable to method: ESM combines the best of qualitative and quantitative methods; it allows for highly individualized experiences to be collected in a random way. Of course, it does not control for response bias: more "positive" or optimistic individuals may respond differently when beeped than those who have a more "negative" perspective. Further, the importance of the design of the diaries cannot be overestimated. Respondents can only check off tasks and feelings delineated for them. With the exception of ethnography, however, no research exists without these constructed biases.*

*The implications of the research reported in this chapter are interesting: men and women do not differ much on how educated they are, how they behave at work, how they feel about work and home, and how self-directed they are. These are important similarities, and they help to remind us that although men and women often occupy different roles, when they occupy the same roles, they often have similar feelings and attitudes.*

*Further, as work–family researchers, we have moved from thinking about work–family balance as being entirely the individual's responsibility to thinking largely about the need for structural change – interventions delivered in part by organizations, in part by government and society as a whole. In the research described in this chapter, we also see some possibilities for helping individuals as well: the more self-directed one is, the more likely one is to be able to navigate potentially conflicting roles. And this can be taught: the more informed adolescents and young adults are about the possible impending conflicts between home and work, the more self-aware they become, and the more conscious their choices can be. Conscious choices are more likely to result in more nuanced identities, greater self-direction, greater internalization of the meaning of work and family, and higher engagement, positive affect, and self-esteem.*

*Luckily, this education does not require vast changes in curriculum. As more and more families of all stripes participate in the labor force, children are increasingly exposed to the realities of two working parents. Working mothers are now the norm; they are the role models for future workers, and research suggests that when working women's mothers have worked themselves, they experience less work–family conflict than when no prior role models have been in their lives at home (Raskin 2002). This shift in the labor force is already having an effect: most young men and women expect to work, and men increasingly expect their wives to continue in the labor force even after having children (Wilkie 1993). There is a strong likelihood that this trend will continue.*

*Sexton has nicely contributed to what will undoubtedly be an on-going dialogue: How do American parents adjust to and cope with both imposed and freely chosen roles, and to what extent are those adaptations associated with individuals, families, organizations, and/or the interactions among them? We see here that men and women have a lot in common when it comes to feelings about work and home. We probably have known that for some time; it's reassuring to have data to support that hypothesis.*

# 4 Women's intrinsic and extrinsic motivations for working

*Sylvia Martinez*

Over the past several decades, there has been a dramatic increase in the employment of married and single women with children. In 1963, 60 percent of children lived in traditional families, where one parent worked outside the home (typically the father) and another took care of the household (Waite and Nielsen 2001:30). In contrast to the 1960s, 67 percent of children now live in families with more than one earner (*ibid.*). Not only are more women working outside the home, a growing number of them are choosing traditionally male professional careers such as medicine and law (Spain and Bianchi 1996).

With more women working full time outside the home, and many choosing demanding careers, work has become a larger part of women's lives. Many women now manage the multiple roles of spouse, mother, and worker. Recognizing these multiple responsibilities, researchers in the area of work and family have emphasized the importance of describing women's work experiences and examining the relationship between women's work lives and their emotional experiences at work and at home (Perry-Jenkins, Repetti, and Crouter 2000). Although this field continues to grow, there is still much to be learned about how women think about their jobs and careers and what rewards they seek from their work experiences.

This chapter investigates these questions using a sample of middle- and upper-middle-class dual-earner families. In contrast to much of the previous research on women's work, which distinguishes between women with careers and women with jobs, the chapter focuses on women's reasons for working, taking into account both the intrinsic and extrinsic rewards they derive from their jobs. The relationship between reasons for working and factors such as job conditions, family characteristics, and emotional states at work and at home are also examined.

## Conceptualizing women's careers

The sociology of work and occupation literature often distinguishes between jobs and careers. Women with careers are typically employed in prestigious occupations and have higher incomes than those with jobs. Career women also enjoy certain levels of job stability and can expect promotions throughout their employment. While useful, this distinction forces one to describe women's work lives as either careers or jobs, which can limit descriptions of women's work experiences and motivations for working.

An example of research that has focused on career women is Goldin's (1997) study of women professionals over several decades. She attempts to incorporate a career path or trajectory model into her exploration of which "career tracks" allow women to successfully manage both a family and a career. She does so by tracing the work experiences of four cohorts of college women over the past century. Goldin identifies "career women" as those who have worked full time for at least two consecutive seven- to ten-year periods (i.e., those who have worked enough years to accrue returns on their job experience). This definition is refined by including only women who have at least college-level educations and whose hourly earnings exceed those of college-educated men in the 25th percentile of earnings.

Goldin's conceptualization of career women is an improvement on other models, and makes distinctions among educational attainment, length of career, and income for understanding women's career trajectories. However, Goldin bases her definition of career women on men's careers or experiences, which overlooks important differences in men's and women's career and life course trajectories. In addition, Goldin does not include women who are not in traditional career tracks in her analyses.

Since few women can actually achieve careers under male standards, some researchers have acknowledged the importance of looking at how women's careers may differ from men's. Han and Moen (1999) argue that not only have the decisions men make about when to retire become more variable, the decision-making process looks very different for women. More importantly, they provide evidence that suggests that women have very different career paths than men. Women, for example, are more likely to have delayed entry (return to paid work after raising children), intermittent, and steady part-time career pathways, while men tend to have orderly or high-geared career pathways.

Regardless of whether women pursue careers or have jobs, they may have similar concerns about balancing work and family obligations. In understanding women's work choices, it is important to examine women's reasons for working and the benefits that motivate their decisions. For example, are women more likely than men to stay in a job because of the health and childcare benefits? Are they more or less likely to value intrinsic job rewards such as feeling challenged by work tasks?

## Job rewards: intrinsic and extrinsic

The idea that there are both extrinsic and intrinsic rewards from work is not a new one; it is embedded in the job satisfaction literature (Kalleberg 1977; Morse 1953). Morse (1953) first suggested that intrinsic job satisfaction – defined as "the degree of satisfaction obtained by the individual employee from performing those tasks which constitute the content of his job" – is one of four crucial indices of overall job satisfaction (14). The other three indices include satisfaction from and identification with the company in which the worker is employed, financial and job status satisfaction, and pride in group performance. While Morse does not explicitly label her financial and job status index as an extrinsic component of work motivation, it seems reasonable to include these measures in models of extrinsic job satisfaction.

In trying to develop a more comprehensive theory of job satisfaction, Kalleberg (1977) examined the relationships among job satisfaction, work values, and job rewards. Unlike Morse's four indices, Kalleberg found six dimensions to job rewards and, ultimately, overall job satisfaction. Among them, he identified an intrinsic dimension, which refers to those characteristics associated with the task itself. This may include, for example, whether the task is interesting or allows the worker to develop and use his or her abilities. The next four dimensions are actually part of an extrinsic component. Kalleberg's extrinsic component, however, includes not only the common notion of financial rewards, but also has a convenience dimension (i.e., good hours, convenient travel to and from work); relationships with co-workers; and career opportunities. The final dimension of work is resource adequacy, which taps into whether workers have the adequate equipment to complete their job tasks. A common theme in Morse and Kalleberg's work is that fulfilling work experiences are not solely based upon receiving monetary rewards, as traditionally conceptualized, but include fulfillment in the tasks performed on the job.

Few researchers however have included benefits (e.g., employer-provided health insurance) in their conceptualizations of extrinsic job rewards. With the rising costs of health care, Americans have become particularly concerned about how their medical needs will be served (Jacobs, Shapiro, and Schulman 1993). Buchmueller and Valetta (1998), for example, found that women who are not covered by health insurance through their husband's employer are willing to work longer hours to acquire health insurance, despite wanting to work part time. Other research has found that employer-provided health insurance reduces job mobility because employees fear that another employer might not provide the same health care plan or coverage (Buchmueller and Valetta 1996).

Such evidence suggests that more attention should be given to the benefits provided at work as an attractive component of a job for extrinsically motivated workers.

## Intrinsic and extrinsic job rewards and family life

In addition to examining the relationship between intrinsic and extrinsic work experiences and job satisfaction, researchers have also examined the effects of work experience on family life. Perhaps the topic of greatest debate centers on how parents' work lives affect children's well-being (Perry-Jenkins, Repetti, and Crouter 2000). Many would agree that parents with extrinsically rewarding jobs are quite capable of providing their children with material resources to ensure their future success.

Researchers have also begun to examine the effects of intrinsic work experience on family life. In exploring the relationship between social class and parents' valuation of self-direction (internal standards of behavior) or conformity (externally imposed rules), Kohn (1969) argued that among the many social conditions explaining this relationship, occupational conditions are of primary importance. He found that fathers who experience occupational self-direction – the absence of close supervision, doing complex work, and working with data or people rather than things – come to value self-direction in other aspects of their lives. Specifically, these fathers value self-direction rather than conformity for their children, meaning that what they most desire from their children is that they show consideration, self-control, and curiosity, rather than behavioral conformity (obedience and neatness, for example).

As an extension of Kohn's work, Parcel and Menaghan (1994b) looked at how both mothers' and fathers' work conditions affect the environments they create for their children and thus influence child outcomes. Like Kohn, they find support for the idea that parents with complex jobs serve as resources for their children. Children of mothers whose jobs are high in occupational complexity, for example, experience better home environments than children of mothers with low job complexity.

## Gender differences in work motivation: work and family influences

Research suggests that men and women may be motivated by different types of job rewards, but the findings are mixed. Those who study job satisfaction have been perplexed by the consistent finding that although women receive fewer job rewards, men and women do not differ significantly in their levels of job satisfaction (Bokemeier and Lacy 1986; Phelan 1994). One explanation is that men and women value different aspects of work. While financial rewards seem to be the most important factor determining job satisfaction among men, women are much more likely to value intrinsic job rewards (Bokemeier and Lacy 1986). Phelan (1994), however, found that for both men and women, job satisfaction is more closely connected to subjective job rewards (intrinsic rewards, recognition of work, social support) than financial rewards.

Research examining the effect of family responsibilities on women's work motivations has also produced mixed results. One line of research, often referred to as "the gender model," suggests that women's work motivations and job perceptions are more strongly influenced by family responsibilities than are men's (Feldberg and Glenn 1982). Filer (1989), for example, argues that women take jobs that offer low wages because these jobs compensate workers with alternative extrinsic rewards such as flexible work hours. These less common extrinsic rewards are offered as a substitute for high wages because having flexible work hours helps women balance work and family responsibilities. Glass and Camarigg (1992), however, have found little support for the idea that women choose jobs because they allow for greater work–family balance. They found that mothers working over 30 hours a week are no more likely to be in jobs that offer flexible work hours, easy work, and the like. In examining job perceptions, Phelan et al. (1993) found that the impact of family-related factors (being married and having children) on worker's assessments of job stresses and benefits is similar for men and women. Similarly, Tolbert and Moen (1998) found that for both men and women, the number of children is unrelated to preferences for specific job characteristics such as short hours, high income, meaningful work, chances for promotion, and job security.

Feldberg and Glenn (1982) have noted that researchers almost always include family variables (e.g., number of children) in models examining women's work experiences, but fail to include such variables when examining men's work experiences, which may account for some of the inconsistencies in research on gender differences in job perceptions and work motivation. Despite such inconsistencies, few would argue that women's work lives are not affected by family demands and obligations; working women are still responsible for the majority of childcare and household responsibilities and to some extent experience conflicts between work and family obligations (Gerson 1985).

### Research focus

This chapter attempts to clarify some of the issues with respect to gender differences in work motivation. First, the chapter examines whether married men and women differ in their motivations for working. Second, the chapter tests whether family responsibilities (in this case, having a preschooler) affect women's and men's work motivation differently. Unlike the research that Feldberg and Glenn (1982) discuss, it is not assumed that family responsibilities only affect women's work motivation; their potential effect on men's work motivation is also examined. Finally, while research has explored the relationship of certain emotions or psychological states to work motivation (e.g., interest and challenge), this chapter expands this focus by examining relationships between work motivation and emotions experienced both at work and at home.

### Hypotheses

*Hypotheses 1a and 1b. Level of autonomy at work will be positively associated with intrinsic work motivation and negatively associated with extrinsic work motivation; the relationship between intrinsic work motivation and job autonomy, however, will be stronger than that between extrinsic motivation and job autonomy.* Having autonomy over work tasks means that workers can control the pace or content of their work. Workers who can make independent decisions about work tasks may feel more challenged by their jobs and thus be more intrinsically motivated (Ross and Mirowsky 1992). If workers are primarily motivated by the extrinsic rewards of work, having responsibility for work decisions may be perceived as burdensome. However, such responsibilities may also be viewed as simply a job requirement and be weakly related to extrinsic work motivation.

*Hypothesis 2. Feelings of stress and boredom at work and of anger and fatigue at the end of the workday will be negatively associated with intrinsic work motivation.* By definition, intrinsic work motivation involves some degree of engagement with work tasks. Workers may find their tasks interesting, challenging, or enjoyable, and derive some degree of satisfaction from using their skills. Consequently they may be less likely to feel stressed or bored with their jobs or to leave work feeling angry and drained. Although some workers may be motivated by both extrinsic and intrinsic job rewards, workers who are primarily motivated by extrinsic job rewards are less likely to have an inherent interest in work tasks and may be more likely to experience negative emotions such as boredom.

*Hypothesis 3a. Mothers with preschoolers may be more likely than those with older children to say that they are working for extrinsic reasons such as flexible work hours and employer-provided benefits.* The evidence regarding the impact of family responsibilities on women's work motivations and job preferences is mixed. If such responsibilities do have an impact on women's job choices and reasons for working, one might expect these preferences to be most evident among mothers of young children. Compared with older children, young children are less likely to spend time at school or in other structured activities. Consequently, many mothers prefer to spend more time at home when their children are young.

*Hypothesis 3b. Fathers with preschoolers may also be likely to say they are working for extrinsic reasons because of their financial obligations to the family.* Some studies suggest that men's job perceptions are rarely influenced by family responsibilities – or are less often influenced than women's job perceptions (Feldberg and Glenn 1982). However, family responsibilities may influence men to seek out jobs that offer high salaries and good benefits, allowing them to fulfill the traditional breadwinner role in the family.

*Hypothesis 4. Regardless of whether they have high intrinsic work motivation, men and women who earn high salaries will view extrinsic work rewards as important.* The consensus is that, for men, high income is the single most important job reward (Major and Konar 1984). Thus men with higher salaries will be more likely to describe their work experiences as extrinsic when compared to men with lower salaries. Ross and Mirowsky (1996) have found that women value high pay just as much as men. Thus women with high salaries should also score high on extrinsic motivation. Although many jobs may offer both high salaries and intrinsic rewards, such as interesting work and the opportunity to use skills and talents, salary is often viewed as validation of such skills and will be perceived as important motivation for working.

## Method

### Sample

The sample consists of 437 women and 358 men who participated in the 500 Family Study (see Hoogstra, this volume, for a description of the study). All are currently employed and have at least one child.[1] Among women in the sample, the average age is 45 years, the average level of education is 16.88 years, and the average annual salary is $46,857. The mean number of hours worked per week for women is about 35 hours. As shown in table 4.1, educational attainment, annual salary, and job prestige scores are higher for the men in the sample. Men also work longer hours, have longer commutes, and are asked to work on short notice more frequently than women.

Table 4.1 *Summary of variables*

| Variable | Total | Women | Men | t statistic |
|---|---|---|---|---|
| Demographics | | | | |
| Age | 45.52 | 44.89 | 46.50 | 3.34*** |
| | (6.12) | (6.00) | (6.18) | |
| Education | 17.26 | 16.88 | 17.71 | 5.37*** |
| | (2.21) | (2.29) | (2.03) | |
| Job characteristics | | | | |
| Annual salary | 64,446 | 46,857 | 85,552 | 15.45*** |
| | (38,887) | (32,127) | (35,691) | |
| Hours worked | 40.53 | 35.44 | 47.16 | 14.20*** |
| | (13.19) | (13.44) | (9.36) | |
| Occ. prestige | 57.65 | 56.27 | 59.34 | 3.25*** |
| | (13.37) | (12.97) | (13.67) | |
| Commute to work | 28.59 | 24.51 | 33.25 | 6.34*** |
| | (18.27) | (17.59) | (17.95) | |
| Works on short notice | 1.28 | 1.08 | 1.53 | 6.25*** |
| | (1.01) | (0.95) | (1.03) | |
| Autonomy | 9.70 | 9.55 | 9.88 | 1.80+ |
| | (2.54) | (2.65) | (2.39) | |
| Family characteristics | | | | |
| Preschooler present | 0.16 | 0.15 | 0.18 | 1.09 |
| | (0.37) | (0.36) | (0.39) | |
| Emotional states | | | | |
| *At work* | | | | |
| Stressed | 2.14 | 2.11 | 2.17 | 1.05 |
| | (0.79) | (0.82) | (0.76) | |
| Bored | 1.16 | 1.16 | 1.16 | −0.02 |
| | (0.92) | (0.99) | (0.83) | |
| *After work* | | | | |
| Angry | 1.34 | 1.33 | 1.36 | 0.60 |
| | (0.76) | (0.79) | (0.71) | |
| Drained of energy | 2.22 | 2.29 | 2.13 | −2.78** |
| | (0.81) | (0.81) | (0.80) | |

*Notes:* Standard deviations appear in parentheses.
+ p < .10; ** p < .01; *** p < .001

### Dependent variables

Measures of *intrinsic* and *extrinsic work motivation* were constructed based on a survey question that asked respondents why they were currently working at their main jobs. Respondents rated each of eight items as being "not true at all," "somewhat true," "true," or "very true" of their reasons for working: (1) the money; (2) the benefits; (3) job security; (4) to become well known in the profession; (5) because they enjoy the tasks involved; (6) to contribute to knowledge in the field; (7) because they like the challenge; and (8) to help people. These items were factor analyzed using principal components analysis with varimax rotation. Separate analyses were conducted for men and women. Analyses resulted in a 2-factor solution.[2]

For women, working because of the challenge presented at work, to contribute knowledge in the field, because of the enjoyment of the tasks involved in the job, to help people, and to become well known in a particular profession had the highest loadings on factor one. These items can be accurately defined as the intrinsic benefits of work. In contrast, the items with the highest factor loadings on factor two can be defined as the extrinsic factors or reasons people typically work – for job security, benefits, or money. These findings are in line with past research that indicates that for women, at least, the intrinsic rewards of work are particularly relevant because they often outweigh extrinsic rewards received (Bokemeier and Lacy 1986; Phelan 1994).

For men, factor loadings for each of the survey items did not differ significantly from those of women. The three highest factor loadings for factor one were currently working to contribute knowledge to the field, because of enjoyment of the tasks involved in the job, and because of the challenge of work. Like the factor analysis for women, the highest factor loadings on factor two for men were working for benefits, job security, and the money.

### Independent variables

*Demographic characteristics*  *Age* and *level of education* were used as controls in all analyses since it was assumed that older and more highly educated women might be more likely to have jobs that allowed them to exercise autonomy and thus might be more intrinsically motivated. Age of respondents is based on year of birth, reported in the parent survey. Level of education was initially measured as a categorical variable, but was recoded into years of education completed.[3]

*Job characteristics*  It was assumed that job characteristics – income, occupational prestige, hours worked per week, length of commute to work, being asked to work on short notice, and job autonomy – might also influence men's and women's experiences of work and their intrinsic and extrinsic work motivations. These variables were thus included in analyses.

*Annual income* was originally coded using the following categories from the survey: $0–$20,000; $20,001–35,000; $35,001–50,000; $50,001–$75,000; $75,001–$100,000; and more than $100,000. This variable was recoded using the midpoint of each category. In other words, the women who reported having annual salaries between $0 and $20,000 dollars were recoded as having annual salaries of $10,000. The midpoint for the last category (more than $100,000) was estimated at $125,000.

Job titles reported by the respondents were matched with *occupational prestige* scores using the 1980 Census prestige codes. Initially, job titles were coded employing the 1990 Census occupation codes. However, since the 1980 Census prestige scores are the most widely used and are the most reliable (Nakao and Treas 1994), job titles were recoded using the 1980 Census occupation codes. These were then easily matched to 1980 Census prestige scores.

To measure *hours worked per week*, respondents were asked to estimate how many hours they spent working at their main job in a typical week, using the following response options: 1–15 hours; 6–25 hours; 26–37 hours; 38–45 hours; 46–50 hours; 51–60 hours; and more than 60 hours. To estimate the average number of hours worked per week by men and women in the sample, this variable was recoded using the midpoint of each category. The difference in hours for the fifth category is five hours (46 to 50), while the difference in the sixth category is ten hours (51–60). These differences were averaged to obtain the upper limit for the seventh category (61 to 67.5); the midpoint for the last category was then estimated at 64.25.

To measure *length of commute to work*, respondents were asked how long it took to get to work on a typical day. Response options were as follows: (1) 1–5 minutes; (2) 6–10 minutes; (3) 11–19 minutes; (4) 20–29 minutes; (5) 30–60 minutes; and (6) more than an hour. A midpoint approximation was used to obtain the average number of minutes it took men and women to get to work. The upper limit on the sixth category was estimated at 90 minutes; thus the midpoint for the last category was estimated at 75 minutes.

The following question was used to assess how often men and women in the sample were asked to *work on short notice*: "How often do you have to do work on short notice for your job or business at times when you had not expected to work or weren't scheduled to work?" Response options ranged from 0 to 4, where 0 = Never; 1 = Once or twice a year; 2 = Once or twice a month; 3 = Once or twice a week; and 4 = Almost daily.

*Level of autonomy at work* is a composite variable that was constructed by summing responses to the following survey items: (1) "I have a lot of opportunity to make my own decisions [at work]"; (2) "I have a lot of say over what happens at my job"; and (3) "I can design or plan most of my daily work." Response options for these items were as follows: 1 = Not true at all; 2 = Somewhat true; 3 = True; 4 = Very true. Composite scores for the sample range from three to twelve; however, the mean for this variable is 9.6, indicating a relatively high level of job autonomy.

*Family characteristics*   Family responsibilities (e.g., presence of a young child in the family) can also be expected to influence women's and possibly men's job choices and work experiences and is included as a predictor in logistic regression models. *Presence of preschooler* indicates whether respondents have a child under the age of five in the home. The variable was coded as a dummy variable, with 1 indicating that fathers or mothers have a child under the age of five, and 0 indicating that they do not.

*Emotional states*   Since individuals who are intrinsically motivated are those who are typically interested in and enjoy what they are doing at work, they may experience lower levels of stress, boredom, anger, and fatigue. Respondents were asked to report their level of *stress* and *boredom* at work, as well as their levels of *anger* and *fatigue* after work. These emotional states were rated on a five-point scale, where 0 = Never; 1 = Hardly ever; 2 = Sometimes; 3 = Often, and 4 = Always. It appears that women in the sample are more likely to say that they experience stress at work and feel drained after work than they are to report feeling bored with their job or angry at the end of the workday (see table 4.1).

### Analyses

To predict how likely currently employed women are to describe their motivations for working as intrinsic or extrinsic, two separate logistic regression analyses were conducted (Long 1997). The first predicts the likelihood of reporting intrinsic motivations for working, while the second predicts the likelihood of extrinsic motivations for working. Both logistic regressions rely on the same four sets of explanatory variables: (1) demographic variables (age of respondent and educational attainment); (2) job characteristics (annual salary, hours worked per week, occupational prestige, length of commute to work, frequency of working on short notice, and level of job autonomy); (3) family characteristics (presence of a preschooler at home); and (4) emotional states (feeling stressed and bored at work and feeling angry and drained of energy after work).

For logistic regression analyses, it was necessary to choose a specific standardized score from the factor analysis as a cutoff point for classifying individuals as having intrinsic and/or extrinsic motivations for working. Theoretically, it seems sound to classify respondents as having a particular orientation to work when their scores are higher than one standard deviation above the mean. That is, respondents with scores above one standard deviation above the mean for factor two would be classified as having an extrinsic work orientation. Given the composition of the sample, however, scores above the mean were chosen as the cutoff point. A more inclusive cutoff point was chosen because respondents in the sample come primarily from middle- and upper-middle-class backgrounds. Had the sample been more varied with respect to socioeconomic status, using one standard deviation above the mean may have been an appropriate cutoff point because it would probably include individuals in the current sample who have scores above the mean. Because this sample is of a higher socioeconomic status, however, the cutoff point has been lowered to include more individuals in each of the two classifications.

## Results

### Correlations among variables

Table 4.2 presents the correlation matrix for variables used in analyses. Because the primary focus of the chapter is on women's motivations for working, the table presents correlations among variables for women in the sample. Of particular interest are the correlations between intrinsic and extrinsic work motivation and job characteristics. Intrinsic motivation is positively and significantly correlated with salary, hours worked per week, and occupational prestige as well as age and educational attainment. Because individuals who are intrinsically motivated are those who work because of the challenge that work offers, the positive correlations between intrinsic work motivation and extrinsic rewards such as salary and job prestige are somewhat surprising. However, it can easily be argued that women who view the intrinsic benefits of work as important are likely to hold jobs that require more education and are rewarded accordingly. As expected, salary and hours worked per week are positively correlated with extrinsic work motivation. However, extrinsic work motivation is negatively correlated with educational attainment and positively correlated with commute time.

An additional relationship of interest is that between level of autonomy at work and work motivation. There is a relatively strong positive correlation between job autonomy and intrinsic work motivation. While the relationship between job autonomy and extrinsic work motivation is not significant, it is negative as expected. Also as expected, there is a fairly strong and negative correlation between boredom and intrinsic motivation. Feelings of anger at the end of the workday are also negatively, though less strongly, correlated with intrinsic work motivation. Boredom

Table 4.2 *Intercorrelations among variables*

| Measure | 1 | 2 | 3 | 4 | 5 | 6 | 7 | 8 | 9 | 10 | 11 | 12 | 13 | 14 | 15 |
|---|---|---|---|---|---|---|---|---|---|---|---|---|---|---|---|
| 1. Intrinsic | – | | | | | | | | | | | | | | |
| 2. Extrinsic | .00 | – | | | | | | | | | | | | | |
| 3. Age | **.12** | .01 | – | | | | | | | | | | | | |
| 4. Education | **.22** | –.13 | **.24** | – | | | | | | | | | | | |
| 5. Salary | **.20** | **.33** | .05 | **.29** | – | | | | | | | | | | |
| 6. Hours | **.26** | **.31** | .14 | .07 | **.54** | – | | | | | | | | | |
| 7. Prestige | **.27** | .00 | .07 | **.45** | **.24** | **.17** | – | | | | | | | | |
| 8. Commute | .01 | .15 | .02 | **.22** | **.27** | **.18** | .09 | – | | | | | | | |
| 9. Short notice | .04 | .02 | –.03 | .08 | **.17** | .12 | .07 | –.02 | – | | | | | | |
| 10. Autonomy | **.40** | –.09 | .02 | **.20** | **.22** | .15 | .09 | .05 | .02 | – | | | | | |
| 11. Preschool | –.04 | –.001 | **–.45** | .02 | .02 | –.11 | .05 | .06 | –.05 | .04 | – | | | | |
| 12. Stress | .05 | **.16** | .00 | **.14** | **.25** | **.26** | **.24** | .09 | **.23** | –.03 | **.10** | – | | | |
| 13. Bored | **–.45** | **.17** | .02 | **–.10** | –.05 | –.06 | **–.13** | .04 | –.02 | **–.29** | –.06 | .06 | – | | |
| 14. Angry | **–.13** | **.11** | .01 | –.04 | **.16** | **.23** | –.03 | .06 | **.21** | –.09 | –.03 | **.46** | **.20** | – | |
| 15. Drained | –.07 | **.15** | .09 | –.01 | .09 | **.26** | .08 | .03 | **.14** | –.09 | –.05 | **.39** | .09 | **.38** | – |

*Note:* All significant correlations (p < .05) are in bold.

and anger are in turn positively correlated with extrinsic work motivation. Although feeling stressed at work and drained at the end of the day are not significantly correlated with intrinsic work motivation, they are positively and significantly correlated with extrinsic work motivation. These correlations suggest that job autonomy and feelings of boredom at work may predict whether women describe their work motivations as intrinsic or extrinsic.

Correlations were also analyzed for men. The pattern of correlations between intrinsic motivation and other variables was similar to that of women. Men with higher intrinsic motivation scores are more educated, have higher salaries, work longer hours, have higher job prestige rankings and greater job autonomy, and experience lower levels of boredom at work. There were no significant correlations with extrinsic work motivation for education, hours worked, commute to work, levels of stress and boredom at work, and levels of anger or fatigue after work. This absence of significant correlations with extrinsic work motivation may indicate that most men view their primary role in the family as that of breadwinner.

### Women's intrinsic work motivation

Table 4.3 presents the results for the logistic regression models predicting high intrinsic and extrinsic motivation for women; coefficients for intrinsic motivation appear in the first column of results. As in the correlation matrix presented in table 4.2, job prestige is positively and significantly associated with high intrinsic work motivation. The coefficient for job prestige is quite small, but it should be noted that occupational prestige scores range from 22 to 86; thus, for every one point increase in occupational prestige, the likelihood of scoring above the mean on intrinsic work motivation increases by 3 percent. More prestigious occupations, such as upper management or professional jobs (e.g., doctors and lawyers) can be characterized as jobs that provide mentally stimulating tasks on an everyday basis. It is no surprise, then, that women with more prestigious positions are more likely to have an intrinsic work orientation.

As hypothesized, women with higher levels of job autonomy and lower levels of boredom at work are more likely to have an intrinsic work orientation. For every unit increase in level of autonomy at work, the odds of having an intrinsic work orientation increase by 40 percent. In turn, for every unit increase in level of boredom at work, the odds of having an intrinsic work orientation decrease by 51 percent. Anger is negatively though marginally associated with high intrinsic work motivation, when controlling for other variables in the model. For women who say they

Table 4.3 *Summary of logistic regression analyses predicting intrinsic and extrinsic work motivation for women*

| Variable | Intrinsic work motivation | Extrinsic work motivation |
|---|---|---|
| Demographics | | |
| Age | 0.03 | 0.02 |
| Education | −0.02 | −0.47*** |
| Job characteristics | | |
| Salary | 0.02 | 0.49*** |
| Hours worked | 0.21 | 0.28* |
| Job prestige | 0.03* | 0.01 |
| Commute | 0.02 | 0.16+ |
| Work short notice | 0.07 | −0.06 |
| Autonomy | 0.34*** | −0.09 |
| Family characteristics | | |
| Presence of preschooler | −0.52 | 0.47 |
| Emotional states | | |
| *At work* | | |
| Stressed | 0.01 | 0.02 |
| Bored | −0.67*** | 0.33* |
| *After work* | | |
| Angry | −0.37+ | −0.36+ |
| Drained | −0.23 | 0.30 |
| Intrinsic motivation | – | 0.17 |
| Extrinsic motivation | 0.11 | – |

*Note:* + p < .10; * p < .05; ** p < .01; *** p < .001

often feel angry at the end of the workday the odds of scoring above the mean on intrinsic work motivation are about 30 percent lower than for women who say they sometimes feel angry. However, conclusions about the findings for emotions should be made with caution since one could easily argue that work experiences are better predictors of emotional states.[4]

### Women's extrinsic work motivation

Results of the logistic regression model used to predict high extrinsic work motivation for women are presented in the second column of table 4.3. Consistent with the correlations presented earlier, education, salary, and hours worked per week appear to be most strongly associated with an extrinsic work orientation. The negative coefficient for education indicates that the probability of having an extrinsic work orientation decreases as years of education increases. For every unit increase in level of education, the odds of having an extrinsic work orientation decrease by a factor of .63 ($e^{-0.47} = .63$). For women with four-year college degrees, for example, the odds of having an extrinsic work orientation are 37 percent lower relative to women with some college education. One explanation for this finding could be that women with higher levels of education are more intrinsically motivated than are women with lower levels of education. However, when controlling for intrinsic motivation (intrinsic scores were added to the model), the education effect remains.

Another explanation for this finding may be that more highly educated women have spouses who are highly educated and earn relatively high incomes. Therefore, the wife might not feel pressured to work for extrinsic reasons. Surprisingly, controlling for spouse's salary in secondary regression analyses did not significantly change the negative association between educational attainment and extrinsic work motivation. Controls for marital status (married versus single, divorced, or widowed) and full- versus part-time work status were also added to the model. Neither variable was significant, and the education effect remained virtually the same.

To explore whether occupation might account for the negative association between education and extrinsic work motivation, extrinsic work orientation was crosstabulated with occupation. Results indicate that, among women, managers are most likely to have an extrinsic work orientation.[5] Approximately 66 percent of the women managers can be classified as having an extrinsic work orientation. In contrast, lawyers and judges were the least likely to report having an extrinsic work orientation. A dummy variable identifying managers was thus added to the logistic regression model predicting high extrinsic work motivation for women. The variable was significant (coefficient = 1.103, $p < .001$). Managers were about three times ($e^{1.103} = 3.01$) more likely than those in other occupations to score above the mean on extrinsic work motivation. These results suggest that the negative coefficient for education in the original model was due to managers in the sample, whose jobs typically do not require advanced degrees.

Finally, to evaluate the theory that extrinsic motivation might be driven more by the benefits of healthcare and/or retirement options, extrinsic work orientation was crosstabulated with a variety of benefits available at respondents' jobs. The benefits most frequently available to women with an extrinsic work orientation were health insurance, paid absences, retirement plans, and stock options. Secondary logistic regressions were then conducted with extrinsic work orientation as the dependent variable and job benefits as predictors, controlling for occupation. Lawyers and judges were used as the referent category. All four work benefits were positively associated with high extrinsic work motivation. For example, women who have health insurance available on the job are about 9.56 times more likely to have an extrinsic work orientation than are women who do not have access to health insurance on the job. Similarly, when retirement plans are available on the job, women are 6.69 times more likely to score above the mean on extrinsic work motivation than are women without retirement plans at work. Additionally, for all regression models including benefits as predictors, being a manager was always marginally significant ($p < .10$) or significant ($p < .05$), showing a positive association with high extrinsic work motivation.

As hypothesized, women who have higher incomes are more likely to have an extrinsic work orientation than women with lower incomes. Women who make annual salaries between $50,001 and $75,000 for example, are 1.63 times more likely to score above the mean on extrinsic work motivation than women who make annual salaries between $35,001 and $50,000. Because these women are well compensated, they are more likely to include income as a reason for working at their main jobs.

Working more hours per week also increases the likelihood that women have an extrinsic work orientation. For example, women who work 46 to 50 hours per week are about 1.32 times more likely to have an extrinsic work orientation than women who work 38 to 45 hours per week. As shown in the correlation matrix, there is a relatively strong and positive correlation between salary and work hours, suggesting that women who are extrinsically motivated may be willing to devote more hours to work if they are compensated for their efforts. Alternatively, women who are extrinsically motivated may work longer hours to qualify for job benefits such as health insurance, which may not be available to employees who work part time.

Job autonomy is not a significant predictor of extrinsic work motivation, although the direction of the effect is negative, as expected. The overriding importance of monetary rewards for those scoring high on extrinsic work motivation may explain the lack of effect for job autonomy. Contrary to expectations, having a preschooler at home has no significant association with high extrinsic work motivation. As suspected, boredom at work is positively associated with high extrinsic work motivation. Women who indicate that they are often bored at work are about 1.39 times more likely to score above the mean on extrinsic work motivation than women who say they are sometimes bored at work. As in the model for intrinsic work orientation, the coefficient for anger is negative and marginal. Since the coefficient for anger is virtually the same in both models, anger does not help to distinguish between women with intrinsic versus extrinsic work orientations.[6]

Table 4.4 *Summary of logistic regression analyses predicting intrinsic and extrinsic work motivation for men*

| Variable | Intrinsic work motivation | Extrinsic work motivation |
|---|---|---|
| Demographics | | |
| Age | −0.01 | 0.00 |
| Education | 0.36+ | −0.26 |
| Job characteristics | | |
| Salary | −0.03 | 0.33* |
| Hours worked | 0.13 | 0.17 |
| Job prestige | 0.02 | 0.01 |
| Commute | −0.11 | 0.03 |
| Work short notice | 0.29+ | 0.04 |
| Autonomy | 0.33*** | −0.08 |
| Family characteristics | | |
| Presence of preschooler | −0.22 | −0.15 |
| Emotional states | | |
| *At work* | | |
| Stressed | −0.26 | −0.50* |
| Bored | −0.59** | 0.20 |
| *After work* | | |
| Angry | −0.004 | 0.68** |
| Drained | −0.08 | −0.30 |
| Intrinsic motivation | – | −0.09 |
| Extrinsic motivation | −0.12 | – |

*Note:* + p < .10; * p < .05; ** p < .01; *** p < .001

### Gender and work orientation

While the primary focus of this chapter has been on women's motivations for working, the same logistic regression models were replicated for men in the sample to test whether women's motivations for working are more strongly influenced by family obligations than men's. Results for logistic regression models predicting extrinsic and intrinsic work orientations for men are presented in table 4.4. Including family characteristics as predictors of men's work motivation offers no support for the suggestion that women's work experiences are shaped by family obligations more so than men's. The presence of a preschooler is not significant in predicting intrinsic or extrinsic work orientation for either women or men.

Overall, results of analyses predicting intrinsic and extrinsic work motivation are quite similar for men and women. Like the results for women, the strongest predictors of high intrinsic motivation for men are job autonomy and boredom experienced at work. On average, men with higher levels of autonomy and lower levels of boredom at work are more likely to score above the mean on intrinsic work motivation. One difference, however, is education is a stronger predictor of an intrinsic experience of work for men than women, though the effect is marginal. Men with college degrees, for example, are 1.46 times more likely to report having an intrinsic experience of work than men with only some college education.

In predicting extrinsic work motivation, annual salary is significant for men as it was for women. Men with higher annual incomes are more likely to score above the mean on extrinsic work motivation. While level of anger experienced after work was only marginally significant in predicting high extrinsic motivation among women, it is significant in the model for men. The direction of effect, however, differs. For women, lower levels of anger are marginally associated with high extrinsic work motivation. In contrast, men reporting higher levels of anger at the end of the day are more likely to score above the mean on extrinsic work motivation. For example, men who report sometimes feeling angry after work are almost twice as likely to have an extrinsic work orientation as men who report rarely feeling angry after work. Despite the monetary rewards of their jobs, men who lack autonomy or challenge at work may become more easily frustrated than women. Interestingly, men with lower levels of stress at work are more likely to have an extrinsic work orientation than men with higher levels of stress.[7] Perhaps extrinsically rewarding jobs typically lack high levels of autonomy and entail less responsibility (over others, for example) and thus are less stressful.

### Discussion

This chapter shows that there are two distinct components to women's and men's work motivation. Factor analysis of eight items regarding respondents' reasons for working at their main job revealed two factors, identified as intrinsic and extrinsic work motivation. Items with high factor loadings on intrinsic work motivation included wanting to become well known in their profession, enjoying the tasks involved, contributing to knowledge in the field, being challenged at work, and helping people. Items with high loadings on extrinsic work motivation include monetary rewards, benefits, and job security.

Predictors of intrinsic and extrinsic work motivation were identified using logistic regression analyses. As expected, job autonomy was a significant positive predictor – and boredom a significant negative predictor – of intrinsic work motivation for both men and women. For women, high job prestige was also a positive and significant predictor of intrinsic work motivation. As suggested, more prestigious occupations may offer more challenging work and thus be more intrinsically rewarding. Although job prestige is not a significant predictor of intrinsic motivation for men, the direction of effect is also positive.

As hypothesized, annual earnings were a strong positive predictor of extrinsic work motivation for both men and women. For women, educational attainment was a significant negative predictor of extrinsic work motivation, an effect that can be attributed to occupation. Women managers are more likely than women in other occupations to have an extrinsic work orientation and are less likely to have advanced degrees. In addition, for women, hours worked per week were also a significant predictor of extrinsic work motivation, even after controlling for salary. Although women are more likely to work part time than men, and many prefer to work part time so that they can spend more time with their children, women who work primarily for extrinsic reasons may choose to work full time so that they can qualify for employer-provided benefits.

The results of supplementary analyses show that job benefits such as health insurance and retirement plans have become particularly valued extrinsic job rewards for women. At a time when healthcare costs are high, many women are choosing to work primarily for extrinsic reasons. Women who score high on extrinsic work motivation are much more likely to report that they have jobs with health insurance, paid absences, retirement plans, and stock options.

By providing a better understanding of women's motivations for working, this chapter is a first step toward understanding the potential impact of women's work experiences on family life. Research has suggested that women's work can affect child outcomes such as academic achievement and emotional development (Perry-Jenkins, Repetti, and Crouter 2000). Results of this research are inconsistent, but researchers generally agree that mothers are now spending less time with their children because more of them are working and more are choosing to work full time.

Research has also shown that the nature of women's work can affect child outcomes. In investigating how parents' work conditions affect the home environments they create for their children and thus impact subsequent child outcomes, Parcel and Menaghan (1994b) find that parents with complex jobs provide richer home environments for their children. With respect to this chapter, women who work primarily for extrinsic reasons such as pay or job benefits appear to be less likely to have jobs that allow for job autonomy and complexity, which could have negative consequences for how these women manage their family lives and thus negative consequences for their children.

NOTES

1. Of the 508 women who participated in the 500 Family Study, 439 indicated that they were currently employed (as opposed to retired, disabled, looking for work, or unemployed and not looking); two currently employed women were eliminated from the sample because of coding errors in the response to the age of the youngest child in the home. Of the 376 men who participated in the study, 358 were currently employed.

2. Factor loadings and eigenvalues for work orientation (intrinsic and extrinsic) are presented below.

| | Women | | Men | |
| | Factor loadings | | Factor loadings | |
| Item | 1 | 2 | 1 | 2 |
| --- | --- | --- | --- | --- |
| **Factor 1: Intrinsic work motivation** | | | | |
| Currently working because I like being challenged at work | .83 | −.01 | .78 | −.02 |
| Currently working to contribute to knowledge in my field | .82 | −.03 | .83 | −.04 |
| Currently working because I enjoy the tasks involved in my job | .81 | −.10 | .79 | −.01 |
| Currently working to help people | .70 | −.04 | .63 | −.14 |
| Currently working to become well-known in my profession | .62 | .10 | .69 | .18 |
| **Factor 2: Extrinsic work motivation** | | | | |
| Currently working for the job security it provides | .15 | .85 | .16 | .75 |
| Currently working for the benefits | −.03 | .83 | .01 | .87 |
| Currently working for the money | −.14 | .67 | −.22 | .71 |
| Eigenvalues | 2.94 | 1.89 | 2.87 | 1.88 |

3. Respondents were asked to report their level of education by selecting one of the following response categories: (1) did not finish high school; (2) graduated from high school or equivalent (GED); (3) after graduating high school, attended a vocational school, junior college, or another type of two-year school, but did not complete a degree; (4) after graduating high school, completed a degree at a vocational school, junior college, or another type of two-year school; (5) after graduating high school, went to college but did not complete a four-year degree; (6) graduated from a four-year college; (7) completed a master's degree or equivalent; or (8) completed a Ph.D., MD, JD, or other equivalent professional degree.

This variable was recoded to estimate the average number of years the women in the sample completed. It was assumed that respondents who reported not finishing high school had attended some high school and were therefore coded as having 10 years of education. Respondents who reported having graduated from high school or the equivalent were coded as having

12 years of education. Those who attended a vocational school or junior college but failed to complete a degree were coded as having 13 years of education. Respondents who reported having completed a two-year degree at a vocational school or junior college were coded as having 14 years of education. Respondents who attended a four-year college but did not complete four-year degrees were coded as having 14.5 years of education. Respondents with four-year college degrees were coded as having 16 years of education. Recipients of master's degrees or the equivalent were coded as having 18 years of education. Those with Ph.D.s or other professional degrees were coded as having 20 years of education.

4. Survey items ask only about negative emotion states (feeling stressed, bored, angry, or drained). To examine the relationship between positive emotional states and intrinsic work motivation, additional analyses were conducted using measures from the Experience Sampling Method (ESM; see Hoogstra, this volume for a description). Specifically, analyses examined the relationship between "flow" and intrinsic work motivation. Conceptualized by Csikszentmihalyi (1990), "flow" is defined as a balance of skills and challenges in the completion of tasks. Csikszentmihalyi has found that when individuals are in flow, they experience a sense of deep concentration and enjoyment. Since individuals who have an intrinsic work orientation are by definition those who enjoy their work and feel challenged by it, it was assumed that they might be more likely to experience flow when engaged in work tasks.

An ESM beep was identified as a "flow beep" when an individual's rating of the challenges of particular activities and his or her ability to deal with those challenges was above his or her own mean for all activities. A proportion of overall flow beeps was obtained by dividing the number of flow beeps by the number of total beeps. The proportion of flow beeps in work contexts was obtained by dividing the number of flow beeps that occurred at work by the number of work beeps. This allowed a calculation of a ratio of flow beeps at work to the proportion of flow beeps overall. A ratio that is greater than one indicates that a person experiences more flow at work than overall. This measure of work flow was added to the logistic model predicting intrinsic work motivation for women. Although the relationship between work flow and intrinsic work motivation was positive, it was not significant.

5. Occupations were coded into eleven categories: Executive/Managerial; Physician; Nurse/Therapist/Counselor; Engineer/Architect; Professor/Scientist/Social Scientist (Ph.D.); Scientist/Social Scientist/Technician (non-Ph.D.); Lawyer/Judge; Teacher/Librarian/Religious Worker; Writer/Artist; Sales/Public Relations; and Service/Clerical/Manual.

6. The relationship between work flow and extrinsic work motivation was also examined (see note 4 above for a description of this variable). It was assumed that individuals who score high on extrinsic work motivation might be less likely to experience flow when engaged in work tasks. As expected, when work flow was added to the logistic regression model predicting extrinsic work motivation for women, the coefficient for this variable was negative and significant ($-0.80$, $p < .01$). Women who experience above-average levels of

flow at work are thus less likely to score above the mean on extrinsic work motivation.

7. The relationship between work flow and work motivation (intrinsic and extrinsic) was also examined for men (see notes 4 and 6 above). Among the men, flow at work was associated with work experiences in the expected directions (positive for intrinsic work motivation and negative for extrinsic work motivation), but was not significant in either logistic regression model.

# Commentary

## Phyllis Moen

*This chapter aims to move beyond simply assessing gender differences to look at within-gender workforce heterogeneity. Specifically, Martinez describes variations in the motivations animating the occupational and life choices of contemporary working women. In doing so, she contributes to our understanding of the complexity of the "work–family" interface and to a finer grained portrayal of women in the workforce.*

*By looking at intrinsic as well as extrinsic motivations for employment, Martinez builds upon and extends a body of work that has traditionally focused more on men than women. Subsequent analyses should model potential clusters of motivations, since we have yet to know whether extrinsic and intrinsic goals are simply two ends of a continuum, or orthogonal to one another. Martinez finds low correlations between them, suggesting that the latter may be the case. This paves the way for investigating the empirical placement along these two coordinates of women with various resources, constraints, and skills at various points. For example, are there some women who score high on both extrinsic and intrinsic motivation? Or, conversely, score low on both? What distinguishes these women from those who score high on one dimension, and low on the other?*

*As a life course scholar, I would like to see how location along these two coordinates varies over time, as women (and men) move through the years of career and family building. Martinez finds that having a preschooler does not predict motivation. But it may be that the transition to parenthood changes women's motivation for employment. Documenting continuity and change around this and other transitions (such as divorce, returning to school, having children leave home) would clarify whether such orientations are for the most part stable characteristics of individuals, or whether they shift in tandem with shifts in resources and prospects at different points in the life course.*

*Understanding women's work experiences is a laudable goal, and the findings in this chapter are suggestive of directions for an even broader research agenda on women's lives. Most important would be looking at various dimensions of work: how they are allocated, how they change. For example, Martinez finds that mothers with higher levels of job prestige and autonomy are more apt to describe work as an intrinsic experience, while those who work long hours, have higher salaries, and lower levels of education have higher odds of describing work as an extrinsic experience. What I would like future research to address is whether these factors are independent or interconnected, and the kinds of jobs and work environments that have certain sets of attributes but not others. For example, data from the Ecology of Careers Study (Moen and Roehling 2005), as well as considerable other extant research, show that women with high levels of job prestige are also apt to have higher salaries and to work longer hours. And, given homogamy in choice of marriage partner, they are apt to be married to men in similar high demand occupations.*

*Employment at every life stage is a qualitatively different experience for men and for women: Two examples are the transition from school to work (Heinz et al. 1998) and the transition from work to retirement (Kim and Moen 2000; Moen, Kim, and Hofmeister 2001). But gender operates as well in the microcosm of social relations and social expectations. Many couples adopt strategies that, in effect but not necessarily in intent, reproduce a variant of the traditional gendered division of labor. This typically involves neotraditional arrangements in which husbands pursue careers largely in the manner of good providers, with their wives arranging their own employment around their husbands' careers (Moen 2003). We know that women are more apt to "scale back" on their hours and their career goals when they have young children (Becker and Moen 1999). How do these actions reflect or initiate changes in how they view their jobs and their job motivations? Are women with intrinsic or extrinsic orientations more or less apt to do the scaling back? What role do husbands' own motivations play in couples' strategic decision-making on whether and when to have children, to change work hours, jobs, or even to leave the workforce?*

*Studying this complex interplay between subjective meanings and objective circumstances through a gender lens (Bem 1994) is crucial to the advancement of our understanding of the work–family interface and its dynamics, as well as career interfaces and dynamics as they play out in various relational contexts and over time. Similar to Martinez, I believe it is important to focus on careers as trajectories, but also focus as much on subjective as well as objective experiences, and invariably separate by gender. In agreement with Martinez, I believe it is less fruitful to model differences between "jobs" and "careers" than to consider various dimensions of the work experience. And like her, I too think that the payoff of such lines of analysis will be an understanding of the implications of various orientations for subsequent outcomes. For example, Martinez suggests that extrinsic factors (such as income) may be important for children's development, while intrinsically rewarding work experiences may matter for children's socialization. But is it the objective circumstances (salary, level of self-direction, etc.) or the subjective assessments of these experiences in terms of intrinsic or extrinsic motivations that matter, or both, and what are the mechanisms by which both parents' circumstances and motivations matter for their children's lives? How do these factors, as they play out on work and family coordinates, emerge and shift over time? Other value orientations could also be charted as they both influence and are influenced by conditions and experiences on and off the job.*

*Several other lines of work are also suggested by this chapter. For example, how does the issue of objective control over aspects of one's job relate to women's (and men's) experiences of them? Martinez finds that working more hours predicts a higher likelihood of the women describing their work as an extrinsic experience. But does it matter whether one is working long hours because of economic need, job demands, the work is pleasant, or because it is "easier" than life at home (Hochschild 1997)? What are the causal relationships between emotional states (such as feeling bored on the job) and cognitive assessments such as extrinsic or intrinsic assessments? Do emotional states precipitate job and/or workforce exits, returns to schooling, or changing jobs?*

*To conclude, in this chapter Martinez has made important strides in looking within, as well as between, gender differences. She has also pointed to the importance of linking objective work conditions with subjective assessments. I see future payoffs to building upon this line of research along three dimensions. The first involves mapping the interrelations among various aspects of jobs and orientations: What constellation of job characteristics are interrelated? What characteristics are unrelated? What groups of people are most apt to hold certain constellations of subjective assessments? Second, what are the dynamics and temporal dimensions to both objective facts of work and subjective orientations? Who moves in and out of certain types of jobs, in and out of certain subjective orientations? Is there a certain path dependence operating, resulting in a cumulative advantage or disadvantage? Third, I encourage a more contextual approach to the study of the links between objective circumstances and subjective assessments. For example, one's family and/or one's spouse's job and orientations become the "context" in which job decisions and assessments are made. But there are other key contexts as well: historical, cohort, class, economic, social, race, and ethnic ecologies that expand or limit both opportunities and expectations. Finally, there are important organizational and policy contexts. Women's typical life courses, and increasingly men's, now involve the integration of work and family roles, but within an occupational structure that presumes that workers are without family responsibilities. Moreover, such double obligations are typically confronted by women without the supports of kin, neighbors, and friends who have historically facilitated the paid work of poor women, but who themselves are now typically in the workforce. The role of public and private sector policies in shaping the nature of objective work and of career paths and workers' subjective assessments of them is perhaps the most crucial item on the work–family research agenda.*

# 5 Momentary emotion and cortisol levels in the everyday lives of working parents

*Emma K. Adam*

In the past few decades, not only has the nature of work and family life undergone profound changes, but methods for understanding the nature of individuals' experiences in their work and family lives have also evolved. Social scientists are increasingly realizing that individuals experience their family and work lives not only at the cognitive and emotional levels, but also at the level of their biology. New "biosocial" perspectives on the family recognize that there are ongoing interactions between the environments in which families live, family and individual functioning, and multiple aspects of biological or physiological functioning (Booth, Carver, and Granger 2000). Thus, aspects of biology, physiology, and health are recognized as one layer of the complex ecological system within which individuals function and develop. There are many examples of the complex interactions between social context and biology, such as the impact of social relationships on cardiovascular functioning, brain development, physical growth, immune functioning, and physical health (Booth et al. 2000; Cacioppo et al. 2000).

Of particular interest have been the effects of social context on stress physiology, especially the activity of the hypothalamic–pituitary–adrenal (HPA) axis, and its major hormonal product, cortisol. There are a number of reasons for this focus. First, the HPA axis is sensitive to social, emotional, and psychological events, including exposure to environmental stressors as well as to social support systems. Second, the activation of the HPA axis has implications for a wide variety of other physiological systems crucial to short-term functioning as well as long-term health outcomes. Finally, cortisol may be non-invasively and reliably measured on a repeated basis in naturalistic settings because it can be measured in small amounts of human saliva (Kirschbaum and Hellhammer 1989).

This chapter reports data relating momentary events and emotions in the everyday lives of working mothers and fathers to the activity of this stress-sensitive physiological system. Results suggest one possible pathway by which daily experiences "get under the skin" to affect physiology, performance, and emotional and physical health.


## Cortisol reactivity to stressful events

When an individual encounters a stressful event (a stressor), a variety of physiological changes occur that are designed to assist the individual in dealing with the stressor (the stress response). The goal of these changes is to promote survival by activating the necessary attentional and energy resources needed to contend with the immediate threat, and suppressing physiological activity that is irrelevant to that goal.

There are two major physiological systems involved in the stress response: the sympathetic–adrenal–medullary (SAM) system and the HPA axis. The SAM system is the rapid-response component of stress-system activation, causing a nearly immediate release of epinephrine (adrenalin) and norepinephrine and the initial increases in vigilance and arousal that accompany the perception of a potential threat (Johnson et al. 1992). Measurement of sympathetic activity requires the collection of blood, urine, or cardiovascular data, and activation of this system is less specific to negative emotional events than is the HPA axis, making it more difficult to measure and interpret this component of physiological stress activation in naturalistic research (Lovallo and Thomas 2000). If evaluation of a threat suggests that a response is warranted, the SAM response is reinforced and extended by the activity of the slower but longer acting HPA axis. A simplified model of the HPA component of the stress response is depicted in figure 5.1.

The HPA response to stress begins in the brain with the release of corticotropin-releasing hormone (CRH) from the hypothalamus, which stimulates the pituitary gland to release adrenocorticotropin (ACTH) into general circulation. ACTH in turn stimulates the release of cortisol from the adrenal cortex into the bloodstream. Most of this cortisol (95 percent) is immediately bound to a corticosteroid binding globulin (CBG) and albumin, making it biologically inactive, while the rest remains active and has effects on tissues throughout the body and feedback effects on the brain (Kirschbaum and Hellhammer 1989). About 20 to 30 minutes after the onset of the stressor, this unbound portion of cortisol is detectable in human saliva (Johnson et al. 1992; Lovallo and Thomas 2000). The signal to decrease stress-related production of cortisol comes from the offset of the stressor and from negative feedback of circulating cortisol to the brain, especially receptors in the

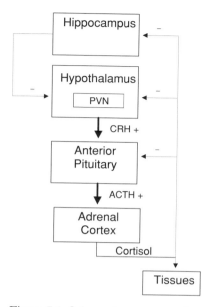

Figure 5.1 Schematic representation of the major components of the hypothalamic–pituitary–adrenal axis
*Note*: Bold arrows with plus signs represent excitatory effects, lighter arrows with negative signs represent inhibitory effects. PVN, paraventricular nucleus of hypothalamus; CRH, corticotropin releasing hormone; ACTH, adrenocorticotropic hormone (corticotropin).

hippocampus, hypothalamus, and pituitary (Chrousos and Gold 1992; de Kloet 1991).

## Short-term effects of cortisol

A major role of cortisol in the stress response is to increase available energy resources through increased gluconeogenesis (glucose production). Cortisol also helps to temporarily suppress the activity of systems that typically operate in the absence of threat, such as digestion, growth, and sexual behavior (Johnson et al. 1992). Increases in cortisol also have complex effects on immune functioning. In the short term, in response to acute stress, cortisol promotes the mobilization of immune resources to the sites in the body where they are required, but over a longer time frame it helps to contain and suppress the immune response (Sapolsky 1998). Cortisol has been shown to suppress the activity of inflammatory cytokines, helping to reduce or contain inflammatory responses to injury or other biological insult (Chrousos and Gold 1992; Miller, Cohen, and Ritchey 2002). Cortisol and the central CRH component of the HPA response also influence cognitive processes such as memory and learning (Chrousos and Gold 1992; de Kloet 1991; Johnson et al. 1992). While HPA activation increases alertness, vigilance to, and memory of threat-relevant stimuli, it impairs more complex cognitive processes. Experimentally increased levels of cortisol are associated with less effective processing of information and poorer memory for new information (Lupien and McEwen 1997).

### What activates the HPA axis?

A variety of factors activate the HPA axis, ranging from internal physical events, such as pain or rapid loss of blood pressure, to external threats to the individual such as the presence or anticipation of physical or psychological harm. The HPA axis is thought to be active when a threat is perceived to overwhelm coping resources. It is not simply the nature of the stressful event (such as its intensity, its duration, or the frequency with which it has occurred) but also the individual's perception of their own ability to cope with it that determines the cortisol response. Any factor which influences individuals' perceptions of themselves and their environments, including their past history, their current emotional and physical state, and the nature of their support systems, can influence the extent to which a cortisol reaction occurs.

### Sex differences in stress reactivity

Some evidence suggests that the HPA response to stress is larger in men than in women (Lovallo and Thomas 2000). While it is possible that this difference is due to differential evaluation of their environments, theorists have suggested that physiological differences in men's and women's stress systems play a role. Taylor et al. (2000) have proposed that in women, levels of oxytocin in interaction with estrogen, may reduce the "fight-or-flight" response, typically associated with stress in men, replacing it with a "tend-or-befriend" response. This "tend-or-befriend" response encourages women to care for rather than abandon their offspring in times of stress, and to develop support networks of other females who may help to protect both offspring and mother. The authors argue that this strategy would have held an evolutionary advantage for women, maximizing the chances of their offspring surviving and passing on their genes. For men, unencumbered by the daily care of offspring, the

SAM- and HPA-mediated "fight-or-flight" strategy remains the most effective approach.

## Basal cortisol activity

In addition to increasing in response to stressors, cortisol exhibits a regular diurnal pattern. That is, cortisol levels are strongly dependent on time of day. In adults, cortisol levels are typically highest in the morning in the hour after waking, drop off rapidly in the first few hours after waking, continue to drop more slowly across the day, and reach a low point or nadir around midnight (Kirschbaum and Hellhammer 1989). There is a pronounced increase in cortisol levels in response to awakening; levels 30 to 45 minutes after waking are higher than those measured immediately upon waking (Pruessner et al. 1997).

It is important to take time of day into account when designing studies and analyzing cortisol data, but individual differences in cortisol diurnal rhythms are also a variable of interest in research (Adam and Gunnar 2001; Smyth et al. 1997), with researchers attempting to identify social-contextual, personality, and mental and physical health factors associated with different daily patterns of cortisol. Measures examined have included differences in average levels of cortisol as well as the degree of change in cortisol levels from morning to evening (the steepness or slope of the cortisol curve). Chronically elevated or suppressed average cortisol levels, as well as flattened diurnal cortisol curves have all been considered to be dysfunctional patterns of cortisol activity (Chrousos and Gold 1992; Gunnar and Vasquez 2001; Heim, Ehlert, and Hellhammer 2000).

Research shows that approximately 72 percent of the variation in cortisol levels across the whole day is explained by time of day in a sample of adult women (Adam and Gunnar 2001). At any one time point in the day, some of the variance in cortisol levels will be due to the typical basal or "trait" levels of cortisol expected at that time of day, while some of the variance will be due to situational or "state" factors (Kirschbaum et al. 1990; Shirtcliff et al. forthcoming). One estimate of the trait versus state contributions to individuals' morning cortisol levels found that approximately 24 to 36 percent of variation in morning cortisol levels was due to stable or trait factors, about 62 to 74 percent was due to state factors, and the rest was due to measurement error (Shirtcliff et al. forthcoming). Thus, although the total variability in cortisol levels across the whole day is to a large part explained by the basal or diurnal cortisol rhythm, at each time point in the day considerable variability remains to be explained by situational factors.

## Cortisol and emotional and physical health

Individual differences in cortisol activity are associated with a variety of emotional and physical health problems (Chrousos and Gold 1992; Heim et al. 2000). Major depression has been consistently associated with higher than average daily cortisol levels in adults (Chrousos and Gold 1992). A variety of physical disorders have been associated with lower cortisol levels (Heim et al. 2000) and a loss or flattening of the diurnal cortisol rhythm, including fibromyalgia (McCain and Tilbe 1989), chronic fatigue syndrome (MacHale et al. 1998), and severe rheumatoid arthritis (Neeck et al. 1990). Flattened daily cortisol curves have also been found in adults with insecure attachment relationships and less effective marital functioning (Adam and Gunnar 2001), in children who have experienced maltreatment, and in orphans who have suffered severe maternal deprivation (Gunnar and Vasquez 2001). Internalizing problems in children and adolescents (social withdrawal, depression, anxiety) have been associated with increases in cortisol reactivity to stressful events (Granger et al. 1996; Smider et al. 2002). Externalizing problems (delinquent, aggressive, and risk-taking behaviors) have been related to low basal cortisol (Shirtcliff et al. forthcoming) and dampened reactivity to stress (Smider et al. 2002).

Recently, researchers have started to investigate whether maladaptive patterns of cortisol activity might have emerged over time from the normal functioning of the stress-response system gone awry. While in the short term, activation of the HPA and other physiological stress systems is adaptive, over the long term, frequent or chronic activation can be harmful. Evidence from animal models has demonstrated that chronic elevations in glucocorticoids may cause first temporary alterations and then permanent damage to the neurons in the hippocampus involved in the negative feedback regulation of the HPA axis. This in turn causes further elevations in basal glucocorticoid levels and further hippocampal damage (Sapolsky, Krey, and McEwen 1986).

In the "allostatic load" model (McEwen 1998), when physiological stress activation (called allostasis) is too frequent or chronic, it is thought to cause harmful wear and tear on the body (called "allostatic load"). Chronic underactivity of stress systems may also cause allostatic load, as a result of harmful overcompensation by the systems typically suppressed or contained by stress hormones (McEwen 1998). There have been few empirical tests of the allostatic load model in humans. In one study, Seeman et al. (2002) related cumulative exposure to social stress to indicators of allostatic load in late adulthood. Individuals with more positive relationship histories and better social support had fewer indicators of allostatic load such as high blood pressure, a higher bad to good choles-terol ratio, a higher waist-to-hip ratio, and higher basal levels of cortisol, epinephrine, and norepinephrine. It was assumed that the individuals with less positive relationship histories had experienced more frequent stress reactivity. The actual events contributing to, and instances of, stress reactivity were not measured. This chapter attempts to identify moments of stress system activity in the everyday lives of parents that could con-tribute over time to allostatic load.

## Cortisol and everyday experience

The majority of prior studies examining cortisol reactions to emotions and events have taken place in a laboratory-based setting. Laboratory studies have the advantage of control – it is possible to observe cortisol activity in a consistent setting and to expose all subjects to the same stress-ful task. Laboratory stressors, however, may not be equally stressful to all individuals or as potent or personally meaningful as stressors encoun-tered in daily life. In addition, individuals may have increases in cortisol in anticipation of their participation in the experiment or as a result of travel to the lab, making it difficult to interpret the data. These problems may account for the relatively inconsistent results that have emerged from this type of research (Nicolson 1992).

Repeated testing of cortisol levels in everyday settings, in conjunction with measurement of real-life events and moods, provides a solution to these problems. These procedures provide minimal disruption of every-day routines and measure events that are relevant to participants' lives, which may therefore be more psychologically meaningful. In pairing cor-tisol levels with randomly selected events and emotions across the day, it is possible to identify factors associated with stress hormone activity, which may be quite different from the limited range of stressors utilized in the lab setting. Studies of this nature help to uncover the types of daily events that, according to the allostatic load model, may over time contribute to the development of stress-related disorders. Such studies also help to identify how stress reactions may be reduced or buffered by aspects of the person or the situation.

Relatively few studies of cortisol reactivity to everyday events have been conducted. Nicolson (1992) studied three samples of college students undergoing a series of typical stressors, such as tests and driver's license examinations. She reported average cortisol increases in anticipation of each of these events, as well as associations between cortisol levels and measures of participants' positive and negative mood states. Van Eck et al. (1996) found that stressful daily events and psychological distress were associated with increased cortisol secretion; events that were relatively long in duration had a larger effect, and familiar stressors were associated with a lower cortisol response than novel ones. Smyth et al. (1998) found increases in cortisol in response to events reported as stressful, as well as greater negative affect associated with higher cortisol levels and greater positive affect associated with lower cortisol levels.

This chapter extends prior work on cortisol reactivity to daily events by breaking down activities and moods beyond the positive and negative emotion distinction that has been analyzed previously, including an examination of parents' feelings about and experiences of their activities at the time of the cortisol sample, and an evaluation of how parents' emotions and cortisol levels differ according to their context – being at home, at work, or in public. Additionally, analyses examine and control for associations between cortisol and medical factors and gender differences, which have been neglected in prior research.

## Hypotheses

It is anticipated that both men and women will show higher levels of cortisol activity at moments when they are experiencing high levels of negative emotion, and lower cortisol levels when they are experiencing positive emotions. Given the Taylor et al. (2000) hypothesis, cortisol reactivity to negative emotions is expected to be greater for men. It is also expected that parents will show lower cortisol levels when they are experiencing feelings of enjoyment, control, and mastery over their activities. Whether cortisol levels are higher or lower at home, at work, or in public will depend on parents' emotional experiences in these contexts.

## Method

### Data collection

The data for this study were collected as a follow-up to the 500 Family Study. Parents who had participated in the 500 Family Study were contacted and asked if they would like to be part of an additional "Physical Stress Study," in which the effects of work and family life on their "physical stress and health" would be examined. Procedures were explained in detail to interested participants (mothers and fathers of kindergarten-aged or adolescent children from primarily middle- to high-income, two-parent, working families). One hundred and twelve parents (69 mothers, 43 fathers) chose to participate.

Participants completed a set of diary entries paired with saliva samples in order to link momentary situations and experiences with stress hormone levels at the time of the diary entry. They were asked to complete six diary-sample pairs across the day (from morning to evening) for two days. These diary-sample pairs were provided in the morning immediately after waking, in the evening immediately before bedtime, and four times during the day when signaled by a specially programmed watch. The watch signals occurred randomly within evenly spaced intervals across the day. Participants were asked to provide each saliva sample 20 minutes after each diary entry, since it takes 20 to 30 minutes after the onset of an event for the associated change in cortisol in saliva. A beep sounded first to signal the diary collection time, then again to signal the associated saliva sample collection time.

The saliva sampling procedure involved chewing a stick of gum to stimulate saliva, then expelling the saliva through a small straw into a vial. Participants refrigerated the saliva samples as soon as possible, then returned them to the research center by courier. Salivary cortisol levels are robust to variations in temperature and motion similar to those experienced in a trip through the postal system (Clements and Parker 1998). Cortisol levels were obtained from the saliva through assays performed by experienced technicians at a laboratory specializing in salivary biomarkers (Salimetrics, State College, PA). Samples were assayed in duplicate for salivary cortisol by enzyme immunoassay. The test used for this study requires only 25 $\mu$l of saliva (for each singlet determination), has a range of sensitivity from .007 to 1.8 $\mu$g/dl, and average intra- and inter-assay coefficients of variation less than 5 percent and 9 percent, respectively. Method accuracy, determined by spike recovery, and linearity, determined by serial dilution, are 105 percent and 95 percent. Salivary cortisol values obtained using this test are strongly positively correlated with serum cortisol values, $r(17) = .94$, $p < .001$.[1] Duplicate cortisol results were averaged, and average values were used in all analyses.

In addition to completing the ESM diary-sample pairs, each participant completed a health survey, in which they reported on a variety of health and lifestyle issues that might affect cortisol levels, such as medication use, consumption of caffeine and alcohol, use of nicotine, timing of menstrual cycle, pregnancy, presence of chronic illness, and their height and weight (used to calculate body mass index). Participants were excluded from the analyses if they were physically ill at the time they completed the study, if they had a serious chronic health condition known to affect endocrine function, were using corticosteroid-based medications for the treatment of asthma, or had extensive missing data.[2]

It was not feasible to eliminate all individuals with a minor ongoing health problem as this would have represented 66 percent of the individuals in the study and severely limited the representativeness of the sample. Only 44 percent of participants reported having no health problems, with 37 percent reporting one health problem, 14 percent reporting two health problems, and 6 percent reporting three health problems. The associations between each of the health variables and basal cortisol, as well as the associations between health variables and cortisol reactivity to daily events, were tested in order to identify and control for the possible influence of these variables. Where associations between health conditions and basal cortisol or cortisol reactivity were found, these variables were included as control variables in all analyses.

### ESM questions and data reduction

The ESM diaries contained a variety of questions about participants: (a) their thoughts and feelings about the main activity they were engaged in at the time of the beep; (b) their current emotions or mood state at the time of the beep; and (c) where they were – their location at the time of the beep. The feelings about the main activity section included the following questions, answered on a four-point scale ranging from not at all (0) to very much (4): Did you enjoy what you were doing? Was this activity interesting? How well were you concentrating? Were you living up to your own expectations? Did you feel in control of the situation? Did the situation allow you to be involved or to act? Did you have the abilities to deal with the situation? Was the activity important to you? Were others expecting a lot from you? Were you succeeding at what you were doing? Did you wish you were doing something else? Did you feel good about yourself? The mood state section asked participants how they were feeling at the time of the beep. Moods were rated on a four-point scale ranging from not at all (0) to very much (4), including: cheerful, lonely, nervous, cooperative, angry, responsible, frustrated, competitive, strained, worried, caring, irritated, relaxed, stressed, proud, friendly, hardworking, and productive.

In order to reduce the number of variables used in analyses and to reduce the possibility of Type-1 error, principal component analyses (with a varimax rotation) were performed on each set of variables.[3] For the "Feelings about Activity" variables, three factors emerged, including an *enjoyment* factor, which was high on enjoyment of the activity and interest in the activity, and low on wishing to do something else; a *mastery* factor, which was high on control of the situation, ability to deal with the situation, and perceived success; and an *involvement* factor, which was high on others expecting a lot from the respondent, degree of concentration, importance of the activity to the respondent, and being involved or being able to act. The analysis of the *Mood State* variables also revealed three factors, including a *negative-stress* factor which was high on stressed, worried, strained, irritated, nervous, lonely, and angry; a *positive-social* factor, which was high on cheerful, cooperative, proud, friendly, and caring; and a *positive-productive* factor, which was high on responsible, hardworking, and productive.

Each participant's location at the time of the beep was answered in an open-ended format and classified into three categories: at home, at work, or in a public setting. The degree of physical activity that was involved in the activity was categorized on a four-point scale ranging from very sedentary to very physical, to test whether the degree of physical exertion involved in the activity might be contributing to cortisol levels.

### Analytic approach

The first step in analyzing the data was to examine cortisol values across the day for each participant. Cortisol values were expected to be high in the morning and decline across the day until evening. But each person will have a slightly different diurnal cortisol pattern, and within each person's data some cortisol values will be higher or lower than would be expected at that time of day for that person. Therefore, the following set of questions can be asked:

(1) How do momentary emotions and feelings about activities relate to cortisol levels, after taking into account the influence of the time of day and health-related variables on cortisol? Are these patterns of association different for men and women?

(2) In which of the primary contexts of parents' lives – at home, at work, or in public – are each of the mood states and feelings about activities experienced most strongly?

(3) Are cortisol levels higher or lower than expected at that time of day when parents are at home, at work, or in public? Are these differences accounted for by the mood states and feelings about activities that were typical of each setting?

The first set of questions was answered using Hierarchical Linear Modeling (HLM) Growth Curve analysis (Bryk and Raudenbush 1992), which is a method used to understand factors affecting how a variable changes over time for each person (in this case, how each person's cortisol levels change from moment to moment across the day). In a Level-1 HLM model, a curve was plotted through the cortisol values across the day for each individual, which provided estimates of the cortisol values expected at each time of day for each participant. Deviations from these expected values were predicted from the mood states and feelings about activities experienced at the time of each beep by adding these variables to the Level-1 model. To test whether these patterns were modified by the health variables or the sex of the parent, these variables were included in a Level-2 HLM model.

The second set of questions, regarding associations between momentary emotions and feelings about activities and location (home, work, public) at the time of each beep were examined using two-way Analyses of Variance (ANOVAs),[4] with location as a within-subject factor and sex as a between-subject factor. When main effects or interaction terms were significant, a series of post-hoc contrasts was conducted comparing the means for the different locations and/or the means for mothers and fathers.

The third set of questions, regarding whether cortisol levels are associated with the location of the parent at the time of the beep and whether these associations are mediated by parents' moods and feelings about activities, were addressed in another HLM model. The momentary location and emotion data were entered in two separate steps at Level-1, and sex of parent and the health control variables were entered at Level-2.

## Results

### Cortisol patterns across the day for mothers and fathers

As seen in figure 5.2, the cortisol data for the parents in the study did show the expected strong diurnal rhythm in cortisol levels – levels are highest in the morning, drop most rapidly in the morning, then continue to decline to near zero values at bedtime.[5] The change in cortisol levels across the day was modeled for each individual separately in a Level-1 HLM model. As this effect was not linear, several curvilinear models were tested. The best fit was obtained by a model that included both linear (time) and quadratic (time of day squared) terms for time of day. Time of day values were expressed as deviations from their mean (centered at their mean) in order to reduce possible multicollinearity between the linear and quadratic terms. Using this model, time of day accounted for 67 percent of the variation in participants' cortisol levels.

*Health control variables*    Even when individuals using steroid-based medications were removed from the sample, having an asthma diagnosis was associated with a slight flattening of the daily cortisol curve ($b = .078$, $t = 2.51$, $p < .05$). The presence of an asthma diagnosis

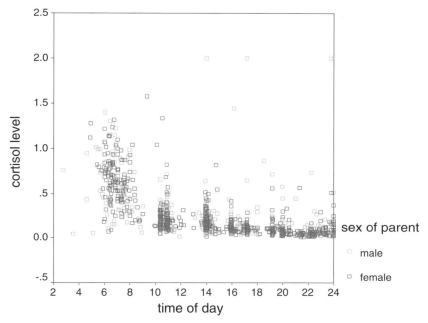

Figure 5.2  Observed cortisol values (in μg/dl) for participants by time of day (on a 24 hour clock, includes both days of measurement)

and having a higher body-mass index (BMI) were shown to modify the strength of the relationships between positive and negative emotion and cortisol (details below). Both asthma diagnosis and BMI were included as control variables in all analyses. Exclusion of these variables did not, however, meaningfully alter the nature of the other study results.

*Momentary emotions and cortisol levels*   The average associations between ESM mood variables and momentary cortisol levels, controlling for time of day and health variables, are presented in figure 5.3.

The bars represent how much higher or lower the cortisol level is than the expected level at that time of day for one standard-deviation change in each mood state factor. The figure suggests that being in a negative emotional state is associated with higher momentary cortisol levels, while being in a positive emotional state is associated with lower momentary cortisol levels.

The HLM analysis (see table 5.1) confirms that higher levels on the negative-stress emotion factor are significantly associated with higher cortisol levels than expected at that time of day (b = .014, t = 2.12, p < .05).

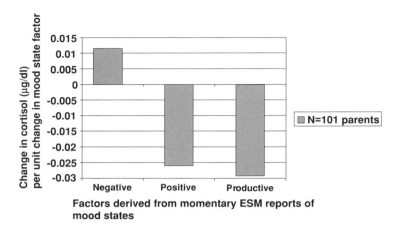

Figure 5.3 Associations between ESM mood state factors and cortisol levels, controlling for time of day

At the average cortisol level (approximately .25 μg/dl), this represents a relatively modest 6 percent increase in cortisol levels per standard deviation increase in negative emotion. The range of coefficients for the association between negative emotion and cortisol, however, was −.07 to .23. Certain individuals, therefore, experienced up to a 92 percent increase in cortisol for each standard deviation increase in negative emotion. Several factors account for these individual differences in cortisol reactivity to negative emotion.

The association between negative emotion and cortisol levels is significantly stronger for men than for women (b = .036, t = 2.26, p < .05 for the test of the difference between men's versus women's coefficients[6]), suggesting that men have significantly greater cortisol reactivity to negative emotion then women. Having an asthma diagnosis, however, is associated with a lesser degree of cortisol reactivity to negative emotion (b = −.021, t = −2.07, p < .05), as is having a higher body-mass index (BMI; b = −.003, t = −3.87, p < .001).

Feeling higher levels of positive-social emotions, such as cheerful, friendly, and caring (b = −.024, t = −3.55, p < .001) is associated, on average, with lower cortisol levels than expected at that time of day. At the average cortisol level of the day (.25) this represents a 10 percent average decrease in cortisol per standard deviation increase in positive-social emotion. The range of coefficients for positive-social emotion was −.29 to .02; some individuals experienced up to 108 percent lower cortisol levels for each standard deviation increase in positive emotion.

Table 5.1 *Hierarchical Linear Model predicting parents' cortisol levels from time of day and mood state factors (N = 101)*

| Fixed effect | Coefficient | SE | df | $t$-value | $p$-value |
|---|---|---|---|---|---|
| Cortisol Intercept | | | | | |
|   Intercept | .165 | .009 | 97 | 17.98 | .000 |
|   Sex | .278 | .002 | 97 | 1.39 | .165 |
|   Asthma | −.017 | .026 | 97 | −.66 | .509 |
|   BMI | .000 | .001 | 97 | .33 | .738 |
| Time of day | | | | | |
|   Intercept | −.166 | .009 | 97 | −18.14 | .000 |
|   Sex | .030 | .021 | 97 | 1.44 | .150 |
|   Asthma | .078 | .031 | 97 | 2.51 | .012 |
|   BMI | .000 | .002 | 97 | .36 | .718 |
| Time of day$^2$ | | | | | |
|   Intercept | .094 | .007 | 97 | 13.05 | .000 |
|   Sex | −.018 | .017 | 97 | −1.05 | .293 |
|   Asthma | −.031 | .021 | 97 | −1.49 | .137 |
|   BMI | −.001 | .001 | 97 | −.09 | .386 |
| Negative-stress | | | | | |
|   Intercept | .014 | .006 | 97 | 2.12 | .033 |
|   Sex | .036 | .016 | 97 | 2.26 | .024 |
|   Asthma | −.021 | .009 | 97 | −2.07 | .038 |
|   BMI | −.003 | .000 | 97 | −3.87 | .000 |
| Positive-social | | | | | |
|   Intercept | −.024 | .007 | 97 | −3.55 | .001 |
|   Sex | −.007 | .016 | 97 | −4.32 | .665 |
|   Asthma | .009 | .030 | 97 | .31 | .759 |
|   BMI | .000 | .000 | 97 | .40 | .691 |
| Positive-productive | | | | | |
|   Intercept | −.027 | .007 | 97 | −3.98 | .000 |
|   Sex | −.025 | .015 | 97 | −1.58 | .112 |
|   Asthma | .009 | .021 | 97 | .45 | .654 |
|   BMI | .002 | .001 | 97 | 1.81 | .070 |

| Random effect | Standard deviation | Variance component | df | Chi-squared | $p$-value |
|---|---|---|---|---|---|
| Intercept | .058 | .003 | 90 | 126.87 | .007 |
| Time of day | .081 | .007 | 90 | 223.52 | .000 |
| Time of day$^2$ | .053 | .003 | 90 | 145.60 | .000 |
| Negative-stress | .036 | .001 | 90 | 79.48 | >.50 |
| Positive-social | .048 | .002 | 90 | 119.59 | .020 |
| Positive-productive | .037 | .001 | 90 | 102.66 | .171 |

*Note:* The time of day and mood state variables were entered as Level-1 (within person, repeated measures) variables and parent asthma, parent sex, and parent body mass were entered as Level-2 (between-person, individual difference) control variables in the HLM model.

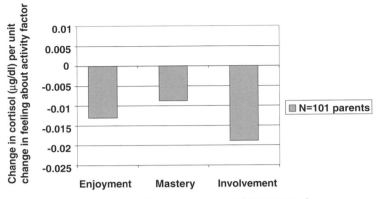

Figure 5.4 Associations between ESM feelings about activities factors and cortisol levels, controlling for time of day

Finally, lower cortisol levels are also experienced when individuals are feeling hardworking and productive (b = −.027, t = −3.98, p < .001). A one-standard-deviation increase on the positive-productive factor is associated, on average, with an 11 percent decrease in cortisol levels. The range of coefficients for the association between the positive-productive factor and cortisol was −.21 to .02; some individuals experienced an 84 percent decrease in cortisol per standard deviation change in feeling hardworking and productive.

Because the three mood variables were entered in the analysis simultaneously, they have been shown to have independent associations with cortisol. That is, the effects for positive-social emotion and feeling hardworking and productive are separate from, rather than simply the opposite of the negative emotion effect. Together, the three mood variables account for 16 percent of the remaining variability in cortisol levels after controlling for time of day.

*Feelings about activity and cortisol levels*    The associations between parents' feelings about their activities at the time of the beep and their cortisol levels are presented in figure 5.4.

The bars represent how much higher or lower the cortisol level is than the expected level at that time of day for one standard-deviation change in each feelings about activities factor. Once again, it appears that positive states, in this case positive feelings about the activity one is engaged in, are associated with significantly lower cortisol levels. Higher enjoyment of present activities is related to lower cortisol levels (b $= -.013$, t $= -3.33$, p $= .001$), with levels 5 percent lower for every standard deviation increase in enjoyment of activities (see table 5.2). The coefficients for this effect ranged from .01 to $-.03$, with effect sizes ranging from a plus 4 percent to minus 12 percent change in cortisol per standard deviation change in enjoyment of activities at the average cortisol level of the day.

There is also a significant negative association between higher feelings of involvement with activities and cortisol levels (b $= -.017$, t $= -2.08$, p $< .05$; b's ranged from $-.27$ to .12). The average decrease in cortisol for every standard deviation increase in task involvement was 7 percent, although for some individuals cortisol levels were up to 108 percent lower for every standard deviation increase in task engagement at the average cortisol level of the day. There was no effect of feelings of mastery or control over the activity on cortisol levels. No significant sex differences were found in the associations between feelings about daily activities and cortisol levels. Together, the feelings about activity variables account for 10 percent of the variation in cortisol levels remaining after controlling for time of day. When both the mood state and feelings about activity variables are entered in the same model, a total of 25 percent of the cortisol variation remaining after controlling for time of day is explained.

### Associations between location and mood and feelings about activity variables

Given the strong pattern of associations between parents' mood states, and their feelings about the activities they are engaged in, the next set of analyses seeks to determine when parents most experience these different moods and feelings. Parents' average levels on each of the emotion and mood state factors in each of three settings (home, work, and public) were calculated and compared using two-way ANOVAs, with location as a within-subject factor and parent gender as a between-subject factor.[7] Using person-level data rather than the data for all the individual beeps is preferable because it avoids the correlated error and exaggerated degrees of freedom that can be a problem with beep-level data. It also weights each individual equally rather than giving greater influences to individuals who have completed more beeps (Larson and Delespaul 1992, see also Jeong in the technical appendix A). In addition, using a within-subject comparison ensures that the effect is not accounted for by between-subject differences on these variables. When overall ANOVAs were significant, post-hoc comparisons were made between the individual groups, and effect size statistics (Cohen's $d$) were calculated. Effect size statistics provide additional information beyond significance levels because they are

Table 5.2 *Hierarchical Linear Model predicting parents' cortisol levels from time of day and their feelings about activity factors (N = 101)*

| Fixed effect | Coefficient | SE | df | $t$-value | $p$-value |
|---|---|---|---|---|---|
| Cortisol Intercept | | | | | |
|   Intercept | .155 | .009 | 97 | 17.86 | .000 |
|   Sex | .004 | .019 | 97 | .21 | .834 |
|   Asthma | −.007 | .030 | 97 | −.23 | .817 |
|   BMI | .002 | .001 | 97 | 1.05 | .296 |
| Time of Day | | | | | |
|   Intercept | −.163 | .009 | 97 | −18.54 | .000 |
|   Sex | .019 | .020 | 97 | .92 | .358 |
|   Asthma | −.069 | .024 | 97 | 2.91 | .004 |
|   BMI | .000 | .001 | 97 | .26 | .796 |
| Time of Day$^2$ | | | | | |
|   Intercept | .101 | .008 | 97 | 12.32 | .000 |
|   Sex | .001 | .019 | 97 | .04 | .969 |
|   Asthma | −.025 | .017 | 97 | −1.47 | .141 |
|   BMI | .002 | .001 | 97 | 1.98 | .048 |
| Enjoyment | | | | | |
|   Intercept | −.013 | .004 | 97 | −3.33 | .000 |
|   Sex | .013 | .010 | 97 | 1.43 | .154 |
|   Asthma | .001 | .010 | 97 | .36 | .721 |
|   BMI | .001 | .000 | 97 | 1.78 | .074 |
| Mastery | | | | | |
|   Intercept | −.007 | .006 | 97 | −1.15 | .251 |
|   Sex | .011 | .013 | 97 | .85 | .397 |
|   Asthma | .014 | .017 | 97 | .78 | .435 |
|   BMI | .002 | .001 | 97 | 1.98 | .048 |
| Involvement | | | | | |
|   Intercept | −.017 | .008 | 97 | −2.08 | .038 |
|   Sex | −.000 | .019 | 97 | −.01 | .993 |
|   Asthma | .022 | .013 | 97 | 1.67 | .095 |
|   BMI | .001 | .002 | 97 | .71 | .477 |

| Random effect | Standard deviation | Variance component | df | Chi-squared | $p$-value |
|---|---|---|---|---|---|
| Intercept | .047 | .002 | 92 | 92.94 | > .50 |
| Time of Day | .072 | .005 | 92 | 205.49 | .000 |
| Time of Day$^2$ | .059 | .003 | 92 | 164.49 | .000 |
| Enjoyment | .004 | .000 | 92 | 69.05 | > .50 |
| Mastery | .022 | .000 | 92 | 100.49 | .256 |
| Involvement | .059 | .003 | 92 | 97.43 | .329 |

*Note:* The time of day and feelings about activity variables were entered as Level-1 (within person, repeated measures) variables and parent asthma, parent sex, and parent body mass were entered as Level-2 (between-person, individual difference) variables in the HLM model.

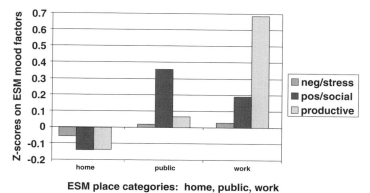

Figure 5.5 Associations between ESM reports of parent location (home, public, work) and ESM mood states

not dependent on sample or cell sizes, and are therefore more comparable across studies.[8]

As shown in figure 5.5 and table 5.3, there are significant associations between location and parent mood state, for both the positive-productive factor [$F(2,103) = 78.4$, $p < .001$], and the positive-social factor [$F(2,103) = 25.6$, $p < .001$]. Post-hoc contrasts reveal that parents feel significantly more hardworking/productive at work than in public ($d = .99$) or at home ($d = 1.64$), and more hardworking/productive in public than at home ($d = .34$). In addition they feel more positive-social in public settings than either at work ($d = .24$) or at home ($d = .69$), and more positive-social at work than at home ($d = .46$).

There are also significant effects of gender on negative affect [$F(1, 104) = 6.4$, $p = .01$] and significant interactions between parent gender and location in predicting negative affect [$F(2,103) = 5.61$, $p = .005$]. Averaging across all contexts, post-hoc contrasts revealed that men experience higher levels of negative emotion than women ($d = .51$), but that women experienced higher levels of negative affect at work than at home ($d = .34$) or in public ($d = .45$), whereas there are no significant differences in negative affect by location for men (although they experienced their highest levels when in public).[9]

There were significant main effects of location for mastery [$F(2, 103) = 7.1$, $p = .001$] and involvement [$F(1,103) = 75.0$, $p = .000$] (see figure 5.6 and table 5.3). Higher levels of mastery are experienced at work and in public than at home ($d = .45$ and $d = .28$ respectively). Levels of involvement are higher at work than in public settings ($d = .67$)

Table 5.3 *Associations between parents' emotions, feelings about activities, and location by parent gender, controlling for time of day*

| | Location at time of beep | | | | |
|---|---|---|---|---|---|
| ESM Variable | Home | Public | Work | F | Contrasts[a] |
| **All Parents** | | | | | |
| Negative-stressed | −.05 (.06) | .02 (.07) | .03 (.06) | 1.0 | |
| Positive-social | −.14 (.07) | .36 (.07) | .19 (.07) | 25.6*** | P>W>H |
| Positive-productive | −.14 (.05) | .07 (.07) | .69 (.05) | 78.4*** | W>P>H |
| Enjoyment | −.07 (.06) | .13 (.08) | .08 (.05) | 4.5** | P, W>H |
| Mastery | −.07 (.07) | .12 (.06) | .21 (.05) | 7.1*** | P, W>H |
| Involvement | −.22 (.06) | .22 (.06) | .60 (.05) | 75.0*** | W>P>H |
| **Mothers** | | | | | |
| Negative-stressed | −.17 (.08) | −.24 (.08) | .05 (.08) | 5.0** | W>H, P |
| Positive-social | −.20 (.09) | .45 (.08) | .27 (.08) | | |
| Positive-productive | .02 (.07) | .09 (.08) | .74 (.08) | | |
| Enjoyment | −.10 (.07) | .32 (.09) | .21 (.06) | 15.4*** | P, W>H |
| Mastery | −.02 (.09) | .18 (.08) | .13 (.06) | | |
| Involvement | −.17 (.07) | .24 (.08) | .58 (.06) | | |
| **Fathers** | | | | | |
| Negative-stressed | .06 (.10) | .28 (.11) | .00 (.10) | .17 | n.s. |
| Positive-social | −.08 (.12) | .26 (.11) | .11 (.10) | | |
| Positive-productive | −.29 (.09) | .04 (.11) | .63 (.08) | | |
| Enjoyment | −.05 (.08) | −.05 (.11) | −.05 (.08) | .00 | n.s. |
| Mastery | −.12 (.11) | .06 (.10) | .29 (.08) | | |
| Involvement | −.27 (.09) | .20 (.10) | .62 (.08) | | |

*Notes:* *p < .05; **p < .01; ***p < .005

Values outside parentheses are means, inside are standard errors. H = home, P = public, W = work. DF's for all parents ANOVAs are (2,103); for mother and father ANOVAs are (1,104).

[a] Contrasts are provided for all parents when a significant main effect is present, and separately for mothers and fathers in the case of a significant interaction. Contrasts are paired sample t-tests, presented when significant at *p < .05* or less.

and at home ($d = 1.44$), and higher in public than at home ($d = .77$). On average, women experience higher enjoyment of activities than men [$F(1,104) = 5.2$, p = .03; $d = .45$], but there was also an interaction between gender and location in predicting enjoyment [$F(2,103) = 5.0$, p = .009]. While there are no differences between work, public, and home for enjoyment for men, women experience significantly higher levels of enjoyment of activities in public settings and at work than at home ($d = .65$ and $d = .59$, respectively).

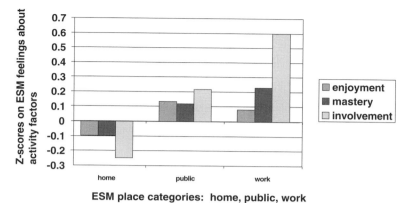

Figure 5.6 Associations between ESM reports of parent location (home, public, work) and ESM feelings about activities

*Associations between location and parent cortisol levels*

The results of the HLM model predicting parents' cortisol levels from parent location at the time of the beep, controlling for time of day, are presented in table 5.4. Dummy (0 1) variables for being in public and for being at work were entered in the Level-1 HLM model after the time of day variables (being at home was excluded as the comparison group). Given the fact that feeling hardworking and productive and enjoying and feeling engaged in activities are strongly associated with lower cortisol (and parents report higher levels of these experiences in the work setting), it is not surprising that cortisol levels are significantly lower than expected for that time of day when parents are at work (b = −.080, t = −5.89, p < .001). This corresponds to a 32 percent decrease in average/midday cortisol levels; see table 5.4, model 1. Being in public is not associated with any systematic difference in cortisol levels (b = −.005, t = −.33, n.s.). When the mood state and feelings about activity variables are included in the Level-1 model after the location dummy variables, the association between being at work and cortisol levels is reduced by almost a third, but being at work remains a significant independent effect (b = −.055, t = −3.76, p = .001; 22 percent lower than expected at average/midday cortisol levels; see table 5.4, model 2). Thus, parents' mood states and feelings about their activities at the time they were beeped partially mediate the association between being at work and cortisol levels. Although a variety of other characteristics of the individual and the workplace environment (amount of control in the workplace,

Table 5.4 *Associations between location and cortisol controlling for time of day and health variables (Model 1) as well as mood state and feelings about activity variables (Model 2)*

| | | Model 1 | | | |
|---|---|---|---|---|---|
| Fixed effect | Coefficient | SE | df | *t*-value | *p*-value |
| In public | −.005 | .016 | 97 | −.33 | .740 |
| At work | −.080 | .014 | 97 | −5.89 | .000 |
| Random effect | Standard deviation | Variance component | df | Chi-squared | *p*-value |
| In public | .076 | .006 | 49 | 42.44 | >.500 |
| At work | .063 | .004 | 49 | 48.97 | >.500 |
| | | Model 2 | | | |
| Fixed effect | Coefficient | SE | df | *t*-value | *p*-value |
| In public | .006 | .016 | 97 | .36 | .718 |
| At work | −.055 | .015 | 97 | −3.76 | .000 |
| Random effect | Standard deviation | Variance component | df | Chi-squared | *p*-value |
| In public | .080 | .006 | 33 | 31.73 | >.500 |
| At work | .070 | .005 | 33 | 40.79 | .165 |

*Note:* Coefficients for control variables not shown in order to preserve space. Home is the excluded (comparison) group.

level of physical activity, level of income and occupational prestige) were tested, no other factors mediating or moderating this association were identified.

## Discussion

Clearly, parents' momentary emotions and how they feel about their daily activities are related to their physiological state, in this case their levels of the stress-sensitive hormone cortisol. In this study, all three factors found for participants' moods and two out of three factors found to describe participants' feelings about their activities in their daily lives are significantly related to their cortisol levels twenty minutes later. More specifically, controlling for time of day and medical factors, higher levels of a negative emotion are associated with higher levels of cortisol (an effect which was significantly stronger for men than for women), and higher levels of a positive-social emotion and a hardworking-productive factor were associated with lower levels of cortisol twenty minutes later. When examining parents' feelings about their main activities at the time of the beep, higher levels of the enjoyment and involvement are both independently associated with lower levels of cortisol than expected at that time of day. Parents experience greater feelings of productivity and higher levels of involvement (both mothers and fathers) and enjoyment (mothers only) when they are at work than when they are at home. Cortisol levels are correspondingly lower when parents are at work.

Several medical variables are significantly related to either basal cortisol patterns or cortisol reactivity to momentary events. The presence of an asthma diagnosis is associated with flatter diurnal cortisol rhythms, even after individuals using steroid based medications were excluded. In addition, the presence of asthma is associated with lower cortisol reactivity to negative emotion. A dampened association between negative emotion and cortisol is also found in individuals with a greater body-mass index (a measure of body weight per unit height).

### Negative emotion and higher momentary cortisol

The association between negative emotion (e.g., stressed, strained, angry, and worried) and higher cortisol is in accord with the few prior studies using a momentary methodology (Nicolson 1992; Smyth et al. 1998; van Eck et al. 1996). Understanding factors in the everyday lives of families that contribute to higher cortisol levels is important, because of the potential short-term negative effects of cortisol on functioning, and also because frequent or prolonged exposure to increased cortisol levels may have harmful long-term effects on health. Results suggest that the momentary stresses of parents' daily working lives are indeed related to small increases in cortisol. The extent to which this momentary reactivity adds up over time to contribute to long-term health problems requires further study. In future research, it will be important to identify which individuals are characterized by more frequent and/or more extreme cortisol responses to negative emotion, as there was considerable variability in the size (and even direction) of the association between negative emotion and cortisol levels.

Gender is one factor associated with significant variations in cortisol responses to negative emotions. The positive association between negative emotion and cortisol was significantly larger for the men in the present study compared to the women. This result provides some support for the theory put forward by Taylor et al. (2000), which suggests that women's physiological response to stressors is different than men's.

### Positive emotion and lower cortisol

Some of the more novel findings of this study involve the associations between positive-social and positive-productive moods and lower levels of cortisol. Positive-social moods involve feeling happy, cheerful, social, cooperative, and caring, and positive-productive moods include feeling responsible, hardworking, and productive. The association between positive-social emotions and lower cortisol to a certain extent fits with the Taylor et al. (2000) idea of a social coping component to the stress response, but the fact that this association was not significantly stronger for women does not fit with their idea that this is a characteristically female response. The possibility that social relationships may be important in modulating cortisol activity for both men and women in their everyday lives deserves further attention. In particular, with a larger sample size or larger number of beeps per person, further examination of who the person is with at the time of the beep, and the effect of the quality of the respondents' relationships with those individuals on cortisol, could be a fruitful approach.

### Productivity, engagement, and enjoyment of activities and lower cortisol

The findings of lower levels of cortisol when individuals are engaged in activities that they find to be enjoyable, and in which they feel highly involved, active, engaged, and have high levels of concentration are also novel. A similar association between engagement in activities and lower cortisol has been reported in one prior laboratory study (Frankenhauser 1979); however, this question has not been previously examined or reported in naturalistic settings.

Although involvement in challenging activities might be expected to be associated with higher cortisol levels, prior evidence suggests that cortisol does not increase in situations of successful effort, but rather increases under conditions where challenges are perceived to be beyond one's abilities to successfully cope with the situation (Kirschbaum and Hellhammer 1989). The concept of challenge being associated with positive emotional experience has been investigated in detail in Csikszentmihalyi's (1990) theory of "flow." According to this line of research, a positive emotional experience of "flow" occurs when individuals are faced with tasks that incorporate an appropriate balance between challenge and skill such that the task is neither boring (when challenge is too low or skill too high) or anxiety-provoking (when challenge is too high or skill too low). Findings suggest the possibility that flow states may be accompanied by lower cortisol levels.

One implication of this finding is that daily challenges are not inevitably physiologically stressful,[10] but may in fact make positive contributions to physical health and psychological well-being. In future research it may be important to differentiate between "good" stresses, which exercise and stretch a person's abilities but lead to reward and success, and "bad" stresses, which challenge a person beyond his or her coping abilities and result in negative emotion and activation of the HPA axis. Just as a certain amount of cortisol is necessary for basic daily functioning, a certain amount of challenge may be an important part of healthy living.

### Mood states and feelings about activities in different contexts

Although there are some complex interactions with gender, in general parents experience their highest levels of feeling productive and involved in the work setting, along with high feelings of enjoyment and mastery. Parent cortisol levels are also significantly lower in the work setting than would be expected given the time of day. The lower cortisol levels in this setting were partially but not fully accounted for by parents' emotions or feelings about their activities at the time of the beep. One possible reason for this finding is stress-induced cortisol levels do not decay very quickly such that the levels of cortisol at any one point in time may reflect cumulative experiences over the past hour rather than the emotional experience at that moment (as captured in each ESM diary report). Future research could explore alternative wordings of the ESM that ask individuals to reflect back over a larger period of time. With a larger sample size, research could also identify in more detail the particular work conditions associated with positive engagement and lower cortisol levels.

Experiences at home are characterized by lower levels of feeling positive-social emotions, feeling hardworking and productive, and lower levels of enjoyment, mastery, and engagement in activities. This effect may be partially accounted for by the data collection procedures. To properly capture the cortisol daily rhythm, cortisol samples and diary entries were required immediately after waking and immediately before bedtime, when participants may be less alert and less positively engaged with family members. Supplementary analyses show that parents feel significantly less social and productive and have lower levels of enjoyment and involvement in activities during these waking and bedtime periods than at other times at home.[11] Future research should attempt to collect data both on weekdays and weekends to sample a broader range of home-based experiences (although these morning and late evening periods are certainly a part of participants' daily experiences of their home lives).

### Which comes first, the emotion or the hormone?

The question of the direction of effect of cortisol and momentary experience is not definitively answered here. One of the age-old debates in emotion theory is whether emotional experience causes a change in physiological state or whether the emotion *is* the experience of the physiological state. A similar directional question could be asked regarding the feelings about activity variables. Does an individual's engagement in activities cause a change in his or her levels of cortisol, or does the individual's hormonal state influence his or her experience of and ability to engage in an activity? There is evidence in prior research for both of these arguments. A large body of experimental evidence shows that exposure to a stressful situation increases cortisol levels (Kirschbaum and Hellhammer 1989), and one experimental study found that "confident task involvement" leads to a drop in cortisol levels (Frankenhauser 1979: 136). However, there is also evidence that experimentally increased cortisol levels can cause changes in immediate functioning, including impairments in cognitive and memory processes (Lupien and McEwen 1997).

Perhaps these variables are dynamically interacting over time, with experiences and activities altering personal emotions and hormone levels, and hormone levels influencing an individual's interpretation of environments and either hindering or facilitating his or her engagement with activities. Future studies using a greater number of data points per day could use a time-lagged or sequential approach to gain more insight into these questions. This study built in a lag of twenty minutes between the diary report and the measurement of cortisol, making it more likely that the cortisol level is a reflection of the prior emotional state, however without more frequent measurement, no strong conclusions about these dynamics can be made. This chapter provides evidence that complex transactions between personal activities, emotions, and hormones are an ongoing part of everyday life.

### Associations between asthma and body mass and cortisol

While a flattening of the cortisol diurnal rhythm has been previously reported for several other stress-related disorders (see Adam and

Gunnar 2001), the flattened cortisol rhythms found in the current study for asthma have not previously been reported. The finding of dampened cortisol reactivity to negative emotion in asthmatics is also novel. These results should be interpreted with caution, since they are based on only six people, but they are nonetheless of interest given the known anti-inflammatory properties of corticosteroids in the body. Perhaps lower morning cortisol levels and a weakened cortisol response to stress in asthmatics contribute to a weakened ability to contain the inflammatory response in the airways that is part of the asthmatic disorder. Miller, Cohen, and Ritchey (2002) suggest that a reduced sensitivity of inflammatory cytokines to suppression by glucocorticoids may contribute to the etiology of disorders involving excessive inflammation. The study suggests the possibility that reduced stress-induced levels of glucocorticoids may also play a role, at least for asthma.

The finding of decreased cortisol reactivity to negative emotion among individuals with higher body mass has also not been reported in previous studies. One possible explanation for this finding could be a difference in the time course of cortisol reactivity, with a time delay to peak level in people with higher body mass, due to higher blood volume. Another possibility could be differential rates of absorption of cortisol by fatty tissue versus muscle. Reduced physiological responsiveness of the HPA to psychological events, CRH, or ACTH among individuals with higher BMI is also a possibility. Clearly, all of these interpretations are speculative, and results need to be replicated before drawing conclusions about the possible significance of these health-related findings.

### Conclusion

This chapter represents just one window into the ongoing and complex interplay between environments and human biology. It nonetheless provides evidence that the simultaneous examination of activities, emotions, and physiology in families' everyday lives is a fruitful approach that yields insights on how the events of daily life can "get under our skin." This research exemplifies the biosocial perspective, which views individual biology and health as embedded in, and interacting dynamically with, social contexts. Evidence that social environments can influence a person not just at the level of his or her thoughts and emotions, but also at the level of his or her biology and health, makes a powerful case for the importance of social science research. In the long run, information on how daily experiences of social settings influence an individual's physiology may provide insights on how to change these environments to improve the emotional, cognitive, and physical well-being of parents and children.

NOTES

1. To determine the reliability of using salivary cortisol, eighteen individuals provided both blood and saliva samples. Correlations between salivary and serum cortisol values for these eighteen individuals were calculated.

2. Of the 112 parents who completed the procedures, two participants' data were not used due to the presence of serious medical conditions, five were eliminated due to use of steroid-based asthma medications, and four other participants were eliminated as a result of extensive missing data, leaving a total of 101 participants (64 mothers, 37 fathers). The average number of ESM-cortisol pairs completed by these participants was 10.01 out of the requested 12 pairs. When the cortisol data were present, but occasional ESM values were missing, missing ESM values were replaced with each person's mean value for that variable. Less than 5 percent of the ESM data were replaced in this manner.

3. Components were retained if they had an eigenvalue greater than 1, and the appropriate number of components was also confirmed through visual inspection of a scree plot.

4. ANOVAs provide information on whether the differences between groups (e.g., men and women) or conditions (e.g., home, public, or work) on a particular variable (e.g., enjoyment or cortisol) are significantly larger than the variation within groups on that variable, such that one can be reasonably certain that between-group differences are not due to random variation. Main effects represent the effect of a single variable on the outcome variable; interactions are the effect of the intersection between two variables on the outcome (e.g., whether the effects of gender vary by location). Within-subject factors involve change within an individual over time (e.g., location or time of day), between-subject factors are factors defining different groups of individuals (e.g., gender).

5. In order to reduce a positive skew in the cortisol data, a windsorizing procedure was used in which cortisol values greater than 2 were replaced with values of 2. Windsorizing procedures enable the analyst to eliminate the influence of extreme values without losing data. In addition, all HLM models are reported using standard errors that are robust to slight violations of normalcy. A log transformation of the raw cortisol values across the entire day was not performed because this would have influenced the accuracy of fit of the diurnal cortisol curves. Time-controlled residual cortisol values were not substantially skewed.

6. Gender was represented as a dummy (0, 1) variable in the model, with women having a score of 0 and men having a score of 1, such that a positive coefficient represents a higher score for men, however the gender variable is centered such that the value for the intercept represents the weighted mean of the scores of the two groups.

7. The sample size is slightly larger for these analyses because the five individuals taking corticosteroid-based medications were not excluded for these comparisons, which relied purely on self-report data. As shown in figures 5.5 and 5.6, z-scores were used for the mood states and feelings about activities. Z-scores standardize the individuals' values on a distribution where the

mean = 0 and standard deviation = 1. For this chapter, the composite scores were computed for each beep. These scores were then standardized within individuals and averaged across each location. A value of 0.5 for productive at work would thus indicate that the individual was above his or her mean on productivity (across all contexts) when at work.

8. Cohen (1988) defined $d$ as the difference between means ($M_1 - M_2$) divided by the standard deviation of either group, assuming the variances of the two groups are homogeneous. In practice, the pooled standard deviation is commonly used. Thus, $d$ is the standardized difference between two groups. Cohen also provided guidelines for interpreting effects sizes, suggesting that a $d$ of .2 can be considered small, .5 medium, and .8 or above to be a large effect size for social science research.

9. The smaller sample size for men than women may be contributing to fewer significant comparisons for men.

10. There is, however, both experimental and naturalistic evidence, that increases in catecholamines (epinephrine, norepinephrine) are typically associated with task-related effort. It is this distinction between challenge and threat that typically differentiates between the activity of the SAM system and the activity of the HPA.

11. For positive-social emotion paired-sample t (105) = 6.66, p < .001; for hardworking-productive t (105) = 6.14, p < .001; for enjoyment of activities t (105) = 5.88, p < .001, for involvement in activities, t (105) = 7.26, p < .001.

# Commentary

*Douglas A. Granger, Elizabeth A. Shirtcliff*

*Conceptual advances of the past two decades, as well as technical developments that enable the non-invasive measurement of many physiological markers in saliva, have created new opportunities to integrate biological constructs into behavioral research. At the cutting edge of this endeavor biosocial models have emerged that consider individual differences in biobehavioral relationships to be a product of independent and interactive influences among environmental, social, and biological processes (e.g., Booth, Carver, and Granger 2000; Gottlieb 1992; Raine 2002). The work described by Adam is in many ways exemplary of this biosocial perspective. Her effort to characterize the relationship between momentary differences in stress-related biological activity and emotion in the context of everyday social life is innovative, and the findings are noteworthy. Adam reveals that higher levels of positive social emotions (cheerful, friendly, caring) and reports of working hard, engagement in activity, and productivity are associated with lower cortisol levels, whereas negative emotions (i.e., nervous, stressed, irritated) are associated with higher cortisol levels. Taken together, momentary emotions and feelings accounted for 26 percent of the variance in cortisol levels. Other findings reveal that the relationship between moment-to-moment change in negative emotionality and cortisol levels was stronger for men than for women, and cortisol levels were lower when adults were at work than at home. These observations are among the first to describe how daily experiences in naturalistic social settings are associated with the psychobiology of the stress response.*

*Generally, the observations support previous literature of linkages between negative emotionality and the activity of the hypothalamic–pituitary–adrenal (HPA) axis. That these effects occur in everyday social ecologies validates observations made in analog and laboratory settings. That gender moderates the link between negative emotion and cortisol is a very important observation and supports the argument by Taylor et al. (2000) that biological and behavioral stress responses may be fundamentally different by sex. To the best of our knowledge, the association between feelings of productivity and engagement and lower cortisol levels are novel. The observation that cortisol levels are higher at home than at work for parents is interesting. By contrast, in young children the opposite may be true. Higher cortisol levels are reported in young children in daycare environments than at home (Watamura et al. 2003). The findings underscore the need to extend our understanding of how cortisol-behavior relationships are attenuated or potentiated by the immediate social context of the family (Booth, Carver, and Granger 2000).*

*As Raine (2002) notes, the establishment of these biobehavioral associations represents a first step in a long process. The mechanisms underlying these interaction effects must be explained before we can derive their meaning for physical and mental health. In our opinion, the search for these "mechanisms," should not automatically focus on discovery of the "biological determinants" of behavior. Indeed, the biosocial perspective argues that our understanding of how behavioral, cognitive, and social variables shape individual differences in biological processes holds the key to extending our knowledge to new limits. Critical questions that remain unanswered include: Are these changes in salivary cortisol a consequence of intrinsic stable individual differences in negative emotionality? Are these effects shaped by unique features of specific social ecologies or determined by factors associated with social landscapes more generally? Do individual differences in cortisol-behavior-context associations confer risk or resilience? What is it about different social environments that permits or obscures cortisol-behavior associations? Clearly, answers to these types of questions are needed before we can speculate regarding the implications of the biosocial phenomenon described by Adam.*

*As behavioral scientists our assessments typically involve multiple methods and informants. Granger and Kivlighan (2003) note that it is surprising that most behaviorally trained investigators employ only a single measure (e.g., salivary cortisol) of the activity of a biological system, such as the HPA axis, in biosocial studies. Fifty years of research defines this system as an interconnected network of glands that communicate via soluble chemical messengers that can have opposing functions (Nelson 2000). In addition to cortisol, the adrenal gland secretes dehydroepinandrosterone (DHEA) in response to activation of the HPA axis. It is likely that DHEA is co-released with cortisol in response to events and psychological states typically studied in relation to cortisol secretion. Whereas cortisol is associated with learning and memory impairment, social inhibition, internalizing behavior problems, and immunosuppression (Chrousos and Gold 1992; McEwen and Sapolsky 1995), research suggests that DHEA may enhance learning, memory, and immunocompetence; protect neurons against the toxic effects of cortisol; and reduce anxiety and depression (see Majewska 1995; Wolf and Kirschbaum 1999).*

*Theorists speculate that the risk for initiation and progression of diverse pathological processes, potentiated by cortisol hyperactivity, is directly related to the ratio of cortisol to DHEA released by the adrenal. Individuals with the highest cortisol and lowest DHEA may be at the highest risk (Hechter, Grossman, and Chatterton 1997). With respect to Adam (this chapter), it would seem valuable to know whether moment-to-moment variation in DHEA is related spontaneously to expressed emotions and feelings in the everyday social world, and whether DHEA moderates the potential "negative effects" of cortisol secretion. Interestingly, studies show that females have higher DHEA levels than males (Granger et al. 1999) raising the possibility that DHEA moderates the sex difference in the strength of the association between cortisol and negative emotionality. Adam notes that cortisol may be independently related to both positive and negative emotions and feelings simultaneously. Without corresponding information about DHEA (and perhaps other products of the HPA axis), the interpretation of individual differences in cortisol secretion in relation to emotion and feelings seems limited. This illustration implies that the "bio" in our biosocial models may not always be operationalized in a manner consistent with the dynamic and integrative nature of biological systems (Granger and Kivlighan 2003). Exploration of ways in which to integrate multiple measures of key biological systems into biosocial research seems worthwhile.*

*The integration of measures of the HPA axis into behaviorally oriented research has focused research attention on the measurement and interpretation of individual differences in salivary cortisol. Traditionally, the activity of the HPA axis has been operationalized using cortisol levels, the diurnal rhythm of cortisol production, or cortisol reactivity and recovery to discrete stimuli or events. Interestingly, each of these perspectives shares a basic assumption of an inherent value of individual differences in cortisol "levels" or "change from pre-challenge baseline." The analytical approach employed by Adam to study correlates of moment-to-moment variation in cortisol "levels" is innovative because it uses Hierarchical Linear Modeling (HLM) to evaluate an individual's cortisol variability relative to their expected diurnal rhythm. In a recent study (Shirtcliff et al. 2003), we also approached the issue of HPA-behavior relationships using a novel analytical strategy. In contrast to Adam, we hypothesized that key behavioral features would be linked to stable or consistent "trait-like" variation in the activity of the HPA axis. Thus, our approach favored estimating individual differences in stable trait-like components of the variation of HPA axis activity. Latent state-trait modeling techniques were used to estimate components of variance in cortisol attributable to consistency, specificity, and measurement error. Briefly, early morning saliva samples were obtained from 654 youth (ages 6–16 yrs) on two successive days one year apart. After controlling time of day, LST modeling revealed 70 percent of the variance could be attributed to state-like sources, and 28 percent to trait-like sources. Higher levels of externalizing behavior problems were associated with lower cortisol levels across three years of behavioral assessments, but only for the component of variance attributable to trait-like sources, and only for boys. These findings raise the possibility that links between trait cortisol and behavior may be obscured if the effects of situational influences on adrenocortical activity are not accounted for. By contrast, Adam's findings suggest the magnitude of the effect between cortisol and momentary emotions and feelings may best be studied when the participants choose the social environments they engage rather than when standard social constraints are imposed on participants by researchers. Taken together, these studies highlight the value of applying two very different measurement and analytical strategies to address cortisol-behavior relationships. Shirtcliff et al. (forthcoming) confirm that the majority of variance in cortisol levels is linked to situationally specific factors. The approach employed by Adam was successful in measuring meaningful situationally specific variance in cortisol levels and relating a large portion of that variance to momentary differences in emotion and feelings.*

*The next generation of biosocial research needs to go beyond simple description of interaction effects and research the fundamental mechanisms and processes underlying them (Raine 2002). Before our knowledge can be extended to new limits using the biosocial perspective, theoretical advances are needed to help guide and interpret the findings of future research. The appropriate measurement tools and statistical strategies necessary move this endeavor toward explaining and understanding the nature of biosocial phenomenon. Yet, discussion of biosocial observations often falls short because investigators digress to focus on mechanistic micro-level detail of the biology of the HPA axis. The immediate need is for the development of mid-level theories that will enable us to specify, test, and refine hypotheses regarding the integration of biological processes with behavioral and social-contextual levels of analysis (Granger and Kivlighan 2003).*

# 6 Emotional transmission between parents and adolescents: the importance of work characteristics and relationship quality

*Jennifer L. Matjasko and Amy F. Feldman*

Dual-earner families are now a normative part of American society. Labor force participation rates among married women almost doubled between 1966, when 35 percent of married women were employed, and 1994, when 61 percent of married women were in the labor force (Winkler 1998). By 1997, 71 percent of women with school-age children were employed (Bianchi 1999). In comparison, fathers' rates of employment have remained relatively unchanged. Both mothers and fathers now fill multiple roles: worker, spouse, and parent. It is likely that this shift in maternal employment has changed the emotional context of contemporary family life (Senécal, Vallerand, and Guay 2001).

Generally, work stress and job autonomy have been linked to both marital quality and parent–child relationships (Westman, Etzion, and Danon 2001). One way that researchers characterize parental employment is in terms of job autonomy, or the extent to which workers have control over the day-to-day activities of their jobs. It is commonly assumed that individuals with job autonomy are intrinsically motivated by their work. In other words, their jobs provide them with a sense of satisfaction that goes beyond monetary rewards, which in turn boosts individuals' career aspirations and productivity on the job. As a result, workers' emotions might be tightly linked with day-to-day fluctuations in job circumstances.

With recent changes in maternal employment and the status of women in the workplace, it might be the case that an increasing proportion of mothers are intrinsically motivated by their jobs; employed mothers with high career aspirations might invest both time and emotions in the workplace. Among such mothers, emotions associated with workplace demands might also be carried over into the home and influence the emotions of other family members. Because women have been investing time in the workplace, fathers have taken a more active role in household tasks and childrearing (Gottfried, Gottfried, and Bathurst 1995). This transformation requires a better understanding of the impact, both positive and negative, that maternal and paternal employment has on day-to-day family processes, specifically, the extent to which job characteristics and the quality of the parent–adolescent relationship influences the transfer of emotions between parents and their adolescents.

Few studies have investigated the relationship between work characteristics and the daily flow of emotions between parents and adolescents (i.e., work–family crossover; see Larson and Richards 1994 for an exception). Studying the impact of parental work on adolescents is critical because most teenagers are concretely formulating their own future educational and career aspirations (Castellino et al. 1998), making this a period in the life course when they might be sensitive to their parents' day-to-day job-related stressors. As a result, both positive and negative emotional experiences associated with parents' employment may influence adolescents' own future career trajectories (see Schneider and Stevenson 1999 on this point).

## Work–family crossover: emotional transmission between parents and adolescents

Emotional transmission, or the extent to which the day-to-day feelings of one family member influence the feelings of another, has recently begun to capture the attention of scholars. Most notably, Larson and Richards (1994) describe the emotional context of working- and middle-class families with adolescents. In studying the transfer of emotions in father–adolescent and mother–adolescent dyads, they find little evidence of emotional transmission between fathers and adolescents. Emotional transfers between mothers and adolescents occur more frequently, although adolescent emotion is more likely to be passed on to mothers (as opposed to the other way around). One exception to this direction of influence is seen when mothers return home from work, a time when mother's mood is found to influence her adolescent's mood. Thus, a high degree of emotional transmission between mothers and adolescents and a lack of emotional transmission from fathers to their adolescents might be expected. On the other hand, the patterns of emotional transmission within father–adolescent and mother–adolescent dyads may be changing due to the evolving roles of women in the workplace and of fathers at home.

## Moderators of work–family crossover: work characteristics and relationship quality

Based on prior research, we expect to find some general patterns of emotional transmission between parents and adolescents; these patterns may differ for mothers and fathers. However, given recent changes in work and family roles of mothers and fathers, it might be the case that family processes vary by the kinds of jobs parents have. A useful concept that can be used to gauge the quality of jobs and the potential for work–family emotion transfer is *intrinsic work motivation* (Bond, Galinsky, and Swanberg 1998; Warr, Cook, and Wall 1979). Jobs that allow for autonomy, require a variety of skills, and that contribute significantly to the quality of the product attract workers who view their work as an end in itself and encourage the development of intrinsic motivation (Fried and Ferris 1987; Hackman and Oldham 1980; Tiegs, Tetrick, and Fried 1992). These same characteristics are associated with "quality jobs" and better worker functioning as defined by Bond et al. (1998). It is likely that parents who are intrinsically motivated by their jobs invest more of their emotional lives in the workplace. They might also bring their workplace emotional experiences home with them and transfer these emotions to other family members.

The relationship between parents' intrinsic work motivation and work–family emotion transfer has not been adequately addressed in the literature, making it difficult to predict how work motivation might affect the relationship between parents' emotions at work and their transfer to adolescents at home. By definition, individuals scoring high on intrinsic work motivation derive more satisfaction from work which might result in better moods at work and at home. Alternatively, if parents are highly invested in and highly value their work, they might be more vulnerable to daily fluctuations in work-related demands and stress, thus increasing negative moods at work and at home that may be transferred to their adolescents.

In addition to intrinsic work motivation, it is important to account for other factors that have been related to work–family emotion transfer. Prior studies indicate that the number of hours that parents work and the amount of time that they take for themselves are related to emotional transmission between family members. Long work hours may take both time and energy away from the family and influence the extent to which positive and negative emotions are transferred between family members. Prior research has found that increased work hours acts as a stressor and may increase the frequency with which negative emotions experienced at work are transferred to the home and to other family members (Schor 1991). Research has also shown that time for self is associated with better parent adjustment (Repetti 1989), which may increase the frequency with which positive emotions are transferred from parents to other family members. Particularly for mothers, time for self may lessen the burdens of household tasks after work, which might increase the rates at which positive emotional transmission occurs between family members.

Adolescent gender and the nature of the parent–adolescent relationship may also influence emotional transmission within parent–adolescent dyads. Larson and Richards (1994) found that daughters are more likely to experience their parents' emotions, especially within the mother–adolescent dyad. Mother–adolescent closeness is also related to greater positive and negative emotional transmission from mothers to adolescents (Larson and Gillman 1999). Given that fathers' roles within contemporary families are evolving, we might also expect to find the same pattern for fathers and adolescents. It would thus be reasonable to expect that gender and parent–adolescent closeness might be important determinants in emotional transmission within parent–adolescent dyads.

## Research focus

We examine two models of work–family crossover in this chapter. Specifically, we assess the extent to which parents' emotions upon returning home from work influence their adolescent's mood. For example, when a father comes home from work feeling angry, does his adolescent also react with anger? Second, we assess the extent to which work characteristics, parental time for self, adolescent gender, and parent–adolescent closeness moderate the transmission of emotions between parents and adolescents. Specifically, the following research questions are addressed: (1) Are anger, anxiety, and happiness transmitted from mothers to adolescents and from fathers to adolescents when parents return home from work? (2) What factors moderate the transmission of emotion from parents to adolescents?

## Hypotheses

*Hypothesis 1.* There will be a high degree of emotional transmission between mothers and adolescents and there may be a lack of emotional transmission between fathers and adolescents (Larson and Richards 1994).

*Hypothesis 2.* Intrinsic work motivation may enhance emotional transmission between parents and adolescents.

*Hypothesis 3.* The more hours that parents work, the greater the likelihood of negative emotional transmission between parents and adolescents.

*Hypothesis 4.* Parental time for self will serve as a "cooling off period" and result in less negative and more positive emotional transmission from parents to adolescents.

*Hypothesis 5.* Gender and parent–adolescent closeness will determine emotional crossover for both mother–adolescent and father–adolescent dyads. This hypothesis is based on previous findings that daughters are more likely to experience their parents' emotions (Larson and Richards 1994) and that adolescents have closer relationships with their mothers (Larson and Gillman 1999).

## Method

### Sample

This study uses data from dual-earner families with adolescents who participated in the 500 Family Study. Only families in which mothers, fathers, and adolescents completed surveys and participated in the Experience Sampling Method (ESM) were selected for analysis. The 143 families in this subsample do not significantly differ from the omitted families with respect to parents' occupations, hours worked, family income, and parent–adolescent relationship quality.

### Measures

*Moderators of work–family crossover*  Moderators of parent-to-adolescent emotional transmission include intrinsic work motivation, number of hours worked, time for self, adolescent gender, and parent–adolescent relationship quality. These five variables were constructed similarly for mothers and fathers.

A series of five survey items was used to assess *intrinsic work motivation*: the degree to which parents work for challenge, for enjoyment, to become well known, to contribute to knowledge, and to help people. The selection of these terms as measures of intrinsic work motivation is based on the work of Hackman and Oldham (1980). To form the intrinsic work motivation scale, separate factor analyses for mothers and fathers were performed using principal components analysis on these five items. One factor emerged representing intrinsic work motivation.[1]

*Parents' work hours* is based on categorical responses to a survey question that asked parents how many hours per week they typically work at their main job. Response options ranged from 1 (1–15 hours per week) to 7 (more than 60 hours per week). Fathers and mothers did not significantly differ on the number of hours per week that they reported working ($\chi^2 = 27.35$; p = .61).

*Time for self* measures how often parents routinely make time to focus on themselves during the week, a variable which has been related to parental well-being (Repetti 1989). Survey responses to this question ranged from 0 (never or rarely) to 3 (several times a week). Mothers and fathers did not significantly differ from each other in the amount of time they set aside for themselves ($\chi^2 = 11.06$; p = .27).

*Parent–adolescent relationship* scales were constructed from a series of survey items designed to assess the mother–adolescent and father–adolescent relationships. These items are from the Armsden and Greenberg parent and peer inventory (1987), which describes the extent to which mothers or fathers accept, talk with, have expectations of, and attend to their adolescents. The inventory also measures adolescents' level of trust and anger with their mothers and fathers. The mother and father scales were factor analyzed separately. Each is based on nine items that loaded on a dimension of the scale termed *closeness*.[2]

*Adolescent gender* was coded as a dummy variable (0 = male and 1 = female). Male and female adolescents were equally represented in the subsample (71 males and 72 females).

### Parent and adolescent emotions

ESM data were used to measure paternal, maternal, and adolescent emotions. The emotions analyzed in this chapter include positive emotions, such as cheerfulness and friendliness, and negative emotions, such as irritability and anger. The ESM items were rated on a 0-to-3 scale (0 = not feeling that emotion; 3 = very much feeling that emotion). The eighteen emotions were factor analyzed using varimax rotation to form three distinct emotionality scales: anger, anxiety, and happiness.[3] Mothers, fathers, and adolescents did not significantly differ on their mean levels of anger, anxiety, and happiness.[4]

ESM responses were also coded by the respondents' locations when beeped. Over 160 specific locations (e.g., in the kitchen, in class, at the office) were originally coded. For purposes of analysis, these specific codes were collapsed into four categories: (1) *home* for beeps that occurred at home for parents and adolescents; (2) *work* for beeps that occurred at work for parents; (3) *school* for beeps that occurred at school for adolescents; and (4) *other* for beeps that did not occur at home, work, or school. Among all participants, approximately 49 percent of ESM responses occurred at home, while 22 percent occurred in contexts other than home, work, or school. Among mothers, about 19 percent of their ESM responses occurred at work; among fathers, 35 percent of responses occurred at work. For adolescents, 35 percent of ESM responses occurred at school.

*Analyses*

Multivariate analyses were used to estimate the extent to which mothers' and fathers' intrinsic work motivation, job hours, time for self, adolescent gender, and the quality of the parent–adolescent relationship moderate parent–adolescent crossover in emotions. Specifically, these models estimate the extent to which the parent's emotion (the sender) at Time 2 (during the first at-home beep) is related to the adolescent's emotion (the receiver) at Time 2 after the parent's return from work, controlling for the adolescent's emotion at Time 1. These analyses were performed by further refining the "transfer occasions" to include times when both parents and adolescents were at home during the first parental after-work beep (i.e., a "contact occasion"; Larson and Gillman 1999) as well as times when adolescents responded to the beep immediately preceding this contact occasion (regardless of context) so that adolescent emotion could be adequately controlled for prior to exposure to the parent's emotional state. Because of these conditions, the number of transfer occasions in the crossover models was limited.[5]

A "prospective model" was used to examine parent–adolescent crossover. This model estimates similarity in the parent's and adolescent's emotions, providing a coefficient that measures parent-to-adolescent crossover in emotional states (Larson and Gillman 1999). The prospective model was estimated using two-level Hierarchical Linear Modeling (HLM; Bryk and Raudenbush 1992). HLM is particularly advantageous for this analysis because it nests emotions (at home and at work) within dyads. Adolescents' emotion at Time 2 is the outcome, and both parents' emotions at Time 2 and adolescents' emotions at Time 1 are predictors.

*Level-One (within dyad):*

$$Y_{ij} = \beta_{0j} + \beta_{1j} + \beta_{2j} + r_{ij} \qquad \text{(Equation 1)}$$

where $Y_{ij}$ = predicted Time 2 adolescent emotion after parents' return from work; $\beta_{0j}$ = coefficient for Time 2 adolescent emotion (holding all variables constant); $\beta_{1j}$ = coefficient for parent emotion at Time 2 upon returning home; $\beta_{2j}$ = coefficient for adolescent emotion at Time 1; $r_{ij}$ = error term.

*Level-Two Intercept Model (between dyad):*

$$\beta_{0j} = \gamma_{00} + \gamma_{01} + \gamma_{02} + \gamma_{03} + \gamma_{04} + \gamma_{05} + u_{0j} \qquad \text{(Equation 2)}$$

where $\beta_{0j}$ = predicted coefficient for Time 2 adolescent emotion; $\gamma_{00}$ = intercept coefficient (holding all other variables constant); $\gamma_{01}$ = coefficient for intrinsic work motivation; $\gamma_{02}$ = coefficient for parents' work hours; $\gamma_{03}$ = coefficient for parents' time for self; $\gamma_{04}$ = coefficient for adolescent gender; $\gamma_{05}$ = coefficient for parent–adolescent closeness; $u_{0j}$ = error term.

*Level-Two Slope Model (between dyad):*

$$\beta_{1j} = \gamma_{10} + \gamma_{11} + \gamma_{12} + \gamma_{13} + \gamma_{14} + \gamma_{15} + u_{1j} \qquad \text{(Equation 3)}$$

where $\beta_{1j}$ = predicted coefficient for Time 2 parent emotion; $\gamma_{10}$ = slope coefficient (holding all other variables constant); $\gamma_{11}$ = coefficient for intrinsic work motivation; $\gamma_{12}$ = coefficient for parents' work hours; $\gamma_{13}$ = coefficient for parents' time for self; $\gamma_{14}$ = coefficient for adolescent gender; $\gamma_{15}$ = coefficient for parent–adolescent closeness; $u_{1j}$ = error term.

Level-1 estimates within-person adolescent emotion at Time 2, taking into account parent emotion at Time 2 and adolescent emotion at Time 1. Level-2 estimates the influence of the parent (in the mother–adolescent or father–adolescent dyad) on adolescent emotion at Time 2 (e.g., level of parental intrinsic motivation). The Level-2 model tests whether there are between-dyad differences in the relationship between parent emotion upon returning home from work and Time 2 adolescent emotion, taking into account the influence of parents' intrinsic work motivation, work hours, time for self, adolescent gender, and parent–adolescent closeness.

## Results

Results from two general models are presented. First, general mother–adolescent and father–adolescent emotional transmission models were estimated. In the basic models for these analyses, adolescent reports of happiness, anger, and anxiety after the parent returns home from work is the dependent variable (Time 2 adolescent emotion at home). Two measures serve as independent variables: parent emotion upon returning home from work, as well as a control for adolescent emotion prior to the parent's return (Time 1 adolescent emotion). The models test whether parent emotion at Time 2 predicts adolescent emotion at Time 2, with separate models for fathers and mothers. The second set of models shows the extent to which the key moderators influence emotional transmission between parents and adolescents.

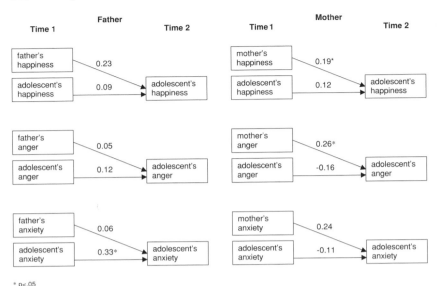

Figure 6.1 Transmission of emotions between parents and adolescents (Level-1 coefficients)

*Emotional crossover: general transmission between parents and adolescents*

Three separate HLM analyses – one for each emotion – were estimated to gauge the transmission of emotions within mother–adolescent and father–adolescent dyads. Hypothesis 1 suggests that there will be a high degree of emotional transmission between mothers and adolescents and a lack of emotional transmission between fathers and adolescents. Figure 6.1, which presents the Level-1 slope coefficients for the basic parent–adolescent transmission models, shows different patterns of emotional transmission for fathers and mothers, providing partial support for the hypothesis. There is some degree of emotional crossover between mothers and adolescents, but there is no evidence of significant emotional transmission between fathers and adolescents.

Both happiness and anger are transmitted from mothers to adolescents. Maternal reports of happiness and anger upon returning home from work are positively related to adolescent happiness and anger at Time 2. The addition of maternal happiness to the mother–adolescent happiness model explains 3 percent of the within-dyad variance in adolescent happiness at Time 2; the addition of maternal anger to the mother–adolescent anger model also explains 3 percent of the within-dyad variance in adolescent anger at Time 2.[6] In the mother–adolescent anxiety model, maternal anxiety is not significantly related to Time 2 adolescent anxiety, which suggests that anxiety may be a less visible and thus less transmittable emotion in this subset of mother–adolescent dyads. In the father models, the small number of transmission occasions may explain the lack of emotional crossover between fathers and adolescents.

### Predictors of emotional transmission between parents and adolescents

The second set of analyses examined the extent to which parents' happiness, anger, and anxiety influenced adolescents' happiness, anger, and anxiety upon parents' return home from work, using parents' work characteristics, adolescent gender, and parent–adolescent relationship factors as Level-2 variables. Despite the lack of evidence for direct emotional crossover from fathers to adolescents, certain factors might serve to strengthen the transmission for father–adolescent dyads with certain dyad-level characteristics. Table 6.1 presents the results for the happiness, anger, and anxiety models for both mothers and fathers.[7]

As table 6.1 shows, the intercept coefficients for the slope models (parents' emotion at Time 2) are significantly associated with adolescents' emotion at Time 2 only for the father–adolescent models. Both fathers' anger and anxiety at Time 2 are negatively associated with adolescent anger and anxiety at Time 2 when all other variables are held constant ($\gamma_{10} = -8.58$, p < .001 and $\gamma_{10} = -7.70$, p < .001, respectively). Higher levels of paternal anger and anxiety at Time 2 (when first returning home from work) are thus associated with decreases in adolescents' anger and anxiety at Time 2. Fathers' happiness at Time 2 is also negatively but marginally associated with adolescent happiness at Time 2 ($\gamma_{10} = -1.91$, p < .10). Adolescents may view their father's emotions as work related rather than personally directed, which could account for the lack of synchrony between fathers' and adolescents' emotions. Alternatively, fathers may be unlikely to communicate their emotions to their adolescents.

*Intrinsic work motivation and work–family crossover*   Hypothesis 2 assumes that intrinsic work motivation may enhance emotional transmission between parents and adolescents. Results from the HLM suggest that the relationship is more complex. In the father–adolescent happiness crossover model, intrinsic work motivation is negative and significant in the slope model ($\gamma_{11} = -0.36$; p < .01), which indicates that the relationship between fathers' happiness at Time 2 and adolescent happiness at Time 2 is more asynchronous for fathers who score high on intrinsic motivation. The addition of intrinsic work motivation on the slope

Table 6.1 *Multilevel crossover models – Time 2 adolescent emotion at home as a function of parent emotion at home (Level-2 coefficients)*

| Variable | Fathers | | | Mothers | | |
|---|---|---|---|---|---|---|
| | Happiness | Anger | Anxiety | Happiness | Anger | Anxiety |
| Time 2 Emotion for adolescent ($\gamma_{00}$) | −0.66 | 0.88 | 0.05 | 0.17 | 0.79 | 0.25 |
| | (0.75) | (0.70) | (0.76) | (0.42) | (0.37) | (0.48) |
| Work motivation ($\gamma_{01}$) | 0.11 | −0.04 | −0.27 | 0.01 | 0.14+ | 0.03 |
| | (0.10) | (0.17) | (0.27) | (0.08) | (0.08) | (0.10) |
| Work hours ($\gamma_{02}$) | 0.06 | −0.04 | 0.05 | 0.04 | −0.07 | 0.04 |
| | (0.10) | (0.09) | (0.09) | (0.07) | (0.05) | (0.07) |
| Time for self ($\gamma_{03}$) | 0.12 | −0.18+ | −0.16 | −0.21** | −0.07 | −0.10 |
| | (0.09) | (0.10) | (0.12) | (0.07) | (0.08) | (0.08) |
| Adolescent gender ($\gamma_{04}$) | −0.03 | −0.17 | 0.10 | 0.01 | −0.22 | −0.19 |
| | (0.21) | (0.27) | (0.30) | (0.16) | (0.16) | (0.18) |
| P–A relationship ($\gamma_{05}$) | −0.06 | −0.09 | −0.03 | 0.20* | −0.09 | −0.10 |
| | (0.11) | (0.11) | (0.31) | (0.09) | (0.08) | (0.11) |
| Time 2 Emotion for parent ($\gamma_{10}$) | −1.91+ | −8.58*** | −7.70*** | 0.13 | −0.70 | −0.11 |
| | (0.98) | (0.73) | (2.15) | (0.45) | (0.72) | (1.10) |
| Work motivation ($\gamma_{11}$) | −0.36** | −1.04*** | −1.39 | −0.14+ | 0.07 | 0.04 |
| | (0.13) | (0.15) | (0.89) | (0.08) | (0.12) | (0.24) |
| Work hours ($\gamma_{12}$) | 0.28** | 0.58*** | 0.03 | 0.04 | 0.35*** | −0.03 |
| | (0.10) | (0.06) | (0.21) | (0.07) | (0.10) | (0.15) |
| Time for self ($\gamma_{13}$) | 0.30** | 1.56*** | 0.94** | 0.10 | 0.12 | −0.28 |
| | (0.11) | (0.20) | (0.32) | (0.09) | (0.13) | (0.21) |
| Adolescent gender ($\gamma_{14}$) | 0.28 | 1.25*** | 2.46** | −0.16 | −0.29 | 0.57 |
| | (0.31) | (0.13) | (0.79) | (0.20) | (0.36) | (0.50) |
| P–A relationship ($\gamma_{15}$) | 0.68*** | −0.23* | 4.18*** | 0.10 | 0.59*** | −0.26 |
| | (0.16) | (0.10) | (0.96) | (0.10) | (0.15) | (0.24) |
| Time 1 Emotion for adolescent ($\gamma_{20}$) | 0.06 | 0.07 | 0.50* | 0.09 | −0.21 | −0.07 |
| | (0.17) | (0.13) | (0.22) | (0.12) | (0.14) | (0.07) |

*Note:* Standard errors are in parentheses.
+p < .10; *p < .05; **p < .01; ***p < .001

explains 11 percent of the between-dyad variation in the relationship between the father's happiness upon returning home from work and the adolescent's happiness after his return.[8] Intrinsic work motivation is negative and marginally significant in the mother–adolescent happiness slope model ($\gamma_{11}$ = −0.14; p < .10).

In the father–adolescent anger slope model, intrinsic work motivation is negative and significant ($\gamma_{11}$ = −1.04; p < .001). The negative coefficient indicates an increase in the negative relationship between fathers' anger at Time 2 and adolescents' anger at Time 2 for fathers who score higher on intrinsic work motivation. Fathers who are highly invested in their jobs may be less involved with their children and thus less emotionally "in sync" with them. The addition of intrinsic work motivation to the father–adolescent anger slope model explains 9 percent of the between-dyad variation in the relationship between father and adolescent anger.[9] In the mother–adolescent anger intercept model, intrinsic work motivation is positive and marginally significant ($\gamma_{01} = 0.14$; p < .10), indicating that adolescents' mean anger at Time 2 is marginally higher when their mothers score higher on intrinsic work motivation. Intrinsic work motivation is not significant in the mother–adolescent anxiety and father–adolescent anxiety intercept or slope models.

*Parental work hours and work–family crossover*  Parents' work hours were hypothesized to act as a parent stressor, increasing the likelihood of negative emotional transmission and decreasing positive transmission between parents and adolescents (Hypothesis 3). This hypothesis is partially supported. In the father–adolescent happiness slope model, the relationship between father and adolescent happiness varies by paternal work hours ($\gamma_{12} = 0.28$; p < .01). The relationship between father happiness when first returning home and adolescent happiness after his return is less asynchronous for fathers who work more (the intercept coefficient for the slope model indicates a negative relationship between fathers' emotion at Time 2 and adolescents' emotion at Time 2). The addition of work hours to the father–adolescent happiness slope model explains 14 percent of the between-dyad variation in the relationship between father and adolescent happiness.[10] In contrast to fathers, maternal work hours has no significant association with the relationship between maternal happiness at Time 2 and adolescent happiness at Time 2.

In the parent–adolescent anger crossover models, hours worked is positive and significant in both fathers' and mothers' slope models ($\gamma_{12} = 0.58$; p < .001 in the father slope model; $\gamma_{12} = 0.35$; p < .001 in the mother slope model). This indicates that the negative relationship between parent and adolescent anger is weaker for parents who work more hours. Parents who work longer hours thus appear to be more likely to transmit their anger to their adolescents. The addition of work hours explains 9 percent of the between-dyad variation in the relationship between father and adolescent anger and 12 percent of the variation in the relationship between mother and adolescent anger.[11] In both the fathers' and mothers' anxiety crossover models, parent work hours does not explain significant between-dyad variation in adolescent anxiety at Time 2. Work hours also does not explain between-dyad variation in the relationship between parent and adolescent anxiety.

*Time for self and work–family crossover*     Hypothesis 4 suggests that parents' time for self may serve as a "cooling off period" and result in less anger and anxiety emotional transmission and more happiness emotional transmission from parents to adolescents. There is partial support for this hypothesis. In the happiness crossover model for fathers, the coefficient for time for self is positive and significant on the slope ($\gamma_{13} = 0.30$; $p < .01$). In essence, the negative relationship between father happiness when first returning home and adolescent happiness after his return is not as strong for fathers who take more time for themselves, suggesting that time for self does contribute to positive emotional transmission between fathers and adolescents. The addition of time for self to the father–adolescent happiness slope model explains 14 percent of the between-dyad variation in the relationship between parent and adolescent happiness.[12] In the happiness intercept model for mothers, time for self is related to between-dyad differences in Time 2 adolescent reports of happiness. Adolescents whose mothers report taking more time for themselves have lower mean happiness scores at Time 2 ($\gamma_{03} = -0.21$; $p < .01$). The addition of time for self to the mother–adolescent happiness intercept model explains 16 percent of the between-dyad variation in adolescents' reports of happiness at Time 2.[13] In the slope model, mothers' time for self does not explain significant variation in the relationship between mothers' happiness at Time 2 and adolescents' happiness at Time 2.

While time for self is not significant in either the mother–adolescent anger crossover intercept or slope models, it is marginally significant in the father–adolescent intercept model ($\gamma_{03} = -0.18$; $p < .10$). The more time that fathers report taking for themselves, the lower the Time 2 reports of adolescent anger. In the father–adolescent anger crossover slope model, time for self explains significant between-dyad variation in the relationship between father and adolescent anger. The negative relationship between paternal anger upon returning home from work and Time 2 adolescent anger is not as strong for fathers who report taking more time for themselves ($\gamma_{13} = 1.56$; $p < .001$). The addition of time for self to the father–adolescent crossover slope model explains 11 percent of the variation between dyads in the relationship between paternal anger upon returning home from work and adolescent reports of their own anger after his return.[14]

Finally, in the anxiety father–adolescent crossover model, the coefficient for fathers' time for self is positive and significant on the slope model ($\gamma_{13} = 0.94$; $p < .01$), indicating that the negative relationship between paternal and adolescent anxiety is not as strong for fathers who report more time for self. The addition of time for self to the father–adolescent anxiety slope model explains 18 percent of the between-dyad variation.[15] Time for self is not significant in either the mother-adolescent anxiety intercept or slope models.

*Adolescent gender and work–family crossover*    Based on prior research, Hypothesis 5 proposes that positive and negative emotional transmission will be more likely to occur in mother–daughter dyads. Analyses indicate that adolescent gender is a significant factor in the transfer of emotions only in the father models. Specifically, the coefficient for adolescent gender is positive and significant in the father–adolescent anger and anxiety slope models ($\gamma_{14}$ = 1.25, p < .001 and 2.46, p < .01, respectively), indicating that the negative relationship between fathers' and adolescents' anger and anxiety is not as strong for girls. The addition of adolescent gender to the father–adolescent slope model explains 14 percent of the between-dyad variation in the relationship between father and adolescent anger, and 19 percent of the between-dyad variation in the relationship between father and adolescent anxiety.[16]

*Parent–adolescent relationship quality and work–family crossover* Hypothesis 5 also suggests that the quality of the parent–adolescent relationship might lead to greater synchrony in parent and adolescent emotions, making the transfer of all emotions more likely in parent–adolescent relationships that are rated higher in acceptance and warmth. In the father–adolescent happiness crossover models, the quality of the parent–adolescent relationship is positive and significant in the slope model ($\gamma_{15}$ = 0.68; p < .001), which indicates that the negative relationship between paternal and adolescent happiness is not as strong for adolescents who feel closer to their fathers. The addition of the parent–adolescent closeness to the father–adolescent happiness slope model explains 16 percent of the between-dyad variation in the relationship between paternal and adolescent happiness.[17] In addition, the parent–adolescent relationship is positive and significant in the mother–adolescent happiness intercept model ($\gamma_{05}$ = 0.20; p < .05). Adolescents who feel closer to their mothers report significantly higher levels of happiness at Time 2. The addition of parent–adolescent closeness to the mother–adolescent happiness intercept model explains 10 percent of the between-dyad variation in adolescent happiness at Time 2.[18]

Relationship quality is not significant in the father–adolescent and mother–adolescent anger intercept models, but is significant in both the father–adolescent and mother–adolescent slope models. In the father–adolescent model, parent–adolescent closeness is negative and significant ($\gamma_{13}$ = −0.23; p < .05). Thus, greater parent–adolescent closeness strengthens the negative relationship between father and adolescent anger at Time 2. The addition of parent–adolescent closeness to the father–adolescent anger slope model explains 6 percent of the between-dyad variation in the relationship between paternal and adolescent anger.[19] In contrast to the father–adolescent model, the parent–adolescent relationship coefficient in the mother–adolescent anger slope model is positive and significant ($\gamma_{15} = 0.59$; $p < .001$), indicating that negative relationship between maternal and adolescent anger is not as strong when adolescents feel closer to their mothers. The addition of parent–adolescent closeness to the mother–adolescent anger slope model explains 12 percent of the between-dyad variation in the relationship between maternal and adolescent anger at Time 2.[20]

Parent–adolescent closeness does not significantly predict between-dyad differences in Time 2 adolescent anxiety in either the father–adolescent or mother–adolescent intercept models or in the mother–adolescent slope model. However, parent–adolescent closeness is positive and significant in the father–adolescent anxiety slope model ($\gamma_{13} = 4.18$; $p < .001$). In other words, the negative relationship between paternal and adolescent anxiety is not as strong when adolescents report feeling close to their fathers. The addition of parent–adolescent closeness to the father–adolescent anxiety slope model explains 21 percent of the between-dyad variation in the relationship between paternal and adolescent anxiety at Time 2.[21]

## Discussion

Even though the two-working-parent family has become the societal norm, few studies have explicitly considered day-to-day emotional transmission between working parents and their adolescents (see Larson and Richards 1994 for exceptions). This chapter aimed to fill this gap by examining the transmission of parental emotion upon returning home from work – in the form of anger, anxiety, and happiness – to their adolescents. In the basic parent–adolescent transmission models, it was assumed that there would be a high degree of emotional transmission between mothers and adolescents, while there might be a lack of transmission between fathers and their teenagers. Generally, results provide evidence for emotional transmission between mothers and adolescents, but not between fathers and adolescents. Despite the increasing involvement of women in the workplace and men in the household, the present findings do not differ from those of Larson and Richards (1994). They found that while fathers were not in tune with their adolescents' emotions, mothers were. It seems that fathers may still be a "shadowy presence," spending time with their adolescents but not necessarily interacting with them. On the other hand, both maternal happiness and anger are significantly related to adolescent happiness and anger. However, in these mother-to-adolescent transmission models, maternal emotion explains only a small proportion of the within-dyad variance in adolescent happiness and anger. Other factors, not captured in the models, may be important in explaining the transfer of emotions between parents and adolescents. It is possible that accounting for activities such as doing housework or for the presence of other family members might explain more within-dyad variation in the emotional transmission process.

A second set of parent-to-adolescent emotional transmission models investigated whether intrinsic work motivation, work hours, time for self, adolescent gender, and the parent–adolescent relationship explain between-dyad differences in adolescent happiness, anger, and anxiety. The two work factors, intrinsic work motivation and work hours, are significant in the paternal happiness slope model but operate in opposite directions: the relationship between father and adolescent happiness is more asynchronous for fathers scoring high on intrinsic work motivation. In other words, when fathers report higher levels of happiness upon returning home from work, adolescents are likely to report lower levels when their fathers rate themselves as high on intrinsic work motivation. The relationship between mother and adolescent happiness is also more asynchronous for mothers who are high in intrinsic motivation, but the effect is only marginally significant. One explanation for this finding could be that those parents working in jobs for personal satisfaction may invest less in other roles, particularly the parent role, which could lead to a lack of emotional synchrony between parents and adolescents.

Paternal work hours has the opposite effect. For fathers who report working more hours, the relationship between parent and adolescent reports of happiness are more in line with each other. Work hours also has the same effect in the father–adolescent and in the mother–adolescent anger transmission models. It may be that putting in the extra time at work limits the amount of time that parents and adolescents can spend together, making their time together more intense. In a sense, these families might be trading quantity for quality of time together. The happiness or anger that parents express upon returning home from work may bring adolescents' own sense of happiness and anger more in line with their parents.

The third parent factor, time for self, is significant in all of the father–adolescent models and is similar in effect to work hours: father and adolescent reports of happiness, anger, and anxiety are more in line with each other when fathers report taking more time for themselves. When this is considered along with the findings related to the number of hours worked per week, it could be that when fathers and adolescents spend more time apart, the time that they do spend together is more intense and emotionally laden. If this is the case, then parents' and adolescents' emotions might be less asynchronous. Maternal time for self is also related to lower values for adolescent happiness. Mothers who report taking more time for themselves may be less invested in their parenting role which may in turn induce lower levels of adolescent happiness when they return home from work.

Fathers' and adolescent girls' reports of anger and anxiety are more in line with each other compared to boys. Girls may be more "in tune" with their fathers' negative moods, causing their own moods to be more similar to their fathers'. Parent–adolescent closeness is also associated with less emotional asynchrony in father and adolescent happiness and anxiety. Perhaps father-to-adolescent emotional happiness and anxiety are less asynchronous when adolescents feel close to their fathers because their relationship allows these emotions to be expressed and shared. In the case of father-to-adolescent anger transmission, the quality of the father–adolescent relationship is related to greater asynchrony. When fathers return home from work angry, adolescents with close relationships with their fathers may understand that the workplace is the source of the anger; as a result, adolescents may be less likely to respond with anger. Further work is needed to explore the origins and mechanisms related to this aspect of emotional transmission between fathers and adolescents.

In the mother-to-adolescent emotional transmission models, adolescents who feel closer to their mothers report small but significantly higher levels of happiness. This suggests that adolescents may feel happy to see their mothers at the end of day because they enjoy spending time together. In the mother-to-adolescent anger model, mother–adolescent closeness operates differently compared to the father-to-adolescent anger model: closeness is related to less asynchrony in anger between mothers and their adolescents. What might explain these findings? Adolescents may have different role expectations for mothers and fathers. Fathers might be expected to place more importance on their work roles. When the father returns home from work feeling angry, the adolescent may understand that work is stressful for him and be less likely to report being angry when he gets home. In contrast, adolescents may expect mothers to put work aside and care for the family when they return home from work. Thus when mothers feel angry upon returning home from work, adolescents may respond with anger as well. Future research should consider adolescents' role expectations for their parents when examining the dynamics of parent–adolescent relationships.

There are several general limitations to this chapter. First, only between-person transmission of the same emotions was explored. In other words, parent anger was examined in relation to adolescent anger. Models of emotional contagion generally predict that emotions in one person translate into similar emotions in others (Hatfield, Cacioppo, and Rapson 1994). However, Larson and Gillman (1999) found exploratory evidence for maternal anger resulting in adolescent anxiety within a sample of single-mother families. Their finding highlights the need to consider alternative models of emotional transmission that allow for different emotional responses among receivers.

Second, while it is important to understand the consequences that work characteristics and the quality of the parent–adolescent relationship has for short-term family dynamics, understanding their consequences for long-term adjustment patterns at the individual and family level is also important. For example, will the adolescents who grew up in families in which fathers work more and also transmit more happiness view their work more positively when they are adults? Will they structure their work and family lives differently from those whose fathers did not structure their work schedules in the same manner? Making connections between short-term dynamics and long-term processes is important for understanding the impact of work factors on individuals and families.

This chapter provides a useful first step in assessing the influence of work factors, specifically intrinsic work motivation, on family processes using time-sequence ESM data. However, the chapter also highlights many new questions that remain to be answered in understanding the impact that intrinsic work motivation has on families. Understanding this relationship is crucial so that employers can boost employee productivity and well-being, as well as the well-being of employees' families.

## NOTES

1. The factor loadings and eigenvalues for *intrinsic work motivation* are as follows:

|  | Fathers | Mothers |
|---|---|---|
| Well known | 0.58 | 0.53 |
| Enjoyment | 0.74 | 0.81 |
| Contribute | 0.72 | 0.74 |
| Challenge | 0.76 | 0.81 |
| Help people | 0.49 | 0.59 |
| Eigenvalue | 2.14 | 2.56 |
| Alpha | 0.80 | 0.82 |

2. The factor loadings and eigenvalues for the *parent–adolescent relationship* scales are as follows:

| Fathers | | Mothers | |
|---|---|---|---|
| I depend on my father for help. | 0.75 | My mother accepts me as I am. | 0.60 |
| I like to get my father's point of view. | 0.75 | Talking over my problems with my mother does not make me feel ashamed or foolish. | 0.53 |
| I tell my father about my problems. | 0.81 | My mother does not expect too much from me. | 0.65 |
| I get a lot of attention from my father. | 0.53 | My mother knows how often I am upset. | 0.47 |
| My father helps me to talk about my feelings. | 0.72 | My mother cares about my point of view. | 0.52 |
| My father depends on me for help with his problems. | 0.41 | I don't feel that I can't bother my mother with my own problems. | 0.42 |
| I spend a lot of time listening to the plans and dreams of my father. | 0.50 | I don't feel angry with my mother. | 0.58 |
| I trust my father. | 0.55 | I trust my mother. | 0.57 |
| My father cares about my point of view. | 0.56 | My mother understands what I am going through. | 0.62 |
| Eigenvalue | 1.59 | | 5.27 |
| Alpha | 0.87 | | 0.85 |

3. The factor loadings and eigenvalues for the emotion measures (anger, anxiety, and happiness) are as follows:

| Emotions | | | | | |
|---|---|---|---|---|---|
| Anger | | Anxiety | | Happiness | |
| Anger | 0.77 | Nervousness | 0.67 | Cheerfulness | 0.70 |
| Frustration | 0.75 | Strain | 0.50 | Friendliness | 0.69 |
| Irritation | 0.69 | Worry | 0.65 | | |
| | | Stress | 0.62 | | |
| Eigenvalue | 3.82 | | 0.76 | | 0.46 |
| Alpha | 0.84 | | 0.81 | | 0.76 |

4. Similar to Larson and Gillman (1999), the spillover and crossover models in this chapter used values for all three emotion scales that are standardized within-person (i.e., z-scores). Therefore, the z-scores used in the analyses represent each person's level of anger, anxiety, and happiness compared to his or her average level on each emotion across time and place. A z-score greater than zero represents above average reports on anger, anxiety, and happiness while scores less than zero signify below average reports on each respective emotion.

5. For mother-to-adolescent transfers, there were a total of 88 anger crossover, 81 anxiety crossover, and 89 happiness crossover occasions. There was

within-family variation in the number of occasions; some had none while others had up to three. For fathers, there was a total of only 72 anger crossover, 57 anxiety crossover, and 67 happiness crossover occasions, with some father–adolescent dyads having four and others having no transfers.

6. To assess how much mothers' emotion at Time 2 explains adolescent emotion at Time 2, models that include only reports of maternal emotion upon returning home were contrasted with unconditional models in which Time 2 adolescent emotion is the dependent variable. This makes it possible to determine the proportion of within-person variance in Time 2 adolescent emotion that was explained by reports of maternal emotion. The same procedures were used in examining percent variance explained in father models.

7. To contrast these intercept and slope models with the basic crossover models presented in the previous section, chi-square difference tests between the deviance estimates for each pair of models (e.g., basic mother-adolescent crossover without Level-2 predictors versus the full mother-adolescent crossover model) were computed. For all of the mother-adolescent models, the chi-square difference tests were significant, indicating that the maternal intercept and slope models fit the data better than the basic models. In the father-adolescent models, the chi-square difference tests were not significant. The deviance statistics were: father-adolescent happiness ($\chi^2 = 3.20$, $p < .20$); father-adolescent anger ($\chi^2 = 4.01$, $p < .15$); father-adolescent anxiety ($\chi^2 = 5.41$, $p < .10$); mother-adolescent happiness ($\chi^2 = 16.19$, $p < .001$); mother-adolescent anger ($\chi^2 = 6.58$, $p < .05$); mother-adolescent anxiety ($\chi^2 = 5.98$, $p < .05$).

8. Variance in slope model with intrinsic work motivation $= 0.00353$, reduced from $0.00398$ in an alternative paternal happiness slope model without intrinsic work motivation: $(0.00398-0.00353)/0.00398 = .11$.

9. Variance in slope model with intrinsic work motivation $= 0.06001$, reduced from $0.06583$ in an alternative paternal anger slope model without intrinsic work motivation: $(0.06583-0.06001)/0.06583 = .09$.

10. Variance in slope model with work hours $= 0.00353$, reduced from $0.00412$ in an alternative paternal happiness slope model without work hours: $(0.00412-0.00353)/0.00412 = .14$.

11. For fathers, variance in slope model with work hours $= 0.06001$, reduced from $0.06600$ in an alternative slope model without work hours: $(0.06600-0.06001)/0.06600 = .09$. For mothers, variance in slope model with work hours $= 0.01672$, reduced from $0.01894$ in an alternative slope model without work hours: $(0.01894-0.01672)/0.01894 = .12$.

12. Variance in slope model with time for self $= 0.00353$, reduced from $0.00409$ in an alternative slope model without time for self: $(0.00409-0.00353)/0.00409 = .14$.

13. Variance in intercept model with time for self $= 0.04818$, reduced from $0.05723$ in an alternative intercept model without time for self: $(0.05723-0.04818)/0.05723 = .16$.

14. Variance in model with time for self $= 0.6001$, reduced from $0.06764$ in an alternative slope model without time for self: $(0.06764-0.06001)/0.06764 = .11$.

15. Variance in slope model with time for self = 0.02913, reduced from 0.03565 in an alternative slope model without time for self: $(0.03565 - 0.02913)/0.03565 = .18$.

16. Variance in slope model for anger with adolescent gender = 0.06001, reduced from 0.06981 in an alternative slope model without adolescent gender: $(0.06981 - 0.06001)/0.06981 = .14$.

17. Variance in slope model with parent–adolescent closeness = 0.00353, reduced from 0.00418 in an alternative slope model without parent–adolescent closeness: $(0.00418 - 0.00353)/0.00418 = .16$.

18. Variance in intercept model with parent–adolescent closeness = 0.04818, reduced from 0.05368 in an alternative intercept model without parent–adolescent closeness: $(0.05368 - 0.04818)/0.05368 = .10$.

19. Variance in slope model with parent–adolescent closeness = 0.06001, reduced from 0.06387 in an alternative slope model without parent–adolescent closeness: $(0.06387 - 0.06001)/0.06387 = .06$.

20. Variance in slope model with parent–adolescent closeness = 0.01672, reduced from 0.01904 in an alternative slope model without parent–adolescent closeness: $(0.01904 - 0.01672)/0.01904 = .12$.

21. Variance in slope model with parent–adolescent closeness = 0.02913, reduced from 0.03692 in an alternative slope model without parent–adolescent closeness: $(0.03692 - 0.02913)/0.03692 = .21$.

# Commentary

## Reed Larson

*Long neglected as a topic of study, scholars are beginning to recognize that emotions are an important part of the social ecology of a society and its institutions. Researchers across the fields of sociology, anthropology, and psychology are coming to see emotional give and take as an important component of the daily processes of societal metabolism. Daily stresses and satisfactions create emotions in individuals and in groups of individuals. These emotions in turn shape behavior: they influence consumer decisions, voting, and parenting; they can be passed from one person to another, thus potentially having expanding effects within a system. Therefore, to understand the functioning of an institution such as the family, one needs to understand these patterns of emotional experience and emotional exchange.*

*The American family, as Matjasko and Feldman point out, has been changing dramatically over the last fifty years; and studying daily family emotional patterns provides an important window on how families are adjusting to these changes. Parents are working longer hours, with many more mothers employed. The nature of the workplace has also been shifting – including downsizing, more team work, and more focus on work quality – creating new stresses as well as new opportunities for satisfaction at parents' jobs. Furthermore, role relationships within families have been changing, with a shift from authoritarian to more democratic and child-centered modes of parenting. Evidence suggests that most families remain strong; they have adapted and been resilient in the face of change. Nonetheless the alterations in parents' work and family roles have created new rhythms and arrhythmias in daily life. Knowledge of families' daily patterns of emotion are essential to comprehending the functioning and resiliency processes of these families.*

*The chapter by Matjasko and Feldman provides important contributions to understanding these processes. The 500 Family Study furnishes a large sample, with a rich set of variables to consider, including variables dealing with parents' experiences of their jobs. The dual-career parents in the sample represent a population of managerial and professional workers who have experienced substantial changes in the workplace over recent decades. Matjasko and Feldman's analyses focus on the time of day when parents are coming home from these jobs,*

159

*a period that can be stressful, when negative emotional exchanges may be likely, and is thus a period that may be crucial to family adjustment. I will comment on a select set of new findings in the chapter that I find to be particularly valuable to our understanding of family emotional dynamics.*

## Positive emotions are transmitted between family members

*Past research has shown only the transmission of negative emotions in families. In our review of this literature, David Almeida and I (Larson and Almeida 1999) worried that positive emotions may not be as readily shared, and that negative emotions of family members "trump" positive emotions. This suggests a bleak picture of American family life in which other family members are not likely to cheer you up but they can bring you down: a family system with a tendency toward what might be called emotional entropy.*

*But this study, at last, shows the opposite dynamic as well. It shows quite robustly that parents and adolescents do sometimes transmit positive emotions to each other. Family interactions can have positive outcomes, family members can bring each other up. Matjasko and Feldman's measure of happiness assesses feelings of cheerfulness and friendliness – and it makes sense that these expressive social emotions are more easily transmitted. A next question is how these get transmitted in families. One psychological theory, is that emotions are passed through a passive process of "contagion" in which receivers unconsciously mimic the emotions in the facial expression, voice, and bodily posture of the sender, leading the receiver to progressively internalize the emotions they are enacting (Hatfield, Cacioppo, and Rapson 1994). It is possible, however, that this transmission occurs through more active processes in the receiver. Research indicates that people experiencing positive emotions are more expansive, generous, and tolerant (Isen 1987), and this expansiveness in parents, for example, may create a context for active, empathic, and cheerful thought processes in their adolescent children. Another important finding, however, is that emotions do not just pass from parents to adolescents, but they are transmitted in the other direction as well.*

## Emotional transmission goes both ways between parents and adolescents

*In our research summary, Almeida and I (Larson and Almeida 1999) were also led to hypothesize that emotional transmission follows the hierarchy of power in families, with emotions flowing from more powerful family members to less powerful ones, for example, from parents to adolescents. What is interesting in Matjasko and Feldman's findings, then, is the approximate equivalence in the coefficients of transmission between parents and teens. Mothers and adolescents are equally likely to pass anger and happiness to each other. Fathers and adolescents are equally likely to pass anxiety to each other.*

*These results suggest that emotional transmission in these middle-class families is not about power; it is not about the one-way imposition of emotions onto another. Possibly affluence, education, and democratic child-centered parenting create a climate in which power is less salient and parents and adolescents are equally attuned and sensitive to each others' emotions. A puzzle, however, is why mothers and adolescents are likely to pass happiness and anger to each other, while this is not the case for fathers. In a study of one-parent families, we found that both anxiety and anger (but not positive emotions) were transmitted from mothers to adolescents (but not from adolescents to parents) (Larson and Gillman 1999). So there are inconsistencies between studies. Possibly the different patterns for mothers and fathers found in the 500 Family data reflect distinct dynamics for this population of two-parent families. Indeed, Matjasko and Feldman's findings show other interesting differences in patterns between mothers and fathers.*

### Transmission of emotions from fathers to adolescents are moderated by how close the relationship is

*The study of moderators of emotional transmission is vital, and Matjasko and Feldman's analyses focus on moderators of the paths from parents to adolescents. The first general pattern one sees is that, while the main effects for transmission are stronger for mothers, there are more and stronger interaction effects for fathers. This suggests that emotional transmission is a more consistent phenomenon across mother–adolescent relationships, and is more conditional for father–adolescent relationships.*

*Importantly, transmission of emotion from fathers to adolescents was moderated by how close the adolescent perceives the relationship to be. Research shows a great deal of variability in the quality of the father–adolescent relationship in two-parent American households, with substantial numbers of youth describing their fathers as distant and detached (Youniss and Smollar 1985). It makes sense that this variability would influence whether and which emotions are transmitted. When the relationship is close Matjasko and Feldman found more transmission of happiness and less transmission of anxiety. These closer fathers and adolescents may spend more time together, be more attuned to each others' realities, and thus be more responsive to each others' joys and worries. Indeed it is possible that this attunement and responsiveness may influence whether the adolescent perceives the relationship as close.*

*But life is more complicated. What is interesting is that the closeness of the relationship between fathers and adolescents also moderates the transmission of anger and anxiety. When relationships are close, fathers may do more to shield adolescents from their anxiety. Hauser (1991) argues that competent parenting involves blocking expression of untoward emotions to adolescents. Again, it is possible that adolescents' experience of closeness is partly shaped by their past experience of this kind of transmission. Repeated experiences of fathers' anger may push teens away. These findings also lead to questions about the conditions under which both parents bring home emotions from their jobs.*

### Parents' intrinsic motivation in their job reduces their transmission of emotion to their adolescent children

*Intrinsic motivation in work is generally found to be a win–win situation for employers and workers. It is good for the employer because intrinsically motivated employees are more productive. It is good for employees because they are happier, more invested and satisfied. As a result of these findings, modern management theory has focused on how to make jobs more intrinsically rewarding.*

*The findings here, however, suggest that parents' intrinsic motivation in their jobs is a mixed bag for families. On the negative side, mothers who are more motivated at their jobs tend to report slightly more anger at home (as well as at their jobs). Being invested – getting wrapped up in their jobs – can have negative effects on parents' emotional states, as we have found elsewhere (Larson and Richards 1994). The good news, however, is that the negative emotions of these intrinsically motivated parents do not necessarily get transmitted to children.*

*As a whole the findings of Matjasko and Feldman's chapter suggest that patterns of emotion exchange in American middle-class families are complex and dynamic. Although Euro-American culture places a high value on emotional independence and self-sufficiency, emotions appear to be passed readily within American families. Curiously, in our ESM study conducted in India – a collectivist culture – we found no evidence of emotional transmission. We attributed this pattern to the more leisurely pace of life in India and to the influence of stronger cultural norms prescribing mothers' and fathers' family roles (Larson, Verma, and Dworkin 2001). We do not know what the pattern would have been had this study been done on American families in the 1950s, but there is reason to speculate that the patterns seen in Matjasko and Feldman's data reflect characteristics of contemporary families, including time scarcity, fluid roles, and relationships between parents and children that have become more egalitarian. Further study of these patterns, particularly the exploration of additional moderators of emotional transmission, would provide knowledge that might help families to better adapt to the challenges of modern life to reduce conditions that lead to negative transmission and increase conditions that permit transmission of positive emotions.*

## Acknowledgments

*Preparation of this commentary was supported by the Pampered Chef Family Resiliency Program at the University of Illinois, Urbana-Champaign.*

*Part III*

# Marriage and family

# Overview

*Alisa C. Lewin*

Economists have argued that the traditional division of labor in the family maximizes efficiency because it is based on trade and specialization. In the traditional family, one parent specializes in market production while the other specializes in home production. This specialization maximizes the gains from marriage, thereby contributing to marital stability. In contrast, deviation from this model reduces the gains from marriage. Given that roles within dual-earner families are not specialized with respect to market work and housework, are these families less stable than traditional families?

Scholars have linked the increase in divorce rates with the rise in women's participation in the workforce and have maintained that women's employment provides them with economic independence from their husbands. The underlying assumption is that economically independent women are able to free themselves from unhappy marriages. Similarly, women in unhappy marriages anticipating divorce may seek employment to facilitate their transition into financial independence. But this focus on the relationship between women's economic independence and marital dissolution has shifted attention away from what may be the central question: Why are so many marriages unhappy?

It seems unlikely that economic dependence itself fosters marital bliss, whereas it is possible that the stress of women's employment creates conflict and unhappiness in marriages. In fact, it is probably not women's increased investment in market production that generates conflict, but rather the reduction in women's investment in home production. The need for home production persists even when both parents are invested in economic production. In the case of dual-earner families, traditional gender roles must be negotiated and renegotiated on a daily basis. Juggling home and work responsibilities may create stress and conflict in the lives of both men and women in dual-career couples. Does this inevitable work–family stress weaken dual-earner marriages?

The focus on stress and conflict within marriages shifts the discussion from changes in economic gains from marriage to the emotional well-being of married men and women. The chapters in this section examine emotional well-being and marital satisfaction in dual-career families. Results suggest that spouses' emotional well-being is determined by the quality of their marital relationship and that the management of work–family conflict is nested within the marital relationship. The quality of this relationship determines how work–family stress is handled. What are the implications of these findings? The traditional family is no longer the dominant family pattern, and most married women are involved in market production. This new reality requires a new research agenda. Instead of lamenting the loss of the traditional family and focusing on the negative ramifications of women's employment, we should examine couples' strategies for coping with the work–family tension, and we should explore the benefits for their marriage of combining family and work.

# 7     The everyday emotional experiences of husbands and wives

*Chi-Young Koh*

What does the internal emotional world of husbands and wives look like as they move through different locations and activities in their daily life? How do they feel about themselves, others, and the activities that they are engaged in? In this chapter, dual-career couples' emotional experiences during a typical week are explored. Spouses' emotional states are described along the following dimensions: how good or bad they feel (positive or negative affect), how strong or active they feel (activation), how responsible they feel about the situation and its importance to them (role salience), how able and in control they feel, how good they feel about themselves (self-esteem), and whether they enjoy and willingly participate in the activities that they are engaged in (intrinsic motivation). Additionally, variations in these emotional experiences by location, companions, and activities are investigated. For the most part, analyses are conducted at the level of the individual. Emphasizing the need for understanding the lives of married couples, the last set of analyses examines spouses' emotional experiences at the couple level. Similarities as well as differences in the emotional experiences of husbands and wives are analyzed.

## Why emotion?

Dramatic changes in American marriage and family behavior in recent decades have led to a focus on marital quality. Because both non-marital unions and divorce rates are increasing, understanding stability and happiness in marriage is important for theoretical and practical reasons. Research in recent years has pointed to the centrality of emotion in accounting for variability in the quality of marriage (see reviews in Bradbury, Fincham, and Beach 2000; Gottman 2001). For instance, after more than twenty years of research on intimate relationships, Gottman (2001) concludes:

[W]e . . . have been compelled to study emotion by necessity, because the emotional life of people in close relationships turned out to be the most productive source of information for predicting relationship outcomes, and for understanding how relationships work or fail. Other aspects of relationships, like communication clarity, have been suggested as important, but they have all been studied and none of them has proven as productive in predicting and understanding relationships as emotion. (79–80)

Despite such evidence, the details of the association between marital quality and emotions remain unexplored. Little is known about the emotional states that husbands and wives experience in their daily lives. Further, the processes through which the more mundane daily experiences accumulate, if they do, into spouses' overall sense of marital quality or psychological well-being are not well understood. The lack of research on these issues underscores the need for description and theoretical development of the "epidemiology" of emotions in the general population (Thoits 1989). This chapter is a first step in addressing this gap in the literature.

## Emotional tensions in dual-career marriages

Research has documented the tensions within and between partners brought about by the transformation of marriage and family life. At the personal level, marriage and family functioning have become fundamentally personal choices and responsibilities, making the maintenance of both more vulnerable. At the cultural level, while traditional values such as gender role ideologies are constantly being challenged, values related to the importance of marriage and family still persist, at least in the US (Waite and Gallagher 2000).

Evidence of such tensions is abundant in the literature on working families. As the number of dual-earner families has increased, more parents have had to deal with the anxieties of balancing work and family life. Families may no longer be the source of emotional and personal satisfaction, but rather a burdensome extension of work, especially for working mothers (Hochschild 1997). Other researchers, on the contrary, contend that two-income families are happy, healthy, and thriving (Barnett and Rivers 1996). The discrepancy in these interpretations may be due in part to diversity *within* and *across* families. An examination of both is necessary to better understand the nature of tensions in diverse family structures. In both arguments, a common thread is apparent: that trying to balance work and family creates emotional dilemmas for both spouses. What needs to be explained is the nature of such emotional dilemmas and how they are dealt with in different families.

According to Gottman (2001), positive and negative emotions during conflict situations are governed by patterns of affective behaviors in non-conflict – that is, ordinary – contexts. Therefore, it is important to understand the totality of daily emotions and not just those of conflict situations. What do spouses actually feel as they routinely encounter different domains of life such as workplace and home? What do they actually feel as they do paid work or various activities at home? What do spouses feel about each other while they interact with one another, and how do they express their feelings? Do husbands and wives differ in their overall levels of affect within different spheres or while engaging in different activities or with different people?

## Emotion and the gender question

The choice of gender as a thematic framework of this study is guided by the findings of past research on emotion, or psychological well-being as it is more customarily referred to, within family life. It has been found that men and women differ in their emotional behaviors as well as in their psychological outcomes. At the behavioral level, it is said that women are more "emotional" (Carstensen, Gottman, and Levenson 1995) or do more "emotion work" (DeVault 1999). Similarly, the emotional transmission literature reports that "[I]n married couples, daily emotions . . . flow from husbands to wives more often than from wives to husbands . . . This finding suggests a process through which husbands exert power over their wives" (Larson and Almeida 1999: 13). At the level of psychological outcomes, Almeida and Kessler have found that "women consistently report more extreme levels of distress and are almost two to three times more likely to report a history of affective disorder than are men" (1998: 1). In the context of marriage, Jacobson (quoted in Waite and Gallagher 2000: 5) claims that "marriage protects men from depression and makes women more vulnerable."

Past research has largely focused on psychological distress or on general health issues rather than on diverse dimensions of emotion in daily life. For instance, what does everyday life feel like to husbands and wives in terms of excitement or boredom? How cheerful do they feel while doing routine tasks at work or with the family? Is there a clear gap between spouses in the experience of daily life? The gender question still remains complex, and detailed study of the workings of inner lives is needed.

## Centrality of emotion in today's marriages

In thinking about systems of emotion in married partners, what needs to be explained is the centrality of emotion for stability and happiness in marriage, as recent research has suggested. Why is it that what partners *feel* toward one another or how they feel about their marriage determines marital fulfillment and stability more than other factors? Answering this question requires a theory of the nature of marriage in contemporary society.

Glenn (1996) has pointed out that in modern Western marriage, and in American marriage in particular, emotional satisfaction from the partnership more than any other aspect of the family system has become the central criterion of marital success. Glenn writes: "the single-minded pursuit of marital happiness through the attraction and retention of an intrinsically desirable spouse received strong and virtually unqualified social encouragement" (30). Empirical research provides ample evidence of emotional satisfaction and/or emotional sharing between spouses as the central criterion of marital quality (see Berscheid and Ammazzaolorso 2001; Faust and McKibben 1999; Swidler 2001). In this vein, the emotional flux of married partners in daily life is not just a set of random experiences triggered by situations and events, but may reveal spouses' internal evaluations of the marital relationship – the expectations and disappointments that contribute to the reproduction of intimacy in marriage.

This latter view – that feelings are evaluative – is evidenced in several psychological studies of emotion (see the recent collection on appraisal theory in Scherer et al. 2001). According to Frijda (2000), the most basic feature of feelings is that they are good or bad, or imply (non-) acceptance of the experience or of the antecedent event as "promoting or obstructing one's well-being, concerns, motives, or current goals" (2000: 63). In Frijda's words, feeling states introduce "value in a world of fact" (2000: 63). The evaluative nature of emotions together with the centrality of emotion in marriage suggests the importance of the study of daily emotions to research on marital quality.

## Themes and structure of the chapter

The discussion thus far has spanned several broad themes related to the topic of spouses' daily emotions: gender, dilemmas of work–family balance, cultural characteristics of contemporary marriage in the West, and the nature of emotions themselves. All of these themes are potentially associated, independently or interactively, with the experience of emotions in working parents' daily lives. Simply put, stimuli and events in the world, as well as personal experiences, are diverse, complex, and multi-dimensional. The task of the sociology of family emotions is to explore patterns of diverse experience within and across groups, showing them to be comparable and having substantive social meaning. This chapter is an initial step in this endeavor, beginning with a presentation of husbands' and wives' self-reports of their daily emotional experiences.

Two themes are emphasized in presenting the emotional experiences of husbands and wives. First, multiple aspects of emotion are explored. As past research has shown, the workings of emotion within a person are complex in several respects. For example, people can feel happy and sad at the same time. The arousal of affect also has many dimensions, as documented in Heise's (1988) affect control theory: a good–bad dimension (evaluation), a strong–weak dimension (potency), and a lively–quiet dimension (activity). And, as suggested by the notion of "affect balance" in earlier studies of marital happiness, positive and negative affect might be independent dimensions, requiring an understanding of how each dimension works (Orden and Bradburn 1968). Based on these findings, spouses' emotions are explored along multiple dimensions: positive affect, negative affect, and activation. In addition, dimensions of emotion that are suggestive of role salience, self-esteem, and intrinsic motivation are analyzed. Husbands' and wives' daily experiences are compared across all of these dimensions.

Second, variations in emotions by location, companions, and activities are analyzed. It is assumed that emotions are not fixed, but vary across contexts. Emotional variations *within* persons as they move through these contexts across a week are also of interest. Because so little is known about the daily emotional experiences of husbands and wives, such contextual analyses of emotion are important in documenting patterns of variation in emotional experience.

In large part, the investigation of the above themes is conducted at the individual level; husbands' and wives' experiences are examined separately, with a focus on gender differences. However, spouses' emotions also need to be understood at the couple level. The absence of couple-level analysis is a serious shortcoming in past research on emotion within families. Therefore, analyses of husbands' and wives' emotions at the couple level are also conducted.

## Method

### Sample

This chapter draws upon data from dual-career couples from the 500 Family Study, and analyses are based largely on the couples' responses to the Experience Sampling Method (ESM). Since analyses are geared toward observing each spouse's daily emotional variations at the same time on a given day, only those beeps where the husband's and the wife's reports are both available were selected for analysis. Since the focus is on emotions in *marriage*, reports of couples in non-marital relationships were excluded. The above selection procedures resulted in a total of 7,504 time-matched observations for 235 couples. Each couple had an average of 31.9 time-matched beeps over a period of 6.6 days (standard deviations = 12.1 and 1.0, respectively), or an average of 5.4 beeps per day (standard deviation = 1.3).

### Measures

*Dimensions of emotion*     To capture the emotional experiences of couples, the following measures were constructed: positive affect, negative affect, activation, role salience, self-esteem, and intrinsic motivation. These are composite measures in which several emotion items from the ESM are combined. Psychological and sociological theories on the nature of emotion guided the selection of these six dimensions. The composite measures of positive and negative affect, activation, and intrinsic motivation are based on Heise's (1988) model of affect control theory as well as mood scales constructed by Csikszentmihalyi and Larson (1984). The measures of role salience and self-esteem are not usually included in "basic emotion" categories (see, e.g., Plutchik 2001); however, they are included here for their sociological significance in explaining human actions (Thoits 1995). Table 7.1 shows the factor loadings and eigenvalues for all composite measures for husbands and wives.

*Positive affect* includes feeling happy, cheerful, relaxed, and friendly when signaled (Cronbach's alpha = .84).[1] *Negative affect* includes loneliness, nervousness, anger, frustration, strain, irritation, stress, and feeling worried ($\alpha$ = .90). Level of *activation* is measured by how strong, active, and excited respondents felt when beeped ($\alpha$ = .87). *Role salience* is a measure of how responsible and caring respondents felt about the event, whether they felt the activity they were engaged in was important, and how proud they felt to be doing it ($\alpha$ = .82). *Self-esteem* captures ways in which husbands and wives evaluate themselves: how good they felt about themselves, whether they felt that they were living up to their own expectations, and their feelings of ability, control, and success ($\alpha$ = .90). Finally, *intrinsic motivation* is a measure based on how much respondents wished to be doing the activity they were engaged in, were interested in it, and enjoyed doing it ($\alpha$ = .76).

*Contextual variations in emotions*     Variations in emotional dimensions are examined by husbands' and wives' locations, companions, and

Table 7.1 *Factor loadings of composite measures*

|  | Husbands | Wives |
|---|---|---|
| **Positive affect** | | |
| Cheerful | 0.90 | 0.88 |
| Friendly | 0.78 | 0.72 |
| Happy | 0.72 | 0.72 |
| Relaxed | 0.62 | 0.71 |
| Eigenvalue | 2.31 | 2.32 |
| **Negative affect** | | |
| Angry | 0.77 | 0.77 |
| Frustrated | 0.90 | 0.90 |
| Irritated | 0.86 | 0.83 |
| Lonely | 0.47 | 0.46 |
| Nervous | 0.78 | 0.79 |
| Strained | 0.71 | 0.59 |
| Stressed | 0.81 | 0.84 |
| Worried | 0.82 | 0.80 |
| Eigenvalue | 4.81 | 4.61 |
| **Activation** | | |
| Active | 0.77 | 0.75 |
| Excited | 0.75 | 0.79 |
| Strong | 0.80 | 0.84 |
| Eigenvalue | 1.79 | 1.89 |
| **Role Salience** | | |
| Caring | 0.80 | 0.80 |
| Importance of current activity | 0.60 | 0.61 |
| Responsible | 0.83 | 0.78 |
| Proud | 0.69 | 0.67 |
| Eigenvalue | 2.17 | 2.07 |
| **Self-esteem** | | |
| Ability to deal with situation | 0.78 | 0.79 |
| Control | 0.80 | 0.84 |
| Feel good about myself | 0.77 | 0.70 |
| Living up to my expectations | 0.87 | 0.82 |
| Succeeding | 0.89 | 0.88 |
| Eigenvalue | 3.38 | 3.27 |
| **Intrinsic motivation** | | |
| Enjoy doing current task | 0.83 | 0.88 |
| Interested | 0.83 | 0.85 |
| Wish to be doing current task | 0.37 | 0.56 |
| Eigenvalue | 1.51 | 1.82 |

activities. For *location*, emotions at home, at work, and at places other than home and work are compared.[2] With respect to *companions*, variations in husbands' and wives' emotions are examined when they are alone, with spouse, with child, with family (both spouse and child), with co-workers, and with all others. Companionship contexts are mutually exclusive. Finally, emotions while doing various *activities* are investigated. These include paid work; activities involving family life, such as talking with family members, doing things with the child, and housework; and more general activities such as eating, watching television, hobbies/sports, and social activities.

*Comparison of emotions at the couple level*    Spouses' emotions at the couple level are also compared. That is, differences in emotions *between* spouses are examined. Emotional differences between spouses are measured by calculating an average for each spouse for each emotion in each context, yielding scores for both spouses in all 235 couples. To generate an inter-spousal difference score, a difference of means was calculated by subtracting the wife's from the husband's average score, yielding a single positive or negative value for each couple.

## Results: daily emotions of husbands and wives

### Overall experience

Summarizing the emotions experienced by husbands and wives over the course of a week is no easy task. The *average* level of emotions husbands and wives experienced during their week of ESM participation is first examined. As shown in table 7.2, emotions are categorized along six dimensions.

One of the most notable features of husbands' and wives' emotional experiences over the course of the week is their low levels of negative emotion. On a 4-point scale (0 to 3), mean negative affect is 0.36 for husbands and 0.34 for wives. In other words, both husbands and wives report having experienced, on average, almost "zero" negative affect during the week. Negative affect, and anger in particular, has the lowest standard deviation compared to other emotions. This relative absence of negative affect could mean several things. It could indicate that husbands and wives indeed experience few negative emotions in their daily lives. Alternatively, people may be controlling their negative emotions by reinterpreting the situations or themselves less negatively. Social desirability may also influence their responses to negative emotion items.

Table 7.2 *Overall means and standard deviations of emotions during the week for husbands and wives*

| | Husband (N = 235) | | Wife (N = 235) | |
|---|---|---|---|---|
| | Mean[a] | S.D. | Mean | S.D. |
| Positive affect | 1.70 | (0.40) | 1.68 | (0.41) |
| Cheerful | 1.58 | (0.52) | 1.69 | (0.52) |
| Friendly | 1.60 | (0.59) | 1.51 | (0.59) |
| Happy | 2.00 | (0.30) | 2.05 | (0.34) |
| Relaxed | 1.59 | (0.50) | 1.49 | (0.50) |
| Negative affect | 0.36 | (0.26) | 0.34 | (0.29) |
| Angry | 0.17 | (0.20) | 0.14 | (0.17) |
| Frustrated | 0.49 | (0.37) | 0.46 | (0.37) |
| Irritated | 0.39 | (0.30) | 0.35 | (0.31) |
| Lonely | 0.15 | (0.23) | 0.08 | (0.20) |
| Nervous | 0.29 | (0.32) | 0.25 | (0.29) |
| Strained | 0.36 | (0.42) | 0.32 | (0.37) |
| Stressed | 0.57 | (0.43) | 0.60 | (0.43) |
| Worried | 0.43 | (0.36) | 0.46 | (0.39) |
| Activation | 1.91 | (0.28) | 1.93 | (0.29) |
| Active | 1.94 | (0.31) | 1.98 | (0.32) |
| Excited | 1.82 | (0.33) | 1.84 | (0.28) |
| Strong | 1.95 | (0.34) | 1.97 | (0.37) |
| Role salience | 1.65 | (0.44) | 1.66 | (0.43) |
| Caring | 1.52 | (0.58) | 1.66 | (0.59) |
| Importance of current activity | 2.10 | (0.41) | 2.21 | (0.37) |
| Proud | 1.08 | (0.66) | 0.88 | (0.63) |
| Responsible | 1.87 | (0.48) | 1.88 | (0.52) |
| Self-esteem | 2.26 | (0.35) | 2.30 | (0.33) |
| Ability to deal with situation | 2.57 | (0.33) | 2.61 | (0.31) |
| Control | 2.15 | (0.40) | 2.17 | (0.42) |
| Living up to own expectations | 2.10 | (0.46) | 2.17 | (0.40) |
| Feel good about self | 2.17 | (0.47) | 2.17 | (0.47) |
| Succeeding | 2.32 | (0.36) | 2.36 | (0.35) |
| Intrinsic motivation | 1.83 | (0.33) | 1.84 | (0.37) |
| Enjoy doing current task | 1.85 | (0.37) | 1.89 | (0.40) |
| Interested | 1.66 | (0.41) | 1.63 | (0.45) |
| Wish to be doing current activity | 1.98 | (0.47) | 2.00 | (0.44) |

*Note:* [a] Person-level averages are reported for all data points during the week. All measures are on a 4-point scale: 0 = not at all, 1 = a little, 2 = somewhat, 3 = very much. The mid-point is 1.5 for all measures.

Second, across all six dimensions of emotional experience, ratings are highest for self-esteem for both husbands and wives, with an average of 2.28 for both. Examining individual self-esteem items separately – that is, feeling able to deal with the situation, in control, living up to one's expectations, feeling good about oneself, and succeeding at the activity – ratings are relatively high compared with other emotions. Husbands and wives report feeling these emotions "somewhat" (above 2 on the 0-to-3 scale), while they report feeling less positive (below 2) for most other emotions. When it comes to evaluating one's own ability, performance, and sense of self, husbands and wives have highly positive opinions about themselves. Of all single emotion items, husbands and wives rate themselves highest on the perceived ability to deal with the situation (2.59 on a 0-to-3-scale for both).

Other emotion dimensions range on average between "a little" (1) and "somewhat" (2) on a 0-to-3 scale, and husbands and wives are almost identical in their emotional experiences in the four remaining dimensions: 1.92 for activation; 1.83 for intrinsic motivation; 1.69 for positive affect; and 1.65 for role salience for both husbands and wives. Sense of role salience – that is, caring, feeling the current activity is important, and feeling responsible and proud – has the lowest values of the four dimensions. In particular, *pride* is the emotion that was experienced least compared with other positive emotions: 1.08 and 0.88 for husbands and wives, respectively. The relatively low values for pride are somewhat surprising given the high levels of self-esteem reported by both husbands and wives.

Finally, comparing husbands and wives, there are very few differences in their overall emotional experiences. Based on the composite measures, there are no gender differences in emotions. Individual emotion items, however, do show some gender differences. For instance, wives report feeling more cheerful (t = 2.61, p < .01), more caring (t = 2.76, p < .01), and say what they were doing is more important to them (t = 3.13, p < .01) than husbands. Husbands, on the other hand, report greater loneliness (t = 4.25, p < .001), relaxation (t = 2.45, p < .05), and pride (t = 3.55, p < .001) than wives. In sum, husbands and wives differ in their experience of positive affect and role salience in their daily lives. These differences are statistical and given the small raw-score differences, it is unclear whether such differences are substantively meaningful. Given well-known gender differences in emotional well-being, the relative absence of gender differences in this study is somewhat surprising. Since these couples have been married on average for eighteen years, however, one might expect their emotional experiences to be more similar than those who are newly married.

Table 7.3 *Husbands' and wives' average emotions in different locations*

| | All contexts | Home | Work | Public | F-value[a] | Post hoc Comparisons[b] |
|---|---|---|---|---|---|---|
| **Husbands** | | | | | | |
| Positive affect | 1.70 | 1.74 | 1.59 | 1.78 | 9.81*** | H,P > W |
| Negative affect | 0.35 | 0.29 | 0.43 | 0.33 | 12.05*** | W > H,P |
| Activation | 1.92 | 1.84 | 2.00 | 1.91 | 12.21*** | W > H,P |
| Role salience | 1.65 | 1.59 | 1.74 | 1.62 | 5.72** | W > H,P |
| Self-esteem | 2.26 | 2.23 | 2.32 | 2.24 | 3.35* | |
| Intrinsic motivation | 1.81 | 1.85 | 1.79 | 1.80 | 0.83 | |
| Number of cases | 235 | 232 | 222 | 225 | | |
| **Wives** | | | | | | |
| Positive affect | 1.70 | 1.64 | 1.63 | 1.83 | 11.51*** | P > H,W |
| Negative affect | 0.34 | 0.32 | 0.39 | 0.32 | 3.18* | |
| Activation | 1.96 | 1.87 | 2.04 | 1.98 | 13.06*** | W,P > H |
| Role salience | 1.69 | 1.61 | 1.74 | 1.72 | 4.30* | W > H |
| Self-esteem | 2.31 | 2.27 | 2.36 | 2.31 | 2.57 | |
| Intrinsic motivation | 1.85 | 1.78 | 1.86 | 1.92 | 4.32* | P > H |
| Number of cases | 235 | 235 | 204 | 228 | | |

*Note:* All measures are on a 4-point-scale: 0 = not at all, 1 = a little, 2 = somewhat, 3 = very much.
[a] Differences in means across home, work, and public places were tested using one-way Analysis of Variance.
[b] H = Home, W = Work, P = Public. All comparisons noted are significant at p < .05.
* p < .05; ** p < .01; *** p < .001

### Emotion in different contexts

*Location*   Emotions vary significantly from one place to another for husbands and wives. Across the three locations of home, work, and public, there are significant differences in most emotions. However, the magnitude of differences varies across emotional dimensions. For example, positive affect and activation vary significantly across locations for husbands (F = 9.81 and 12.21, respectively; p < .001) and wives (F = 11.51 and 13.06, respectively; p < .001). Patterns of variation, however, are weaker for role salience, self-esteem, and intrinsic motivation. For some emotions, such as intrinsic motivation for husbands (F = 0.83) and self-esteem for wives (F = 2.57), there are no significant differences across locations (see table 7.3).[3]

For husbands, average levels of emotion at *home* and in *public* do not differ for any of the six composite variables. With the exception of intrinsic motivation, emotions are slightly lower at home than they are in public, but these differences are statistically negligible. When *work* is compared with either home or public, however, significant differences emerge. Husbands feel significantly lower levels of positive affect and far greater negative affect at work than they do at home or in public. At work they also feel greater activation and role salience than they do in other locations (all differences significant at $p < .05$).

The patterns of emotional variation for wives differ from those of husbands in several respects. In particular, emotions at home and at work are similar in most cases. Wives report similar levels of positive affect, negative affect, self-esteem, and intrinsic motivation in these two places. Feelings of activation and role salience are exceptions and are greater at work than at home as they are for husbands (both significant at $p < .05$). Positive affect is much higher in public than at home or at work ($p < .05$). Intrinsic motivation is also higher in public than at home. For all other emotions there is little difference between being at work and in public.

Overall, husbands' and wives' emotions appear to be most different in public locations. For husbands, there are no significant differences in emotions between home and public; emotional variations occur primarily between work and other locations. Wives, however, experience similar levels of emotion at home and at work. In public, however, they experience greater positive affect, activation, and intrinsic motivation than at home.

What accounts for these gender differences? For instance, why is it that husbands' emotions change little while wives experience a significant change in emotions in public locations? One speculation is that it is a matter of time allocation. That is, since wives spend more time than husbands in public locations ($t = -3.9$, $p < .001$),[4] they may simply encounter more situations that arouse emotion. It may be that the activities or people wives encounter in public locations are different in kind – that is, personally more meaningful for wives than husbands, thus affecting their emotions differently. Public locations may also provide an opportunity for wives to get away from the more demanding tasks of home or work life.

A more general implication of these findings is that emotions work in complex ways. Feeling positive affect does not preempt the experience of negative affect. For example, the experience of negative emotion does not mean people care less about the tasks at hand, experience lower self-esteem, or feel less strong or active, suggesting that situations where experiences are either all positive or all negative may be deviant cases.

*Companionship* Companions are important because the emotions people experience in different situations are to a large extent a reaction to the expectations and behaviors of others with whom they are interacting. In this next set of analyses, variations in husbands' and wives' emotions are explored when they are alone and when they are with others, including their spouse, their child, their families (spouse and child), their co-workers, and others (i.e., those individuals who are not specified in any of the previous categories). As shown in table 7.4, husbands' and wives' emotions vary by whom they are with.

Emotional variations for both spouses appear to be primarily driven by situations in which the individual is alone in comparison to all other situations. Both wives and husbands experience less positive affect and more negative affect when they are alone, and this is most striking when contrasting being alone with spending time with family. There are, however, gender differences with respect to both positive and negative affect.

Positive affect for husbands is significantly higher when spending time with their child or their family than with co-workers or others. For wives, however, positive affect remains similar across all companions. Similarly, for wives negative affect does not appear to differ by companions. Negative affect for husbands is highest when alone and with co-workers in comparison to family situations. This finding supports the earlier analysis that shows that husbands have higher negative affect at work than they do at home.

The differences seen for activation, role salience, and intrinsic motivation by companions are also similar for husbands and wives. For both spouses, role salience is significantly lower when they are either alone or with their spouse compared to situations in which they are with their child, family, co-workers, or others. Therefore, both husbands and wives experience similar levels of role salience when they are alone and when they are with their spouse. Potentially, this similarity is a result of husbands and wives not feeling the need to fulfill a "role" when they are with their spouse. Husbands and wives also experience significantly lower levels of activation when they are alone or with their spouse compared to when they spend time with co-workers or others. Finally, intrinsic motivation is lower for both spouses when they are alone versus all other situations.

The emotions of husbands and wives exhibit similar patterns; however, close examination reveals subtle differences in husbands' and wives' emotional experiences across companions. Gender differences are perhaps most pronounced when the comparison is simplified to two groups: family versus non-family. For husbands, family contexts seem to generate more positive experiences than non-family contexts, while for wives family and non-family contexts are both experienced positively.

*Activities*  Although the data set contains over one hundred different activity codes, for the current analysis activities are classified into eight categories: work (job), talking with family, childcare, housework,

Table 7.4 Husbands' and wives' average emotions with different companions

| | All contexts | Alone | With spouse only | With child only | With family (spouse and child) | With co-workers | With others | F-value[a] | Post hoc comparisons[b] |
|---|---|---|---|---|---|---|---|---|---|
| **Husbands** | | | | | | | | | |
| Positive affect | 1.74 | 1.47 | 1.80 | 1.88 | 1.95 | 1.67 | 1.79 | 21.65*** | A < S,C,F,CW,O; CW < C,F;O < F |
| Negative affect | 0.34 | 0.42 | 0.27 | 0.25 | 0.26 | 0.46 | 0.34 | 11.83*** | S,C,F < A,CW; O < CW |
| Activation | 1.91 | 1.83 | 1.79 | 1.96 | 1.92 | 2.00 | 1.99 | 8.41*** | A,S < C,CW,O; S < F |
| Role salience | 1.67 | 1.49 | 1.47 | 1.90 | 1.79 | 1.74 | 1.69 | 18.46*** | A,S < C,F,CW,O; O < C |
| Self-esteem | 2.25 | 2.23 | 2.16 | 2.30 | 2.27 | 2.27 | 2.29 | 2.22* | |
| Intrinsic motivation | 1.88 | 1.61 | 1.92 | 1.92 | 2.05 | 1.83 | 2.04 | 16.60*** | A < S,C,F,CW,O; C < F,O |
| Number of cases | 235 | 230 | 195 | 187 | 195 | 178 | 169 | | |
| **Wives** | | | | | | | | | |
| Positive affect | 1.72 | 1.47 | 1.75 | 1.75 | 1.83 | 1.75 | 1.89 | 15.73*** | A < S,C,F,CW,O |
| Negative affect | 0.33 | 0.36 | 0.27 | 0.32 | 0.32 | 0.36 | 0.29 | 2.46* | |
| Activation | 1.93 | 1.84 | 1.81 | 1.94 | 1.92 | 1.99 | 2.06 | 10.35*** | A,S < CW,O; S < C; F < O |
| Role salience | 1.68 | 1.47 | 1.45 | 1.85 | 1.74 | 1.80 | 1.81 | 23.68*** | A,S < C,F,CW,O |
| Self-esteem | 2.29 | 2.29 | 2.26 | 2.28 | 2.23 | 2.30 | 2.38 | 2.42* | F < O |
| Intrinsic motivation | 1.87 | 1.64 | 1.97 | 1.83 | 2.00 | 1.86 | 2.05 | 14.27*** | A < S,C,F,CW,O; C < F,O; CW < O |
| Number of cases | 235 | 231 | 188 | 207 | 196 | 228 | 176 | | |

*Note:* All measures are on a 4-point-scale: 0 = not at all, 1 = a little, 2 = somewhat, 3 = very much. There is no overlap in companions across categories.

[a] Differences in means across companions were tested using one-way Analysis of Variance.

[b] A = Alone, S = With spouse only, C = With child only, F = With family (spouse and child), CW = With co-workers, O = With others. All comparisons noted are significant at p < .05.

* p < .05; *** p < .001

watching television, eating, hobbies or sports, and social activities. As shown in table 7.5, variations in emotion across several activity categories are similar for husbands and wives. In fact, husbands and wives look much more similar with respect to emotional variations across activities compared with variations by location or companions.

For both husbands and wives, positive affect is significantly lower and negative affect significantly higher when engaged in housework or work-related activities compared to most other activities. In contrast, sports or hobbies and social activities are associated with higher levels of positive affect and lower levels of negative affect. Not surprisingly, hobbies or sports and social activities are also associated with significantly higher levels of activation and intrinsic motivation for both husbands and wives when compared to other activities. Both spouses also report significantly lower levels of intrinsic motivation when engaged in housework or work-related activities. Once again results show that time spent with family is positive for both husbands and wives. For husbands, time with their child is associated with higher role salience than other activities. Husbands also experience higher positive affect relative to their overall means when with their child.

### Emotions at the couple level

Thus far, husbands' and wives' daily emotions have been examined at the individual level, taking the individual husband or wife as the unit of analysis. It is also important to examine emotional experiences at the couple level. As a preliminary step, differences in average emotions between spouses are analyzed across different locations and companions.[5] A difference score was computed for each couple (husbands minus wives) in each context.[6]

*Emotional differences between spouses*     Is one spouse more positive, negative, or more intrinsically motivated at home than the other, or do spouses feel the same way when they are together? Similarly, do spouses experience similar levels of responsibility or feel that time with children is equally important to them? Earlier, it was found that emotions vary significantly depending on where individuals are, whom they are with, or what they are doing. In this section, similar questions are explored for couples.

Spouses overall do not differ in their daily experience of positive affect, negative affect, activation, role salience, self-esteem, or intrinsic motivation (see table 7.6). These results seem to contradict the general findings on gender differences in emotional well-being in much of the literature

Table 7.5 *Husbands' and wives' average emotions while engaged in different activities*

| | All Contexts | Work | Talking with Family | Activities with Child | Housework | Watching Television | Eating | Hobbies/ Sports | Social Activities | F-value[a] | Post hoc Comparisons[b] |
|---|---|---|---|---|---|---|---|---|---|---|---|
| **Husbands** | | | | | | | | | | | |
| Positive affect | 1.82 | 1.56 | 1.98 | 1.92 | 1.58 | 1.82 | 1.94 | 2.01 | 2.16 | 23.09*** | H,W < TV,E,F,C,SP,SO; TV,C < SO |
| Negative affect | 0.29 | 0.46 | 0.23 | 0.31 | 0.35 | 0.16 | 0.25 | 0.24 | 0.25 | 13.15*** | TV,E,F,C,SP,SO < W; TV < C,H; F < H |
| Activation | 1.94 | 2.01 | 1.95 | 1.99 | 1.90 | 1.59 | 1.90 | 2.29 | 2.11 | 27.81*** | TV < E,F,C,H,W < SP; TV,H,E < SO |
| Role salience | 1.69 | 1.77 | 1.81 | 2.01 | 1.62 | 1.21 | 1.65 | 1.76 | 1.82 | 22.20*** | TV < E,F,C,H,W,SP,SO; E,H,W < C |
| Self-esteem | 2.26 | 2.31 | 2.25 | 2.29 | 2.26 | 2.07 | 2.24 | 2.38 | 2.37 | 5.35*** | TV < E,F,C,H,W,SP,SO |
| Intrinsic motivation | 1.96 | 1.80 | 2.08 | 2.03 | 1.38 | 2.00 | 2.14 | 2.51 | 2.35 | 52.16*** | H < W < TV,F,C < SP, SO; H,W < E < SP |
| Number of cases | 235 | 226 | 193 | 119 | 207 | 159 | 180 | 89 | 89 | | |
| **Wives** | | | | | | | | | | | |
| Positive affect | 1.77 | 1.61 | 1.84 | 1.71 | 1.56 | 1.74 | 1.85 | 1.98 | 2.14 | 17.15*** | W,H,C < SO,SP; TV,E,F < SO; W,H < E,F |
| Negative affect | 0.29 | 0.38 | 0.29 | 0.38 | 0.35 | 0.16 | 0.24 | 0.22 | 0.23 | 9.15*** | SO,E < C,H,W; TV < F,C,H,W; SP < C,W |
| Activation | 1.95 | 2.05 | 1.92 | 1.93 | 1.93 | 1.61 | 1.91 | 2.30 | 2.10 | 24.70*** | TV < E,F,C,H < SO < SP; TV, E < W < SP |
| Role salience | 1.69 | 1.75 | 1.77 | 1.90 | 1.64 | 1.28 | 1.67 | 1.79 | 1.80 | 15.25*** | TV < E,F,C,H,W,SP,SO; H,E < C |
| Self-esteem | 2.31 | 2.36 | 2.26 | 2.24 | 2.27 | 2.25 | 2.35 | 2.44 | 2.40 | 3.67*** | |
| Intrinsic motivation | 1.96 | 1.88 | 1.94 | 1.85 | 1.42 | 2.15 | 2.15 | 2.47 | 2.31 | 44.12*** | C,H,W < TV,E,SP; F,C,H,W < SP, SO;H < F,C,W; F < E; |
| Number of cases | 235 | 220 | 199 | 134 | 223 | 145 | 183 | 80 | 134 | | |

*Note:* All measures are on a 4-point-scale: 0 = not at all, 1 = a little, 2 = somewhat, 3 = very much.

[a] Differences in means across activities were tested using one-way Analysis of Variance.

[b] W = Work, F = Talking with Family, C = Activities with Child, H = Housework, TV = Watching Television, E = Eating, SP = Hobbies/Sports, SO = Social Activities. All comparisons noted are significant at p < .05.

*** p < .001

Table 7.6 *Differences in emotions of spouses by location*

|                      | Overall | Home    | Work     | Public    |
|----------------------|---------|---------|----------|-----------|
| Positive affect      | 0.02    | 0.10**  | −0.05    | −0.07     |
| Negative affect      | 0.02    | −0.03   | 0.07*    | 0.04      |
| Activation           | −0.02   | −0.02   | −0.05    | −0.07*    |
| Role salience        | −0.01   | −0.02   | −0.02    | −0.10*    |
| Self-esteem          | −0.04   | −0.03   | −0.05    | −0.08*    |
| Intrinsic motivation | 0.00    | 0.07*   | −0.09*   | −0.12**   |

*Note:* Reported are the average differences in means for spouses' emotions in each context, which were calculated by subtracting the wife's mean from the husband's. Positive values indicate higher levels of emotion for husbands; negative values indicate higher levels of emotion for wives.

* $p < .05$; ** $p < .01$ (on two-tailed t-tests of differences relative to zero)

and suggest the need for more in-depth investigation of the question of emotion and gender, especially in the family context. Some gender differences do emerge in comparing spouses' emotions across different locations.

At the couple level, husbands experience more positive affect ($t = 2.94$, $p < .01$) and greater intrinsic motivation ($t = 2.05$, $p < .05$) at *home* than their wives. Compared with their husbands, wives are slightly higher in negative affect as well as in activation, role salience, and self-esteem at home. However, with the exception of positive affect and intrinsic motivation, these differences are not statistically significant. Comparing emotions at *work*, spouses' experiences are different in two dimensions: negative affect and intrinsic motivation. At work, husbands are higher in negative affect ($t = 2.00$, $p < .05$) and are less motivated ($t = −1.99$, $p < .05$) than their wives; for all other emotions, the differences between spouses are negligible. Spouses' emotions are most different in *public* locations. In public, wives are higher than their husbands in the experience of activation ($t = 2.28$, $p < .05$), role salience ($t = 2.27$, $p < .05$), self-esteem ($t = 2.39$, $p < .05$), and intrinsic motivation ($t = 2.7$, $p < .01$).

Finally, emotions between spouses by different companions are explored (see table 7.7). The ways emotional experiences vary by different companions are very similar between spouses in the following three contexts: when alone, when with spouse only, and when with spouse and child together. In these contexts, spouses are very similar in their experience of emotions in all dimensions.

In other contexts, however, there are some differences in spouses' emotional experiences. When with child alone, husbands report greater

Table 7.7 *Differences in emotions of spouses by companions*

|  | Alone | With spouse only | With child only | With spouse and child | With others |
|---|---|---|---|---|---|
| Positive affect | 0.01 | 0.06 | 0.11* | 0.08 | −0.18** |
| Negative affect | 0.06 | 0.00 | −0.05 | −0.04 | 0.05 |
| Activation | −0.01 | −0.04 | −0.01 | −0.03 | −0.08 |
| Role salience | 0.02 | 0.03 | 0.03 | 0.07 | −0.19** |
| Self-esteem | −0.06 | −0.08 | 0.02 | 0.01 | −0.13* |
| Intrinsic motivation | −0.03 | −0.10 | 0.12* | 0.03 | −0.08 |

*Note:* Reported are the average differences in means for spouses' emotions in each context, which were calculated by subtracting the wife's mean from the husband's. Positive values indicate higher levels of emotion for husband; negative values indicate higher levels of emotion for wives.
* $p < .05$; ** $p < .01$ (on two-tailed t tests of differences relative to zero)

positive affect ($t = 2.08$, $p < .05$) and intrinsic motivation ($t = 2.01$, $p < .05$) than their wives. Husbands are also higher in feelings of role salience and self-esteem than their wives when with the child, although these differences are not statistically significant. Wives, on the other hand, experience slightly more negative affect and greater activation than their husbands when with the child, but these differences are negligible. The companionship of non-family, non-work-related others tends to yield the largest difference in spouses' emotions. When with others, wives' emotional levels are higher than their husbands' for all emotions except negative affect. Compared with their husbands, wives feel significantly greater positive affect ($t = 2.71$, $p < .01$), greater role salience ($t = 2.85$, $p < .01$), and greater self-esteem ($t = 2.35$, $p < .05$) when with others. Wives also experience greater activation and intrinsic motivation than their husbands when with others, but these differences are negligible.[7]

When husbands' and wives' experiences are compared at the couple level, their emotional worlds appear to be even more similar than when comparisons are made at the individual level. This could mean several things. It may be a selection effect. That is, people who are similar in emotional make-up tend to marry each other. Alternatively, over many years of sharing life together, spouses may become more alike in their emotional experiences.[8]

## Discussion

With respect to understanding emotions, a primary finding of this study is that emotions are not fixed but vary depending on different situations.

This may sound too obvious a claim, but in popular psychology the opposite is often assumed. That is, emotions are viewed as being more dispositional and are seen as rooted in genes, personality, or other seemingly enduring qualities that individuals are born with or develop over time. For example, men and women are often seen as having different emotions, and such differences are assumed to be gender-based. Although gender differences are found in daily emotional experiences, internal variations *within* husbands or wives are as substantial as the differences *between* them. These findings point to the need for examining emotions contextually, investigating the mechanisms that produce variations rather than pursuing a general theory of emotion using a single variable such as gender.

Another implication for emotion research is that emotions have multiple dimensions. For example, an individual may be fully relaxed at home after work, but at the same time feel absolutely bored, or angry with the children, or wishing to be somewhere else. An individual may also feel highly motivated and happy to be doing a particular activity but feel stressed or lonely at the same time. This chapter has found that emotional lives are full of such complexities. These findings suggest that emotions could perhaps be better conceptualized in terms other than the *intrinsic quality of experience*. To elaborate, various interpretations or evaluations of stimuli or oneself may occur in the arousal of emotion at any given moment. Factors that influence one's views about the given situation may come from many sources, such as one's own needs, demands from others, and beliefs about life. These multiple and often conflicting emotions suggest the need for more qualitative, in-depth investigations of the ways in which both internal and inter-relational needs and conflicts are experienced at each moment and how they change and develop over time.

Overall, husbands and wives are not so different in terms of the average level of emotions experienced in daily life. When comparing experiences in different contexts, however, some gender differences in emotion are evident. One of the most consistent differences between husbands' and wives' emotions occurs when interacting with children. For husbands, spending time with children is in many respects a more positive experience compared with paid work or housework. For wives, on the other hand, spending time with children is no different from paid work or housework along several emotional dimensions. This pattern is also found in comparisons across locations, companions, and activities.

What accounts for husbands' more positive emotional experiences when spending time with children, and how crucial are these differences in understanding the relationships between spouses in dual-career marriages? The task of raising children seems to be at the heart of work–family dilemmas, particularly for wives. With respect to housework, for example, despite a rather large discrepancy in the division of household labor, spouses' emotions are affected by housework in much the same way.[9] The greater emotional dilemmas for wives concerning childcare could mean that wives are not free from traditional gender ideology, feeling more responsibility than their husbands. Wives also spend more time with children than their husbands. The way spouses deal with the task of raising children is a topic that needs to be explored more fully when examining the emotional dynamics of married couples.

Finally, as noted in the beginning of the chapter, emotional fulfillment from marriage occupies a central place in examinations and explanations of marital stability. As has been shown, family life does not seem to be uniformly positive compared with other aspects of peoples' lives. However, the couples in this study have been married a relatively long time (an average of eighteen years), suggesting that their marriages are stable. In the absence of a comparison group – for example, those who are divorced – the relationship between emotional satisfaction and marital stability is difficult to explore. Given the long relationships of the couples, however, spouses apparently find ways to resolve the emotional needs in their marriage. A task for future research is to investigate how emotional differences become accommodated within and between spouses.

## NOTES

1. The internal consistency of measures was separately analyzed for husbands and wives. Reported here are the average scores for both.
2. The ESM data include more detailed place codes. If at home, place codes include bedroom, dining room, garage, laundry, etc.; if at work, codes include one's office, one's boss's office, the mail room, etc.; if in public, codes include the car, the park, the store, etc. For purposes of analysis, all places were recoded into home, work, and public.
3. Results reported in tables 7.3, 7.4, and 7.5 are based on one-way Analysis of Variance (ANOVA) tests that compare emotions across different locations for husbands and wives separately. Multiple post hoc comparisons with Bonferroni corrections were performed for all significant F-values. Additionally, to verify the main effects and gender differences for all three sets of analyses (location, companions, and activities), two-factor ANOVAs were performed with gender as the second factor. These results are not specifically presented in the tables, but are elucidated in the text.
4. On average, husbands and wives spend 12.9 percent and 16 percent of their time, respectively, in public locations across the week. Time spent at home and at the workplace also differs for husbands and wives. Husbands spend 42.4 percent of their time at home, and wives 52.1 percent, ($t = -7.2$, $p < .001$). In turn, husbands spend 33.9 percent of their time at the workplace and wives only 22.3 percent ($t = 8.7$, $p < .001$).

5. The analyses in this section include comparisons by location and by companions. Comparisons by activity are not included because the results are similar to those for the first two analyses. Since the activities people engage in are likely to vary depending on where they are or whom they are with, this similarity in results is not surprising.

6. To determine whether the mean emotions of spouses were significantly different, difference scores for each emotion in each context were tested against zero, using a one-sample t-test of means; the null hypothesis assumes that spouses experience similar levels of emotion and therefore do not differ in their levels of emotion (i.e., husband − wife = 0).

7. For this analysis, data for co-workers were analyzed but not presented. Husbands have higher negative affect when with co-workers than their wives.

8. It is possible that couples who have been together for a longer period of time have more similar emotions. In order to evaluate this possibility, chi-square tests were performed on the mean difference values by length of marriage. The difference measures for the six primary emotion measures (overall positive affect, negative affect, etc.) and the length of marriage for each couple were categorized into quartiles. Six chi-square tests of independence were performed between the quartiles for the length of the marriage and each of the emotion difference values. A significant chi-square test would suggest that there was an effect of marriage length on the degree of discrepancy between husbands' and wives' emotions. However, there were no significant chi-square tests (all $\chi^2 < 4.96$, ns). This suggests that, for this sample, the length of the marriage does not have a significant relationship with the similarities or differences in couples' emotions.

9. Overall, wives spend 25.2 percent of their time on housework during the week, including weekends, whereas husbands spend 17.9 percent of their time on housework ($t = 7.5$, $p < .001$).

# Commentary

## Elaine Wethington

*It has become almost a cliché to say that a new paradigm is emerging in research on the integration of work and family. The shift, briefly stated, is from the now-classic role strain and conflict perspectives that focused on the power of institutions to shape lives, expectations, norms, and behavior to "bottom-up" perspectives that focus on the dynamic, interactive, and negotiated boundaries (or not) between the public institution of work and the private realms of home and feeling. Like all emerging paradigms, this more contemporary perspective leads researchers to seek new answers to the old questions, and to ask new ones. The Experience Sampling Method (ESM) provides an opportunity to integrate many different lines of research: research on role expectations in couples and how they vary by spouses' personal histories; the daily life of couples; research on adaptation and coping at the boundary of family and work; and the impact of changing social conditions on family life.*

*Koh takes an important step toward addressing the second of these three questions in this chapter. She describes her study as an epidemiology of everyday life and emotions in married couples. The chapter's major accomplishment is its contribution to understanding how couples experience the daily demands of work and family in their lives at the micro-emotional level. First, the analyses capture the daily rise and fall of moods as men and women go about their daily tasks. Within individuals, mood varies across role settings, varying by the context and nature of the tasks.*

*The second contribution of this chapter is that it focuses on the positive as well as the negative emotions that people feel as they adapt to everyday demands. Too often, research on work and family has concentrated on negative emotions alone, in parallel to general research on stress, coping, and appraisal (Somerfield and McCrae 2000). The analyses presented in this chapter capture the positive outcomes of being "under demand" such as the perceptions of personal benefits even in potentially stressful situations (Lazarus 1999). Most data on the positive impacts of stress rely on retrospective measures of emotion that can be easily distorted by subsequent events and emotions.*

*Third, these analyses consider a much more comprehensive range of emotions and affects than have been assessed in previous research. They also raise the possibility that the ESM can be used to demonstrate that positive emotions can counterweigh negative emotions in specific situations, contributing not only to adaptation to the situation but also to persistence and accomplishment under more difficult circumstances. As Folkman and Moskowitz (2000) recently observed in a review of intensive studies of stress and appraisal, positive emotions can serve as a powerful resource for adaptation in daily life, as people actively balance the negative in their lives with positive emotions such as control, pride, and self-esteem.*

*Perhaps one of the more intriguing observations in this chapter is that gender differences in mood are very small, at least within a sample of married couples. Variations across individuals across time and in different situations are wider than the average differences between the emotions of men and women in the same types of situations. There are a number of explanations for this. As Koh points out, forces of selection are at work. Because of the nature of mate selection, those who marry have similar personalities, goals, attitudes, and backgrounds. As time goes on they become even more similar; and as well they encounter similar situations in everyday life. Yet I would also venture that the traditional theories on the relationship between work and family have led researchers to predict much larger gender differences than may have ever existed, most particularly at the micro-level of adaptation observed in this study. It is informative to reflect on the types of studies in which gender differences in mood appear much larger. Those where the outcome is depression or depressive affect; those using retrospective designs, often over six-month to one-year periods; and those focusing on rare and severe life events rather than events at the daily level. In fact, two recently published studies that reported gender differences in daily mood (and using different daily diary samples) converge with the Koh study. Almeida and colleagues (Almeida and Kessler 1998; Almeida, Wethington, and Kessler 2002) found that gender differences on the daily level in mood and exposure to work and family stressors were very modest. In short, situation and context are more associated with variations in emotions than gender, at the daily level of observation.*

*The gender differences in mood found in Koh's study are not pervasive, yet those that emerged underscore the power of work and family role expectations to affect the appraisal of daily events, as predicted by transactional theories of appraisal (Lazarus 1999). The underlying pattern seems to be that both men and women feel more positively engaged in those situations which are more novel and counter to their socially normative roles, specifically, fathers interacting with their children, and mothers interacting in public situations. In general, obligations seem to be associated with lower levels of emotional engagement; however, an alternative explanation is that the context for obligatory actions produces more ambivalence, or mixed emotions. An important follow-up to the current study would be the explicit analysis of mixed emotions. Are they associated with activities that represent fulfilling obligations rather than exercising freer choice?*

*The ESM holds promise to translate transactional theory on stress and adaptation (e.g. Lazarus and Folkman 1984) into research designs that capture changes in individuals across time and context. A further step that a couple-level analysis could take is toward the study of mutual coping and adaptation, by focusing on changes in mood of family members in the same households rather than just individual change (see also Bolger, Zuckerman, and Kessler 2000). A full-scale analysis of the impact of one spouse's mood on the other was beyond the stated intentions of this chapter. However, Koh's analysis does point the way to a more detailed series of analyses that could influence research on emotions and appraisal.*

*One important way in which this study might contribute is to document the interaction in daily life between role expectations and responses to daily demands. Serido and colleagues (2004) found that there is an association in daily life between the chronic demands in employment and family and the daily hassles experienced in those roles, as predicted by conventional theories of stress. However, this association was not very large, suggesting that reports of daily stressors and reports of chronic strains have different origins. The study reported here raises the possibility of examining these findings on a deeper level. How do contexts and normative expectations combine to affect the appraisal of daily stressors and demands?*

## *Norval D. Glenn*

*Koh presents a wealth of descriptive information about the everyday emotions of persons in dual-career marriages and highlights some of the most important and interesting dimensions of that information. The findings are so numerous and detailed, however, that, in spite of Koh's competent efforts, the trees to some extent obscure the forest. The most valuable contribution I can make, therefore, is to extend Koh's efforts to extract the most important findings from the morass of information and to draw implications from those findings.*

*Koh uses six categories of emotions, one negative and five positive, and correctly deals with the different kinds of positive emotions separately because each kind relates differently to other variables. However, it is also useful to construct a summary measure of the positive emotions to be used in addition to, rather than instead of, measures of the different kinds. One rather crude such measure is simply the mean of the scores on the five different kinds of positive emotions, which I call the Index of Positive Emotions (IPE). The IPE values by location and by identity of companions are presented in the figure.*

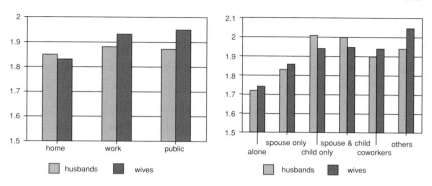

Index of positive emotions (IPE) by locations and companions

*Arguably the most important of the findings are those concerning differ-ences between husbands and wives in the way they feel at home and at work. Both husbands and wives reported higher levels of positive emotions at work, but the difference is considerably greater for the wives. (I am unable to cal-culate the statistical significance of differences between IPE scores, but the .04 difference between home and work for husbands may not be significant.) Both husbands and wives reported more negative affect at work than at home (table 7.3), but this difference is greater for husbands than for wives (.14 and .07 points, respectively). Husbands reported greater negative affect at work than wives, and wives reported greater negative affect at home than husbands (table 7.3). Which sphere is better overall is not entirely clear for either hus-bands or wives, but the data suggest that home is better than work for husbands and that work is better than home for wives, the latter being in accordance with Hochschild's thesis that work has become a haven from family life (Hochschild 1997). What is clearly indicated by the data is that home life is slightly better for husbands than for wives and that work is distinctly better for wives than for husbands.*

*The persistence of traditional gender roles in dual-career families provides a plausible explanation for this pattern of differences. There is an abundance of fairly recent evidence that even when both spouses work outside the home, the husband tends to assume the role of primary breadwinner and the wife tends to be the primary parent and homemaker. Each of these roles carries burdens, which are likely to be felt mainly at work by husbands and at home by wives. It is obvious how this division of responsibility may affect wives' emotions as they spend time with children and in other domestic settings. Somewhat less obvious is how the husbands' being the primary providers allows wives greater freedom to work or not work, and if they do, to choose work on the basis of non-pecuniary considerations. It is informative that, compared with the husbands, the wives reported distinctly lower negative affect, higher positive affect, and higher intrinsic motivation at work, the latter being essentially enjoyment of work.*

*If my explanation is correct, a shift toward more androgynous roles in marriage is not likely to result in substantial net gains in the emotional quality of life for either husbands or wives. Gains at work are likely to be offset by losses at home and vice versa. For instance, if wives take more responsibility for breadwinning, they are likely to begin emphasizing earnings to the detriment of enjoyment of work and other non-monetary work rewards. This same change would allow husbands to place more emphasis on intrinsic work rewards, to their benefit, but their taking more responsibility for child rearing and domestic chores would almost certainly lower the quality of their emotions at home.*

*Given the time pressures faced by most dual-career couples with children, time to spend alone or only with one another must typically be scarce, and thus, one might speculate, precious and conducive to positive emotions. It is surprising, therefore, that "alone" and "with spouse only" rank last and next-to-last in the IPE among the companion situations. It is not surprising that these two companion situations are low in activation and role salience, but for both husbands and wives "alone" is very low, and "with spouse only" no more than moderately high, in positive affect and intrinsic motivation (table 7.4). In the case of "with spouse only," the low level of positive emotions is offset somewhat by low negative affect, but "alone" is characterized by high negative affect for both husbands and wives.*

*The human need for human companionship is well documented, but the poor emotional showing of "alone," even among people who must on average have a high level of social interaction, suggests that this need is stronger than it is generally understood to be. On the other hand, people in dual-career marriages may on average have unusually high social needs. These marriages may tend to be selective of "people who need people," or a high level of social interaction may engender intolerance for solitude.*

*The relatively low level of positive emotions for "with spouse only" must be discouraging to anyone concerned about the quality of marriages in American society, but this finding should not be over interpreted. This companion situation fares somewhat better in positive affect and intrinsic motivation (arguably the most crucial of the kinds of positive emotions) than in the IPE. Both husbands and wives at least apparently tend to enjoy the company of their spouses more than that of their co-workers. Furthermore, the psychological benefits of marriage extend beyond enhancing positive emotions when one is alone with a spouse. For instance, sexual gratification can improve a person's mood when the sexual partner is not present, and as I point out above, a primary-breadwinner husband may enhance a wife's quality of work life. Still another consideration is that these dual-career couples with children may not be typical of all married couples in the emotions they experience when they are with one another. The time pressures faced by the studied couples may tend to prevent them from spending quality time together, for instance time when they are not fatigued.*

*One of the most interesting aspects of the data is that the highest IPE is for wives in the presence of persons who are neither co-workers nor members of their immediate families. These "others" no doubt consist of a variety of kinds of persons, including friends and relatives but also such persons as clerks and service providers with whom the wives had rather impersonal relationships. What may distinguish these persons from co-workers and immediate family members is that interaction with them is generally voluntary rather than obligatory and is less burdened by feelings of duty and obligation. One might even speculate that low-investment social relationships tend to be more relaxed and more pleasurable in some other respects than relationships in which a great deal is at stake.*

*According to these explanations, companionship with "others" should be about as important to husbands as to wives, but apparently that is not the case. Wives probably have, on average, better social skills to relate to persons outside the family and work settings, and associating with various persons in public settings may provide wives with a haven from family responsibilities to an even greater extent than does work.*

*Koh's seminal study suggests a number of topics for future research. For instance, it would be useful and interesting to compare the emotions at work of women without husbands, or without earner husbands, with the emotions of the wives studied here. If my reasoning is correct, the quality of work life of these primary-breadwinner women should be lower on the average than that of women in dual-career marriages. It would also be useful and interesting to compare the emotions experienced while alone of unmarried persons and stay-at-home wives with those of the persons studied by Koh. And so forth. The possibilities are numerous. I look forward to seeing the results of the research that will be prompted by Koh's study.*

# 8 Couples making it happen: marital satisfaction and what works for highly satisfied couples

*Mark R. Nielsen*

Nine out of ten Americans choose to marry, providing strong evidence that marriage remains an important life goal for adults in the US (Cherlin 1992). This trend has held for at least three cohorts born between 1950 and 1964 (Goldstein and Kenney 2001). Goldstein and Kenney (2001) report that marriage tends to occur later among college graduates than non-college graduates, but by the time adults are in their thirties the marriage rate is about the same for both groups. Despite changes in the timing and duration of marriage – increased incidence of cohabitation, later age of first marriage, and higher divorce rates – they conclude "marriage remains a normative part of adult life" (Goldstein and Kenney 2001: 517).

Most people marry because they believe their lives will be better than if they remain single (Becker 1991). The expected benefits of marriage include economic gain from shared expenses, affection, and sexual relations that usually come with marriage, establishing a home and family – including raising children – and a certain sense of security. In addition to such social and economic benefits, men and women marry because they want and expect a relationship that is satisfying for each of them (Fowers 2000). This expectation is fulfilled for the majority of married couples. Although Glenn (1996) finds evidence for a decline in marital satisfaction over the past three decades, most husbands and wives still say they are satisfied with their marriage relationship (Waite and Nielsen 2001).

Numerous studies of marital satisfaction have been conducted, but the factors that contribute to a more or less satisfying marriage remain unclear. What parts of the marital relationship do couples include in their assessments of marital satisfaction? How do husbands and wives differ in their assessments of aspects of their relationship? What factors contribute to a more satisfying marital relationship?

Using a subset of items from the ENRICH[1] marital inventory (Olson, Fournier, and Druckman 1987), this chapter examines the relationship between spouses' positive agreement on various aspects of the marriage relationship (e.g., communication, intimacy, finances, parenting, and decision-making) and their self-reported levels of marital satisfaction. Analyses are based on data from couples who participated in the 500 Family Study. Both husbands and wives completed surveys, including a fifteen-item abbreviated ENRICH inventory. It is thus possible to compare their responses to the same set of items. In addition to determining couples' level of positive agreement about their marital relationship, analyses consider individual characteristics that may affect marital satisfaction, including number of depressive symptoms, self-esteem, and whether husbands and wives come home from work feeling angry, exhausted, or emotionally drained.

### Assessing marriages

Historically, marital appraisal has been an assessment by each spouse about how he or she thinks the marriage is going. This approach is the result of decades of research grounded in early studies that interviewed couples about their marriage to discover what enhances the quality of the relationship (Terman 1947). Later research examined the marital relationship in greater depth (see, e.g., Bradburn and Caplovitz 1965), finding that marital happiness has two dimensions: a "negative feeling state" and a "positive feeling state." Although both dimensions are correlated with marital happiness, the dimensions are uncorrelated with each other. In explaining this finding, Bradburn and Caplovitz note that "negative feelings do not necessarily at the same time diminish positive feelings, nor do experiences producing positive feelings affect the number of negative feelings" (1965: 19–20). In examining the different contributions of positive and negative feelings to overall happiness, they found that individuals scoring high on the positive dimension and low on the negative were more likely to report being very happy or satisfied, while those scoring high on the negative dimension and low on the positive were more likely to report being unhappy or dissatisfied. Based on these findings, they conclude that it is the relative balance of the two dimensions that defines and predicts marital happiness.

Offering a different perspective on marital satisfaction, Bradbury, Fincham, and Beach argue that "[marital] satisfaction is appropriately conceptualized not simply as a judgment made by spouses at one point in time but as a trajectory that reflects fluctuations in marital evaluations over time" (2000: 974). They view marital satisfaction as a long-range assessment, rooted in prior marital interactions, that considers the future of the relationship with all of its expressed and tacit expectations. This does not mean that marital satisfaction is fixed. They note that it can vary as the dynamics of the marital situation change, but tends to be relatively robust. Factors shown to be associated with marital satisfaction – and changes in marital satisfaction – include income, financial situation, educational attainment, family structure, religiosity, values, communication, decision-making, spouse's habits, emotions, employment status, and spillover and conflict between work, family, sex, and health (Burleson and Denton 1997; Williams and Alliger 1994).

## Marital satisfaction and couple disagreement

Most married people would probably agree that married life can sometimes be difficult. For husbands and wives, particularly those who are both employed, juggling work responsibilities, childcare, social and family obligations, and the necessities of maintaining a home can be a challenge that requires negotiations over priorities and division of responsibilities. Married couples faced with these demands may find themselves "coming up short" on time, energy, and other resources needed to fulfill their responsibilities. Not being able to fulfill their responsibilities – to each other, their children, work, friends, and others – may lead to disagreements or problems between spouses.

Such problems may pose a threat to marital satisfaction. But how much of a threat? Olson, Fournier, and Druckman (1987) suggest that the higher the level of disagreement among couples on how well they do in various areas of their marital relationship, the less satisfied husbands and wives will be with their marriage. Gottman (1994b) maintains that disagreement is a precursor to divorce, but elsewhere (Gottman and Notarius 2000) states that not all disagreement is counter to having a *happy* marriage. He describes three *styles* of marriage – validating, volatile, and avoidant – that indicate how couples settle disagreements. Couples who calmly work out their disagreements in a mutually satisfying way have a validating style. Spouses can disagree but still acknowledge the validity of the other person's position. Couples with a volatile style have disagreements that can be loud and passionate. They resolve their conflicts with yelling and shouting while still being happy with their marriage. Couples with an avoidant style agree to disagree and rarely confront their differences. Gottman reports that all three styles are found in happy marriages.

Couple disagreement is not necessarily bad for marriage. What is important is the balance in the relationship. Gottman and Notarius (2000) finds that couples can have a happy and long marriage as long as the positive aspects of the relationship outweigh the negative. These results are consistent with Roberts (2000), who finds that couples can be very passionate in their disagreements as long as they are passionate in their affection. Going a bit further, Gottman points out that this balance cannot be a simple majority. He suggests that there should be, on average, five times more positive than negative aspects in the relationship for a marriage to succeed. His assessment is consistent with Olson, Fournier, and Druckman's (1987) finding that the more areas of the marriage couples positively agree on, the better off the marriage.

### Hypotheses

Couples with high levels of marital satisfaction may be those who not only agree that their relationship is going well, but also agree on more areas of their relationship. The particular areas on which couples agree may also be important to marital satisfaction. The fifteen items that comprise Olson, Fournier, and Druckman's (1987) abbreviated ENRICH inventory include areas specific to the couple and the management of their relationship (e.g., affection and intimacy, communication between spouses, the handling of role responsibilities, and conflict resolution) as well as areas that involve the couple's relationships and responsibilities to others (e.g., children, parents, in-laws, and friends). Gottman's (2001) work suggests that spouses' relationship with each other, particularly their ability to communicate effectively and resolve conflicts, may be more important to marital satisfaction than the couple's relationships with others. This research suggests the following hypotheses:

*Hypothesis* 1. Highly satisfied couples will likely agree that they do more things well than couples who are less satisfied.

*Hypothesis* 2. Highly satisfied couples will engage in activities that maintain and strengthen their relationship.

*Hypothesis* 3. The quality of the relationship between spouses is more important for marital satisfaction than the quality of the couple's relationships with others (e.g., children, parents, and friends).

### Method

#### Sample

Analyses are based on 330 couples who participated in the 500 Family Study. Only married couples in which both the husband and the wife completed the parent survey were selected for study. In addition, only couples who had no missing data on the items of interest were selected.

*Measures*

*Dependent variable*   Marital satisfaction, the dependent variable, is based on the following item from the parent survey: "Overall, I am satisfied with my relationship with my spouse/partner." Respondents were asked to indicate the extent of their agreement with this statement using the following scale: 1 = strongly disagree; 2 = moderately disagree; 3 = neither agree nor disagree; 4 = moderately agree; and 5 = strongly agree. For several analyses, responses were recoded into three categories: highly satisfied (those who responded 5 on the above scale); moderately satisfied (3 or 4), and not satisfied (1 or 2). This item is similar to marital satisfaction items used in the General Social Survey (GSS) and the Current Population Survey (CPS).[2]

*Independent variables*   Independent variables include gender, number of years married, and items assessing respondents' psychological health and emotional well-being. The following measures were used to assess psychological well-being: the twenty-item CES-Depression Scale,[3] several items measuring self-esteem,[4] and three questions asking how angry, exhausted, and emotionally drained respondents feel at the end of the workday. Historically, scholars have found that gender and mental health – especially depressive symptoms and self-esteem – affect marital satisfaction. When one or both spouses are depressed, couples may be less satisfied with their marriage. In fact, depression has been shown to influence the way couples resolve conflict, thereby affecting marital satisfaction (Marchand and Hock 2000). Work stress may also affect marital satisfaction. Roberts and Levenson (2001) show how emotional spillover from work can negatively impact marriage. The number of years married is one of the control variables in regression analyses because length of marriage has been associated with decreases in marital satisfaction (Bradbury, Fincham and Beach 2000).[5]

The ENRICH inventory is frequently used by counselors to help couples with their marital relationship (Olson, Fournier, and Druckman 1987). A fifteen-item ENRICH abbreviated inventory was included in the 500 Family Study parent survey as an additional measure of the quality of the marital relationship; these items have been shown to be reliable and valid for research and clinical practice (Fowers and Olson 1989, 1993). The Positive Couple Agreement score, based on a subset of ten items in the ENRICH abbreviated inventory, is used to assess the extent to which husbands and wives agree that they do well in ten areas of their marriage. If a husband and wife both say they do well in any area of their marriage and their ranking is within one point on the positive end of the five-point scale, the couple is considered to positively agree on that item. A Couple Agreement composite score was computed across all ten items indicating the level of positive couple agreement about the marital relationship; couples with higher scores will be more satisfied with their marriage.[6]

### Analytic approach

Descriptive analyses compare husbands' and wives' levels of marital satisfaction. The ranking of marital agreement items by spouses is also compared by level of marital satisfaction and gender. These analyses are designed to answer the following questions: Do husbands and wives have similar levels of marital satisfaction and do they assess their marriage differently across marital satisfaction categories?

The next set of analyses examines factors associated with marital satisfaction using ordered logistic regression, the appropriate method for ordered categorical data (DeMaris 1992). Two ordered logistic regression models are compared. The first model examines the effect of individual psychological characteristics on marital satisfaction. The second model examines the influence of couple characteristics on marital satisfaction, controlling for individual characteristics.

## Results

### Opposites don't necessarily attract

Do husbands and wives agree on how satisfied they are with their marriage? To create a couple score for marital satisfaction, the wife's score was subtracted from her husband's. The range of the couple score is minus four to plus four. A value of zero means that wives' and husbands' responses to the ten marital agreement questions were the same. The wife's score was coded as "similar" to her husband's if her response was the same or 1 point above or below her husband's score on the five-point marital satisfaction scale. Wives whose responses were 2 to 4 points higher than their husbands' on this scale were coded as "more satisfied." Wives whose responses were 2 to 4 points lower than their husbands were coded as "less satisfied." Table 8.1 shows the extent to which couples report similar levels of marital satisfaction. Columns indicate husbands' level of marital satisfaction; rows indicate wives' marital satisfaction relative to their husbands' (i.e., similar, more satisfied, less satisfied).[7]

Most highly satisfied and moderately satisfied couples have similar assessments of marital satisfaction. Nearly 98 percent of highly satisfied

Table 8.1 *Husbands' marital satisfaction and percent of wives who agree*

| Wives' marital satisfaction relative to their husbands' | Husbands' marital satisfaction | | |
|---|---|---|---|
| | Highly satisfied | Moderately satisfied | Not satisfied |
| More satisfied | – | 5.9 | 42.9 |
| Similar | 97.5 | 86.3 | 57.1 |
| Less satisfied | 2.5 | 7.8 | – |
| Total | 100.0 | 100.0 | 100.0 |
| Number of cases | 200 | 102 | 28 |

husbands are married to wives who rate their marriage similarly. Just over 86 percent of the moderately satisfied husbands are married to wives who rate their marriage in the same way. The pattern among couples who are not satisfied with their marriage is very different, however. Slightly more than half of the couples whose husbands are not satisfied with their marriage have wives who rank their marriage similarly, while 43 percent of wives are more satisfied with their marriage than their husbands.

### Marital relationship assessment

While many husbands and wives have similar levels of marital satisfaction, do they agree on *other* dimensions of their relationship? Table 8.2 shows the couple scores for each of ten areas by couple's marital satisfaction level. If a couple has a score of 5, both the husband and wife have a score of 5, both husband and wife *strongly agree* that they do well in that area of their relationship; if a couple has an average score of 1, both strongly *disagree* that they do well in this area. For all ten items, highly satisfied couples have higher scores than moderately satisfied and less satisfied couples. Moderately satisfied couples score higher than less satisfied couples in all but one area – relationships with relatives and friends. For highly satisfied couples, the highest areas of positive agreement are communication, spouse's personality, decision-making, and how spouses carry out their roles. The highest areas of positive agreement for moderately satisfied couples are finances, parenting, relationships with relatives and friends, and religion and values. For less satisfied couples, the highest areas are the same as those for moderately satisfied couples, but the order is different: relationships with relatives and friends, religion and values, parenting, and finances. Couples who are highly satisfied with their marriage thus appear to have greater positive agreement on areas specific to their own dyadic relationship, while couples with lower levels of marital satisfaction focus on external relationships.

Table 8.2 *Mean couple scores by level of marital satisfaction (n = 330)*

| | Marital satisfaction | | |
| --- | --- | --- | --- |
| Relationship items | Highly satisfied | Moderately satisfied | Not satisfied |
| Communication | 4.4 | 3.1 | 2.0 |
| Spouse's personality and traits | 4.4 | 3.4 | 2.2 |
| Decisions | 4.3 | 3.1 | 2.2 |
| Roles | 4.3 | 3.1 | 2.4 |
| Parenting | 4.2 | 3.7 | 3.0 |
| Relationship with relatives and friends | 4.2 | 3.6 | 3.7 |
| Religion and values | 4.0 | 3.5 | 3.4 |
| Affection and sex | 3.9 | 3.0 | 1.8 |
| Finances | 3.9 | 3.8 | 2.7 |
| Leisure | 3.7 | 3.0 | 2.4 |
| Sum of mean scores | 41.3 | 33.3 | 25.8 |

### Marital satisfaction and couple agreement

To assess the extent to which couples positively agree on ten areas of their relationship, the Positive Couple Agreement score was used. When a husband and wife score an item such as "I am very pleased about how we express affection and relate sexually" within one point (plus or minus) of each other on the *positive* end of the scale, they are considered to positively agree on the item. This means that one spouse must rate the item either 4 or 5 (i.e., agree or strongly agree with the item) and the other spouse must rate the same item 3, 4, or 5. For each of the ten items in the scale, couples received one point for an item if they rated that item within one point of each other on the positive end of the scale; they received a score of zero on that item if they did not. The Positive Couple Agreement score is additive and is created by summing the ten item scores. Scores from 6 to 10 indicate a *high* level of positive agreement, suggesting a stronger marital relationship. A score of 5 indicates a *medium* level of positive agreement; perhaps suggesting a balance of strengths and weakness in their marital relationship. Scores of 4 or lower indicate a *lower* level of relationship agreement, suggesting a weaker relationship.

Table 8.3 shows the distribution of positive relationship agreement (high, medium, and low) within each of the three marital satisfaction categories for both husbands and wives. Some of the patterns in table 8.3 suggest common sense explanations, while others do not. One might expect that spouses who are highly satisfied with their marriage would say they agree that they do most things well, while those who are not

Table 8.3 *Marital satisfaction and percent of relationship agreement for husbands and wives*

| Positive relationship agreement | Marital satisfaction | | | | | |
| | Highly satisfied | | Moderately satisfied | | Not satisfied | |
| | Husbands | Wives | Husbands | Wives | Husbands | Wives |
|---|---|---|---|---|---|---|
| High | 68.0 | 68.5 | 22.5 | 18.6 | 0.0 | 4.0 |
| Medium | 9.0 | 9.9 | 14.7 | 11.8 | 0.0 | 4.0 |
| Low | 23.0 | 21.7 | 62.7 | 69.6 | 100.0 | 92.0 |
| Total | 100.0 | 100.0 | 100.0 | 100.0 | 100.0 | 100.0 |
| Number of cases | 200 | | 102 | | 28 | |

satisfied with their marriage would agree that they do few things well. Table 8.3 provides evidence for this supposition. More than two-thirds of husbands and wives who are highly satisfied with their marriage agree that they do most things well. In contrast, over 90 percent of husbands and wives who report low levels of marital satisfaction agree that they perform well in *four or fewer* areas of their marital relationship.

Contrary to expectation, however, more than 20 percent of highly satisfied spouses score low on relationship agreement; 23 percent of the husbands and 22 percent of the wives agree they do well in four or fewer areas. An additional 9 to 10 percent of highly satisfied husbands and wives agree they do well in only half of the relationship areas. The distribution of relationship agreement for moderately satisfied spouses is almost the reverse of that for highly satisfied spouses as seen in table 8.3.

Overall, husbands and wives with high levels of marital satisfaction tend to agree that they are doing well in more areas of their relationship than those with lower levels of marital satisfaction. Most husbands and wives who are not satisfied with their marriage agree that they are doing well in only a few areas of their relationship. Results for spouses with moderate levels of marital satisfaction are mixed, with 30 to 40 percent agreeing that they do well in five or more areas of the marriage and the remainder agreeing that they do well in four or fewer areas. Husbands' and wives' self-reported levels of marital satisfaction thus appear to be associated with the extent of agreement between couples on how well they are doing in several areas of their marriage.

### What makes most couples satisfied?

What are the similarities and differences in agreement areas among couples with high, moderate, and low levels of marital satisfaction? Table 8.4

Table 8.4 *Marital satisfaction and ranking of marital areas by husbands and wives*

| | Highly satisfied | | Moderately satisfied | | Not satisfied | |
| --- | --- | --- | --- | --- | --- | --- |
| | Husbands | Wives | Husbands | Wives | Husbands | Wives |
| | Roles | Roles | Parenting | Parenting | Parenting | Relationship with others |
| | Decision-making | Decision-making | Roles | Relationship with others | Finances | Religion/values |
| | Communication | Communication | Religion/values | Finances | Relationship with others | Parenting |
| | Spouse's personality/ traits | Spouse's personality/ traits | Spouse's personality/ traits | Religion/values | Religion/values | Finances |
| | Parenting | Parenting | Relationship with others | Spouse's personality/ traits | Spouse's personality/ traits | Leisure time |
| | Relationship with others | Relationship with others | Decision-making | Roles | Roles | Roles |
| | Affection and sex | Affection and sex | Communication | Communication | Decision-making | Decision-making |
| | Religion/values | Finances | Finances | Decision-making | Communication | Spouse's personality/traits |
| | Leisure time | Leisure time | Leisure time | Affection and sex | Leisure time | Communication |
| | Finances | Religion/values | Affection and sex | Leisure time | Affection and sex | Affection and sex |

compares husbands' and wives' rankings of the ten different relationship areas by level of marital satisfaction.[8] The similarities and differences across levels of marital satisfaction are striking. Highly satisfied husbands and wives individually agree on the ranking of nearly every area. There are only two areas – practice of religion or values and finances – where highly satisfied husbands and wives differ in their rankings. The highest ranked areas for highly satisfied couples – those they are most likely to agree on and respond positively to – are roles, decision-making, communication, and spouse's personality and traits.

Moderately satisfied husbands and wives are most likely to agree that they parent well. For most other areas, moderately satisfied husbands and wives differ somewhat in their rankings. Areas that are highly ranked by both include parenting, religion and values, relationships with others, and spouse's personality and traits. Lower ranked items for both moderately satisfied husbands and wives include leisure time, affection and sex, communication, and decision-making. The areas on which there appears to be least agreement among moderately satisfied husbands and wives are role performance and finances: husbands rank role performance second while wives rank it sixth; in turn, wives rank finances third while husbands rank it eighth.

Husbands and wives with low levels of marital satisfaction are most divergent in their rankings. Less satisfied husbands and wives rank only three areas the same: roles (ranked sixth), decision-making (ranked seventh), and affection and sex (ranked tenth). Consistent with table 8.2, the higher ranked areas for less satisfied husbands and wives are parenting, relationships with others, religion and values, and finances.

Table 8.4 shows not only that couples with high, moderate, and low levels of marital satisfaction rank areas of their relationship differently, but also that husbands and wives with moderate and low levels of marital satisfaction identify different areas of strength in their relationships. This pattern contrasts sharply with that of highly satisfied spouses who rank eight of the ten areas identically. In general, the level of agreement between spouses decreases across levels of marital satisfaction.

### Other influences on marital satisfaction

The next set of analyses examines the relationship between marital satisfaction and husbands' and wives' psychological well-being, as measured by depressive symptoms and level of self-esteem. The relationship between marital satisfaction and work stress – coming home from work feeling angry, exhausted, or emotionally drained – is also examined.

Table 8.5 *Depressive symptoms and self-esteem by marital satisfaction and gender*

| | Marital satisfaction | | | | | |
|---|---|---|---|---|---|---|
| | Highly satisfied | | Moderately satisfied | | Not satisfied | |
| | Husbands | Wives | Husbands | Wives | Husbands | Wives |
| Mean depressive symptoms score[a] | 6.6 | 6.2 | 9.7 | 8.9 | 12.9 | 10.9 |
| Mean self-esteem score[b] | 39.1 | 39.0 | 36.9 | 36.0 | 34.4 | 34.2 |
| Number of cases | 200 | 203 | 102 | 102 | 28 | 25 |

[a] The depressive symptoms score is the sum of responses to the the twenty-item CES-D scale. Higher scores indicate higher number and/or higher frequency of depressive symptoms. The range for composite scores is 0 to 60. Composite scores of 16 or higher are considered high (Radloff, 1977).

[b] The self-esteem score is the sum of responses to fourteen self-esteem items. The range for the composite measure is 0 to 56. Higher scores indicate higher self-esteem.

*Depressive symptoms and self-esteem* Table 8.5 shows the average number of depressive symptoms and the average self-esteem scores for husbands and wives by level of marital satisfaction. Highly satisfied husbands and wives have, on average, fewer depressive symptoms than moderately satisfied and less satisfied husbands and wives. Similarly, moderately satisfied spouses have fewer depressive symptoms than spouses who are not satisfied with their marriage. The most striking difference is that husbands have more depressive symptoms on average than wives. These differences increase as marital satisfaction decreases. Among husbands, there are no statistical differences between adjacent categories, but the difference between highly satisfied and not satisfied husbands is statistically significant. For wives, differences between each of the categories are statistically significant ($p < .001$).

Table 8.5 also shows the average self-esteem scores for husbands and wives by their level of marital satisfaction. Results are as expected. More satisfied husbands and wives have higher self-esteem scores than less satisfied husbands and wives. Within each category of satisfaction, husbands' and wives' scores are extremely close, but there are differences across satisfaction categories. For husbands, there is a significant difference between those who are highly satisfied and not satisfied, but there are no differences between adjoining categories. For wives, there are significant differences between those who are highly or moderately satisfied and those who are not satisfied ($p < .001$), but there is no difference between wives with high and moderate levels of satisfaction.

Table 8.6 *Percent of husbands and wives who come home from work feeling exhausted, emotionally drained, and angry by level of marital satisfaction*

| | Marital satisfaction | | | | | |
|---|---|---|---|---|---|---|
| | Highly satisfied | | Moderately satisfied | | Not satisfied | |
| | Husbands | Wives | Husbands | Wives | Husbands | Wives |
| Come home exhausted | | | | | | |
| Seldom | 18.8 | 21.8 | 18.8 | 17.0 | 7.4 | 16.0 |
| Sometimes | 46.2 | 43.0 | 50.5 | 42.6 | 40.7 | 60.0 |
| Often | 35.0 | 35.2 | 30.7 | 40.4 | 51.9 | 24.0 |
| Total percent | 100.0 | 100.0 | 100.0 | 100.0 | 100.0 | 100.0 |
| Come home drained | | | | | | |
| Seldom | 15.8 | 16.4 | 20.8 | 12.9 | 14.8 | 12.0 |
| Sometimes | 50.0 | 45.2 | 47.5 | 46.2 | 33.3 | 48.0 |
| Often | 34.2 | 38.4 | 31.7 | 40.9 | 51.9 | 40.0 |
| Total percent | 100.0 | 100.0 | 100.0 | 100.0 | 100.0 | 100.0 |
| Come home angry | | | | | | |
| Seldom | 58.9 | 70.2 | 53.5 | 55.9 | 48.1 | 56.0 |
| Sometimes | 39.1 | 24.7 | 42.6 | 38.7 | 40.7 | 36.0 |
| Often | 2.0 | 5.1 | 4.0 | 5.4 | 11.1 | 8.0 |
| Total percent | 100.0 | 100.0 | 100.0 | 100.0 | 100.0 | 100.0 |
| Number of cases | 197 | 179 | 101 | 94 | 27 | 25 |

There appears to be a stronger relationship between depressive symptoms and lower marital satisfaction for husbands compared to wives. Dehle and Weiss (1998) point out that the likely causal path runs from low marital satisfaction to an increase in depressive symptoms which suggests, perhaps, that those with the highest number of depressive symptoms might be on their way out of the relationship. Yet Waite and Gallagher (2000) have found that when "unhappily married" spouses stay together for a while, they become happier with their marriage. What is surprising is that depressive symptoms tend to be slightly higher for husbands, while self-esteem scores are similar for husbands and wives. These results are not consistent with other studies. Previous studies have found that the number of reported depressive symptoms is higher for women and self-esteem scores are higher for men. Because of these differences, number of depressive symptoms and self-esteem scores are included in logistic regression analyses to evaluate their effect on marital satisfaction.

*Coming home from work*    After a day at work spouses may come home angry, exhausted, or emotionally drained by the events of the day. Often, the workday can spill over into the life of the family. Table 8.6

shows the percentage of husbands and wives, by level of marital satisfaction, who come home from work feeling exhausted, emotionally drained, or angry. Few husbands and wives say that they seldom come home from work physically exhausted; most say that they are sometimes or often exhausted after work. Similarly, most husbands and wives indicate that they sometimes or often feel emotionally drained after work. In contrast, most husbands and wives indicate that they seldom come from work feeling angry. However, in looking across levels of marital satisfaction, husbands and wives who are not satisfied with their marriage are more likely to report that they often come home feeling angry.[9]

### What really matters?

Since marital satisfaction is a three-level categorical variable with ordered response options, two ordered logistic regression models were used.[10] The first model includes psychological characteristics and years of marriage. This model tests the association between individual characteristics and level of marital satisfaction. The second model adds the ten couple agreement items to the first model. The effects of these variables on marital satisfaction are modeled for the combined sample (husbands and wives together) and for husbands and wives separately.

Each panel in Table 8.7 reports the coefficient of association, its statistical significance, and the odds ratio. The odds ratio is included for ease of interpretation and indicates the percent change in the dependent variable for those who are one unit apart on an independent variable, net of other predictors in the model. It also indicates the likelihood of being one level higher or lower on marital satisfaction when other variables in the model are taken into account, and helps to describe the importance of a particular variable in increasing or decreasing marital satisfaction. If the ratio is higher than 1.0, that variable increases the likelihood of higher marital satisfaction. If the ratio is lower than 1.0, that variable decreases the likelihood of higher marital satisfaction.

In table 8.7, when looking at results for husbands and wives together, both self-esteem and the number of depressive symptoms are significantly related to level of marital satisfaction. Higher self-esteem is associated with higher levels of marital satisfaction, while higher number of depressive symptoms is associated with lower levels of marital satisfaction. The odds ratio indicates that each one-unit increase in self-esteem (on a 56-point scale) increases the likelihood of having a higher level of marital satisfaction by approximately 5 percent. Similarly, a one unit increase in depressive symptoms (on a 60-point scale) increases the likelihood of having a lower level of marital satisfaction by 4 percent. Coming home from

Table 8.7 *Ordered logistic regression of marital satisfaction on emotional well-being and years married for husbands and wives*

| | Marital satisfaction | | | | | |
|---|---|---|---|---|---|---|
| | Husbands and wives | | Husbands | | Wives | |
| | Coef. | Odds ratio | Coef. | Odds ratio | Coef. | Odds ratio |
| Self-esteem score | .050[**] | 1.051 | .034 | 1.034 | .069[**] | 1.072 |
| Depressive symptoms | −.042[**] | .959 | −.046[*] | .955 | −.036 | .965 |
| Come home from work drained | .083 | 1.086 | .092 | 1.097 | .118 | 1.125 |
| Come home from work angry | .033 | 1.033 | −.023 | .977 | .044 | 1.045 |
| Years married | −.014 | .986 | −.006 | .994 | −.022 | .978 |
| Constant 1[a] | −.981 | | −1.545 | | −.260 | |
| Constant 2 | 1.029 | | .436 | | 1.794 | |
| LR $\chi^2$ (16) | 42.37 | | 17.60 | | 26.29 | |

[a] The STATA procedure combines the constant and the threshold parameters.
+ p < .1; *p < .05; ** p < .01; *** p < .001

work feeling angry or drained does not have a significant effect on marital satisfaction, nor does number of years married, although the effect of this variable is in the expected direction: the longer one is married, the lower one's marital satisfaction.

When husbands and wives are analyzed separately, the results differ in two ways from those for the combined sample. For husbands, self-esteem is no longer significant, but the number of depressive symptoms remains significant. The reverse is true for wives. The number of depressive symptoms is not significant for wives, but self-esteem remains significant. Husbands who score one point higher on depressive symptoms are about 5 percent more likely to have a lower level of marital satisfaction. For wives, a one-point increase in self-esteem increases the likelihood of having a higher level of marital satisfaction by approximately 7 percent.

The model presented in table 8.8 includes the ten couple agreement items in addition to the variables included in the previous analysis.[11] Once these items are added to the model, self-esteem and number of depressive symptoms are no longer significant either for the combined sample or for husbands and wives separately. For husbands and wives together, eight of the ten items are statistically significant.[12] The variable with the largest coefficient is affection and sex. An increase in one unit of agreement between husbands and wives that they do well in this area increases the likelihood of having a higher level of marital satisfaction by

Table 8.8 *Ordered logistic regression of marital satisfaction on individual ratings of marital functioning for husbands and wives*

| | Husbands and Wives | | Husbands | | Wives | |
|---|---|---|---|---|---|---|
| | Coef. | Log odds | Coef. | Log odds | Coef. | Log odds |
| Relationship items | | | | | | |
| Roles | .488*** | 1.629 | .526* | 1.692 | .532** | 1.703 |
| Spouse's personality and traits | .508*** | 1.662 | .510** | 1.666 | .512** | 1.668 |
| Parenting | −.177 | .838 | −.118 | .889 | −.166 | .847 |
| Decision-making | .541*** | 1.717 | .427+ | 1.533 | .599** | 1.820 |
| Communication | .489*** | 1.631 | .529** | 1.697 | .486** | 1.626 |
| Relationship with relatives and friends | .242* | 1.273 | .285+ | 1.330 | .145 | 1.156 |
| Practice of religion and values | .260* | 1.297 | .265 | 1.303 | .286+ | 1.332 |
| Leisure time | .265* | 1.304 | .475** | 1.608 | .124 | 1.132 |
| Affection and sex | .587*** | 1.798 | .667*** | 1.948 | .498** | 1.646 |
| Finances | .036 | 1.036 | −.046 | .955 | .094 | 1.099 |
| | | | | | | |
| Self-esteem score | −.001 | .999 | .010 | 1.010 | −.003 | .997 |
| Depressive symptoms | −.006 | .994 | −.021 | .979 | .001 | 1.001 |
| Come home from work angry | .074 | 1.077 | .282 | 1.325 | .015+ | 1.015 |
| Come home from work drained | .188 | 1.207 | .208 | 1.231 | .192 | 1.212 |
| Years married | −.020 | .980 | −.009 | .991 | −.039 | .961 |
| | | | | | | |
| Constant 1[a] | 7.624 | | 9.433 | | 6.562 | |
| Constant 2 | 11.482 | | 13.363 | | 10.513 | |
| Number of cases | 540 | | 283 | | 257 | |
| LR $\chi^2$ (16) | 407.68 | | 214.58 | | 201.89 | |

[a] The STATA procedure combines the constant and the threshold parameters.

+ p < .1; * p < .05; ** p < .01; *** p < .001

nearly 80 percent. The second highest coefficient is decision-making. An increase of one unit in agreement on decision-making increases the likelihood of having a higher level of marital satisfaction by over 70 percent. Three items in the model have similar effects – personality and traits, communication, and role performance. For each of these areas, the odds ratios range from 1.629 to 1.662. Each variable increases the likelihood of having a higher level of marital satisfaction by over 60 percent. Finally, leisure time, practice of religion and values, and relationship with relatives and friends have odds ratios that range from 1.273 to 1.304, indicating that these items slightly increase the likelihood of higher marital satisfaction. Financial situation and parenting are not significantly associated with marital satisfaction.

These results suggest that what is important for marital satisfaction is the relationship between husband and wife. What is important to a satisfying marital relationship is how husbands and wives work out their roles, communicate, resolve differences, mediate their personalities, express affection, and relate sexually. When there is agreement on these items, marital satisfaction is significantly higher.

Separate models for husbands and wives indicate that five items are predictive of higher marital satisfaction for husbands and wives; four of these items are significant in both models. For husbands, the variable with the largest odds ratio is affection and sex. A one-unit increase in affection and sex increases the likelihood of having a higher level of marital satisfaction by 95 percent. An increase of one unit in communication, role performance, and spouse's personality and traits, holding other variables constant, increases the likelihood of having higher marital satisfaction by about 70 percent. Finally, husbands' rating of leisure increases marital satisfaction by approximately 60 percent. The three items that are not statistically significant in the husbands' model, but were in the combined model, are decision-making, relationship with family and friends, and practice of religion and values.

The model for wives shows that affection and sex is high on the list in predicting marital satisfaction, but is not highest. For wives, the variable with the largest coefficient is decision-making (which is not significant in the husband model). A one-unit increase in decision-making increases the odds of having a higher level of marital satisfaction by about 82 percent. Role performance, spouse's personality and traits, affection and sex, and communication have similar effects, increasing the odds of higher marital satisfaction by approximately 63 to 70 percent. The three items that are not significant in the wives' model, but were in the combined model, are relationships with relatives and friends, practice of religion and values, and leisure time.

The separate husband and wife models are similar on four dimensions: role performance, spouse's personality and traits, communication, and affection and sex. The differences between husband and wife models are two-fold. The odds are different for some of the variables, and each model includes one item that is not in the other. For husbands, leisure time is significant, and for wives decision-making is significant. The similarity of the two models suggests that couples have a consensus on what is important for a satisfying marriage. Both husbands and wives agree that affection and sex are important to a satisfying marriage, although it is more important for husbands. Husbands and wives consider how they perform their roles and their spouse's personality and traits to be equally important. Wives think making decisions with their husbands is more important, while husbands say communication between husband and wife is more important. Perhaps communication and decision-making refer to the same dimension, but there is a gender difference in perception. The results show the importance of the dyadic relationship between husband and wife for a satisfying marriage.

### Discussion

This chapter offers insights on marital satisfaction through a couple's perspective. Studies on marital satisfaction rarely conduct analyses at the couple level. When considering both the husband's and wife's perceptions of marital satisfaction, a more complex picture emerges that places greater emphasis on the couple relationship. Couples with low levels of marital satisfaction are less likely to agree that they do the following things well: affection and sex, communication, and decision-making. In contrast, highly satisfied couples agree that they do all of these things well and rank decision-making and communication, together with roles, highest on their list. Couples who agree on the ranking of *internal* areas of their dyadic relationship appear to be more satisfied with their marriage than couples who agree that they do well in areas *external* to their relationship.

Assessments of marital satisfaction appear to be associated with relational characteristics, though in different ways for husbands and wives. Husbands with lower levels of marital satisfaction report a higher number of depressive symptoms than husbands with higher levels of marital satisfaction. In contrast, wives with lower levels of marital satisfaction score lower on self-esteem than wives with high levels of marital satisfaction. These findings were confirmed in the logistic regression analysis.

When couple agreement items were added to the ordered logistic regression models, however, depressive symptoms and self-esteem were no longer significant. Depressive symptoms and self-esteem appear to be mediated by aspects of the couple's relationship, particularly roles, spouse's personality and traits, communication, and affection and sex. This suggests that couples who are less satisfied with their marriages may be unhappy and have difficulty in communicating and resolving conflict. It also may be that their intimate relationship with each other is unsatisfactory. These results seem to suggest that marital satisfaction involves not only role clarity but intimacy and communication.

Highly satisfied couples appear to be those who have mastered the intricacies of the husband and wife relationship. In contrast, couples with lower levels of marital satisfaction tend to rank inter-couple agreement areas much lower and relationships with others much higher. These results suggest that couples who wish to have high levels of marital satisfaction need to make the dyadic husband-and-wife relationship a high priority.

Findings suggest that couples and their families, even their extended families, need to understand the importance of the "internal" relations between husbands and wives. Couples could set aside resources, especially time, to tend to their relationship with each other. Results of supplementary analyses (available from the author) suggest that if couples spend 90 minutes a day alone together, or 10.5 hours a week, they are likely to be more satisfied with their marriage than couples who spend less than an hour a day alone together. Time alone may not make a more satisfied marital relationship, but couples spending time with each other may be a mediating factor that provides an opportunity for couples to talk, resolve conflicts, and enjoy each other's company on a more intimate level.

NOTES

1. ENRICH is an acronym for Evaluation and Nurturing Relationship Issues, Communication, and Happiness.
2. The General Social Survey is a bi-annual survey based on a representative sample of 3,000 households in the US (see General Social Survey 2000). The Current Population Survey (CPS), conducted by the Bureau of the Census, is a monthly survey based on a representative sample of about 60,000 households across the US (US Bureau of the Census 1998).
3. See Hoogstra, this volume, and Radloff, 1977, for a description of the CES-D.
4. Self-esteem is a composite measure based on the following items from the parent survey:

   (1) I feel good about myself; (2) I feel I do not have much to be proud of; (3) I feel on edge, like something awful is about to happen; (4) I forget things readily; (5) I feel nervous for reasons I can't put my finger on; (6) I have trouble concentrating; (7) My

anger is unpredictable; (8) I get more angry than I should; (9) I express my anger easily; (10) I feel on top of things; (11) I feel stressed; (12) I feel I can't cope with everything I have to do; (13) I feel confident about my ability to handle personal or family matters; (14) I feel confident about my ability to handle work-related matters.

Respondents were asked to ask to indicate how often each statement applied to them. Response options range from 0 to 4 where 0 = never and 4 = very often. Items referring to negative emotional states (e.g., anxiety, anger, stress) are reverse coded. To construct the composite measure, the items were summed. Composite scores range from 0 to 56.

5. The parent survey asks respondents to report the month and year when they and their current spouse/partner began living together. The survey does not ask for date of marriage or length of marriage. For purposes of analysis, length of marriage is estimated by subtracting the date the couple began living together from the date of the survey.

6. The fifteen items in the ENRICH abbreviated inventory are as follows:

(1) I am not pleased with the personality characteristics and personal habits of my partner; (2) I am very happy with how we handle role responsibilities in our relationship; (3) I am not happy about communication and feel my partner does not understand me; (4) I am very happy about how we make decisions and resolve conflicts; (5) I am unhappy about our financial position and the way we make financial decisions; (6) I am very happy with how we manage our leisure activities and the time we spend together; (7) I am very pleased about how we express affection and relate sexually; (8) I am not satisfied with the way we each handle our responsibilities as parents; (9) I am dissatisfied about our relationship with my parents, in-laws, and/or friends; (10) I feel very good about how we each practice our religious beliefs and values; (11) My partner and I understand each other perfectly; (12) My partner completely understands and sympathizes with my every mood; (13) Our relationship is a perfect success; (14) I have some needs that are not being met by our relationship; (15) I have never regretted my relationship with my partner, not even for a moment.

Response options for these items range from 1 to 5 where 1 = strongly disagree and 5 = strongly agree.

The last five items are considered social desirability items and are excluded from analyses. The first ten items comprise the Positive Couple Agreement items. Negatively worded items were reverse coded.

7. Nearly 61 percent of the couples report they are highly satisfied, 31 percent report they are moderately satisfied, and 8.5 percent say they are not satisfied with their marital relationship.

8. For each column in table 8.4, and for each item, individual ratings of items (on a five-point scale) were averaged and then ranked. For example, the responses of highly satisfied husbands were averaged for each item; all items were then ranked from high to low based on those scores. The same procedures were used for all groups represented within the table. There were no ties on average scores for any of the items.

9. Chi-square tests comparing expected and observed frequencies were conducted for each response for each variable (exhausted, drained, and angry). Results of these tests showed that husbands with low levels of marital satisfaction had higher than expected frequencies for often feeling angry, while

husbands with high levels of marital satisfaction had lower than expected frequencies for this response ($\chi^2 = 6.11$, p < .05). Wives with low and moderate levels of marital satisfaction had higher than expected frequencies for this response, while wives with high levels of satisfaction had lower than expected frequencies ($\chi^2 = 6.36$, p < .05).

10. The dependent variable has three ordered categories represented by the integers 1, 2, 3. If $\beta$ is the vector of the ordered logistic regression coefficients, then the exponent $\{-\beta_k\}$ is the odds ratio or the proportionate change in the odds of being in any one category or less that is produced by a one-unit increase in value of one person's response or score for the independent variable. A coefficient with a positive sign can be interpreted as reducing the odds of being in a given category of marital satisfaction or a lower one. Alternatively, the coefficient can be interpreted in a more conventional way. A positive regression coefficient means that an increase in values of the explanatory variables is associated with an increase in the respondent's marital satisfaction.

11. Because the analysis presented in table 8.4 focuses on gender differences in marital satisfaction, husbands' and wives' *individual* ratings of the ten Positive Couple Agreement items were entered as predictors in the logistic regression models.

12. Taken individually, many of the ten ENRICH items have a statistically significant association with individuals' levels of marital satisfaction (results not shown).

# Commentary

## William J. Doherty

*This study puts one more nail in the coffin of Tolstoy's famously inaccurate aphorism, "All happy families resemble one another; each unhappy family is unhappy in its own way." Only such a famous writer could get away with such a misleading influence on a century of conventional wisdom. For their part, marriage researchers and therapists seem to have shared Tolstoy's opinion because they have showed far more interest in marital dysfunction and distress than in marital health and happiness. We assumed, when we uncovered negative patterns associated with marital distress and divorce, that satisfied couples would simply show an absence of these negative characteristics. It is the classic medical model of interest in disease more than health, with health being thought of as the absence of disease rather than as a state of human flourishing.*

*As Nielsen notes, John Gottman was among the first researchers to empirically demonstrate multiple pathways to marital happiness (Gottman and Notarius 2000). He and his colleagues showed how couples succeed with three strikingly differently communication styles: validating, volatile, and avoidant. This research extended the much earlier work of Bradburn and Caplovitz (1965) on mood states; they emphasized the different valences of positive and negative moods, with each having a different effect on emotional well-being. We are now considering the possibility that many people can put up with negativity and avoidance if they also feel loved and cared for by their spouse.*

*Into this line of research comes the current chapter by Nielsen. His study embodies two methodological advances in research on marital satisfaction. First is the emphasis on dyadic measurement. The area of marital satisfaction research has been dominated by individual self-reports by married people not sampled as couples, as opposed to dyadic analyses of marriages. Many of the major data sets used to study marriage do not sample married couples but individual spouses. This study is clearly focused on married dyads by using both dyadic data and individual data.*

*The second methodological advance is the use of Olson's Positive Couple Agreement (PCA) scores. I have long thought that this innovative way to assess couple relationships has been underused in the field outside of Olson's own research with Fowers and others. It is a hard approach to get one's mind around:*

*the measure is of the couple's consensus on positive areas of their relationship, not just their consensus on any aspect of their relationship. Thus, the PCA provides a dyadic measure of spouses' joint perceptions of their strengths. It is unique in the field, and I am glad that Nielsen decided to use this assessment method in his study.*

*Using the PCA provided one of the more interesting findings in the study: that 20 percent of highly satisfied couples agreed they do few things well in their marriage. This certainly deserves follow up. Seemingly, it fits with prior research on the varieties of marital success. Perhaps these couples have something going for them in a few key areas that are most salient to them. Generally our measures assume additive, linear relationships between key variables, in this case between number of agreed-upon strengths and satisfaction with the marriage. Results from this study suggest that we need to look for non-additive and non-linear relationships as well. I am reminded of a woman married 63 years who told a group of couples that every night her husband holds her in bed, strokes her head, and tells her he loves her. This one positive interaction might overwhelm a plethora of other areas of strength and weakness in the relationship.*

*This leads me to my principal suggestion for future research based on this study. These intriguing quantitative research findings call out for in-depth qualitative research to understand what is going on beneath the statistical relationships. There is no better way to understand the dynamics of the 20 percent low PCA/high satisfaction couples than to interview them about their relationships. I would even want to go through the ENRICH instrument with them to understand what they were thinking as they answered it. The explanation could be as simple as a response orientation in which couples don't like to "brag" about their marriage. Or it could uncover patterns such as the one I suggested before: the strengths they agreed on might be the keys to how they assess their marriage, with the others areas not nearly as important to them.*

*This reminds me of how people answer global questions about their health: Many people with serious chronic illnesses rate their health as very good because of their own internal standard for health, or because they see themselves as very good "for their age," or because they are better off than others around them. What is interesting is that these self-reports of health are good independent predictors of subsequent mortality. My point is that we don't really know much about what goes into married people's assessments of their marriages, and that qualitative research could open some doors.*

*We also need more research, quantitative and qualitative, to follow up on the intriguing finding of this study that "couples who agree on the ranking of internal areas of their dyadic relationship appear to be more satisfied with their marriage than couples who agree that they do well in areas external to their dyadic relationship." The highly satisfied couples do indeed see strengths in external areas such as parenting and religion, but they also see themselves as strong in areas such as affection and sex. This suggests once again that it is not an additive list of strengths that counts but what kinds of strengths. Perhaps we will learn that having strengths in the external areas is a necessary but not sufficient condition for a highly satisfied marriage, or is a building block for some couples but not others to a highly satisfied marriage.*

*Further research is also needed to determine how specific the findings of this study are to the population of dual-earner couples raising children. David Olson has data on tens of thousands of couples using the same inventory, which would make the comparisons relatively straightforward. Perhaps we will learn that agreement on external strengths is of first importance mainly for working couples with young children. Alternatively, replicating the findings of this study with a much larger population of couples would add considerable confidence to Nielsen's notion of differential importance of internal and external strengths for marital satisfaction.*

*Since marital strengths have been a central focus of this commentary, I want to conclude by re-emphasizing that I think we still know relatively little about the idiosyncratic positive interactions that occur within marriages. In my own clinical and educational work on marital "rituals" – defined as repeating, coordinated, and emotionally significant couple interactions – I have been struck with the seemingly limitless variety of rituals that couples in strong marriages have evolved (Doherty 2001). These range from greeting rituals at the end of the workday, to cute terms of affection spouses share with only each other (and would be embarrassed to tell anyone else about), to cuddling while watching television, to putting love notes in a lunch bag. I have a hunch that when both spouses agree that they are good at prioritizing their relationship in these ways, which means they keep at it even if they are feeling distant or stressed, they stay at the top of the heap in terms of marital satisfaction. This would be consistent with Nielsen's finding that "affection and sex" was the strongest predictor of marital satisfaction. I am suggesting that we should start unpacking the deeper meanings and real-world examples of positive interactions in marriage, just as we have done for negative interactions. It is time to get over the Tolstoy effect.*

## Scott M. Stanley

*As Nielsen notes in this chapter, there is a long history of attempts to understand satisfaction in marital relationships (e.g., Bradbury, Fincham, and Beach 2000). Satisfaction is an important construct because it is one of the two defining characteristics people look for in marriage, the other being longevity. The chapter raises a number of key issues that are at the center of efforts in the field to better understand this construct, including:*

*The differences between those who are highly satisfied vs. anything less, especially with regard to key aspects of couple functioning.*

*The role that positives vs. negatives play in satisfaction and dissolution.*

*The ways in which the contexts of life, especially work, affect the quality of life at home.*

The measures used to assess the quality of relationships in this sample limit Nielsen in the hypotheses he can test and the conclusions he can draw, yet there are insights to be gained which he enumerates in his chapter. I will comment on those I found most interesting of all.

## Highly satisfied or not

Nielsen's analytic strategy of examining those who are highly satisfied, moderately satisfied, or not satisfied as separate groups implies that there is more than merely a linear difference in satisfaction when it comes to these levels. It has been suggested in various places (e.g., Glenn 1998) that those who are anything less than highly satisfied on this type of one-item scale are qualitatively different than others. Further, there is a growing interest in delineating the nature and possible typology of those lowest in satisfaction (e.g., Beach and Fincham 2003); this interest is driven in part because of data suggesting that, in some situations, there can be a return to greater levels of happiness among those who were, at one time, most unhappy in their marriages (Johnson et al. 2002; Waite et al. 2002).

My impression is that there are two key ways to think about what table 8.4 demonstrates. First, relative to the rankings derived from the highly satisfied, the moderately satisfied and not satisfied respondents are reporting they do relatively well on parenting, religion and values, and relationships with others. This suggests that dimensions related to the meaning of marriage in the social context could be playing a strong role in the definition and continuation of these marriages that are otherwise less satisfying. In contrast, those who are highly satisfied reported the highest agreement with items suggesting that they do well on dimensions more directly tied to the quality of their relationships: roles, decision-making, communication, and personality.

In contrast to the intriguing hypothesis above, the second way to view the data in table 8.4 is that it merely reflects the very high salience of communication, decision-making, roles, and personality in determining who is happy and who is not in marriage. Indeed, the more robust analysis using logistic regression presented in table 8.8 favors this second interpretation. People who say they do well on those dimensions tend to be very happy and people who do not say they do well on those tend to be unhappy. In that light, these findings parallel an extensive literature demonstrating that such dimensions are strongly *associated with marital quality and/or divorce (e.g., Gottman 1993; Stanley, Markman, and Whitton 2003). Nevertheless, I find it intriguing that these data might be showing that less happy couples are staying together on the basis of their relative success on dimensions related to meaning and social context compared to interpersonal qualities. This would be a productive avenue for future research.*

## The role that positives vs. negatives play in satisfaction

*There is a growing consensus that unsatisfying marriages are not simply marriages on the low end of the satisfaction scale. In other words, positive dimensions and negative dimensions are not mirror images, but each reflects different aspects of marital quality (e.g., Fincham and Linfield 1997). While Nielsen argues this point well, the measures available to him in this data set do not allow for much of a test of this notion because the Positive Couple Agreement (PCA) measure does not easily lend itself to being divided into positive and negative affective judgments about the respondents' marriages.*

*However, as noted earlier, the data that he presents are quite consistent with the broader literature demonstrating the large roles that communication, responsibilities/roles, personality, and affection/sex play in overall relationship satisfaction. In various studies, communication – especially conflict and negative interaction – seems to play a particularly strong role in predicting both divorce (e.g., Gottman 1994a) and thinking and talking about divorce (e.g., Johnson et al. 2002). Indeed, the 5:1 ratio of positive to negative found by Gottman (1994b), or the similar 20:1 ratio found by Notarius and Markman (1993), is specifically in respect to the likelihood of divorcing. Along with my colleagues, I believe that negative interaction plays such an important role in tendencies toward divorce because such poorly controlled, caustic negative interchanges actively erode satisfaction over time (Stanley, Blumberg, and Markman 1999), making divorce more likely to result. Of course, there are other ways that satisfaction erodes, in line with Nielsen's comments related to making one's relationship a high priority, which I will comment on at the end.*

## The ways in which the contexts of life, especially work, affect the quality of life at home

*The sample that is the focus of this book is dual-earner couples who are relatively well-off financially. That, perhaps, explains why the level of discontent or disagreement about financial matters was relatively unimportant in understanding overall marital satisfaction. This may mean that these couples who tend to be doing well financially are simply not very stressed about finances.*

*However, there is a more compelling explanation for this. Nielsen finds that neither finances nor parenting were associated with satisfaction in the most robust analysis. Given that money and children are the two most common argument starters for couples (Stanley, Markman, and Whitton 2003), that seems odd at first blush. Yet, the logistic regression findings may well mean that, when the variance related to the level of agreement about roles and how decisions are made is accounted for, there is relatively little variance left to money or parenting to explain marital satisfaction. In other words, how couples handle key issues in life is far more important than what those key issues actually are, as long as there is an adequate financial base to avoid the strains of poverty. In the data that Nielsen analyzes here, the PCA areas of role, communication, decision-making, and affection and sex all reflect how well partners stay connected in the stream of life, in comparison to dimensions that are more content specific (e.g., finances, parenting, in-laws). Put another way, it is the way couples relate to one another that is far more important than specific content domains such as finances or parenting (Stanley, Markman, and Whitton 2003).*

*The analyses presented by Nielsen highlight a very interesting finding related to spillover from work to quality of life at home. In these dual-earner relationships, both males and females were likely to report that they "sometimes" or "often" come home from work weary. Both males and females were less likely to report coming home angry, suggesting perhaps that weariness from work is far more likely to impact the day-to-day home life than negative emotional turmoil from work. These couples are in what I call the "heavy-lifting" years of family development, where career demands, financial needs, and child-rearing tasks can take a toll on the ability of a husband and wife to stay connected – perhaps through simple weariness. As with depression and self-esteem scores, coming home from work drained of energy most likely fails to show a significant association with satisfaction in the logistic model. This seems likely because there are many other variables entered that are more proximal to marital satisfaction.*

*Nielsen closes his chapter by concluding that ordered logistic regression supports the findings that couples who want to be "Highly Satisfied" in their marriage need to make the dyadic husband and wife relationship a high priority. While there is no specific measure of commitment in the form of priorities in this study, I would concur. These data suggest that there is something very important in how spouses come to agreements about roles and decision-making, as well as in the degree to which they are able to communicate well and respectfully, that determines whether they will be highly satisfied or less satisfied in marriage. The couples who are doing the best probably have mutually defined priorities that facilitate their agreements in how to live life. Furthermore, how couples protect and preserve the marriage relationship as a high priority, with all the competing and wearying demands of children and work, is crucial to success in life. A key question in our field is whether or not couples can actually be taught how to develop and act on protective priorities. If it is possible to teach people such values – and associated actions – we might be able to help more couples remain closer to the higher end of satisfaction throughout life as partners.*

*Part IV*

# Making it work at home

# Overview

*Shira Offer*

Fragmentation has become a major challenge for families in contemporary Western society. With family members involved in different, and often loosely connected, spheres of activities, there is growing concern that the core functions of the family are being eroded. Today, parents spend longer hours at work, which often crowd out family activities, leisure, and involvement in local communities. Some scholars argue that the workplace has marginalized family life by becoming the major source of support and personal fulfillment (e.g., Hochschild 1997).

Not only are family members physically distant from each other for most of the day, but even when at home they do not necessarily spend time *together* or engage in joint activities. Often each family member is absorbed in his or her personal matters – parents crunching several more hours of work at home during the evening, children skipping dinner to surf the web. This compartmentalization of family members' activities threatens family interactions and creates a potential risk of family erosion.

Rather than becoming a fragmented entity, family can serve important integrative functions, helping to shield both parents and children from the stress and tension associated with competitive labor and educational markets. In light of global changes in the economy and the nature of work, the role of the family as a central institution in daily life could be reaffirmed; specifically, family life can facilitate the achievement of tasks and promote individual well-being by providing emotional resources and social support.

The changing nature of family requires that researchers closely examine how daily activities promote or constrain family functioning. Additionally, the strategies families use to increase interactions and strengthen family bonds require further systematic study. By examining activities such as household labor, the outsourcing of domestic tasks, religious participation, and television viewing, the chapters in this section demonstrate how family members can strengthen social ties and emotional bonds.

# 9    Measuring the gender gap in household labor: accurately estimating wives' and husbands' contributions

*Yun-Suk Lee*

Although today most married women work for pay and beliefs about the roles of men and women have undergone noticeable shifts toward gender equality, married women still perform the bulk of household tasks. Employed wives spend approximately twice as much time as their husbands on family work, according to many estimates (Axinn and Thornton 2000; Bianchi 1995; Lennon and Rosenfield 1994; Presser 1994), even though women do less and men do slightly more now than twenty years ago (Bianchi et al. 2000). Researchers from a wide range of disciplines have attempted to isolate the causes and consequences of this division of household labor for men and women (Coltrane 2000; Shelton and John 1996). To fully understand the causes and consequences of time allocated to household labor, obtaining accurate measures of how much time husbands and wives spend on housework is fundamental.

Currently, researchers estimate household labor using different measures and methods, which often lead to conflicting conclusions about the absolute and relative amounts of time husbands and wives allocate to household tasks (Mederer 1993). Regarding married men's contribution, some scholars argue that husbands have substantially increased the time they spend on household labor (Bianchi et al. 2000). Others contend that the observed increases in husbands' time on housework are derived mainly from husbands' overestimation of their own contribution (Press and Townsley 1998). Concerning married women's housework, some researchers conclude that wives have reduced their time on housework (Bianchi et al. 2000; Sayer 2001). Others, however, point out that most estimates exclude household management and the planning and organizing of household tasks – mental labor for which wives take primary responsibility – and that inclusion of this "invisible" labor may lead to a different conclusion (Barnett and Baruch 1987; Daniels 1987; DeVault 1987). According to some arguments, wives are more likely to "multi-task," doing several things at once, perhaps leading to an underestimate of the time they spend on housework (Hochschild 1989, 1997).

Using different measures of housework, such as the inclusion of mental labor, poses multiple problems for investigators, especially when comparing their results to other studies.

This chapter compares various estimates of the time spent on housework using data from couples in the 500 Family Study. Estimates of hours spent on housework by self and spouse are calculated from responses to survey questions asked of both husbands and wives. Survey estimates are then compared to estimates from the Experience Sampling Method (ESM), which produces a random sample of primary and secondary daily activities measured over a one-week period also obtained from each spouse. The ESM estimates include three separate measures: (1) time spent on housework as the primary activity; (2) time spent on household tasks as either the primary or the secondary activity; and (3) time spent thinking about or planning housework tasks. These different ESM estimates of time spent on household labor are also compared and evaluated.

## Issues in the measurement of household labor

Most researchers define household labor as unpaid work that contributes to the well-being of family members and the maintenance of their home. For example, Shelton and John (1996: 300) define housework as "unpaid work done to maintain family members and/or a home." Berk (1985: 2) defines household labor as "all household and family maintenance activities undertaken by family members on a routine basis." Under this definition, housework includes physical activities such as cleaning, laundry, and cooking, emotional labor such as providing encouragement or advice, and mental labor such as planning or household management (Erickson 1993; Mederer 1993).

To estimate the amount of time spent on household labor, most previous studies use either survey questions or time diaries (Coltrane 2000; Shelton and John 1996). In surveys, respondents are asked to estimate the number of hours they or their spouses spend on housework (see, e.g., Panel Study of Income Dynamics and Quality of Employment Survey, Hofferth 1977) or on selected household tasks (e.g., National Survey of Families and Households). In time diary studies, participants are asked to report all of their activities, usually for the previous day (see, e.g., Americans' Time Use Study).[1] Comparisons between the surveys and time diaries indicate that time diary data provide more accurate estimates of time spent on activities that happen frequently, like household labor (Juster and Stafford 1991; Marini and Shelton 1993). Surveys produce estimates that are often 25 to 50 percent higher than time diary estimates, especially for daily domestic tasks like cooking and washing the dishes, perhaps due to social desirability bias or to double-counting of simultaneous activities (Marini and Shelton 1993; Press and Townsley 1998).

In addition to the amount of time spent on housework, the size of the gender gap in household labor depends on the methods used to collect the information, on who the respondent is, and on the researcher's definition of housework. The gender gap is generally larger in estimates from survey data than from time diary data. Examining 1985 time diary data, Robinson (1985) finds that the gender gap in time spent on housework for married men and women is 11.3 hours per week. But using the 1987–88 National Survey of Families and Households (NSFH), South and Spitze (1994) report a gap of 18.8 hours, which is about 40 percent larger than Robinson's estimate. When the survey method is employed, husbands and wives also differ in the estimates of their contributions. Using the 1987–88 NSFH, Marini and Shelton (1993) find wives estimate that they spend 21.7 more hours per week on housework than their husbands, whereas husbands estimate that their spouse spends 18.3 more hours on housework. Finally, some scholars criticize estimates of the gender gap that do not consider the mental labor of household tasks, arguing that the organizing and planning of household labor is disproportionately done by women, and that ignoring such activities underestimates the time differential between husbands and wives (Thompson 1991).

Disagreements about the size of the gender gap in housework raise three key issues about the measures and methods used for studying time spent on household chores. First, does the data collection method affect the estimates obtained? Previous studies that compare estimates of time spent on housework obtained from surveys with those obtained from time diaries show substantially higher estimates for surveys. This finding suggests that respondents, especially males, tend to overestimate their contribution to housework (Marini and Shelton 1993; Press and Townsley 1998). Since *both* the samples and approaches differ in these comparisons, the contribution that each makes to discrepancies in estimates of time spent on housework cannot be distinguished. Comparisons of survey questions and time diary measures for a single set of respondents make it possible to resolve this issue.

Second, to what extent do estimates of the gender gap in housework depend on how one treats simultaneous or secondary activities? Even though respondents report one "simultaneous" or "secondary" activity in most time diary studies, estimates of time spent on housework usually do not consider the secondary activity (Bianchi et al. 2000; Robinson and Godbey 1997). Time diary researchers have suggested that counting simultaneous activities is an important source of overestimation in time spent on daily activities. If secondary activities are included in estimates, the time spent on all activities exceeds 24 hours per day or 168 hours per week (Juster and Stafford 1991). Moreover, time spent on secondary housework activities may be negligible, amounting to "less than an hour per week" (Bianchi et al. 2000: 201). Therefore, some argue that in estimates of "the amount of time spent on household work, the inclusion of secondary activities would be inappropriate" (Marini and Shelton 1993: 366).

However, ethnographic studies suggest that wives spend substantially more time multi-tasking than husbands – cooking while taking care of children, for example (Hochschild 1989, 1997). To the extent that this is the case, ignoring secondary activities may underestimate the gender gap in housework. This bias could be sizeable; some studies find that respondents spend about 3 to 4 hours per day doing more than one activity, and most of these hours are spent on social activities, personal care, or "nonmarket work" (Stinson 1999, INSTRAW– International Research and Training Institute for the Advancement of Women 1995).[2] The number of hours spent on secondary activities suggests that it is important to assess the impact of including these activities when estimating the gender gap in time spent on household labor.

Because husbands and wives may differ in which activity they regard as primary or secondary, including secondary activities may also be important for estimating the gender gap. Some scholars suggest that men tend to inflate the time they spend on household labor more than women due to "cognitive biases relating to salience effects and ego enhancement" (Coltrane 2000: 1217), while many wives do not even consider some household tasks as work (Daniels 1987; Shaw 1988). These studies suggest that if wives and husbands participate in both household tasks and other activities, husbands may be more likely than wives to report household tasks as their primary activity. If this is the case, ignoring the secondary activity may lead to an underestimate of the time married women spend on household work.

Third, to what extent is the size of the gender gap sensitive to the inclusion of mental labor, such as household management, planning, and organization?[3] Housework tasks generally require the inputs of time, skill, and goods, which must be coordinated. Many housework tasks must be done at a particular time or on a fairly rigid schedule. Thus, planning, scheduling, organizing, and coordinating are essential features of household labor (DeVault 1991; Robinson 1977; Warner 1986). However, studies based on time diaries or surveys tend to approach family work as a set of physical activities (Thompson 1991) and do not generally consider the time spent on making shopping lists, planning for meals, supervising paid help with cleaning or yard care, or other management tasks (Coleman 1988). Independent of task accomplishment, household management affects perceptions of fairness in the division of labor and conflicts over division of household labor (Mederer 1993), and consequently, subjective well-being for husbands and wives (Bird 1999; Glass and Fujimoto 1994; Robinson and Spitze 1992). This invisible orchestration of the household may also be important for family bonding (DeVault 1991). For example, many wives report that they often tailor the dinner menu to accommodate different tastes of family members and arrange family members' schedules in order to make dinner time an enjoyable family event.

In addition to its significance to the well-being of individuals and families, mental or organizational household labor may account for a substantial amount of time. In qualitative studies, many husbands and wives report spending a sizeable amount of time on planning and managing household tasks for which wives take primary responsibility (DeVault 1991; Hochschild 1989, 1997). Mothers also spend more time and energy thinking, worrying, and planning than fathers when they are away from their children (Walzer 1998). Therefore, whether this "invisible" labor is included or excluded may be influential in estimating the gender division of housework. However, surveys and time diary methods typically focus on physical labor and cannot assess how much time married women and men spend managing and planning household chores.

## Method

### Sample

The data used in this chapter are drawn from a subsample of 265 married couples with children ages 5 to 18 who participated in the 500 Family Study. These were couples in which both the husband and wife completed the survey and the ESM. Of these 265 couples, 152 have children ages 12 to 18, and 98 have children ages 5 to 6. The remaining 15 couples have both kindergarteners and teenagers.

In this subsample, the families are economically advantaged compared to married parents in the US as a whole, and more of them are non-Hispanic whites (90.5 percent of husbands and 88.5 percent of wives). The educational levels are high (89.8 percent of husbands and 85.2 percent of wives are college graduates) relative to the population of the US, and more wives (87.6 percent) are employed than among married women in the US (Waite and Nielsen 2001). The median household income ($80,001–$100,000) is also higher than the national average.

The married couples who agreed to participate in this study may also differ from those in the nation as a whole with respect to the amount of time they spend on housework. The burden of data collection may have acted to select some families and exclude others. Since all families in the subsample consist of two working parents with children, they tend to be busy. Those who agreed to complete the surveys, interviews, and week-long ESM data collection may also be somewhat more organized than average. Compared to families with lower incomes, high-income working families tend to purchase more services to replace the parents' time in housework, and women with high earnings generally spend less time on housework than those with lower earnings (Goldscheider and Waite 1991). Thus, the wives and husbands in the 500 Family Study may spend less time on housework than those with fewer years of education and lower earnings.

### Advantages of this data set

There are several aspects of the 500 Family Study that make it particularly useful for examining estimates of time spent on housework. For example, the survey includes detailed information about the sociodemographic background and home and work experiences of the two spouses. The survey also asks respondents to estimate the number of hours usually spent on various household tasks completed by themselves and their spouses. In most cases, both the husband and wife in each family completed a survey. Thus, independent estimates of time spent on housework tasks by self and by spouse are reported by both the husband and wife.

The ESM provides yet another method for estimating differences in time spent on housework by couples. The ESM is a variant of time diary methods (Coltrane 2000), and comparisons of ESM and time diary data point to the validity of the ESM for measuring time use (Juster and Stafford 1991; Mulligan, Schneider, and Wolfe 2003). Research also concludes that, in general, ESM data are reliable and valid when compared with data obtained from other instruments (see Hoogstra this volume for a discussion of these issues). Because the majority of the respondents participated in both the survey and the ESM, the 500 Family Study provides unique information that is unavailable in studies based either on surveys or time diary methods. The study design thus makes it possible to compare estimates from survey questions about time spent on household chores with those from time diaries for the same sample and so verify conclusions of previous studies that compare estimates from different samples (Marini and Shelton 1993; Press and Townsley 1998).

This comparison of ESM and survey data provides an opportunity to examine the reliability of each respondent's estimates as well as their spouse's estimates across methods. It is possible to examine the extent to which each spouse either under- or overestimates the other spouse's contribution and whether this differs by gender.

The ESM data also provide reliable information on secondary as well as primary activities. When beeped, ESM respondents are asked to report their primary activity ("What was the main thing you were doing?") and their secondary activity, if any ("What else were you doing at the same time?"). Because respondents record their activities at the time that they are doing them, the information from the ESM about secondary activities may be more reliable than information from other time diary methods. Recall errors are a basic problem in time estimates (Robinson 1999); the issue of accurate memory may be even more serious for recording secondary versus primary activities. While time diaries are generally retrospective and open to this problem of recall errors (Warner 1986), the ESM minimizes such errors since activities are recorded at the time they occur.

The ESM, unlike other methods, asks respondents directly about mental labor. ESM participants are asked to report what they are thinking about when signaled ("What was on your mind?"). This distinction between what the person is thinking and what the person is doing allows investigators to examine instances when the wife or husband is thinking about household tasks while at home and elsewhere. This combination of responses can create an estimate not only of how much time husbands and wives engage in household tasks, but also the amount of time they spend thinking about them.

### Measures

*List of household tasks*    Most researchers agree that major household tasks include "(a) meal preparation or cooking, (b) housecleaning, (c) shopping for groceries and household goods, (d) washing dishes or cleaning up after meals, and (e) laundry, including washing, ironing, and mending clothes" (Coltrane 2000: 1210). These tasks are included in the estimates of time spent on housework. There is an additional set of tasks that researchers may or may not include in their definition of household labor: driving, financial paperwork, yard maintenance, and making repairs. With the exception of driving, these tasks are included in the current measure of housework because they are domestic activities that are important in the management of a household. Driving is excluded because it includes giving rides to children, which is viewed here as a

Table 9.1 *List of household tasks: survey and ESM*

| Survey | ESM |
|---|---|
| Washing the dishes | Dishes |
| Cleaning the house | General cleaning |
| | General organizing |
| Laundry | Laundry |
| Cooking | Non-intensive cooking |
| | Intensive cooking |
| Shopping for household | Buying food |
| Family paperwork | Financial affairs |
| Yard and home maintenance | Repairing |
| | Yard maintenance |
| | Unspecified/other Household maintenance/ chores |

childcare activity. Table 9.1 shows the specific tasks included in the measure of time spent on housework.

*Survey measures of own time and spouse's time spent on housework* In the survey, respondents are asked, "How many hours per week do you personally spend on the following tasks?" and "How many hours per week does your spouse spend on the following tasks?" A list of tasks, including the seven tasks in table 9.1 is given to respondents. Seven Likert-type scales are used as the responses to these questions, ranging from "0 hours" to "21+ hours." Midpoints are assigned to the first six categories ("0 hours" to "16–20 hours"), and a value of 21 is given to the last category ("21+ hours"). The number of hours spent on housework per week is calculated by summing the values for the seven tasks in table 9.1. One variable measures the individual's estimate of his or her own time spent on housework, while another measures the individual's estimate of his or her spouse's time spent on housework.[4]

*ESM time dairy measures of own time on housework activities* In the ESM, signals occur at random, making it possible to obtain a representative sample of how each respondent spends his or her time. The time spent on household labor is measured by the ratio of the number of beeps for which the respondent reports doing household tasks to the total number of beeps he or she responds to. The ratios are transformed into the number of hours by multiplying by 105 (i.e., 7 days × 15 hours per day).[5] The most restrictive and conservative measure of time spent on housework is based only on beeps for which respondents indicate that housework was the primary activity. A more liberal measure of time spent on housework includes beeps where respondents report doing housework either as a primary or secondary activity. This measure adds a full hour to housework time for each hour spent doing the laundry while cooking dinner, for example; the respondent would thus get "credit" for two hours of housework time – one for laundry and one for cooking – for a single hour spent on housework. Clearly, this measure provides an upper-bound estimate of housework time.[6]

The ESM data also provide a measure for how often respondents think about the household tasks listed in table 9.1, which allows for the calculation of time spent on the mental labor of housework. The ratio of the number of beeps for which participants report thinking about household tasks to the total number of beeps is estimated and then transformed into the number of hours by multiplying by 105. These estimates exclude the times during which respondents report that they are *doing* household tasks.

Response rates to the ESM vary by characteristics of the individual, and by time of day and day of week. These differential response rates may distort ESM estimates. Therefore, weights have been developed to adjust for differential response rates using the method described by Jeong (see technical appendix A).

## Results

### Time use estimates from the survey

Table 9.2 shows the self report and the spouse's report for the amount of time that married men and women spend on selected household tasks. This table indicates that husbands and wives agree that wives spend more time on household labor than husbands. Estimates based on self reports indicate that wives account for about 60 percent of the total time spent on housework by both spouses, which is consistent with previous studies using nationally representative samples (Presser 1994).

Husbands and wives agree on the amount of time that women contribute to household labor. There is only about a one-hour difference between husband's and wife's estimates of the number of hours that women allocate to household tasks per week, although wives' estimates are higher. But the similarity of husbands' and wives' estimates of the amount of time wives spend on housework does not mean that these estimates are accurate. Husbands and wives both overestimate their own contribution to household labor, and husbands often overestimate their wives' contributions to family work, especially for tasks that husbands do not perform well (Kamo 2000). Therefore, it would be helpful to compare

Table 9.2 *Number of hours spent on housework per week: survey*

|  | Husbands | | | Wives | | |
|---|---|---|---|---|---|---|
|  | Self report | Spouse's report | t-test | Self report | Spouse's report | t-test |
| Washing the dishes | 2.9 | 2.0 | ** | 3.4 | 3.1 | * |
| Cleaning the house | 2.4 | 1.3 | ** | 4.4 | 4.1 |  |
| Laundry | 1.6 | 1.1 | ** | 4.3 | 4.2 |  |
| Cooking | 3.0 | 2.0 | ** | 6.3 | 5.9 | * |
| Shopping for household | 1.9 | 1.5 | ** | 3.1 | 3.4 | * |
| Family paperwork | 2.3 | 2.1 | * | 2.2 | 2.5 | * |
| Yard and home maintenance | 3.6 | 2.8 | ** | 2.4 | 1.9 | ** |
| Total | 17.7 | 12.8 | ** | 26.0 | 24.9 |  |

* p < .05; ** p < .01

these estimates calculated from surveys with estimates calculated from the ESM.

Although spouses agree on the approximate amount of time that wives spend on housework, they differ much more in their views of the amount of time husbands spend. As shown in table 9.2, on average, husbands report that they spend about 18 hours on household chores, while wives report that their husbands spend only 13 hours. Previous studies suggest that this five-hour discrepancy may come from husbands' overestimation of their time on household labor (Press and Townsley 1998). A comparison of survey and ESM estimates makes it possible to test this reasoning.

### Time use estimates from the ESM

Table 9.3 provides ESM estimates of the time that husbands and wives in the sample devote to household labor. These estimates first include primary activities only, and then include both primary and secondary activities.

*Primary and secondary activities*    Measures of time spent on housework that include only the primary activity show that husbands and wives spend about 10 and 15 hours respectively on household labor per week. The estimate for married men is similar to other time diary studies that count only the primary activity; however, the estimate for married women is lower than other time diary estimates based only on the primary activity (Bianchi et al. 2000). This lower estimate for wives may be

Table 9.3 *Number of hours spent on housework per week: the ESM*

| | Husbands | | | | Wives | | | |
|---|---|---|---|---|---|---|---|---|
| | Primary | Secondary | Primary + secondary | Proportion of secondary[a] | Primary | Secondary | Primary + secondary | Proportion of secondary[a] |
| Washing the dishes | 0.9 | 0.1 | 1.0 | 0.09 | 1.2 | 0.5 | 1.6 | 0.28 |
| Cleaning the house | 1.8 | 0.8 | 2.5 | 0.30 | 3.3 | 1.7 | 5.0 | 0.34 |
| Laundry | 0.7 | 0.4 | 1.0 | 0.35 | 1.4 | 1.1 | 2.5 | 0.45 |
| Cooking | 2.9 | 0.8 | 3.8 | 0.22 | 5.2 | 1.7 | 7.0 | 0.25 |
| Shopping for household | 0.5 | 0.0 | 0.5 | 0.08 | 0.9 | 0.2 | 1.1 | 0.16 |
| Family paperwork | 0.9 | 0.3 | 1.2 | 0.25 | 0.8 | 0.3 | 1.1 | 0.26 |
| Yard and home maintenance | 2.3 | 0.6 | 2.9 | 0.20 | 2.2 | 0.8 | 3.0 | 0.26 |
| Total | 10.0 | 3.0 | 13.0 | 0.23 | 15.0 | 6.3 | 21.2 | 0.30 |

[a] Proportion of Secondary Activities = Secondary / (Primary + secondary)

due to sample characteristics; recall that most women in our sample are employed, all have children in the household, and most have a college degree or higher.

The ESM data show that husbands spend approximately three hours per week, and wives spend about six hours per week performing household tasks while engaged in another activity that they consider "primary." Because women are more likely than men to multi-task, the gender gap in housework is about 3 hours greater when indexed by the time spent on household chores done as a primary activity *plus* time spent on housework as a secondary activity. If time spent on both primary and secondary activities is considered, married women report spending about 30 percent of their time on housework as a secondary activity, and married men a little more than 20 percent. In particular, wives more frequently report washing clothes (45%) and dishes (28%) as their secondary activities than husbands (35% and 9% respectively). Both women and men often consider cleaning the house as their additional activity (34% and 30% respectively). The gender difference in time on housework is about eight hours per week if both primary and secondary activities are counted, whereas the difference is about five hours per week when only the primary activity is counted.

*Multi-tasking on housework*    What are husbands and wives doing when they are performing household tasks as a secondary activity? Preliminary analysis shows that the most frequently reported primary activity when household tasks are reported as secondary is another household task. Multi-tasking wives and husbands are stirring the spaghetti and washing the dishes, folding the laundry and sweeping the laundry room floor, working in the yard and cleaning out the garage. The ESM data indicate that mothers spend more than two hours per week, and fathers about one hour, performing two household tasks at the same time. Although wives multi-task on housework twice as often as husbands, the absolute number of hours involved is small.

*Management of household tasks*    Previous studies that rely on surveys or time diaries do not take into account mental labor; here, however, respondents are asked to report what they are thinking about when beeped. Responses to this question are examined to show how much time husbands and wives spend on mental household labor.

Table 9.4 indicates that wives and husbands spend a significant amount of time thinking about household labor when they are not performing household tasks. Married men and women devote about two and three hours per week, respectively, to thinking about family tasks. If this mental

Table 9.4 *Number of hours spent on thinking about housework per week: the ESM*

|  | Husbands | Wives |
|---|---|---|
| Washing the dishes | 0.0 | 0.0 |
| Cleaning the house | 0.3 | 0.4 |
| Laundry | 0.1 | 0.2 |
| Cooking | 0.3 | 0.9 |
| Shopping for household | 0.2 | 0.4 |
| Family paperwork | 0.7 | 0.5 |
| Yard and home maintenance | 0.8 | 0.7 |
| Total | 2.3 | 3.1 |

Table 9.5 *Estimates of number of hours spent on housework per week: survey and the ESM*

|  | Husbands | Wives | Difference | Wives' portion (%) |
|---|---|---|---|---|
| Survey |  |  |  |  |
|   Self-Report | 17.7 | 26.0 | 8.3 | 59 |
|   Spousal Report | 12.8 | 24.9 | 12.1 | 66 |
| The ESM |  |  |  |  |
|   Primary | 10.0 | 15.0 | 5.0 | 60 |
|   Primary + secondary | 13.0 | 21.2 | 8.2 | 62 |
|   Primary + secondary + Management | 14.1 | 23.5 | 9.4 | 63 |

labor is considered as an independent category of household labor, husbands and wives spend more time on coordination and management of household tasks than on laundry or washing the dishes (see table 9.3). Because couples spend a sizeable amount of time on the orchestration of domestic labor, consideration of this mental labor may be important in estimates of time spent on housework.

### Comparisons of survey and ESM time use estimates

Table 9.5 provides five different estimates of the amount of time that married women and men in the sample spend on household labor based on survey responses and ESM data. These results show that, regardless of the measure employed, wives spend more time on housework than husbands. Wives account for between 59 and 66 percent of the couple time devoted to household tasks, depending on the measure used. However, the absolute gender gap ranges from five hours to twelve hours, depending on the way that time spent on housework is measured. The lowest estimate of hours spent on housework comes from the ESM, when only primary activities are included.

These findings are similar to those of studies that assume that time diary estimates are accurate and that the larger gender difference found using survey questions comes mainly from the tendency to overestimate time spent on housework (Marini and Shelton 1993; Press and Townsley 1998). Results in table 9.5 point to another explanation for at least part of the discrepancy. When compared to husbands' housework, a greater portion of wives' housework is done as a secondary activity (see table 9.3), so the gender gap is larger when these secondary activities are counted. If full credit is assigned for housework done while doing another activity, the gender gap in estimates increases from five to eight hours, and the proportion of housework done by wives increases from 60 to 62 percent. The eight-hour gap is almost identical to the gender difference in the estimate based on self reports, suggesting that respondents answering survey questions tend to count their time on secondary as well as primary activities.

Self reports and spouse's reports in the survey show that husbands and wives agree about wives' contribution to housework but disagree about husbands' time on housework (see table 9.2). Both, however, probably overestimate the amount of time wives spend on housework, as table 9.5 shows. This is true using survey estimates, ESM estimates that count only the primary activity, and ESM estimates that include both primary and secondary activities. Wives' estimates of their own housework time (26.0 hours) and husbands' estimates of their wives' time (24.9 hours) are both substantially greater than ESM estimates that include simultaneous activities (21.2 hours) or ESM estimates including the primary activity only (15.0 hours). Wives provide relatively accurate estimates of the amount of time that husbands devote to housework; their estimates of husbands' hours of housework (12.8 hours) are almost identical to the ESM estimates that include simultaneous activities (13.0 hours), suggesting that wives give husbands full credit for housework done while doing something else.

Husbands and wives have different perceptions of the gap in their contributions to household labor as table 9.5 shows, even though they agree that wives spend more time on housework than husbands. On average, the difference in husbands' reports of their own and their spouse's time on housework is about seven hours ($24.9 - 17.7 = 7.2$), whereas for wives the difference is about thirteen hours ($26.0 - 12.8 = 13.2$). Compared to the thirteen-hour gap reported by wives in the survey, the seven-hour gender gap seen in husbands' survey reports is closer to the gap obtained from ESM estimates that include the primary activity only ($15.0 - 10.0 = 5.0$) or both the primary and secondary activities ($21.2 - 13.0 = 8.2$). While husbands overestimate both their own and their spouse's time on housework, wives overestimate their own time but not their husband's.

## Discussion

Using data collected through surveys and the ESM for husbands and wives in the same families, this chapter develops and compares a series of estimates for the division of household labor, which range from restrictive to inclusive. Results show that wives account for about 60 percent of the couple's time devoted to household labor regardless of the estimation measure employed. But the results also show that the absolute size of the gender gap in time spent on housework varies substantially across the various measures and types of data employed. In particular, this chapter suggests that estimates based on time diary data that include housework done only as a primary activity provide the lowest estimate of hours spent on household labor per week and the smallest absolute gender gap in housework. These estimates may underestimate the gender difference by ignoring housework tasks done while doing something else as a primary activity. ESM data show that wives are more likely than husbands to report performance of household tasks as their secondary activities. Therefore, exclusion of the secondary activities leads to estimates of the gender gap in household labor that are biased downward.

Including secondary activities of time spent on housework is not, however, a complete solution for accurately measuring the gender gap in household labor. Men and women appear to differ in their designation of primary and secondary activities when they participate in two activities at the same time. Time diary estimates including and excluding simultaneous activities may differ for men and women not because of the activities they do but because of how they report them. Future research might explore this gender difference and its role in measurement of time spent on housework.

This chapter finds that husbands and wives provide similar estimates of wives' time on household labor but divergent estimates of husbands' contributions. Previous studies often assume that husbands overestimate their own contribution (Press and Townsley 1998) but assume that both husbands and wives make accurate assessments of the wife's time (Kamo 2000). Little evidence is found to support this view. Analyses of the data from surveys and the ESM support the argument that wives make accurate estimates of husbands' time on housework, whereas husbands overestimate their own time. But the results also suggest that both wives and husbands quite substantially overestimate the amount of time wives spend on housework. These biases lead men and women to have different perceptions about the size of the gender gap in household labor. If wives think that the gender gap in housework is much larger than husbands do, this may lead to marital conflict regardless of the absolute amount of time that husbands and wives allocate to household labor.

Implications of the findings reported in this chapter are clear: conclusions about the size of the gender gap in housework depend substantially on *who* provides the information about time spent on housework, *what* information that person is asked to provide, and *how* housework is defined. Results show large differences between self reports of housework time and those estimated from the ESM. This suggests that researchers should be quite cautious in their use of measures that simply add together respondent reports on the amount of time spent in a typical week on a series of housework tasks. Clearly, this method of assessing total hours spent on housework leads to substantially inflated estimates. Perhaps more worrisome, wives appear to inflate their own time substantially more than they inflate their husbands', whereas husbands overestimate more consistently. This means that studies that use both the wife's report of her own time on housework and her report of her husband's time on housework (Goldscheider and Waite 1991) contain substantial bias that differs for the husband and wife.

Results reported here also suggest that researchers should give considerable thought to the treatment of housework done as a secondary activity. A sizeable proportion of time spent on housework is done in conjunction with other activities, often other housework tasks. A researcher might decide to count only time spent primarily on housework to limit total time spent to a twenty-four hour day. Alternatively, a researcher might decide to give full credit for time spent on housework while doing another activity, thereby allowing a respondent to get credit for two hours of housework when only one hour of total work was done. Clearly, a person who folds the laundry while talking to a client on the phone *is* spending the time doing housework, and housework done intermittently over several hours while visiting with a neighbor or playing with the children does take up some portion of those hours but not all of them. Estimates that ignore housework done as a secondary activity provide a conservative, lower bound of time spent. Perhaps more important, estimates of housework as a primary activity suggest that dual-career, middle- and upper-middle-class mothers and fathers spend modest amounts of time on housework in an average week – only about fifteen hours for women and about ten hours for men. If a researcher decides to include housework done as a secondary activity, the weight it is given must be considered, although the results presented here suggest that the size of the gender gap is not sensitive to the weighting of secondary activities.

The most innovative feature of this research is, perhaps, the measurement of time spent *thinking about* household tasks. Some scholars have argued that women spend substantially more time and energy than men in the organization, planning, and coordination of their households. This mental labor is difficult to capture and hard to measure. The ESM questions that ask what the respondent was thinking about at the moment signaled provide an estimate of the amount of time that husbands and wives spend thinking about household tasks and precisely what tasks they were thinking about. Researchers studying time spent on housework must first decide whether to include time spent thinking about housework and then decide whether to add it to the time spent doing housework or to consider it separately, and, as with secondary activities, what weight to give it. The choice must depend on the questions that the research is designed to answer.

Although the study reported here presents measures of a number of dimensions of housework, it does not consider emotional labor – the time and effort spent in maintaining and repairing the relationships between family members and in maintaining and promoting their psychological well-being. A number of scholars suggest that women do much of the emotional labor in families (Di Leonardo 1987; Umberson et al. 1996). If this is the case, then measures of household labor that include emotional labor would show a larger gender gap than those that ignore it.

The findings presented in this chapter have implications for future studies of time spent on housework. The division of household labor has changed in complicated ways over the last several decades (Bianchi et al. 2000; Gershuny and Robinson 1988). Descriptions of these changes and analyses of them require measures of housework that are valid and reliable, with well-known measurement properties. However, most measures currently being used are based either on respondents' estimates of the time they spend on various household tasks reported in response to survey questions, or on time diaries, generally for the previous day (Juster and Stafford 1991). Both have limitations and biases. To use these data appropriately, researchers need to understand the nature of the bias.

The data used in this study are limited in ways that may affect the results. The married couples in the sample were selected from a small number of communities, so the sample is not nationally representative. And because only families with kindergarteners or teenagers participated in the study, newly married or older couples without children are not studied. A larger and perhaps more important issue is that most husbands and wives in the sample are drawn from middle- or upper-middle-class communities, with relatively high levels of education and income compared to the population of the US as a whole. Highly educated men and women tend to hold more liberal attitudes than others toward gender roles and toward the division of household labor. These families purchase more services to replace the spouses' time in housework than most families in the US (see Stuenkel, this volume). The presence of teenagers in many of these families may reduce parents' housework time because the adolescents may perform some of the household tasks (Goldscheider and Waite 1991). For these reasons, with a more nationally representative sample, the gender gap may be more pronounced.

Measuring housework, much like measuring other family activities, is more complex than has been portrayed in the literature. The striking differences, across various measures, in both estimates of wives' and husbands' time spent on housework and in the gender gap, suggest that researchers need to be aware of several conditions when designing studies examining the division of household labor. It is important not only to assess who does what, but also *who* is asked, *how* they are asked, and *what* they are asked.

NOTES

1. The Panel Study of Income Dynamics (PSID) is a longitudinal survey of a representative sample of US individuals and the families in which they reside. For further details see http://www.isr.umich.edu/src/psid and Hofferth et al. 2002. The National Survey of Families and Households (NSFH) is a multi-wave cross-sectional and longitudinal national study of representative households, beginning in 1987 (see Sweet and Bumpass 1996). The Quality of Employment Survey 1977, 1991, is a cross-sectional study designed to evaluate job characteristics and satisfaction; this study is related to the Quality of Employment Survey, 1973–77 (Quinn and Staines 2001). The Americans' Time Use Study, collected in 1985, is part of a nationally representative longitudinal, cross-sectional group of time-diary studies (see Robinson 1999; Ver Ploeg et al. 2000).
2. According to Stinson, time diary participants "reported nearly two hours of either social or personal activities and an additional hour of nonmarket work occurring simultaneously with other activities per day" (1999: 18).
3. Management of household labor is restricted to the mental labor that is part of typical household tasks such as cooking or cleaning. Wives and husbands may provide emotional support to other family members – offering encouragement or advice. This chapter does not include this "emotional work" as part of the concept of management of household labor.
4. Measures of time spent on housework were also calculated using data from the National Survey of Families and Households 1987–88 (analyses available from author). These NSFH questions asked respondents to estimate the number of

hours they spend on a variety of household tasks. For each task, the number of hours reported by NSFH respondents was used to calculate the means for each category used in the 500 Family Study. Substitution of the mean number of hours calculated from NSFH respondents for the midpoint in the 500 Family Study data does not affect the conclusions, suggesting that the midpoint is an adequate estimate of respondents' answers to questions on housework hours.

5. Fifteen hours is used rather than 16 or 18 because it is assumed that housework is unlikely to be performed in the half-hours immediately following waking or prior to falling asleep.

6. Estimates of time spent on housework that combine primary and secondary activities give full housework credit for each hour spent doing housework at the same time that the respondent reported doing something else. This is unrealistic. Secondary activities are therefore assigned half value if they are done in conjunction with non-housework activities and are not counted at all if they are done with primary housework activities.

# Commentary

## Glenna Spitze

*This chapter provides a very useful comparison between measures of husbands' and wives' household labor time, using a unique data set based on two complementary methodologies. Given that researchers tend to assume time budget data are more accurate than survey data but more expensive to collect (Coltrane 2000), and that measures based on survey items (particularly the NSFH) are the most widely used in the literature, it is extremely helpful to know how they compare.*

*The chapter poses several important questions. First, how accurately do husbands and wives report on their own and each other's housework time? Second, what difference does it make if secondary activities are included in measures of housework time? And third, how can we take into account the kinds of planning and management that have been well described in both qualitative and survey-based studies (DeVault 1991; Mederer 1993) but have never been combined with other time-based measures?*

*The chapter's conclusions about accuracy of reporting and the size of the gender gap are contrary to those from past studies that were based on comparisons across different samples. Both husbands and wives overestimate wives' housework time, while wives report husbands' time more accurately than husbands do. Further, the husbands' estimate of the actual gender gap is closest to that found in the ESM data. Previous studies have concluded that only husbands overestimate their contribution, and they are the ones whose perceptions need to be explained (e.g., Marini and Shelton 1993). This chapter provides a strikingly different picture. Now we need a different kind of explanation: why do both husbands and wives exaggerate what wives do? And why do wives seem to have a clearer idea about husbands' time than do the husbands themselves?*

*A second contribution of the chapter is its focus on the problematic issue of "secondary" activities. There is no obvious solution to this problem – our desire to count housework time accurately, even if it is spent doing something else as well, runs counter to our knowledge that there are only twenty-four hours in every day. The author provides alternative estimates, based on counting time spent in secondary activities in several different ways, and it is reassuring that the conclusions do not depend on which alternative is chosen. Generally, the inclusion of secondary activities increases both husbands' and wives' housework time and increases the gap between them, but does not change (by much) the proportion of the total done by the wife.*

*These data not only tell us how the division of total work changes with the inclusion of secondary activities, but also whether husbands and wives tend to report housework differentially as primary or secondary, and what kinds of multi-tasking are done by each spouse. It would be fascinating to learn more, perhaps using in-depth qualitative interviews, about how respondents decide which task to designate as primary or secondary at a given point in time. We might also ask what are the consequences, for people's experience of particular household tasks and for psychological well-being in general, of this multi-tasking? Is it fulfilling because one derives a greater sense of accomplishment from making the best use of one's time, or frustrating because one cannot focus total attention on, say, creating a gourmet meal?*

*Third, the chapter focuses on the invisible mental labor of thinking and planning about housework. It is interesting that, of all the tasks to which thought and planning are devoted, cooking is the most time-intensive. This makes sense based on everyday experience – it would be difficult to prepare a meal without having decided what to cook and made certain that the ingredients are in the house. DeVault (1991) describes this planning process eloquently. In contrast, it is quite possible to plunge into dishwashing or housecleaning or laundry without much advance thought.*

*This discussion of mental labor raises some interesting conceptual issues. One relates to the distinction between "emotion work" and various other kinds of mental labor. Certainly "emotion work" as described by Erickson and Hochschild is central to family dynamics and, as this chapter points out, is distinct from thinking about housework. However, the boundary between the two may become fuzzy at times. Certainly the "emotion work" of being supportive to partner and children and "working" on a relationship are not a part of housework, and the "mental labor" of thinking about a shopping list or planning a meal are. But what about spending time thinking about family members' food preferences and what topics should be raised at the dinner table to best promote family cohesion?*

*Such thoughts may bridge the gap between planning housework and more general emotion work. The same could be said for various aspects of "kin-keeping" such as planning family get-togethers, keeping track of birthdays and purchasing cards and presents, and so on. The author has chosen to limit the measure used in this chapter to thinking about particular household tasks, rather than a broader definition including planning family activities. This seems quite reasonable, but it would be worth examining further where this line belongs. And one might explore whether these data could be used to create quantitative measures of the kinkeeping role, which have been examined in the past using qualitative (Di Leonardo 1987) or survey-based measures (Rosenthal 1985). Although beyond the bounds of most definitions of household labor, this would be an intriguing addition to our knowledge about family dynamics.*

*Although the gender differences in time spent thinking about (largely female-typed) household tasks are hardly surprising, one could pose questions about validity that may have implications for these gender differences. When people are beeped and are asked what they are thinking about, how honest are their responses, and how might they be influenced by (gendered) social desirability? How often, for example, do respondents report having a sexual fantasy, or an angry thought about a spouse or child? Might they be inclined instead to report thinking about the grocery list, especially if female, and perhaps this had been on their mind an hour ago? These are undoubtedly the best data we can get on people's mental labor, but they should still be viewed with a small dose of caution.*

*The data presented in this chapter are uniquely useful not only because they provide a credible answer to questions about the aggregate gender gap in housework, but also because they could allow us to ask questions at the individual and couple level about agreement and accuracy of reporting. These average estimates necessarily mask a lot of individual variation – some couples agree, some disagree in each direction. Some individuals provide a reasonably accurate survey report of their own time, while some overestimate it and perhaps a smaller number underestimate it. Who are the people in each of these groups and what does their level of accuracy or agreement tell us about other aspects of their marriages?*

*Some previous studies have looked at couple agreement in reporting. For example, Huber and Spitze (1983) found that more highly educated and younger couples agreed more in their reports of relative housework contributions and shared decision-making. Also, employed wives and their husbands were more inclined to overestimate their own contribution, perhaps because housework became more contentious in such households. Gager and Sanchez (2003) find that spousal disagreements about marital quality and time together have implications for marital dissolution. The data reported in this chapter could be used to discover, for example, whether couples' reports are more divergent when they are less happy, when they spend less time together, or when they are more gender-segregated in their division of tasks.*

*Even more useful, because such parallel measures have not existed previously for respondents in the same sample, would be comparisons across individuals of accuracy in reporting their own housework. It would seem reasonable that some kinds of people (perhaps those who are more highly educated or professionals, who may be more aware of time-management issues in their paid work) report time use more accurately and thus have more consistency between the survey* and ESM measures. What kinds of people tend to be most aware of their own time use patterns?

The focus here is on the "gender gap" and it is worth noting that the fuller measures create less change in the proportion than in the gap. While it may be the proportion that affects people's sense of equity, both figures are worthy of our attention, if only because an increased gap in one component in time must be made up in another component (such as sleep). However, discussion of the housework gap might be usefully placed in the context of the "paid labor gap." When both paid labor and unpaid household labor are summed, husbands' and wives' contributions tend to be approximately equal (e.g., see Spain and Bianchi 1996: 189). Clearly men are still viewed as responsible for breadwinning to a greater extent than wives. At the same time, to the extent that husbands resist sharing housework, women's options for increasing their own paid work hours are limited.

In sum, this analysis, incorporating both multiple measures and reports from both spouses, provides more convincing answers to questions about accuracy of reporting and the size of the gender gap in housework than have ever been available in this literature. The additional measures incorporating secondary activities and mental labor are also major contributions to our ability to measure household labor more accurately. I would echo the author's suggestion that this kind of study be conducted for a nationally representative sample. And I look forward to seeing these data used to answer some of the additional questions they are uniquely able to answer.

# 10   A strategy for working families: high-level commodification of household services

*Carolyn P. Stuenkel*

Dual-earner families enjoy the additional income generated by a wife in the workforce, but they tend to find life more hectic than single-earner families, in part because neither partner is at home to run the household. It is difficult for these families to carve out the time necessary to maintain their homes, shop for necessities, cook meals, and care for family members. Obtaining help with domestic responsibilities from extended family members is problematic because families are smaller and more geographically dispersed than they once were (Eggebeen 1992; Merrill 1997). However, middle-class families can now use their disposable income to purchase a wide variety of household services much like they buy any other commodity (Hochschild 1989; Schor 1998).

In an expanding service-oriented economy, many tasks traditionally performed by family members are now available in the marketplace (Bittman, Matheson, and Meagher 1999; Spitze 1999). Families who prefer not to perform a particular chore can likely find someone they can employ to do it for them. Outsourcing of time-consuming, labor-intensive, or unpleasant tasks such as cleaning, yard work, laundry, meal preparation, and grocery shopping can help to alleviate the everyday strain of maintaining a household and caring for children. This coping strategy, referred to in this chapter as *commodification of household services*, is particularly attractive to busy middle-class, dual-earner couples who have ample financial resources but lack the time, energy, or interest to complete all of their household chores.

The study of commodification of household services is important for three reasons: (1) to learn which services appeal to families; (2) to determine how families go about purchasing them; and (3) to identify factors that shape outsourcing behavior. Existing studies of outsourcing concentrate on a limited range of services, and the majority of studies focus on only a few services at a time. Despite the nearly universal experience of purchasing household services, there are few, if any, studies that examine the social nature of the process as a series of discrete steps. Little is known about how families identify the need for a service, locate a service

252

provider, set up a service transaction, and monitor and evaluate service delivery. In addition, it is unclear how families differentiate among household responsibilities. Why are some tasks easily outsourced while others are jealously retained? Using a sample of middle- and upper-middle-class, dual-earner families from the 500 Family Study, this chapter examines what services families purchase and how they make decisions about the number and types of services they will buy. The primary goal of the chapter is to conceptualize and investigate why middle-class, dual-earner families adopt high-commodification strategies.

## Situating the question

Commodification of household services – also known as purchasing services, hiring out, or outsourcing – is a practice that has existed in a variety of culturally and historically specific forms for centuries. In the twentieth century, as more women have entered the labor force, an increasing number of market-based services has become attractive to working families. Hochschild (1989) identifies five strategies that working women use to manage their household responsibilities. These strategies include: getting husbands to help with housework, doing all of the work themselves ("supermomming"), reducing commitments at work, cutting back on tasks at home, and seeking help from outside the family. The last of the strategies, seeking outside help, is the focus of this chapter.

Research indicates that families with higher household incomes are more likely to purchase all types of services. The types of services purchased vary by parents' employment status, with dual-earner families typically purchasing more services such as meals (Bittman, Matheson, and Meagher 1999), childcare, (Yang and Magrabi 1989), and elder care than do single-earner families. Similarly, there is a positive relationship between women's earnings and the purchase of services such as meals (Cohen 1998), house cleaning (Cohen 1998; Oropesa 1993), childcare, home repairs, and exterior painting (Weagley and Norum 1989).

Although previous studies have identified important relationships between service purchasing and family characteristics, most have not looked at the process of service purchasing in depth or considered why families choose to purchase certain types of services. The current study addresses these gaps in the literature through qualitative analysis of interviews designed to investigate these questions. The interviews, conducted with a subset of families in the 500 Family Study, ask about a variety of services not examined in previous studies; interviews also include extensive information on how and why families purchase certain types of services.

### Learning to commodify

Research suggests that outsourcing of household services is a behavior individuals learn from three sources: personal experience, peers, and parents. The crucial first step in learning to commodify is understanding the potential to exchange money for almost any household service imaginable. The second step is recognizing that similar services are available at a number of different price points. Generally, the more a service costs, the more "comprehensive" or "inclusive" it is. For example, a basic exterior car wash costs only a few dollars, but for an additional cost, many establishments include hand drying and interior vacuuming. Families who have more disposable income often opt for the more expensive version of a service because they equate price with quality (the more expensive car wash does a better job of cleaning the car) or convenience (paying for the more expensive car wash means not having to use the awkward coin-operated vacuum to clean the interior, see Schor 1998). Regardless of the motivation, consistently choosing the more comprehensive version of a service gradually cultivates a higher level of dependence upon outsourcing. In essence, high income can serve as a portal into high-level commodification by allowing families to become accustomed to and develop a taste for the "hidden commodification" that often accompanies more inclusive versions of a service.[1]

Individuals also learn to commodify from their reference group, or those friends, neighbors, and co-workers whom they consider to be their peers. Whether researching a commodity, such as a car, or a service, like house cleaning, families turn to their social networks for new ideas, norms, and trustworthy referrals (Lichtenberg 1996; Schor 1998). Because network members often share common resources and consumption patterns as well as cultural notions of what is "good" or "important," it is no great surprise that families who belong to the same networks tend to outsource similar services in a comparable manner. However, the types of information available within a family's social network vary depending upon the values and norms shared by network members. For example, if a woman belongs to a high-commodifying social network, inquiries about SAT tutoring for a teenager will likely result in referrals to private tutors; if she belongs to a low-commodifying social network, however, the same inquiries are much more likely to produce recommendations for SAT preparation materials or group tutoring sessions. Shared among a family's reference group, a common understanding of what it means to manage a household and care for children shapes commodification behavior by influencing exposure to new services, assessments of which services are necessary, and access to referrals for service providers (Ball and Vincent 1998; Bourdieu 1984; Lichtenberg 1996).

Intergenerational transmission of values is a third way in which many individuals, especially women, learn to commodify. Girls who grow up in high-purchasing families are often socialized with three values in mind: first, mental labor is more important than physical labor; second, it is less stressful to hire help than to perform one's own domestic work; and third, there is no reason to feel obligated to perform these tasks without help. In contrast, girls who grow up in low-purchasing households are often instilled with nearly diametrically opposed values – that physical labor is honorable and satisfying, that it is easier to do their own housework than to find someone else who will do it well, and that competent wives and mothers do not need help (Willis 1977). In an economic context in which the ability to afford services distinguishes families of different means, an upbringing geared toward outsourcing is an undeniable marker of status that many upper-middle-class parents are eager to impart to their children (Bourdieu 1984; Chin 2000; Newman 1993).

### Hypotheses

In this chapter, three hypotheses are tested regarding pathways to high-level commodification of household services:

*Hypothesis 1 (Hidden Commodification/Childcare Choice).* Families with higher incomes are more likely to choose the more comprehensive form of a service (in this instance, in-home childcare) than a less inclusive version (e.g., center care or occasional care by relatives or others) and to develop a taste for high-level commodification as a result.

*Hypothesis 2 (Social Network Norms).* Families in which the wife participates in social networks where a high level of commodification is the norm will purchase more services than families in which the wife participates in social networks where a low level of commodification is the norm.

*Hypothesis 3 (Intergenerational Transmission of Values).* Families in which the wife grew up in a household with a high level of outsourcing will purchase more household services than families in which the wife grew up in a household with a low level of outsourcing.

Hypothesis 1 proposes that families who choose in-home childcare, the most comprehensive form of care, are more likely to outsource household services than families who choose other childcare arrangements.

High income initially enables families to choose in-home care, but it is hidden commodification that increases the likelihood of a high-commodifying lifestyle. Hypothesis 2 argues that women who belong to high-commodifying social networks are likely to purchase more services, due to the sharing of good ideas, service purchasing norms, and reliable referrals, than women who belong to low-commodifying social networks. Hypothesis 3 suggests that cultural capital specific to outsourcing house-hold services is transmitted from parents to daughters. When girls mature and marry, they bring with them expectations formed during childhood about which household tasks families should perform themselves.

## Method

### Sample

*Survey subsample*   The sample analyzed in this chapter consists of 552 parents from 276 families who participated in the 500 Family Study. Only married, dual-earner couples with children were selected for analysis.[2] Of the 276 families analyzed, 158 had children between the ages of 12 and 18, 107 had children who were 5 or 6 years old, and 11 families had both teenagers and young children.

*Follow-up interview sample*   From the 276 families described above, thirty-one completed intensive follow-up interviews that focused on the purchase of household services. Several criteria were used in select-ing these families. First, to allow for face-to-face interviews, only families living in three communities in close proximity to Chicago were eligible. Second, to ensure variability within the subsample, several types of fam-ilies were selected: high- and low-level service purchasers; higher- and lower-income families; families in which both parents were employed full-time and those in which a parent was employed part time; families with teenagers and families with young children. Selected families were contacted by phone to inform them of the follow-up study and to schedule an interview. Only mothers participated in follow-up interviews.

### Measures

Follow-up interviews with the subsample of thirty-one mothers focused on the outsourcing of household services as well as the role of val-ues, work-related demands, family, and social networks in outsourcing decisions. To address the variety of services now available to families, respondents were presented with a list of approximately forty-five services including services for children, elders, families, homes, and pets, and asked which of these they purchased.[3] In addition, interviews included a series of open-ended questions that allowed respondents to identify services they had purchased that are not yet widely available (e.g., services for organizing the household). Particular attention was given to the process of purchasing a service, from the initial decision, to locating a provider, setting up a service transaction, and monitoring and evaluating service delivery. In addition to interview responses, the following items from the 500 Family Study parent surveys were included in analyses: household income, parents' work hours, and the purchase of seven household services.

### Analysis of follow-up interviews

Interview transcripts were analyzed and coded using an inductive approach.[4] The primary purpose of the coding was to examine respondents' attitudes and motivations regarding outsourcing of household services. Five interviews were initially coded using open coding. Potential codes were created as salient topics were encountered. These codes were then organized and refined, and thematic categories and relationships between codes were identified. Under-utilized codes were eliminated, and overlapping codes were combined and redefined. The resulting set of codes was then used in conjunction with Atlas Ti qualitative software to code all thirty-one transcripts.

## Results

### Descriptive statistics

In the 500 Family Study, parents indicated whether or not their family purchased seven types of services, including house cleaning, yard work, laundry, order-in/take-out meals, tutoring for children, grocery shopping, and other household maintenance. Families purchasing at least four of the seven services were defined as high-level purchasers; families purchasing only one or no services were defined as low-level. A descriptive analysis showed that the average number of services families purchased was 2.5. Even among middle-class families for whom the median annual household income is between $100,000 and $150,000, paying for more than a few household services is not a widespread strategy for managing household responsibilities.

The popularity of different services among the sample varies widely; the percentage of families purchasing a given service ranges from more than 90 percent of families paying for order-in/take-out meals to only about

10 percent paying for tutoring. These results suggest that the factors influencing decisions about outsourcing differ depending upon the type of service being sought. If nearly all families purchase meals, but only half purchase house cleaning, and a fifth purchase laundry services, then clearly commodifying cooking, cleaning, laundry, and other tasks involves diverse kinds of considerations.

In addition to the number and types of services that families buy, how often they pay for these services also varies considerably. Some services are purchased more often than others. For example, if a family is to avoid running out of groceries or clean laundry, these tasks require almost constant vigilance. As a result, families who pay others to do their grocery shopping or laundry are likely to do so at least once a week or even several times a week. House cleaning, yard work, order-in/take-out meals, and tutoring also show patterns of regular, but slightly less frequent, purchasing. Apparently families can benefit from purchasing these services once a week or even a few times a month. "Other maintenance," and for some families, yard work, are the only services that can be purchased as infrequently as once a month without impairing household functioning. Families may choose to purchase services with greater frequency for a number of reasons, including greater income, particularly high standards, or an inability, or unwillingness, to perform the task. Another way to think about the significance of frequency is to consider how disruptive the discontinuation of a service would be for the everyday lives of high-purchasing versus low-purchasing families.

### Pathway 1: choosing in-home childcare

The first hypothesis predicts that families who choose in-home childcare are more likely to be or become high-level purchasers than families who choose other types of childcare arrangements. Although it is possible that the direction of causality is reversed, with high-commodifying parents being more likely to opt for in-home care, it seems likely the process of employing a nanny or babysitter leads to the outsourcing of a greater number of household services.[5] While conceding the difficulty of making a causal argument with cross-sectional data, respondents' recollections suggest that hiring a nanny pushes their commodification to a new level.[6]

In examining parents' decisions to hire a nanny, it is important to keep in mind the childcare options available to dual-earner, middle-class parents. The four main alternatives are care by relatives, center care, daycare in a private home, and in-home care by a non-relative (England 1996). According to the literature, in-home care by a non-relative is the most popular choice among more affluent dual-earner families (Johansen,

Liebowitz, and Waite 1996). This preference is reflected in the childcare arrangements of the high-income families in the subsample of thirty-one families; of the fourteen families earning over $150,000 per year, ten selected nannies for their childcare needs. Parents often cite several disadvantages associated with other types of care as reasons for choosing a babysitter or nanny: many relatives are unavailable to care for children because they live too far away or are employed themselves; daycare centers are too inflexible and suffer from high caregiver turnover rates; and daycare in private homes can be unregulated and overcrowded (Folk and Yi 1994; Wrigley 1995). In contrast, parents view in-home care as advantageous because they believe it is the best for their children and the most convenient for themselves (Hertz and Ferguson 1996).

The strong and trusting relationship that parents build with their nannies allows for the gradual development of a high-commodification strategy (Wielers 1997). As parents gain more confidence in their employees, and as children grow older and require less constant attention, caregivers begin to assume responsibility for a number of household tasks that go well beyond formal childcare duties. Of the thirteen families in the subsample currently or formerly employing in-home caregivers, twelve had turned over at least some additional household tasks to them, such as meal preparation, transportation of children, laundry, housecleaning, and errands (including grocery shopping). These types of services are examples of "hidden" commodification.

The term *hidden commodification* is chosen for two reasons: (1) families are not locating or paying additional service providers to accomplish these tasks; and (2) parents are not doing the tasks themselves. The gradual development of the nanny's role to encompass additional traditionally female-typed tasks, such as cooking, cleaning, laundry, and errands, is an example of the evolution of hidden commodification. Through this evolution, in-home care becomes the most comprehensive form of childcare.

The evolution of the role of the in-home caregiver can be so seamless that parents may not even be aware that they are sharing certain tasks. For example, when Caroline Goldblatt,[7] a full-time attorney and high-level purchaser,[8] was asked if anyone ever helped her with meal preparation, she replied, "Oh, no." But when asked if her nanny was ever responsible, she conceded:

Oh, well, I guess she was . . . After a while she learned our standard recipes and I would come up with a menu for the whole week before I do the grocery shopping. And then I would post it and so she would know what was there, and at least she could get it started. And if I wasn't coming home, she would do it by herself. (Caroline, 5/31/01, p. 10)

Clearly, the relationship between Caroline and her nanny had progressed to a point where handing over a household task, such as making dinner, was so routine that the commodification was nearly hidden from Caroline herself. Hidden commodification is quickly exposed, however, when there is no longer a nanny in the home to pick up the slack. As Alexandra Thompson, a high-level purchaser and owner of a real-estate rehab business, lamented:

> I think the situation that we have now, which is really nothing except evening and weekend babysitters, is not real satisfactory because I think there's a lot of pressure that I didn't have before [when we had a nanny] just to be home and to take care of all of the details. (Alexandra, 9/6/01, p. 10)

Without a nanny engaged in hidden commodification, Alexandra was again primarily responsible for keeping her household and her children's lives running smoothly. Both Caroline's surprise and Alexandra's disappointment suggest that neither family had hired their nannies with hidden commodification in mind; over time, however, their caregivers' helpful presence had lured these mothers into an even higher level of outsourcing.

While hidden commodification may not be the driving motivation behind the selection of in-home childcare, there are at least three positive consequences for families that arise from the practice.[9] The first benefit families enjoy is greater efficiency in completing household tasks; a nanny who is willing to take on responsibilities beyond childcare can help families save time and effort by reducing the seemingly endless to-do lists that plague busy families. Elena Pizzi, a part-time vice president of public relations and a high-level purchaser, enthusiastically describes all that her nanny does beyond caring for her three boys:

> We have a nanny who comes in so she'll do, she's actually great at cleaning and she's really good at, well she's not really good at doing the laundry, but she does my laundry, and so that's just great in itself . . . I mean it's not like paying her to do that because she's paid to do something else, but she is awesome, and she takes our library books back and she takes our movies back and she'll go to the cleaners. Yeah, she's the best! And she'll go to the grocery store for me. (Elena, 6/06/01, p. 2)

Because Elena feels that she is paying her nanny only for childcare, she considers the cleaning, laundry, and errand running to be a special bonus.

Denise Harris, a full-time marketing manager and high-level purchaser, not only appreciates all her nanny does, but recognizes the incredibly stressful alternative:

If Nina wasn't there, I just think how crazed my life would be . . . She's doing a lot. It's a pretty hectic day for her . . . The alternative would be getting up in the morning, taking children now both who go to school at 8 o'clock, getting them both dressed, getting them up, having then to worry about someone getting my son or both of them from school to a daycare place, having to be home no later than 6 o'clock because a lot of these places are just – "You will be here at 6 o'clock." So having no flexibility, and then during the course of the day; you're getting home, and dishes are still in the sink from breakfast, clothes are still in the, you know, clothes are piling up all throughout the week because you don't have time to do them during the week. Then you're preparing or trying to fix meals and do lunches at night. And then you have to clean the house. [Nina] is the one that saves me the most time and effort and sanity. (Denise, 7/13/01, p. 26)

Elena and Denise are both professionals with unpredictable schedules and husbands who work even longer hours; without the hidden commodification taking place in their homes courtesy of their nannies, they would undoubtedly have to devise new strategies for managing their households and caring for their children (Arat-Koc 1989).

The second benefit of hidden commodification is a byproduct of the first: when nannies save parents time and energy, parents then have the opportunity to spend this additional time and energy with their children. Most parents in dual-earner families would prefer to spend their free time with their children rather than engaged in household chores. As Vanessa Rest, a full-time teacher and high-level purchaser, explains:

Today I actually took all three of the kids to swimming lessons and she [the nanny] did grocery shopping because the kids wanted me to take them and I'm sort of keeping the baby with me because I'm breast feeding and everything. I thought, "This is silly, I'm paying Ellen, and I've got all three kids with me!" But I thought, you know, "This is actually great because I'd almost always rather have the kids and have her do the grocery shopping." So, she's been happy to do that. (Vanessa, 7/16/01, p. 12)

In this instance, Vanessa eagerly trades grocery shopping for the chance to spend some time with her three children at the pool. This trade-off is only possible because her nanny is amenable to doing household tasks beyond childcare.

Similarly, Kimberly Hughes, a part-time manager at a local museum and high-level purchaser, acknowledges that the gradual expansion of the caregiver's role has enabled her to spend more time with her children:

It's increasingly helpful to me that the [nanny] also does some things around the house, like laundry and ironing and walking the dog, because [my children] are in school or . . . they can entertain themselves, they don't need to be played with. It's more helpful to the entire family if I can get some of the housework done and have more time for them than to arrive home and find . . . that I have to spend my evenings picking up. So my needs for this childcare person have turned from just strictly childcare to childcare/housekeeper. (Kimberly, 7/17/01, p. 5)

Now that her children are older, Kimberly fully expects that her nanny will split her focus between childcare and other household chores.

The hidden commodification equation is simple but powerful; any "free time" – that is, time without immediate childcare responsibilities – that nannies spend on household tasks translates into more time mothers can spend with their children. This equation is based on findings in the literature and interview data which confirm that in-home caregivers essentially substitute for mothers in the household division of labor (Hochschild 1989; Rollins 1985; Wrigley 1999).

A third benefit of hidden commodification is the opportunity for families to develop intimate, supportive relationships with their service providers. Long-term service relationships can evolve to a point where family members consider childcare providers to be fictive kin engaged in a type of tag-team parenting (Wrigley 1999). Denise explains that because she thinks of her nanny's two children as her own, she hired a tutor for one of them:

Nina's son spoke Spanish as his first language. I hired a tutor for him. It's a reading tutor, actually, through my son's school. [The tutor] has experience in kind of foreign language, in terms of children who spoke Spanish as a foreign language, English as a second language and kind of getting them to read a lot more fluidly in English. . . . It's like I have four kids. She takes her son to the tutor, but I actually found the tutor for her. . . . I do [pay for the tutor] because it was something that I thought was important. And understanding what her situation is . . . it just seemed to be the right thing to do. (Denise, 7/13/01, pp. 12–13)

Denise feels Nina acts as a mother to her own children, and it pleases her to be able to reciprocate by taking a motherly interest in Nina's children. Especially when children are involved, intimate relationships between employers and service providers can become quite intense (Kousha 1995).

Patricia Jones, a law library consultant and high-level purchaser, recalls her nanny with great fondness, not just for what she did, but for who she was:

Well she gave me the flexibility to work and also to have some free time but yet to feel comfortable that my children were safe and happy. My kids loved her. And she loved my kids and we . . . I mentioned it before, she was like a family member. She would go on vacations with us. All my family knew her; she was like a family member. (Patricia, 7/30/01, p. 28)

Over time, parents benefit from sharing the joys and challenges of parenting with someone whom they consider to be part of their family (Kaplan

1987). The benefits of hidden commodification can thus transcend the practical and enter the emotional realm.

### Pathway 2: social network norms

The second hypothesis assumes that women share information about household services within their social networks and that this information influences purchasing behavior. This hypothesis draws upon two related strands of the sociological literature: analysis of consumption practices and the role of social capital in shaping those practices. A long line of social theorists (Bourdieu 2000; Schor 1998) suggests that an important reason why individuals consume commodities is simply because other people around them are doing so. This same theoretical framework can be applied to the consumption of services. The focus in this section is on purchasing services to improve the quality of life and maintain a sense of equality with peers, examining how purchasing household services can produce and reproduce social distinction.

According to Lichtenberg (1996), the "demonstration effect" is a powerful motor of consumption. When families see friends, neighbors, or co-workers using an appealing service, the demonstration of the utility of the service stimulates a desire to consume it. Put another way, membership in a high-commodifying social network can increase outsourcing of household services through the contagion of good ideas among people who respect, or at least consider, one another's opinions. Women may learn about new services or even change their mind regarding services they had discounted simply by encountering a member of their social network who shares a positive experience or somehow redefines a particular service as something that is acceptable, worthwhile, or even valuable.[10] Many respondents report hearing about new services by word of mouth. Elena admits that she relies on her ties to a network of stay-at-home mothers to find out about activities for her sons:

The summer camp stuff . . . I find that the stay-at-home moms are really, they're really on top of that because they are on all the mailing lists and they get the stuff from the Park District and they know all the *good* classes. And you know those classes fill up fast, so I do know a couple of moms who stay at home so I always call them up and see how I'm doing . . . that's how we found out about the summer camp stuff. (author's emphasis, Elena, 8/2/01, p. 9)

Without her network, it seems quite likely that Elena would never hear about the best classes.

Another method of discovering new services is through observation. Vanessa explains that it was through observing her neighbors that she and her husband got the idea to hire a yard service for a spring clean-up:

The landscaping thing came up sort of like when they come and do a spring clean up. They came and did our neighbor's lawn and we're like, "That looks nice. We should do that." So I'd say more it becomes a *good idea* when we see somebody else doing something that maybe it hadn't occurred to us to do. (author's emphasis, Vanessa, 8/7/01, p. 29)

As well as introducing her family to a new service through demonstration, Vanessa recalls the influential part her social network played in changing her mind about a particular service:

Yeah actually like the nanny thing I remember feeling very influenced by that, thinking it was something I didn't think I'd want to do and I had friends who were doing it. It just seemed like it was making their life a lot easier. So I'd say, yeah, I was influenced by friends on that. (Vanessa, 8/7/01, pp. 29–30)

The experiences of her friends provided positive examples where none existed before, thus effectively convincing Vanessa to redefine in-home childcare as a good idea worth trying. When women observe others in their social networks already consuming and ostensibly benefiting from particular services, they are likely to want to try these services themselves.

In addition to using their social networks as a source of good ideas, families rely on these networks for an understanding of purchasing norms – the services "everybody" is buying. Everybody, of course, does not mean literally everyone, but rather the people to whom a family compares themselves, or their reference group (Schor 1998). Reference groups are typically composed of friends, neighbors, and co-workers and tend to be somewhat economically homogeneous. A family's desire to maintain equality with their reference group invokes the concept of relative deprivation (Lichtenberg 1996). So long as a family is able to consume the same sorts of services as their reference group, there is a sense of equal social status and belonging. However, if a family begins to fall behind their reference group, even if their purchasing level has not changed in absolute terms, they will feel relatively deprived.

Anything from a walk around the neighborhood to the scuttlebutt at the local PTA meeting is potential fodder for mothers' perceptions of what other families are outsourcing. Impressions of what "everybody else is doing," regardless of their accuracy, can convince families that certain services are absolutely essential to maintaining and conveying social status (Bourdieu 1984). Asked whether she had ever used a contractor, Denise, who owns a home in an older upper-middle-class suburb, responded:

Oh, absolutely. I live in Maple! *Everybody* does. Absolutely. As a matter of fact, I'm in that process now. . . . Two houses [on our block], one is undergoing major renovation, the other is having some tuck pointing done, but it's *constant*, you know, it's just *constant*. There was actually one week . . . where there were just so many contractor trucks on the block where it was almost dangerous. As you were walking across the street, you couldn't see someone in between those cars or trucks. Yeah, it's just *constant* activity from a contractor standpoint. I think that's pretty *typical* of Maple these days. (author's emphasis, Denise, 7/13/01, pp. 20, 35)

Because her family is in the process of using a contractor, and because everybody else in Maple uses contractors, Denise seems to be suggesting that her family belongs in the community.

In addition to confirming membership, another motivating factor for seeking popular services is the fear of falling behind. For example, Patricia, a resident of a newer, more exclusive suburb, reports, only partially in jest, that failing to outsource certain services in her neighborhood is a sure way to become conspicuous for all the wrong reasons:

Home delivery, I mean the standard joke [with] the neighbors on the street, if the Domino's car isn't in one of their driveways at least every night something's wrong. Some nights he goes from house to house. I mean you know that's one example. I think basically *everyone* here has cleaning help, *almost everyone* has a yard service. The standing joke now is that if you don't have a yard service, what's wrong? (author's emphasis, Patricia, 7/30/01, p. 41)

Patricia's comment illustrates how the fear of falling behind looms large because there are so many different fronts on which high-commodifying families feel pressured to keep up (Chin 2000). If the observation is that everybody has a contractor, delivery dinners, a yard service, and a housekeeper, then it is very clear that high-commodifying families need to consider outsourcing to keep pace with their social networks.

Another way in which high-commodifying social networks encourage outsourcing is through the use of social capital. Portes, in a recent review, reports that "the consensus is growing in the literature that social capital stands for the ability of actors to secure benefits by virtue of membership in social networks or other social structures" (1998: 5). In the case of purchasing services, the benefit network members receive is information in the form of reliable referrals for a wide variety of services. The ability to tap into a pre-screened pool of service providers makes outsourcing more likely because it decreases the risk and research associated with locating a provider and increases the chances of a satisfactory experience.

Referrals from members of high-commodifying networks facilitate outsourcing because most families who are thinking of hiring a service provider prefer "hot" information gathered from a trusted network to "cold" information garnered from the phone book, newspaper, or other source (Ball and Vincent 1998; Granovetter 1973). Having many contacts who routinely purchase a wide variety of services increases the chances of receiving a good referral, thus significantly decreasing the chances of hiring a poor-quality provider. Denise, in her search for a contractor, explains how reassuring it is to know exactly whom to ask for a referral:

I have a neighbor who lives to the right of me. She is just very, very picky. The running joke I have is well, if it's good enough for Julie, sure, it's great for me. Who am I? So, you know, Julie uses just about all the contractors. It's good enough for Julie, it's good enough for me. So Julie's like the barometer. She's the litmus test. Good enough for her, who am I? (Denise, 7/13/01, pp. 28–29)

Effectively mining a high-commodifying social network for recommendations can also considerably reduce the time, effort, and risk involved in locating a service provider. Vanessa found this to be the case when searching for her nanny:

It's amazing, sort of, once you have kids and they're a little bit older, and you know through school and sports, and this and that, it's amazing how many [people] are like, "Oh, I'm going to have to get rid of my nanny because I'm not going back to work," or "My kids are old enough now they don't need her," so there is that good word of mouth network out there. I don't think people have to go through agencies or newspaper ads necessarily. (Vanessa, 8/7/01, p. 4)

While a lack of "hot" information may not have prevented Denise from finding a contractor or Vanessa from hiring a nanny, access to trusted sources of information definitely expedites the process. Outsourcing is a self-reinforcing behavior; if families are satisfied with the providers they obtain through referrals from their social networks, they are more likely to take the plunge the next time they are considering a service.

### Pathway 3: intergenerational transmission of values

The third hypothesis predicts that women will reproduce in their own marriages a level of service purchasing similar to that which they witnessed as children. In the previous section, it was argued that service purchasing is actually a form of consumption, which according to Bourdieu (1984) is the very type of cultural practice that serves to create and reproduce class boundaries. One method middle- and upper-middle-class families can use to distinguish themselves from lower-status families is to purchase a high level of household services. Undoubtedly, parents who enjoy this status strive to pass it on to their children (Schor 1998). In the case of domestic chores, passing on social status means ensuring that daughters are aware of the stress-reducing benefits of outsourcing, value mental labor above physical labor, and are unencumbered by the belief that they must perform their own household tasks. This specialized knowledge parents teach daughters is a form of cultural capital, or "competence in a society's high status culture, its behaviors, habitus, and attitudes" (Chin 2000). Cultural capital in combination with adequate economic capital places girls from high-purchasing families on a pathway to high-level commodification in their own marriages.

The follow-up interviews with mothers are particularly well-suited to the task of understanding the complexities of the transmission process. During the interviews, respondents were specifically asked about the types of services they remember their parents purchasing. They were also asked how growing up with, or without, certain services might influence their own purchasing decisions. The majority of respondents feel that their parents' values and methods for completing household tasks had directly shaped their own attitudes and behaviors. Of the nine women who recall high levels of outsourcing in their childhood homes, six are currently high-level commodifiers, one is a moderate-level commodifier, and only two are low-level commodifiers. From a theoretical standpoint, it is possible to see how the cultural capital transmitted across generations and the middle- or upper-middle class consumption patterns these women experienced as girls play an important role in explaining this relationship.

The intergenerational transmission of values within high-commodifying families appears to operate through three main mechanisms to encourage the continuation of a high-commodification strategy. Girls' observation of and parental instruction regarding the stress-reducing benefits of outsourcing is the first mechanism which helps transmit a high-commodification strategy between generations. Janet Heller, whose purchasing has become more moderate since recently selling her house-cleaning franchise, reflected that her parents' penchant for outsourcing made her aware of the availability and convenience of a whole host of services:

[B]abysitters, if my parents were going out at night, summer camp, after school activities, tutors if we needed it . . . take-out or delivery dinners, catering, dry cleaning, alterations, financial planning, accountant, travel agent, house cleaning, rug cleaning, painting, wallpapering, handy man, exterior painting, yard work, snow removal, car wash, grooming, boarding for the dog – these are all things that my parents used. . . . It's probably influenced me because I know that [these services] exist and that they make life easier. (Janet, 7/25/01, p. 25)

For Janet, childhood exposure to a world of service-related possibilities has helped her to appreciate how she can use outsourcing to her advantage. Alexandra learned from her parents how she can employ commodification to simplify her life:

I think the attitude I got from [my parents] was use your time where it's best spent, and I think that's how Randy and I both, that's one thing that we both agree on, that rather than driving ourselves crazy – and we're overcommitted too much as it is, as a lot of people are – I think to ease that, we both agree that some of the more basic household functions are better handled by outsourcing: the house cleaning, the yard, the car washing, the household repairs. There are a lot of things that we could do, but we'd rather spend the time with the kids or spend the time with each other. (Alexandra, 9/6/01, p. 36)

Alexandra, with her parents' guidance, realizes that she can use outsourcing to successfully combat the time bind that plagues many busy, dual-earner families. First-hand knowledge of how outsourcing can serve as an effective strategy to manage households and care for children is a type of cultural capital that flows from high-commodifying parents to their daughters.

Second, by routinely purchasing certain household tasks, parents may fail to teach their daughters how to do these tasks while simultaneously teaching them that they are not worth learning, especially at the possible expense of more cerebral tasks. Just as working-class boys are trained to embrace physical labor, middle- and upper-middle-class girls are taught to shun it (Willis 1977). Instead, their parents consciously and unconsciously encourage them to hire someone to do their physical household labor. Caroline unapologetically attributes her lack of skills in the areas of yard work and house cleaning to her parents' outsourcing and attitudes:

I think if we had grown up taking care of the yard ourselves, I might feel differently about it, but since we didn't, and I never learned how to do it, I didn't do it. . . . When I got out of law school, my mother told me, "You don't like to clean. If you can afford it, why don't you pay someone to do it?" And so I did, and I always have. I think the things that my parents bought, I didn't learn to do, and I didn't particularly see them as things I should do, so I didn't do them. (Caroline, 5/31/01, pp. 3, 26)

A professional whose salary has helped her to afford a sizeable home on a generous plot of land, Caroline has neither the skills nor the desire to care for her house and yard on her own.

Michelle Summers, a part-time attorney and high-level purchaser, remembers a similar indoctrination to the value of learning housework skills:

We always had a dry cleaner, and we always had cleaning people and they would do some of the laundry. . . . My mother taught school, so we always had house-cleaners, likewise with rug and furniture cleaning. . . . My mother had a real bias against housework, so I probably have the same bias. She said one could be a trained monkey and do housework. (Michelle, 9/20/01, p. 35)

Michelle learned from her parents' outsourcing and attitudes that housework consists of simple, routine tasks that are easy to learn, but not worth learning. In both examples, physical labor, consisting of yard work and house cleaning, is abandoned in pursuit of mental labor, law practice and teaching pursuits, which are more valued in middle-class culture. Partially, as a result of their childhood experiences and what they have grown up to view as worthy of their limited time and effort, Caroline and Michelle have become high-commodifiers, apparently just as their parents intended.

Finally, when daughters know that their mothers favor the use of certain services, they tend to feel less pressure to perform similar household tasks themselves. Lack of guilt or obligation is thus a third mechanism that allows for the transmission of high-level commodification from one generation to the next. Vanessa recalls how her parents' use of a nanny, cleaning lady, laundress, and handyman have enabled her to pay for many of the same services without guilt: "It has probably made it easier, I guess, to do it. It is not like there is any financial or family pressure saying, 'Oh, I never had a cleaning lady,' or 'I don't know why you can't do that yourself.' So, it has probably made it easier" (7/16/01, p. 21). For Vanessa, her mother's implicit approval is important in allowing her to pursue a high-commodification strategy without self-doubt. Similarly, when Denise was asked if her mother approved of all of the services she outsources, she replied, "My mother thinks that I should have more!" (7/13/01, p. 34). Like Vanessa, Denise purchases services freely; neither woman feels the guilt sometimes experienced by women whose mothers disapprove of a high-commodification strategy. It appears that these women do not possess traditional gender role attitudes that mandate "doing gender," or perhaps they have discovered that doing gender does not necessarily require doing housework, but rather making sure that it gets done.

## Conclusion

Commodification of household services is a useful strategy that enables busy middle-class, dual-earner families to complete all of their household tasks and care for their children. However, despite the availability, practicality, and affordability of outsourcing for a relatively high-income sample, half of the married couple, dual-earner families participating in the Sloan 500 Family Study are low-level purchasers. This chapter identifies families at the high end of the commodification spectrum and tests hypotheses about the pathways these families may have followed to high-level commodification – childcare choice, social network norms, and intergenerational transmission of values.

Results show that families who choose in-home childcare do strengthen their commitment to high-level purchasing. Busy dual-earner, middle-class families initially choose in-home childcare because they believe it is the best situation for their children and the most convenient arrangement for themselves. Over time, the role of the nanny evolves through hidden commodification to encompass household tasks beyond childcare, such as cooking, cleaning, errand running, and pet care. As a result of a reduced burden at home, parents, especially mothers, can enjoy more family time as well as a supportive and fulfilling relationship with the service provider who makes this time possible. Because of these benefits, parents steadily become more committed to and dependent upon a high-commodification strategy to manage their households and care for their children.

Analyses also show that consumption of services is a social process in the sense that families look to their reference group for good ideas, to learn service purchasing norms, and for reliable referrals. Hiring a service provider is not just a method of taking care of household responsibilities, it is also an opportunity for families to improve their quality of life, communicate their social status, and reap the benefits of shared information in a high-commodifying social network. Membership in a high-commodifying social network thus appears to be a well-traveled pathway to high-level commodification of household services.

Finally, the data illustrate how a parental penchant for outsourcing is successfully transmitted across generations. High commodification is successfully transmitted from one generation to the next when daughters appreciate the stress-reducing potential of outsourcing, value mental labor over physical labor, and do not feel obligated to perform their own household tasks. Parents who enjoy middle- or upper-middle-class social status and subscribe to its cultural models undoubtedly want their daughters to enjoy similar status when they mature and marry. In order to prepare their daughters to adopt a high-commodification lifestyle, parents attempt to convey the necessary cultural capital to their daughters. In addition to making sure their daughters possess the knowledge and values compatible with high-level commodification, parents also reassure their daughters through their own example that outsourcing is not a source of embarrassment or guilt. Instead, outsourcing is presented as an effective strategy that can help women to manage their households and care for their children.

This chapter only begins to tap the potential of qualitative interviews analyzed in conjunction with survey data to shed light on both the process of purchasing services and the values that motivate individual families in their outsourcing choices. Future research could pair multivariate statistics with analysis of qualitative data to attempt to answer a number of questions generated by this study. What are the pathways to low-level commodification? How do resources, such as money and time, affect the number of services that families choose to outsource? What is the role of personal preference and family values in determining which services families hire out and which they choose to retain? Commodification of household services can be conceptualized as a strategy with monetary, temporal, psychological, and interpersonal costs and benefits, all of which require investigation. Commodification also raises larger questions about the kinds of group activities that define family functioning and the importance of family, neighborhood, and class culture in shaping commodification behavior.

Future research might also broaden the scope of this study to address additional family types, geographic areas, and methodologies. Clearly the number of parents in a family and the nature of their relationship influences family income, the division of labor, and the meaning of gender – all of which are important to the study of commodification. A second factor to consider when researching outsourcing is the effect of place. It seems likely that outsourcing functions differently in urban versus rural areas, and in different regions of the US and abroad. Local norms and labor markets as well as regional culture may determine the types of services that families choose to outsource and the availability of service providers. Finally, it might be fruitful to consult census data at the tract level to locate purchasing norms within particular community contexts or to use time diary data to provide a more accurate account of exactly whose labor time outsourcing replaces. Longitudinal data could be used to examine the effects of major life changes, such as job loss, the birth of additional children, family illness, or divorce on commodification behavior. Regardless of the methodology used, further study can help to educate families about how to better utilize outsourcing of household services as a strategy to manage their households and care for their children.

NOTES

1. The term *hidden commodification* is used to refer to additional services performed by service providers that may not always be obvious to the purchaser (e.g., a nanny washing the dishes while the children watch television).
2. The families were selected based on the following criteria: (1) both mothers and fathers in each family had completed parent surveys; (2) the parents in each family are married (as opposed to being divorced, separated, cohabiting, or never married); and (3) both parents are either currently employed or have been employed.

3. **Services for Children:** Day Care/Nanny, Baby Sitters for nights/weekends, After-school activities, Summer camp, Transportation, Tutors, ACT/SAT test prep, College counselors (for college applications), Driving instruction
   **Services for Elders:** In-home care, Elder day care, Residential care facilities, Transportation
   **Services for Families:** Grocery shopping services, Milk delivery, Take-out or delivery dinners, In-home meal preparation, Catering (for parties/ holidays), Laundry (in-home or drop-off), Dry cleaning (for pressing), Clothing alterations, Financial planning, Accountant, Travel agent, Errand service, Personal shopping services (for clothing/gifts), Internet for gifts (gift registries, delivery of gifts), Computer help, Therapy/Counseling
   **Services for Homes/Cars:** House cleaning, Rug/furniture cleaning, Interior decorator, Interior painting, Wall papering, Personal organizer, Household maintenance (Handyman), Contractor (Remodeling), Exterior painting, Yard work, Leaf removal, Snow removal, Car wash
   **Services for Pets:** Grooming, Boarding, Walking/Exercise
4. The approach used in this chapter is a version of "grounded theory" (see Strauss 1987).
5. Mothers in the interview subsample referred to in-home caregivers as both babysitters and nannies. To avoid confusion, for the remainder of this chapter, the term *nannies* refers to regular in-home care providers, while the term *babysitters* refers to caregivers hired occasionally, often for nights or weekends.
6. Longitudinal data would make it possible to test this hypothesis with greater certainty. However, the complexity of the qualitative data provide an opportunity to pursue and develop a compelling idea.
7. Pseudonyms are used for all participants, their communities, and family members or others mentioned in their interviews.
8. When conducting the follow-up interviews, it became apparent that the original method for determining purchasing level, based on survey items, was inadequate. Thus, the forty-five services asked about during follow-up interviews were used to distinguish high and low purchasers. Using this method, the interview subsample included thirteen high-level purchasers, five moderate purchasers, and thirteen low-level purchasers. For a more detailed description of this method, see Stuenkel 2002.
9. This is not to say that hidden commodification is necessarily a positive arrangement for in-home caregivers. The caregivers' perspective is beyond the scope of this chapter. See Rollins (1996) and Kaplan (1987) for discussions of how women negotiate roles with their household employees.
10. Thanks to Tom Fricke for pointing out that a "good idea" is much more than that; it is a cultural model of "the good" – what is considered valuable within a social network or society.

# Commentary

## Tom Fricke

*Stuenkel's chapter is a wonderful example of the interpretive richness that qualitative materials can lend to already existing survey data. The subtlety of her analysis raises too many potential points for discussion to address here. For that reason, I want to pursue two issues that are implicit in her discussion and that, from the point of view of an anthropologist anyway, deserve some further highlighting. The first of these begins as the methodological issue of how we can treat the kinds of material that come from long, discursive interviews of the type considered by Stuenkel. But this apparently methodological theme quickly elides into the second issue, that of culture. I had, in an earlier comment on this chapter, referred to these as the arguments that lurked just around the corner without getting made. My intent was not to disparage those arguments that <u>are</u> made in the analysis – one of the great strengths of this chapter is, in fact, that its richness allows the reader to push the data further along his or her own paths. Rather, my comment was meant to highlight the different kinds of questions that an anthropologist might ask about the same material.*

*The methodological contribution here is to link open-ended interviews resulting in discursive transcripts with quantified material from a social survey. Stuenkel's conversations with her respondents were themselves motivated by processual questions arising from the data on the outsourcing of services. The earlier survey lacked detailed data on the content of services, the reasons for engaging in them, and the contexts of their provision. While long interviews can also be done by trained staff, Stuenkel makes clear that some of the advantages of the researcher herself conducting these discursive interviews include the ability for quick follow-up and a sensitivity to the way respondents make their points. What I think is also true is that analyses of data based on interviews done by the primary researcher confer a different level of trust in the quality of data than in other popular models of open-ended interview collection. An analysis achieves part of its warrant from the simple fact of the researcher "being there" to observe the non-verbal clues to meaning that seldom appear in the transcripts themselves. Anthropologists conducting participant-observation are at one extreme of this continuum. At the other end of the qualitative side (we might think of this as the "thin" side) would be those transcripts gathered by a team of interviewers other than the primary analyst.*

*Even at that thin side, where all that is available is the text, there are multiple analytic possibilities. Stuenkel's use of her transcripts stays pretty close to the ground as is appropriate for the questions of process and strategy she addresses. This use of the transcripts takes them at more or less face value, very much as the responses to the original survey questionnaire are taken. It's easy to imagine, in fact, a close-ended survey getting at very much the same kind of information, given enough time and a prescient enough constructor of questions. The background assumptions, both those of the investigator and those of the respondent, remain in the background. This is where methodology elides into culture.*

*It is precisely those background assumptions that draw the attention of the anthropologist. Stuenkel documents some compelling behavioral changes involving shifts in the performance of what used to be called "family functions" in older sociological models of the family. These shifts occur in the domain of kinship. A recent resurgence in anthropological attention to this domain has tended toward more cultural, rather than behavioral, questions. One of the bracing characteristics of the transcripts in this chapter is how directly they offer clues to answering questions about cultural meaning. Two very general elements for defining culture have to do with its role in providing a view of the world and its role in providing motivation for acting in conformity to that view. What gets called a family, what counts as good – these are some of the questions that are cultural. And underlying them at yet another remove are questions about personhood and relationships with others. Let me develop two examples of the kinds of cultural questions that arise from the data in this chapter.*

*We could begin with Stuenkel's point that outsourcing "is a practice that has existed in a variety of culturally and historically specific forms for centuries." Here, outsourcing is explicitly defined in terms of commodification and purchase. That, of course, is to already narrow the frame from a larger set of possible comparisons that direct our gaze to different kinds of questions. Childcare outside of the family is far from being an unusual practice. Similarly, the practices of bringing in people to clean and maintain households, to prepare food, and to run errands are also widespread. But less widespread is the peculiar practice of monetary payment and the different degrees of relationship with those service providers that seem to go along with that payment.*

*We are all familiar in this country with the occasional and episodic childcare provided by grandparents and other non-residential kin. Historical sociologists of European families describe residential servants as something more than mere household members. In some contexts, they were regarded as family members. In my work in Nepal, I'm familiar with middle-class families taking in unrelated servant girls who become, in some sense, family members. Often they are unpaid in the sense of having a regular salary or wage. The interesting point here is not to establish a list of all the varieties of outsourcing, monetary and non-monetary. Rather it is to draw attention to the question of what it means to have these activities, once familial in the American context, performed for money. What does it say about family? What does it say about the relationships between employer and employee? And how does all this connect to the intensely cultural notion of what it is good for a person to be?*

*Stuenkel's interviews already show the difficulty of holding job descriptions to neatly defined tasks. It might be worth asking if these additional tasks are considered outsourced in the same sense of being purchased. Take the full-time attorney Caroline Goldblatt's sudden realization in the course of the interview itself that her nanny was, in addition to childcare, preparing meals. Or Vanessa Rest's swapping of tasks with her childcare provider, letting the provider do the grocery shopping while she spends time with her own children. In addition to Stuenkel's excellent and novel point about hidden commodification, I was equally struck by how stealthily these employees take on an almost familial flexibility in their activities. The job configuration begins to sound less joblike. In an earlier comment, I referred to this as "hidden familification." We shouldn't let that tongue-in-cheek phrasing obscure the disciplinary differences between an anthropologist interested in background meanings and a sociologist focused on strategic processes. While a focus on commodification turns us toward an examination of behaviors, it is possible to use the same data to formulate questions about relationships between people. I think it would be a mistake to emphasize one to the exclusion of the other. (I should make clear that I am speaking of a whole research program rather than a discrete analysis such as the very fine one in this chapter!)*

*This parallel process revealed in the relationships between service purchasers and providers brings us back to old questions about family definition. And this is my second example. On the one hand, we take it for granted that the families referred to here are defined in terms of structure – two parents and at least one child. But on the other hand, it is difficult to not read something into the emotive content that comes through the various transcripts:*

*. . . I mean it's not like paying her to do that because she's paid to do something else, but she is awesome. . . . Yeah, she's the best!*

*If Nina wasn't there, I just think how crazed my life would be. . . . [Nina] is the one that, you know, saves me the most time and effort and sanity.*

*My kids loved her. And she loved my kids and we . . . I mentioned it before, she was like a family member. She would go on vacations with us. All my family knew her; she was like a family member.*

*These kinds of relationships suggest other scales for typing the various tasks that are outsourced. In addition to specialization or pleasantness or required intellectual skill, we might think of scales that use continua of intimacy or degree of closeness to the culturally defined sense of personal being. Access to children is one indicator. There are obviously others that need to be discovered.*

*One of the pleasures of reading Stuenkel's analysis is how it opens into these very themes that so excite the anthropological imagination. That it does so while presenting a compelling argument for process makes it doubly fine.*

# 11　Television use and communication within families with adolescents

*Nicholas P. Dempsey*

Television is often thought of as an isolating medium in that individuals, whole families even, sit down in front of the television and watch inertly, silently throughout an evening of viewing. Though there are undoubtedly times when many individuals fulfill this stereotype, research has shown that this inactivity is not representative of all time spent watching television, perhaps not even the majority (Alexander 1993; Kubey and Csikszentmihalyi 1990; Lull 1990). These studies suggest television viewing is associated with more active states. A number of activities, from doing housework to eating dinner, frequently accompany television viewing. Since its introduction, watching television has become an almost indispensable part of the home life of most Americans (Leichter et al. 1985). Not just an activity to fill up the precious little leisure time of busy people, television viewing has been integrated into the complex fabric of families' lives at home.

This chapter examines the relationship between television viewing and communication among family members. Data obtained through the Experience Sampling Method (ESM) are used to test the hypothesis that a key role of television is to foster communication among family members, providing them with a relaxed atmosphere for interaction and discussion (see, e.g., Kubey and Larson 1990; Lull 1990). Both the frequency with which families interact while watching television and how they feel during this interaction are considered. Family members' emotions while interacting and watching television are compared to their emotions in other leisure activities to determine whether the experience of family interaction is enhanced by television viewing relative to other leisure activities. This hypothesis stems from the idea that television viewing is now so pervasive that it can be used as stress-reducing background noise, cheap therapy for busy families, or a backdrop for other activities. This contrasts with the way television was watched during the first twenty or so years after its introduction when watching was an event demanding great concentration from viewers and its novelty helped to fixate attention on the television set and isolate people from interactions with others (Brown and Hayes 2001).

## Family television viewing

In contrast to early perspectives on television, which were primarily concerned with the content of television programs and which saw viewers as passively absorbing this content (see, e.g., Adorno 1953, 1975; Minow and LaMay 1995), more recent studies have a different take on the role of television in people's lives. They view television, implicitly or explicitly, as one activity among the myriad of other activities in people's lives – from the consumption of other media, to leisure and exercise, to housework and market work. These studies are considerably less negative than earlier studies, taking more or less for granted that the content of television programming has not led to the wholesale destruction of Western civilization. Instead, they see television as potentially positive, an easy activity around which families may coalesce. ESM studies by Kubey, Larson, and Csikszentmihalyi have shown that television viewing may harmonize with other family activities (Kubey and Csikszentmihalyi 1990; Kubey and Larson 1990). These studies find that individuals tend to watch television with other family members, and that they combine television viewing with a variety of activities. The data suggest that one activity that individuals tend to engage in when watching television is talking with family members. These studies also have found that for adolescents, television viewing appears to be an activity that they largely engage in with their parents. If adolescents want to engage in media consumption of a more individual nature or more valued by their peer group, they are likely to listen to music rather than watch television (Kubey and Larson 1990).

The finding that television plays a role in family interactions is born out by ethnographic data. Television viewing can serve as a source of entertainment and may provide background noise during other activities. Due to the regularity of programming, television can even help people schedule their days: Hochschild (1997) found that some families ease their children into their daily routine by turning on their favorite programs each morning. Moreover, television can create an immediate agenda for conversation or discussion where there might otherwise be none, with plots, characters, and actors' personal lives providing rich ground for lively discussions (Luil 1990; May 1999). Reviewing the body of literature which considers the role of television in familial interactions, Alexander (1993) concludes that "directly and indirectly, television provides bases for family interaction" (56). She not only discusses the facilitative role television may play as a medium, as Lull (1990) and Hochschild (1997) do, but also shows that the messages conveyed by the medium provide context for making sense of our lives and interactions: "[I]ndividuals and families selectively take the raw material of life and put it into narratives (or stories) and, through that process, come to understand our life or some component of it" (Alexander 1993: 58).

Research on television and how it interacts with family life shows a general shift in views from worried denouncements of its effects to a cautiously positive stance on television's role in people's lives. This positive outlook stems from observations that television can potentially help bring family members together and help them organize their busy lives. Though recent studies have answered many questions about television's role in family life, more questions remain unanswered. New data from the 500 Family Study make it possible to update the ESM work of Kubey and his colleagues with data specifically taken from families, and to more directly consider how television influences the frequency of family interactions, and the emotions that are experienced during such interactions. These data also provide a novel opportunity to consider the television viewing habits of entire families. Never before has such comprehensive time use data been available from multiple members of the same family.

## Hypotheses

This chapter uses the 500 Family Study data to test several hypotheses that have been raised in previous studies.

*Hypothesis 1. Time spent watching television within families will frequently be accompanied by a range of other activities, including interactions among members of the family.* Television may provide a background to a variety of activities that take place in the household. Not only conversation, but housework, homework, or even dinner may occur concurrent with television viewing. Television viewing should thus be compatible and perhaps even conducive to family interaction.

*Hypothesis 2a. Compared to other activities that families do as a group, such as eating or playing games, television viewing will be less frequently associated with interaction.* Some researchers have termed conversation and family interactions that occur in front of the television "quasi-interaction" (Johnson 1984: 173). Although family members are talking to one another, the rules of conversation are altered to accommodate the television (e.g., people may only talk during commercial breaks). Conversations that occur while watching television may also be limited in their content to themes directly relating to the programming being watched. There is also a decrease in the level of attention paid to one another by interactants when the television is on versus when it was not. These findings suggest that family members will spend more of their time interacting when doing activities other than watching television (e.g., concentrating only on talking to other family members, eating a meal, or engaging in recreational pursuits together).

*Hypothesis 2b. An alternative hypothesis, consistent with the theories of Lull and the research of Kubey, Csikszentmihalyi, and Larson, is that individuals who spend more time watching television will spend more time interacting with family members since television provides an atmosphere that eases conversational discomfort.*

*Hypothesis 3. People will have a lower level of affect during their interactions with family members when watching television – particularly when television is the main focus of their activity – compared to interactions that take place while not watching television.* There is significant evidence that television may affect individuals' emotional states. Kubey and Csikszentmihalyi (1990) found that when watching television versus doing other activities with their families, people were more relaxed, but less challenged, alert, strong, or active. In general, they found that affect – happiness, sociability, cheerfulness, and friendliness – was lower when watching television compared to other leisure activities. The present study, with a slightly different set of emotional measures and a new ESM sample, will attempt to replicate these findings.

## Method

This chapter uses data from parents and adolescents in the 500 Family Study who participated in the ESM. The ESM is a useful tool for answering the questions posed by this study. It not only provides estimates of the amount of time people spend in particular activities such as watching television, but also provides information regarding who they are with, the quality of their experiences, and which activities tend to co-occur. The calculations of time spent on various media and other activities are reliable (Kubey, Larson, and Csikszentmihalyi 1996) and help to overcome the overestimation observed when questionnaires are used to determine how much time people spend watching television (Bechtel, Achelpohl, and Akers 1972). The ESM should ameliorate this overestimate because it requires that people record what they are doing *as they do it*, and thus obtains a probability sample of the activities a given individual engages in over the course of a day.[1]

*Sample*

Analyses were performed on a subsample of 309 families with adolescents who responded to at least 15 ESM signals. This provided data on 196 fathers, 280 mothers, and 298 adolescents (between the ages of 12 and 18). It should be noted that this is not a representative sample of US families, since there are higher proportions of dual-earner, high-income families in the sample than in the nation as a whole. According to the estimates produced by Bianchi and Robinson (1997), families in which the mothers work and have spent as much time in school as those in the 500 Family Study should watch less TV on average than families in the population as a whole.

*Measures*

*Primary and secondary activities*    Individuals' responses to the ESM questions "What was the main thing you were doing [when beeped]?" and "What else were you doing [when beeped]?" were recoded into several categories of interest, such as watching television or doing housework. These categories were then used to generate dummy variables indicating whether an individual was engaged in a given activity when beeped. For example, when an individual reported that his or her primary activity was watching television, the variable for television viewing as a primary activity was assigned a value of 1. Otherwise, the variable was assigned a value of 0. These variables were used to estimate the amounts of time people spend in various activities, the frequency with which certain activities coincide (in particular, how often family communication and television viewing coincide), and the emotions individuals experience during certain activities or combinations of activities. They were also used to estimate whether there are any relationships between the television viewing habits of different family members. Regression analyses described below use these measures of time use to estimate the amount of time family members spend talking, watching television, and working.

*Parenting experiences*    The amount of time adolescents spend talking with their parents or watching television may be influenced by a number of factors, including their parents' attitudes toward parenting. Measures of positive and negative parenting experiences are thus included in regression analyses. *Negative parenting* is a composite variable based on the following items from the parent survey: "Being a parent is harder than I thought it would be"; "My child does things that really bother me"; and "I find myself giving up more of my life to meet my child's needs than

I ever expected." Responses to these items range from 1 (never true) to 5 (always true). *Positive parenting* is another composite variable based on six different statements about parenting, also from the parent survey which begin, "In general I am a parent who . . .": "makes my children feel better when they talk over their worries with me"; "likes to talk with my children and be with them much of the time"; "enjoys talking things over with my children"; "enjoys doing things with my children"; "cheers my children up when they are sad"; and "has a good time at home with my children." Responses to these items also range from 1 (never true) to 5 (always true).[2]

*Emotion measures*    For analyses of the emotions individuals experience while doing various activities, the following emotion measures from the ESM were used: sad/happy, involved, stressed, enjoying activity, feeling good about self, and interested. One of the items (sad/happy) was measured on a 7-point semantic-differential scale, where 1 indicates very sad and 7 indicates very happy. The remaining items were measured on a 4-point scale, with 0 indicating that the respondent did not experience the emotion at all, and 3 indicating that he or she experienced it very much. Raw scores for each emotion were transformed into standardized (z) scores at the individual level (with each respondent's mean score set to 0, with a standard deviation of 1) to compensate for individual differences in scale use and response style. Positive scores indicate people's responses are higher than their personal means, on average, during these activities; negative scores indicate their responses are lower than their personal means.

## Results

### Time use

On average, individuals spend a significant proportion of their time watching television. Combining the estimates of time spent watching as either a primary or secondary activity, both mothers and fathers watch about 9.1 hours of television each week, while their adolescents watch about 13 hours.[3] These estimates are consistent with earlier results obtained from ESM studies that found that individuals watch an average of about 9.8 hours of television per week (Kubey and Csikszentmihalyi 1990: 70). As expected, based on the work of Bechtel, Achelpohl, and Akers (1972), these estimates are considerably lower than estimates provided by surveys.[4]

These results resonate with Bianchi and Robinson's (1997) finding that dual-earner families watch less television than average families. As was found in previous ESM studies, much of the television viewing done by individuals takes place with other family members. In fact, for all family members, less than half of their television viewing is solitary; everyone spends a few hours each week on average watching with other members of their family (individuals also report watching some television with friends or co-workers). Further analysis reveals that mothers report watching television an average of 2.43 hours each week with their spouse and child, fathers report doing so for about 2.26 hours, and adolescents report watching with both parents about 2.24 hours per week.

Television viewing, however, is not uniformly distributed across individuals. For the purposes of some of the analyses reported below, individuals who watched no television were placed into their own group, as they represent a sizable proportion of the sample.[5] Teenagers in all groups watch more television than their mothers or fathers, who watch similar amounts of television. The median hours of television viewing fell at 6.2 hours per week for fathers, 7 hours for mothers, and 10.9 hours for adolescents. On the other hand, in the heaviest viewing quartile, fathers watched at least 13.2 hours of television each week, mothers 12.9 hours, and teenagers 17.8 hours. Thus there is a substantial proportion of mothers and fathers watching two or more hours of television each day, and a large group of teenagers who approach three hours on average each day.

Television viewing occurs primarily in the evening hours, beginning around 5:00 p.m. and rapidly dropping off at about 11:00 p.m. This is the case for all family members, and the distribution of time spent watching television alone is very similar to the distribution of time spent watching television with other family members. Adolescents distribute their viewing more evenly across the evening hours than their parents, who tend to watch television around eight or nine o'clock, and spend a greater proportion of their television viewing time in the 10:00–11:00 p.m. hour. During the 10:00–11:00 p.m. period, adolescents appear to spend a large proportion of their time doing schoolwork, listening to the radio, and talking with friends (results not shown). The largest single time slot during which family members watch television, both alone and with other family members, is the hour between 9:00 and 10:00 p.m. About 35 percent of mothers' television viewing occurs during this hour, while about 30 percent and 20 percent, respectively, of fathers and adolescents' television viewing occurs during this period.[6]

*Concurrent activities*

Is television viewing compatible with, perhaps even conducive to, communication between family members? At least as evidenced by what

Table 11.1 *Percent of time spent in secondary activities when television watching is the primary activity, by family member*

| | Father | $z^a$ | Mother | z | Adolescent | z |
|---|---|---|---|---|---|---|
| TV exclusively | 30.65 | −5.51*** | 24.51 | −2.47* | 28.06 | −10.33*** |
| Talking with family | 17.47 | − | 19.80 | − | 10.54 | − |
| Eating/drinking/smoking | 12.91 | 2.62** | 10.98 | 6.37*** | 17.95 | −5.12*** |
| Reading/writing | 10.75 | 4.18*** | 7.85 | 10.03*** | 2.27 | 14.71*** |
| Sleep/rest | 6.18 | 9.04*** | 9.41 | 8.04*** | 10.97 | −0.37 |
| Other | 5.38 | 10.34*** | 4.90 | 15.59*** | 8.40 | 2.04* |
| Housework | 4.30 | 12.52*** | 8.24 | 9.49*** | 2.99 | 11.74*** |
| Child/family care | 2.69 | 17.62*** | 3.33 | 20.73*** | 0.28 | 51.45*** |
| Socializing (non-family) | 2.42 | 18.89*** | 2.94 | 22.54*** | 7.97 | 2.51* |
| Exercise/playing | 2.15 | 20.37*** | 1.77 | 30.88*** | 1.00 | 24.40*** |
| Thinking | 1.88 | 22.14*** | 2.75 | 23.55*** | 1.42 | 20.42*** |
| School/work | 1.61 | 24.30*** | 0.78 | 48.83*** | 5.41 | 6.01*** |
| Computer | 0.81 | 35.85*** | 0.00 | ∞*** | 0.85 | 27.97*** |
| Personal maintenance | 0.54 | 44.56*** | 2.55 | 24.71*** | 1.42 | 20.42*** |
| Sum | 99.74 | | 99.81 | | 99.53 | |
| N (number of beeps) | 372 | | 510 | | 702 | |

[a] z measures the significance of the difference in proportions between a given secondary activity and talking with family members.
* $p < .05$; ** $p < .01$; *** $p < .001$

family members do while watching television – or while talking – it appears that it is. As table 11.1 shows, most of the time that people are watching television (69.35 percent for fathers, 75.49 percent for mothers, and 71.94 percent for adolescents), they are also engaged in other activities, from housework and childcare to reading or playing.[7] Only about one-third of television viewing time is spent in what might be termed a "couch potato" mode – watching television and doing nothing else (30.65 percent for fathers, 24.51 percent for mothers, and 28.06 percent for adolescents).

A wide range of other activities accompany television viewing, including reading and writing, doing paid work or schoolwork, and doing housework (see table 11.1). One of the most frequent activities family members engage in while watching television is talking with other family members. On average, for about six minutes of every hour an adolescent spends watching television (10.54 percent of his or her television viewing time) he or she is talking with family members. Note that adolescents spend about another five minutes of every television viewing hour talking with their friends (7.97 percent of viewing time). Clearly, watching television can be a social activity. For mothers and fathers, the time they spend

Table 11.2 *Percent of time spent in secondary activities when interacting with family members is the primary activity, by family member*

| | Father | $z^a$ | Mother | z | Adolescent | z |
|---|---|---|---|---|---|---|
| Talking with family exclusively | 31.09 | −7.69*** | 24.59 | −7.38*** | 24.60 | −6.87*** |
| Eating/drinking/smoking | 16.21 | −3.64*** | 12.07 | −1.78+ | 10.71 | −2.44* |
| Other | 12.16 | −2.26* | 13.70 | −2.67** | 27.38 | −7.63*** |
| Housework | 7.66 | −0.25 | 14.39 | −3.02* | 3.97 | 1.62 |
| TV | 7.21 | – | 9.28 | – | 5.96 | – |
| Transit | 4.95 | 1.55 | 4.18 | 5.29*** | 4.37 | 1.24 |
| Child/family care | 4.50 | 1.95+ | 1.62 | 12.60*** | 2.38 | 3.73*** |
| Reading/writing | 4.50 | 1.95+ | 5.33 | 3.65*** | 1.59 | 5.55*** |
| Thinking | 2.70 | 4.15*** | 2.32 | 9.60*** | 4.76 | 0.90 |
| Socializing (non-family) | 2.25 | 4.98*** | 3.02 | 7.59*** | 2.78 | 3.07** |
| Personal maintenance | 2.25 | 4.98*** | 2.32 | 9.60*** | 2.38 | 3.73*** |
| School/work | 1.80 | 6.06*** | 2.55 | 8.86*** | 3.97 | 1.62 |
| Sleep/rest | 1.35 | 7.57*** | 2.78 | 8.21*** | 1.98 | 4.54*** |
| Computer | 0.45 | 15.05*** | 0.70 | 21.37*** | 0.40 | 13.98*** |
| Exercise/playing | 0.45 | 15.05*** | 1.16 | 15.74*** | 2.78 | 3.07** |
| Sum | 99.53 | | 100.01 | | 100.01 | |
| N (number of beeps) | 222 | | 431 | | 252 | |

[a] z measures the significance of the difference in proportions between a given secondary activity and watching television as a secondary activity (when talking with family members is the primary activity).
+ p < .10; * p < .05; ** p < .01; *** p < .001

watching television is even more family oriented. Mothers spend about twelve minutes of every hour they watch television in direct interaction with their families, fathers about ten minutes (19.80 percent and 17.47 percent of viewing time, respectively). These findings are comparable to those of Kubey and Csikszentmihalyi (1990), who found that about 21 percent of all television viewing beeps – twelve minutes of every hour – occurred concurrent with talking to family members (although they did not break their results down by family member).

The converse also holds true. Table 11.2 shows what activities coincide with talking with family members, including the proportion of time family members are also watching television.[8] Adolescents spend about three and a half minutes of every hour watching television when talking with family members is their primary activity (5.96 percent of talking beeps). For parents, this proportion is even higher – a little over four minutes per hour for fathers, and about five and a half minutes for mothers (7.21 percent and 9.28 percent, respectively). Though there is

Table 11.3 *Amount of time spent talking to other family members (summed proportion of primary and secondary activities), by family member by television use, with results of one-way ANOVAs*

|  | No TV | Some TV to median | Median to 75th centile | 75th to 100th centile | F |
|---|---|---|---|---|---|
| Father | 0.13 | 0.12 | 0.13 | 0.11 | 0.64 |
| Mother | 0.13 | 0.16 | 0.15 | 0.15 | 1.87 |
| Adolescent | 0.11 | 0.08 | 0.07 | 0.07 | 3.15* |

* $p < .05$

considerable evidence for Hypothesis 2a, which assumes that families will interact more while doing activities other than watching television, it should be noted that only two activities appear to accompany interaction more than watching television: consuming food, drink, or tobacco, and doing housework (for mothers and fathers).[9]

### Heavy viewers, lighter viewers, and non-viewers

People spend widely varying amounts of time watching television. As noted earlier, a considerable proportion of this sample watches no television at all. Though the average individual watches a little more than ten hours of television in a week, there are individuals who report spending nearly a third of their waking hours – upwards of six hours per day – watching television. To explore the varying experiences of people whose television viewing habits differ, individuals were categorized into one of four groups based on the amount of television they watched per week. Individuals who watch different amounts of television are very similar to one another with respect to demographic characteristics such as income. However, there are some significant differences between them with regard to time use (results not shown). For example, fathers who watch more television tend to spend less time at work than those who watch less, and adolescents who watch more television tend to spend less time doing school-related activities.[10]

The amount of time spent talking with other family members was calculated for individuals in each of the four television use groups. Table 11.3 presents results of comparisons for mothers, fathers, and adolescents of time spent talking to family members by amount of television watched. For fathers and mothers, there is no significant association between time spent watching television and time spent talking to their families. For adolescents, however, those who watch the most television spend the least

Table 11.4 *Regression of adolescents' time spent talking to parents on family members' time spent watching television, working, and parents' experiences of parenting*

|  | Coef. | Beta |
|---|---|---|
| Own time watching | −0.105** | −0.264 |
| Father's time watching | 0.060 | 0.118 |
| Mother's time watching | 0.071 | 0.124 |
| Father's negative parenting | −0.004** | −0.246 |
| Mother's negative parenting | 0.000 | 0.010 |
| Father's positive parenting | −0.001 | −0.129 |
| Mother's positive parenting | 0.001+ | 0.163 |
| Father's time working | −0.054* | −0.204 |
| Mother's time working | −0.035+ | −0.146 |
| Constant | 0.117** | – |

*Note:* $F_{(9,108)} = 3.61***$; adj. $R^2 = .167$
+ $p < .10$; * $p < .05$; ** $p < .01$

time talking to their family. Adolescents who were above the median for television viewing reported talking to other family members during 7 percent of their total beeps, while those who watched no television reported talking with other family members during roughly 11 percent of their beeps.

Regression analysis provides further evidence for this trend. Table 11.4 presents the results of an ordinary least squares regression with the amount of time an adolescent spends talking to his or her parents as the dependent variable. The independent variables include the amount of time an adolescent watches television and the amount of time his or her mother and father watch television. Mothers' and fathers' reports of both negative and positive parenting and the amount of time each spends working were also included as independent variables because it is suspected that television is associated with family interactions. Adolescents with more unsupervised free time may be likely to spend more time watching television and less likely to spend time talking to their parents. This appears to be the case.

While the amount of time an adolescent's father or mother spends watching television does not appear to have a significant effect on how much time the adolescent spends talking to them, the amount of time the adolescent spends watching television does appear to have a significant negative effect. On average, each hour increase per week in the amount of time an adolescent spends watching television is associated with a decrease of a little over six minutes of time talking to his or her parents.

The regression also suggests that adolescents whose fathers report negative experiences of parenting spend somewhat less time talking to their parents, while those whose mothers report positive parenting experiences tend to spend a bit more time talking with their parents. The amount of time both fathers and mothers spend at work tends to be associated with a decrease in the amount of time they spend talking with their adolescents – about three fewer minutes of talking for every hour a father works, and about two fewer minutes for every hour a mother works.

While the absolute values of these effects appear relatively small, if beta coefficients are considered, these differences prove important. In fact, the largest effect is for the amount of time an adolescent spends watching television. On average, a change of one standard deviation in an adolescent's television viewing time – about twelve hours per week – results in a change of about 0.26 standard deviations in the amount of time he or she spends talking to parents.[11] That is equivalent to about 1.2 hours per week – a reasonably large effect considering that adolescents in the sample average about 4.9 hours of talking with their parents on average.[12] These associations show that while television appears to play some role in adolescents' communication with their families, it cannot be considered independently of more general family dynamics. Parental characteristics – how parents feel about parenting and how they spend their own time – are a large part of the story.

To investigate whether the television viewing habits of individual family members are associated with those of other family members, bivariate regressions were conducted on a subsample of 118 families.[13] The results of these regressions show positive associations of mother's time spent watching with father's time spent watching ($\beta = 0.4371$, $p = .000$, $R^2 = 0.1911$), mother's time with adolescent's time ($\beta = 0.2073$, $p = .024$, $R^2 = 0.0430$), and father's time with adolescent's time ($\beta = 0.1604$, $p = .083$, $R^2 = 0.0257$). For example, if a father watches two hours of television each day while another father watches just one hour daily, his wife can be expected to watch an extra twenty-three minutes of television each day on average compared to the spouse of the father who watches less television. That same father's daughter would be expected to watch an average of twelve more minutes of television each day, compared to the daughter of the father who watches less television. With respect to mothers' impact on their children's television viewing time, a mother who watches an additional hour of television could be expected to have a daughter who watches on average about eighteen minutes more per day. As in the old public service announcements that spoke of the risks to adolescents of parental drug use, parents who watch a lot of television have children who watch a lot of television.[14]

Table 11.5 *Emotions when watching television and engaging in other leisure activities while talking with other family members, by family member*[a]

| | TV | Other leisure | t |
|---|---|---|---|
| Happy | | | |
| Father | 0.22 | 0.70 | −2.67** |
| Mother | 0.27 | 0.56 | −2.36* |
| Adolescent | 0.10 | 0.19 | −0.64 |
| Involved | | | |
| Father | −0.46 | −0.04 | −2.24* |
| Mother | −0.55 | 0.02 | −3.41*** |
| Adolescent | −0.29 | 0.20 | −3.26** |
| Stressed | | | |
| Father | −0.40 | −0.30 | −0.62 |
| Mother | −0.39 | −0.31 | −0.67 |
| Adolescent | −0.20 | −0.27 | 0.50 |
| Good about self | | | |
| Father | −0.05 | 0.38 | −2.64** |
| Mother | −0.05 | 0.25 | −2.16* |
| Adolescent | −0.06 | 0.12 | −0.97 |
| Enjoy | | | |
| Father | 0.50 | 0.63 | −0.78 |
| Mother | 0.58 | 0.57 | −0.84 |
| Adolescent | 0.36 | 0.46 | −0.84 |
| Interested | | | |
| Father | 0.34 | 0.39 | −0.37 |
| Mother | 0.53 | 0.58 | −0.50 |
| Adolescent | 0.32 | 0.39 | −0.55 |

[a] Raw scores of responses were transformed into standardized (z) scores at the individual level (with each respondent's mean score set to 0, with a standard deviation of 1) to compensate for individual differences in scale use and response style. Positive scores thus indicate that people are answering higher than their personal means, on average, during these activities; negative scores indicate they are responding lower than their personal means.

*p < .05; ** p < .01; *** p < .001; two-tailed test

*Emotions and television*

Hypothesis 3 posits that people will feel lower levels of affect when watching television with their families than when doing other activities. Table 11.5 shows the emotional reports of family members while watching television and talking with other members of their family, and compares the responses to other leisure activities engaged in while talking to family members.[15] The emotion values presented in table 11.5 represent the difference from individuals' average emotional levels. Thus, a positive value for "happy" denotes that people feel happier doing the activity in question than they normally would.

Across the board, family members report that watching television vis-à-vis other leisure activities provides them with less of an opportunity to be involved or active, as has been found in previous ESM studies (Kubey and Csikszentmihalyi 1990). Mothers and fathers also report that they are significantly less happy when watching television while talking to family members than when participating in other leisure activities. Their adolescent children, however, feel about equally happy when watching television or participating in other leisure activities while talking to members of their family. The same holds true for feeling good about oneself: mothers and fathers report feeling significantly less good about themselves while watching television compared to other leisure activities when they are talking with family members, but there is no significant difference for their adolescents. Television viewing is also associated with lower than average experiences of stress among all family members, and higher than average experiences of both enjoyment and interest. These levels are not significantly different from those reported while engaging in other leisure activities.

The next analysis examines whether it makes any difference what people consider their "main activity" when they are both talking and watching television. The ESM asks people both "What was the *main thing* you were *doing*?" and "*What else* were you doing at the same time?" A significant difference was found in emotional state if an individual reported television viewing as his or her primary activity while talking to family members versus television viewing as a secondary activity when talking to family members is the primary activity. This is well documented in earlier work by Kubey and Csikszentmihalyi (1990). The emotions family members experience when they report that television viewing is the only thing they are doing are also different from the times that they report that they are talking and watching television concurrently. These results are shown in table 11.6.

These results show that for several of the emotions under consideration, the quality of the experience of watching television as a primary activity while talking to other family members lies between the quality of experience of watching television exclusively and watching television while the main activity is talking to one's family. In general, individuals feel less happy, less involved or active, adolescents and fathers feel less stressed, and mothers feel less good about themselves, experience less enjoyment, and feel less interested as they go from talking as a main activity to watching television exclusively.

Table 11.6 *Emotions when watching television, with talking as primary or secondary activity, compared to exclusively watching television, by family member*

| | Talk primary/ TV secondary | TV primary/ Talk secondary | Just TV | F |
|---|---|---|---|---|
| Happy | | | | |
| Father | 0.43 | 0.17 | 0.00 | 1.60 |
| Mother | 0.37 | 0.23 | −0.17 | 4.59*** |
| Adolescent | −0.51 | 0.20 | 0.03 | 2.24+ |
| Involved | | | | |
| Father | 0.35 | −0.65 | −1.26 | 73.00*** |
| Mother | 0.02 | −0.76 | −1.16 | 78.79*** |
| Adolescent | 0.14 | −0.37 | −0.70 | 36.83*** |
| Stress | | | | |
| Father | −0.10 | −0.47 | −0.49 | 11.94*** |
| Mother | −0.30 | −0.42 | −0.46 | 15.77*** |
| Adolescent | 0.48 | −0.33 | −0.30 | 9.51*** |
| Good about self | | | | |
| Father | 0.14 | −0.09 | −0.31 | 3.97** |
| Mother | 0.32 | −0.18 | −0.34 | 7.22*** |
| Adolescent | 0.31 | −0.13 | −0.05 | 1.05 |
| Enjoy | | | | |
| Father | 0.74 | 0.45 | 0.31 | 11.13*** |
| Mother | 0.78 | 0.50 | 0.41 | 23.84*** |
| Adolescent | 0.03 | 0.42 | 0.41 | 16.07*** |
| Interested | | | | |
| Father | 0.54 | 0.29 | 0.24 | 5.74*** |
| Mother | 0.68 | 0.47 | 0.40 | 20.54*** |
| Adolescent | 0.22 | 0.34 | 0.31 | 9.91*** |

$+ \; p < .10; \; ** \; p < .01; \; *** \; p < .001$; two-tailed test

To more closely explore adolescents' displeasure with talking to family members while also watching television, adolescents' responses to a question asking if they were doing this activity because they wanted to, had to, or had nothing else to do were examined. During those beeps when talking to their family is primary and television viewing secondary, adolescents only report that they want to be doing the activity about 31 percent of the time. In contrast, when watching television is primary and talking to family is secondary, adolescents report wanting to do the activity 61 percent of the time. That they do not wish to talk to family members resonates with the findings that adolescents are less interested and happy about this activity. They may not want to engage in talk as a primary activity because of simple adolescent hesitance to talk with their parents or because they may feel their television viewing time is being interrupted by parents or siblings. Alternately, their parents may be dominating the choice of programming during these times. The literature on adolescent development suggests that in trying to gain greater independence from their parents, adolescents often seek out opportunities to exercise personal control (Csikszentmihalyi and Larson 1984; Erikson 1968).

## Discussion

This chapter offers new empirical insights into the dynamics of television viewing in families: how much they watch, what they do while watching, who watches together, how they feel about it, and how the dynamics of individual members' viewing habits are related to the habits of other family members. Some of the substantive implications may relate to wider social processes and are addressed below.

Some evidence is found to support Hypothesis 1 – time spent watching television is accompanied by various activities, including talking to family members. As would be expected from Lull's hypotheses about television, families spend a good deal of time talking in front of the television. With respect to Hypothesis 2a – television watching is less frequently associated with interaction than other family activities – there is mixed evidence. Table 11.2 shows that there are a range of activities that accompany such interaction, and while television is not at the top of that list, it is high on the list.

Contrary to what would be expected from Lull's theory and Hypothesis 2b, adolescents who watch more television end up spending *less* time talking to their family. This is particularly interesting in light of the fact that there is no significant difference in the amounts of time spent with other family members among teenagers in this sample. The teenagers who are heavy viewers are physically with their family as much as lighter viewers, they are just not talking to them. Note that Kubey and Larson (1990) found that teenagers who spend more time watching television spend more time with their families overall, although they did not consider the impact of this time investment on communication within families. The current findings of no significant difference may suggest that there have been changes in the role of media in adolescents' lives over the last twenty years that are not at all straightforward. Factors such as the broadening of television programming choices, the ubiquity of personal computers, and a concomitant rise in access to the Internet present an array of potential media effects that needs to be disentangled.

Analyses also show that television does not appear to provide an overwhelmingly positive emotional context for family members, confirming

Hypothesis 3. While findings indicate that watching television while talking with family members is more interesting, less stressful, and more enjoyable than other activities in their lives, it does not make them as happy as other kinds of leisure activities, nor do they tend to feel as good about themselves or as involved in the activity. If television plays any role in facilitating interactions within families, or providing a context for conversations, it is a relatively small one.

There are a number of reasons to be concerned about the amount of time families spend together and the effect of that time on family communication patterns. Time spent with children by parents, including time within leisure activities such as television viewing, has been shown to be important for the transmission of human capital (Bryant and Zick 1996), which is vitally important to a child's future life chances. Theories of social capital have pointed out the deleterious effects of parents spending inadequate amounts of time with their children, due in part to parents overinvesting in their own human capital (e.g., spending excess time doing market work; Coleman 1987). Over time, this yields a diminution of social capital – "the norms, the social networks, and the relationships between adults and children that are of value for the child's growing up" (Coleman 1987: 36) – and a decline in the ability of society to retain core cultural values. Bianchi and Robinson (1997) speculate that children who spend more time watching television may not be accruing as much social capital as those whose parents tend to limit television viewing. Perhaps more importantly, this chapter has shown that those adolescents who watch more television spend less time talking to their families. These adolescents lack the opportunities of their peers who watch less television and interact more with their parents to accrue or strengthen their social capital. Further research should consider in more depth the determinants of adolescents' television viewing habits, and whether there are steps their parents can take to spend more time interacting with them.

There are a number of questions still to be answered about the relationship of television viewing to family interactions. Of particular interest is what is transmitted during conversations that take place during television viewing. Based on Lull's hypotheses, one would expect television to provide a context in which family members may feel more comfortable discussing sensitive topics such as sex, smoking, drugs, and alcohol. More direct observation of families in the context of television viewing could help answer this question. It would also be worthwhile to explore whether parents can use television to help reinforce the messages they wish to transmit to their children.

While this study suggests some negative aspects of television use, it should also be noted that television need not be regarded as entirely detrimental to contemporary family life. People enjoy watching television, and it may provide a much needed relief from everyday stress. Though it does not provide as positive a context for family interactions as other leisure activities, watching television requires much less effort than other activities, from assembling and concentrating on a board game to leaving the home to play sports. In the busy, dual-earner families that this study examines, a bit of time in front of the television each day may be just what is needed.

Despite this potentially positive aspect of television viewing in families of adolescents, the analyses presented above suggest that increased television use by adolescents is associated with lower levels of communication within families, and that adolescents' viewing habits are strongly associated with the viewing habits of their parents. The 500 Family Study is the first ESM study that allows analysts to link parental time use habits to the habits of their children. The new findings of this study suggest that parents who wish to moderate their adolescent's television viewing should not only take steps to change their children's viewing habits, but concentrate on reducing the amount of time they spend watching television themselves. It follows logically from the findings of this study that if they replace time spent watching television with other family-oriented activities, parents could enhance the potential for communicating with their adolescents.

## NOTES

1. This study has the advantage of using data from all of the respondents' waking hours in contrast to previous ESM studies of television viewing which stopped at 10 pm.
2. The positive parenting variable was constructed by summing responses to six items, with a reliability coefficient (Cronbach's alpha) of .87. The negative parenting variable was constructed using three negatively worded items (Cronbach's alpha = .71).
3. The dummy variables for activities were averaged across all of an individual's beeps to determine the fraction of total time spent in a given activity (the proportion of primary beeps were added to the proportion of secondary beeps to estimate the total amount of time spent in that activity). These summed proportions were averaged for mothers, fathers, and adolescents, and multiplied by 16 (the number of waking hours in the average person's day) and by 7 (the number of days in a week) to obtain estimates of the amount of time spent weekly in given activities.
4. The General Social Survey (GSS) estimates that individuals watch 20.8 hours of television per week (2000): for example, Nielsen Media Research (2000: 14) estimates that individuals watch more than 28 hours of television each week.

5. 17.86 percent of fathers, 20.71 percent of mothers, and 14.09 percent of adolescents reported watching no television.

6. Estimates of when television was watched were obtained by cross-tabulating the dummy variable for primary television viewing with the time of the ESM beep.

7. For these estimates, dummy variables for various secondary activities were averaged for only those beeps when individuals responded "watching television" was their primary activity.

8. For these estimates, dummy variables for various secondary activities were averaged for only those beeps when individuals responded "talking with other family members" was their primary activity.

9. The concurrence of oral activities such as eating and drinking with television viewing has been noted by Kubey and Csikszentmihalyi (1990).

10. Two one-way ANOVAs were used to examine the relationship between television viewing and: (1) time spent at work by fathers; and (2) time spent on schoolwork by adolescents. Both analyses yielded statistically significant results (available from the author upon request).

11. Recall that the amount of time individuals watch television varies widely, which accounts for the relatively large standard deviation.

12. These findings are somewhat in contradiction to those of previous ESM studies of television viewing. Kubey (1990) found that the amount of television an adolescent watched was positively correlated with the amount of time he or she spent with other family members (he did not separately consider whether or not they were talking). Analyses of the 500 Family data suggest that among adolescents there is no such correlation: the average number of family members present and the amount of time an adolescent watches television only show a non-significant correlation of 0.009. The reasons for this marked difference from earlier ESM research are open to speculation. It could be due to a cohort effect – adolescents in the late 1990s may have had a very different relationship to media than their counterparts in the 1970s and 1980s (e.g., the introduction of the Internet and the proliferation of cable television channels). The difference might also be attributable to the fact that in the 500 Family Study, the mothers *and* fathers of the adolescents work, whereas adolescents in prior ESM studies came from both dual-earner and single-earner families.

13. The sample is reduced to 118 families because these were the only families in which there were ESM responses from a mother, father, and at least one adolescent child. Comparisons of demographic characteristics of these families to those in the rest of the sample suggest that they are representative of the whole.

14. To explore these associations, families were divided into quartiles based on the combined amounts of television watched by different family members. The television viewing habits of individuals in these families were then tabulated to see if certain family members were skewing the average total viewing times of families upwards; that is, if families in the upper quartiles had members who watched an average amount of television while another member watched an unusual amount of television. That is not the case. On average,

the individual mothers, fathers, and teenagers in the families that watch the most television watch more television than those in families that watch less television. In families in the bottom quartile of total television viewing, 2 percent of mothers' and fathers' beeps and 4 percent of adolescents' beeps occurred while watching television. In the highest quartile, 17 percent of mothers' beeps, 15 percent of fathers' beeps, and 19 percent of adolescents' beeps occurred while the respondents were watching television. This is further evidence that the total amount of time a family watches television is determined by the habits of the entire family, not just of individual family members.

15. Specifically, other leisure activities include watching movies, socializing with others, listening to the radio, play (such as practicing music or playing board games), exercise, and sports. This closely parallels the categorizations used by Kubey and Csikszentmihalyi (1990: 121, note). Emotions during these activities tend to be quite similar (results not shown).

# Commentary

*Mihaly Csikszentmihalyi*

*Social scientists have written about few other topics as much as they have about television viewing, and with so little effect. Despite literally thousands of articles written on the subject by experts in communication, psychologists, social scientists, and sociologists, the medium goes its merry way unfazed by academic kudos or critiques. Part of the problem is that the public is very adept at turning a deaf ear on scientific demonstrations that interfere with its pleasures as, for example, it does with warnings against tobacco, fast food, gambling, or excessive alcohol. But part of the problem is with the studies themselves, which typically sacrifice scientific objectivity on the altar of ideology and opinion. Even when the study is very rigorous and careful, the data are often interpreted within the context of taken-for-granted assumptions about whether TV is good or bad for you. In their rush to judgment, investigators often forget that, first and foremost, scientific understanding requires the painstaking, careful measurement of relevant facts.*

*It was in part to provide a more balanced account of the role of television in human experience that we decided to apply the method developed in my lab at the University of Chicago, the Experience Sampling Method (ESM), to the study of how people actually use this medium in everyday life. Thirteen years ago my then student Robert Kubey and I wrote up the results in a book entitled* Television and the Quality of Life, *which critics hailed as the most important contribution to the topic since McLuhan's (1964) celebrated* Understanding Media. *Our findings did not present a very positive view of the effects of television viewing on the human psyche, but as we were careful to note, one cannot blame the medium entirely for its blandness – after all, never in history, to my knowledge, have people shone in how creatively they used free time. For instance, according to the historian Emmanuel Le Roy Ladurie (1979), in twelfth-century France the most popular free time activity was to sit on one's stoop and pull lice from a friend's hair. Compared to that, television viewing is probably a step up, even if the gossip exchanged while de-lousing a friend was probably more useful to the lives of people than the news one gets nowadays on television.*

*Be that as it may, in the years since the book appeared not many studies have used the ESM to study television (and most of them are referenced in this chapter). The reason is that while the ESM provides a uniquely accurate and nuanced picture of how people use their time and how they feel about what they are doing, the method is time consuming and difficult to use. On the basis of expediency alone, it cannot compete with the majority of studies that use surveys or narrowly focused experimental designs. However, it makes up for that weakness in terms of the wealth of information it provides.*

*Dempsey's chapter is a good illustration of the detailed understanding of daily life that the ESM can make available. Of the studies of television viewing done in the last decade, this is certainly one of the most informative and well executed. Its virtue in part is that it is clearly focused on a central question: What is the relation between watching TV and family interaction? This simple question – with important theoretical and practical consequences for parents and scholars alike – would be difficult to answer with the research tools that most studies employ.*

*What Dempsey shows is an intricate but meaningful set of relationships. In the first place, his findings confirm previous studies in reporting the time people actually spend watching TV (less than generally thought), and the feelings people have when they watch (worse than generally thought). These replications, astonishingly close to previous reports, are in fact extremely valuable, especially in a field where due to constant changes in methods and theories it is very difficult to achieve the first step of scientific process, namely the replication of findings.*

*The original contribution of Dempsey's chapter is the fine-grained analysis of how parents and their teenagers experience television, and how viewing relates to the quality of their experience. Here the most important finding is the generational split between parents and children: fathers and mothers in general feel better when they are talking and doing other leisure activities, but children prefer to watch TV to talking. Table 11.6 especially gives a vivid picture of the generational differences: while both parents enjoy those moments when talk is primary and TV is in the background, their children enjoy much more the moments when TV is the main focus and talk is either absent or of secondary importance. At the same time, the nuanced responses to the ESM indicate that even the teenagers are aware that watching TV may have its downside. For instance, all three members of the family, regardless of generational differences, report that they feel much less active and involved when TV is the primary focus (0.4 to 0.7 of a standard deviation below their own weekly average for children, 0.6 to 1.3 of a standard deviation below for their parents).*

*It would be difficult to argue from Dempsey's data – as other researchers have done – that watching television encourages interaction and strengthens family bonds. Children clearly abhor their parents' attempts to intrude into their viewing experience, and prefer to take their virtual reality straight, rather than filtered through conversation. Of course this is not necessarily the fault of the medium. Those of us who grew up reading will remember how irritating it was when mom or dad recalled us from the steamy jungles of an adventure story to drab quotidian realities.*

*The more insidious effect of television is difficult to document: the problem is that as a medium it is too good, too realistic, too complete in the information it provides – and therefore, it requires too little effort to decode and interpret. It is because of this feature of the medium that viewers in Dempsey's study – and all others as well – report low levels of concentration, activity, involvement, and challenge when watching TV. The cognitive demands of viewing – the demands on imagination, curiosity, concentration – are typically so low as to make the experience of viewing truly a low-impact cognitive task (Kubey and Csikszentmihalyi 2002). Of course we cannot be always in top form, mentally engaged, and involved. As the lice-picking French farmers remind us, a certain amount of relaxation is necessary to round out the daily cycle. And that function television undoubtedly provides.*

*Dempsey's study rightfully belongs among the few studies of television viewing that are worth remembering. Will it actually make a difference in the way we live our lives? I should hope this will be the case, although if past experience is to be any indication, that might be too much to hope for.*

## Robert Kubey

*It is intriguing to see the Experience Sampling Method (ESM) applied to recent adolescent use of television, and to find more than two decades after the first work that things do not appear to have changed very much in how young people experience television.*

*In 1976 when I first began using the ESM to look at the experience of television in everyday life, I was struck by the uniformity of the experience by age, gender, and by country. The more I worked with beeper data, the more I came to respect the considerable reliability and validity of the findings produced. After a time, I could predict with fair precision how different activities would be experienced by individuals and groups and under different social circumstances.*

*I came, over time, to be sensitive to minute perturbations in beeper data. If people were watching television by themselves, one pattern emerged. If they were watching with others, family or friends, then I would see a different experience. If it was a primary versus a secondary activity, once again, one would find predictable results. This was not a tribute to my abilities as an observer but to the nature of the method and the great number of observations that ESM data provide the researcher. Multiplied across, say, 500 people, and 40 to 50 separate observations on each individual, and 40 to 50 measures on each observation, one might well obtain an extraordinarily dense and rich ESM database of 1,250,000 entries. And it is from this richness and the simplicity of asking people how they feel when signaled that the depth and validity of ESM data arise. It is to these factors that I attribute the considerable symmetry between what Dempsey has found in the current study and what I found in work that I did on my own, and with both Larson and Csikszentmihalyi in the 1980s and 1990s.*

*One of the more intriguing findings, I think, and one that seems different from what Larson and I found is that heavier viewing adolescents spent less time talking with their parents than would have been predicted from our earlier work. We were not able to look at time spent talking with parents as readily as Dempsey could, as the ESM used in this study involved signaling adolescents and their parents simultaneously. The question does arise whether more viewing truly "causes" less talk with parents. The regression analysis does point in this direction but we do not know whether a third, or other, intervening variable might explain the results. As Dempsey says, "While television appears to play some role in adolescents' communication with their families, it cannot be considered independently of more general family dynamics."*

*We had consistently found that teenagers who watched more television spent more time with fellow family members and that they generally enjoyed time spent with family. The current study does not test for precisely these same relationships and it would be interesting to conduct a specific replication.*

*Dempsey raises the question as to whether the difference he observes might lie in changes in the nature of media and its availability. Clearly, in the late 1970s and very early 1980s, VCRs had only begun to enter homes. Numerous cable channels were not yet available. Video games were in their infancy, and the Internet had not yet been substantially developed.*

*The questions also arise as to whether something has actually changed in the relationship of teenagers to TV, or in teenagers themselves, or whether there is some difference in the samples. Exploration of adolescent experiences with other media, especially the new media that have altered most everyone's lives to lesser or greater degrees, would also prove fruitful.*

*It comes as little surprise that parents report "that they are significantly less happy when watching television while talking to family members than when participating in other leisure activities." After all, television experience is often subdued and passive relative to most everything else that people do on a daily basis. Thus, since most other leisure activities are more activating than is television viewing, it is not surprising that when combined with talking with a family member, the experience is not as happy a one for the parents as compared to more active leisure pursuits. Worth noting is that "their adolescent children, however, feel about equally happy when watching television or participating in other leisure activities while talking to members of their family." But the level of happiness for the teenagers is not very high in either condition. It seems that talking with other family members when watching TV or engaged in other leisure activities is not a time when adolescents often report feeling happy. The story on the enjoyment variable, by contrast, is more optimistic. Family talking time is generally enjoyed by adolescents, just not as much as by parents.*

*These findings might take on new meaning when others look at what experiences were most associated with adolescent happiness and enjoyment. From Larson's and my work, one would surmise that it is when they are engaged in leisure activities of their own choosing, especially when socializing with friends.*

*What is suggested in Dempsey's work is that family contact in general for many of these teenagers is experienced in a state of subdued emotion. And they certainly do not feel "good about self" when watching TV and talking with their family. We might wonder if when families do sit down to watch television together whether the parent might be making the choice of which program to view with greater frequency than was the case in the 1970s and 1980s when Larson and I were exploring these questions. It is also quite possible that the media activities that are most enjoyed contemporarily by adolescents are playing video games, instant messaging, and other computer and Internet activities. Our earlier research certainly points in this direction (Kubey and Larson 1990). These media activities are interactive, done by the teenager with his friends or siblings and rarely with parents, and by contrast to the rest of everyday life, television viewing done with family members is perhaps of a slightly different character than it was 20-plus years ago. It certainly is the case in our early explorations of affective response to new media that Larson and I found that adolescent boys' affect when playing video games and watching music videos was quite positive both relative to the rest of their daily experiences and especially relative to girls' experience with these same media. Only when boys and girls were watching TV via VCR (most likely they were watching movies on tape, often with friends) do both genders report significantly higher affect in new media activities. Still, even this difference was much greater for the boys than the girls. In short, we need to know more about the social–emotional ecology of the rest of these young people's media experiences. Interactive media are very much the fancy of contemporary adolescents, more so than are older media like television. And then, when they are viewing, if their parents have made the choice of what to view and are talking with/at them, they may experience viewing more negatively.*

*I also wonder whether it is possible that some of the adolescents that Larson and I studied who watched more TV and generally felt good with family members might also have said that they did not feel quite so good when someone was talking. Talking during TV, while a very common phenomenon and often an enjoyable way for family members to share experience, can also fly in the face of another's viewing. If parents are talking, and especially if they are telling the adolescent to do something (such as to not watch television or to complete their homework or some chore), it would come as no surprise that teenagers (especially the heavier viewers) might report more negative experiences when talking with parents while viewing. Perhaps this is why, in table 11.6, we see such a high stress rating (.48) for "Talk primary/TV secondary" and a rather unstressed experience when teens rate "TV primary/Talk secondary" (−.33) or when they are just watching TV and there is no talking (−.30). Indeed, the .48 rating is the only stressful rating we see for any group or for any condition in table 11.6.*

*It is important to point out that the parent may not be co-viewing; they may simply be talking with/at their child while the child is viewing. It is particularly telling, I think, that teenagers reported "wanting to do" the activity only 31 percent of the time when talking with the family was the primary activity and TV secondary. In contrast, when viewing is primary and when talking with the family is secondary, the adolescents want to do the activity 61 percent of the time. The question arises whether some of the instances of primary talking are not about pleasant things, or are perceived by the adolescent to be the agenda of the parent − or a sibling − rather than the teenager.*

*If I think about my own interactions with my 9 and 17 year-olds, insofar as each sometimes watches more television than I would like them to, and insofar as most of this viewing is done in the main room of our home, I am often suggesting they turn off the set at the end of a program and that they get back to their homework, or to a chore left undone. Not to paint too negative a picture, we also immensely enjoy various programs that we have picked to view together and we have a lot of fun both with and without the TV. Both my kids, I think, would "test out" as pretty happy with their parents and they would also report a happy home and family life, but I would also bet that a lot of the time that they have chosen to watch something on their own − which is often the case − and I am nearby and talking to them, that a percentage of that time I am working on them not to be watching, and at those times I think it quite possible that they would say that the main thing they were doing was talking (or listening) to me and the secondary thing was watching TV precisely because I had interrupted their viewing. Not only do they resent having their viewing interrupted (who doesn't?), but they are being told they need to go back to work on something that is rarely as relaxing and effortless as television viewing. And if we were beeped during such times, our interactions would sometimes be less than relaxed and more unpleasant than at many other times.*

*Unless the parent is also viewing television, one wonders whether some of these new observations might be tapping such a phenomenon, where discussion about viewing itself, or about chores and obligations not being done because of viewing, is what is going on and so, by looking at parents and kids talking during TV, we may be bound to observe a higher frequency of such negative experiences. And we might be particularly likely to observe this phenomenon in those homes where children are viewing heavily.*

# 12 Religiosity, emotional well-being, and family processes in working families

*Jennifer A. Schmidt*

Although religions vary in their emphasis on the transcendent versus worldly benefits of a religious life, most religions hold that their beliefs and practices are "good" for people in their practical living. This view is reflected in conventional wisdom, and recent decades have produced a considerable body of research to support this claim. Studies conclude that religious people are happier, healthier, and have more positive relationships with others, including their children. A commitment to religion, however, is a commitment, and requires some degree of investment by those involved. Time and energy are precious resources, particularly in dual-earner families, and parents and children must make choices about what takes priority in family life.

This chapter explores the place of religion in dual-earner households in the 500 Family Study. Using a number of indicators of religiosity, a description of religious commitment among mothers, fathers, and adolescents is presented. Among their many obligations, do parents and teenagers consider themselves to be religious and align themselves with a specific religious tradition? If so, how often do they make time in their daily lives for formal religious practices? Variations in religious commitment associated with sociodemographic factors such as gender, socioeconomic status (SES), or work hours are discussed. The chapter also examines whether religiosity has any association with parents' or children's emotional well-being. Are religious people happier people? Do they feel differently than non-religious people about themselves or others? Is there evidence of a psychological benefit to a religious life? Finally, do religious parents interact with their children differently than non-religious parents? Do they spend more time with their children and provide greater levels of support or challenge and more frequently discuss rules and values? The answers to these questions add to a growing body of research on the role of religion in modern families and the impact it has on parents and children.

## Dimensions of religiosity

Religion figures prominently in the landscape of American life. A 1995 Gallup Poll estimates that 70 percent of Americans identify themselves as having some type of religious affiliation; more than 40 percent report attending religious services in the week prior to the survey (Gallup Poll 1995). Even by more conservative estimates, however, religious participation in the United States is relatively high. Some estimate that approximately 60 percent of Americans claim a religious affiliation, while only about 25 percent report weekly attendance at religious services (Hadaway, Marler, and Chaves 1993).[1] Over half of the US population identifies with a particular religious denomination. Therefore, it is important to determine whether families in the 500 Family Study have similarly high rates of affiliation and attendance as those in national surveys since such high rates would indicate families' religious commitment and the emphasis they place on religion in everyday life.

Religiosity can be defined in a variety of ways (for a review see Hill and Hood 1999). Different definitions convey varying perspectives on what it means to be religious and what benefits religiosity has for the individual. In their review of religiosity and psychosocial well-being, Ellison, Gay, and Glass (1989) identify three distinct forms of religious commitment. These forms of religious commitment include: (1) *personal faith*; (2) *participation in organized religious activities*; and (3) *identification with a particular religious community*.

*Personal faith* refers to devotional intensity, individual belief, or personal religious experience that exists independent of organized religious activity. Scholars believe that a sense of personal faith "may facilitate a comprehensive interpretive framework through which the individual can make sense of the totality of human existence" (Ellison, Gay, and Glass 1989: 103). This personal framework may exert the most influence on individuals' feelings about themselves and their orientation toward others. An examination of this type of personal faith may be particularly important in studying families because personal faith may serve as a framework for parenting and for daily interactions among family members.

*Participation in organized religious activities* includes attending religious services. Such participation is a source of social interaction and support within a community of individuals who share similar value orientations. Churches and synagogues offer an institutional framework for developing social ties, while providing shared experiences that are intended to reinforce members' individual beliefs (Roof and Hoge 1980). It is expected that the social supports provided by regular participation in organized religion may promote a sense of well-being among parents and children.

*Identification with a particular religious community* involves both the strength of an individual's identification with this community and his or her affiliation with a set of cultural traditions. While the first two forms of religiosity pertain to personal or formal religious commitment in a general way, this dimension allows for an exploration of the impact that a particular set of cultural traditions may have on individuals. Studies of denominational and institutional affiliation indicate that the demands placed upon individuals by a community vary widely, and it is assumed that this variation may affect personal beliefs, practices, or well-being (Hoge 1979).

## The effects of religiosity on well-being

Empirical research has found support for the conventional wisdom that religion is "good for people." Much of this research examines the links between religiosity and positive behavioral or health-related outcomes. Studies of adults and children support the association between religious commitment and psychological well-being, positive self-concept, and good physical health (Cochran and Beeghley 1991; Donahue and Benson 1995; Ellison 1991; Oleckno and Blacconiere 1991; Poloma and Pendleton 1989). Research on adolescents suggests a connection between religious commitment and reduced incidence of drug use, sexual activity, and delinquency (Hays et al. 1986; Woodroof 1985).

Scholars have proposed a number of ways in which religion may affect well-being and health, including health behaviors and individual lifestyles, social integration and support, and positive emotions and healthy beliefs.[2] Most religious communities discourage participation in risky or deviant behavior, which may result in lifestyle patterns that promote better health. Religious involvement may also regulate behavior in ways that reduce the risk of illness or disease by encouraging moderation or dietary restrictions. The benefits of a religious life may be rooted in the social ties that are established through regular participation in religious activities. Religious communities provide support for individuals, particularly in times of stress, and this support is likely to produce measurable health and psychological benefits. Finally, the personal relationship with "divine others" (gods) fostered by religious traditions may enhance feelings of personal efficacy, self-esteem, and optimism, thus promoting a sense of security that is psychologically and physiologically beneficial.

## Religion and the family

Religion in the US is primarily a family-oriented endeavor; religious participation is highest among adults with school-age children (Stolzenberg, Blair-Loy, and Waite 1995). Parents often begin or renew their affiliation with a religious institution with the expectation that the institution will help them instill desirable values in their children. In a study of Protestant parents, Ammerman observes that "[parents] are eager for what churches can contribute to the task of bringing up their children and are convinced that churches offer something uniquely valuable not present in other kinds of community and social activities" (1997: 207). Parents may feel that religion provides an institutionalized framework of values for children to internalize, and a road map of good parenting for them to follow. Indeed, religious institutions in the US have made significant contributions to "family culture" by emphasizing the importance of family life (Ammerman and Roof 1995; Wuthnow 1998).

A primary concern of this study is to determine whether religious parents interact with their adolescents in measurably different ways than non-religious parents. The focus in this chapter is on *family processes*, which refer to the amount of time parents and adolescents spend together, the frequency with which they discuss rules and values, and the degree of challenge and support that families provide to their adolescents. Sociological research on the family has tended to focus on *family structure* (e.g., family size, composition, single- versus two-parent families), social class, and social ties (see, e.g., Lareau 2000, 2002). In contrast, psychologists, such as Baumrind (1987) have examined different parenting styles and their influence on young peoples' social and cognitive development. The term *family processes* moves beyond a focus on parents to include all family members, their interactions, and the quality of their relationships. As discussed earlier, what values parents instill in their children and how much time parents and children spend together appear to be related to religiosity. What has yet to be explored is how more intensive relationships among family members are affected by religion. The two aspects of family relationships of particular interest here are support and challenge.

Family support refers to the degree of parental and familial responsiveness to the child. Children in supportive families feel loved unconditionally, spend time with family members, and feel comfortable in their home. Family support has been linked to children's positive affective experiences (Rathunde, Carroll, and Huang 2000). Family challenge refers to the degree of stimulation a family provides for a child, and to the expectations family members have for each other. Children in a challenging family environment are encouraged and expected to take on greater responsibility, to develop autonomy, and to learn new skills. Family environments characterized by such expectations have been linked to greater engagement in purposeful, goal-directed activities, including higher school performance (Hoge, Smit, and Crist 1997; Rathunde, Carroll, and Huang 2000). An optimal family environment is one in which both challenge and support are present; when such conditions exist children feel good about themselves and are likely to confront responsibilities with competence and enthusiasm (Csikszentmihalyi and Rathunde 1993). In families where there is a religious framework for parenting and family interaction, one might expect to see higher levels of family support and challenge.

### Hypotheses

Overall, it is expected that religiosity will be positively associated with emotional well-being and specific family processes among the working families in this study.

*Hypothesis 1.* Religiosity will be associated with increased happiness, self-esteem, and caring among parents and children.

*Hypothesis 2.* Among dual-earner families, religious parents will *parent* differently from non-religious parents. Religious parents are more likely to (a) spend more time with their children; (b) have more frequent discussions with their children; and (c) provide a more supportive and challenging environment for their children.

*Hypothesis 3.* Parent religiosity will be positively associated with children's emotional well-being, and with family support and challenge regardless of the child's own religiosity. The expectation is that family processes are shaped to some degree by parents' beliefs and behaviors and that these effects will exist independent of the child's religiosity.

### Method

#### Sample

This chapter analyzes a subsample of 264 two-parent families with adolescent children who participated in the 500 Family Study.[3] Although most families in the study have multiple children, in most cases only one of these children participated in the study. The average age of adolescent participants in the subsample is fifteen and a half.

*Measures*

*Religiosity*    Several indicators of religiosity from parent and adolescent surveys are used. *Personal faith* is based on participants' responses to the question "Do you think of yourself as a religious person?" Response categories for this item were "not at all," "somewhat," and "very much." The personal faith measure is essentially an indicator of religious self-identification or subjective religiosity. *Religious participation* refers to the frequency with which participants reported attending religious services in the past year. Participants who attended services three times a month or more were considered "regular" attenders, while those who attended services less often were categorized as having only occasional participation. A third group was comprised of those who reported that they never attend religious services. *Religioius affiliation* is characterized as Protestant (Baptists, Methodists, Lutherans, Presbyterians, Episcopalians, Pentecostals, Eastern Orthodox, and Other Protestants), Roman Catholic, Jewish, and Other ("other Christians," Mormons, Muslims, Eastern religions such as Buddhism, Hindu, Tao, and anyone who defined themselves as "other religion").[4]

*Emotional well-being*    Measures of the emotional well-being of mothers and their adolescent children are taken from the Experience Sampling Method (ESM). *Happiness, self-esteem,* and feelings of *caring* toward others are measured using Likert-type scales. Overall levels of happiness, feeling good about self, and caring are computed as the average of an individual's ratings on these items over the course of the entire week.

*Family processes*    The analyses employ four different measures of family processes – two based on reports from mothers and two based on adolescent reports. *Time with child* is computed as the proportion of a mother's ESM responses for which she indicates being with her child. *Discussion of rules and values* is constructed by summing seven survey items in which mothers report the frequency with which they discussed a variety of values and rules with their children on topics such as love, money, and independence.[5]

Survey data provided by teenagers are used to construct measures of *family support* and *family challenge* using procedures developed by Rathunde in previous studies (Rathunde 1996; Rathunde, Carroll, and Huang 2000). *Support* is measured using sixteen survey items in which teenagers are asked to endorse statements such as "In my family I feel appreciated for who I am," or "We enjoy having dinner together and talking." *Family challenge* uses another sixteen items on the adolescent survey in which teenagers are asked to endorse statements such as "In my family I am expected to do my best," or "We express our opinions about current events even when they differ."[6]

*Sociodemographic indicators*   Parents' occupation was coded according to the Socio-Economic Index (SEI) developed by Nakao and Treas (1994). The family socioeconomic status indicator (SES) is the higher SEI score of either the mother or father. Controls for family structure are included in the model, such as *number of children* in the household and the *age* of the child participating in the study. Indicators of adolescents' *gender* and *mothers' weekly work hours* are also included in analyses.

### Analyses

The analyses proceed in three phases. The first set describes the role of religion in the lives of the families and examines links between personal faith, religious participation, and religious affiliation. Correlations between the religiosity of members of the same family are examined, and variations in religiosity by family characteristics such as SES and number of children are described.

The second phase of analysis explores the relationship between religiosity and the emotional well-being of parents and children, while the third phase examines the association between religiosity and family processes such as time use, discussions of rules and values, and family support and challenge. In both sets of analyses, personal faith ("Are you a religious person?") is used as the primary indicator of religiosity. Because the measures of personal faith and religious participation are highly correlated, it is not possible to independently consider both factors in statistical models given the sample size. Identification with a particular religious community is included in all models as a statistical control, but is not of primary interest in the analyses.

The second and third phases of analysis focus on mothers' religiosity rather than fathers'. This choice was made for several reasons. First, there are virtually no detectable effects of fathers' personal faith on fathers' emotion or their interactions with their children, which is consistent with previous research (Hunsberger and Brown 1984).[7] Further, participation rates in our sample are considerably lower among fathers than among mothers, and presenting analyses of fathers would further decrease the sample size. While the descriptive analysis includes fathers, the predictive analyses focus on the association between personal faith, emotion, and family processes between mothers and their children.

## Results

### Personal faith

Approximately half of the adults and children in our sample identify themselves as somewhat religious, and an additional 20 percent identify themselves as very religious. This pattern is consistent with more liberal estimates from nationally representative surveys conducted in the past decade (Gallup Poll 1995). There is a moderate amount of inter-family agreement about personal faith. The correlation between mothers' and fathers' personal faith is highest ($r = .42$, $p < .001$), followed by mothers' and children's ($r = .38$, $p < .001$), then fathers' and children's ($r = .29$, $p < .001$). In general, mothers report more often than their children or their husbands that they are very religious. While 30 percent of mothers in this sample say they are very religious, only 21 percent of fathers and 16 percent of teenagers make this same assertion. About a third of the fathers and a third of the teenagers in the sample indicate that they are not at all religious, while only about a fifth of all mothers report this. These findings are also consistent with other national studies of adult religiosity that find greater religiosity among women as compared to men by virtually every conventional indicator (Hout and Greeley 1987; Miller and Hoffmann 1995; Stolzenberg et. al. 1995). The gender difference in religious identification observed between mothers and fathers is not apparent in the younger generation; teenage boys and girls do not differ from one another in their self-reported level of personal faith.

The degree of one's personal faith is not related to the number of children in the household, the age of the child participating in the study, or the number of hours worked by mother or father. There is a relatively strong association between personal faith and SES. Mothers, fathers, and children in more affluent families tend to consider themselves less religious, while those in less affluent families have a stronger sense of personal faith.

### Religious participation

Not surprisingly, religious participation is related to personal faith. Mothers, fathers, and teenagers who identify themselves as more religious are also more likely to participate regularly in formal religious practices such as attending religious services. The correlation between personal faith and religious participation is .64 for mothers ($p < .001$), .62 for fathers ($p < .001$), and .54 for teenage children ($p < .001$). When the responses of mothers, fathers, and children regarding attendance at religious services are examined more closely, however, some interesting patterns emerge in the discrepancies between reports of personal faith and formal participation. The data suggest that family members "walk the walk" of a religious person through attendance at services to a *greater* extent than might be suggested by reports of their own personal faith.

A number of individuals report attending religious services even though they do not consider themselves to be religious. For example, one-third of the teenagers in the sample report that they are not at all religious, but about half of this group reports attending services at least occasionally, if not regularly. Considering that these are adolescents, this finding is not surprising; it is likely that many teenagers who lack a personal conviction about religion are being forced to attend religious services occasionally, or even regularly, by their parents. What is interesting, however, is that this same pattern exists, though not quite as strongly, for mothers and fathers. Over a quarter of the mothers who claim they are not at all religious report that they attend religious services occasionally or regularly. Among non-religious fathers, approximately 46 percent report attending services occasionally or regularly. Some parents may choose to attend religious services not out of personal faith but primarily because they believe it will benefit their children or because they recognize the potential benefits of social interaction and support that religious attendance provides.

When religious participation is examined through the lens of different demographic characteristics, the general pattern looks similar to that described for personal faith. Mothers in the sample attend religious services more regularly than fathers. Mothers, fathers, and teenagers from wealthier families attend religious services less regularly, while less affluent families attend more frequently. There is no consistent variation in religious attendance by number of children, hours worked per week, child's age, or child's gender.

### Religious affiliation

Of those individuals in the sample who identify themselves as religious, approximately 40 percent self-identify as being of some Protestant faith. The vast majority of these are mainline Protestants (Methodist, Episcopal, Lutheran, and Presbyterian). About a third of mothers, fathers, and teenagers identify themselves as Catholics, while approximately 15 percent identify themselves as Jewish. Approximately 10 percent of mothers and fathers identify themselves as being of an "other" religion, while just over 20 percent of teenagers identify themselves this way.

Forty percent of the couples studied identified themselves as mixed-faith couples. It is also not uncommon for teenagers to identify with a religious tradition that differs from their parents. Even when looking at those marriages in which husbands and wives profess the same faith, one quarter of these couples have a child who identifies with a different religious denomination. The proportion of adolescents identifying with "other" religions such as "other Christian," Muslim, Hindu, or Tao is double the proportion of mothers or fathers who identify with these faiths. This pattern is perhaps indicative of the process of identity development that characterizes the period of adolescence.

While the unusually high percentage of teenagers in the "other religion" category may be explained in part by identity exploration, it is also possible that the distribution of adolescents' reports of religious affiliation reflect teenagers' limited knowledge of religious denominational categories. The large percentage of teenagers who self-identify as "other Christian" suggests that some adolescents may not have been able to accurately distinguish between the many Christian denominations listed in the survey. This denominational self-report problem is a concern in many nationally representative surveys as well. It is important to approach findings regarding denomination (particularly among adolescents) with a somewhat skeptical eye because of these potential inaccuracies in adolescents' self-reporting.

There is some evidence in the data to suggest that one's religious affiliation is associated with both personal faith and attendance at religious services. Parents and children who identify themselves as Protestants are the most likely to view themselves as very religious, and are the most likely to regularly attend religious services. Parents and teenagers who identify themselves as Jewish are the least likely to say they are religious, and are the least likely to attend services regularly.

### Religiosity and emotional well-being

The data suggest fairly strongly that even though the families in the sample are extraordinarily busy, they are making time for some sort of religious life. Given the presence of religious commitment (in its many forms) among these families, it makes sense to ask, "What are the benefits of a religious life?"

*Mothers' emotional well-being*  The ordinary least squares (OLS) regression models presented in table 12.1 suggest that personal faith is consistently associated with maternal emotion. Compared to mothers who are not at all religious, those who are somewhat religious report greater levels of overall happiness in daily life. Mothers who identify themselves as very religious report still higher levels of happiness. The

Table 12.1 *Associations between maternal religiosity and maternal emotion*

| Variable | Mothers' happiness | Mothers' self-esteem | Mothers' caring |
|---|---|---|---|
| Maternal religiosity (vs. not at all) | | | |
| Somewhat religious | .21** | .04 | .11 |
| Very religious | .31** | .25** | .25** |
| Religious denomination (vs. Protestant) | | | |
| Catholic | .05 | .11 | .06 |
| Jewish | −.09 | −.06 | .02 |
| Other | .01 | −.01 | .01 |
| None | .06 | .12+ | .02 |
| Family Structure | | | |
| Age of focal child | .09 | .16* | .04 |
| 3+ children in household | −.08 | .02 | .16* |
| SES & work hours | | | |
| Family socioeconomic index | .01 | −.01 | −.10 |
| Mom works over 38 hrs/week | −.04 | −.09 | −.08 |
| Adjusted $R^2$ | .09 | .11 | .10 |

*Note:* Coefficients presented are standardized betas.
+ p < .1; * p < .05; ** p <.01

association between personal faith and happiness is independent of religious affiliation. In fact, the religious denomination with which one affiliates appears to have no measurable association with happiness. Neither family structure, family SES, nor mother's work hours is significantly associated with maternal happiness.

To provide a better sense of what the regression coefficients in table 12.1 mean, the standardized coefficients were transformed to reflect actual differences in mothers' overall happiness ratings, and the estimates for religious and non-religious mothers were compared so that the data could be interpreted in terms of relative increases or decreases in happiness for one group as compared to the other.[8] This transformation indicates relatively small differences in happiness: mothers who are somewhat religious are 6 percent happier than non-religious mothers, while mothers who consider themselves very religious are more than 10 percent happier than their non-religious counterparts.

In addition to being happier, mothers who are religious also tend to have higher self-esteem compared to non-religious mothers. This association is only apparent when comparing very religious mothers to those who are not at all religious. Mothers who are somewhat religious do not feel significantly better or worse about themselves compared to non-religious mothers. However, self-esteem among very religious mothers is nearly

20 percent higher than that of non-religious mothers. Religious affiliation appears to have little association with positive feelings toward oneself, although those claiming no specific denomination report marginally
higher self-esteem compared to Protestants. The only significant result
among the remaining control variables is that mothers with older children
tend to have higher self-esteem than those with younger children.

As expected, strong personal faith is also associated with feelings of caring toward others. Mothers who are religious report feeling significantly
more caring in general than mothers who are not religious. This difference is only statistically significant when comparing the non-religious to
the very religious, though the coefficient for somewhat religious mothers is in the expected direction. In comparison to non-religious mothers, somewhat religious mothers report feeling 9 percent more caring
and very religious mothers report feeling 22 percent more caring. As was
observed with happiness and self-esteem, religious affiliation has no association with mothers' level of caring. However, mothers who have several
children in the house tend to report feeling more caring compared with
mothers who have fewer children.

*Adolescents' emotional well-being*    Results from the analyses modeling adolescents' emotion look remarkably similar to the findings for
maternal emotion (see table 12.2). Among adolescents, those who report
being very religious are happier, feel better about themselves, and feel
more caring compared with their non-religious peers. Similar to the pattern observed for mothers, these differences are clearly discernable among
the extremes – very religious versus non-religious adolescents – while
results often fall short of statistical significance for somewhat religious
adolescents.

As is observed in the analysis of mothers' happiness, the real difference
in the happiness of religious and non-religious teenagers is statistically
significant, but somewhat small. Very religious teenagers feel 6 percent
happier than their non-religious peers. The differences in self-esteem
and caring levels of religious versus non-religious teenagers are considerably greater. Very religious teenagers report self-esteem levels that are
13 percent higher than non-religious adolescents. The effect sizes for
adolescents' caring are even more striking. Somewhat religious teenagers
report feeling 14 percent more caring toward others compared to non-
religious teenagers, though this difference only approaches statistical significance. Very religious teenagers, however, report caring levels that are
43 percent higher than those reported by non-religious teenagers.

While there are consistent associations between adolescent religiosity
and adolescent emotion, there are no discernable independent effects

Table 12.2 *Associations between religiosity and adolescents' emotion*

| Variable | Adolescents' happiness | Adolescents' self-esteem | Adolescents' caring |
|---|---|---|---|
| Adolescent religiosity (vs. not at all) | | | |
|   Somewhat religious | .11 | .12 | .13+ |
|   Very religious | .22* | .22* | .31*** |
| Maternal religiosity (vs. not at all) | | | |
|   Somewhat religious | −.04 | .06 | .01 |
|   Very religious | −.07 | .05 | −.13 |
| Religious denomination (vs. Protestant) | | | |
|   Catholic | .20* | .06 | .05 |
|   Jewish | −.04 | .01 | .03 |
|   Other | −.04 | .05 | −.01 |
|   None | .13 | .12 | .03 |
| Family structure | | | |
|   Age of adolescent | −.19* | −.09 | −.06 |
|   Adolescent is female (vs. male) | .01 | −.05 | .25*** |
|   3+ children in household | −.11 | −.06 | .03 |
| SES & work hours | | | |
|   Family socioeconomic index | .02 | −.01 | −.12 |
|   Mom works over 38 hrs/week | −.14+ | −.05 | −.04 |
| Adjusted $R^2$ | .10 | .05 | .14 |

*Note:* Coefficients presented are standardized betas.
+ $p < .1$; * $p < .05$; *** $p < .001$

of maternal religiosity on adolescents' emotional well-being. Contrary to what was predicted, when the adolescent's own personal faith has been taken into account, mother's religiosity does not add any explanatory power to the models. While mothers' religiosity undoubtedly has some influence on adolescents' religiosity (as evidenced by a correlation between the two of .38, $p < .001$), the potential emotional benefits of greater happiness, self-esteem, and caring appear in adolescents only when personal faith has been internalized.

Several other aspects of the models in table 12.2 deserve mention. While religious affiliation is not related to any aspect of maternal emotion, Catholic adolescents report significantly greater levels of happiness compared with their Protestant peers. It is not clear why this is the case, and this positive association is not replicated in the other models of adolescents' emotion. An explanation of this finding will require further inquiry that is beyond the scope of this chapter. The analysis also reveals that older adolescents tend to be less happy than younger adolescents, and teenagers whose mothers work more than 37 hours per week are slightly less happy than their peers whose mothers work fewer hours.

While table 12.2 shows a significant association between adolescents' religiosity and self-esteem, it is necessary to point out that, as a whole, the model has almost no explanatory power. Analyses presented in table 12.1 are at least marginally successful at explaining variance in mothers' self-esteem, however, the independent variables of interest do little to explain adolescent self-esteem. The model explains only 11 percent of the variance in maternal self-esteem (indicated by the adjusted $R^2$ in table 12.1); the similar model for adolescent self-esteem explains only half that much. So while there appears to be a relationship between religiosity and self-esteem among adolescents, it is important to point out that the proportion of variance being explained in the analysis is extremely small.

The model for adolescents' caring toward others has more explanatory power relative to the self-esteem model, explaining about 14 percent of the variance in caring. In addition to the positive relationship with religiosity, there is a significant association between gender and caring; on average, girls report feeling much more caring than boys.

### Family processes

The importance of family is a common theme across many religious traditions, and one might wonder whether this value is reflected differently in religious and non-religious families. Both somewhat and very religious mothers spend greater proportions of time with their children, though the association for very religious mothers is only marginally significant. There is no association between religious denomination and the amount of time mothers spend with their children. Not surprisingly, mothers tend to spend more time with younger children, and mothers with three or more children report spending more time with their children than mothers with smaller families. Because the outcome variable here refers to the time spent with the child who participated in the study the observed increase in *time with child* for mothers with more children is not simply a reflection of having more children. Rather, the data suggest that mothers who have more children still manage to spend more time with individual children in the family. The regression model shows that mothers who work over 37 hours per week spend less time with their children compared to mothers who work fewer hours. Note that the standardized regression coefficients for religiosity and work hours are roughly similar in magnitude, though opposite in direction (.19 and −.17, respectively). This means that, on average, mothers who are somewhat or very religious may gain enough time with their children to compensate for the time they lose due to work. Translated into real terms, mothers who work over

Table 12.3 *Associations between maternal religiosity and parenting*

| Variable | Time with child | Discussion of rules & values[a] |
|---|---|---|
| Maternal religiosity (vs. not at all) | | |
|   Somewhat religious | .19* | .10 |
|   Very religious | .14+ | .32*** |
| Religious denomination (vs. Protestant) | | |
|   Catholic | .08 | .04 |
|   Jewish | −.09 | −.06 |
|   Other | .10 | −.01 |
|   None | .10 | −.05 |
| Family structure | | |
|   Age of focal child | −.15* | −.02 |
|   3+ children in household | .34*** | .01 |
| SES & work hours | | |
|   Family socioeconomic index | −.07 | .03 |
|   Mom works over 38 hrs/week | −.17** | −.11+ |
| Adjusted $R^2$ | .24 | .11 |

*Note:* Coefficients presented are standardized betas.

[a] Measure constructed by summing 7 survey items regarding frequency of discussion with child

$+ p < .1$; $* p < .05$; $** p < .01$; $*** p < .001$

37 hours per week lose an average of 7 hours per week with their children, while the net effect of being religious is a 6 to 7 hour per week increase.

But what about the quality of time parents spend with their children? The parent survey asks a variety of questions about how often parents talk with their children about values and rules regarding concepts such as love, money, and independence. The data suggest that religious parents spend considerably more time than non-religious parents discussing these rules and issues with their children. Here the relationship is clearly linear, with very religious mothers saying that they discuss these issues most frequently with their children. The nature of the responses to survey questions about rules and values prevents the translation of these results into real hours or minutes; however, the regression coefficients indicate that very religious mothers report discussing these issues with their children 48 percent more often than non-religious mothers. While the degree of personal faith is associated with the frequency of discussion of rules and values, religious affiliation is not; controlling for personal faith, mothers of Protestant, Catholic, Jewish, and other faiths are equally likely to discuss rules and values with their children. Again in this model there

Table 12.4 *Associations between religiosity and family dynamics*

| Variable | Family support | Family challenge |
|---|---|---|
| Adolescent religiosity (vs. not at all) | | |
|     Somewhat religious | .15* | .22** |
|     Very religious | .20** | .24*** |
| Maternal religiosity (vs. not at all) | | |
|     Somewhat religious | −.11 | −.06 |
|     Very religious | −.15 | −.18+ |
| Religious denomination (vs. Protestant) | | |
|     Catholic | .04 | .10 |
|     Jewish | .04 | .04 |
|     Other | −.06 | −.01 |
|     None | −.01 | .04 |
| Family structure | | |
|     Age of adolescent | .10 | .12+ |
|     Adolescent is female (vs. male) | .05 | .16* |
|     3+ children in household | −.08 | −.05 |
| SES & work hours | | |
|     Family socioeconomic Index | .20** | .28*** |
|     Mom works over 38 hrs/week | −.08 | −.09 |
| Adjusted $R^2$ | .06 | .16 |

*Note:* Coefficients presented are standardized betas.
$+ p < .1;$ * $p < .05;$ ** $p < .01;$ *** $p < .001$

is some evidence of the influence of full-time employment on mothers. Mothers who work full-time report having fewer discussions with their children about values and rules, though this association is only marginally significant.

Table 12.4 indicates that adolescents who are religious perceive greater levels of support and challenge in their family environment. In comparison to non-religious teenagers, those who are somewhat or very religious report significantly greater levels of family support and challenge. Somewhat religious teenagers report levels of family support that are 35 percent higher than reported by non-religious teenagers, while adolescents who are very religious report levels of family support that are 63 percent higher than those of their non-religious peers. The patterns for family challenge are similar. Somewhat religious teenagers report levels of family challenge that are 35 percent higher than the levels of those who are non-religious; in turn, very religious adolescents report levels of challenge that are 53 percent higher than those who are non-religious.

Contrary to expectations, maternal religiosity has no independent association with teenagers' reports of family support and challenge after controlling for the adolescent's own personal faith. The one exception to this pattern is an unexpected but only marginally significant association in which teenagers with very religious mothers perceive slightly *less* family challenge than those from non-religious families. The relative absence of a relationship with maternal religiosity may at first seem surprising, since one would expect parents to be the primary providers of a supportive and challenging home. It stands to reason that if parents do indeed create such an environment for their children, and if the creation of such an environment is associated with religiosity, the association would appear when we consider *parents'* religiosity, not children's. It is important to note, however, that the constructs of family support and challenge refer to broader processes within the family unit, not just to parenting styles. These findings then suggest that, as members of a family unit, adolescents may play a crucial role in creating and maintaining a supportive and challenging home-life, and their degree of religiosity may play some role in this process. Fathers' religiosity may also contribute to the degree of support and challenge adolescents perceive in the family.

In the model for family support, neither religious affiliation nor family structure has any significant association with the outcome of interest. Adolescents from higher SES families, however, report substantially higher levels of support compared with their less advantaged peers. It should be noted that the model presented in table 12.4 explains only 6 percent of the variance in family support.

The second model in table 12.4 explains a greater proportion of the variance in family challenge – approximately 16 percent. In addition to the significant association with adolescents' religiosity, older adolescents perceive marginally greater family challenge than younger adolescents, and girls feel significantly greater family challenge than boys do. Finally, higher SES families tend to provide greater levels of family challenge than less affluent families.

Looking across the support and challenge models it is noteworthy that the coefficients for adolescent religiosity are of approximately the same magnitude as the coefficients for family SES. It is not surprising that families with more social and economic resources might be able to provide a more supportive and challenging environment for children. It is remarkable, though, that similar effects might be achieved through the development of a strong personal faith.

## Discussion

Despite the many commitments and obligations of today's working families, people are still making time for religion. Most parents and teenagers in the sample consider themselves to be at least somewhat religious, and there is evidence to suggest these families are making substantial commitments to religion in terms of time as well. Nearly half of the parents and children in the sample report regularly attending religious services, even if they do not necessarily view themselves as religious. As previously noted, even non-religious parents (particularly fathers) may attend religious services because they believe formal participation will help them instill desirable values in their children (Becker and Hofmeister 2001; Sandomirsky and Wilson 1990; Stolzenberg, Blair-Loy, and Waite 1995).

Mothers and adolescents also appear to be reaping some emotional benefits from their personal faith; those with relatively strong personal faith experience greater happiness, have higher self-esteem, and feel substantially more caring toward others. The magnitude of these associations is particularly striking compared to the size of other associations in the models. It is rather noteworthy, for example, that having strong personal faith appears to have a stronger association with mothers' daily emotion than the hours they spend at work, their socioeconomic status, or the number of children they have. In nearly all analyses predicting mothers' and adolescents' emotional well-being, the coefficients for personal faith are among the largest in the models.

The data also suggest a connection between religiosity and family processes. Mothers who are more religious spend slightly more time with their children in general, and spend more time engaging their children in discussions about rules and values. These findings are consistent with those of Wilcox (2001), who identified a broad range of family-centered practices (particularly child-centered practices like engaging in activities with the child) as hallmarks of a religious life. Such family-oriented practices might reflect a more authoritative parenting style among religious parents. Parents who take the time to articulate and discuss values and rules with their children may establish clearer expectations for their children, while the discussion of these expectations, coupled with greater time spent with children in general, may indicate a particular responsiveness to the children as well.

Examinations of family support and challenge provide mixed evidence regarding the link between religiosity and family processes at the level of the family unit. Controlling on maternal religiosity, adolescents who themselves are more religious report a family environment that is both more challenging and supportive than that reported by non-religious adolescents. These findings suggest that religion may indeed be related in a more general way to family dynamics, and that the adolescents themselves play an important role in this process. On the other hand, mothers' religiosity is not independently associated with adolescents' perceptions of support or challenge, suggesting that maternal religiosity alone may not be enough to affect these aspects of family dynamics.

Because these data are cross-sectional, it is not possible to make any firm assertions about the directionality of any of the associations discussed here. It may be that having a strong personal faith elicits positive emotions in parents and children, and adherence to a religious tradition leads parents to interact more with their children and spend more time discussing values. On the other hand, there may be some self-selection into religion such that those who are happier, feel better about themselves, and are more caring, are more likely than others to turn to religion in the first place. In an examination of religion and family involvement, Wilcox (2001) argues that positive relationships observed between religiosity and parenting are not entirely attributable to selection effects. In order to untangle the direction of causality in the ever-growing list of associations between religiosity and positive outcomes, longitudinal research is required.

As expected, there are only minimal and inconsistent associations between mothers' or children's religious affiliation (denomination) and the outcomes of interest. These non-findings may indicate that the strength of one's personal faith to a given religion may be far more important for emotional well-being and for family processes than the particular set of cultural and religious practices and values to which one chooses to subscribe. There are, of course, many other aspects of well-being and parenting that may be more strongly influenced by specific religious traditions, but these data indicate far stronger and more consistent associations for one's level of personal faith. Consistent with these findings, some studies of parenting and family outcomes have also revealed larger effects for generic religiosity measures, such as frequency of religious attendance, than for specific denominational factors (Pearce and Axinn 1998). However, other researchers find substantial denominational differences (Ellison and Bartkowski 2002; Ellison and Sherkat 1993; Wilcox 2002).

The present study has several limitations that prevent a more comprehensive inquiry into the impact of religious affiliation. The sample is not entirely representative of the diversity of religious traditions in the US, and this restriction limits the range of religious traditions both across and within the religious affiliations studied. Also, the small sample size prevents a more discrete analysis of many religious traditions (e.g., Muslim, Tao) that, because of their rarity in the sample, have to be characterized as "other religious denominations." In light of this limitation, it is recommended that future research on religious affiliation use larger, more representative samples.

A second interesting caveat to consider is that mothers' personal faith has no independent effects on adolescents' emotional well-being or perceptions of family support and challenge. While adolescents' own personal faith is associated with higher levels of happiness, self-esteem, caring toward others, and family support and challenge, mothers' personal faith does not have any influence beyond this. It appears then that simply being a religious mother may not measurably affect her children's emotional well-being unless the child has developed his or her own sense of personal faith. One might have assumed that regardless of the personal faith of adolescents, the more positive emotional states experienced by religious mothers might be transmitted to their children, or that more frequent interactions between religious mothers and their children might provide a greater sense of love and attention that would result in more positive emotional states among adolescents. One might expect that the seemingly positive interactions between religious mothers and their children would be reflected in the adolescent's perceptions of support and challenge, regardless of whether the adolescents were themselves religious. There is no evidence to suggest that this is the case.

It is possible that maternal religiosity influences both family support and challenge and adolescent religiosity, and that once adolescent religiosity is controlled for, this may reduce the estimated net effect of maternal religiosity. Another possibility is that maternal religiosity has longer-term independent effects on adolescents that are not discernable in a cross-sectional analysis (Pearce and Axinn 1998). The data suggest that religious mothers may interact with their children in slightly different ways, by spending a little more time with them, and having more frequent discussions of rules and values. Over time, these parenting practices may have measurable effects on children's behavior or well-being that are independent of the child's own personal faith.

The correlation between mothers' and adolescents' personal faith is moderate, suggesting that religious beliefs come partly, but not entirely, from parents. The nature of this study does not allow for an investigation of other sources of adolescents' religious beliefs, but it is important to acknowledge the likelihood of other influences such as the role of peers, personal life experiences, and relationships with the larger religious community. It is likely that the influence of parents' religiosity operates in much more complex ways than could be captured in the analyses presented here. For example, children may gain faith and its positive consequences not only from their parents' views, but also from the communities to which their parents connect them through participation in religious and even secular activities. Due to the sample size and the correlation between the measures of religiosity, only the influence of personal faith and religious affiliation are explored in this chapter. Future analyses should focus on participation in religious activities and other indicators of religiosity that, together with personal faith, may provide a more complex understanding of how religiosity influences adolescents.

As a final point of discussion, it is important to stress that personal faith is only one of several factors that may influence emotional well-being and family processes. Results should not be interpreted as suggesting that personal faith is the only influence – or even the most important influence – on the outcomes studied here. After all, most of the models explain only 10 to 20 percent of the variance in the outcomes of interest. Clearly, there are many other factors associated with emotional well-being and family processes that could not be adequately addressed in this study. The point of this work is not to provide an exhaustive account of the many factors that influence one's happiness, the amount of time parents and children spend together, or adolescents' perceptions of family support and challenge. Rather, the goal is to explore whether the personal faith of mothers and their adolescent children have some measurable association with these factors, particularly in the context of dual-earner families where the time parents and children can spend together is likely to be limited. While the personal faith of mothers and their adolescent children does not entirely explain the variation in the outcomes of interest, the results show consistent associations between religiosity on the one hand, and emotional well-being and family processes on the other. Just as religiosity is not the only important influence on well-being or family processes, well-being and family processes are not the only family factors likely to be influenced by religion. Future research might examine how religion affects other factors such as gender role attitudes, the distribution of domestic responsibilities in homes, specific parenting practices, marital satisfaction, and spousal relationships.

Despite these limitations, the findings regarding the importance of religion for working mothers and their children should be emphasized. As results of this study show, when mothers work full-time they spend less time with their children. However, the data indicate that some of this lost time may be regained through developing a sense of personal faith, as mothers who have a strong sense of personal faith spend more time with their children. Personal faith also seems to benefit adolescents. Strong personal faith appears to be related both to adolescents' overall emotional well-being and their positive perception of family dynamics.

NOTES

1. Differences in estimates are due to variations in wording of questions across surveys, and to a tendency to over-report church attendance (see Woodberry 1998 for a review).
2. For a discussion of these and other mechanisms see Sherkat and Ellison (1999).
3. The following criteria were used in sample selection: (1) parents are married; (2) both parents are employed; and (3) families have at least one adolescent.
4. Ideally, analyses would have distinguished mainline Protestants from conservative Protestants, but there were too few self-identified conservatives in the sample to conduct analyses using this distinction. Similarly, it would be informative to individually explore the "other" religions, but this was not possible given the sample size.
5. Seven items were used to construct *discussion of rules and values*. Mothers were asked how often they or their spouse talk with their teenager about: (1) religion/faith/spirituality; (2) expressing love or caring; (3) standing up for oneself; (4) becoming independent; (5) staying out late; (6) breaking rules; and (7) spending money. Responses were on a five-point scale, with 0 indicating "never" and 4 indicating two to three times a week. Internal consistency as indicated by Cronbach's alpha was .79.
6. Internal consistency for the support and challenge measures, as indicated by Cronbach's alpha, was .87 and .77, respectively.
7. Few studies have focused on the role of fathers in the religion–family connection. For exceptions, see Bartkowski and Xu (2000) and Wilcox (2002).
8. This transformation is calculated as follows: (1) the unstandardized coefficients are used so that reported increases or decreases are in the same metric as the original variables, and (2) the value of the unstandardized coefficient is subtracted from the intercept value and then divided by the intercept value to obtain a percent change calculation. This format is used for all effect size calculations.

# Commentary

## Don S. Browning

*My response to Schmidt's insightful chapter is based on my own academic disciplines. This means my angle of vision will come from the fields of religious studies and theology rather than the social sciences. I approach this with deep appreciation for the social sciences and with the conviction that they have much to contribute to both religious and theological studies. As a scholar in religious studies, I ask how consistent her assumptions about religion are with the best historical and comparative work in the academic study of religion. As a theologian interested in the health of both religious institutions and families, I ask what religious institutions and families have to learn from this chapter.*

*Before answering these questions, I want to highlight the importance of this study for both families and religious institutions. Much of contemporary social science predicts the eventual marginalization in modern societies of both families <u>and</u> religion. The German social theorist Jürgen Habermas (1975, 1981) argues that technical rationality in the form of both market forces and government bureaucracy increasingly can intrude upon the lifeworld of neighborhoods, families, and religious institutions. It disrupts the mutual dependencies of these spheres with demands for efficiency and gradually pushes both families and religion to the margins of modern societies.*

*Schmidt's article addresses the first half of this thesis – the market's possible marginalization of religion as a resource for families. Modernization theory suggests that families simply will not have time for religion. Her findings state rather emphatically, "Not so fast." Religion may have more influence, and offer more resources, than the theory suggests, even to families embattled by the pressures of technical rationality in the market, that is, the world of paid employment. Indirectly, the chapter addresses other aspects of this thesis as well; families may survive better within the context of modernity than theory suggests, partially due to the resources of religion. This chapter has a positive message, both for families and for religion.*

*Furthermore, from the standpoint of religious studies, this chapter handles the category of religion with nuance. Notice that Schmidt claims that most religions "value" families; she does not say that families are central to religion or that family cohesion is the main business of religions. The latter claim, often thought* to be the message of the Religious Right (Dobson and Bauer 1990), is disturbing to informed scholars of religion and theology. Religions vary considerably as to how central they consider families to be for their main objectives. Judaism and Islam assign great value to families, progeny, and lineage; however, they also are aware how families and children can become objects of idolatrous preoccupation that can obscure one's faithfulness to God's wider rule or kingdom (Browning et al. 2000). Christianity historically has been even more ambiguous about families; for some of its history it subordinated the goods of family life to the sacrality of celibacy, although even then it still valued marriage and families as worthy vocations (Witte 1997). In addition, Christianity always has been fearful that family commitments could interfere with one's obligation to do God's will. Hinduism and Buddhism value families, but also view them as transitional commitments on the way toward deeper renunciations in the later stages of life (Neusner 2001). Nonetheless, Schmidt is right: these religions valued families as long as they were properly located within a larger scheme of commitments. Furthermore, we learn from her that these religions may still be supporting families today – even dual-earner families – in spite of the pressures of the market.

From my perspective as a theologian actively interested in the strength of both religious institutions and the families they serve, I will disseminate the findings of Schmidt's research to the audiences I address. This information will come as a surprise to some religious leaders who are worried about the competition between paid work and religion. Many will be surprised to hear that a majority of adults and children in dual-earner families in Schmidt's study consider themselves "somewhat" to "very" religious. The situation of two parents in the work world does not completely squeeze out religiosity in families. These leaders will be reassured to learn that religiosity, primarily measured for methodological reasons as the personal faith of mothers, makes a positive difference. It makes a difference in these mothers' sense of emotional well-being, their self-esteem, and their sense of caring for others. And children who are religious also perceive themselves as happier, more self-confident, and more caring as well. Religious mothers take more time for their children, discuss rules and values with them more, and both challenge and support their children more. And adolescents who perceive themselves as religious report more time spent with parents, more discussion with parents, and more challenge and support from parents.

Religious leaders are advised to take seriously, however, Schmidt's extremely important observation that these effects obtain only if children have internalized their own personal religious faith; they are not a direct result of the mother's faith alone. Furthermore, ministers, priests, rabbis, and lay people – who sometimes see religion as the only important factor in people's lives – should attend with care to Schmidt's subtle demonstration that other non-religious factors *are important for these outcomes as well. In fact, religiosity, Schmidt tells us, explains roughly only "10 to 20 percent of the variance in the outcomes of interest." For example, authoritative parenting – that combination of challenge and support – is not only a characteristic of mothers with personal faith; parents with high socioeconomic status also tend to provide high expectations and warm support for their children, and do so in a way that is measurably independent from their religiosity. But in an age when the social sciences have learned so much about the positive benefits of education and income, it is, as Schmidt points out, "rather remarkable though, that similar effects might be achieved through the development of a strong personal faith." In a world where many families are not well-educated and affluent, it is extremely important to know that religion can count as well. One wonders what would happen if religiosity, education, and financial strength could be combined?*

*I conclude with several general comments. First, in my role as a theologian, I should mention that measuring religiosity by the values of emotional well-being, happiness, and self-esteem will seem to many religious adherents as insensitive, if not destructive, to the very core of their faith. Many theologians and philosophers of religion interpret the Western religious traditions as divine command traditions; the task of the faithful in these traditions is to remain obedient to God no matter what the results – even if this obedience leads to pain, unhappiness, and self-doubt. Sometimes faith, health, and other satisfactions will coincide, but often they will not. And when they do not, religious adepts – from Abraham to Job, from Jesus to the Catholic martyrs, from Luther to Kierkegaard – have said that faithful obedience should be dominant. The value of "care" seems more consistent with the self-understanding of most religions. The family process values of time with children, discussions with children, and challenge and support are more ambiguous; both utilitarian reasons or appeals to obedience to God could be given to support these values. It is perfectly legitimate for social scientists to assess the effects of religiosity by these measures of the goods of life. It should be recognized, however, that from the perspective of some respected interpretations of these religions, these measures are in reality secular and utilitarian views of life used to judge religions based on quite different understandings of the purposes of life. In view of these differences, a tone of epistemological humility should permeate such social science analyses.*

*Second, it should be remembered that Schmidt is primarily measuring perceptions, that is, subjective assessments of emotional well-being and family process. We do not know for sure whether these religious people are actually doing better in their lives in dual-earner families than the non-religious. For this reason, we should take as tentative the finding that such features as family structure and denomination have little influence on these perceptions. Findings by McLanahan and Sandefur (1994) and Amato and Booth (1997) and many other researchers suggest family structure does have a behavioral consequence for*

*the objective school performance of children, their rates of pre-marital pregnan-
cies, their delinquency rates, and their later employment success. Maybe religious
people simply assess themselves more favorably even though these judgments
may have little to do with their actual performance. Maybe family structure
and denominational affiliation make a difference in performance even though
they make little difference in the way people assess themselves.*

*As Schmidt herself indicates at the end of her important chapter, there are
many good questions that beg for more research. These questions, I hope, would
lead to an analysis of actual behavior and performance as well as attitudes and
perceptions. My own list of questions for future research parallels her own. Does
religiosity have an impact on perceptions of gender in families and also does
it influence genuine behaviors of equal regard between husbands and wives,
parents and children? Does religiosity help dual-earner families devise actual
behavioral strategies for coping with their busy lives? Do religious parents measurably spend more time with their children and actually talk and discuss with
them more in comparison to the non-religious? If so, why? Is it because these parents have more confidence that they actually have something to share with their
children and hence something more for them to discuss and mutually interpret?
Does religiosity help families find realistic and objectively measurable ways to
contain or even resist the spread into their lives of technical rationalilty in the
form of market forces? And since the market is not the only source of the disruptions of technical rationality, does religiosity help families deal with those
stemming from governmental and other forms of bureaucratic reason? Good
research of the kind found in this informative chapter always leads to further
questions.*

*Part V*

# Parenting and adolescent development

# Overview

*Phillip L. Hammack*

Post-industrial life in the West has radically altered the cultural landscape of human development. The economic forces which shape both social and individual consciousness have shifted away from an emphasis on *material* production (in the Marxist sense) and toward a focus on *informational* production, which relies heavily on interpersonal processes. The middle-class jobs of the West have become increasingly tied to service and information. With these economic changes emerge new contexts for individual engagement with productive work and reformulations of social roles and identities.

Over the past half-century, the sharp increase in dual-earner families has caused a fundamental cultural shift fueled in part by social movements and the permeation of feminist philosophy into popular discourse. How has this shift in the nature of families affected the development of adolescents? How does the larger cultural ethos toward dual-earner families impact the ideological concerns of youth? How do *parents* – those in the first generation of dual-earner families – influence their adolescents' identities? During adolescence, individuals further develop their identity by synthesizing understandings from childhood with the social system in which they are culturally embedded (Erikson 1959). How do youth integrate their parents' identities into their own?

This section of the book seeks to address this broad question by focusing on parental influence. Through an examination of critical factors such as role management, occupational identity, gender role ideology, and education-related beliefs and values, results show that adolescents do indeed form their identities through a dynamic engagement with the qualities of their parents.

The life course of individuals is always historically and culturally situated (Elder 1998; Shweder 1998), but it is first and foremost located within the family system. In adolescence, as the social sphere of influence extends to an exosystem outside the home, the formation of self assumes primacy. Adolescents attempt to resolve parents' examples and influence with expanding social ideology in order to create the adult self. Examination of youth from this first generation of dual-earner families illuminates this larger process of self-development in social and historical perspective and thus provides insights into the next generation of working parents.

# 13 Adolescents' assessments of parental role management in dual-earner families

*Elaine Marchena*

Many parents, especially those in dual-earner families, experience work–family role conflict (Crouter et al. 2001; Greenhaus and Beutell 1985; Kandel, Davies, and Raveis 1985). While this conflict can affect all members of the family, not just the workers, relatively little is known about how work–family conflict is experienced by other members of the household, particularly children. This is an important omission because just as parents' occupations can shape adolescents' career aspirations (see Kalil, Levine, and Ziol-Guest, this volume), parents' ability to role manage – to negotiate the demands of work and family – may also influence adolescents' goals for work and family life. As such, it is important to know what aspects of parental work and children's family life enter most prominently into adolescents' assessments of parents' work–family role management.

The last few decades have brought significant changes to the family context in which children are raised, especially with regard to the work patterns of two-parent families (US Bureau of the Census 2001). In the majority of two-parent families both parents are employed,[1] and both remain fairly committed (either out of desire or economic necessity) to their work roles throughout their adult lives. This demographic shift first drew attention to how children's well-being was affected by mothers' employment, with a particular focus on the impact of mothers' absence on children's emotional and cognitive development. Early studies tended to contrast working and non-working mothers (see Spitze 1991 for a review). However, questions regarding variation in the experiences of children *within* the population of children raised by working mothers – and, in particular, the experiences of adolescents in dual-earner families – have been largely left unanswered.

In this chapter, the focus on adolescents is motivated by the realization that adolescence is an important period of identity formation and a time when children start thinking about future personal, occupational, and ideological commitments (Erikson 1964; Taylor 1989). Parents provide the most immediate role models for their children's social learning, and the way parents manage their work and family roles may help to shape

333

adolescents' work and family values and provide learning examples of how adolescents can manage role conflict in their own lives.

Adolescents experience their parents' jobs within the context of the family. Thus, to understand how adolescents are influenced by their parents' employment, this context must be considered. While adolescents may know their parents' job titles and have a sense of their parents' general job duties, they are more apt to experience their parents' jobs through the impact these jobs have on their own daily lives. However, in parental work research, this intersection of work and family life from the *adolescent's perspective* remains largely unexplored.

This chapter uses a role-conflict framework to examine the intersection of work and family life. This framework expands the scope of inquiry and refocuses attention from whether children are affected by mother's employment to how children's lives are shaped by the work experiences of mothers *and* fathers. A particular drawback of previous research is that it has examined mothers' employment status outside the context of the family. This abstraction treats mothers the same regardless of whether they are married with a working spouse, single with additional social and economic support, or single without any support. Such a paradigm is potentially problematic, particularly when looking at two-parent families. First, because couples may make employment decisions jointly, the simple working versus non-working mother distinction is unable to ascertain whether or not associations with maternal employment are in part associations with characteristics of *paternal* employment. And second, it does not consider how parents are managing both work and family roles and thus treats all working families as equal.

To examine how parents and their adolescents experience parental work–family conflict, this chapter uses data from surveys administered to parents and adolescents in the 500 Family Study. The first set of analyses examines how parents' subjective experiences of work–family role conflict are associated with time constraints and strain in both the work and family domains. This preliminary step towards understanding adolescents' assessments reveals significant differences in the way that mothers and fathers experience role conflict. Parental work characteristics are then used to model *adolescents'* assessments of each parent's ability to manage work and family roles. This part of the analysis examines adolescents' own perceptions of conflict between work and family, and adds their perspective on family relationships. These analyses show that although parents experience moderate to high levels of work–family conflict, their adolescents make rather favorable assessments of their ability to manage work and family roles. This finding may stem from the fact that parents' experiences of role conflict and adolescents' assessments of their parents' ability to manage conflict are fundamentally rooted in fairly similar aspects of the work–family experience.

## Defining work–family conflict

A discussion of adolescents' assessments of parental role management begins with the closely related concept of *role conflict*. Role conflict occurs when there are two or more sets of demands or expectations that are difficult to meet simultaneously (Kahn et al. 1964). These conflicts can arise because: (1) two sets of actors make competing demands on the individual; (2) one actor makes multiple demands that conflict with one another; or (3) the individual's own actions conflict with his or her expectations or values. More specifically, inter-role conflict is experienced when membership in one group makes it difficult to fulfill obligations in another.

Greenhaus and Beutell (1985) apply this notion of inter-role conflict to define the experience of work–family role conflict (WFRC). They describe WFRC as "a form of inter-role conflict in which the role pressures from work and family domains are mutually incompatible in some respects" (1985: 77). They elaborate on the concept by making distinctions between three forms of work–family role conflict, two of which are relevant to this analysis. The first, *time-based* conflict, occurs because of competing time demands made on parents by family and work domains. Time spent on work-related activities translates into time away from children, spouses, and less time for individual pursuits; similarly, family obligations may conflict with career pursuits. The second, *strain-based* conflict, arises when stress produced in one domain is carried over to the other, making it difficult to fulfill the role obligations of the second domain. For example, this can take the form of coming home from work (or going into work) feeling tired, depressed, or irritable.

This model of role conflict conceptualizes WFRC as being potentially bi-directional. That is, work can intrude on home and home can intrude on work. However, the few studies that include bi-directional effects consistently find that compared to family intrusions on work, work intrusions on home life are more frequent and pervasive (Eagle, Miles, and Icenogle 1997). Thus, how work shapes family life has been the focus of most role conflict research.

## Work–family conflict as experienced by men and women

Given the multiple tasks involved in the roles of wife, mother, and worker, it is surprising that research does not always find higher levels of work–family conflict among women compared to men (higher: Hammer, Allen, and Grisby 1997; lower or no difference: Eagle, Miles, and Icenogle 1997). This lack of consistent evidence might stem from the degree to which dual-earner couples follow traditional gender role patterns in accommodating careers of spouses. When WFRC exists in a given household, wives may be more likely than husbands to restructure their work in order to meet family needs (Karambayya and Reilly 1992). Studies have also shown that women are more likely than men to relieve their role conflict by relying on their social networks (Jones and Fletcher 1993).

However, the absence of large gender differences in WFRC might also stem from differences in the way men and women experience work–family conflict. If the primary factors that influence women's WFRC are related to concern over childcare or household task burdens, women can reduce WFRC by making alternative child care arrangements or by purchasing household services (see, e.g., Stuenkel, this volume). On the other hand, if men's experience of conflict is tied to the emotional demands and physicality of work, then the family strategies for reducing role conflict are not as readily apparent.

To move past simple speculations, WFRC research needs to be reframed to include the work and family experiences of couples. Early research inferred couples' experiences by using the reports that men and women gave of their spouses' work schedules. Data sets that included married couples and contained multiple measures of work and family domains were rare; thus, only a handful of studies on WFRC have been able to examine the couple as a unit. These studies suggest that there are crossover effects, such that characteristics of a spouse's job also influence one's own experiences of WFRC (Hammer, Allen, and Grisby 1997; Parasuraman, Greenhaus, and Granrose 1992). Additional analyses of daily psychological states suggest that the crossover effects may be greater for women since the flow of negative emotions runs predominantly from husbands to wives (Larson and Richards 1994).

## Parents' work and children's well-being

The earliest studies concerning work and children's well-being focused on young child outcomes, primarily because it was believed that children's emotional and cognitive development was being jeopardized by their working mothers' absence (Perry-Jenkins, Repetti, and Crouter 2000). While some researchers uncovered a relationship between maternal employment during children's infancy and children's subsequent cognitive and social outcomes (Han, Waldfogel, and Brooks-Gunn 2001), others found that either maternal employment had no direct effect or, in some cases, enhanced cognitive outcomes for children (Vandell and Ramanan 1992).

Relatively few studies have examined how work is related to adolescent outcomes. Much of the research on parental work and adolescents has focused on the link between parental work stress and parent–child relationships, since the quality of parental relationships are important for healthy adolescent psychological adjustment (Crouter et al. 1999). Data collected from surveys and time diaries provide evidence that parents' work stress does affect parental–child interaction. Fathers' work-related stress is particularly pervasive; fathers' negative emotions are more likely than mothers' to spill over to other family members (for a review of emotional transmission literature, see Larson and Almeida 1999). Perhaps in an attempt to decrease the impact of stress on children, parents are also more likely to withdraw from children after particularly stressful days at work (Repetti and Wood 1997).

The demands of work, particularly hours of work, also tend to decrease parents' knowledge about their adolescents' lives, especially among fathers (Crouter et al. 1999). Interestingly, fathers know more about their children's daily experiences the more time mothers spend working – a finding that is consistent with studies that indicate an increase in father's involvement the more time mothers spend at work (Coltrane 1996). Compared to fathers, however, mothers maintain a rather high level of involvement and knowledge about children's lives regardless of their work commitments.

Such behavior may stem from gender differences in parenting and family roles, even in families where parents hold fairly egalitarian views about general household management. These differences in family roles should reveal themselves in the ways parents experience role conflict. Being an economic provider is still a major aspect of men's family role, while for women adoption of the worker role is considered a matter of choice (Coltrane 1996). Contributing time and energy to work – even if it means less time with children or spouses – is consistent with expectations of men's family roles.

In contrast, a major part of women's family roles is devoting time and energy to the management of household affairs and overseeing the well-being of other family members. Regardless of their work status, women are still primarily responsible for housework and childrearing (Bianchi et al. 2000). Perhaps even more important, their status as wage contributor does not exempt them from taking on the burdens of being the family manager. Even in egalitarian households women are still primarily responsible for paying bills, scheduling doctor appointments, attending school meetings, arranging for household repairs, and maintaining family ties to extended kinship networks and the community (Goldscheider and Waite 1991). Add to this the less-visible work of caring, which makes psychological demands on women. Women's role conflict is thus likely to be high and deeply rooted in aspects of both work and family life.[2]

### Children's perspective

Why should children's views on the matter be examined? Children's perspective on work–family conflict provides a point of contrast to how mothers and fathers define their levels of work–family conflict, while still being tied to the gender role expectations of the teen. Adolescents may have a different perspective on work–family conflict because their desires and expectations for parenting roles may not be the same as those that parents hold for themselves.

While the majority of parents report having too little time with their children, their teens are much less likely to report that they spend too little time with their parents (Galinsky 1999). This discrepancy may stem in part from having different generational perspectives. The older generation may mark time in relation to the past; thus time is a precious commodity that passes too quickly. Among youth, time may be marked by reference to the future; time seems to stretch out endlessly before them. In addition, adults are socialized to feel guilty about spending time away from children, while children are socialized to think of time away from parents as an expression of independence. There is no doubt that children expect a minimal amount of parental presence – ethnographic data show that children are particularly starved for interaction with fathers (Galinsky 1999). However, teenagers' lives may be filled with school, recreational activities, peer group interactions, romantic interests, and even their own work. Adolescents (especially older ones) may be less likely to notice parental absence than parents are to notice theirs.

Parents may also not realize that their work can have positive socializing benefits on family life. Wilson (1996) argues that employment has more than just economic benefits for children. Work schedules provide neighborhoods and homes with a daily rhythm that structures children's lives. While Wilson makes this argument primarily to emphasize the importance of work in poor communities, his argument suggests that work has the potential to structure family life if work itself is patterned and predictable. In addition to organizing time, certain types of jobs can help build skills that might translate into more effective parenting at home.

For instance, researchers theorize that exposure to job autonomy discourages authoritarian parenting styles, leading to better parenting and possibly fewer adolescent problem behaviors (Galinsky 1999). Similarly, the level of job task complexity has been found to be related to a mother's ability to provide a positive home environment (Parcel and Menaghan 1994a).

Another reason that adolescents may have a different perspective on work–family conflict may be that parents may actually *do* a better job than they think at managing work–family conflict. Figures from the Gallup Youth Survey (Bezilla 1993) indicate that the majority of teens acknowledge that parents face problems and pressures that are greater than their own (65 percent), but most of them assess their parents as handling these problems and pressures very well (54 percent). An overwhelming majority of adolescents also report that they get along at least fairly well with their parents (96 percent), suggesting that most parent–child relationships are not particularly strained. Although children's assessments of parents may be biased upwards – they may be reluctant to make negative assessments of parents – the way their assessments relate to characteristics of parents' jobs and parents' own reports of role conflict could still provide reliable information about the degree to which parents moderate the effects of work on family life.

## Hypotheses

### Parents' perceptions of work–family role conflict (WFRC)

Role conflict theory provides a useful framework for deriving hypotheses about how role conflict is related to both characteristics of work and circumstances at home. Specifically, predictions can be made about how work–family role conflict derives from both time-based conflict and strain-based conflict:

*Hypothesis 1P.* Parents will perceive higher levels of WFRC when they work longer hours, work non-standard shifts, are often on call, have lower job autonomy, or experience higher levels of work strain.

*Hypothesis 2P.* Parents will perceive lower levels of WFRC when they work in family-friendly environments. Some work environments are more family-friendly than others, and those parents who work in family-friendly environments should feel less pressure to choose work over family.

*Hypothesis 3p.* Net of their own work characteristics, wives and husbands will report higher WFRC when their spouse also expresses high levels of WFRC. When work and family conflict, a spouse may be called upon to take on more of the home responsibilities – essentially increasing the demands that the family makes on the spouse.

*Hypothesis 4p.* Parents will express higher levels of WFRC when there are shortages in time spent with family members. At first glance, this hypothesis may seem little more than stating a definition: role conflict is a shortage of time and strain in roles. However, net of work characteristics – that is, net of the actual structural aspects of work–family conflict – parents experience role conflict because certain aspects of family life are not meeting their ideals. Since the focus in the media has been on family time, this analysis considers how involvement with children and shared spousal leisure time enters into parents' experiences of role conflict.

*Hypothesis 5p.* Compared to fathers, mothers should report higher levels of WFRC since role responsibilities attached to parent, spouse, and worker potentially conflict more often for women than for men.

*Hypothesis 6p.* The associations between WFRC, work characteristics, and family life will be stronger among mothers than among fathers since mothers are more likely than fathers to be family managers.

### *Adolescents' perceptions of work–family role management (WFRM)*

Because there is relatively little research that focuses on adolescents' perceptions of work and family life, there is not much by way of theory to predict which family experiences enter most prominently into adolescents' assessments of parents' ability to manage both work and family responsibilities. While public attention has tended to focus on the negative impact that work has on family time, it is not known whether adolescents are more inclined to make their assessments based on quality of relationships or on quantity of interactions.

The literature on work–family conflict has found little direct relationship between parents' job characteristics and various family outcomes. This is likely because parents act in ways to intervene or moderate the effects of work on family life. However, when making assessments of parental role management, adolescents should still be particularly sensitive to those aspects of work that impinge on the daily routines of family life.

*Hypothesis 1$_A$.* The greater the frequency of work interruptions on family life, the poorer adolescents rate their parents' role management.

*Hypothesis 2$_A$.* The more maternal and paternal acceptance, the better assessments children make of their parents. Given that adolescence is marked by increasing independence, children are likely to be more sensitive to the interpersonal aspects of their relationships with parents, rather than the amount of quality time they spend together.

*Hypothesis 3$_A$.* Home-life characteristics will be more significant predictors of the assessments adolescents make of mothers' WFRC compared to those they make of fathers' WFRC. Very little is known as to whether adolescents hold their mothers or fathers more responsible for certain aspects of family life. However, mothers are more often the managers of children's day-to-day activities, while a father's work is central to his role in the family.

## Method

### Sample

The sample consists of 226 adolescents and their parents who participated in the 500 Family Study. Of the 361 adolescents in the study with available survey information, just under 68 percent were from two-parent, dual-earner families (some parents were looking for work at the time of the survey, but are not included in this analysis). Dual-earner families were defined as any household consisting of two parents (biological, adoptive, or fictive) who were both employed for pay at the time of the study. An additional 5 percent of the sample was dropped due to parent non-response. After exclusions, the adolescent–parent sample analyzed in this chapter consists of 226 mother–adolescent dyads and 198 father–adolescent dyads from dual-earner families.

The sample is predominantly non-Hispanic white (86 percent of adolescents), with slightly more adolescent females (52 percent) than males (48 percent). The average age of adolescents is 15½ (range = 11–19). Parents in the sample are highly educated (more than 50 percent of mothers and fathers hold at least a master's degree) and have relatively high incomes (mothers' average salary = $44,000; fathers' = $74,000). The average family size is 4.5. Results do not vary by any of these variables. Descriptive statistics for the measures used in analyses appear in table 13.1

Table 13.1 *Variable descriptive statistics – mothers, fathers, and adolescents*

| Variable | Range | Mothers | | | Fathers | | | |
|---|---|---|---|---|---|---|---|---|
| | | Mean | % in highest cat. | Std. dev. | Mean | % in highest cat. | Std. dev. | Diff – sig[a] |
| **Dependent** | | | | | | | | |
| Work–family role conflict (WFRC) | 1–3 | 2.26 | 39.27 | .68 | 2.19 | 31.96 | .64 | |
| Work–family role management (WFRM) | 1–3 | 2.49 | 63.18 | .73 | 2.23 | 47.25 | .81 | *** |
| **Independent – parent perspective** | | | | | | | | |
| # of work hours | 8–85[b] | 37.52 | – | 13.46 | 49.10 | – | 8.46 | *** |
| Non-standard work schedule | 0–1 | – | 27.35 | .45 | – | 17.10 | .37 | * |
| Work autonomy | −2.8–1.24 | −.03 | – | .94 | .08 | – | .90 | |
| Work strain | −3.3–2.6 | .00 | – | .80 | −.05 | – | .88 | |
| Work on demand | 1–3 | 1.40 | 7.69 | .63 | 1.69 | 18.46 | .77 | *** |
| Family friendly work environment | 0–1 | – | 86.61 | .34 | – | 88.06 | .33 | |
| Satisfied leisure time w/spouse | 1–5 | 3.44 | – | 1.19 | 3.46 | – | 1.06 | |
| Shared activities with adolescent | 10–30 | 21.41 | – | 1.87 | 21.03 | – | 1.99 | ** |
| Marital satisfaction | 1–3 | 2.44 | – | .73 | 2.48 | – | .71 | |
| Ease of parenting | 1–5 | 3.32 | – | .73 | 3.37 | – | .72 | |
| **Independent – adolescent perspective** | | | | | | | | |
| Brings work home/feels ignored | 0–2 | .62 | 9.18 | .65 | .66 | 10.80 | .66 | |
| Family work-interruptions | 0–4 | 1.00 | – | .70 | 1.31 | – | .80 | *** |
| Shared activities with parents[c] | 10–30 | 20.60 | – | 2.12 | 20.60 | – | 2.12 | |
| Organization of the household[c] | 0–3 | 1.94 | – | .53 | 1.94 | – | .53 | |
| Parent makes time for adolescent | 0–4 | 1.93 | – | 1.13 | 1.88 | – | 1.09 | |
| Maternal/paternal closeness | 8–32 | 21.10 | – | 3.84 | 19.76 | – | 3.38 | *** |

[a] t-tests for significant differences between mothers and fathers.

[b] One father, an occupational therapist, holds 2+ jobs and has a wife that is employed part-time. Without his work hours, the range for this variable is 8–66. Results are the same with and without this case included in the analyses.

[c] Some measures are collected in reference to both parents at the same time, or in reference to the household. Averages and standard deviations are listed in the table as identical for mothers and fathers. Testing for differences was not applicable in these instances.

* p < .05; ** p < .01; *** p <.001

*Measures*

*Work–family role conflict (WFRC) and work–family role manage-ment (WFRM)*     The primary dependent variables are work–family role conflict (WFRC) as reported by each parent, and work–family role management (WFRM) as reported by the adolescent for each parent. Parents were each asked how often they felt that work and family roles conflict (WFRC); adolescents were asked how well their parents balanced work and family life (WFRM).

Parents' reports on conflict clustered at the center, with very few parents reporting that they experience work–family conflict either "never" or "always." The five categories for this set of variables were collapsed into three, distinguishing between parents who experienced "low," "medium," and "high" WFRC. Ideally, multiple items would be used to measure this construct – especially if there is interest in both the degree of work–family conflict (missing important family events, having trouble picking up children, being late for work because of family tasks, missing workdays because of child's illness, etc.) as well as the frequency. However, since such variables are lacking, a single global question regarding work–family role conflict is used. This question varies in the degree to which it correlates with other psychological variables (moderate correlations with variables such as coping and control) as well as other structural variables (such as work schedules and job flexibility). The patterns of correlation suggest that this measure captures both psychological dimensions of conflict (feeling role strain) as well as actual reports of occurrences (given the wording of the question).

Although adolescents were asked to rate their parents' WFRM on a five-point scale, fewer than 6 percent of cases appeared in the bottom three categories. These three categories were collapsed into a single category. The final variable thus has 3 categories that group adolescents' responses into "never/rarely/sometimes," "often," or "always." These categories were renamed to reflect three levels of performance: 1 = Fair; 2 = Good; and 3 = Excellent. T-test statistics indicate that mothers and fathers do not experience significantly different levels of conflict, but that adolescents are more likely to report better WFRM by mothers than by fathers ($p < .001$).

*Parents' perspective: job characteristics*     To assess time constraints imposed by job responsibilities, a measure of total work hours is used. This measure is the sum of hours spent on work (including offsite hours and weekends) and hours from second jobs. While work hours may be a constraint on family time, the way these hours are scheduled may produce an even more significant effect. Non-standard day schedules (or shift work) make adult family members unavailable just when other members are likely to be at home. Work schedules are categorized using a dummy variable that contrasts parents who work within regular business hours (6 a.m. to 6 p.m.) against those who work outside those hours.

Since the freedom to structure one's work environment and schedule can mediate the impact of work hours, a measure for work autonomy is also included. This variable, along with the measure of job strain, was constructed using factor analyses. The factor for work autonomy reflects items dealing with the opportunity to make one's own decisions; to have a say over what happens at one's job; and the freedom to plan one's day. The factor for work strain reflects finishing a work day feeling physically exhausted; coming home from work feeling angry or hostile; coming home from work feeling drained of energy; and, finding work stressful.

Parents may also feel less role conflict when they work in environments that are more tolerant of family–work interruptions. The extent that a work place is tolerant of family–work interruptions is measured using parents' responses regarding being able to make family-related phone calls without feeling guilty. This item was part of a series of "yes–no" questions regarding tolerance of family matters in the work place, but this was the only item that showed variance in responses.

The patterns of family life may also be disrupted when parents are asked to work on demand. A variable was created to distinguish among parents who were called in to work (1) once or twice a year or less; (2) once or twice a month; and (3) once or more a week.

*Home characteristics*    Home characteristics are entered into models in order to capture how perceptions of family time and strained family roles are associated with WFRC. Time constraints and strains as they relate to spousal roles are first considered. Although a measure of the *amount* of time couples actually spend together is not available from survey data, a single item from a marital satisfaction scale was used to measure how satisfied wives and husbands were with the way they and their spouses managed leisure activities and the time they spend together. *Marital satisfaction* is also measured, using the global statement "Overall I am satisfied with my relationship with my spouse/partner." Both satisfaction with leisure time and marriage were measured using a five-point Likert scale (1 = Strongly Disagree to 5 = Strongly Agree). However, given the heavily skewed responses to the marital satisfaction item, the "disagree" and "neutral" ratings were collapsed into one category. Although leisure and marital satisfaction are correlated ($r_m$ = .38; $r_f$ = .42), they make unique contributions to the models.

Time constraints and role strain as they pertain to parenting are captured using scales that measure each parent's report of sharing activities with their adolescent, and each parent's report of their parenting ease. The measure of *shared activities* was constructed using Rasch rating-scale analysis (Wright and Masters 1982) on ten items that asked how frequently each parent engaged in particular activities with their adolescent.[3] Each item was measured on a rating scale of 1 = Rarely to 3 = Almost everyday. According to parents, they and their adolescents engaged most frequently in talking and eating meals together, and least frequently in sports/athletic activities. The final scale of ten items ranges from 10 to 30.

For each parent, a measure of *ease of parenting* was constructed using four items that deal with various dimensions of parenthood, including items such as how their parenting experiences compared to their expectations, and how difficult it is to parent their particular adolescent. These items were reverse coded to reflect parenting ease (alpha: mothers = .70; fathers = .71).

Summary measures on the independent variables reveal significant differences between mothers and fathers. Mothers work fewer hours (p < .001), are less likely to get called into work unexpectedly (p < .001), and report a greater degree of interaction with their adolescent (p < .01).

*Adolescents' perspective: parents' jobs and home-life characteristics*
Parents' own reports of WFRC, hours of work, schedules, job autonomy, and work strain are used in the analyses of adolescent global assessments of WFRM. However, adolescents provided their unique perspective on the intersection of work and family by responding to questions on the occurrence of certain events as they relate to each of their parent's work. Adolescents were asked how often each parent brought work home from the office and, if their parents worked from home, whether adolescents felt ignored while their parents worked. They were combined to construct a variable that contrasts (0) adolescents who observe their parents work at home never/rarely; (1) adolescents who observe their parents work, but do not feel ignored while their parents do so; and (2) adolescents who observe their parents work and feel ignored.

The extent that work interrupts daily routines was measured using the average frequency with which each parent (1) worked longer than expected; (2) was called into work unexpectedly; and (3) missed school meetings or special events in which adolescents participated. The items were rated on a scale ranging from 0 = Never to 4 = Every day (alpha reliability for mother's job = .53; for father's job = .65). Higher values on the scale indicate more work-to-family interruptions.

A measure of the organizational climate of the home was constructed from the average agreement with the items (1) "Day-to-day life is disorganized and unpredictable" (reverse coded); (2) "We compromise when schedules conflict"; (3) "We are willing to help each other out when something needs to be done"; and (4) "There are many fights and arguments" (reverse coded). Each item was rated on a scale ranging from $0 =$ Never to $3 =$ Every day. Higher values on the scale indicate better organization of the home.

The remaining variables were all derived from questions based on adolescents' reports of their family life. Using the same items as those that appear in parents' reports of shared activities, a scale for *shared activities with parents* is composed for adolescents. Unfortunately, this measure comes from adolescents' reports on engaging in particular activities with *either* of their parents, and as such is not the best indicator for children's involvement with each parent. Nevertheless, Rasch analysis reveals a pattern in item ordering that is fairly similar to that of the scale constructed for parents' shared activities with adolescents. Adolescents are most likely to report sharing meals and talking about everyday events with parents, and least likely to report partaking in athletic activities with parents.[4] The item rating scale ranges from $1 =$ Rarely to $3 =$ Almost every day. The final scale of ten items ranges from 10 to 30.

The last two scales are based on identical items regarding adolescent–parent relationships. Each set of questions was asked about mothers and fathers separately. Rasch analyses revealed the same construct map for both maternal and paternal closeness. That is, the eight items that describe both maternal and paternal closeness are ordered identically. Adolescents were most likely to report that their mother/father accepts them for who they are, and least likely to say that their mother/father helps them to talk about their problems. Finally, adolescents' reports of how often each parent takes a day off from work to spend time with them are used to test whether adolescents are responsive to their parents' gestures of foregoing work to be with them.

A summary of the measures indicates that work interruptions from father's jobs were more frequent than those from mothers ($p < .001$). Adolescents also indicate closer relationships with mothers than with fathers ($p < .001$).

### Analytic strategy

Analyses were conducted in two separate stages. The first focuses on parental reports of work–family role conflict (WFRC). The second examines how adolescents assess their parents' work–family role management (WFRM). Given the categorical nature of the dependent variables, the models are estimated using ordinal probit analyses. The model assumes that the ordinal variables serve as indicators of a normally distributed latent variable, and that a particular response is observed in the measure when the latent variable reaches a certain threshold. The model takes the form:

$$\text{Prob } (y = 1) = \Phi\left[ -\sum_{k=1}^{k} \beta_k x_k \right]$$

$$\text{Prob } (y = 2) = \Phi\left[ \mu_2 - \sum_{k=1}^{k} \beta_k x_k \right] - \Phi\left[ -\sum_{k=1}^{k} \beta_k x_k \right]$$

$$\text{Prob } (y = 3) = \Phi\left[ \mu_3 - \sum_{k=1}^{k} \beta_k x_k \right] - \Phi\left[ \mu_2 - \sum_{k=1}^{k} \beta_k x_k \right]$$

where $\Phi$ is the normal cumulative distribution function, $\mu$s are the unknown threshold parameters (cutoff points) that separate the categories of the dependent variable, $\beta$s are the effect coefficients to be estimated, and k is the number of variables.

Models for mothers' and fathers' reports of their WFRC are estimated separately, as are adolescents' assessments of each parent. To provide a sense of the size of effects, the transformed coefficients are reported to reflect the change in probability (with all other variables held at the mean) of reporting a high level of WFRC (in the models for parents) or an excellent assessment of WFRM (in the models for adolescents). Effects are calculated in terms of a one standard deviation change in independent variables that are treated as continuous, and in terms of a discrete change in categorical variables.[5] Since standard errors are different for mothers and fathers, the calculated probabilities for changes in variables are not directly comparable. However, the scales of the independent variables are equivalent across the parent models, and thus coefficients can be compared.

### Results

*Predicting work–family conflict of mothers and fathers*

*Mother's self-reported WFRC*    Table 13.2 displays the coefficients from two different sets of ordered probit models: one predicting mothers' reports of WFRC, the other predicting fathers' (categories for WFRC are

Table 13.2 Ordered probit models predicting mothers' and fathers' self-reported work–family role conflict (WFRC) from work and family characteristics – coefficients and changes in probabilities of predicting "high" conflict at the mean[a,b]

| | Mother's self-reported WFRC | | | | | | Father's self-reported WFRC | | | | | |
|---|---|---|---|---|---|---|---|---|---|---|---|---|
| | [1] Coef | Δ prob. | [2] Coef | Δ prob. | [3] Coef | Δ prob. | [1] Coef | Δ prob. | [2] Coef | Δ prob. | [3] Coef | Δ prob. |
| Work characteristics | | | | | | | | | | | | |
| # of work hours | .00 | –.03 | | | .00 | –.02 | –.01 | –.02 | | | –.01 | –.02 |
| Non-standard work schedule | .85 | .13*** | | | .93 | .15*** | –.33 | –.04 | | | –.29 | –.04 |
| Job autonomy | –.26 | –.10** | | | –.29 | –.12** | –.18 | –.05 | | | –.11 | –.03 |
| Work strain | .24 | .07 | | | .27 | .08* | .59 | .17*** | | | .52 | .15*** |
| Family-friendly work environment | –.37 | –.05 | | | –.48 | –.06 | –1.04 | –.11*** | | | –1.19 | –.13*** |
| Work on demand – less than monthly [ref] | | | | | | | | | | | | |
| Work on demand – monthly | .35 | .06 | | | .41 | .07 | –.04 | .00 | | | .07 | .01 |
| Work on demand – weekly | 1.31 | .13** | | | 1.23 | .12* | .42 | .06 | | | .60 | .09* |
| Spouse's WFRC – Low [ref] | | | | | | | | | | | | |
| Spouse's WFRC – Med | .52 | .08 | | | .49 | .07 | .13 | .02 | | | .25 | .04 |
| Spouse's WFRC – High | .79 | .13** | | | .93 | .15** | .43 | .07 | | | .45 | .07 |
| Home life characteristics – parents reporting | | | | | | | | | | | | |
| Leisure time w/ spouse | | | –.10 | –.04 | .03 | .02 | | | –.30 | –.12*** | –.25 | –.09** |
| Marital satisfaction | | | –.02 | .01 | .02 | .02 | | | .09 | .03 | .17 | .04 |
| Time with adolescent | | | –.13 | –.08** | –.12 | –.08** | | | –.03 | –.03 | –.06 | –.04 |
| Ease of parenting | | | –.39 | –.13** | –.51 | –.16** | | | –.35 | –.08** | –.35 | –.08** |
| Ancillary parameters | | | | | | | | | | | | |
| cut 1 | –.88 | | –5.62 | | –5.06 | | –2.47 | | –3.98 | | –5.37 | |
| cut 2 | .73 | | –4.18 | | –3.32 | | –.47 | | –2.21 | | –3.27 | |
| N | 175 | | 175 | | 175 | | 179 | | 179 | | 179 | |
| Likelihood ratio | 55.48 | | 24.14 | | 77.52 | | 54.70 | | 21.57 | | 69.53 | |
| Df | 12 | | 4 | | 16 | | 12 | | 4 | | 16 | |
| Pseudo R² | .16 | | .07 | | .22 | | .16 | | .06 | | .21 | |

[a] Parent's reports of WFRC: 1 "Low" 2 "Medium" 3 "High"

[b] For dummy variables probabilities contrast against omitted category; for continuous variables, 1 std. error change in X. All other variables are held at their mean values.

* p < .05; ** p < .01; *** p < .001

low, medium, and high). Each set of analyses consists of three models, each predicting WFRC from: (1) work characteristics, including spouses' reports of their own WFRC; (2) characteristics family life only; and (3) characteristics of both work and family life.

In the first set of models, mothers' reports of role conflict are predicted from their total work hours, type of work-shift, job autonomy, work strain, the work environment, working on demand and their husbands' self-reported WFRC. The first model shows that mothers who report having greater work autonomy are less likely to experience a high level of WFRC. In contrast, higher WFRC is associated with having a non-day shift schedule; working on demand on a weekly basis; and being married to a husband who also experiences a high level of WFRC. Net of these other variables, WFRC is not associated with total weekly working hours, degree of work strain, or the family-friendliness of the work environment.

Model 2 shows the association between mothers' reports of WFRC and characteristics of their home lives. WFRC is not related to mothers' levels of satisfaction with the amount of leisure time they have with their husbands, nor with their overall satisfaction with their marriages. However, when a mother is less likely to report high WFRC she is more likely to share in activities with her adolescent, and the easier she finds her parenting role. Compared to the average mother, mothers who are about one standard deviation higher in their level of involvement are about 8 percent less likely to report high WFRC. Compared to the average mother, one who scores one standard deviation higher on parenting ease is about 13 percent less likely to report high WFRC.

Model 3 shows that controlling for variables across both work and family domains does not change the associations between WFRC and any of the variables mentioned earlier. The one exception is work strain, which becomes significant after controlling for home characteristics. This suggests that if it were not for particular family characteristics, mothers with high work strain might have reported higher levels of WFRC. However, this apparent suppression effect of family characteristics is rather small, given that work strain is significant at the $p < .05$ level. This final model explains approximately 22 percent of the variance in mother's work–family conflict.

*Father's self-reported WFRC*  The right half of table 13.2 displays models predicting fathers' self-reported WFRC. Model 1 predicts WFRC using fathers' work characteristics. Of all the work characteristics considered, WFRC is only significantly associated with the degree of work strain a father experiences and working in a family-friendly environment. Fathers who report a work strain level that is one standard deviation above the mean are about 17 percent more likely than the average father to experience a high level of WFRC, while those who work in a family-friendly environment are about 11 percent less likely to experience a high level of WFRC.

Considering only home characteristics (model 2), fathers' perceptions of WFRC are related to both satisfaction with the amount of leisure time they spend with their wives and reported ease of parenting. Increasing a father's satisfaction with his leisure time with spouse by one standard deviation would decrease the probability of having high WFRC by 12 percent, while a similar increase in parenting ease would decrease this probability of high WFRC by 8 percent.

Finally, model 3 shows that associations mentioned earlier remain significant when controlling for variables across both the work and family domains. The significance of spousal leisure time decreases slightly, suggesting that part of the association between leisure time and work–family conflict stems from its association with certain work characteristics. Overall, this final model explains about 21 percent of the variance in fathers' reports of work-family role conflict.

### Predicting adolescents' reports of parental work–family role management

Two separate sets of ordered probit models are used to predict adolescents' assessments (fair, good, and excellent) of each parents' performance in managing work and family roles. Each set of analyses consists of three nested models that enter the following blocks of variables in turn: (1) work characteristics as reported by parents; (2) parents' reported WFRC; and (3) home-life characteristics as reported by adolescents.

Table 13.3 displays the coefficients from ordered probit models that predict adolescents' assessments of parents' work–family role management. Model 1 predicts WFRM from characteristics of parents' jobs. For mothers and fathers, the more hours spent on work, the less likely adolescents are to assess their role management as excellent. Interestingly, job autonomy only predicts assessments made of fathers, with those having greater job autonomy also being assessed more positively by their adolescents. The models explain about 5 percent and 4 percent of the variance, respectively, in adolescents' assessments of parental WFRM.

Model 2 adds to the first model parents' self-reported WFRC. In the model predicting WFRM of mothers, the greater the role conflict reported by mothers, the less likely adolescents are to make favorable assessments of their management. Compared to adolescents who have mothers with low WFRC, those who have mothers with medium or high levels of WFRC are about 15 percent less likely to rate their mothers as having excellent role management. This relationship is similar for fathers' WFRC, although among fathers, role conflict is an even more significant predictor of adolescents' assessments ($p < .01$).

Model 3 adds characteristics of adolescents' home life, including variables that capture how work might have a direct bearing on the adolescent's daily life. First, with respect to these new variables, the pattern of effects is somewhat different for the assessments made of mothers and fathers. While working from home does not significantly affect adolescents' assessments of fathers, mothers are penalized when they work from home and the adolescent feels ignored. Compared to adolescents whose mothers do not work from home, those who feel ignored while their mothers work from home are about 11 percent less likely to assess their mothers' role management as excellent. Interestingly, it appears that mothers (but not fathers) are also held responsible for the organization of the home. The more organized the home, the more likely an adolescent will rate their mother positively.

However, adolescents' assessments of mothers and fathers are similarly predicted from the way that work intersects with family life, as well as aspects of the parent–child relationship. Parents are less likely to receive positive assessments for role management the more often work interrupts family routines. A one standard deviation increase in work–family interruptions decreases the likelihood of an excellent assessment by about 11 percent for mothers and 27 percent for fathers. For assessments of both mothers and fathers, adolescents also take into account whether parents take time off to be with them. Compared to the average adolescent, those whose parents take time off an average of one standard deviation more often are about 11 and 14 percent more likely to assess their parents as having excellent role management. In addition, adolescents also take into account the quality of their relationships with their parents. The better the parent–child relationship, the better the adolescents' assessments of parents' role management.

Interestingly, in this final model the association with parents' reports of WFRC is significantly reduced, although mothers with medium levels of role conflict and fathers with high levels of role conflict are still less likely to receive positive assessments. Fathers' level of autonomy is also among the work variables that become non-significant, although now work hours become more significant in adolescents' assessments of fathers. Each of these models explains between 27 and 29 percent of the variance in adolescents' reports of parental role management.

## Discussion

### *Men's and women's experiences of work–family role conflict*

Although the last few decades have brought significant changes to the work patterns of two-parent families, how these new patterns challenge parents to manage their multiple roles of worker, spouse, and parent, and how this affects children are just beginning to be understood. This chapter suggests that although mothers' and fathers' experiences of work–family role conflict differ in how they are rooted in work and family life, adolescents assess their mothers and fathers' management of their roles in ways that are fairly similar – yet in ways that also reveal their gendered expectations of parenting roles.

Contrary to predictions, mothers and fathers show no significant differences in their overall levels of work–family role conflict. This may stem from the fact that less than 5 percent of these families had young children present in the home, a factor that is associated with higher WFRC and likely increases the WFRC gap between spouses. Another consideration is that the parents in the sample are in the middle stages of their family cycle. As such, they have probably established work and family patterns that provide an acceptable arrangement of equity. Newly (re)married couples may have yet to reach this point of "equilibrium" and as such may display more gender-inequality with regard to who shoulders more of the household's work–family conflict.

While differences in overall levels of WFRC are not significant, the subjective experiences among mothers and fathers are tied to different aspects of work and family life. Mothers' feelings of conflict are closely tied to aspects of work that might impinge on their ability to manage the household. Mothers experience less role conflict when they have more autonomy at work, although admittedly, this might reflect a spurious relationship with mothers' management skills. However, other aspects of work that might constrain the opportunity to manage family life are important. For instance, although role conflict is unrelated to hours of work, the way these hours are distributed over the day and the predictability of these hours are significant for mothers. When a mother works a non-standard shift, or must work on demand on a weekly basis, she is more likely to express higher levels of role conflict. Since both work schedules and working on demand remain significant even after controlling for characteristics of family relationships, these aspects of work may matter because both make it difficult to plan for and manage household activities. This may be especially true for working a non-standard day shift, which often means working a rotating shift as opposed to a steady evening shift.

Table 13.3 Ordered probit models predicting adolescents' assessments of mothers' and fathers' work–family role management (WFRM) – coefficients and changes in probabilities of predicting "excellent" assessment at the mean[a,b]

| | Adolescents' assessments of Mother's WFRM | | | | | | Adolescents' assessments of Father's WFRM | | | | | |
|---|---|---|---|---|---|---|---|---|---|---|---|---|
| | [1] Coef | Δ prob. | [2] Coef | Δ prob. | [3] Coef | Δ prob. | [1] Coef | Δ prob. | [2] Coef | Δ prob. | [3] Coef | Δ prob. |
| Parental work characteristics (parent reporting) | | | | | | | | | | | | |
| # of work hours | −.02 | −.10** | −.02 | −.10* | −.01 | −.03 | −.03 | −.09** | −.03 | −.10** | −.04 | −.12** |
| Non-standard work schedule | .40 | .06 | .45 | .07* | .63 | .09** | .02 | .00 | −.09 | −.01 | −.13 | −.02 |
| Job autonomy | .18 | .07 | .17 | .07 | .18 | .08 | .32 | .11*** | .33 | .12*** | .20 | .07 |
| Work strain | .02 | .01 | .07 | .03 | .03 | .02 | −.12 | −.04 | −.01 | .00 | .02 | .01 |
| Parents' personal perceptions of WFRC | | | | | | | | | | | | |
| Parents' WFRC – Low [ref] | | | | | | | | | | | | |
| Parent's WFRC – Med | | | −.76 | −.15* | −.86 | −.11* | | | −.95 | −.18** | −.59 | −.12 |
| Parent's WFRC – High | | | −.77 | −.15* | −.57 | −.05 | | | −1.07 | −.19*** | −.79 | −.14* |
| Intersection of home & work | | | | | | | | | | | | |
| Parent rarely works from home [ref] | | | | | | | | | | | | |
| Parent works from home often | | | | | −.36 | −.08 | | | | | .07 | .01 |
| Parent works from home often and feels ignored | | | | | −.87 | −.11** | | | | | .14 | .02 |
| Work-Family interruptions | | | | | −.53 | −.11** | | | | | −.86 | −.27*** |
| Shared activities with either parent | | | | | .06 | .06 | | | | | −.02 | −.02 |

(cont.)

Table 13.3 (*cont.*)

| | Adolescents' assessments of Mother's WFRM | | | | | | Adolescents' assessments of Father's WFRM | | | | | |
|---|---|---|---|---|---|---|---|---|---|---|---|---|
| | [1] Coef | Δ prob. | [2] Coef | Δ prob. | [3] Coef | Δ prob. | [1] Coef | Δ prob. | [2] Coef | Δ prob. | [3] Coef | Δ prob. |
| Parent takes time off | | | | | .26 | .11** | | | | | .31 | .14** |
| Organization of the household | | | | | .53 | .12** | | | | | .22 | .05 |
| Positive relationship with parent | | | | | .13 | .17*** | | | | | .15 | .20*** |
| Ancillary Parameters | | | | | | | | | | | | |
| cut 1 | −1.88 | | −2.57 | | 2.09 | | −2.05 | | −3.02 | | −.86 | |
| cut 2 | −1.02 | | −1.68 | | 3.30 | | −1.31 | | −2.26 | | .17 | |
| N | 190 | | 190 | | 190 | | 168 | | 168 | | 168 | |
| Likelihood ratio | 16.45 | | 22.45 | | 95.29 | | 15.47 | | 25.53 | | 93.88 | |
| Df | 5 | | 7 | | 15 | | 5 | | 7 | | 14 | |
| Pseudo R² | .05 | | .07 | | .29 | | .04 | | .07 | | .27 | |

[a] Adolescent assessments of parent's WFRM: 1 "Fair" 2 "Good" 3 "Excellent"

[b] For dummy variables probabilities contrast against omitted category; for continuous variables, 1 std. error change in X. All other variables are held at their mean values.

* p < .05; ** p < .01; *** p < .001

Unlike mothers' role conflict, fathers' role conflict is most closely tied to the emotional and physical stress of their jobs, as well as the extent to which their work environment is family-friendly. These effects remain significant even after controlling for aspects of family relationships, suggesting that they either enter directly into fathers' notions of role conflict, or that they impact family experiences in ways not captured in the model – perhaps by affecting a father's ability to pursue personal leisure activities. It seems that working in a family-friendly environment translates into less work–family conflict among men more often than among women, perhaps indicating differences in status and power at the work place. As Hochschild notes in *The Time Bind* (1997), work places vary in the degree of family-friendly policies that are offered, but so does workers' access to them and the degree to which they feel comfortable using them.

Not only is parents' role conflict tied to different aspects of work, but mothers' and fathers' subjective experiences of work–family role conflict are rooted in different aspects of family life. Mothers' experiences of work–family role conflict can be described as child-focused, while fathers' appear to be focused on both spouse and child. After controlling for work characteristics, mothers and fathers are both more likely to express high WFRC when they find it difficult to parent. However, mothers are also more likely to perceive work–family conflict the less they share in activities with their adolescents, while fathers' perceptions of WFRC are more closely tied to their satisfaction with the time they spend with their spouse.

Just as in previous research, these results indicate that mothers' role conflict is related to that of their husbands', but not vice versa. There are three reasons why this relationship is uni-directional. First, since this relationship remains significant even after controlling for aspects of the marital relationship, it may reflect the tendency for wives to have to adjust their work to that of their husbands, as well as to accommodate work to meet the needs of the family. Thus, the greater the work–family conflict of husbands, the more likely wives are to take on more of the household responsibilities, in turn increasing their own work–family conflict. Second, this relationship could arise from the emotional aspects of role conflict, since father's role conflict is best predicted from his level of work-related stress. The psychological literature on emotions shows that the direction of the "contagion" effect is from husbands to wives (Larson and Richards 1994). As such, a husband's role conflict could increase the emotional management that mothers have to do at home. Third, the relationship may arise from a reporting bias among wives. For instance, if wives are more likely to think of the collective experiences of the couple when responding to these types of survey questions, then their reports of work–family conflict will also capture their spouses' experiences. It is likely that all three phenomena play a part in these findings.

### Adolescent views on parental role management

The inclusion of adolescents' perspectives in these analyses provides an even better understanding of how parents' work shapes the daily experiences of other family members, and how work–family conflict is experienced within the household. In general, adolescents' assessments of their parents are rather favorable, despite moderate to high levels of role conflict reported by parents. This finding may be due in part to adolescents' reluctance to speak poorly of their parents. However, it is also true that many adolescents accept their parents' work roles as part of family life; the majority of the adolescents in this study (68 percent males; 70 percent females) expect to be part of a *dual-full-time*-earner family when they themselves have adolescent children (everyone expects to be at least in a part-time/full-time-earner family).

Although adolescents may accept their parents' roles as workers, their assessments of how parents manage work and family roles vary by work characteristics, and even more importantly, by how work intersects with family life. Among the most significant predictors of adolescents' assessments were whether they felt ignored when their mothers worked from home, and whether their parents' jobs caused family interruptions by keeping parents at work longer than expected, calling parents into work unexpectedly, or causing parents to miss important events in the adolescent's life.

Note also how beliefs about gender roles emerge from adolescents' assessments. Adolescents expect to have many of their daily needs met by their mothers since mothers (but not fathers) are penalized for ignoring them while working from home. In addition, adolescents also appear to hold mothers responsible for the organization of home life since this variable also increased the likelihood of better WFRM for mothers, but not fathers.

But perhaps just as intriguing is the absence of gender differences where one might expect them to be. Given the focus on the importance of maternal bonding, it is surprising that having a close relationship with fathers is just as important in adolescents' assessments of role management. Because work is an important part of the men's family roles, it is also surprising that work interruptions are no more tolerated when they stem from fathers' jobs than when they come from mothers'. Apparently while work roles are important for fulfilling family roles, adolescents expect that home life will be protected from the intrusions of both mothers' and fathers' work.

Further, net of work characteristics, adolescents' assessments of their parents are also related to their parents' own perceptions of WFRC. Adolescents whose mothers experience medium levels of conflict are less likely to believe that their mothers do an excellent job of balancing work and family. In the case of fathers, high levels of conflict are associated with poorer assessments of their work–family role management. These findings suggest either that (1) these levels of parental WFRC are associated with other aspects of work (left out of the models) that also influence adolescents' assessments; or that (2) these parents are more inclined to negotiate work and family demands in ways that do not meet adolescents' expectations. The latter is suggested by the findings of Crouter et al.'s (1999) study on working fathers and their children. Their research shows that adolescents of fathers who experience greater work overload are more likely to see their fathers as less accepting and as being less able to take their perspective.

Finally, heightened concerns about whether parents are spending enough "quality time" with children may be closely associated with parents' own feelings of work–family conflict. But these analyses allay these fears to some extent. Either parents are *jointly*[6] doing an excellent job of sharing in activities with children despite challenging work circumstances, which is consistent with studies that find rather small differences in the amount of child-parent interaction among employed and non-employed mothers (for a review, see Bianchi et al. 2000), or adolescents are just not as concerned about spending time together as they are about sharing a close relationship with parents. Although that goal is met more easily when parents spend time with their children, at this stage of their childhood, adolescents assess their parents' management of roles by putting greater stock in having a patterned home life that has few interruptions, and having parents present during special moments in their lives than in necessarily sharing many activities with them. The one exception to this pattern of results may be in the case of fathers' total work hours. The significant effect of fathers' work hours on adolescents' assessments suggests that adolescents are sensitive to fathers' *presence*, even if that presence does not translate into sharing in activities. It may be that as children's economic needs are met by the wages of *both* parents, adolescents may see little justification for the extra hours that fathers seem to be putting in at work. Children may begin to believe that fathers are working long hours by choice rather than necessity. It would be interesting to test this hypothesis using a more economically heterogeneous sample of families.

Mothers and fathers tend to report moderate to high levels of work–family conflict. Yet most adolescents make very positive assessments of parents – especially of mothers. It was suggested that parents' experiences of role conflict and adolescents' assessments of parents' role management are fundamentally rooted in similar aspects of the work–family experience. This relationship may be even more applicable to mothers and adolescents than to fathers and adolescents. Although it is true that fathers' work imposes more on family life than mothers' work (via work–family interruptions), a shared notion of work–family conflict may direct mothers' and adolescents' attention to similar aspects of family life. This might explain why mothers are rated more positively than fathers, even though mothers experience higher (although not significant) levels of conflict.

To elaborate, setting aside the issue of whether mothers actually *do* manage their work and family roles better than fathers, there is an even more compelling story when the adolescents' point of view is also considered. Adolescents are concerned with the intrusions that work can have on family experiences, and their focus is on having the attention of their mothers and having a close relationship with them. That mothers are similarly sensitive to work factors that constrain their ability to manage family life, and that they are centrally focused on their relationships with their adolescents, suggest that mothers and adolescents share a perspective of what it means to balance work and family life. On the other hand, while fathers' perceptions of role conflict are also associated with their ability to parent, their perceptions are more closely related to their experiences with spouses and the emotional and physical aspects of their work. Fathers may not realize that their adolescents expect to have them present more often (even if not necessarily engaged in shared activities) and that their adolescents are affected by the intrusions that their work brings to family life and the quality of the relationship they share. If anything, this analysis suggests that while mothers play an important role in managing an adolescent's family life, adolescents hold their fathers to similar standards with regard to how they should manage their responsibilities of work and family.

### Study limitations and other considerations

The small sample size and the unique characteristics of the sample (families with parents who have high levels of income and education) limit the ability to generalize these results to a more heterogeneous population. The intersection of work and family domains may give rise to a considerably different pattern of role conflict in families that are more economically distressed, and where children are particularly vulnerable to adverse adolescent outcomes due to the communities in which they live. However, the absence of such confounding factors provides an opportunity to discover some of the fundamental differences (and similarities) in how mothers, fathers, and adolescents experience the intersection of work and family life. These families most likely represent the best case scenario – the favorable economic circumstances of these families certainly provide the means for relieving work–family conflict through the purchase of goods and services.[7] Nevertheless, it is noteworthy that even in such a small, homogeneous sample, significant relationships can be found between work, family, and the subjective experiences of role conflict, and that these relationships follow a pattern that is consistent with what is known about family dynamics. Perhaps this research will inspire scholars to examine work–family conflict in families from more diverse backgrounds, and to broaden the scope of work–family research by taking into consideration the perspective of children.

## NOTES

1. According to 2001 figures from the US Bureau of Labor Statistics, roughly 68 percent of married-couple families with children under the age of eighteen were families where both parents were employed.
2. Responses to the Experience Sampling Method from the 500 Family Study also indicate that compared to fathers, mothers spend much more of their time thinking about their children, even when not directly involved with them.
3. Rather than taking a raw sum, the Rasch measurement model uses observations and probabilities of responses to construct a hierarchical ordering of items on a scale (thought to describe a single dimension), and the relative "strengths" of the persons who complete them. Thus, items at the "easy" end of the scale are those that almost all of the respondents would be able to give high responses to, while items at the "difficult" end are those to which almost all of respondents would give low responses. Rasch computes scores as logits, but for ease of discussion, the scores have all been rescaled to reflect a sum of the original item rating scale.
4. Because adolescents were asked to report in reference to *one or both* parents, the variable cannot capture the extent to which adolescents interact with each parent personally. However, the stronger correlation with mothers' reports of shared activities (as opposed to fathers') suggests that the variable captures the degree of interaction with mothers more so than with fathers. As such, caution should be used when interpreting how this variable operates in models predicting WFRM of fathers.
5. Standard deviations were calculated before model estimation. This is because list-wise deletion selected on a few independent variables. Effects are described

as they would occur in the complete sample in order to more accurately describe average differences in a similar population of families.

6. Recall that this variable references "parents" and does not provide a separate measure for mothers and fathers.

7. Perhaps this would explain why different measures of household labor (mothers' reports, fathers' reports, and ratios between the two) were never significant in any of the models.

# Commentary

## Rena L. Repetti, Tali Klima, and Tamar Kremer-Sadlik

### How might parents' work and family roles contribute to adolescents' future roles?

*Marchena's chapter addresses an important and largely overlooked topic in the work–family literature, the experience of parents' role conflict from the perspective of a child living in the family. Using survey data from over 400 parent–adolescent dyads in the 500 Family Study, she examined how often teens thought their parents did a "good job of balancing work and family life." Overall, the teens gave their parents high marks, with the average response falling between "often" and "always." The generally positive impression conveyed by these teens is consistent with findings from another recent survey study involving over 1,000 children (Galinsky 1999). Interestingly, Marchena found differences in the teens' descriptions of mothers' and fathers' skill at role management. Whereas 63 percent said that their mothers "always" did a good job, fewer of the teens (47 percent) described fathers in this way. Marchena's analysis goes beyond descriptive findings to test hypotheses about the way that differences among adolescents in their perceptions of parents' role management are linked to aspects of their home lives and characteristics of their parents' jobs. For example, parents who devoted more hours to work were less likely to be seen as doing a good job of balancing roles. In this and many other ways Marchena's chapter suggests new avenues for work–family researchers to explore. We restrict our comments here to a single line of inquiry, one that is prompted by Marchena's focus on the adolescent offspring's perspective on work–family role management (WFRM). We ask: How might teens' evaluations of their parents' role management influence their thoughts about their own future roles?*

### Adolescents' thoughts about their future roles

*The chapter calls our attention to the rather unique position of adolescents in the family. While teens observe and evaluate their parents as children within the current family system, they are at the same time approaching and preparing for their own adult roles in a future family. Marchena notes that the role*

361

*management children observe in their home may also influence their future work and family goals. Do working families reproduce themselves? Do some children expect to adopt the same patterns that they observe at home, while others anticipate using different strategies in order to improve on their parents' performance?*

*Galinsky's (1999) survey data provide a clue. In her study, most children said that they wanted to manage work and family life in a way that is "very similar" or "somewhat similar" to their parents. Galinsky also examined how adolescents' perceptions of parents' roles related to their hopes and expectations for their own future roles. Children were most likely to want to emulate their parents' role management if they believed their parents liked their work and put family before their jobs. Despite what appears to be a commonly held wish to model parents' role choices, the amount of time that children said their parents spent at work was inversely related to the amount of time that they hoped to spend at work as adults. Marchena's finding that adolescents believed their parents were doing a poorer job of balancing work and family life when they devoted more hours to work may help to explain this finding.*

### Adolescent girls' expectations

*We know that men and women experience the balance of work and family roles differently (Kiecolt 2003). For example, even though women spend less time on household chores when their working hours increase, they still do more housework than men (Coltrane 2000; Hochschild 1997). Some estimates suggest that, in families with two employed parents, the fathers' proportion of child caregiving is about half the size of the mothers' proportion (Wood and Repetti 2004). In addition, women report feeling more torn between demands of work and family, and feel more responsible for their home and children (Hochschild 1989). Today, most adolescent girls are growing up in homes with mothers who juggle the roles of parent, worker, and spouse. As daughters they are privy to the challenges and the rewards that their mothers' experiences present for both mothers and their families. It is thus plausible that adolescent girls will turn to their mothers as models for how to manage their own work and family roles in the future. In fact, Galinsky found just that: boys and girls did not differ in their desire to emulate their fathers' WFRM, but daughters were more likely than sons to want to emulate their mothers' style of managing work and family. As they look toward adulthood, will adolescent girls expect their husbands to share equally in the running of the household and childcare? Do those who are planning to pursue demanding careers also anticipate feeling torn between work and home? Recall that Marchena reported differences in the teens' evaluations of how well mothers and fathers balanced work and family life. Do daughters expect to be better than their partners at managing work and family? In the work–family* realm, the expectations, hopes, and goals of adolescent girls strike us as having particular importance.

Studies of adolescent girls' gender role attitudes and career orientation and aspirations reveal that girls hold less traditional attitudes toward work and family roles than do boys (Bohannon and Blanton 1999; Ex and Janssens 1998; Galinsky 1999). One study found that adolescent girls were more inclined than adolescent boys to view a wife's career as equal in importance to her husband's, and to believe that men and women should share household and child-rearing duties (Tuck, Rolfe, and Adair 1994). At the same time, potential conflicts between their future work and family roles are inherent in the narratives that girls construct of their futures. For instance, while young females express a desire for careers, they also report strong maternal obligations and a willingness to move for their husbands' jobs at the expense of their own (Novack and Novack 1996). In another study, girls expected to start a career, get married, and become a parent within a time span of two years (Greene and Wheatley 1992). This projected life course was associated with girls' concerns about the temporal constraints of work and family, as well as pessimism about their futures. Thus, it seems that even as adolescent girls are planning ambitious careers, the seeds of work–family role conflict (WFRC) are already planted in their goals and plans.

### The role of the developing self-concept

Adolescent girls' perceptions of their parents' role management, especially the ways in which they perceive their mothers' balancing of work and family responsibilities, may not have only a direct impact on their expectations, hopes, and goals for their future work–family roles. These perceptions may also indirectly influence their future roles through the developing self-concept. Self-concept refers to the way in which an individual describes herself. Developmental psychologists have found that during adolescence the self becomes increasingly differentiated into role-related multiple selves (Harter et al. 1997). This proliferation of selves is generally attributed to cognitive advances that allow adolescents to make greater and more subtle distinctions, as well as to handle the complex demands placed on adolescents in varying social contexts. Harter (1999) has demonstrated that individuals have different self-concepts in different social contexts. At times, these self-concepts may be contradictory or in conflict with one another, and contradictory self-concepts are associated with negative affect (Harter and Monsour 1992).

Interestingly, girls report more conflicting self-concepts than do boys in middle school and high school (Harter and Monsour 1992). Could the greater conflict felt by adolescent girls be shaped in part by perceptions of their mothers' WFRC? Perhaps a girl who sees her mother effectively balancing her two roles without *much conflict is more likely to believe that two role-related selves can coexist harmoniously. In contrast, a girl who sees her mother struggling with her work and family roles may come to feel that two role-related selves will inevitably generate internal conflict. It is important to ask whether the processes through which role-related multiple selves are formed during adolescence and the contradictions that at least some girls sense in the various aspects of their self-concept could impact their expectations for their own futures. That is, would girls who have internalized a harmonious coexistence of role-related selves expect to hold fulfilling jobs while simultaneously experiencing a satisfying family life? Conversely, would girls who have conflicting selves express pessimism regarding the coordination of roles in the future?*

*Marchena's chapter brings to the forefront the importance of adolescents' perceptions of their parents' WFRC and WFRM. This commentary expands on Marchena's study by focusing on adolescent girls and their perceptions of their mothers' balancing of work and family responsibilities. In particular, we suggest that adolescent girls' perceptions of their mothers may influence their expectations, hopes, and goals for their own future work and family roles. We further propose that adolescent girls' perceptions of their mothers may affect their developing self-concept, which can, in turn, impact their expectations and goals. We believe this is a research direction worth pursuing as it may shed light on the development of both girls' and boys' expectations and goals for their future education, professional aspirations, marriage, and parenthood.*

# 14    Imagining family roles: parental influences on the expectations of adolescents in dual-earner families

*Matthew N. Weinshenker*

In the US in recent years, the majority of two-parent families with children have become two-income families (Cherlin 1992; Perry-Jenkins, Repetti, and Crouter 2000). In contrast to the post-war era, when it was normative for husbands to work for pay while wives cared for home and children, today the average married woman is employed. In addition, her husband may be more involved in housework and childcare than before (Bianchi et al. 2000; Demo and Acock 1993). Given that parental influence on children's gender socialization is well established (e.g., see Eccles 1993; Thornton, Alwin, and Camburn 1983), a key question is what kinds of gender-related attitudes children in dual-earner families have. One might expect them to think in relatively egalitarian terms as they begin to form ideas about how they will organize their lives, particularly with respect to the major responsibilities for earning an income, childcare, and household chores. Further, one might expect the strength of children's egalitarian orientation to vary systematically depending on whether parents are equal partners, or whether the husband remains the primary earner while the wife retains most of the responsibility for the home and children.

This chapter investigates the accuracy of the above predictions, as well as several related ones. The phenomenon to be explained is how the children of dual-earner couples believe they will divide responsibility for the "breadwinner" role and the "homemaker" role when they are adults. This is related to, but distinct from, the more commonly studied issue of children's gender role norms, which is a question of how children feel they *should* behave, as opposed to how they think they *will* behave. The focus here is on how variations in expectations relate to parental influence. What effects do the gender attitudes, role behavior, and parenting styles of mothers and fathers have on their children's expectations about the future marital division of labor? Both qualitative and quantitative data from mothers, fathers, and adolescents who participated in the 500 Family Study are used to investigate this question.

## Recent trends in American marriages

Contemporary American adolescents are growing up in an era when typical parental roles have undergone a fifty-year process of transformation. The "traditional" family, consisting of a breadwinner father and a stay-at-home mother, has become increasingly rare. The key change in two-parent families has been the entry of married women with children into paid employment. This trend has combined with the rise of the single-parent family to considerably increase the proportion of mothers in the labor force.

In married couples, men also appear to have taken on more housework in recent decades (Bianchi et al. 2000). Research, however, suggests that men's participation in housework has not changed to an extent comparable to their wives' increasing presence in the workforce. The current situation is one where the average wife and mother works, but continues to do the lion's share of the household chores (Demo and Acock 1993). For Hochschild, this is one component of a "stalled revolution," a contradiction between equality in the work place and inequality in the home. The stalled revolution arises from the fact that "the exodus of women into the workforce has not been accompanied by a cultural understanding of marriage and work that would make this transition smooth" (Hochschild 1989: 12).

Scholars have devoted considerable thought to explaining why men have not increased their participation at home in a way that comes close to compensating for women's increased work responsibilities. Several mechanisms have been proposed, including relative power, early socialization, and gender as performance. In the latter explanation, associated with the symbolic interactionist school (Berk 1985; West and Zimmerman 1987), housework is an opportunity for both sexes to "do gender." By taking responsibility for the housework, women confirm their femininity. Just as importantly, their husbands demonstrate their masculinity by holding themselves aloof from such tasks.

On the other hand, not every family is average. Although many dual-earner couples divide the housework in a way consistent with the predictions of the performative theory of gender, at least a few have pioneered highly egalitarian housework arrangements. These couples tend to be distinctive both ideologically and structurally. Ideologically, they believe in equality and are "child-centered"; structurally, they are likely to have middle-class standards of living and to be highly educated (Coltrane 1989; Risman and Johnson-Sumerford 1998).

## Parental influence on family role expectations

If teens' family role expectations are influenced by their parents, the above considerations suggest that children in middle-class, dual-earner families would be more likely than others to have egalitarian expectations. But is such a conclusion warranted? Do parents influence their children's expectations about future family roles? Children's expectations about how they will divide roles within their future marriages are conceptually different from their norms about how marriages ought to be arranged. However, the two constructs are similar enough that one would expect factors that predict the latter to predict the former as well. In the literature on transmission of gender norms, the three most important explanatory variables are attitude transmission, the division of household labor, and maternal employment. In addition, this chapter explores the influence of a fourth predictor: parenting style.

### Attitude transmission

It is well-established that parents, and mothers in particular, transmit their gender role attitudes to their children. Mothers' current beliefs about proper gender roles have a strong influence on their children's contemporary attitudes (Cunningham 2001a; Thornton, Alwin, and Camburn 1983). Additionally, mothers' beliefs when their children are young continue to influence them over time (Moen, Erickson, and Dempster-McClain 1997).

In general, past studies have focused on mother–child influence because many data sets include limited information from fathers. An advantage of the 500 Family Study is that data were collected from both parents in each family. Thus, in this chapter the gender role attitudes of mothers and fathers are included in statistical models in order to see whether both have a significant effect on adolescent expectations. The initial supposition is that they both do.

*Hypothesis 1.* The more liberal (egalitarian) the mother's or father's gender role attitudes, the more likely his or her children will be to expect equal sharing of breadwinning and homemaking roles.

### Division of household labor

Aside from attitude transmission, scholars have found that parents influence their children's gender-related attitudes and beliefs by modeling behavior. This has two components. One is housework modeling, specifically the question of how much female-typed housework the father does. The other is work modeling, which comes down to the question of whether the mother works, and secondarily, the prestige and other characteristics of her job.

Although Booth and Amato's (1994) study of the effect of parental "non-traditionalism" on children used the amount of housework done by the father in the family as one index of non-traditionalism, it has been rare for scholars to consider parental housework as a factor predicting children's gender role attitudes. An exception is Cunningham (2001a), who looks at the relationship between parental housework and children's opinions about the ideal division of housework; he finds 18-year-olds' beliefs about responsibility for both female-typed chores and childcare to be significantly related to the parents' earlier division of these tasks. This result holds even when controlling for the parents' gender role attitudes.

Another advantage of the 500 Family Study is that, as in Cunningham's work, it is possible to relate parents' housework to children's attitudes while controlling for the parents' attitudes. Thus, it is possible to corroborate Cunningham's finding by testing the following hypothesis about role modeling.

*Hypothesis 2.* The larger the father's share of female-typed housework, the more likely his children will be to expect equal sharing of tasks.

### Maternal employment

On the question of whether maternal employment affects children's gender attitudes, the existing research is not unanimous. On the positive side, Dennehy and Mortimer (1993) report that high school boys are more likely to accept the notion of wives returning to work after giving birth if their own mothers are employed. Similarly, Stephan and Corder (1985) find that high school students whose parents are both employed in "high-prestige occupations" are more likely than others to expect to form families in which the wife combines career and family.

Maternal employment may also affect children's expectations about role sharing at home. Stephan and Corder report that the children of dual-career couples are more likely to expect that the husbands in their future families will participate in childcare. Cunningham finds that women are more likely to share housework with their husbands if their own mothers were employed. Maternal employment, Cunningham suggests, "might operate [by] minimizing the extent to which sons and daughters make an association between gender and the performance of particular kinds of work" (2001b: 186).

The proposition that maternal employment affects children's attitudes is not universally supported. Moen, Erickson, and Dempster-McClain (1997) find that children's gender role attitudes are explained by parental attitudes, but not by the mother's employment behavior. In an earlier paper, Thornton, Alwin, and Camburn (1983) reached the same conclusion. However, it must be noted that these authors are trying to explain broad indices of child gender role attitudes. For example, Moen et al.'s gender role attitude scale contains items not directly related to work, such as whether it is acceptable for a woman to "argue with a man not her husband at a social gathering" or "travel long distances by herself" (1997: 285). Among those who found an effect for maternal employment on children's attitudes, the dependent variable is more focused – children's expectations about work and childcare in the future. It seems reasonable that these specific expectations would be more influenced by maternal employment than a child's diffuse feelings about proper gender roles. Since it is precisely expectations about the future marital division of labor that are of interest here, the following hypothesis is suggested.

*Hypothesis 3.* The greater the mother's relative responsibility for paid work, the more likely children will be to expect equal sharing of tasks.

### Parenting style

Aside from attitude transmission and role modeling, is there any other way in which parents influence teens' gender and family expectations? Although it is less often considered in the literature, parents also influence teenagers' orientations through their style of interaction. Rathunde and colleagues (Csikszentmihalyi, Rathunde, and Whalen 1993) identified two dimensions of parenting practice – family support and family challenge – which are particularly consequential for adolescents' views about their futures. Family support is defined as "the parents' responsiveness to the child. In a responsive family, the child is comfortable in the home, spends time with other family members, and feels loved and cared for." Family challenge, by contrast, "refers to the stimulation, discipline, or training that parents and other family members direct towards the child. Challenge also includes the expectations the child perceives family members to have of him or her and the child's desire to fulfill those expectations" (Rathunde, Carroll, and Huang 2000: 115–16). Rathunde and colleagues found that family support promoted optimism in teenagers, family challenge promoted motivation, and the combination of the two encouraged an achievement orientation. Corroborating evidence was provided by Schneider and Stevenson (1999) who found that adolescents of both genders tended to have high educational and occupational aspirations if their parents were supportive and challenging.

These results suggest that daughters of parents who are both supportive and challenging would expect to be heavily invested in the world of paid work. They may also expect to have husbands who do a considerable share of the household labor and childcare if they recognize that accepting traditional female responsibility for the home makes it difficult to pursue a career, suggesting the final hypothesis.

*Hypothesis 4.* The higher the parents' scores on family support and challenge, the more likely girls will be to expect equal sharing of the breadwinner and homemaker roles.

### Gender-specific effects

Of the four hypotheses offered, only the last makes any mention of the child's gender. Considering that men and women continue to play somewhat different roles in the vast majority of families, it seems reasonable to suppose that adolescent boys' and girls' expectations about the future are influenced by different sets of factors. Yet when researchers have explicitly asked whether parental effects on gender socialization vary by gender of the child, more often than not they have found no difference (see e.g., Cunningham 2001b; Thornton, Alwin, and Camburn 1983). Still, the occasional findings of gender-specific effects means one can hardly ignore them. Without explicitly hypothesizing where they might occur, it is prudent to test for gender-specific effects in relation to all hypotheses.

## Method

### Sample

For this research, the unit of analysis is the family triad, consisting of father, mother, and adolescent child. Accordingly, the survey data provided by each parent and by the teenaged child are matched with one another. If more than one teenager in the same family completed a survey, only one triad of father, mother, and child was selected for analysis. Using two or more triads from a single family would give the parents disproportionate influence over the results.

Largely because of the use of family-matched data, some cases are not included in the analysis. Of the families who participated in the

500 Family Study, 379 have adolescent children, defined as children between the ages of 12 and 18. In 142 of these families, one member of the triad (either the adolescent or a parent) failed to complete a survey. These cases were excluded. In addition, since the surveys were filled out by the respondents and mailed to the research center, there was no way to guarantee that all questions were answered. Consequently 58 additional families were dropped due to missing data.[1] Finally, since the focus of this analysis is the effect of dual-earner parents on children's expectations, a small number of two-parent families in which one parent was out of the labor force at the time of the survey were excluded. Following the standard definition, an individual is out of the labor force if he or she is neither working nor actively looking for work.

After exclusions, the final sample size is 160 families. Considering the number of families that were excluded, it is important to ask whether they differ from those who remain. Two-sample t-tests comparing the included and excluded families show a few differences at the 95 percent confidence level, but more similarities. Included adolescents are about half a year older than those excluded. Included parents are also older on average, which reflects the fact that older adolescents tend to have older parents. Mothers and fathers in included families work a slightly longer workweek than others (an average difference of about two hours per week for men and four hours for women). Further, the ratio of father's to mother's work hours is lower on average in included versus excluded families. This suggests that included parents share the burden of earning income in a relatively equal way, which may be consequential for their children's gender-related expectations.

In many other ways, however, the included and excluded families are not significantly different. The two groups of parents do not differ in terms of educational attainment, gender role attitudes, housework (either absolute number of hours or the relative share performed by each parent), income (either absolute value or relative share earned by each parent), and parenting style. In addition, teens in the two groups have about the same gender composition, and they are no more or less likely to have egalitarian expectations about their future marriages.

It is not possible to draw definitive conclusions from these t-tests. The majority of the excluded families are excluded because one family member did not take part in the study, and it is impossible to say whether such people differ in important ways from individuals who chose to participate. Based on the data that are available, however, it seems that the included families are not much different from the other dual-earner families in the 500 Family Study.

*Dependent variables*

The dependent variables were constructed based on three questions about teens' family role expectations: the first question concerns the future division of housework or chores; the second, taking care of children; and the third, responsibility for providing financial support for the family. In each case, teens were asked, "In the future, who do you expect will take responsibility for these tasks, you or your spouse?" There were five response options: "mostly you," "you slightly more than spouse," "you and your spouse/partner equally," "spouse slightly more than you," and "mostly your spouse."

For each item, at least 89 percent of respondents of each gender selected either the egalitarian answer ("you and your spouse/partner equally") or the slightly traditional answer to these questions. (A boy who says his wife will do slightly more than half the housework is an example of a slightly traditional answer.) Therefore, each of the dependent measures was recoded into a dummy variable distinguishing teens with egalitarian versus traditional expectations. In most cases, a response of one indicates that the adolescent expects to share the role in question (housework, childcare, or earning money) equally with his or her spouse. A response of zero indicates expectations more or less in line with traditional gender roles.

*Explanatory variables*

Parents' gender ideologies are measured by a construct consisting of four questions. Participants were asked to rate the following statements on a five-point Likert scale: "It should not bother the husband if a wife's job sometimes requires her to be away from him overnight." "If his wife works full-time, a husband should share equally in household chores such as cooking, cleaning and washing." "It is more important for a wife to help her husband's career than to have a career herself." "Parents should encourage just as much independence in their daughters as in their sons."[2]

On the survey, parents were asked how many hours per week they spent working at certain "core" household tasks that have traditionally been assigned to females. These include shopping for the household, cooking, washing dishes, cleaning the house, and doing laundry. The original response options were categorical but have been recoded into continuous variables using the median number of hours in each category. The percentage of both parents' housework that is performed by the father was then calculated. This percentage is used as an index of the parental division of labor at home.

The mother's relative share of work hours was calculated in a similar way. On the survey, each parent was asked to report hours spent at his or her main job. A separate series of questions asked about hours at second jobs, if any. The original, categorical response options were recoded based on the category medians. After adding together hours at each job, the percentage of total parent hours logged by the mother was computed. This percentage is used as a measure of relative parental responsibility for the breadwinner role.

Family support and family challenge are measured using the Support/Challenge Questionnaire that has been employed on several occasions by Rathunde and colleagues. Each construct reflects adolescents' levels of agreement with sixteen statements about their family life and their parents' parenting practices. Examples of support statements are "We enjoy having dinner together and talking" and "If I have a problem, I get special attention and help." "I'm expected to do my best" and "We enjoy playing competitive games" are typical statements from the challenge scale. Negatively worded items were reverse scored to match with the positive items and then an overall mean for each measure was calculated.[3]

Finally, a number of demographic measures are included as controls because they may explain part of the variation in adolescents' gender-related expectations or parents' attitudes, division of labor, and parenting styles. The controls utilized are the teenager's gender and age, the mother's age, and household income.[4] In addition, considering that the dependent variables are children's expectations about marital life, including the issue of who will do childcare, it is reasonable to suppose that teens who do not plan to get married or to have children will have different attitudes than those who do. Fortunately, the survey asks adolescents about their future family plans. A dummy variable was created to index adolescents who indicate the odds are "low" or "very low" that they would get married and/or have children. This dummy variable is also used as a control.

## Results

### Descriptive findings

Table 14.1 provides adolescents' responses to the three questions about family role expectations. The last row below each question shows the percent egalitarian, which represents those who expect to share a given task equally with their spouse, as well as the small number who expect to divide tasks in a "role reversal" way (such as the 2.6 percent of boys who expect to do more housework than their spouses).

Table 14.1 *Distribution of responses to family role expectation questions by gender of respondent*

|  | Boys % | Girls % |
|---|---|---|
| Who will do housework/chores? | | |
| Mostly you | 0.0 | 6.0 |
| You slightly more than spouse | 2.6 | 26.2 |
| You and your spouse equally | 67.1 | 66.7 |
| Spouse slightly more than you | 26.3 | 1.2 |
| Mostly your spouse | 4.0 | 0.0 |
| Percent "egalitarian" | 69.7 | 67.9 |
| Who will take care of your children? | | |
| Mostly you | 0.0 | 2.4 |
| You slightly more than spouse | 2.6 | 32.1 |
| You and your spouse equally | 75.0 | 65.5 |
| Spouse slightly more than you | 22.4 | 0.0 |
| Mostly your spouse | 0.0 | 0.0 |
| Percent "egalitarian" | 77.6 | 65.5 |
| Who will earn money to support the family? | | |
| Mostly you | 5.3 | 0.0 |
| You slightly more than spouse | 47.4 | 2.4 |
| You and your spouse equally | 42.1 | 73.8 |
| Spouse slightly more than you | 5.3 | 23.8 |
| Mostly your spouse | 0.0 | 0.0 |
| Percent "egalitarian" | 47.4 | 76.6*** |

*Notes:* Total number of cases is 160.
Not all columns sum to 100 percent due to rounding.
*** $p < .001$ (difference between groups)

As table 14.1 shows, the majority of teenagers expect to share family tasks in an egalitarian fashion: 70 percent of boys and 68 percent of girls have egalitarian expectations about housework; 78 and 66 percent respectively have egalitarian expectations about childcare. The difference between genders is not significant in either case. Earning money for the family, however, is a different story. While 77 percent of girls expect to share the breadwinner role equally with their husbands, only 47 percent of boys have a similar expectation ($p < .001$). It appears that while boys have absorbed cultural messages telling them that they need to take an active role at home, they have not relinquished plans to be their family's primary earner. Given the principle of marital homogamy, which posits that individuals from similar backgrounds tend to marry, this is troubling. The numbers suggest that disagreements over the work role may be a source of conflict in these respondents' future marriages.

Means and standard deviations of all independent variables are presented in table 14.2. The numbers are first shown for the total sample, and then separately for adolescent boys and girls. The adolescent sample is almost evenly split by gender (53 percent female, 47 percent male); this closely tracks the numbers for the entire 500 Family Study. The mean age is 15.6. A full 92 percent of respondents feel they are likely to marry and have children. The average adolescent in the sample lives in a family with a household income above $100,000. This is not surprising given that these are dual-earner households, and that many parents have individual incomes close to, or above, that figure (see chapter 2).

Parents' gender role attitude scores are, on average, quite far towards the egalitarian end of the scale. This finding is not surprising given that these parents share the characteristics of those who have led national gender attitude trends in a liberal direction (Brewster and Padavic 2000). Specifically, the mothers in the sample all work, and most parents of either gender are highly educated.[5]

While some fathers in the sample do no female-typed housework, the average father does about one-third of the work performed by either parent, meaning the mother does the other two-thirds. This is a good deal more egalitarian than the national average (Bianchi et al. 2000). The average mother in the sample in turn logs about 40 percent of the hours worked by either parent, with her husband accounting for the other 60 percent. Finally, teens rate their parents as high on both supportive and challenging dimensions of parenting, although girls tend to give their parents higher scores than boys.

### Predicting adolescents' role expectations

Do any of the parent characteristics discussed above explain adolescent expectations? Results from a series of logistic regression models estimated to answer this question are shown in table 14.3. All coefficients are presented as odds ratios.

There are five models reported in table 14.3. Models 1, 2a, and 3a use only the main effect of each explanatory variable to predict adolescents' expectations about doing housework/chores, taking care of children, and earning money to support the family, respectively. It is possible that parents' effects on their children's family role expectations vary by the gender of the child. Accordingly, models were estimated to allow for interaction effects between gender and the other explanatory variables. All possible gender interactions were tested, but only interactions significant at

Table 14.2 *Means and standard deviations of independent variables*

| | All adolescents | | | | Boys | | Girls | |
|---|---|---|---|---|---|---|---|---|
| | Mean | S.D. | Minimum | Maximum | Mean | S.D. | Mean | S.D. |
| Teen's gender (dummy=1 if female) | 0.53 | 0.50 | NA | NA | – | – | – | – |
| Teen's age | 15.60 | 1.60 | 12 | 18 | 15.72 | 1.66 | 15.48 | 1.53 |
| Mother's age | 47.26 | 4.54 | 29 | 56 | 46.67 | 4.76 | 47.79 | 4.29 |
| Household income (thousands) | 116.05 | 43.55 | 12.5 | 175 | 112.99 | 43.60 | 118.81 | 43.58 |
| Teen unlikely to get married or have kids (dummy) | 0.08 | 0.26 | NA | NA | 0.07 | 0.25 | 0.08 | 0.28 |
| Mother's gender role attitude scale (1–5) | 4.39 | 0.56 | 1.75 | 5 | 4.28* | 0.60 | 4.49 | 0.51 |
| Father's gender role attitude scale (1–5) | 4.34 | 0.55 | 2.5 | 5 | 4.31 | 0.55 | 4.36 | 0.54 |
| The percentage of "female" housework performed by dad | 35.73 | 16.79 | 0 | 80.56 | 36.30 | 17.54 | 35.21 | 16.18 |
| The percentage of family work hours logged by mom | 41.87 | 11.90 | 12.00 | 65.34 | 41.43 | 13.02 | 42.28 | 10.85 |
| Family support (0–3) | 2.26 | 0.44 | 0.25 | 2.94 | 2.16** | 0.50 | 2.35 | 0.36 |
| Family challenge (0–3) | 2.25 | 0.34 | 0.75 | 2.81 | 2.14*** | 0.39 | 2.35 | 0.26 |
| N | 160 | | | | 76 | | 84 | |

*p < .05; **p < .01; *** p < .001 (t-test for the difference in means between boys and girls)

Table 14.3 *Logistic regression coefficients (expressed as odds ratios) from regressions predicting whether teenaged children of dual-earner parents expect to share tasks equally*

| Independent variable | Doing housework/chores Model 1 | Taking care of your children Model 2a | Taking care of your children Model 2b | Earning money to support the family Model 3a | Earning money to support the family Model 3b |
|---|---|---|---|---|---|
| Female | 1.17 | .63 | .08* | 4.53*** | 712.24 |
| Teen's age | 1.21 | .79 | .77 | .91 | 1.23 |
| Mother's age | .92 | 1.04 | 1.03 | 1.03 | 1.02 |
| Household income (thousands) | .99* | .99 | .99 | 1.00 | 1.00 |
| Teen unlikely to get married or have kids | 2.22 | 3.39 | 3.67 | 3.61 | 3.81 |
| Mother's gender role attitude scale | .91 | .38* | .42 | .79 | .79 |
| Father's gender role attitude scale | 1.50 | .88 | .78 | 1.77 | 1.63 |
| Percentage "female" housework performed by dad | 1.03* | 1.02 | .99 | 1.00 | 1.00 |
| Percentage work hours logged by mom | .98 | 1.02 | 1.03 | 1.01 | 1.01 |
| Family support | 1.12 | 16.05*** | 15.85*** | 2.22 | 3.59 |
| Family challenge | .77 | .05** | .05** | .21 | .05** |
| Female*–father's housework interaction | – | – | 1.06* | – | – |
| Female*–teen's age interaction | – | – | – | – | .45** |
| Female*–family challenge interaction | – | – | – | – | 25.47* |
| Likelihood-ratio chi-square (df) | 20.26 (11) | 30.71 (11) | 35.94 (12) | 25.42 (11) | 37.20 (13) |
| Prob>chi2 | .04 | .00 | .00 | .01 | .00 |
| Pseudo R$^2$ | .10 | .16 | .19 | .12 | .18 |

*Note:* Total number of cases is 160.

*p < .05; **p < .01; ***p < .001

the .05 level were retained in the final models.[6] The childcare and earning regressions with interaction terms are labeled models 2b and 3b. In the case of the housework regression, no interaction effects were significant at the p < .05 level. Therefore, there is only a single model predicting housework expectations.

In model 1, only one of the four expected paths of parental influence is evident. The father's share of female-typed chores has a significant effect as predicted by hypothesis 2. Note that while the odds ratio is only slightly larger than 1, this is because the father's share of housework is measured in percentage units. To understand the model, consider two hypothetical households: in one, the father does only 10 percent of the chores; in the other, the father does 50 percent. According to model 1, in the latter home children would be $1.03^{40} = 3.26$ times more likely to expect an egalitarian division of housework when they get married, all else being equal. Thus, in a home where the father does a large share of the core tasks, children are much more likely to expect to share the chores.

In models 2a and 2b, parenting style has a significant effect on adolescents' expectations about childcare. Supportive parenting makes teens more likely to expect an equal division of responsibility for childcare, but challenging parenting appears to have the opposite effect. Since the coefficients are of similar magnitude, these effects would appear to cancel each other out if parents are high on both dimensions of parenting. However, to the extent that parents are challenging but not supportive, this seems to contribute to less egalitarian outlooks among their children.

In the "main effects only" model (model 2a), the father's share of chores does not affect teenagers' expectations about childcare. In model 2b, the main effect remains insignificant, but there is a significant interaction between father's housework and gender. When fathers do a large share of "female" tasks, girls are likely to expect their future husbands to participate in *all* tasks done around the house, including childcare. Boys are also influenced by their fathers' participation in housework, but this influence apparently does not carry over to participation in childcare.

In model 2a, the mother's gender role attitude has a significant effect on expectations about childcare. However, the coefficient is in a direction contrary to hypothesis 1: mothers with more egalitarian attitudes have children who are less likely to expect to share childcare duties equally. In model 2b, the significance of this term is suppressed by the inclusion of the interaction between gender and father's housework, although the odds ratio does not change much in substantive terms. This unexpected finding seems to suggest that whatever influence maternal gender egalitarianism has on teens' expectations, it is not the simple attitude transmission that was discussed earlier in this chapter.

What about expectations about the breadwinner role? In model 3a, the teenager's gender is the only significant predictor. The significance of gender is not remarkable considering that many more girls than boys expect to share the breadwinner role equally with their spouses (see table 14.1). What is more surprising at first glance is that none of the measures of parent influence appear to have an effect. As it turns out, model 3b shows that there are several gender-specific effects on breadwinning expectations that are hidden when one looks only at "main effects." Family challenge is associated with less egalitarian earnings expectations for boys, but not girls. (For girls, the main effect of challenge is offset by the interaction between challenge and gender. The odds ratio is 0.05 * 25.47 = 1.27, which is not statistically significant at the p < .05 level.) Although the coefficient for family support is not significant (p < .08), there is a trend for adolescents in supportive families toward more egalitarian expectations about earning money.

In model 3b, age is shown to be the only factor predicting girls' earning expectations. Specifically, older girls are less optimistic about the extent to which their future spouses will allow them to perform the breadwinning duties. One way to read this result is that girls who initially hope to find a husband willing to share become more "realistic" over time.[7]

If the teenager believes that he/she is unlikely to marry and have children, this has a large (but insignificant) effect on the odds of holding an egalitarian outlook in all of the models. This appears to be consistent with the theory of Goldscheider and Waite (1991), who fear that young people – especially women – whose gender beliefs are egalitarian will opt for "no families" rather than risk falling into traditional breadwinner–homemaker marriage patterns. However, only 8 percent of adolescents do not believe they will marry and have children, and most favor shared housework and childcare. Thus respondents seem more supportive of egalitarian "new families" rather than "no families."

To review, how well did the four hypotheses about parents' influence on adolescents' expectations fare? Hypothesis 1 – parents with egalitarian gender role attitudes will tend to have children with egalitarian role expectations – is not borne out. If anything, the opposite notion – that egalitarian parents have adolescents who desire more traditional families – is suggested by the coefficient for mother's gender role attitude in model 2a. Considering that this is the only instance where either parent's gender role attitude is significant, the evidence is too equivocal to draw strong conclusions.

Hypothesis 2 predicted that adolescents would have more egalitarian expectations when the father does female-typed housework. This is confirmed, especially for girls. When the father participates in these tasks, children of both genders tend to be more egalitarian in their housework expectations, and girls are also more likely to expect an equal division of childcare responsibilities. By contrast, in none of the three regression equations does the percentage of work hours logged by the mother have any effect on adolescent expectations. Furthermore, the odds ratio is always very close to 1.0, suggesting that among adolescents in dual-earner families, family role expectations are independent of relative time spent in paid work. Consequently, hypothesis 3 – the more equal the parents' responsibility for paid work, the more likely children will be to expect equal sharing of tasks – is not confirmed.

Finally, hypothesis 4 predicted that parental support and challenge would affect girls' expectations; no predictions were made regarding boys. In fact, these dimensions of parenting style are shown to have more effects on boys than on girls.

## Discussion

### The central role of the division of housework

It was initially expected that parents influence their adolescents' family role expectations through attitude transmission, modeling paid work, and modeling household labor. In fact, the only consistent source of influence among these variables is the parents' division of household tasks. Because these other factors were hypothesized to matter, various alternate model specifications were tested. Parents' paid work and attitudes did not have the predicted effects in any of these alternate models.[8]

How can these null findings be interpreted? In part, they may be due to the homogeneity of the sample. In a more ethnically, racially, and economically diverse sample, variation among parents' attitudes and work behaviors would be greater, leading to more robust effects on adolescent expectations. For example, past literature (Cunningham 2001b; Stephan and Corder 1985) suggests that single-earner families, who are not represented in the sample analyzed, may exert a more traditional influence by virtue of parent role modeling. Children whose mothers work may form more egalitarian expectations than those whose mothers stay home; all the mothers in this sample, however, are employed (or at least looking for work).

Findings that parents' division of housework affects children's expectations about housework is, of course, perfectly in line with conventional social learning theory, as well as the symbolic interactionist concept of "doing gender." Since it is done at home, by definition, housework is a realm of activity in which children of dual-earner couples are easily able to observe their parents engaged in gender-differentiated role performances. Thus, it is not surprising that children in the bottom 10 percent of this sample's families, where the husband does less than one-eighth of the core housework, tend to construct different notions about appropriate gender roles than children in the top 10 percent, in which the husband does more than half of it.

Social learning theory and symbolic interactionist theory would both probably lead one to predict that parents' relative work hours should also affect adolescent expectations. However, there is at least one theoretical perspective that helps explain why dual-earner couples' housework might influence their children's family role expectations when their division of paid work does not. This is Hochschild's notion of the "stalled revolution" (1989). As Hochschild argued, it has become quite normative for two-parent families to have "transitional" gender roles, meaning that the husband accepts the wife's entry to the world of work so long as she continues to assume primary responsibility for home and children. If this is correct, and mothers are expected to "do it all" in our culture, then female participation in breadwinning will not seem nearly as unusual to children as a father who helps around the house. The latter remains much less normative, and thus far more likely to make an impression.

### Explaining the effects of parenting style

Besides housework, the data show that parental support and challenge influence adolescents' family role expectations. According to the findings, family challenge reduces teens' odds of expecting an egalitarian division of childcare when they marry, and is also associated with boys expecting to keep the breadwinner role for themselves. Recall that challenge involves parents holding high expectations of their children. Perhaps boys who are challenged are more likely to internalize high expectations for themselves, and to have ambitious career plans. They come to realize that it is easier to be career-oriented if one has a traditional wife who puts her husband's career before her own, so they plan to marry this type of wife.

What about the girls? Challenging parents tend to encourage girls to think about and explore the world of work. In the course of this exploration girls may observe the unfortunate fact that women, rather than men, are most often the ones who make difficult choices between career and family, especially when children arrive. Thus, they may become less optimistic about sharing childcare in their own marriages. Other authors have conjectured that girls who become aware of the trade-off between career and family are likely to reject marriage and children entirely in favor of personal achievement (Goldscheider and Waite 1991), but the low odds ratio for family challenge in the childcare regression suggests that the girls in this sample are planning to sacrifice career to some extent in order to raise children.

In contrast to family challenge, family support is associated with more egalitarian expectations about the division of childcare by adolescents of both sexes. How can this be explained? The odds ratio for support has an obvious interpretation where girls are concerned. As discussed earlier, teens from supportive families are more optimistic about the future. This optimism may carry over into girls' hopes for egalitarian childcare arrangements. However, this line of reasoning cannot account for the significant relationship between family support and boys' egalitarian expectations about childcare. The relationship between parenting practices and teens' gender attitudes and expectations is far from straightforward, and is an area ripe for future research.

### Qualitative illustrations

Qualitative interviews, conducted with mothers, fathers, and adolescents in the 500 Family Study, help to illustrate the results of the regression models. The following four families were chosen in part because they comment explicitly on expectations for the future, parenting, and/or housework. Parenting style is not an explicit part of the interview protocol, and when teens were asked about their future plans, most were vague. While comments of the four families are not necessarily typical of the interviews conducted with families in the study, their responses to the survey questions reflect general trends in the data.

#### An active father and an egalitarian son: the Fleming-Colemans

In the Fleming-Coleman family, the father does a large share of the housework. Despite working full-time as a lawyer, Samson Fleming does about half of core household tasks according to his and his wife's reports. "The uniqueness in our family," Samson notes, "is the amount of workload that I carry in this family. I am the one that does the laundry. I'm the one that does the shopping and those kinds of outside activities that normally one would associate primarily with a woman, or the wife of the house." His wife, Marge Coleman, a college professor, concurs: "Well, I had a sense that my husband's a lot more involved in the home – in all the home-associated work. You know, like the laundry and the cooking. Well, none of us cook, but the dishwashing and the lunch packing. He does at least his share. I think that's pretty rare."

Samson's large contribution to the housework seems to have made an impression on his son Lewis, a twelfth-grader. He is already in the habit of helping out, particularly by driving his two younger siblings from place to place. "I feel it's my responsibility, and I love it," he claims. "I'm the big brother and I love being the big brother. You know, sometimes it's kind of irritating with being the one that has to shuttle everybody around. I'm almost like a soccer mom some weekdays. You know, I'm dropping my brother off at soccer and basketball. I'm picking my sister up from band, or driving her to swimming. We're in so many activities."

The family's perspective is consistent with the performative theory of why housework matters. In Lewis's mind, chores and gender do not seem to be strongly associated. Although he likens the job of chauffeuring his siblings to that of a "soccer mom," he also sees it as an appropriate responsibility for a big brother. Furthermore, on the survey he reports that he expects to do half the housework and the childcare when he gets married. Considering how non-traditional the Fleming-Colemans' division of labor is, it seems likely to be influential in Lewis's thinking.

### Reproducing the second shift: the Lieberthals

In contrast, families in which the father does a relatively small proportion of the housework tend to produce children who expect the same unequal division of labor when they marry. Tenth-grader Tanya Lieberthal plans to play the homemaker role when she marries. When asked who should do the housework, she replies, "The wife. In my family, it's the wife. You know, there's this understanding that she's supposed to take care of the house. And frankly, she's the only one of the two who should take care of the house. So, she's got to worry about coming home and vacuuming and doing laundry and fixing things."

What makes Tanya remarkable is that she has these plans despite circumstances that would seem to encourage her to be more career-oriented. According to her father, she is at the top of her class at a highly competitive magnet school. An overachiever, she participates in a variety of extracurricular activities. As her father tells it, "She does a million things in high school. She's on the debate team. She's on the JV soccer team. She's on the newspaper. There are probably three or four other things that she does. I just can't think of them right now." In addition to this, she has liberal beliefs about gender; her gender attitude scale score is 5, the most egalitarian score possible.

Despite all of this, Tanya's stated plans involve working part time and taking primary responsibility for home and children. This is close to the path followed by her mother, who stayed home when Tanya and her two siblings were young, and now continues to do nearly all the chores while working part time. Thus, just as was the case with Lewis Fleming, Tanya Lieberthal's story strongly suggests that dual-earner parents' division of housework affects their children's expectations.

Of particular interest is the way Tanya justifies her surprisingly gender-traditional plans. Asked whether she would rather have a husband who shares the chores, she observes, "I'm a bit of a control freak. So, I might tend towards [saying], 'I'll do everything just as long as I'm the one who decides how it gets done.'" Here, she is essentially saying that she should do the chores because she is an overachiever. This is highly reminiscent of Hochschild's concept of the "cultural cover-up." As Hochschild writes, "The common portrayal of the supermom working mother is that she is 'energetic' and 'competent' because these are her *personal* character-istics, not because she has been forced to adapt to an overly demanding schedule" (Hochschild 1989: 24, emphasis in the original). Apparently doubting that she has any choice but to do the housework in the future, Tanya justifies it in terms of being a "control freak" – a personal char-acteristic. Although still a teenager, she has been effectively socialized to accept the second shift.

### High support and a strong father–daughter bond: the Castilles

Roger Castille is a professional actor and musician who now combines his performing career with steady work teaching drama at a four-year college. Daughter Candice, a tenth grader, is drawn to this way of life. Not only does she act, play music, and sing in choirs at her local high school, but she also hopes to follow in her father's footsteps and make a career out of one or more of these pursuits. Her expectations are quite egalitarian; she hopes her future husband will share in housework and childcare, thereby allowing her to make a significant contribution to family income.

Although Candice reports that her father does a good deal of house-work, what is equally telling is that she indicates that her parents are very supportive and not too demanding of her. "I know that I get along bet-ter with my parents than a lot of people do . . . my parents respect us and listen to us and give us reasonable rules and not very many of them compared to other families I know." Roger agrees that he and his wife have been more supportive than challenging of Candice and her brother Victor, particularly when it comes to housework. During the interview, which took place in a basement cluttered with musical instruments, he says, "Well, you know, we have a very close relationship with our kids. We still go on vacation with them, and their friends envy their relation-ship with us, blah, blah, blah. But in some ways we have spoiled them.

We haven't demanded a lot of housework out of them, you know, which explains why the basement looks like this."

High family support seems to be an important part of the explanation for Candice's aspirations and expectations. Supportiveness fosters a strong father–daughter bond. As Candice notes, "Mom and daddy admit that I'm daddy's favorite . . . he tells me all the time that he just like thinks of me, and goes, 'Oh, she's so cute.'" While not explicit in the interview, this close relationship may have encouraged her to follow in her father's footsteps. And if she is to pursue the demanding life of a musician or an actor, it would be reasonable to expect to have egalitarian arrangements in her marriage. This, then, could be one mechanism by which high family support leads to egalitarian expectations.

### High challenge and a son who aims high: the Summers

A good illustration of the effects of high family challenge on teenage boys is provided by Kendall Summers, a twelfth grader. On the survey, Kendall reported that when he gets married, he hopes to be the primary breadwinner while his wife does most of the childcare. While he is unsure about his future occupation, he sees himself in the traditional provider role. "My dad works because it makes him feel good to keep us happy and to support us as a family. And I think it would do the same for me. You know, hard work . . . would be fulfilling for me knowing that I was helping keep the family together." As this comment indicates, Kendall's plans are influenced not just by parental challenge but also by the division of roles between his father, a small business owner, and his mother, who had just recently found part-time work after spending many years as a housewife and volunteer worker. Even though parents' relative work hours have no influence on adolescent expectations in the aggregate, the fact that his father has been more attached to the workforce than his mother seems to influence Kendall's expectations.

When asked what values his parents have tried to instill in him, Kendall immediately mentions the work ethic and responsibility: "Mainly that nothing is just handed to anyone. Hard work is the way to get everything." Since encouragement to work hard is a component of Rathunde's challenge scale, Kendall's comment is consistent with rating his parents as high on challenge.

Kendall's mother concurs that she and her husband push him, particularly to do well in school. "I know he probably feels stressed from that. With his grades, it's probably a big stress for him because we have just always told him that it's an unfortunate thing that the world out there has become competitive, and a lot of the competitiveness is unfair that's out there now. And so you really do need to strive to be at the top or do something to distinguish yourself."

While it may seem that the case of Kendall Summers merely shows that adolescent sons in dual-earner families aspire to be like their fathers, recall that mothers and fathers in the subsample analyzed are not equal participants in the workforce. As seen in table 14.2, fathers work more hours per week, on average, than mothers. A fact not shown in the table is that on average they also earn nearly twice as much as mothers. Also, some families such as the Summers became dual-earner families only recently, when the mother, formerly a full-time homemaker, entered the workforce. Nevertheless, 47 percent of boys expect to share responsibility for family income equally with their wives, and 78 percent expect equal sharing of childcare. The factor that appears to distinguish Kendall from these other adolescents is parental challenge. The boys whose parents push them hardest tend to orient themselves toward achievement in the workplace. While this is speculation, such boys may conclude that they would prefer a traditional wife who will support their aspirations.

### Conclusion

It is important to offer some cautions about these results. First, particpants in the 500 Family Study are not representative of the American population in general, but only of middle- and upper-middle-class dual-earner families with children. The results cannot be generalized beyond this population. Furthermore, the data are cross-sectional, making attributions of causality problematic. For example, it may seem that parents' gender role attitudes are shaping their children's attitudes. As Glass and her co-authors have shown, however, the pattern of influence can also proceed in the other direction (Glass, Bengtson, and Dunham 1986).

Despite these limitations, the study has several strengths relative to the existing research on gender role socialization. The sample includes as much data for fathers as for mothers or children. This allows analysis of both parents' influence on their children, rather than merely the mothers' influence, as is commonly done. Also, systematic consideration is given to the ways in which socialization effects vary by the gender of the child. Finally, the availability of matching qualitative and quantitative data allows greater insight into results than would be possible in a purely quantitative study.

Several suggestive findings have emerged from this study. When fathers participate in traditionally female household tasks, children are more likely to expect to share housework in the future; girls are also more likely to expect that their husbands will share childcare with them. On the other hand, mother's relative participation in work outside the home has no effect. Viewed as a deviation from the normative "transitional" arrangement in dual-earner families, where mothers retain primary responsibility for housework, the father's contribution to housework appears to make a particularly deep impression on children.

Another noteworthy finding is that parenting style affects teens' gender role expectations, even when parental attitudes and role modeling are controlled. Family support appears to lead children to expect a more egalitarian division of childcare, while family challenge has the opposite effect. When parents are perceived as challenging, boys are more likely to expect to be their family's primary breadwinner. It was speculated, with some corroborating evidence from the qualitative data, that boys who aspire to challenging careers hope for wives who will be supportive of them rather than pursuing their own careers. This is troubling, especially given the finding that more boys than girls expect the husband to be the main breadwinner in their marriages. Given the principle of marital homogamy, the work role may remain a source of conflict in middle-class marriages in the future. Of course, these conclusions would be bolstered if they were backed by similar findings using other samples. While the effects of parental attitudes and role modeling are the subject of a considerable literature, this is a relatively new area for research and requires additional investigation.

## NOTES

1. Conservative attempts were made to fill in missing data based on the *respondent's* own answers. For example, on the support and challenge scales, if an adolescent answered 14 or 15 of the relevant 16 items, missing values were set equal to the mean of the respondent's non-missing items. No attempt was made to impute values for any variables based on *sample* means.
2. A construct based on these four items has a Cronbach's alpha of .62 for fathers and .58 for mothers.
3. In the subsample of 160 families, Cronbach's alpha is .87 for support and .74 for challenge.
4. Several other controls were considered but not used. Father's and mother's age are very highly correlated ($r = .77$); of the two, mother's age was chosen because there is less missing data. Parent educational attainment was not used because it is highly correlated with household income ($r = .49$ for mother's education and .52 for fathers). Finally, while race could presumably have a powerful effect on family role expectations, the effect of a dummy variable for non-white or mixed racial membership was never significant, and excluding it had no appreciable effect on any of the other coefficients in the models, perhaps because 84 percent of adolescents in the sample are white. Therefore, to preserve a degree of freedom, race is not included in the analysis. Income

was calculated based on procedures developed by Casey Mulligan and Yona Rubenstein (see technical appendix B).

5. Among the families used in this analysis, the median education for a parent of either gender is a master's degree or equivalent.

6. Generally it is best to test all theoretically interesting interaction terms at once, rather than including and excluding them on the basis of significance. The problem is that gender could plausibly interact with parents' gender role attitudes, division of labor, parenting style, or even the teenager's own age. Given the sample size, there are not enough degrees of freedom in the model to test all these interactions at the same time. Running separate regressions for adolescent boys and girls was not feasible. By including all main effects in the models, but selectively including interaction terms, an appropriate balance is sought between methodological correctness and the difficulties of working with a small sample.

7. The large but statistically insignificant main effect for gender in model 3b needs to be understood in relation to the gender-by-age and gender-by-challenge interaction effects. In model 3b, it appears that girls are 712 times more likely than boys to expect to share breadwinning responsibility equally with their future spouses. But in fact, the true difference in odds ratios between boys and girls is $712 * 0.45^{\text{age}} * 25.47^{\text{challenge}}$. Thus, a 14-year-old girl who rates her parents as being at the mean on family challenge is predicted to be 14.49 times more likely than the average boy in the sample to expect an equal division of breadwinning responsibility. Change the girl's age to 18, however, and she is predicted to be only 0.59 times as likely as a boy to have this expectation. Manipulating the girl's family challenge rating would have similarly dramatic effects on the odds ratio.

8. It seemed possible that multicollinearity between the four indicators of parental attitude transmission and role modeling is raising the standard errors of the estimates, and thereby preventing some coefficients from reaching significance at the .05 level. This is to be expected if couples with egalitarian beliefs about gender roles are likely to put their beliefs into practice by sharing housework and income-earning responsibility. Inspection of the correlation matrix did reveal significant correlations among the four variables. To test for distortions in results due to multicollinearity, logistic regression models were estimated again with fewer predictors. Each of the the main effects models was run four times in succession, each time including only one of the four indicators of parental influence. In no cases did these variables achieve statistical significance at the .05 level, except where they were already found to be significant in the complete models.

# Commentary

## Mick Cunningham

*Understanding contemporary adolescents' perspectives on the intersection of work and family holds tremendous import for future trends in family life. The extent to which contemporary adolescents are aware of work–family issues is not well-understood, and this is especially true for boys. We know that many girls receive messages from multiple sources about the centrality of marriage and children for their adult lives, but the extent to which boys ever contemplate these topics is unclear.*

*The chapter by Weinshenker offers us an exemplary use of multi-source data on families in the service of enhancing our theoretical and empirical understanding of the nexus of work and family life. Weinshenker uses several types of measures of family, employment, and their intersection to illuminate the ways that adolescents envision their lives in the future. The analysis of multiple data-gathering modalities from multiple family members offers great potential for helping us better understand the day-to-day context of family life.*

*The investigation of the relationships between parenting style and gender-related outcomes in Weinshenker's chapter constitutes an important step forward in an emerging area of research. I begin by examining how integration of quantitative and qualitative data holds the potential to allow researchers to make significant strides in the construction of theories of family. I then argue that Weinshenker's findings about the importance of parenting style for adolescents' expectations about future family life may provide an important missing piece in the development of theories of gender socialization in families.*

### Does Lewis Fleming "do gender?"

*The collection of in-depth interviews provides an excellent opportunity to "go behind" survey responses so that those responses may be interpreted in terms of the respondent's "life space" and the sense that the respondent makes of it (Cain 1973: 9). Indeed, Weinshenker's analysis does a remarkable job of linking statements from adolescents' in-depth interviews to existing sociological research on gender in families. However, an integrated analysis of information drawn from in-depth interviews and survey data is complex; Weinshenker could take his analysis even further by specifically identifying ways that his multi-source findings combine to support, refute, or modify existing theoretical explanations of the phenomena under study. Below is one example of how Weinshenker's analysis could be used as the basis for further theoretical development.*

*Given the 500 Family Study research design, it is an interesting and highly interpretive exercise to search for quotes relevant to a particular topic when the topic may not have been specifically and consistently addressed in the in-depth interviews. For instance, there is an evocative quote in Weinshenker's analysis of the Fleming-Coleman family in which Lewis, a twelfth-grade son in an egalitarian family, refers to himself as a "soccer mom." Weinshenker uses this self-description to argue that chores and gender are not strongly linked in Lewis Fleming's mind. He then infers that Lewis's description provides support for a performative theory of gender.*

*While I strongly agree that Lewis Fleming's own understanding of gender-appropriate tasks is shaped by his parents' relatively egalitarian actions, it seems likely that, contrary to Weinshenker's interpretation, Lewis makes a strong association between gender and specific types of chores. Indeed, his use of the term "soccer mom" suggests that Lewis is well aware of cultural definitions of masculine and feminine work. West and Zimmerman (1987), among others, argue that everyone is accountable for "doing gender." Further, as Weinshenker points out, in my research on intergenerational patterns in the division of housework I argue that paternal modeling of routine housework or maternal modeling of paid employment might work by "minimizing the extent to which sons and daughters make an association between gender and the performance of particular kinds of work" (Cunningham 2001b: 186). However, Lewis's comments offer a potential critique of this argument.*

*Rather than being unaware of the connection between gender and family work, Lewis is clearly cognizant of the fact that his role as a caretaker for his siblings could be interpreted as "feminine" work. For some reason, Lewis is both willing and able to ignore these cultural definitions of gender. Understanding his decision to "un-do gender" provides an excellent opportunity to re-evaluate the limitations of theories of gender performance, showing that parental socialization may have the potential to override the strong influence of context that performative theories place at the center of gendered interactions. It seems likely that his father's example is likely to be critical to Lewis's actions. Lewis's mother and father also express awareness that their own family patterns conflict with widely shared cultural understandings of gender. It seems that what is being "transmitted" from parents to children is the acceptability of breaking cultural stereotypes in the service of some other goal. The question of what that other goal might be remains to be answered.*

## The potential importance of family relationship dynamics

*Fortunately, Weinshenker's analysis of parenting styles suggests a potentially rich source of theorizing about what some of the personal or familial goals that "trump" gender might be. The role of family relationships and parent–child dynamics in shaping gendered family patterns is not well understood, although a small number of disparate studies have pointed to the potential importance of family relationship dynamics for gender-related outcomes. For instance, in his qualitative study of couples who participate equally in family work, Coltrane (1989) argues that many sharing couples are best characterized not so much by their feminist gender ideologies as by their "child-centeredness" and "equity ideals." This finding suggests a potential theoretical mechanism through which the effects of parental support and/or challenge operate. Lewis's parents may reason that their children's well-being, given their particular circumstances (context), will be best served by following an unconventional model of household arrangements. It is possible that Lewis's recognition of the importance of ensuring children's well-being (in this case, his siblings), in combination with his father's significant participation in housework and/or his mother's central economic role in the family, interact in such a way that Lewis has the personal resources to ignore prevailing cultural definitions of gender. Together, Weinshenker's analyses of parental modeling and parenting styles combine to point toward an emerging research agenda regarding the determinants of egalitarian ideals and practices among children.*

*There are several aspects of Weinshenker's measures of family challenge and family support that suggest areas for future investigation. First, measures of fathers' and mothers' independent contributions to each of these might be enlightening. For instance, it may be especially important to understand the extent to which the father, in particular, is responsible for fostering a supportive or challenging environment. Weinshenker's findings suggest that fathers' participation in housework holds particularly strong significance for adolescent girls' expectations about future responsibility for childcare. In an investigation of "child-centered fathering," Coltrane and Adams (2001) showed that men's participation in child-centered activities, including helping children with homework, driving children to activities, and having private talks with children, was associated with greater relative participation by men in the kinds of routine housework Weinshenker uses as his indicator of the parental division of labor. It is unclear whether this type of child-centered fathering would be linked to adolescent children's perceptions of family support, but it seems likely that fathers' involvement in child-centered family work might shape children's future expectations about housework and childcare. Future research examining the connections between fathers' day-to-day interactions in families, their level of commitment to children's well-being, and changes in fathers' gender-related attitudes and behaviors may offer additional insights into our understanding of contemporary family practices.*

*The findings regarding the influence of family challenge are also worthy of future investigation. Again, it may be important to know not only which parent is the primary source of adolescents' perceptions of challenge, but also whether this sense of challenge is communicated equally to sons and daughters. Weinshenker finds that children, especially boys, who are frequently challenged by their parents have less egalitarian expectations about their future family roles. The individual family challenge measures suggest that children who report high levels of family challenge probably generalize this challenge to the world of paid work and economic success more than to raising healthy children or having successful family relationships. Therefore, it seems likely that the prevalence of the "ideal worker" ideology among middle-class families is likely to continue to produce gender-stratified family responsibilities (Williams 2000). Given these possibilities, it may be fruitful for future investigations to consider interactions between parenting styles and each parent's gender ideology and contributions to family work.*

*Combined with consideration of the consistent influence of fathers' relative participation in routine housework, research on parenting styles and family relationship dynamics offers the potential for the formulation of a comprehensive model of the influences that lead to "sharing couples." Despite some continuing evidence of a "stalled revolution" (Hochschild 1989), there is also growing evidence that men are becoming more involved in the kinds of family work that have historically been performed by women. Weinshenker's powerful and provocative analysis suggests a number of new directions researchers should thoroughly investigate in the search for mechanisms that may provide a "jump start" for the stalled revolution.*

## *Jennifer Glass*

*Weinshenker has done an admirable job of summarizing the existing theories about how parents influence their children's anticipated division of labor between spouses – direct transmission of parents' ideas and beliefs about gender roles, and modeling both fathers' actual participation in housework and childcare and mothers' employment and earnings outside the home. His analyses also shows the limitations of these theories, which fail to take into account the character of the relationship between parents and their teenagers. Developmental psychologists have paid much more attention to the ways in which the quality of parent–child relationships affect children's social and intellectual development; it is not surprising that those same characteristics might influence how adolescents plan to organize their own family lives.*

*I find it particularly intriguing that parental warmth and support encourage both young women and young men to anticipate more egalitarian divisions of childcare and breadwinning, although the latter does not quite attain statistical significance. The items in this scale suggest that the adolescents who scored highest on this measure received a great deal of love and attention from their parents – presumably both parents, although the scale items are unclear on the exact referent. Even if one parent put in more time on childcare tasks than the other, the scale clearly measures the emotional atmosphere created by both parents. If there was tension in the household over one spouse's inadequate participation in family life, or if one parent was clearly not supportive of the adolescent although the other was, scale scores would remain low. Given the traditionally greater involvement of mothers in childcare and the difficulties in American culture with distant or uninvolved fathers, high scores on the family support measures are likely to indicate a family in which the father is involved in his adolescents' daily lives and demonstrates affection and appreciation for them. Irrespective of his participation in daily housework, such a father creates a role model for involved fatherhood that leads daughters to expect similar involvement from their future husbands and sons to expect to be equally involved in their children's lives. Those adolescents who felt nurtured and cherished see the nurturing of children as a positive enriching experience they want to share with their future spouses. The nurturing of boys in particular during adolescence may be important in predisposing them to share childcare in the future.*

*The finding that girls alter their expectations about shared breadwinning as they age is also interesting but not surprising. Perhaps girls learn more about the gender wage gap as they age and their naive belief that gender equality has been "achieved" fades away. Perhaps their own experiences as young wage workers demonstrate the gender wage gap in a more visceral way. Given the wage differential between male-dominated and female-dominated jobs even in the low wage service sector, it may be quite reasonable for girls to anticipate marrying someone who earns more than they are capable of earning, no matter how egalitarian their intentions. This seems particularly plausible when one considers the modal "traditional" response to the breadwinning item – that one's spouse would earn slightly more than the respondent. Weinshenker is quite right that this is movement toward a more realistic assessment of young women's statistical chances of marrying someone with higher earnings than their own. However, I am not sure that this indicates women are lowering their own career aspirations or planning on reducing their work involvement following marriage. It may simply be a reflection of the way that shared breadwinning is operationalized here – as equal earnings rather than equal involvement or effort in the labor force. In dual-earner households where both partners work full time, women's earnings constitute about 40 percent of household income. Most households could not afford a 40 percent cut in income, meaning that these households are highly dependent on wives' earnings even though they are not equivalent to husbands'.*

*Finally, the findings that high levels of parental challenge encourage adolescent boys to form more traditional expectations regarding their responsibility for breadwinning and their role in childcare are troubling. High levels of parental challenge affect girls differently – increasing both their expectation that they will have primary care for their children and their expectation that they will provide financial support for their family, although the latter effect falls just short of statistical significance. Parental challenge thus seems to prepare boys for traditional male careers that require a supportive secondary earner spouse, but prepares girls to become "superwomen" who carry responsibility for both breadwinning and childcare simultaneously.*

*What could be the psychological mechanism driving these results? Turning to the actual scale items, the parental challenge items reflect youth's engagement in a wide variety of activities in high challenge households (interests and hobbies, extracurricular activities, competitive games), the high level of achievement and hard work expected of them in this wide range of pursuits (use time wisely, do your best, be a hard worker, expect to be good at what you do, make family members proud), and the value placed on individualism (self-confidence, self-discipline, independence, individual accomplishment, and responsibility). Although Weinshenker rightly supposes that such households should nourish high aspirations for success in both sons and daughters, there is nothing in the scale items that challenges the traditional sex typing of adult social roles. Given his portrait of the parents in this sample as typifying Hochschild's (1989) "stalled revolution" in gender roles, perhaps the high achieving children in these households understand success in very gender-biased ways. For the sons, this parental pressure to succeed results in a very traditional orientation toward achievement outside of home and family. Given cultural conceptions of masculinity that view successful fatherhood as synonymous with financial provision, these young ambitious men may see no contradiction between their roles as workers and fathers (Simon 1995). For daughters, the pressure to achieve combined with an ideology of individualism and self-discipline results in an orientation toward both career and family involvement with only minor assistance from a partner. Because traditional definitions of successful motherhood require enormous investments of time and energy in children (Hays 1996), these young women may see heavy maternal involvement as imperative while expecting relatively less involvement from their future husbands.*

*If correct, this interpretation suggests that a possible interaction between gender egalitarianism among parents and a high level of parental challenge may be necessary to translate parental challenge into aspirations for shared childcare* and mutual career support. Until achievement in childrearing becomes part of the general cultural lexicon for success among both genders, parents may need to do more explicit role modeling and direct teaching of such expectations to their sons, while deemphasizing them among their daughters, if they expect to see greater egalitarianism among their children.

Weinshenker has done a good job of working with the available measures in the data set to understand the determinants of adolescents' work and family aspirations, but other measures might help illuminate some of the more perplexing findings here. For example, parents' gender role attitudes had virtually no impact on their children, and even the direct example of father's participation in domestic labor had only limited impact. If measures of the amount of parental conflict over housework and childcare were available, I wonder if they might not condition the effects of parents' attitudes and behavior. Adolescents watching their parents fight continually over a more equitable division of housework might view fathers' housework as bought at too high a price, or might make egalitarian attitudes seem less attractive.

I also wonder about the differential impact of time use versus responsibility for domestic labor. Some literature suggests that even when fathers contribute substantially to the total time spent in domestic labor, mothers continue to shoulder the responsibility for thinking about and organizing domestic tasks and childcare activities. While time use measures tap one dimension of the division of household labor, this hidden labor of planning and worrying about domestic life and children's well-being is often transparent to children. Children pick up fairly quickly on who in the household can be relied upon to make sure that activities get planned and tasks get done. When this responsibility is truly shared by both parents, it might make a bigger difference in their children's future expectations than time use alone.

What these interpretations share is an emphasis on the emotional climate in the family rather than just the actual behavior of parents. Adolescents who feel both their parents are involved in their lives, both can be counted on to keep the household running smoothly, and both accept their roles with equanimity instead of reluctance or hostility, are more likely to expect shared childcare and breadwinning in their own future relationships. Weinshenker's significant contribution here is the attention he draws to the psychological elements of family life that often get missed in sociologists' focus on the structural organization of family life. Future research on adolescents' family and career aspirations would be well advised to pick up on the intriguing start that Weinshenker's analysis provides.

# 15 Transmitting educational values: parent occupation and adolescent development

*Kimberly S. Maier*

The unique culture of math and science professions is likely to influence how parents in these occupations interact with their children and what resources and encouragement they are willing and able to provide for them. Bourdieu (1977) conceptualized this intergenerational transmission of knowledge, skills, and interests as cultural capital. The requirements and expectations of parents' work environments impact parents' values; these values in turn influence parenting practices (Kohn, Slomczynski, and Schoenbach 1986; Mortimer and Kumka 1982) and the cultural capital parents provide for their children.

Parenting practices that challenge adolescents to do their best, encourage them to use their time wisely, and support post-secondary attendance and career choices are practices that most parents, regardless of their social status or income, value and engage in. The educational expectations that parents have for their children are typically quite high, with an overwhelming majority expecting their children to graduate from college (Schneider and Stevenson 1999). However, it is expected that parents employed in scientific fields interact differently with their adolescents in subtle ways, influenced by the distinct culture of their professions. In particular, these parents are likely to incorporate parenting behaviors in tune with the values and norms of their professions. Such differences should be apparent in daily interactions between parent and child as well as in the educational planning process, creating somewhat different cultural capital in these homes that influences adolescents' educational values as well as their psychological attributes (Ryu and Mortimer 1996).

In this chapter, day-to-day interactions and family dynamics are examined to understand how parents transmit educational values to their children. Family members typically have multiple interactions regarding educational goals, motivations, and time use, providing an opportunity to examine the process of transmission in detail. This chapter investigates whether the transmission process via parenting practices differs by occupational field and parent gender and what effect these practices have on adolescents' educational values, happiness and enjoyment at home and at school, their motivation to succeed, and their sense of meeting their own expectations and the expectations of others.

## Intergenerational transmission of values

The process of the intergenerational transmission of values and the effect of family characteristics on the occupational success of children and parents has been studied extensively. Drawing on the early work of Blau and Duncan (1967), two related strands of research have been developed that examine how families influence the formation and transmission of educational values. The first strand, based on the theory of status attainment, relates adolescents' educational expectations to parents' values and encouragement (Sewell, Haller, and Ohlendorf 1970). The second strand focuses more specifically on values that are specific to parents' work experiences and their influence on parenting practices. The association between value transmission and aspects of parents' jobs, such as prestige, occupational sector, and complexity of occupational tasks, has been studied in detail (Kohn 1969; Kohn and Schooler 1969; Mortimer 1975; Mortimer and Kumka 1982; Ryu and Mortimer 1996). However, no research has focused specifically on this process for science and mathematics professionals.

Examining how values are influenced by individuals' work experiences, Kohn and colleagues argue that personality and work are intertwined and have a reciprocal effect on one another (Kohn and Schooler 1969). This idea has been extended beyond the individual to the realm of the family to include attitudes about marital roles and labor division, parenting styles and practices and the nature of interactions between parents and children (Curtner-Smith, Bennett, and O'Rear 1995; Greenberger, O'Neil, and Nagel 1994; Klute et al. 2001; Kohn et al. 1986; Luster, Rhoades, and Haas 1989; Menaghan and Parcel 1995; Mortimer and Kumka 1982). While much of the previous research has examined job complexity, autonomy, or prestige, this chapter focuses on how the culture of parents' professions – specifically science and mathematics professions – affects value transmission from parent to adolescent.

## The culture of science and its implications for parenting

Math and science professions have characteristics that are unique to their fields of expertise. Merton (1973) characterized the culture of science (including the discipline of mathematics) as valuing rational and logical thought and analysis. The values and norms of science are transmitted by example and precept and reinforced through sanctions within the profession. Those engaged in professions such as engineering and mathematics internalize these values and norms through their educational and work experiences (Becker and Carper 1962). As parents, these professionals may model values and norms at home with their children through the habitus they have developed in part as a consequence of their professions.

Habitus, or an individual's view of the world and his or her place in it, influences how individuals use available cultural resources (Bourdieu 1977). A person's professional identity plays an important role in the development of his or her habitus. Individuals who are employed in science professions have had particular educational and professional experiences that are specific to their fields. These professionals have had the personal experience of early educational pre-planning and understand the significance of taking advanced mathematics and science courses at the secondary level. They are likely to value mathematics and science education, early and informed pre-planning of educational experiences, and scholastic achievement, particularly in the sciences. These particular values are modeled in the home via the parenting choices and activities these parents engage in with their children, providing their children with cultural capital that is influenced by their experiences as science professionals.

Because the field of science has traditionally been dominated by males, the effect of gender must also be considered. Research has shown that schools inequitably distribute resources among girls and boys and has examined the effects such inequities have on student achievement, self-esteem, educational attainment, and occupational choices (AAUW 1992). While the distribution of these resources is changing, and the gender gap between girls and boys appears to be closing, at least with respect to performance on national achievement tests (Dwyer and Johnson 1997), it could be argued that mothers who are math or science professionals were likely recipients of inequitable resources in schools, discouraged from pursuing math or science fields, or perhaps thwarted in their career advancement. These mothers may be particularly sensitive to gender issues and may take extra steps to ensure that their daughters and sons receive similar levels of support, encouragement, and resources for their schoolwork and future plans.

## Values played out in the home: parenting practices and monitoring

The values and norms of parents are instantiated through their parenting and monitoring practices. Through their choice of parenting practices, parents provide particular expressions of challenge and support to their children (Hauser, Powers, and Noam 1991). Parental support facilitates the transmission of values from parent to child (Mortimer and Kumka 1982). Other research has examined parental challenge as a measure of the quality of interaction between parent and adolescent, finding that children of supportive and challenging parents are more likely to succeed in school (Csikszentmihalyi and Schneider 2000).

Parents provide *support* to their adolescents by expressing love for them, which in turn fosters adolescents' feelings of well-being and security. Adolescents who perceive that their parents provide high levels of support are comfortable in their homes and feel loved and cared for by their parents. Parents *challenge* their adolescents by expressing high expectations to their teenager about how to use their time wisely, work hard, and be self-confident and independent. By challenging their adolescents, parents help provide an environment that is beneficial to their adolescents' development and transition to adulthood, encouraging them to become autonomous and self-directed individuals (Csikszentmihalyi and Schneider 2000).

High levels of both support and challenge have been shown to positively impact adolescents' experiences in school and with their families as well as the career planning process, likely facilitating the intergenerational transference of educational values. Csikszentmihalyi, Rathunde, and Whalen (1993) found that teenagers who experience high levels of parental support and challenge are more likely to approach tasks such as schoolwork and planning for the future competently and enthusiastically. Adolescents in these types of families also report high levels of self-esteem, optimism, and motivation, and feel that their current school and life engagements are important for their future goals (Rathunde, Carroll, and Huang 2000).

Parents also engage in a variety of parenting practices that are designed to control their children's behavior. Control, in the custodial sense, involves monitoring and supervising the teenager. Patterson and Stouthamer-Loeber (1984) describe parents who engage in high levels of monitoring as having an awareness of their child's companions and knowing where their children are and what they are doing most of the time. Parents who provide high levels of supervision rarely leave their adolescents at home alone and require their teenagers to obey firmly established curfews (Kurdek and Fine 1993; Thomson, McLanahan, and Curtin 1992).

This chapter focuses on the supervisory and monitoring behaviors of parents as they relate to the social and academic aspects of adolescent life. Since math/science-employed parents have themselves had to formulate goals and persevere in their studies early in their school careers they are more likely to engage in direct supervision of their adolescents' school experiences. These parents are also more likely to employ stricter monitoring of their adolescents' time use and choice of social activities and to be involved in adolescents' academic decisions and activities (Ispa, Gray, and Thornburg 1984).

### Unexplored student outcomes: mood, motivation, and self-esteem

In examining the transmission of educational values, this chapter investigates the impact of this process on the psychological characteristics of adolescents – characteristics that may help them weather the challenges and disappointments of high school. Previous research suggests that adolescents' success in meeting challenges in high school is associated with feelings of control and positive self-attitudes (Amato and Keith 1991). Students who are self-directed are able to monitor their own behaviors and feel efficacious and, thus, are more likely to succeed in meeting academic challenges (Finn and Rock 1997). Adolescents' mood, motivation, and self-esteem are also positively related to their success in advanced courses, extracurricular activities, and their ability to use time alone productively (Hektner and Asakawa 2000). These variables are the focus of analysis.

Wessman and Ricks (1966) formally define mood as the emotional shifts that represent an individual's personal orientation to the world. Conceptually, mood is indicative of an adolescent's engagement or interest in particular activities (Rathunde et al. 2000). High mood states suggest that the adolescent is experiencing positive affect and high energy. Mood has been found to be positively associated with high levels of family support in both middle-class adolescents and talented teenagers (Rathunde et al. 2000). In contrast, lower levels of mood or a high variability in mood could interfere with an adolescent's capacity for concentrated effort, especially at school (Larson, Csikszentmihalyi, and Graef 1980).

Along with mood, motivation plays an important role in adolescents' ability to meet challenges. A motivated adolescent is energized to achieve a specific goal or result. Deci and Ryan (1985) distinguish between two types of motivation: intrinsic and extrinsic. Extrinsic motivation results when forces outside the person encourage him or her to pursue a specific goal. In the case of adolescents, this extrinsic motivation could be parents' demands, or anticipated punishments or rewards for particular behaviors. Intrinsic motivation results when the person finds either the process or the end result to be enjoyable or interesting, which can be driven by the adolescent's long-term goals.

Adolescents' self-esteem also plays an important role in their academic success. Self-esteem is a reflection of the individual's own evaluation of his or her self-worth (Wylie 1979). Parents have been shown to have the largest effect on an adolescent's self-esteem (Yabiku, Axinn, and Thornton 1999). Further, research has found that adolescents who experience high levels of family support typically experience high levels of self-esteem (Rathunde et al. 2000).

### Hypotheses

*Hypothesis 1.* Parents who are employed in math/science professions may be more directly involved in their adolescents' educational experiences and planning and may employ stricter monitoring of their adolescents' social and educational activities. Compared with parents in other occupations, math/science-employed parents will thus be more likely to be perceived by their teenagers as providing supportive home environments.

*Hypothesis 2.* These same parents are expected to provide more challenge to their teenagers because of the value that they themselves place on self-direction and autonomy. Because of their personal experiences within male-dominated occupations, mothers employed in math or science occupations may be more challenging of their adolescents than mothers in other occupations.

*Hypothesis 3.* Differences in parenting practices will affect adolescents' educational values. Specifically, adolescents who come from supportive and challenging family environments will be more likely to earn high grades and to have graduate school aspirations than adolescents from less challenging and supportive home environments. Although family support and challenge and parental monitoring practices are expected to vary by parent occupation, parenting practices are unlikely to account for all differences in the transmission of educational values. Consequently, parent's occupation (math/science versus other) is also expected to be a significant predictor of adolescent outcomes.

*Hypothesis 4.* Adolescents whose parents are employed in math or science professions are expected to have higher levels of mood, self-esteem, and motivation than adolescents whose parents are employed in other occupations (Rathunde et al. 2000).

## Method

### Sample

The sample consists of 315 families with adolescent children who participated in the 500 Family Study. Adolescents in the sample are almost evenly split between males and females. Most are between fourteen and seventeen years old and attend high school (grades nine through twelve). Almost 80 percent of the adolescents are white, approximately ten percent are African American, and the remaining students are Hispanic, Asian, or Native-American. The parents have similar demographic characteristics to those of the full sample.

### Measures

*Adolescent measures*    Measures of adolescent mood, motivation, and self-esteem were constructed from student responses to the Experience Sampling Method (ESM). The items that were used in constructing measures of mood, motivation, and self-esteem employed Likert and semantic-differential scales. Because the chapter focuses on adolescents' responses to the ESM while they were with their parents and when they were at school, only ESM responses that were obtained in these two contexts were selected.

Graduate school plans and students' grades (from the student survey) were used as measures of adolescents' educational values. Because the educational expectations of adolescents in the sample are very high, plans to attend graduate or professional school (rather than college) is used as a measure of educational expectations. A student grade measure was constructed based on adolescents' self-reports of average grades received on their last report card.[1] Adolescent gender was added as a control variable in all models.

*Family and parent measures*    Measures of support and challenge were constructed from adolescents' responses to a series of statements asking them about various aspects of their family environment. The eleven items measuring support inquired about the family's responsiveness to the adolescent.[2] The twelve items measuring challenge include encouragement of competitiveness, decision-making, and high expectations.[3] To construct the measures, a one-parameter logistic item response model was used.[4]

A measure of school guidance was constructed based on parents' responses about the guidance parents provide their children with school and career planning and their levels of involvement in their adolescent's

school experiences and college plans.[5] This measure was constructed separately for mothers and fathers using the item response theory approach
in order to allow for parental gender effects.[6]

A math/science career variable was constructed based on parents'
responses to a question asking what kind of work they do. The descriptions of the parents' job titles were examined to determine (1) whether
the career required substantial math and/or science training for entrance
to that career; and (2) whether persons engaged in this career would be
required to use math and/or science skills to fulfill their job duties. If both
requirements were met, the parent was coded as math/science-employed –
approximately 16 percent of the sample.[7]

Because different occupations vary in their work demands and environments, aspects of job characteristics and work environments are examined. These include work status, hours worked per week, hours spent
commuting per week, hours spent working at home in the evenings, time
away from family due to business travel, and opportunities to communicate with family members while at work.

The types and frequency of parents' interactions with their teenagers
are also based on items from the parent survey. These include the frequency of shared activities, and the frequency parents talk with adolescents about everyday events, news and politics, dating, friends, and
staying out late. Several measures of parents' expectations for their children are used, including expectations regarding adolescents' chances of
graduating from high school, post-secondary educational attainment, getting married, owning a home, enjoying work and family life, and having
a stable marriage.

### Analytic approach

To address the hypotheses, this chapter follows a multi-step process. Descriptive analyses investigate potential work-related differences
between parents in the two employment groups. How the parents interact with their adolescents on a daily basis are also examined. A more
microscopic approach to these interactions is then taken to determine
whether there are any gender-specific effects by parent's occupational
field. Relationships among family support and challenge, parent occupation, parent and adolescent gender, adolescent educational values, and
parent school guidance are examined.

To investigate the effects of parent occupation and parenting practices
on adolescents' psychological attributes, the three measures of mood,
motivation, and self-esteem are used as outcomes in three different
hierarchical measurement models (HMM) (Maier 2000). The HMM was

developed to estimate measures using item response theory and models the effects of multilevel independent variables upon these measures simultaneously.

## Results

### *What work and home look like for parents in different occupations*

Features of parents' jobs and their work environments affect how much time parents can spend with teenagers, and time constraints can affect the socialization process. Descriptive analyses of work characteristics were conducted to examine variations in the work experiences of parents across different occupations.[8]

Overall, both groups of parents report similar experiences at work. Both groups put in similar work hours and commute times, and have similar part-time versus full-time status patterns. While at work, both groups feel comfortable conducting personal business and engage equally in these behaviors. Furthermore, both groups have similar business travel requirements. Generally, parents in each group are equally able to attend to their families' needs, if required, while at work. From these analyses, it appears that the time requirements of both groups are similar, and that parents in each group have the same time available to devote to the family once their work responsibilities are met.

To determine whether family interactions differed for these two groups, parents' expectations for their adolescents and their interactions with them were also examined. As expected, both groups of parents have high educational expectations for their teenagers, and most feel that their teenagers' opportunities will be better than their own opportunities were. Most also indicate that they believe their adolescents have a high chance of graduating from high school and college, getting married, owning a home, enjoying work and family life, and having a stable marriage. Overall, most parents foresee a successful future for their teenagers, and both groups of parents report that they engage in similar amounts of conversation and activities with their teenagers and use comparable monitoring practices.

However, as shown in table 15.1, there are subtle differences in the parenting practices between both groups. First, math/science-employed parents are more likely to engage in activities with their teenagers, such as hobbies and listening to music, than are the other parents (see table 15.1).[9] Although the two groups do not differ in the frequency of conversations they had with their teenager about such topics as time watching TV, where the teenager goes, and how they use their free time,

Table 15.1 *Parental communication patterns with adolescents*

| | Parent employment | | |
|---|---|---|---|
| | Math/Science | Other | |
| Sharing a hobby with teen | | | |
| Rarely/Never | 49.3 | 57.6 | |
| Less than once a week | 44.9 | 29.4 | |
| Once/Twice a week | 5.8 | 11.1 | |
| Every day/Almost daily | 0.0 | 1.9 | |
| $N$ | 69 | 377 | |
| $\chi^2$ (d.f. = 3) | | | 8.00* |
| Listening to music together | | | |
| Rarely/Never | 17.5 | 31.9 | |
| Less than once a week | 40.0 | 33.0 | |
| Once/Twice a week | 32.5 | 23.9 | |
| Every day/Almost daily | 10.0 | 11.2 | |
| $N$ | 80 | 445 | |
| $\chi^2$ (d.f. = 3) | | | 20.13*** |
| Talking to teen about staying out late | | | |
| Never | 10.3 | 17.6 | |
| About once a month | 39.7 | 34.1 | |
| About twice a month | 16.7 | 14.6 | |
| About once a week | 15.4 | 25.1 | |
| Two–three times a week | 17.9 | 8.6 | |
| $N$ | 78 | 431 | |
| $\chi^2$ (d.f. = 3) | | | 11.37* |
| Talking to teen about friends | | | |
| Never | 8.9 | 16.9 | |
| About once a month | 43.0 | 34.6 | |
| About twice a month | 16.5 | 22.7 | |
| About once a week | 12.7 | 19.5 | |
| Two–three times a week | 19.0 | 6.3 | |
| $N$ | 79 | 431 | |
| $\chi^2$ (d.f. = 3) | | | 20.13** |

* $p < 0.05$; ** $p < 0.01$; *** $p < 0.001$

math/science-employed parents tend to talk more to their teenagers about how late they are allowed to be out at night and talk frequently with their teenager about the teenager's friends.

Other interesting patterns emerge when responses are examined separately for each group of parents by adolescent gender (see table 15.2). Parents employed in non-math/science careers have slightly different patterns of interaction with their male and female adolescents. They tend to

Table 15.2 *Parental communication patterns with male and female adolescents*

| | Math/Science | | | Other | | |
| --- | --- | --- | --- | --- | --- | --- |
| | | | **Parent employment** | | | |
| | Male | Female | | Male | Female | |
| Talking about news/politics | | | | | | |
| Rarely/Never | 0.0 | 4.7 | | 3.8 | 6.8 | |
| Less than once a week | 17.1 | 16.3 | | 19.5 | 24.3 | |
| Once/Twice a week | 40.0 | 51.2 | | 46.7 | 52.3 | |
| Every day/Almost daily | 42.9 | 27.9 | | 30.0 | 16.7 | |
| $N$ | 35 | 43 | | 210 | 222 | |
| $\chi^2$ (d.f. = 3) | | | 3.40 | | | 11.86** |
| Preparing meals together with child | | | | | | |
| Rarely/Never | 25.7 | 16.3 | | 37.9 | 24.7 | |
| Less than once a week | 34.3 | 46.3 | | 29.9 | 32.3 | |
| Once/Twice a week | 31.4 | 30.2 | | 28.0 | 37.7 | |
| Every day/Almost daily | 8.6 | 7.0 | | 4.3 | 5.4 | |
| $N$ | 35 | 43 | | 211 | 223 | |
| $\chi^2$ (d.f. = 3) | | | 1.61 | | | 9.70* |
| Decisions about dating | | | | | | |
| Parents decide | 2.9 | 4.5 | | 4.8 | 8.1 | |
| Parents decide after discussion | 20.6 | 25.0 | | 10.1 | 14.0 | |
| Parents and adolescent decide | 20.6 | 40.9 | | 29.5 | 35.3 | |
| Adolescent decides after discussion | 20.6 | 18.2 | | 22.2 | 19.9 | |
| Adolescent decides | 35.3 | 11.4 | | 33.3 | 22.6 | |
| $N$ | 34 | 44 | | 207 | 221 | |
| $\chi^2$ (d.f. = 3) | | | 7.86+ | | | 8.92+ |

$+ p < 0.10$; $* p < 0.05$; $** p < 0.01$

talk with sons more frequently about news and politics, and tend to prepare meals more often with their daughters. This suggests that this group of parents may be involving their daughters in more traditional gender roles. In addition, the analyses seem to indicate that the two groups of parents handle dating decisions with their sons and daughters somewhat differently.

The analyses presented in table 15.3 examine if the adolescents of parents in these two groups differ in their perceptions of support and challenge in the home. The results show no differences in support or

Table 15.3 *Mean of perceived challenge and support by adolescent gender*

| | Challenge | | | | Support | | | |
|---|---|---|---|---|---|---|---|---|
| | Male | Female | t | Effect size[a] | Male | Female | t | Effect size[a] |
| **Adolescents – Full sample** | | | | | | | | |
| Mean | 1.39 | 1.59 | 2.83 | 0.19 | 1.76 | 2.10 | 4.25* | 0.28 |
| N | 146 | 167 | | | 146 | 167 | | |
| **Adolescents of math/science fathers** | | | | | | | | |
| Mean | 1.53 | 1.62 | 0.90 | 0.09 | 1.74 | 2.31 | 0.06 | 0.44 |
| N | 15 | 16 | | | 15 | 16 | | |
| **Adolescents of non-math/science fathers** | | | | | | | | |
| Mean | 1.43 | 1.66 | 2.58 | 0.23 | 1.84 | 2.20 | 3.04 | 0.30 |
| N | 93 | 100 | | | 93 | 100 | | |
| **Adolescents of math/science mothers** | | | | | | | | |
| Mean | 1.59 | 1.60 | 0.33 | 0.01 | 1.80 | 2.07 | 0.01 | 0.21 |
| N | 20 | 28 | | | 20 | 28 | | |
| **Adolescents of non-math/science mothers** | | | | | | | | |
| Mean | 1.38 | 1.60 | 2.84 | 0.21 | 1.77 | 2.12 | 3.83* | 0.29 |
| N | 123 | 132 | | | 123 | 132 | | |

[a] The effect size is calculated as Cohen's d (Cohen, 1988): $d = \dfrac{\overline{X}_1 - \overline{X}_2}{s_p}$

* p < 0.05

challenge provided to adolescents by parents between the two groups when examining the sample as a whole. There are also no differences in challenge and support by father's occupation. Regardless of occupational field, fathers do not differentiate between their male and female children in terms of support and challenge, nor do they offer significantly higher levels of support or challenge to their adolescents than non-math/science fathers.

When looking at mothers and daughters, however, some significant differences emerge. Overall, female adolescents report slightly higher levels of support than their male counterparts. An inspection of the means across occupational categories and parent and adolescent gender reveals that this difference may be attributable to the additional support provided by non-math/science mothers to their daughters.[10] Female adolescents with non math/science-employed mothers seem to get more support than male adolescents in these families. Research suggests that parental support acts as a conduit for the socialization and value transmission processes in the family (Mortimer and Kumka 1982). While this difference may seem beneficial for adolescent girls, the different environments that non-math/science mothers are providing for their adolescents may be communicating different sets of expectations for their sons and daughters.[11]

In the next set of analyses, logistic regression was used to examine the effects of support and challenge and parents' occupation on students' educational values, with student grades and graduate school plans serving as proxies. Grades represent the more immediate values that the adolescent holds, while graduate school aspirations indicate more long-range educational values. As previous research suggests, support and challenge are likely to be strongly related to adolescent educational values because of their effect on the value transmission process. Furthermore, the presence of math/science-employed parents in the home may influence adolescent educational values indirectly via the unique character of the transmission process in these homes. Because females typically earn higher grades than males (Alexander et al. 1982; Riordan 1998), adolescent gender is included as a control variable.

As shown in table 15.4, several variables are significantly associated with student grades. First, adolescents who experience more support are likely to receive higher grades in high school. For each standard deviation change in support, the odds of a student receiving grades in the next highest category increase by a factor of 1.39. Consistent with previous research, gender is also a significant predictor of student grades; female adolescents are almost twice (1.94) as likely as their male counterparts to have higher grades in school. Net of other variables in the

Table 15.4 *Unstandardized coefficients from logistic regression analyses of adolescent grades and graduate school aspirations*

| Variable | Coefficient (S.E.) | |
| --- | --- | --- |
| Grades | | |
| Constant[a] | −1.7604*** | (.262) |
| Constant2[b] | −0.4995* | (.241) |
| Family support | 0.3320*** | (.085) |
| Adolescent female | 0.6609** | (.228) |
| Math/science mother | 0.6054* | (.310) |
| -2log-likelihood | 584.124 | |
| Number of cases | 282 | |
| Graduate school aspirations | | |
| Constant[c] | −0.4172* | (.202) |
| Family challenge | 0.2384* | (.112) |
| -2 log-likelihood | 433.146 | |
| Number of cases | 316 | |

[a] log-odds of attaining mostly As versus A/B or B or less
[b] log-odds of attaining A/B versus B or less
[c] log-odds of aspiring to attend graduate school versus not
* $p < .05$; ** $p < .01$; *** $p < .001$

model, having a math/science-employed mother significantly increases the likelihood of receiving higher grades. Those adolescents indicating that they have a mother employed in a math/science field are almost twice (1.83) as likely to have higher grades compared with those who do not have math/science-employed mothers. The effect of having a math/science-employed mother is almost 1.5 times that of an incremental change in support. The significant positive effect of this variable on student grades suggests that the subtle differences in the home environment identified in descriptive analyses may very well have a positive impact on the formation of short-term educational values, as indicated by student grades.

The impact of these variables on the formation of longer-term educational values, specifically aspirations to attend graduate school, is presented in the bottom half of table 15.4. Results indicate that female adolescents are just as likely as their male counterparts to report that they plan to attend graduate school. Further, having a math/science-employed parent has no significant effect on graduate school aspirations. Challenge, however, is positively and significantly associated with adolescents' graduate school aspirations. The odds that an adolescent plans to attend graduate school increase by 1.27 with each incremental increase in challenge.

Table 15.5 *Regression coefficients from linear analysis of support and challenge*

| Variable | Model 1 | Model 2 |
|---|---|---|
| Support | | |
|    Constant | 1.761*** | 1.794*** |
|    Female | 0.338* | 0.361+ |
|    Father school guidance | | 0.243** |
| Challenge | | |
|    Constant | 1.508*** | 1.367*** |
|    Female | 0.194 | 0.170 |
|    Father school guidance | | 0.211*** |

$+ \text{p} < .10; * \text{p} < .05; ** \text{p} < .01; *** \text{p} < .001$

Various aspects of the home environment and of parent–adolescent interactions were examined to determine which are predictive of perceived challenge and support. Results indicate that the school guidance provided by fathers has a substantial positive relationship with adolescents' reported levels of both support and challenge (see table 15.5). Support increases by a factor of 0.24 for every one point increase in father's school guidance, controlling for adolescent gender. The results for challenge are similar. These results indicate the important impact a father can have on support and challenge.[12]

The results of the descriptive and regression analyses provide some support for the claim that parents in math/science and other occupations differ in their parenting practices, and that these differences have effects on adolescents' educational values. As suggested by the descriptive analyses, non-math/science mothers appear to treat sons and daughters differently, offering greater support to their daughters. In addition, analyses of parent interactions suggest that non-math science parents engage in different types of activities with their sons and daughters (e.g., they are more likely to discuss news and politics with their sons and to engage in meal preparation with their daughters). In contrast, math/science-employed parents appear to be more egalitarian and are more likely to share activities with their teenagers and talk with them more frequently about friends and staying out late, suggesting that they engage in stricter monitoring practices.

Parents' occupations and parenting practices in turn affect adolescents' educational values. Adolescents of math/science employed mothers earn significantly higher grades. Although math/science employed fathers do not appear to differ in the levels of challenge and support they provide to adolescents, results of the regression analyses indicate that adolescents whose fathers provide greater school guidance are more likely to report high levels of support and challenge at home. Higher levels of support are associated with higher grades in school, and higher levels of challenge are associated with graduate school aspirations, suggesting the importance of father's school guidance in the transmission of educational values.

### Teenagers' daily subjective experiences

To examine the relationship between adolescents' emotions and parents' occupations and parenting practices, adolescents' day-to-day experiences while they were with their parents or at school were analyzed using ESM data. Each of the emotion variables was modeled separately for adolescent interactions with their mothers and with their fathers to better capture the unique aspects of these two types of dyads.[13] Adolescents' graduate school aspirations was included in the models to examine the relationship between adolescent educational values and emotions. Adolescent gender was also added as a control variable.

Results indicate that mood is generally low when adolescents are at school or with parents; mood is lowest when adolescents are at school but improves slightly when teenagers are with either parent (see table 15.6). Having a math/science-employed mother has a positive effect on mood. This effect is greatest when the teenagers are at school or with their fathers. Having a math/science-employed father, however, seems to have a negative effect on adolescents' moods at school, regardless of adolescent gender; when the adolescents are with either parent, however, this negative effect disappears.

Self-esteem is generally negative while the teenager is at school or with parents (see table 15.7). As with mood, the mothers' math/science-employed status gives a modest positive boost to adolescents' self-esteem. Students' graduate school plans are marginally significant, suggesting that educational aspirations may also play a minor positive role in adolescent self-esteem.

As with mood and self-esteem, adolescent motivation at school is negative, although to a greater extent than the other two measures (see table 15.8). Unlike mood or self-esteem, none of the variables in this model are significant predictors of motivation. The adolescents' motivation at school is low and persistent, as modeled by parent occupation, adolescent gender, and graduate school plans. Most likely, motivation is closely tied to experiences that the adolescents are engaged in while at school, which are not included in the model.

Table 15.6 *Results of hierarchical measurement modeling for mood*

| Variable | Coefficient | Standardized coefficient | 95% credibility interval |
|---|---|---|---|
| Mood at School | | | |
| Intercept | −0.712* | | (−0.77, −0.65) |
| Math/science Mother | 0.225* | 0.083 | (0.15, 0.31) |
| Math/science Father | −0.114* | −0.040 | (−0.21, −0.02) |
| Female | −0.019 | −0.009 | (−0.08, 0.04) |
| Plans to attend graduate school | 0.058 | 0.029 | (0.00, 0.12) |
| Var.epsn | 0.140 | | (0.11, 0.17) |
| Tau | 0.117 | | (0.08, 0.16) |
| Mood with mother | | | |
| Intercept | −0.679* | | (−0.78, −0.59) |
| Math/science Mother | 0.166* | 0.061 | (0.04, 0.24) |
| Math/science Father | 0.043 | 0.015 | (−0.10, 0.18) |
| Female | −0.033 | −0.016 | (−0.13, 0.06) |
| Plans to attend graduate school | 0.026 | 0.013 | (−0.06, 0.12) |
| Var.epsn | 0.167 | | (0.13, 0.22) |
| Tau | 0.098 | | (0.06, 0.15) |
| Mood with father | | | |
| Intercept | −0.637* | | (−0.74, −0.54) |
| Math/science Mother | 0.213* | 0.078 | (0.07, 0.35) |
| Math/science Father | −0.002 | −0.001 | (−0.16, 0.16) |
| Female | −0.025 | −0.012 | (−0.13, 0.08) |
| Plans to attend graduate school | −0.033 | −0.016 | (−0.14, 0.07) |
| Var.epsn | 0.154 | | (0.11, 0.21) |
| Tau | 0.150 | | (0.09, 0.23) |

* $p < 0.05$

Results of these analyses provide some support for the hypothesis that parent occupation has an effect on adolescents' psychological characteristics. First, although adolescent mood is generally low at school and with parents, it is significantly higher for those with a math/science-employed mother. However, the hypothesis that adolescent mood would be higher in families with a math/science-employed mother or father is borne out only for math/science-employed mothers. Math/science-employed fathers seem to have a slightly negative effect on adolescents' mood, and only when they are at school; when teenagers are at home with their mothers or fathers, this effect disappears. Math/science-employed mothers also have a positive effect on the adolescents' self-esteem, but only when they are at school. There is no evidence to support the hypothesis that adolescents with parents in math or science fields have higher levels of motivation than their peers.

Table 15.7 *Results of hierarchical measurement modeling for self-esteem*

| Variable | Coefficient | Standardized coefficient | 95% credibility interval |
|---|---|---|---|
| Self-esteem at school | | | |
| Intercept | −0.296* | | (−0.35, −0.24) |
| Math/science Mother | 0.106* | 0.040 | (0.024, 0.19) |
| Math/science Father | −0.089 | −0.031 | (−0.18, 0.00) |
| Female | −0.037 | −0.018 | (−0.10, 0.02) |
| Plans to attend graduate school | 0.085* | 0.042 | (0.026, 0.15) |
| Var.epsn | 0.112 | | (0.09, 0.14) |
| Tau | 0.119 | | (0.09, 0.16) |
| Self-esteem with Mother | | | |
| Intercept | −0.229* | | (−0.32, −0.14) |
| Math/science Mother | 0.013 | 0.005 | (−0.11, 0.14) |
| Math/science Father | 0.045 | 0.016 | (−0.09, 0.18) |
| Female | −0.039 | −0.019 | (−0.13, 0.05) |
| Plans to attend graduate school | 0.054 | 0.027 | (−0.03, 0.14) |
| Var.epsn | 0.056 | | (0.13, 0.22) |
| Tau | 0.150 | | (0.10, 0.21) |
| Self-esteem with Father | | | |
| Intercept | −0.196* | | (−0.29, −0.11) |
| Math/science Mother | 0.112 | 0.042 | (−0.02, 0.25) |
| Math/science Father | −0.148 | −0.052 | (−0.30, 0.00) |
| Female | −0.056 | −0.027 | (−0.15, 0.04) |
| Plans to attend graduate school | −0.006 | −0.003 | (−0.09, 0.11) |
| Var.epsn | 0.067 | | (0.04, 0.11) |
| Tau | 0.144 | | (0.09, 0.21) |

* $p < 0.05$

Table 15.8 *Results of hierarchical measurement modeling for motivation*

| Variable | Coefficient | Standardized coefficient | 95% credibility interval |
|---|---|---|---|
| Motivation at school | | | |
| Intercept | −0.850* | | (−0.94, −0.77) |
| Math/science mother | 0.079 | 0.029 | (−0.04, 0.20) |
| Math/science father | −0.139 | −0.049 | (−0.28, 0.00) |
| Female | −0.017 | −0.008 | (−0.10, 0.07) |
| Plans to attend graduate school | 0.058 | 0.028 | (−0.03, 0.15) |
| Var.epsn | 0.384 | | (0.31, 0.46) |
| Tau | 0.109 | | (0.07, 0.16) |

* $p < 0.05$

Additional analyses were conducted to determine whether the effects found for adolescent mood and self-esteem might be a consequence of factors other than the parent's math/science employment status, such as parent's mood or educational attainment. Results indicate that parents generally report positive moods when they are with their adolescents, regardless of parent occupation or adolescent gender.[14] To determine whether math/science employment status might be an artifact of educational attainment, the model for adolescent mood was re-run, replacing the math/science-employed status of each parent with the educational attainment of each parent (coded as having a masters degree or higher versus a lower level of educational attainment). No significant effect was found.[15] As in the original model, adolescents generally experience fairly negative moods while at school.

## Conclusion

From these analyses, it can be seen that parents influence their adolescents in a variety of ways. The subtle nature of family dynamics and the many facets of parent monitoring behaviors required the use of a variety of analytic techniques to thoroughly explore the relationships between parents and adolescents. Three major themes about the transmission of educational values emerge from these analyses.

While differences in support and challenge were expected to be related to parent's occupation, no such differences were found for fathers. Regardless of occupation, fathers provide their daughters and sons with similar levels of support and challenge. For fathers in both occupational categories, perceived challenge and support are positively associated with fathers' school guidance. By taking the time to discuss course-taking and plans for college, fathers not only provide support for their teenagers but also encourage them to achieve. The significant effect of such paternal guidance may be due to its infrequency. Such discussions are more likely to occur on *a daily basis* between mothers and adolescents. Fathers may involve themselves after a majority of the discussions have taken place with the mother. If fathers involve themselves early on in their adolescents' educational planning and goal-setting, they are able to bring additional benefits to their adolescents to aid in goal formation and planning.

Results suggest that mothers' parenting practices do differ by occupation. First, math/science-employed mothers offer their male and female teenagers the same levels of challenge and support. The daughters of these mothers are reaping benefits from this equitable treatment that their peers are not experiencing. By providing their daughters with the same home environments as they do for their sons, these mothers are communicating similar expectations of them. These mothers may also play an important role in encouraging their daughters to pursue math–science careers. Seymour and Hewitt (1997) show that female students readily respond to parental influence in choosing to pursue math or science coursework, majors, and occupations. Math/science-employed mothers also seem especially able to boost their adolescents' mood and self-esteem at school. Daughters of non-math/science mothers receive more support than their brothers, which may communicate different expectations for sons and daughters.

Parental monitoring practices are also used in slightly different ways by math/science-employed parents and parents in other careers. Because these practices are an important mechanism for transmitting values, math/science-employed parents are engaging in somewhat different socialization patterns than the other parents. Parents employed in math/science occupations tend to be stricter with their adolescents than parents in other occupations. These stricter monitoring practices reflect the high expectations they have for their children in concrete ways. This is not to say that non-math/science-employed parents are not expressing high expectations for their children; after all, descriptive analyses indicate that all parents are optimistic and hopeful about their adolescents' future success. However, by employing stricter monitoring practices, the math/science-employed parents are communicating high expectations and providing challenges on a daily basis.

The sample analyzed consists of highly educated and high-status parents who are able to provide their adolescents with a wide range of opportunities and resources. One might expect that if any group of parents were to engage in the equitable treatment of their sons and daughters, it would be this group of parents. The finding that math/science mothers treat their sons and daughters in similar ways while mothers who work in equally high status professions such as the law or business treat their sons and daughters differently is somewhat surprising. Both groups of mothers are highly educated and high achieving, yet pervasive differences in the way these two groups socialize their adolescents can be identified.

These findings suggest that the reproduction of social stratification may be influenced not only by social class, but also by parent occupation, specifically the mother's occupation. By engaging in differential treatment of their teenagers, non-math/science-employed mothers are reinforcing traditional gender roles. As a result, these mothers are helping to reproduce the stratification structure for their sons and daughters.

These results suggest that the transmission of educational values and parent–adolescent socialization dynamics are tied more closely to the occupational experiences of parents than one may expect. Research with a larger and more representative sample is needed to determine whether the socialization of sons and daughters differs by parent occupation in families that are more diverse with respect to race, educational attainment, and income.

## NOTES

1. Because the majority of responses fell within two categories, the variable was recoded into three categories: mostly As; about half As and half Bs; and mostly Bs or below.
2. The items for support:
    1. Others notice when I'm feeling down, even if I don't say anything.
    2. I feel appreciated for who I am.
    3. If I have a problem, I get special attention and help.
    4. I do things I like to do without feeling embarrassed.
    5. I am made to feel special on birthdays and holidays.
    6. No matter what happens, I know I'll be loved and accepted.
    7. We enjoy having dinner together and talking.
    8. We compromise when our schedules conflict.
    9. We are willing to help each other out when something needs to be done.
    10. We try not to offend and hurt each other's feelings.
    11. Our home is full of things that hold special memories.
3. The items for challenge:
    1. We enjoy playing competitive games.
    2. We express our opinions about current events, even when they differ.
    3. We ask each other's ideas before making important decisions.
    4. It's important to be self-confident and independent to earn respect.
    5. Family members expect to be good at what they do.
    6. Individual accomplishments are noticed.
    7. I'm given responsibility for making important decisions affecting my life.
    8. I'm expected to do my best.
    9. I try to make other family members proud.
    10. I'm encouraged to get involved in extracurricular activities.
    11. I'm respected for being a hard worker.
    12. I'm expected to use my time wisely.
4. For construction of the measures of support and challenge, all items were required to have an outfit statistic of 1.35 or less. The distribution of the challenge measures had a mean of 1.47 and a standard deviation of 1.03; the measure of support had a mean of 1.91 and a standard deviation of 1.46.
5. The items for parent school guidance variable:
    How often do you or your spouse talk to your teen about:
    1. Which course or programs to take at school.
    2. School activities or events of particular interest to your teen.

3. Things your teen has studied in class.
4. Your teen's grades.
5. Your teen's plans and preparations for the ACT or SAT tests.
6. Your teen going to college.
7. Your teen's career plans.

6. The school guidance measure has a mean of 0.21 and a standard deviation of 1.01 for mothers and a mean and standard deviation of 0.19 and 1.08, respectively, for fathers.

7. The following job titles were coded as math/science: medicine or health manager; accountant; auditor; agricultural or food scientist; biological or life scientist; medical scientist; physician; dentist; registered nurse; economics teacher; mathematics teacher; computer science teacher; medical science teacher; economist; psychologist; technical writer; radiologist; biological technician; and computer programmer.

8. Because differences in work experiences were not statistically different between these two groups of parents, the results were not tallied in a table.

9. Only statistically significant results are shown in table 15.1.

10. The differences in table 15.3 appear to be rather small. However, the measures of support and challenge are on a standardized normal scale, making even seemingly small differences among means meaningful. Cohen's effect size measure can be applied directly to the differences in means between groups.

11. Because of the small number of math/science-employed parents in the sample, additional analyses were conducted to explore whether the patterns of support and challenge observed for these parents would change if the sample sizes and variances of the measures were comparable to those of the non-math/employed parents. Results of these analyses indicate that all patterns except one would remain the same given a larger sample size and smaller variance. If the sample size of math/science-employed fathers were increased to match that of the non-math/science fathers, the difference in the support they offer their sons and daughters would be statistically significant, with daughters receiving more support from these fathers. In contrast to the greater support offered to daughters by non-math/science mothers, this pattern of cross-gender support between math/science fathers and their daughters might work counter to traditional gender roles.

12. The measures of support, challenge, and father school guidance are standardized and yield small but significant effects sizes, using Cohen's d.

13. For a more detailed description of this methodology, see Maier (2000) and Gelman et al. (1995). To determine whether the value of any coefficient is statistically different from zero, one must examine the limits of the 95 percent credibility interval to determine if zero lies within this range. If the posterior distribution of a parameter approximates the shape of a normal distribution (as was the case with these analyses), the bounds of the 95 percent credibility interval are essentially the 2.5 percent and 97.5 percent quantiles of the data. Statistically significant coefficient estimates are flagged with an asterisk in the tables. Additionally, standardized coefficients are presented so that direct comparisons of predictive variables can be made.

14. A HMM modeling parent mood with adolescent gender and math/science-employment status of mother and father had a single statistically significant coefficient for the intercept (0.108).

15. A HMM modeling adolescent mood with MS/Ph.D. mom, MS/Ph.D. dad, graduate school aspirations, and adolescent gender had two statistically significant coefficients: the intercept (−0.64) and graduate school aspirations (0.064).

# Commentary

## Jeylan T. Mortimer

*The earliest studies of intergenerational occupational mobility proceeded by cross-classifying categorical occupational variables expressing origin and destination states (e.g., Rogoff 1953). Blau and Duncan's landmark study (1967) greatly facilitated the analysis of intergenerational mobility by expressing occupational variability by a single continuous dimension of occupational prestige. Educational attainment was shown to be the crucial mediator of the effects of socioeconomic origins on occupational destinations (Duncan, Featherman, and Duncan 1972). Building on this path-breaking work, subsequent research has incorporated social psychological variables, including significant other influences, educational achievement, and educational and occupational aspirations and plans. The large body of research in this tradition has immensely enriched our understanding of the process of stratification.*

*But lost in the shift in conceptualization of work from categorically diverse occupational positions to continuously varying occupational prestige was the rich variation in types of work and dimensions of work experience that could potentially have profound implications for familial socialization and child achievements. Though researchers have continued to draw attention to other dimensions of work, besides its prestige, that have important consequences for the attainment process (e.g., Kohn 1969; Mortimer 1974, 1975; Ryu and Mortimer 1996), influencing intergenerational value transmission and mobility, the unidimensional consideration of work, as a social status or prestige hierarchy has remained dominant in studies of educational and occupational attainment.*

*Maier, by focusing on differences in home environments and child-rearing practices in math/science and other middle-class families, continues this line of inquiry and challenge to the dominant stratification paradigm. The distinctive patterns of communication, activities, challenge, and support for children that she describes among parents who have math/science related and other occupations draw attention to an important non-vertical feature of work (akin to what was earlier called the situs dimension of occupational structure, see Morris and Murphy 1959). As she observes, persons in scientific and technical occupations have undergone a demanding process of professional socialization emphasizing logical thinking, efficacious action, and positive orientations to learning and knowledge. Their own occupational experiences and tasks are perceived, by themselves and others, as difficult and challenging.*

*Kohn and Schooler (1983) observed that psychological orientations and values developed in the work sphere extend beyond this particular domain, coming to influence attitudes and behaviors in multiple spheres. As part of this "generalization" process, parents try to transmit psychological orientations to their children that they have found to be conducive to success in their own work. If the same process extends to scientists and technical workers, it is likely that they would approach child-rearing in a manner paralleling their own work experiences, viewing this familial task as challenging, perhaps difficult, and deserving of their full engagement. Consistent with these speculations, Maier brings forth evidence that scientific/technical parents are more engaged in activities with their children and in monitoring their adolescent offspring than other middle-class parents (table 15.1). Paralleling the sciences' universalistic achievement values, there are indications that gender is a more prominent consideration in non-science/math parents' activities and interactions with their children (table 15.1).*

*Maier further observes that science/math consequences for parenting are conditioned by the gender of the parent. Whereas fathers are found to provide similar levels of support and challenge to sons and daughters irrespective of their occupations, math/science mothers appear to be slightly less sex-typed than other others in their treatment of their children (table 15.2). Furthermore, math/science mothers are found to promote adolescent children's grades (table 15.3) and to enhance their moods and self-esteem when they are at school (tables 15.5 and 15.6), consequences that would likely promote the children's future success in the educational sphere. The fact that having a math/science mother is related to more positive moods when the adolescent child is with mothers and fathers as well (table 15.5) would perhaps also strengthen the efficacy of both math/science parents as transmitters of educationally relevant and other values (assuming that good adolescent moods promote receptivity to parental socialization attempts). Interestingly, math/science fathers do not appear to enhance adolescents' grades and mood state in these ways, perhaps because fathers are more likely than mothers to inhabit "separate worlds" of work and family, being less engaged in, and responsible for, the family realm.*

*These findings also bear directly on long-term debates regarding the effects of maternal employment on children. Because math/science occupations are particularly engaging and time consuming, one might think that mothers pursuing such demanding careers would be relatively disengaged from their children, and that their children would respond by expressing negative moods. To the contrary, the general pattern of findings in this study indicates that children of math/science mothers may be particularly advantaged.*

*Given the increasing prominence of scientific and technical occupations in the US labor force, and increasing prevalence of women in these fields (though they are still the minority), one might expect increases in the salutary patterns of child-rearing found to be distinctive in math/science families, thereby contributing to children's achievement. But while Maier's study is instructive, the relatively small number of math/science parents in her sample limits the scope of the analysis, particularly the capacity to introduce a variety of pertinent controls. While all families in this study are described as middle and upper-middle-class, the analyses do not control for socioeconomic differences (in education, income, and occupational prestige) that might account for the patterns that are highlighted here. Furthermore, the non-math/science mothers in this study, despite their high levels of education, may be more likely to adhere to traditional, gender-linked work patterns, involving part-time employment, positions of lesser responsibility, and the capacity to be unpaid partners in supporting their husbands' careers. A larger sample of math/science mothers would perhaps enable investigation of these and other potential sources of spuriousness.*

*Notwithstanding these limitations, this research breaks new ground in exploring the manifold ways that pursuit of a scientific or technical career may impact parenting style and adolescent children's educational achievement. Maier's findings indicate the fruitfulness of further research focused on dimensions of occupational variability, occupational subcultures, and family socialization practices across a wide span of the class structure.*

# 16 Following in their parents' footsteps: how characteristics of parental work predict adolescents' interest in parents' jobs

*Ariel Kalil, Judith A. Levine, Kathleen M. Ziol-Guest*

A central aspect of identity development during adolescence involves making decisions about future work roles and, ideally, an eventual commitment to an occupation that best fits one's unique combination of interests, needs, and talents (Erikson 1968). Vocational identity development may begin early in adolescence however, as young adolescents begin to incorporate occupational aspirations into their self-concepts (Super 1990). Theory and research from several disciplines highlight the family's role in this process. In the sociological literature, studies have repeatedly found that parents' level of education and occupational status are associated with children's educational and occupational outcomes (Blau and Duncan 1967; Sewell and Hauser 1975), although the processes by which these linkages occur have not been fully explored. The psychological literature, in contrast, has often focused on the family processes (e.g., parents' role modeling, attitudes, and behaviors) that might contribute to the development of adolescents' occupational identities and the ways in which parents' occupational characteristics shape parenting behavior.

Many developmental studies are concerned with the ways in which the nature of parents' work makes a difference in the lives of parents and children. For example, previous research has focused on the ways in which parental work overload, role strain, and length of the workday are linked to children's psychosocial, behavioral, and cognitive development (Galambos et al. 1995). Other work suggests that parents' work characteristics and attitudes can shape adolescents' work values, meaning the characteristics of occupations that adolescents see as important for themselves (i.e., the extent to which jobs are highly remunerated or prestigious, or offer opportunities to exercise creativity and autonomy) (Galambos and Sears 1998; Mortimer 1976). Especially as children grow older, they can acquire knowledge about their parents' jobs directly, through their conversations with parents about parents' jobs. In this way, parents' jobs can serve as important "laboratories" for children's developing views of the occupational system and their future place within it. Studies that enhance our knowledge about the specific aspects of parents' jobs that shape adolescents' aspirations for the jobs they themselves would like to hold in the future can provide insights into adolescents' eventual occupational trajectories.

This chapter examines the relationships between mothers' and fathers' work conditions and adolescents' interest in having jobs like their mothers' and fathers' in the future. In particular, the chapter focuses on the roles of substantive complexity and autonomy in parents' jobs. Analyses are based on a subsample of dual-earner families with adolescent children from the 500 Family Study. This dual-earner sample provides an opportunity to examine the influence of fathers' as well as mothers' work characteristics. Findings are linked to the literature on the intergenerational transmission of social class status, and also to the psychological literature on the role of parental work in adolescent identity development. Ways in which occupational status might be transmitted across generations through specific characteristics of parents' jobs are also discussed.

## Intergenerational transmission of occupational status

One motivation for the current study is to take a step toward illuminating the mechanisms that drive intergenerational transmission of occupational status. Starting with Blau and Duncan's (1967) classic model of inheritance, the status attainment literature has focused on the route between parental occupation and child occupation. Their five-variable model, in which son's occupation is predicted by father's education and occupation through the mediators of son's education and first job, is one of the first and most basic regression-based treatments of the relationship between parental and child occupation. Several generations of scholars have elaborated the model, paying more attention to mediators between parent and child job (Hauser and Featherman 1973), struggling with the difficulties of incorporating the role of maternal occupation (Sewell, Hauser, and Wolf 1980), and looking to effects in the third generation (Warren and Hauser 1997). Yet, while the literature has established substantial intergenerational correlations in parent and child educational and occupational attainment, it has not fully investigated the more micro-level, within-family mechanisms behind this transmission.[1]

Much of children's access to information regarding future career choices likely flows through their parents and through parent–child interactions that occur at home. This chapter therefore focuses on parent–child discussions about parents' work as an important factor in children's aspirations to hold jobs like their parents in the future. The effect of job traits in one generation on aspirations in the next may be an important mechanism by which occupational status is reproduced across generations. Given the cross-sectional nature of the data, it is not possible to observe children's actual occupational outcomes. The chapter thus examines the first stage of this possible mechanism: the effect of parental job characteristics on children's desire to hold jobs like their parents' in the future.

### Influences of parental job characteristics on family processes

Previous research has shown that parental job characteristics can influence parental mood, attitudes, and behavior, interactions between parents and children, and children's developmental outcomes (Kohn and Schooler 1982; Menaghan 1990; Menaghan and Parcel 1995; Miller et al. 1979; Parcel and Menaghan 1994b, 1997). Much of the existing work, however, focuses on young children and thus misses the important developmental tasks of adolescence, including the formation of adult aspirations. Nevertheless, the findings in the existing literature are robust enough to hypothesize that parental job characteristics might influence the attitudes and behavior of older children as well.

Kohn and colleagues (e.g., Kohn and Schooler 1982; Miller et al. 1979) hypothesized that parents' job characteristics influence behaviors that are valued and encouraged in children, thus providing the link to children's developmental outcomes, including children's own work values. Specifically, Kohn and Schooler (1982) proposed that parents come to value behaviors and attitudes that are adaptive in their employment setting and that these values are subsequently expressed in their parenting practices. Thus, for example, when parents' jobs involve greater self-direction, parents more often tend to use reason (as opposed to power assertion) when disciplining their children and tend to expect their children to internalize adult norms. These child-rearing practices are expected to foster children's own values (of the importance of self-direction, for example), and to shape their occupational aspirations accordingly. This model, which has been termed the "occupational linkage hypothesis," has received empirical support, but studies have rarely considered the entire process in a single investigation (Galambos and Sears 1998).

In a related vein, Mortimer (1976) hypothesized that fathers in professional positions (relative to those in business) would, by virtue of being more concerned with self-reliance and autonomy in their jobs (as opposed to external rewards and standards of achievement), have closer and more communicative relationships with their sons (the study did not include mothers or daughters). Given evidence that children who feel closer to their parent are more likely to want to emulate that parent (Ruble and Martin 1998), one could make the link between parents' level of autonomy at work and the likelihood that children would want to hold jobs like their parents' in the future. Mortimer's evidence suggests that sons with prestigious paternal role models and close father–son relationships are most likely to share vocational values with their fathers.

Menaghan and colleagues (Menaghan 1991; Menaghan and Parcel 1995; Parcel and Menaghan 1994b, 1997) expanded these work socialization models by studying the effects of maternal work and by examining work conditions, parenting processes, and child development outcomes. Like Kohn and Schooler, they proposed that working conditions, such as wages, work hours, and task complexity that mothers experience on the job, can influence their emotional well-being, attitudes and values, and parenting practices, thereby shaping parent–child interactions and, ultimately, children's development. In particular, they hypothesized that occupational complexity, or variety of tasks performed at work leads parents to encourage intellectual flexibility in their children. Menaghan and Parcel (1995) demonstrated that occupational complexity is positively associated with preschool children's home environment, assessed in terms of parental cognitive stimulation and emotional warmth. Piotrkowski and Katz (1982) showed that mothers' job autonomy and skill utilization at work are significantly associated with young adolescents' positive academic behaviors, although the pathways through which these effects occur are not explored. Similarly, Menaghan and Parcel (1990) showed that maternal job complexity is related to children's verbal facility, in part via the associations between occupational conditions and parenting behaviors.

Many of these studies have focused on young children, among whom occupational values and aspirations were not assessed. Galambos and Sears' (1998) study was one of the first to link adolescents' perceptions of parents' work with adolescents' work values. Using a sample of 64 dual-earner couples with 14-year-old children, these researchers found that adolescents base their respect for parents' work on three job features: whether the work is perceived as being depersonalizing, straining, or satisfying. In addition, the study showed that adolescents' respect for fathers' jobs is based on perceptions that fathers are employed in jobs that are financially rewarding. Interestingly, the study found no evidence that adolescents' respect for, or perceptions of, mothers' work are associated with adolescents' work values.

### Hypotheses

The perspectives discussed above regarding the potential relationship between parental work characteristics and children's occupational aspirations suggest the following hypotheses:

*Hypothesis 1.* Parents' substantive job complexity and job autonomy will be positively associated with children expressing a desire to hold jobs similar to each of their parents' jobs in the future. This hypothesis allows for the following possibilities. First, children may absorb societal views of middle-class norms about desirable work conditions. Since job traits such as substantive complexity and job autonomy are correlated with prestige, children may want jobs with these traits in order to achieve the prestige they have learned to value (Mortimer 1976). Alternatively, children may simply make their own independent calculations that these traits are desirable.

*Hypothesis 2.* The relationship between the parental job traits of substantive complexity and autonomy and child aspirations will be stronger if parents and children discuss parents' jobs. Thus, in predicting children's expressed job preferences, there will be a statistical interaction between these parental job traits and parent–child discussion of parents' jobs. This hypothetical relationship is based on the expectation that it is through discussions with parents about parents' work that children learn about the nature of their parents' job traits and the meaning of these traits in one's occupational identity.

*Hypothesis 3.* The nature of the relationship between job traits and child's interest in holding a similar job in the future will not differ appreciably between mothers' jobs and fathers' jobs. Although previous research often examined the role of fathers' jobs only (e.g., Mortimer 1976), there is no obvious reason to expect the pattern of results to differ between predicting desire for mothers' jobs and desire for fathers' jobs in a modern dual-earner family.

*Hypothesis 4.* Based on the literature suggesting that children are more likely to identify with their same-sex parent (see Ruble and Martin 1998 for an extensive summary), we expect a main effect of sex on job preference in the same-sex direction. That is, boys will be more likely than girls to want jobs like their fathers' in the future. Girls will be more likely than boys to want jobs like their mothers' in the future. Further, statistical interactions between child sex and maternal and paternal job characteristics are expected such that the correlation between parental job characteristics and adolescents' expressed job preferences will be stronger in same-sex dyads.

## Method

### Sample

The data analyzed in this chapter are from a subsample of families in the 500 Family Study. Only families in which both parents as well as the teenager completed surveys were selected for analysis. The subsample consists of 191 teenagers from 150 two-parent families in which both resident parents are working at least part time. In addition, only families in which teenagers were living with both biological parents were selected, which resulted in dropping a small number of families (8) in which teenagers were living with a parent and a step-parent. These families were excluded because the survey collects job information on the parents or step-parents who reside with the teenager, while teenagers' responses about aspirations to hold parents' jobs may be based on biological parents who are not in the home.

93 percent of the fathers in the subsample and almost 60 percent of the mothers report working full time. 55 percent of the families consist of two full-time employed parents, and 38 percent of the families consist of a full-time employed father and part-time employed mother. The remaining 7 percent of the subsample consists of families where the mother works full time and the father works part time (4 percent), or both parents work part time (3 percent). The families in the subsample are relatively affluent. 60 percent of the mothers report total annual family incomes of over $100,000, with only 4 percent of all mothers reporting total family incomes of less than $50,000. The parents in these families are also highly educated. 91 percent of the fathers have graduated from college. In addition, 33 percent hold a master's degree, and another 39 percent hold professional degrees. Among the mothers, 83 percent have graduated from college, with 39 percent holding a master's degree and another 19 percent holding professional degrees. With respect to family composition, on average, each family has 2.5 children.

### Dependent variables

The dependent measures of interest are two single-item questions that ask the teenager, "How interested are you in having a job like your mother's (father's) when you grow up?" Each of these single items was coded on a 4-point Likert scale, where $0 =$ Not at all interested, $1 =$ Just a little interested, $2 =$ Quite a bit interested, and $3 =$ Very interested.

### Independent variables

The major independent variables of interest are two characteristics of mothers' and fathers' jobs that reflect the jobs' substantive complexity (i.e., the extent to which jobs are cognitively and interpersonally challenging) and the degree to which jobs afford the opportunity for autonomy or self-direction. The two measures are identical for mothers and fathers and are reported separately in surveys completed by each parent.

In analyzing occupational data, Parcel's (1989) measure of the substantive complexity of occupations is used. Following the methods described in Parcel (1989), her measure of occupational substantive complexity was replicated using the *Dictionary of Occupational Titles* (DOT), and factor loadings identical to those of Parcel were obtained. Two coders trained by the National Opinion Research Center (NORC) assigned Census occupational codes to the job titles provided by parent respondents in the 500 Family survey. These codes were then used to match parents' occupations with the occupational substantive complexity measure. The substantive complexity factor is based on seventeen different items in the DOT (alpha $= .95$) reflecting, for example, the education and training required of people in that occupation, the complexity of working with data and people required of workers in that occupation, the routinization of the work performed in that occupation, and opportunities for abstract and creative thinking in that occupation. The substantive complexity measure is computed as a mean of the standardized items within the DOT. Standardized scores (z-scores) are used in this analysis, with higher scores indicating higher levels of job complexity. For example, substantive complexity scores for doctors, lawyers, elementary school teachers, and truck drivers are 1.53, 1.60, .80, and $-.98$, respectively. This measure has been used extensively in analyses linking parental occupational conditions to family processes (see Menaghan 1991; Menaghan and Parcel 1995; Parcel and Menaghan 1994b, 1997).

The measure of job autonomy is based on the mean of three survey items, all of which begin with "How true are the following statements about your job?" The items include "I have a lot of opportunity to make my own decisions"; "I have a lot of say over what happens on my job"; and "I can design or plan most of my daily work." Parents' responses were based on a 4-point Likert scale ranging from 1 to 4 (Not true at all, Somewhat true, True, Very true), with higher values representing greater autonomy. The internal reliability for mothers is .86 and for fathers is .90.

The measure of the extent to which teenagers and mothers (fathers) discuss parents' work is based on a single item asking the teenager, "How often do the following events happen related to your mother's (father's) work: Your mother (father) talks to you about what she (he) is doing at work." Responses for this item are based on a 5-point Likert scale ranging from 0 to 4 (Never, Rarely, Sometimes, Often, Almost Every Day).

### Control variables

To help isolate the unique effects of the two job characteristics of interest, several demographic, individual, family, and other work-related characteristics were statistically controlled to partial out their effects from those of mothers' and fathers' job complexity and autonomy. First, the teenager's overall relationship with his or her mother (father) was represented with a summary scale created by taking the mean response to sixteen questions, with responses coded on a 5-point Likert scale ranging from 1 to 5 (Never true, Rarely true, Sometimes true, Often true, and Always true).[2] Higher values on the scale indicate more positive parent-child relationships. The internal reliability for the relationship with mother (father) scale is .82 and .83 respectively. It is expected that adolescents who report a closer relationship with their mother and father will be more likely to want to emulate each parent by expressing a greater desire to hold a job like theirs in the future (Mortimer 1976; Ruble and Martin 1998).

Second, parent salaries are used as control variables. Mothers and fathers were each asked to report their current annual salaries using the following categorical choices: $0–$20,000; $20,001–$35,000; $35,001–$50,000; $50,001–$75,000; $75,001–$100,000; and more than $100,000. The midpoint is assigned for each category (a value of $100,000 is assigned to the highest category). Finally, the analyses control for several demographic characteristics of the teenagers, including sex (boys are coded "1" and girls are coded "0"), age (in years), and race (white is coded "1" and others are coded "0").

### Models

Two separate analyses were conducted for the two different outcome measures – the teenager's interest in a job like his or her father's, or like his or her mother's. For each analysis, two models are assessed. Model 1 includes teenagers' demographic characteristics (age, race, and sex), mothers' and fathers' salaries, teenagers' reported relationship with the respective parent (i.e., the regression for "wanting a job like mother" controlled for the teenager's relationship with the mother), and teenagers' reported discussions of parental work with the respective parent. Model 2 includes the two measures of each parents' job characteristics (substantive complexity and job autonomy). Both parents' job characteristics are entered in the regression models to ensure that, given the likelihood of assortative mating, the coefficients on fathers' or mothers' job traits are not expressing the role of the other parent's job traits. Correlations between parents' job traits are not high enough to create a multicollinearity problem.

As described above, virtually all of the fathers, but not all of the mothers, are employed full time. Preliminary analyses (available from the authors) suggest that this variable (mothers' part-time versus full-time work) is unrelated to children's aspiring to hold jobs like their mothers. Because comparable models for mothers and fathers are desired, the variable was excluded in the analyses that follow.

Due to the ordered nature of the dependent variables, the model used for analysis is the ordered probit. The ordered probit is modeled with a latent variable regression. The data suggest the following levels of interest in having a job like either parent:

$$y_i = \begin{cases} 0 \text{ } if \text{ } not \text{ } at \text{ } all \\ 1 \text{ } if \text{ } just \text{ } a \text{ } little \\ 2 \text{ } if \text{ } quite \text{ } a \text{ } bit \\ 3 \text{ } if \text{ } very \end{cases}$$

The underlying latent variable y* is modeled as:

$$y_i = \begin{cases} 0 \text{ } if \text{ } y^* < c_1 \\ 1 \text{ } if \text{ } c_1 \leq y^* < c_2 \\ 2 \text{ } if \text{ } c_2 \leq y^* < c_3 \\ 3 \text{ } if \text{ } y^* \geq c_3 \end{cases}$$

where $c_n$ is an arbitrary cutoff point for the latent variable $y^*$, determining what category the observed ordered variable $y$ will take. The cut point is an unknown parameter that is estimated along with $\beta$. The $y^*$ latent variable in this model can be thought of as the propensity the teenager has for wanting a job like his or her parent. The ordered probit seeks to determine the probability of falling into any of the outcome categories of interest.

Coefficients from the models are presented, together with the robust standard errors of the coefficients, the average marginal effects, and cutoff points used to derive the marginal effects. Marginal effects can be interpreted as the change in the probability of being in a particular category of the dependent variable given a unit change in a particular independent variable. The sum of the marginal effects for all of the outcome categories for a given X, must, by construction, equal zero. The marginal effects are calculated for each person in the sample; the average of these marginal effects is then calculated and presented in the tables.

Also presented in the tables is the Wald chi-square which tests significance of the entire model, the log likelihood, the likelihood ratio chi-square which tests the addition of blocks of variables entered in the model, and the predicted probabilities for each outcome. Predicted probabilities are calculated by estimating the fitted values for individuals based on their individual characteristics and are then averaged across the entire sample. Because the sample includes some children who are siblings and hence are not independent cases, the standard errors are corrected using the Huber-Eicker-White sandwich estimator of variance.

### Results

Before presenting the results of the multivariate analyses, it is useful to describe the types of jobs that these dual-earner couples hold. These middle- and upper-middle-class workers hold a wide variety of jobs, and the job titles of mothers and fathers overlap to a significant degree. Among the fathers, the largest group is classified as managers and administrators (representing more than 25 percent of the sample), with the next-largest groups classified as lawyers (11 percent) and as teachers (11 percent). Fewer than 10 percent of fathers are in sales positions and only about 10 percent are in service or manual labor positions. The remaining fathers are scattered in positions such as editor, systems analyst, physician, urban planner, and accountant.

Among mothers, the largest group is also classified as managers and administrators (representing about 25 percent of the sample). About 20 percent are teachers and around 10 percent are nurses, therapists, social workers, or salespersons. Approximately 10 percent are in female-dominated positions such as secretary, bank teller, or childcare worker.

Descriptive statistics for the study variables are presented in table 16.1. Teenagers in the study average around 15 years of age, with equal numbers of boys and girls. A majority of the sample (86 percent) is white. As can be seen, mothers and fathers each report relatively high average levels of job autonomy, and these average values are not significantly different from one another. Results of a two-tailed paired $t$-test indicate that fathers' occupations exhibit larger values of substantive complexity than mothers', on average. Teenagers expressed fairly positive relationships with both parents, although the teen–mother relationship is more positive than the teen–father relationship, according to a two-tailed paired $t$-test. Similarly, teenagers report significantly more frequent conversations

Table 16.1 *Descriptive statistics of all study variables*

|  | Mean | S.D. | Min | Max |
|---|---|---|---|---|
| Teen's characteristics |  |  |  |  |
| Age | 15.18 | 1.72 | 11.00 | 19.00 |
| Gender (boy) | 0.49 | – | 0.00 | 1.00 |
| Race (white) | 0.86 | – | 0.00 | 1.00 |
| Parent salaries |  |  |  |  |
| Mom's salary mid-point | 42,767 | 26,669 | 10,000 | 100,000 |
| Dad's salary mid-point | 76,617 | 24,454 | 10,000 | 100,000 |
| Teen–parent communication |  |  |  |  |
| Talk with mom about her job | 2.25 | 1.07 | 0.00 | 4.00 |
| Talk with dad about his job | 2.07 | 1.08 | 0.00 | 4.00 |
| Teen relationship with parents |  |  |  |  |
| Overall relationship with mother | 3.65 | 0.53 | 2.00 | 4.75 |
| Overall relationship with father | 3.47 | 0.54 | 2.13 | 4.75 |
| Mother's job characteristics |  |  |  |  |
| Job autonomy | 3.19 | 0.83 | 1.00 | 4.00 |
| Substantive job complexity | 0.64 | 0.54 | −0.88 | 1.60 |
| Father's job characteristics |  |  |  |  |
| Job autonomy | 3.25 | 0.86 | 1.00 | 4.00 |
| Substantive job complexity | 0.81 | 0.56 | −0.98 | 1.63 |
| Outcomes |  |  |  |  |
| Job like mother | 0.65 | 0.81 | 0.00 | 3.00 |
| Job like father | 0.96 | 0.93 | 0.00 | 3.00 |

*Note:* Parental reports of salary and job characteristics are run only on the 150 parent pairs. Range reflects actual responses.

with their mothers about their mothers' jobs, relative to the frequency of conversations with fathers about fathers' jobs.

Finally, with respect to the dependent measures, although the distribution of wanting a job like mothers' or fathers' is generally similar, teenagers are significantly more likely to state that they want a job like their fathers', as indicated by a two-tailed paired $t$-test. Specifically, the proportion of teenagers wanting a job like fathers' (mothers') is as follows: "not at all interested" 37 percent (52 percent); "just a little interested" 40 percent (34 percent); "quite a bit interested" 15 percent (10 percent) and "very interested" 8 percent (4 percent).

Table 16.2 presents the inter-correlations among the study variables. Within mothers and fathers, autonomy and substantive complexity are, not surprisingly, moderately correlated (.23 for mothers and .29 for fathers). The correlation between mothers' job autonomy and fathers' job autonomy is .25, and the correlation between the two parents' substantive job complexity is also .25. Both correlations are significant.

Table 16.2 *Bivariate correlations for all study variables*

| | 1 | 2 | 3 | 4 | 5 | 6 | 7 | 8 | 9 | 10 | 11 | 12 | 13 | 14 | 15 |
|---|---|---|---|---|---|---|---|---|---|---|---|---|---|---|---|
| Teen's characteristics | | | | | | | | | | | | | | | |
| 1. Age | — | | | | | | | | | | | | | | |
| 2. Gender (boy) | 0.06 | — | | | | | | | | | | | | | |
| 3. Race (white) | 0.03 | 0.05 | — | | | | | | | | | | | | |
| Parent salaries | | | | | | | | | | | | | | | |
| 4. Mom's salary mid-point | −0.11 | −0.07 | −0.02 | — | | | | | | | | | | | |
| 5. Dad's salary mid-point | 0.09 | 0.01 | 0.11 | 0.07 | — | | | | | | | | | | |
| Teen–parent communication | | | | | | | | | | | | | | | |
| 6. Talk with mom about her job | −0.02 | −0.11 | 0.09 | 0.06 | 0.10 | — | | | | | | | | | |
| 7. Talk with dad about his job | −0.08 | 0.02 | 0.08 | 0.03 | 0.07 | 0.43* | — | | | | | | | | |
| Teen relationship with parents | | | | | | | | | | | | | | | |
| 8. Overall relationship with mother | −0.12 | −0.17* | 0.17* | 0.08 | 0.01 | 0.09 | 0.14 | — | | | | | | | |
| 9. Overall relationship with father | −0.07 | 0.00 | 0.02 | −0.07 | 0.00 | 0.04 | 0.20* | 0.50* | — | | | | | | |
| Mother's job characteristics | | | | | | | | | | | | | | | |
| 10. Job autonomy | −0.11 | −0.12 | −0.02 | 0.11 | 0.10 | −0.06 | 0.06 | 0.20* | 0.09 | — | | | | | |
| 11. Substantive job complexity | −0.03 | −0.08 | −0.03 | 0.40* | 0.11 | 0.04 | 0.07 | 0.14* | −0.03 | 0.23* | — | | | | |
| Father's job characteristics | | | | | | | | | | | | | | | |
| 12. Job Autonomy | −0.06 | 0.12 | 0.10 | −0.06 | 0.32* | 0.01 | 0.03 | 0.11 | 0.16* | 0.25* | 0.00 | — | | | |
| 13. Substantive job complexity | −0.06 | −0.14 | 0.03 | 0.13 | 0.21* | −0.02 | −0.02 | 0.04 | 0.07 | 0.21* | 0.25* | 0.29* | — | | |
| Outcomes | | | | | | | | | | | | | | | |
| 14. Job like mother | −0.14* | −0.23* | −0.02 | 0.18* | 0.12 | 0.15* | 0.21* | 0.22* | 0.06 | 0.17* | 0.12 | 0.03 | 0.04 | — | |
| 15. Job like father | −0.14* | 0.02 | −0.03 | −0.04 | 0.11 | 0.06 | 0.09 | 0.04 | 0.21* | 0.03 | −0.07 | 0.21* | 0.21* | 0.24* | — |

* p < .05

Table 16.3 *Ordered probit estimates for wanting a job like mother*

| | Model 1 | | | | | | Model 2 | | | | | |
|---|---|---|---|---|---|---|---|---|---|---|---|---|
| | Coeff. | SE | Marginal effects[a] | | | | Coeff. | SE | Marginal effects[b] | | | |
| | | | 0 | 1 | 2 | 3 | | | 0 | 1 | 2 | 3 |
| Teen's characteristics | | | | | | | | | | | | |
| Age | −0.08 | 0.05 | 0.029 | −0.013 | −0.010 | −0.006 | −0.08 | 0.05 | 0.030 | −0.013 | −0.011 | −0.006 |
| Gender (boy) | −0.48** | 0.18 | 0.170 | −0.074 | −0.060 | −0.036 | −0.49** | 0.19 | 0.172 | −0.075 | −0.061 | −0.036 |
| Race (white) | −0.24 | 0.26 | 0.085 | −0.037 | −0.030 | −0.018 | −0.22 | 0.26 | 0.076 | −0.033 | −0.027 | −0.016 |
| Parent salaries | | | | | | | | | | | | |
| Mom's salary mid-point | $6.18\text{e-}06$* | $3.08\text{e-}06$ | $-2.19\text{e-}06$ | $9.53\text{e-}07$ | $7.74\text{e-}07$ | $4.63\text{e-}07$ | $5.75\text{e-}06$ | $3.34\text{e-}06$ | $-2.03\text{e-}06$ | $8.83\text{e-}07$ | $7.25\text{e-}07$ | $4.21\text{e-}07$ |
| Dad's salary mid-point | $6.17\text{e-}06$ | $3.36\text{e-}06$ | $-2.19\text{e-}06$ | $9.52\text{e-}07$ | $7.73\text{e-}07$ | $4.62\text{e-}07$ | $6.89\text{e-}06$ | $3.72\text{e-}06$ | $-2.43\text{e-}06$ | $1.06\text{e-}06$ | $8.68\text{e-}07$ | $5.04\text{e-}07$ |
| Teen–parent communication | | | | | | | | | | | | |
| Talk with mom about her job | 0.13 | 0.08 | −0.046 | 0.020 | 0.016 | 0.010 | 0.13 | 0.08 | −0.046 | 0.020 | 0.016 | 0.010 |
| Teen relationship with parents | | | | | | | | | | | | |
| Overall relationship with mother | 0.41** | 0.17 | −0.147 | 0.064 | 0.052 | 0.031 | 0.37* | 0.17 | −0.132 | 0.057 | 0.047 | 0.027 |
| Mother's job characteristics | | | | | | | | | | | | |
| Job autonomy | | | | | | | 0.13 | 0.11 | −0.044 | 0.019 | 0.016 | 0.009 |
| Substantive job complexity | | | | | | | 0.01 | 0.16 | −0.002 | 0.001 | 0.001 | 0.000 |
| Father's job characteristics | | | | | | | | | | | | |
| Job autonomy | | | | | | | −0.07 | 0.12 | 0.025 | −0.011 | −0.009 | −0.005 |
| Substantive job complexity | | | | | | | −0.07 | 0.17 | 0.024 | −0.010 | −0.009 | −0.005 |
| Wald chi-square | 33.34** | | | | | | 37.80** | | | | | |
| Log likelihood | −186.90 | | | | | | −186.14 | | | | | |
| Likelihood-ratio test chi-square | | | | | | | 1.52 | | | | | |
| cut 1 | 0.91 | | | | | | 0.90 | | | | | |
| cut 2 | 2.05 | | | | | | 2.05 | | | | | |
| cut 3 | 2.82 | | | | | | 2.83 | | | | | |

*Note:* Salary coefficients and marginal effects reported in scientific notation.

[a] Predicted probabilities: $0 = .525$, $1 = .335$, $2 = .102$, $3 = .038$

[b] Predicted probabilities: $0 = .524$, $1 = .336$, $2 = .103$, $3 = .037$

* $p < .05$; ** $p < .01$

Results for wanting a job like mother are presented in table 16.3. The average marginal effects in model 1 indicate the differences between teenagers based on several variables. First, being male increases the probability that one will not want a job like one's mother by 17 percentage points. As illustrated by the average marginal effects, being male decreases the probability that the teenager will want a job like mother's "just a little bit," "quite a bit," and "very much" by 7.4, 6.0, and 3.6 percentage points, respectively. Second, the higher a mother's salary, the more likely her child is to aspire to her job. The marginal effects for salary are very small, largely because salary is in dollars, a very small unit. Third, the quality of the relationship between the teenager and his or her mother is a significant predictor of wanting a job like the mother. Specifically, for every unit increase in the teenager's overall relationship quality, the probability that a teenager wants a job like his or her mother "just a little bit," "quite a bit," and "very much" increases by 6.4, 5.2, and 3.1 percentage points, respectively.

The introduction of the block of job trait variables in model 2 does not add significantly to the model. The measures of parental job autonomy and job complexity do not jointly contribute significantly to the teenager's wanting a job like his or her mother, and none of the coefficients is individually significant. The coefficient for a teenager's overall relationship with his or her mother maintains its significance, as does the coefficient for teenager's sex.

Results for wanting a job like father are presented in table 16.4. As was the case in the regression for mothers' jobs, the teenagers' relationships with their fathers is a significant predictor of wanting a job like one's father, such that better reported relationships are predictive of being more likely to be interested in the father's job. Specifically, a unit increase in the relationship scale decreases the probability of not wanting a job like the father's by 14.1 percentage points, and increases the probability of wanting a job like the father's "just a little bit," "quite a bit," and "very much" by 2.6, 5.5, and 6.0 percentage points, respectively.

The block of parental job characteristics added in model 2 results in a significant improvement over model 1. In contrast to the findings for mothers, the results of model 2 suggest that fathers' job characteristics are significant factors in teenagers' desire to have jobs like their fathers. Children of fathers who report more job autonomy or have higher substantive job complexity are more interested in having jobs like their fathers' in the future. For every unit increase in the father's job autonomy, the probability of the teenager not wanting a job like father decreases by 7.2 percentage points; the probability of wanting the job "just a little bit,"

Table 16.4 *Ordered probit estimates for wanting a job like father*

| | Model 1 | | | | | | Model 2 | | | | | |
|---|---|---|---|---|---|---|---|---|---|---|---|---|
| | Coeff. | SE | Marginal effects[a] | | | | Coeff. | SE | Marginal effects[b] | | | |
| | | | 0 | 1 | 2 | 3 | | | 0 | 1 | 2 | 3 |
| Teen's characteristics | | | | | | | | | | | | |
| Age | -0.10* | 0.05 | 0.037 | -0.007 | -0.014 | -0.016 | -0.09 | 0.05 | 0.031 | -0.006 | -0.012 | -0.014 |
| Gender (boy) | 0.10 | 0.15 | -0.035 | 0.006 | 0.014 | 0.015 | 0.19 | 0.16 | -0.063 | 0.011 | 0.025 | 0.027 |
| Race (white) | -0.22 | 0.27 | 0.076 | -0.014 | -0.030 | -0.033 | -0.29 | 0.27 | 0.098 | -0.017 | -0.038 | -0.042 |
| Parent salaries | | | | | | | | | | | | |
| Mom's salary mid-point | -1.94e-06 | 2.88e-06 | 6.92e-07 | -1.28e-07 | -2.69e-07 | -2.96e-07 | -8.19e-08 | 3.18e-06 | 2.78e-08 | -4.90e-09 | -1.09e-08 | -1.20e-08 |
| Dad's salary mid-point | 6.42e-06 | 3.76e-06 | -2.29e-06 | 4.22e-07 | 8.88e-07 | 9.77e-07 | 1.83e-06 | 4.07e-06 | -6.24e-07 | 1.10e-07 | 2.45e-07 | 2.69e-07 |
| Teen-parent communication | | | | | | | | | | | | |
| Talk with dad about his job | 0.05 | 0.08 | -0.018 | 0.003 | 0.007 | 0.008 | 0.08 | 0.07 | -0.026 | 0.004 | 0.010 | 0.011 |
| Teen relationship with parents | | | | | | | | | | | | |
| Overall relationship with father | 0.40* | 0.19 | -0.141 | 0.026 | 0.055 | 0.060 | 0.34 | 0.19 | -0.116 | 0.020 | 0.046 | 0.050 |
| Mother's job characteristics | | | | | | | | | | | | |
| Job autonomy | | | | | | | -0.07 | 0.10 | 0.025 | -0.004 | -0.010 | -0.011 |
| Substantive job complexity | | | | | | | -0.24 | 0.16 | 0.082 | -0.014 | -0.032 | -0.035 |
| Father's job characteristics | | | | | | | | | | | | |
| Job autonomy | | | | | | | 0.21* | 0.10 | -0.072 | 0.013 | 0.028 | 0.031 |
| Substantive job complexity | | | | | | | 0.42* | 0.18 | -0.143 | 0.025 | 0.056 | 0.062 |
| Wald chi-square | 16.21* | | | | | | 33.32** | | | | | |
| Log likelihood | -226.61 | | | | | | -219.96 | | | | | |
| Likelihood-ratio test chi-square | | | | | | | 13.28* | | | | | |
| cut 1 | -0.17 | | | | | | 0.20 | | | | | |
| cut 2 | 0.96 | | | | | | 1.37 | | | | | |
| cut 3 | 1.62 | | | | | | 2.06 | | | | | |

*Note:* Salary coefficients and marginal effects reported in scientific notation.

[a] Predicted probabilities: 0 = .367, 1 = .399, 2 = .145, 3 = .089

[b] Predicted probabilities: 0 = .367, 1 = .398, 2 = .147, 3 = .088

* p < .05; ** p < .01

"quite a bit," and "very much" increases by 1.3, 2.8, and 3.1 percentage points, respectively. The coefficient for substantive complexity is significant. Recall that substantive complexity is measured as a z-score, hence a unit increase corresponds to a one standard deviation increase. For every standard deviation increase in a father's job complexity, the probability that the teenager does not want a job like his or her father (coded as 0) decreases by 14.3 percentage points, while it increases by 2.5, 5.6, and 6.2 percentage points, respectively, for the remaining categories. Interestingly, in model 2, the relationship variable becomes insignificant, suggesting that fathers' job autonomy and substantive complexity are correlated with the quality of the relationship between the father and his children.

Note that complexity and autonomy are significantly associated with a child's aspirations for a father's job, despite the inclusion of father's salary as a control. Hence, these characteristics seem to appeal to children over and above the financial remuneration often attached to them. In analyses not shown, salary was excluded from the mother's equation to see if complexity and autonomy would have significant coefficients or more sizeable marginal effects in the absence of this control. However, they did not. Thus, while mothers' salaries are associated with children's aspirations for mothers' jobs, the inclusion of salary as an explanatory variable does not explain why complexity and autonomy do not have significant coefficients in the model of aspirations for mothers' jobs.

In Hypotheses 2 and 4, it was proposed that the association of parental job autonomy and complexity would interact with the measure of parent–child discussion about parents' jobs, on the one hand, and child's sex, on the other, to produce different effects. Two different models of interactions were tested. In each of these models, the interaction terms were added as a "Step 3" to the main-effects models described above. First, the interactions of the two job characteristics with the measures of the teenager's talking to the mother (father) about the mother's (father's) job were tested. No significant effects of these two interaction terms in either one of the regression equations were found. Therefore, there is no support for Hypothesis 2 that there would be differences in the role of job characteristics depending on how often the teenager and the parents discuss parents' current jobs. Second, the sex of the teenager was interacted with the two parental job characteristics, and these two interaction terms were entered as Step 3 into the regression model. Results suggested no differences in the effect of the parents' job characteristics on boys versus girls, providing no support for the second part of Hypothesis 4.[3]

## Discussion

The analyses in this chapter show a link between parents' job characteristics and teenagers' expressed preferences for a job like their parents'
when they grow up. However, this "linkage" is only true for the association between fathers' job characteristics and youths' aspirations to hold
jobs like fathers' in the future. When fathers hold jobs that are substantively complex and when they report having higher levels of autonomy
at work, adolescents express greater interest in having a job like their
fathers'. Interestingly, these relationships do not apply to interest in having a job like their mothers'. These results provide some support for the
first hypothesis.

No support is found for the second hypothesis, that parents with higher-
autonomy or substantively complex jobs who also engage in more discussion with their teenagers about their work are more likely to have children
who want jobs like theirs in the future. At the same time, significant main
effects are found for the quality of teenagers' relationships with mothers
and fathers, which indicates a positive association between having a good
relationship with one's parent and aspiring to a job like his or hers in the
future. These findings lend some support to the conjecture that occupational aspirations created through children's connections with their
parents play a key role in the transmission of occupations from one generation to the next. However, results do not show a direct effect of parent–
child discussion of parents' work on child aspirations. Future research
could explore how, in particular, a positive relationship with one's parent
is associated with aspiring to be like that parent in the future.

There is no support for the third hypothesis that job characteristics
would be similarly predictive for mothers and fathers. Neither mothers'
job autonomy nor substantive job complexity are significant predictors of
wanting a job like hers in the future, whereas fathers' job autonomy and
substantive job complexity are significant predictors of wanting a job like
his.

Finally, the fourth hypothesis is partially supported by the finding that
girls are more likely to report wanting a job like the mother's; however,
there are no sex differences in wanting a job like the father's. In addition,
no child sex differences are found in the effects of parental job characteristics on aspirations for parents' job in models with interaction effects.

Taken together, these results provide some insight into the previously established linkages between parents' substantive job complexity
or job autonomy and children's behavioral outcomes, including academic
achievement (e.g., Piotrkowski and Katz 1982). Occupational goals and
aspirations may influence relevant behavioral choices. Perhaps children's

relatively high occupational goals (as reflected in their wanting upper-middle-class, white-collar jobs such as their parents hold) translate into greater effort at school, more concrete plans for pursuing post-secondary education, or relevant extracurricular choices that support these occupational aspirations (i.e., work or internship experiences). In other words, the findings suggest that the previously established linkages between parental job characteristics and children's behavior might be mediated by children's aspirations to hold jobs like their parents'.

One limitation of these analyses is that it is not clear how children interpret the question that was used as the outcome measure. That is to say, it is not known whether children perceive the question as asking about jobs identical or simply similar to those their parents hold. If children are taking the question to literally mean their parent's exact job, then the role that job traits play in intergenerational transmission of occupational status may be underestimated. However, this possibility would simply render the results presented in this chapter a conservative test of the hypotheses regarding intergenerational transmission processes. If, however, children are "substituting" other jobs in their minds that have similar levels of autonomy and substantive complexity (e.g., substituting doctor for lawyer), then the results are capturing a broader notion of status transmission. Given the frequencies on the dependent measures, in which 37 percent of teenagers are "not at all interested" in a job like their fathers' and 53 percent are "not at all interested" in a job like their mothers', it appears that many teenage respondents did interpret the question to mean a job exactly like the parent's job.

There are several possible explanations of why these particular characteristics of fathers' jobs are the ones that shape adolescents' future aspirations. One possibility is that substantive job complexity and job autonomy proxy for job prestige, and, as such, adolescents want jobs like their fathers only if these jobs are prestigious. This possibility was explored. Parents' jobs (identified by Census occupation codes) were coded for occupational prestige (see Nakao and Treas 1994 for scale construction). Occupational prestige scores for the current sample range from 17 (miscellaneous food preparation or dishwasher) to 86 (physician). Job prestige is only slightly correlated with job autonomy (.18 for mothers, .13 for fathers), but it is highly correlated with substantive job complexity (.77 for mothers, .87 for fathers). In regressions substituting job prestige for substantive job complexity, similar results are found, namely that job prestige is significant in the regression for fathers but not for mothers. Regressions do not include measures of both job prestige and substantive complexity since their high correlations pose a multicollinearity problem. Nevertheless, these results indicate a fair amount of overlap between job complexity and job prestige, and suggest that both are important components of youths' aspirations toward having a job like their fathers', but do not play a role in youths' aspirations to hold jobs like their mothers'.

Alternatively, it may be that substantive job complexity and job autonomy are important components of fathers' job satisfaction. Perhaps children base their future aspirations on their interpretations of parents' emotions or mood states when discussing work, or when coming from or going to work (see Matjasko and Feldman, this volume, for an analysis of the home-to-work emotional spillover). Fathers who work in highly autonomous and complex jobs might come home fulfilled and satisfied by a day at work. Teenagers may pick up on these cues. It is possible that characteristics of mothers' jobs other than autonomy and complexity are associated with mothers' job satisfaction.

The results presented in this chapter parallel, in part, those from Galambos and Sears (1998), whose analyses suggest that adolescents' perceptions of mothers' work conditions are not significant in predicting adolescents' work values in dual-earner couples, whereas adolescents' perceptions of fathers' work conditions are. If, despite the substantial occupational achievements of many of the mothers in the current sample, fathers' careers take center stage in these families, conversations about parental work may focus on the work tasks and responsibilities in which fathers engage. This situation would render children relatively ignorant as to the nature of their mothers' jobs or how job traits affect maternal well-being. Recall, however, that results indicate that youth are more likely to talk about their mothers' jobs with their mothers than they are to engage in such conversations with their fathers.

It is also possible that parent–child or family conversations about mothers' and fathers' jobs have different content; in future research it would be helpful to have more detail about the nature and valence of these conversations. For example, Ochs's research (see Ochs and Taylor 1996) on family narrative and collaborative problem-solving practices indicates that mothers' workdays are far more often the focus of attention than fathers' workdays (which echoes the finding in this chapter that youth more often talk with their mothers about their mothers' jobs). However, the content of conversations about mothers' jobs differs markedly from the conversations about fathers' jobs. When the mothers' workdays are the subject of conversation, the family, especially the father, is involved in discussing mothers' workday problems and how to address them. In contrast, fathers in Ochs's research are reluctant to talk about their workdays and, when they do, report how they were able to resolve a problem in the workplace. In other words, mothers raise problems for fathers to resolve, while fathers display how they resolved their own problems. It could be that mothers expose their doubts, frustrations, and vulnerabilities in relation to their job experiences, while fathers tend not to reveal these facets of the workplace to the rest of the family, especially the children. This "gender asymmetrical storytelling" (Ochs and Taylor 1996) could account in part for why fathers' work is perceived more positively by adolescents.

An alternative possibility is that if mothers feel the weight of domestic responsibilities more strongly than fathers, the transition from work to home may create tension for them. Larson, Richards, and Perry-Jenkins's work (1994), which finds that men's emotional states become more positive as they transition from work to home whereas women's become less positive during the same transition, supports this notion. Mothers' tension upon returning home could mask any satisfaction the complexity or autonomy of their work grants them, thus giving children the impression that mothers' job quality does not offer psychological benefits and is therefore not something to which children aspire.

Another explanation for the different results for mothers and fathers in the effect of substantive complexity might have to do with the kinds of jobs men and women hold within the same occupational title. The analysis presented in this chapter, which assigns substantive complexity by occupational title, misses such within-occupation variation. For example, take the case of a dual-earner couple in which both parents are managers. If the parents hold different types of managerial jobs within this occupational category, they may differ in terms of the nature of job tasks and responsibilities they have, such that children do not equate job complexity across the two parents' jobs. The measure used in this chapter, however, codes each parent's job as having the same amount of substantive complexity since they are in the same occupation.

The current study is one of relatively few that has compared how the same characteristics of mothers' and fathers' jobs in dual-earner families are associated with children's vocational aspirations. Results of this study shed some light on the potential intergenerational linkages between fathers' jobs and youths' aspirations; however, the same predictions could not be made for mothers' jobs. Analyses were likely limited by the brevity of some of the measures; for example, the indicator of parent–child conversation about parental work measured frequency, not content, of these conversations.

Future research should gather more information about why youth aspire to hold (or not to hold) jobs like their parents' and pursue answers that explain the intriguing differences demonstrated in this chapter between mothers and fathers. In addition, replication with a larger, more ethnically and socioeconomically diverse, and more representative sample would be useful in generalizing results. Finally, future research should situate this question in the context of other aspirations youth have for their futures (e.g., marriage and childrearing) and examine how parental work in dual-earner families shapes children's visions of their futures, broadly defined (see, e.g., Weinshenker, this volume).

In summary, the findings presented in this chapter support the notion that the qualities of a parent's job might shape children's occupational aspirations and the intergenerational transmission of occupational status, bearing in mind that analyses were not conducted on a representative sample of American families. Results also provide some insight into how parental job characteristics might ultimately be related to children's behavior. In addition, the chapter raises some questions concerning the different nature of these relationships among working mothers and fathers. Future research should explore how children interpret their perceptions of parents' work and how these interpretations shape their occupational identities.

## NOTES

1. A large body of sociological literature, however, has examined the role in children's outcomes of parents' connections to other adults and institutions outside of the family. See, for example, Bourdieu 1986; Schneider and Coleman 1993.

2. The sixteen items measuring the teenager's overall relationship with his mother (father) include eight positively worded items and eight negatively worded items. The positive items include: "My mother (father) accepts me as I am"; "I depend on my mother (father) for help with my problems"; "I like to get my mother's (father's) point of view on things I am concerned about"; "When we discuss things, my mother (father) cares about my point of view"; "I tell my mother (father) about my problems and troubles"; "I get a lot of attention from my mother (father)"; "I trust my mother (father)"; and "My mother (father) helps me to talk about my feelings."

   The negative items, which were reverse coded, include: "Talking over my problems with my mother (father) makes me feel ashamed or foolish"; "My mother (father) expects too much from me"; "I get upset a lot more than my mother (father) knows about"; "My mother (father) has her (his) own problems, so I don't bother her (him) with mine"; "I feel angry with my mother (father)"; "My mother (father) doesn't understand what I'm going through these days"; "My mother (father) depends on me for help with her (his) problems"; and "I spend a lot of time listening to the plans and dreams of my mother (father)."

3. These non-significant results are not presented in the tables but are available from the authors upon request.

# Commentary

## Nancy L. Galambos

*One of the least understood set of processes in research on the influence of parents' work on children concerns the mechanisms that might lead to links between parents' job characteristics and adolescents' vocational development. Interest in this issue dates back to the late 1960s, with several relevant studies published in the 1970s, and others appearing only sporadically since then. The study by Kalil, Levine, and Ziol-Guest adds to the rather small body of research that focuses specifically on how features of parents' jobs are linked with adolescents' occupational preferences. For this, the authors are to be applauded. The authors selected the adolescents' interest in having a job like their mothers' or fathers' as their marker of adolescents' occupational preferences. This was a good choice given the relatively young age of adolescents in this sample, most of whom would not yet have clearly developed ideas about what occupations they might want to enter. The authors are also to be commended for zeroing in on two aspects of parents' jobs that have been identified as important in previous work: substantive complexity and autonomy. Moving beyond the tired formula of asking about the effects of parents' work status per se, they examined whether adolescents' interest in parents' jobs was predicted by substantive complexity and autonomy, as well as support in the parent–adolescent relationship and the frequency of parent–adolescent discussions about parents' experiences at work.*

*Kalil et al. found that substantive complexity and autonomy in the mother's job were unrelated to the adolescent's interest in having a job like mother's. Although the main hypothesis pertaining to job complexity and autonomy, then, was not supported, an interesting result emerged from the analysis. That is, mother's salary, which was examined as a control variable, emerged as a significant predictor of the adolescent's interest in mother's job. Thus, salary is an important feature of the parent's work situation of which the adolescent might be well aware and not just a control variable. This analysis also showed that adolescent gender (being a girl) and higher levels of support in the mother–adolescent relationship were significant predictors of adolescents' interest in mothers' job. This set of findings is consistent with the process of identification, as outlined by Kagan long ago. Kagan (1958) defined identification as a belief that some of the attributes of the model (e.g., mother) belong to the self, and argued that three*

443

*conditions must be met if an optimally strong identification (and role modeling) is to occur: (a) the model (i.e., mother) must be perceived by the child as being warm and nurturant (demonstrated by a supportive mother–adolescent relationship in the Kalil et al. study); (b) the model must be in control of the goals, power, or competence that the child desires (e.g., a higher salary); and (c) the child must already perceive some objective basis of similarity with the model (e.g., same gender). Who follows in mother's footsteps? The additive effects shown in the analysis suggest that it is most likely to be girls whose mothers are well-paid and who enjoy supportive mother–adolescent relations. The pattern of results points to the likelihood that the process of identification plays a role in the development of occupational preferences, at least insofar as those preferences mirror the mother's work situation.*

*Who follows in father's footsteps? The analysis points to adolescent boys and girls whose fathers have jobs characterized by complexity and autonomy, and who share supportive relationships with their fathers. Here again, the results are suggestive of the process of identification in that the first two of Kagan's (1958) conditions are met among adolescents with higher interest in father's job: first, a warm relationship with father, and second, father in an occupational position that is demanding of competence and associated with prestige. It is not clear, however, how the third of Kagan's conditions (i.e., perceived objective basis of similarity to father) was met among adolescents following in their fathers' footsteps, given that boys and girls were similarly interested in their fathers' jobs (excluding gender as a basis of similarity). It could be that there were shared similarities between these adolescents and their fathers, such as personality characteristics or world views, that promoted perceived similarity. The fact that boys and girls were equally likely to express interest in their fathers' jobs but girls were more likely than boys to show interest in their mothers' jobs bears some explanation. The literature on gender roles in adolescence suggests that pressures on boys to engage in behavior consistent with their gender role may be stronger than pressure on girls to do so. Moreover, girls may benefit psychologically from having more masculine than feminine interests (Galambos 2004). In short, it is acceptable and even beneficial for a girl to show interest in either her mother's or her father's job, but boys may be compelled by others' and/or their own understanding of the world to turn away from their mothers' work as a possibility for the future.*

*Why did frequency of discussions with either parent about their jobs have no impact on adolescents' interest in mothers' and fathers' jobs? The authors correctly point out that the measure of discussions did not capture the nature and valence of work-related conversations. It is very likely that a measure that assessed the content of such discussions, whether positive, negative, or neutral, or that indicated whether parents revealed job-related stresses or strains, would yield more insight into how adolescents learn about and come to judge their parents' jobs. We know from other research that adolescents have relatively accurate impressions of their parents' work-related affect (job satisfaction and role strain) and that these impressions are significantly linked to adolescents' respect for their parents' jobs (Galambos and Sears 1998). Looking deeper into parents' communications with their adolescents about work is a priority if we are to learn more about the transmission of occupational preferences from parent to adolescent.*

*In considering who is likely to follow in their parents' occupational footsteps, it is remarkable that, in this relatively affluent sample in which many parents hold professional jobs, more than a third of adolescents found their fathers' jobs of no interest and more than half found their mothers' jobs not at all interesting. Moreover, another 40 percent and 34 percent found their fathers' and their mothers' jobs, respectively, only a little interesting. Undoubtedly, some adolescents reject or prefer their parents' jobs because of realistic assessments of the characteristics associated with those jobs. On the other hand, given the importance in adolescence of establishing an identity that is separate from one's parents, it is perhaps surprising that some adolescents actually admit that their parents' jobs might be of interest! Occupational preferences are likely shaped by many characteristics, including those that are present within the adolescent as well as in the multiple contexts of which the adolescent is a part (e.g., the family, school, peer group, and culture). The challenge for future researchers is to integrate and build on the knowledge that has been generated so far so that we can learn more about the many sources of influence on the development of adolescents' career preferences.*

*Part VI*

Lessons to be learned

# 17 Achieving work–life balance: strategies for dual-earner families

*Kathleen E. Christensen*

With both parents now working, how are dual-earner families coping with the stresses and demands of balancing work and family life? Are parents spending more time working, and are their children suffering emotionally and developmentally? Do mothers feel exploited as they continue to manage the household as well as their work responsibilities? What role are fathers undertaking in family life? How do adolescents perceive their parents' ability to manage their complicated lives? The answers provided by the media and popular press often rely on personal vignettes to describe harried working parents feverishly trying to meet the needs of their children. Mom is often portrayed as overworked, dad as being less than cooperative, and their children as saddled with household chores and eating their meals at fast food restaurants or popping something in the microwave. Recent news stories highlight the plight of professional women who, unable to meet the demands of work and family, are increasingly withdrawing from the labor force (see, e.g., Wallis 2004).

How realistic are the stories in the popular press? Drawing on surveys, time diaries, and extensive interviews with parents and their children, the 500 Family Study was specifically designed to examine how dual-earner couples and their children are coping with their complex lives. At first glance, findings from the 500 Family Study seem to mirror those reported in the media and other research studies. Work plays a significant role in the lives of dual-career families, not only in terms of time spent in work-related pursuits, but also with respect to parents' attitudes toward work when at home and with their children. Nonetheless, having working parents does not negatively influence adolescents' academic goals, well-being, or their relationship with their parents. Adolescents are not resentful of their parents' work unless it interferes with activities that they expect their parents to participate in.

Results from the 500 Family Study diverge from other studies regarding the nature of work and how it affects the husband and wife relationship and the socialization of their children. Work appears to have the strongest influence in the social interactions mothers and fathers have with each other and with their children (Koh and Nielsen), and these relationships can be especially negative if the parents spend long hours at jobs that have little autonomy or self-direction (Adam, Matjasko and Feldman, Marchena). How many hours parents work and the complexity of their job profoundly affect adolescents' views of their future occupational and family roles (Kalil et al., Maier, and Weinshenker).

For most working parents, trade-offs and compromises between family and work obligations appear unavoidable. Having to choose between undesirable alternatives often results in feelings of guilt and regret, particularly for mothers. But work is not an escape from household responsibilities; mothers and fathers are happier at home than at work. For parents, work can be an especially positive emotional experience, providing them with an engaging cognitive challenge and sense of self-esteem not found in other situations (Martinez and Sexton). Work becomes a problem for parents not because it is challenging or even demanding, but because the expectations held of full-time professionals and other workers – 150 percent commitment to the job and a willingness to forego family obligations for the sake of work – collide with and overpower family needs. Given the pressures of full-time work, are there conditions at work and at home that can mitigate work–family conflict?

## Time apart and together: what the results of the 500 Family Study tell us

Dual-earner couples describe their experiences at work as positive, particularly when they are employed in jobs that provide them with considerable status, autonomy, and challenge. These emotional states do not vary by gender, and mothers and fathers feel more cognitively engaged and have a higher sense of self-esteem when at work than at home (Sexton). While finding such jobs intellectually satisfying, many mothers and fathers in these types of jobs are likely to work more than a forty-hour week. Believing that a valued worker is one who is willing to put in extra effort, and that not working additional hours results in being overlooked for promotion, many working parents find themselves conforming to the image of the *unconditional worker*. With cell phones and laptops in tow, working parents come in early, leave late, and take work home. These long hours take a toll, and these parents are the ones more likely to arrive home emotionally drained, stressed, and resenting the intrusion of work into family life.

Despite the good intentions of fathers and children, the responsibilities of the third job – caring for the home – in most families remain with the mother, who finds most household tasks emotionally unsatisfying

(Lee). Mothers spend considerably more time than fathers planning, organizing, and performing household tasks. And, in contrast to their husbands, mothers appear to more accurately estimate how much time their spouses devote to housework. Inaccurate assessments of the time mothers spend on housework, and the lack of appreciation they receive for it, may contribute to interpersonal conflict between spouses and to destabilizing work–family balance.

To reduce the burdens of housework, a growing number of middle-class families are purchasing household services. Undesirable household tasks, such as cleaning, laundry, and meal preparation, are being outsourced to professional service providers (Stuenkel). Easily accessible on the internet, there are now reputable referral services that list purveyors of every conceivable service from lawn care to tutoring. A cost-efficient, although time-consuming, alternative to outsourcing is exchanging services such as childcare or carpooling with other parents.

Few emotional benefits are reported for housework, yet when the whole family engages in tasks that are designed for the maintenance of the household, everyone is happier, more involved, and more relaxed than if they have to do them alone (Lee). It appears that one media message that has validity is the importance of family time. When mothers find themselves highly stressed, spending time with family seems to be the best tonic for improving their state of mind. And when parents, particularly fathers, have close relationships with their children, anger and anxiety experienced at work are less likely to affect their children (Matjasko and Feldman). Participating in religious activities also helps to improve parent and adolescent emotional well-being (Schmidt). Television viewing, when it occurs as a family activity, can also be a positive experience for parents and their children (Dempsey). All in all, quality family time is restorative; it is during this time that parents and children communicate with one another, plan activities, and reinforce values. Recognizing that time with family is important for achieving work–family balance, what suggestions can be offered for improving the lives of working families?

### Barriers to reducing work hours

Full-time workers in the 500 Family Study typically work longer than a standard workday. Much like other workers, they would prefer to work fewer hours per week or fewer weeks during the year (Hart 2003). Findings from the 500 Family Study indicate that the majority of full-time working mothers would rather work part time; those who are not working would also prefer to work part time. Fathers, despite having spouses who work, maintain that they have to work full time, although they would prefer their jobs to be more accommodating to the lives of their families. Such accommodations might include working less overtime, traveling less, or having more control about when to work while maintaining full-time status. Mothers, especially those with young children, express a desire to work a different schedule than their current one; fathers express this preference to a lesser extent. It is understandable that mothers with young children would desire to work fewer hours. Overall, parents want different kinds of scheduling flexibility, and workplaces provide minimal opportunities, particularly for reduced hours.

Although wanting a change in work schedules, most parents are reluctant to request a change in hours from their employers. Nor are many employers willing to institute alternative work schedules. Collectively, American workers and their employers share the belief that what keeps the US economy strong is working long hours. Among professionals, there is a sense that if they work fewer hours, they are not really part of the culture nor would they be seen as a member of the team. Other workers, even those who are managers, cannot afford to reduce their hours since this would result in reduced earnings, health benefits, and job security. However, the financial incentive for full-time work is not, as some have suggested, to acquire luxury items; in many cases, it is to keep pace with the rising costs of childcare, elder care, health services, and education, including tutors, summer learning experiences, and college tuition.

One reason that employers and employees are resistant to change is that they share a sense of inertia, as well as lack a sense that alternative ways of structuring work time are genuinely possible and profitable: "If you want to be promoted at our company that means putting in the long hours, that's how it has been and it is unlikely to change"; "Today, when you become a partner, the expectation is that you will continue to work that 50-hour week, and be available for lunches, dinners, and weekend events" (All quotes in this chapter are abstracted from parent interviews in the 500 Family Study). This is how it is in the US, but it is not how work is organized in other countries. In the Netherlands and other northern European countries, substantial part-time work (20 to 34 hours per week) is quite prevalent, and such workers are more likely to achieve work–family balance (European Foundation for the Improvement of Living and Working Conditions 2003). Although part-time schedules are more common among low-wage workers than professionals in these countries, a shorter workweek makes it easier for many dual-earner couples to fulfill family obligations. If part-time schedules were more widely adopted in the US, however, workers would need assurances that they would not lose career opportunities nor pensions and other benefits, an issue that may be of less concern in countries with comprehensive social welfare systems.

Second, in the US, health insurance and other benefits are tied to employment status. Many part-time workers, for example, pay for a larger proportion of their health insurance than full-time workers. In many countries, health benefits are a right of citizenship. Because health benefits are not available to all citizens in the US, one might expect that individuals would be more likely to work for health benefits than in other countries. There is some indirect evidence for this in the 500 Family Study: the majority of women who work full time in managerial and sales positions cite health benefits as a primary reason for working (Martinez). It is not that their spouses who are working do not have coverage; rather, these mothers claim that full coverage for their children and themselves requires the combination of benefits from two full-time workers. Additionally, couples often desire dual coverage as protection against loss of health benefits should one spouse be terminated from his or her job.

Third, concerns about job security make it difficult for workers to negotiate a change in work schedule with their employers. Too often the worker assumes that a desire to cut back on work hours is a private problem: "It is because my child needs more of my time"; "My aging parent requires more care"; or "I cannot keep up this pace and remain healthy and be a good parent or spouse." These types of problems are easily personalized. Once seen as a private problem, the onus of responsibility rests entirely with the worker, and negotiation with the employer concerning alternative work schedules is less likely. But as seen in the 500 Family Study, this is not simply a personal issue, it is a pervasive structural problem experienced by nearly all working families.

### Creating a public agenda

Throughout this book, the authors provide solid empirical evidence challenging many of the myths about working families – that they are out of control and always stressed, their children suffer, they leave home to avoid the drudgery of housework, and they use their salaries to satisfy a decadent and hedonistic life style. Instead, they show the constraints faced by dual-earner couples and why there is a need to rearrange their work schedules. Not unlike other workers, they want to spend more time with their families but find few opportunities to do so.

The Family and Medical Leave Act of 1993 provides working parents with the opportunity to take unpaid leave from work for up to twelve weeks in the event of the birth or adoption of a child or when they or a family member is seriously ill or injured. Although the policy applies to all workers, for the most part employees cannot take intermittent leave or work part time under this Act unless such leave is medically necessary or the employer agrees to such an arrangement. In addition, employees who are among the highest paid 10 percent in their regional area may be denied restoration of their position following leave due to the disruption or economic burden such leave might cause their employer. Such exceptions help to reinforce highly paid professionals' decisions not to take time off from work for family reasons, as shown in this and other studies (Moen 2003). These professionals realize the importance of spending time with their children, yet are constrained by the pride they take in their work, their commitment to their jobs, and expectations of their colleagues. What seems to be the case is that all parents need to have more time with their families, regardless of whether they work in a law firm or a bakery. Workplace family policies fail to address the invisible strings that tie the professional worker to the workplace and to a demanding work schedule.

Part of what needs to be changed is the culture of the workplace, which currently demands a commitment to work at the expense of commitments to family, especially children. Instead, the culture of work, particularly for professionals, reinforces a dedication to colleagues, clients, and professional standards, regardless of the time required to fulfill these obligations. It is not that the standards need to be lower, but rather that we need to rethink the expectations that parents work nights and weekends, spend a week or more away from their families on company business, and take laptops and cell phones on vacations. Research has shown that relaxation is necessary for productivity and that healthy workers need time away from the job (Csikszentmihalyi 2000).

The parents in the 500 Family Study report that they enjoy their families more than they enjoy their work. But they are willing to work long hours and give in to work demands because that is what they believe the job requires; they are also engaged and challenged by their work. It is not the case that mothers work to avoid household demands and responsibilities so much as it is that they work for the challenge and intellectual stimulation that work gives them. Work and home offer different emotional and cognitive benefits to parents: home, relaxation, and time with family; work, stimulation, and a chance to excel. In an optimal situation, a worker would enjoy the benefits of both experiences. However, work now encroaches on family life, creating emotional spillovers from work that exacerbate stresses at home.

### Rearranging the work schedule

Parents who work full time cannot always afford to reduce their income. They, as well as those who can, must have access to alternative work schedules that make their lives more reasonable. Several flexibility alternatives exist, including flexibility in the scheduling of full-time work hours (including flextime and compressed work weeks); flexibility in the amount of time spent working (including part time, job sharing, and part year); and career flexibility, with effective entry and exit points over the course of a career (including leaves, sabbaticals, and time out).

Hart (2003) shows that many people find the idea of having a large block of time away from work more valuable than reducing the hours worked within each week. However, for employees, the idea of a reduced year is seen as a viable option only for one particular year or a few years, not something that is permanently in place for every year. The option to take several weeks off during the course of a work year *with a reduction in pay* is limited by financial constraints. Those who have college degrees, who are employed as professionals or managers, and are in dual-earner households would be more likely to take advantage of such an alternative were it available. As Hart indicates, older workers would prefer to move to a part-time basis sometime prior to retirement, whereas younger workers have the greatest interest in taking off blocks of time during the year.

For many workers, there is greater interest in reconfiguring the work schedule than in performing less work for reduced pay. Several options are generally seen as desirable. The most popular alternative is a compressed work week – for example, working four ten-hour days and having three days off each week. This alternative is not necessarily relevant for those professionals whose workdays already exceed ten hours. In dual-earner families, fathers express a greater interest in this option than mothers. It may be that mothers, who already shoulder a majority of household responsibilities, do not view an extra day at home as helpful or do not see how they can arrange childcare for such long days. What women, especially mothers, prefer is a schedule that parallels the local school day. For this reason, working from home during the business day is especially appealing to women facing work–family pressures.

One way to increase choice and autonomy in the workplace would be to provide employees with flexibility to set their own work schedules. However, providing choice of work schedules is not without problems. There is an accountability problem in that there are likely to be some employees who will exploit flexible schedule arrangements to avoid work, and others will have to pick up the additional burden for these employees. There is also a performance measurement issue in terms of how to ensure that people are being productive when one cannot rely solely on face time as a measure of productivity. Second, there are other practical concerns for employers. Choice poses major administrative challenges to employers in that it can be more difficult to manage people working diverse schedules; to some extent this difficulty can reinforce an ideological resistance to change. Only by addressing such issues publicly will solutions to these challenges be realized.

The 500 Family Study shows the viability of dual-earner families. Results reveal that these families are not the frazzled, dysfunctional ones that the media portrays, but are solid, functioning families. But the study also makes clear that a new balance needs to be achieved between work and home. Presently, the parents in dual-earner couples tend to be oriented toward work rather than family, not because family is not important, but because the demands on the unconditional worker supersede day-to-day family concerns. At an individual level, these parents feel they have to work: it enhances their self-esteem, they feel challenged when working, they have made sizeable investments in their education and careers, and they feel part of their work culture.

Motivations for working are also family oriented: parents want their children to succeed in life, and substantial resources are needed for that to occur. Middle-class parents worry about their children's education and early on strategize about how to begin and how to sustain their children's schooling careers. Good schools, tutors, special programs, and access to technological resources like the Internet have taken on an importance that is perhaps unprecedented in family life. Given the increased competition for college admissions, parents find themselves working with adolescents on ways to maximize their chances of being accepted to their preferred school. The rising costs of post-secondary education, and the costs of preparing for it, have become the third mortgage for many households.

To bring work and family into a more reasonable alignment will require recognition on the part of both employers and employees that there is a problem. The fact that middle class families with substantial resources are having a difficult time balancing their work and home lives points to the likelihood that parents with more limited resources are struggling with similar issues. A recent study by Barnett and Gareis (2004) shows that many parents with children have work schedules that prevent them from being home when their children arrive home from school and that there are few safe, accessible, high-quality, and affordable afterschool programs to meet the demand. Parents who have concerns about their children's afterschool arrangements are also more likely to report low psychological well-being and to have significantly more job disruptions. On average, parents with high levels of stress due to concerns about their children's afterschool arrangements miss as many as five or more days of work a year compared to parents with fewer concerns. They also frequently make errors, turn down requests to work extra hours and miss meetings and deadlines. What distinguishes the high-stress from the low-stress parents is the availability of flexible work arrangements.

Working environments need to be redesigned so that they allow parents to be available for the care of their children, including their adolescents. How that can be accomplished is a societal challenge, not just a problem for working families.

Bear in mind that the 500 Family Study was conducted in 1999–2000 at a time when jobs were plentiful and the economic outlook was promising. Since then the jobless rate has risen significantly and the prospects for recovery are uncertain. The work conflicts and pressures reported by parents in the 500 Family Study may thus be even more pronounced now than they were when the study was conducted. It is also more apparent that these conflicts are societal rather than individual in nature. With downsizing and layoffs, workers who remain on the job may feel even more pressured as they take over the tasks of those who have left and more fearful that they will be next in line if they fail to perform to expectation. Longer workdays and work weeks and less time with children may be the choices that many workers feel they have to make. But what are the consequences of these choices for the next generation? How are children's well-being, perceptions of work and family life, and views of their own ability to meet these challenges being affected? Even if after-school care and daycare options are considerably improved, parents still need to spend time with their children. There is no substitute for the care parents provide. If these issues are not addressed, we run the risk of having workers resenting their jobs, spouses resenting each other, and children who suffer the consequences.

# Technical appendices

# Appendix A
# Obtaining accurate measures of time use from the ESM

*Jae-Gea Jeong*

Most statistical analysis based on survey research assumes that the data are likely to contain missing records, and different techniques have been developed to adjust for these problems. However, analyses using data from the Experience Sampling Method (ESM) have typically not included techniques to correct for non-response. This is problematic since ESM data generally have a substantial number of missing responses, primarily as a consequence of respondent burden. Missing responses may produce bias in point estimates of variables (e.g., means and proportions of variables X, Y, and Z) and in associations among variables (e.g., regression coefficients) in ESM data analysis. Both the extent of the bias and the method for reducing this bias are contingent upon the relationships between response probabilities and outcome variables. In analyzing ESM data, it is therefore important to understand how missing responses are related to other variables in the data set. Using data from parents in the 500 Family Study, this appendix examines ESM response patterns, identifies variables affecting response probabilities, and presents a method to adjust for non-response bias in these data. The appendix reviews the strengths and weaknesses of the ESM and briefly discusses how the relationship between response variables and response probability affects data analysis.

## The Experience Sampling Method

Time use estimates based on ESM data are generally consistent with those based on data obtained from time diaries, in which respondents are typically asked to report the activity or activities they engaged in during a 24-hour period.[1] Despite this consistency, there are several differences between the ESM and time diary methods. The ESM has been found to be more accurate than the time diary because it is free from recall bias – respondents' inaccurate recollections of prior events or

461

experiences (Bernard et al. 1984). In many ESM studies, more than half of the sample respond to the beep immediately, and about 90 percent of responses are recorded within eighteen minutes of the beep (Hormuth 1986). As a result, ESM responses better reflect the timing of an activity than responses in time diaries. Comparing ESM responses and time diary entries for the same time period, Mulligan, Schneider, and Wolfe (2003) found that about 2 percent of non-identical records seem to occur because respondents do not remember the exact time when they were doing certain activities, especially those that are not work-related. For instance, while ESM records indicate that respondents were eating a meal when signaled, diary entries typically report that they were eating twenty minutes before or after the scheduled signal. Finally, since the ESM covers an entire week, it enables researchers to examine respondents' activities across the week. Considering that people tend to organize their lives on a weekly schedule (Gershuny et al. 1986: 18), this aspect of the ESM becomes very important.

The ESM has limitations, however. Because ESM participants are asked to specify the activity they are engaged in at a given moment, but are not asked to indicate the duration of the activity or to note prior and subsequent activities, the duration and sequence of activities can be better estimated using the time diary method. Other limitations of the ESM are generally related to non-response. The mean response rate of participants in most ESM studies is less than 85 percent (Hormuth 1986). In other words, participants in ESM studies generally fail to respond to one in five beeps. The nature of the ESM is partly responsible for the relatively low response rate. Since respondents are asked to write responses in a booklet upon hearing the beep, the process might disrupt their daily routine, especially when in public (Hormuth 1986). Activities done outside the home tend to be underestimated since respondents are more likely to miss these beeps, either because they forgot to carry the beeper or because it was inconvenient for them to respond when engaged in certain types of activities (e.g., swimming or attending meetings).

### Non-response and its effects

In general, the relationship between an outcome variable such as time allocation and a response probability can be characterized by three assumptions about missing data (Allison 2002):

(1) *Missing completely at random (MCAR)*. If the probability of having missing data on the outcome measure, commonly referred to as Y, is unrelated to the value of Y or to the value of any other variable in the data set, the data are *missing completely at random*. In other words,

if non-response for an activity is unrelated to the activity itself (e.g., being engaged in work as opposed to being engaged in some other type of activity) or to other variables in the data set, the data are MCAR.

(2) *Missing at random (MAR)*. If the probability of having missing data on Y is unrelated to Y after controlling for other variables, the data are *missing at random*. For example, the MAR assumption is satisfied if the probability of having missing data on income depends on marital status, but within each marital status category, the probability of having missing income data is unrelated to income.

(3) *Non-ignorable*. If the parameters that govern the missing data *are* related to the parameters being estimated, then the missing data are *non-ignorable*. If, for instance, people with extremely high incomes are reluctant to report their income, the estimated average income does not represent the characteristics of the population (Heckman 1976).

The relationship between the outcome variable and the response probability determines the extent of influence of non-response on survey data or data from other instruments. The effects of non-response are first discussed for standard surveys, since surveys are more widely used than the ESM. In the typical survey, the bias from non-response is calculated as follows:

$$B(\overline{Y}_r) = \overline{Y}_r - \overline{Y} = \overline{M}(\overline{Y}_r - \overline{Y}_m) \qquad \text{(Equation 1)}$$

where $B(\overline{Y}_r)$ is bias from non-response, $\overline{Y}_r$ is the mean of the outcome variable for the observed sample, $\overline{Y}$ is the mean for the population, $\overline{M}$ is the proportion of non-respondents, and $\overline{Y}_m$ is the mean for non-respondents. Equation 1 shows that the mean for the observed sample $(\overline{Y}_r)$ is an approximately unbiased estimate of the mean for the population if either the proportion of non-respondents is small or the mean for non-respondents is close to that for respondents. Again, if the data are MCAR, the mean for non-respondents is the same as that for respondents $(\overline{Y}_r - \overline{Y}_m)$, and the estimates from the observed sample are not biased. In the MAR assumption, the estimates would be biased without considering differences in response rate. For instance, if married couples are politically more conservative than widowed or divorced individuals and are more likely to respond to the survey, the estimated mean of political attitudes is more conservative than the real mean for the population. But in MAR, which assumes that responses are missing at random within each subgroup, an unbiased estimate of the population mean can be obtained by calculating a weighted average consistent with the population distribution. The unbiased population mean is equal to:

$$Y = \frac{1}{N} \sum_{h=1}^{L} N_h Y_h \qquad \text{(Equation 2)}$$

where $N_h$ is the number of members in subgroup h, $Y_h$ is the mean of available observations in subgroup h, and N equals the number of individuals in the population. In Equation 2, the mean of each subgroup ($Y_h$) is weighted in accordance with its proportion in the total population. Therefore, the point estimates, such as means or proportions, are not biased when appropriate adjusted weights are used for MAR data. However, as Equation 1 suggests, in *non-ignorable* situations, the magnitude of the bias depends on the response rate and the strength of the relationship between the dependent variable and the response rate.

The effect of non-response in the ESM is similar, except that ESM data have a multi-level structure where multiple beeps are nested within persons. Therefore, for the ESM data to be MCAR, the response rate must be unrelated not only to characteristics of respondents but also to characteristics of the contexts in which signals occur, such as time, place, and activity. More specifically, two conditions should be met: (1) ESM participants must respond to the beep randomly, that is, without regard to place, time, and activity; and (2) there must be no difference in response rates across categories of respondents (i.e., response rates must not be influenced by characteristics of respondents such as educational attainment, race and ethnicity, or gender). If these two conditions are met, no bias in point estimates will be observed.

What if these two conditions are not met? Even if ESM response rates differ by time and place, if the probability of response is not influenced by the activity respondents are engaged in within particular categories of time and place (e.g., day of the week, home versus work), the ESM data are MAR. In addition, the MAR assumption is not violated if the activity does not affect response rates within particular respondent categories (e.g., highly educated versus less educated respondents), regardless of differential response rates across these categories.

Assume, for example, that highly educated respondents (1) are more likely to answer the beep, and (2) spend less time watching television than less educated respondents. Also assume that (3) within the same education level, the probability of responding to the beep is unrelated to watching television. In this circumstance, the potential bias in estimates of how much time respondents spend watching television can be eliminated by adjusting for differential response rates across persons. In the same way, the bias from contextual influences on response rates (e.g., the timing of signals) can be adjusted for. For instance, assume that people (1) are less likely to respond to beeps on the weekend, and (2) watch more television on the weekend. If television watching does not affect response rates, the point estimates for time devoted to television viewing are not biased provided they are adequately weighted to adjust for the proportion of beeps responded to on the weekend by each category of respondent (e.g., highly educated versus less educated). In non-ignorable circumstances, where the response rate is directly related to the outcome of interest, the point estimates will be biased. For example, if people are less likely to answer the beep when they are in public, the proportion of an activity performed in public will be underestimated.

The analyses of ESM data presented in this appendix examine both respondent characteristics and contextual variables that may influence response rates. The primary focus of these analyses is on whether the MAR assumption holds for these data. In other words, is the outcome of interest – time allocation – unrelated to response probabilities after controlling for variables that influence response rates? If the MAR assumption holds, then unbiased estimates of time allocation can be obtained by weighting the data to adjust for these influences.

## Method

### Calculating response rates

In analyses of ESM data, response rates are analyzed at two levels: the person level and the beep level. Person-level analyses examine the influence of respondent characteristics (e.g., gender, race and ethnicity, educational attainment) on individual response rates. An individual's response rate is calculated by dividing the person's total responses by the total number of times he or she was signaled. Since individuals were signaled eight times each day for seven days, totaling fifty-six signals for the week of ESM participation, a person who responded to only forty of these signals would have a response rate of 71 percent (40/56).

Beep-level analyses examine the influence of contextual variables (e.g., the time and place at which responses occur) on response rates for a given time slot (e.g., Monday between 8 a.m. and 9 a.m.). The number of potential time slots for the week of ESM participation is dependent on the number of days of the week (Monday through Sunday) and the number of hours per day during which respondents were signaled

(6 a.m. to midnight, for a total of eighteen hours).[2] Multiplying 18 hours per day by the 7 days of the week yields a total of 126 one-hour time slots. However, in addition to occurring during specific hours of the day and on specific days of the week, signals also vary by day of participation. Some ESM respondents begin participation on a Sunday, others on a Monday, and so on throughout the week, and the day on which participation starts and ends can influence response rates.[3]

Because the potential times at which signals can occur are contingent upon the day of participation, the 126 hours of the week are multiplied by the seven days of participation (first through seventh), yielding 882 potential time slots during which signals can occur.[4] In actuality, some of these time slots are empty, since no beeps occurred within a given classification of potential response times by hour of day, day of week, and day of participation. For all existing time slots, response rates are calculated by dividing the total responses occurring within a given time slot by the total number of scheduled beeps for that time slot (determined from the beep schedules of participants).

### Sample

This subsample consists of 784 parents (461 mothers and 323 fathers) who provided a total of 33,346 responses to the ESM. Twenty-seven of these parents (3 percent) did not complete a parent survey.[5]

### Measures

*Person-level variables* The following sociodemographic variables, obtained from parent surveys, were used in analyses of relationships among individual response rates and person-level characteristics: gender, age, race/ethnicity, income, and educational attainment. In addition, thirty-six survey items were analyzed measuring the psychological states of respondents, including twenty items comprising the CES-D depression scale and sixteen items measuring various aspects of self-esteem, anger, anxiety, and attachment to others.

Measures of time allocated to various activities by individual participants were constructed based on responses to an ESM item indicating the main activity engaged in when signaled. Activity codes were collapsed into eleven categories: market work, housework, shopping, childcare, active leisure, passive leisure, social entertainment, education, voluntary organization (e.g., attending church services), personal care, and driving/travel.[6] For each respondent, the proportion of time allocated to each of these types of activities was calculated by aggregating responses within each activity category and then dividing the number of responses within each category by the total number of responses provided by the individual. Thus, if an individual responded to forty ESM signals, and on ten occasions indicated that he was engaged in job-related activities, the proportion of time devoted to market work by this individual would be .25.

*Beep-level variables*   In examining the potential influence of contextual variables on response rates for the 882 time slots described above, several beep-level variables were analyzed, including time, place, momentary psychological states of respondents, and the proportion of responses occurring within specific activity categories. The variables measuring the time at which responses occurred included weekend versus weekday (dichotomously coded), day of participation (first through seventh), and hour of the day (coded in military time). The places at which responses occurred (determined by an ESM item asking where the respondent was when signaled) were collapsed into three categories: home, work, and public. Activities respondents were engaged in were again grouped into the eleven categories used in person-level analyses. To reduce the number of variables to be analyzed, the categories were further collapsed into five categories that occur most frequently in the data: work, personal care, passive leisure, housework, and other (all other categories).

Twenty-two ESM items measuring the momentary psychological states of respondents were used in analyses. Standardized scores for these items were computed. Standardized scores (also known as z-scores) are calculated by subtracting the raw score for a given item from the person's mean for that item and dividing by the standard deviation. By adjusting individual scores to the person's own mean, z-scores allow analysts to distinguish between-person from within-person effects (Reis and Gable 2000). To reduce the number of items used in analysis, exploratory factor analysis was used to identify items measuring similar constructs. Using this procedure, five factors were identified, which can be characterized as hardworking, friendly, frustrated, happy, and nervous.[7]

For each of the existing time slots (classified according to hour of the day, day of the week, and day of participation), the proportion of responses in the time slot that occur within each place category and each activity category, respectively, was calculated. The proportions for place and activity categories and the means for psychological factors are used in analyzing relationships between each of these contextual variables and the response rates for the time slots.

Table A.1 *Mean number of ESM responses by race, educational level, and gender*

|  | Mean number of responses |
|---|---|
| *Race/ethnic group** |  |
| White (636) | 43.61 (11.33) |
| Other race/ethnic group (97) | 38.06 (15.35) |
| *Education*** |  |
| Less than four-year degree (123) | 37.58 (15.34) |
| Four-year college degree (197) | 43.57 (11.40) |
| Graduate/professional degree (428) | 44.21 (10.78) |
| *Gender** |  |
| Male (323) | 40.87 (13.18) |
| Female (461) | 43.69 (11.81) |
| *Overall* (784) | 42.53 (12.46) |

*Note:* Number of respondents in each category is presented in parentheses; standard deviations are presented in parentheses after the mean.
$*p < .01$ in t-test; $**p < .001$ (in ANOVA test)

## Influences on response rates

### *Differential response rates across categories of individuals*

The overall response rate is 76 percent (i.e., $42.53/56 \times 100$), as shown in table A.1.[8] The typical response rate for similar studies ranges from 75 percent to 85 percent (Hormuth 1986; Moneta and Csikszentmihalyi 1996). While ESM data from the 500 Family Study are at the lower end of the range of response rates, there is ample evidence showing the validity and reliability of these data. To identify the respondent characteristics that may influence response rates of individuals in the sample, response rates were compared by gender, educational attainment, income, age, and race/ethnicity. Among these five variables, there are no significant differences in response rates across age or income groups. However, as shown in table A.1, response rates do differ significantly by race and ethnicity, educational attainment, and gender. Response rates are significantly higher among white respondents compared with respondents from other racial/ethnic groups. Response rates are also higher among respondents who have earned bachelor or graduate degrees compared with respondents who have lower levels of educational attainment. In turn, women have higher response rates than men.

Associations between psychological characteristics of respondents and the response rates of individuals were also examined. Considering that the ESM was developed and has been used primarily by psychologists, one might assume a priori that ESM participation is unrelated to a participant's psychological characteristics. However, if ESM participation is related to particular psychological attributes of individuals, the data obtained by the ESM cannot be representative. For example, in an extreme case, if only relatively happy people were to participate in the ESM, the ecological validity of the ESM would be seriously challenged.

Partial correlations for the relationship were computed to examine the relationship between the number of responses participants provided and various indicators of individuals' psychological states from the parent survey. Among thirty-six variables measuring respondents' psychological states, controlling for race/ethnicity, gender, and education, only three variables show statistically significant associations with number of responses. Those who get nervous more frequently and who feel less proud of themselves respond less often, whereas those who feel that they enjoyed life in the last week have higher response rates. Moreover, there is no association between scores of sixteen or higher on the twenty-item CES-D scale and number of responses, indicating that people who score in the depressive range of the scale are not significantly less likely to respond to the ESM. Thus, variations in the psychological attributes of respondents do not appear to produce serious bias in the ESM data.

Relationships between time use estimates and individuals' ESM response rates were also examined. According to the MAR assumption, if responses are missing at random, response probabilities should be unrelated to the outcomes of interest (in this case, proportion of time individuals allocate to various types of activities), after controlling for variables that influence response rates (i.e., gender, race/ethnicity, and educational attainment) and outcome variables.

A series of regression analyses was conducted in which the number of ESM responses provided by each individual was used to predict the proportion of time individuals allocated to eleven different activities, controlling for race/ethnicity, gender, and education. Weighted least squares regression was used because the number of beeps on which these proportions are based varies, producing differences in standard errors and heteroskedasticity that violate the assumptions of ordinary least squares (OLS) regression.

Results of these analyses indicate that the response rates of individuals are related to only two activities: work and passive leisure. In other words, the MAR assumption holds when measuring time use for most activities, with the exception of work and passive leisure.[9] These results suggest that the MAR assumption is not seriously violated with respect to respondent characteristics. However, as noted above, differential response rates across categories of individuals are not the only source for bias due to non-response; variables such as the timing of beeps can also influence response rates.

### Contextual influences on response rates

In this section, the effects of several contextual variables on response rates are examined. A series of OLS regressions is used to examine these effects, with response rates for the 882 time slots serving as the dependent variable, and several contextual variables that could potentially influence these response rates serving as independent variables. These contextual variables include the timing of beeps – weekend versus weekday, day of participation, and hour of participation – the proportion of responses in each time slot occurring within different place and activity categories, and mean psychological factor scores for each time slot. This beep-level analysis may provide clues to understanding the relationship between response rates and activity, place, or psychological states in these different time slots. For instance, if a time slot with a lower response rate also has a lower proportion of respondents who are in public, one might suspect that being in public affects the response rate. Admittedly, such an interpretation may be criticized for ecological fallacy – that is, relationships at the beep level are not consistent with relationships at the individual level (Robinson 1950). However, even without direct observations or individual-level data, such beep-level analyses are useful and can contribute to an understanding of non-response mechanisms in the ESM.

Table A.2 presents the results of this series of regression analyses. Model 1 shows the effects of beeper timing. The significant negative coefficient for day of participation confirms that attrition in response rates across the week of ESM participation is substantial. Controlling for day of participation, the response rate is lower on the weekend. The hour of the day shows a curvilinear effect on response rates; that is, the mean response rate is highest around noon, and gradually decreases on both sides.[10]

Model 2 examines the effects of psychological state on response rates. Among the five psychological factors, three have a significant effect on response rate. The time slots with higher values for being productive, being frustrated, and being nervous exhibit higher response rates. These feelings may be more typical of work settings and of job-related activities, and thus occur more frequently in the workplace where respondents are engaged in market work. That is, certain psychological states may co-occur with certain locations and activities.

Table A.2 *Unstandardized regression coefficients for the effect of time, place, activity, and psychological state factors on response rates (%)*

| | Model 1 | Model 2 | Model 3 | Model 4 | Model 5 |
|---|---|---|---|---|---|
| Time | | | | | |
| Weekend | **−8.55 (−6.89)** | | | | **−8.05 (−5.95)** |
| Day of participation | **−2.79 (−9.93)** | | | | **−2.61 (−10.6)** |
| Hour | **3.59 (5.23)** | | | | **3.08 (3.4)** |
| Square of hour | **−.147 (−6.29)** | | | | **−.13 (−3.94)** |
| Psychological state | | | | | |
| Hardworking | | **2.84 (5.47)** | | | −1.05 (−1.37) |
| Friendly | | .81 (1.55) | | | −.35 (−.67) |
| Frustrated | | **1.85 (3.59)** | | | .54 (1.1) |
| Happy | | −.80 (−1.53) | | | .82 (1.66) |
| Nervous | | **2.32 (4.49)** | | | −.27 (−.49) |
| Place | | | | | |
| Home | | | **−18.4 (−8.51)** | | −6.90 (−1.56) |
| Public | | | **−10.9 (−3.24)** | | −7.72 (−1.50) |
| Activity | | | | | |
| Work | | | | 6.28 (1.78) | −7.64 (−1.38) |
| Personal care | | | | **−7.63 (−2.17)** | −2.09 (−.51) |
| Passive leisure | | | | **−18.70 (−4.24)** | −1.60 (−.31) |
| Housework | | | | −8.46 (−1.76) | −3.40 (−.67) |
| Adjusted R-square | .203 | .071 | .077 | .065 | .230 |

*Notes:* t-values are indicated in parentheses.
Coefficients significant at the p < .05 level are shown in bold.

Model 3 shows the effects of place on response rates. The two dummy variables (at home, in public) have significant negative coefficients, indicating that the baseline, being in the workplace, is related to a higher response rate (consistent with the finding that time slots with higher response rates have higher values for being productive, being frustrated, and feeling nervous). The comparison between being at home and being in public is not significant.

In model 4, the proportion of work activity is positively related to response rates. The other three activities (housework, personal care, and passive leisure), most of which occur in the home, have negative effects on response rates. In other words, when participants are at work, they are more likely to answer the beep, which explains the curvilinear effect for hour of day. When they are home and want to relax, they are more likely to miss the beep.

Model 5 examines the effects of these factors simultaneously. Although model 4 suggests that ESM time use estimates are biased, since the activity itself is related to the response rate, model 5 shows that if relevant timing variables, such as day of participation, occurrence on the weekend, and hour of day, are controlled for, none of the activity variables has a significant relationship to response rates. This result can be attributed to the fact that the proportions for activity categories are highly associated with day of week and hour of day. As Gershuny and colleagues (1986) show convincingly, life today tends to be organized according to a weekly schedule, and even within a day, activities are closely related to the time of day. These results confirm this point. Additional analyses (not shown) indicate that on weekends, the proportion of responses that occur while respondents are engaged in market work is less than 10 percent, whereas it is greater than 24 percent on weekdays. On the other hand, all other activities except childcare are more likely to be done on the weekend. In particular, most of the shopping is done on Saturday, and participation in organizational activities such as religious services is often done on Sunday. Within days, some regularities are also observed. Most work activities are conducted from 9 a.m. to 5 p.m. on weekdays, and males tend not to do housework after 10 p.m. In sum, this regularized pattern of time use in middle-class families explains why once weekend and time of day effects are controlled for, the effect of activities becomes insignificant.

This interpretation supports the MAR assumption since response probabilities are only indirectly related to the proportion of time spent on various activities. These results also suggest that the timing of the responses should be considered in adjusting for differential response rates since timing is related both to the outcome variables of interest – the

proportion of time spent on various activities – and to response probabilities.[11]

## Post-stratification weighting

### Post-stratification and auxiliary variables in the ESM

Post-stratification is primarily used to correct for differential non-
response among sociodemographic groups (Gelman and Carlin 2001).
For post-stratification weighting, one or more qualitative auxiliary variables (i.e., neither ordinal nor ratio variables) that affect the response rate
is selected. The categories of these variables (e.g., married or not, female
or male) or a combination of these variables (e.g., married male, married female) serve as the post-stratum. Post-stratification assigns identical
adjustment weights to all elements in the same post-stratum so that the
proportion of a given stratum in the sample is the same as that in the
population. The weight $W_i$ for an element in stratum h is calculated as
follows:

$$W_i = \frac{N_h/N}{n_h/n} \qquad \text{(Equation 3)}$$

where $N_h$ is the number of individuals in group h in the population, N
is the total number of individuals in the population, $n_h$ is the number of
group h in the sample, and n is the number of individuals in the sample.
This equation shows the weights obtained by dividing the proportion of
a certain stratum in the population ($N_h/N$) by its proportion in a sample ($n_h/n$). In the typical survey, these weights reduce the discrepancies
between the survey sample and the population.

Considering the 500 Family Study's focus on dual-earner middle-class
families, the sample is not adjusted to the general population. Rather,
the purpose is to give adjusted weights so that (1) the proportion of ESM
beeps from each stratum is equal to the proportion of respondents in
that stratum; and (2) a whole week of this stratum can be proportionally
represented in the data. For example, college-educated males comprise
8.3 percent of the sample, so the purpose in weighting the data is to ensure
that (1) the beeps from college-educated males comprise 8.3 percent of
the beep data; and (2) this 8.3 percent of the beeps is representative of
the whole week.

One way to represent the week is to adjust the data so that every hour
of the day of the week has an equal proportion. However, this approach
is problematic for two reasons. First, although the total number of beeps
provided by parents in the 500 Family Study is more than 33,000, if

respondent characteristics are considered in identifying auxiliary variables, the risk of empty strata or strata with too few observations is greater if adjustments are made for each hour of the day as opposed to grouping hours into units. Second, for the weights used in person-level analysis, where estimates for each person are obtained, since the maximum number of beeps (56) is less than the number of hours per week (126), there will be at best one beep for any given hour of the day. To avoid this problem, which makes weights very unstable, the hours of the day of the week should be collapsed into several groups that are relatively homogeneous with respect to both activity type and response probabilities (Bethlehem 2001).[12] These groups function as an auxiliary variable or variables.

In sum, for beep-level analytical weights, which try to reduce bias from differences in response rates both between persons and within person, the auxiliary variable comes from a combination of respondent characteristics and the classification of the hours of the week into groups that are homogeneous with respect to activity type and response probability. On the other hand, for person-level data, where the goal is to obtain variable mean proportions for each individual, the auxiliary variable is based only on the classification of hours of the week into homogeneous groups. In the next section, a method is presented for grouping hours of the day of the week into a few groups that are homogeneous with respect to distribution of activities and response rates.

### Cluster analysis: classifying 126 hours into clusters

Cluster analysis is the generic name for a wide variety of procedures used to create a classification. These procedures empirically form "clusters" or groups of highly similar entities (Aldenderfer and Blashfield 1984). To identify relatively homogeneous groups among 126 sampled hours based on similarity in distribution of activities, hierarchical cluster analysis was used, where 126 clusters is the starting point (i.e., each hour constitutes its own cluster). In successive steps, the two closest clusters are combined, thus reducing the number of clusters by one in each step.

For measuring the similarity among hours, a correlation matrix is used since, unlike distance measures, it is not affected by dispersion and size differences between the variables. The correlation coefficient is defined as:

$$r_{jk} = \frac{\sum (x_{ij} - \overline{x}_j)(x_{ik} - \overline{x}_k)}{\sqrt{\sum (x_{ij} - \overline{x}_j)^2 (x_{ik} - \overline{x}_k)^2}} \qquad \text{(Equation 4)}$$

where $x_{ij}$ is the value of variable i for case j, $\bar{x}_j$ is the mean of all values of the variable for case j, $x_{ik}$ is the value of variable i for case k, and $\bar{x}_k$ is the mean of all values for case k. Since the means for each case are almost identical, this correlation measure represents the relative similarity nearly perfectly (for details, see Aldenderfer and Blashfield 1984).[13] Two cases are closer, or clustered earlier, to the extent that the proportions of activities within the hours are similar.

Cluster analysis does not provide robust criteria for deciding how many clusters are appropriate. Thus, to ensure enough beeps in each stratum in weighting, the minimum number of independent clusters is set at ten. That is, if only two or three hours cluster into one unit, larger clusters are sought that include these hours. However, some hours cannot be combined into larger cells even in later steps. In that case, the hours are assigned to another cluster relatively similar in terms of distribution of activities.

Different time use patterns across categories of respondents should be considered in constructing efficient weights. If the time use patterns of women are different than those of men, the hours combined into the same cluster should be different for men and women. A series of preliminary analyses (not shown) suggest that time use patterns differ significantly by gender.[14] Level of education (less than a college degree versus a college degree and higher) results in different patterns of time use among males. In addition, white females exhibit distinctive time use patterns relative to non-white females. Therefore, cluster analyses were separately conducted for four different groups: males with a four-year college degree or higher; males with less than a four-year college degree; white females; and non-white females. Ultimately, five clusters were obtained for white females and the two male groups, and four clusters were obtained for non-white females. These clusters are interpreted based on modal activities. If the difference between the two most dominant activities is less than 10 percent, the clusters are referred to as "mixed."

Analyses show that there are five major activities for the two male groups and the two female groups. For males with a college degree or higher, the five clusters can be characterized as work, personal care, passive leisure, mixed personal care and housework, and mixed personal care and work. Market work is mostly done on weekdays between 8 a.m. and 6 p.m. This market work cluster is surrounded by times included within the personal care and work cluster. This mixed cluster can be interpreted as a transitional period. While some respondents work, others are at home. A few (16 percent) are actually in transit. After getting home from work, respondents prepare and eat dinner in the personal care and housework cluster, which consists of some weekday evening hours (7–9 p.m.) and most daytime weekend hours. Generally, around 9 p.m. on weekdays and during the evening hours on weekends, highly educated males spend most of their time engaged in passive leisure activities, such as watching television (passive leisure cluster). Early mornings and late nights are devoted to personal care activities, such as grooming and sleeping. This personal care cluster consists of some lunch hours as well.

Compared to the time use patterns of males with college degrees or higher, the time use patterns of males with less than a college degree seem more irregular, though caution should be used in interpreting such patterns since the small number of males in the sample who have less than a college degree may be partly responsible for the irregularity. Time use patterns for less educated males differ in two ways. First, unlike more highly educated males, housework forms a distinctive cluster, and the proportion of housework in other clusters is smaller than the corresponding clusters for college-educated males. Second, market work begins earlier, which reflects the job characteristics of these respondents. In addition, the driving and work cluster includes many late night hours, suggesting that some less educated males have two jobs or work the night shift.

For females, there is no transition period where a substantial amount of time is devoted to driving. The work and non-work divide is still salient, but the number of hours in work clusters is smaller than for males, and the proportion of work activity is also smaller. In non-work clusters, the proportions of time spent on personal care, passive leisure, and housework are relatively similar to the proportions of time spent on these activities by males in non-work clusters.[15] Among the five clusters for white females and the four clusters for non-white females, two are mixed clusters, respectively. Even in the passive leisure cluster, the difference between passive leisure and personal care is only slightly larger than 10 percent. With the exception of the personal care and work cluster, the relative distribution of personal care, housework, and passive leisure is not very different across clusters, although their rank order is somewhat different. The lack of an independent passive leisure cluster explains the smaller number of clusters for non-white females.

Roughly speaking, women spend most of their time doing housework during the day on weekends and around dinner time on weekdays. Men also spend more time doing housework during the day on the weekends than at any other time, and one or two hours after dinner on weekdays. At around nine o'clock, both men and women engage in passive leisure activities (mainly watching television), with slight gender differences in time composition. After these passive leisure activities, men are more often engaged in personal care activities, such as showering or sleep, while more women stay up late doing housework or other activities.

### Post-stratification weighting: an example

The results presented in tables A.1 and A.2 suggest that the goal of weighting responses is to adjust for differential response rates by respondent category and by timing of beeps. The respondent characteristics that influence response rates and the times obtained by cluster analysis based on the similarities in the distribution of activities act as auxiliary variables. There are three educational categories, two race/ethnicity categories, and two gender categories. Therefore, there are twelve strata based on characteristics of respondents. However, some ESM participants did not complete all items on the survey, so information on race/ethnicity and educational attainment is missing in some cases. In these cases, only the gender of respondents is known, so these respondents are placed into one category for each gender. There are thus fourteen strata based solely on differences in response rates across categories of respondents.

Four or five clusters are obtained from the 126 sampled hours across the week, which excludes 6 hours per day. Since the average sleep time of adult Americans is more than seven hours (Robinson and Godbey 1997: 359), half a weight is assigned to the hours between 6 a.m. and 7 a.m. and between 11 p.m. and 12 a.m., so that the average number of hours per day covered by the ESM is 17 hours. The total number of hours covered by the ESM is thus assumed to be 119 hours. As a result, while 23 hours belong to personal care for highly educated males, the beeps from those hours are assumed to represent only 17 hours, since 12 of the hours included are treated as half hours. Since the hours spent sleeping show little difference by demographic and status factors (Robinson and Godbey 1997: 113), every group is assumed to spend the same amount of time responding to the ESM.

Based on the above discussion, table A.3 presents examples of how the adjusted weights are calculated. The upper half of the table shows the beep-level weights for college-educated white males, and the lower half shows the beep-level weights for white females with professional or graduate degrees. From Equation 3, the weights are calculated by dividing the expected proportion by the observed proportion. For instance, the expected proportion of a stratum is obtained by simply multiplying the proportion of persons who have certain attributes by the proportion of hours in a certain cluster. From table A.3, the expected proportion for the work cluster for college-educated white males is 0.032 ($65/784 \times 46/119$), while the observed proportion is 0.037. From Equation 3,

Table A.3 *Examples of procedures used in assigning weights*

| Cluster | | Number of hours (a) | Expected proportion of hours (b = a/119) | Expected proportion of respondents (c) | Expected proportion of beeps (d = b*c) | Observed proportion of beeps (e) | Weights (f = d/e) |
|---|---|---|---|---|---|---|---|
| College-educated white males | Work | 46 | 0.387 | 0.083 | 0.032 | 0.0365 | 0.878 |
| | Personal care | 17 | 0.143 | 0.083 | 0.012 | 0.0075 | 1.586 |
| | Passive leisure | 15.5 | 0.130 | 0.083 | 0.011 | 0.0095 | 1.14 |
| | Personal care and housework | 26 | 0.218 | 0.083 | 0.018 | 0.0197 | 0.92 |
| | Personal care and work | 14.5 | 0.121 | 0.083 | 0.01 | 0.0095 | 1.06 |
| Graduate or professional degree white females | Work | 40.5 | 0.340 | 0.253 | 0.086 | 0.105 | 0.820 |
| | Personal care | 21 | 0.176 | 0.253 | 0.044 | 0.0359 | 1.241 |
| | Passive leisure | 14.5 | 0.121 | 0.253 | 0.031 | 0.026 | 1.192 |
| | Housework and personal care | 23.5 | 0.197 | 0.253 | 0.050 | 0.051 | 0.975 |
| | Personal care and passive leisure | 19.5 | 0.164 | 0.253 | 0.041 | 0.057 | 0.720 |

0.878 (.032/0.037) is obtained as an adjusted weight for this stratum. In this way, adjusted weights are calculated for all strata. The weights for the person-level analysis are calculated by adjusting for the differential response rates across clusters. For each participant, weights are assigned so that each cluster is proportionately represented, given the number of responses provided.

### Efficiency of weights

To examine the efficiency of weights, estimates of time spent on market work and housework were obtained from both the ESM and the parent survey. While self-reports may overestimate work hours (Robinson and Godbey 1997), Jacobs (1998) indicates that self-reported work hours – the standard survey measure of weekly work hours – is a reasonable estimate of work hours. In the 500 Family Study, respondents were asked to report weekly work hours by choosing among seven categorical response options.[16] Because respondents do not provide work hours in real numbers, both the correlation and the improvement in correlation between ESM estimates and self-reported measures may not be very large. When self-reported work hours are compared with non-weighted estimates for hours worked from the ESM, the correlation between the two measures is 0.455. When the survey measures are compared with weighted ESM estimates, the correlation increases to 0.476. If the sample is restricted to individuals who answered more than 25 beeps (90 percent of the sample), the correlation is much improved; the correlation with non-weighted estimates is 0.468, while the correlation with weighted estimates is 0.496. The comparison of correlations shows that the weighted measure is a better fit to self-estimated work hours, even when the MAR assumption does not perfectly hold.

## Conclusion

While the ESM is widely regarded as useful for obtaining estimates of time use, non-response must be addressed. Most ESM studies simply use non-weighted measures. The only previous work addressing this issue concerns differential response rates for the ESM, which only reduces the bias of estimates (see Mulligan, Schneider, and Wolfe 2003). By considering both response rates and the distribution of activities within clusters, the method presented in this appendix reduces both bias and variance.

The weights described in this appendix are based on the MAR assumption. It is assumed that there are differential response rates across strata, but that within each stratum, non-response occurs at random. Although this assumption is not entirely valid, the results show that it improves time use estimates.

One of the limitations of this study is that it does not provide weights for adjusting for distinctive features of the data. In future research examining time use patterns of middle-class families, additional weights will need to be developed to make the data from the 500 Family Study representative of American middle-class families.

The analyses presented in this appendix do suggest a few practical guides for ESM researchers. First, the starting day of ESM participation should be varied across samples, considering the decline in response rates that occurs over the week of ESM participation. Results of these analyses suggest that the participants may need special incentives to participate in ESM studies for an entire week. Second, although non-white racial/ethnic groups and males with less than a college education are underrepresented in the 500 Family Study, the finding that response rates are lower for these respondents compared with respondents from other groups suggests that researchers need to make special efforts to raise response rates among these participants.

## NOTES

1. The ESM is sometimes described as a form of time diary since both methods can be used to study time use. Unlike the ESM, however, traditional time diaries do not use beepers to signal respondents. (For a brief overview of time diary approaches, see Mulligan, Schneider, and Wolfe 2003.)
2. It is assumed that all individuals who participated in the ESM were signaled between the hours of 6 a.m. and midnight. In practice, the beep schedules for each individual were based on information on the respondent's usual sleep hours. If an individual indicated that he or she typically went to bed at 11 p.m. and got up at 6 a.m., then signals were programmed to occur between 6 a.m. and 11 p.m. Despite these individual variations in beep schedules, signals typically occurred between 6 a.m. and midnight.
3. An examination of response rates by day of participation reveals significant attrition over the week of ESM participation. The response rate for the first day of participation is greater than 83 percent, but the response rate gradually declines to 66.7 percent by the final day. Response rates also vary by day of the week, with higher response rates occurring on weekdays compared to weekends. Compared with an overall 75.8 percent response rate, the response rate for Saturday is slightly above 70 percent, and that for Sunday is 72.7 percent. Because the starting day of participation varies across individuals, the effect of day of participation can be distinguished from the weekend effect.
4. For example, the response rate for Sunday between 9 and 10 a.m. is 67.3 percent. However, the response rate for this hour also depends upon day of participation. When ESM participation begins on Sunday, the response

rate for this hour is more than 75 percent. In contrast, if Sunday is the last day of ESM participation, the response rate for this hour is less than 50 percent.

5. In addition, a small percentage of parents who did complete surveys have missing data for some of the survey items used in analyses. Parents who have missing data for these items are therefore excluded from analyses that examine relationships between individual response rates and respondent characteristics (obtained from surveys).

6. The first ten of these activity categories come from Juster and Stafford (1985). The last category (driving/travel) is included because the purpose of travel could not be identified from ESM responses.

7. The principal component method and varimax rotation were used. All factors with eigenvalues greater than 1 were retained. Because varimax rotation was used, the five factors are not correlated with each other.

8. Out of a possible fifty-six beeps, the mean number of responses for individuals in the sample is 42.53.

9. In weighted least squares regression analyses (not shown), the direction of coefficients for number of responses is negative for work, and positive for active leisure. The significant negative association between number of responses and work indicates that individuals who allocate a greater proportion of their time to work activities have lower response rates. In turn, the positive association between number of responses and active leisure (e.g., exercise, hobbies) indicates that individuals who devote a greater proportion of their time to active leisure have higher response rates.

10. Mathematically, the effect of hour of day is expressed as: $-.15$ square of hour $+ 3.59$ hour $+$ constant, which describes the inverted U-shape effect of hour of day on response rates. The peak of this curve is 11.98 (3.59/2/.147) hour.

11. Some might question whether this aggregation of the data ignores the heterogeneity of the sample. For example, individuals' psychological states on weekday mornings could be dependent on employment status. Also, the effect of psychological state on response probabilities might differ across respondent characteristics. To consider heterogeneity in terms of both time use and patterns and psychological states, and their influence on response probabilities across individuals, several logistic regressions were run where the outcome variable for each regression was whether each individual beep was responded to or not. The missing values for place, activity, and psychological state were imputed, using regression imputation methods. The results of these analyses are generally consistent with the discussion in the text, because the imputed values themselves are primarily determined by the timing of the beeps.

12. Post-stratification based on strata that are homogeneous with respect to the target variables reduces both variance and bias. Post-stratification based on strata that are homogeneous with respect to response rates only reduces bias.

13. Because proportions used in cluster analysis include most major activities, the sum of these activities sometimes explains all responses within a given time period. The median and mean of the sum of these activities is 92 percent for highly educated males and the standard deviation is .04. Therefore, the mean of these eleven activities in each time slot is very close to .09.

14. Several logistic regressions were run. The dependent variable in each of these regressions was whether or not a respondent reported a certain activity

(e.g., work). After controlling for gender, race/ethnicity, educational attainment, and the timing of beeps (i.e., weekend versus weekday, hour of the day), interaction terms for timing of beeps by respondent characteristics were added. When these interaction terms are significant, it suggests that time use patterns are somewhat different across different categories of respondents. While this analysis was concerned with the absolute proportion of the activities, the second step in this set of analyses focused on the relative distribution of the activities. Based on a number of clusters extracted from the entire sample for each gender, the proportion of an activity reported in a certain cluster was divided by the total beeps for which the activity was reported. For example, assume that one individual responds to 50 beeps, with 20 of these beeps occurring while the respondent is engaged in work-related activities. Among these 20 beeps, 9 of the beeps fall within the first cluster. In that case, the proportion of work activity in the first cluster is calculated as .45 (9/20). In this way, the relative contribution of each cluster to certain activities is measured. Note that this proportion does not depend on the absolute amount of time spent in a certain activity. In the second step, the relative contribution of each cluster is the dependent variable in a regression in which the effects of race and educational attainment are tested, controlling for gender.

15. Professor Suzanne Bianchi provided this insight after reading an earlier version of this appendix.

16. The seven categories are: 1–15 hours, 16–25 hours, 26–37 hours, 38–45 hours, 46–50 hours, 51–60 hours, and more than 60 hours.

# Commentary

## Suzanne M. Bianchi

*The Jeong appendix does yeoman service in addressing the internal validity and representativeness of the ESM data collection method used in the 500 Family Study. In the process, the appendix sheds light on time use, the difficulties in sustaining respondent cooperation with time use methodologies that collect data over an extended period, and the procedures that can be helpful in correcting data for non-response. The ESM methodology is an important one in the arsenal of time use methods. More so than any other method except direct observation, it captures time use in natural settings and assesses subjective states that accompany daily activity. We learn things from this type of data collection that we cannot ascertain with other methods. Hence, enhancing confidence in the representativeness of this type of data collection is extremely important.*

*Jeong shows that ESM reports are more complete for women than men, for college-educated than less than college-educated individuals, and for whites than for respondents who are members of minority groups. He also shows clearly that timing matters: respondents are less likely to report on weekends, more likely to respond to the beeps at mid-day, and response rates decline with time in the survey (i.e., respondents report over a one-week period and there is decay in response rates over the week). He then incorporates both person-level factors (gender, race, educational attainment) and beep-level factors (clusters of time use periods in which the beeps occurred) to construct post-stratification weights. These weights adjust responses internal to the 500 Family Study so that beeps are "weighted up or down" to adequately represent the "beep protocol" used in the study. Weights appear to improve the estimates, though not as much as might have been expected given the large amount of work involved in constructing the weights. For example, the survey measure of work hours correlates 0.455 with unweighted estimates and a slightly higher 0.476 with weighted estimates.*

*There are a number of unanswered questions in the analysis. One is whether the elaborate cluster analysis that organizes time by similarity in activities is necessary. In table A.2, the overwhelming association between response rates is with three timing factors. Once these are controlled, psychological state, location of the respondent when the beep went off, and activity are reduced to non-significance. Yet, a complex cluster analysis based on timing and activity is used to construct strata. For most groups, strata other than "work" and perhaps "personal care" seem quite heterogeneous in terms of activity. One wonders whether a simpler post-stratification adjustment with additive factors for day of participation, weekend day, and distance from mid-day, might perform as well or better in weighting the sample than the clusters.*

*The main limitation of the appendix is that the major question of representativeness of the time use estimates from the ESM 500 Family Study remains unaddressed even after the careful weighting adjustment. For sure, this appendix takes an important first step. The weights that are constructed help ensure that those who elected to participate in the 500 Family Study have responses that reflect the beep protocol of the study. The weights adjust for the fact that respondents did not answer all beeps and their pattern of non-response was not random – not random in terms of respondent characteristics and not random in terms of when beeps occurred over the study. However, after reading the appendix, one still has an overriding question about the study: how representative was the sample who accepted the beepers in the first place? The ESM methodology is intrusive – who elects not to participate at all and how does this affect time use estimates and the characterization of subjective states that accompany time use categories?*

*If the goal of substantive analyses with these data is to describe what middle-class families do and how they feel about what they do, there are two roadblocks. The first, attended to well in this paper, is that within individuals there is non-random non-response to the beep schedule. The second is not addressed: the threat to accuracy if a non-representative sample of the middle–class families was included in the study in the first place. Generalizable findings from the 500 Family data require an additional set of weights. One can envision a procedure analogous to what is done in this paper in which the Current Population Survey (CPS) is used as the "gold standard" against which to measure population representativeness. The sampling criteria that were employed in the selection of the 500 Family Study – for example, the selection criteria by education, age of children, and so forth – are applied to the CPS to select a comparable CPS sample of families. Then, using the matrix approach to array either individuals or families by gender, age, race/ethnicity, education, and so forth in both the CPS and the 500 Family Study, differences can be assessed and a set of weights constructed that adjust the Sloan families (or parents/adolescents) to match the national distribution of comparable families. Without attention to this weighting issue, one cannot generalize accurately to time use among "middle-class American" families.*

*It is possible that this second set of weights may not make all that much difference to estimates. In fact, it is noteworthy that after all the cluster analysis that is done in this appendix to adjust for non-response and gain efficiency, the weights do not seem to make all that much difference. However, without the additional CPS work to adjust the study population to national totals, findings from the current study will be treated with skepticism because it will not be clear how "select" or non-representative the sample is.*

*A final comparison that needs to be made is between ESM estimates from the 500 Family Study and estimates of time use for a comparable, or roughly comparable sample of individuals and families who keep a time diary. It is noted that the advantage of the ESM method over time diaries is that the ESM elicits an immediate response. When respondents are beeped, they write down what they are doing at the time, whereas in the time diary a respondent must reconstruct the activities of the previous day. However, it is also noted that the ESM methodology has limitations for chronicling the days and weeks of busy American families because the beeper methodology does not collect information on the duration or sequencing of activities. The time diary reports over a 24-hour period have the advantage of capturing these aspects of time use.*

*Rather than competing, the two types of time sampling would seem to be complementary. Repeated beeps over a week and across respondents begin to pick up a picture of time use in middle-class families that can be compared with the picture from time diaries. One can calculate the proportion of (weighted) beeps that occurs during work hours. Is the proportion of waking hours spent at work similar under the two methodologies? How does the percentage of mothers' and fathers' time spent in market work under the two methodologies (ESM and time diaries) compare with the estimates that would be derived from the type of (stylized) questions usually asked in a labor force survey like the CPS? What explains the difference?*

*We need better understanding of time use in families, both objective and subjective aspects of the experience of time. The 500 Family Study provides new data, and the Jeong appendix increases confidence in the internal consistency and quality of these data. The next step is to be able to use the ESM information in conjunction with other data on time use, namely the CPS which provides information on market time allocation for large national samples, and time diaries which provide a way of assessing non-market as well as market time allocation and are beginning to be incorporated into the CPS. To make these comparisons, we need to push beyond the "within-sample" weighting adjustments of the Jeong appendix. The ESM method, with its emphasis on subjective states, enriches what we know about the "meaning" of time. But to realize its full potential to understand how families mesh work and family life, the information from the 500 Family Study must be able to be compared and contrasted to the information in the CPS and time use surveys. We not only need work on the internal consistency and representativeness of the ESM data, we also need careful attention to its external validity and comparability to data on time use collected using other methodologies.*

## Kazuo Yamaguchi

*The appendix by Jeong addresses the most important methodological issue in the analysis of the ESM data: the handling of non-response to the beep. He presents a very informative analysis that sheds light on the issue. The method of weighting he employs is certainly an option for an adjustment for missing data, and he derives a concrete method of weighting after a careful analysis of the data. However, the method he proposes for missing data still has limitations. I clarify these limitations and suggest some alternative methods that avoid the limitations of his approach. More generally, I address three questions regarding his analysis of the ESM data and the consequent proposal. I use the terms MCAR, MAR and NMAR according to Little and Rubin (2002) below.*

*The three questions are (1) whether the evidence that Jeong provides to conclude that the MAR condition is satisfied for the ESM data he analyzed is strong; (2) assuming that the MAR condition is satisfied, whether the weighting method is the best method for adjusting for non-response in the ESM data; and (3) assuming that the MAR condition is satisfied and that the weighting method is adopted for adjusting for non-response, whether there is any weighting method that is better than the particular method for constructing weights that Jeong proposes.*

*I discuss the questions in reverse order. For the discussion, I assume a dependent variable Y, and its covariates X. For the ESM data, we can distinguish three kinds of covariates of Y (1) time-constant covariates; (2) defined covariates; and (3) time-dependent covariates. Time-constant covariates do not change their values for anyone in the sample during a one-week period of observation. Race, gender, education, and age at the first survey date are examples of time-constant covariates. Defined covariates include hour of the day, day of the week, and day of participation in the ESM. They are time-varying variables whose values are predetermined and, therefore, are available even when non-response occurs. The ESM employs an experimental design for those variables such that if there are no missing responses, the distributions of hour of the day, day of the week, and day of participation in the ESM will be independent and uniform in the sample. By time-dependent covariates, I mean covariates whose values change over time but are not predetermined. They include all variables, other than Y, recorded when the beep sounds. An important characteristic of these covariates is that when Y is missing due to non-response to the beep at time t, their values are usually missing at that time as well. Under the assumption that the MAR condition is satisfied, the response rate depends on some covariates X of Y, but not on Y itself, and, therefore, the adjustment of the sample to make the sample distributions of these Xs to be the same as those that would be obtained if there were no missing responses is necessary to eliminate bias in statistics such as means and proportions. Since the use of weights for observations is indeed an option for such an adjustment, I will first discuss this method.*

*Jeong proposes that the weights that adjust sample proportions be made equal to the proportions expected if there are no missing responses for each state distinguished by cross-classifying gender, race, education, and the cluster of activities (which consist of work, personal care, passive leisure, etc.) He adjusts the weights by gender, race, and education not only because the response rate significantly differs (as shown in Jeong's table A.1) among people with different race, gender, or education, but also because the distribution of hours spent in a week for activities varies with each combination of the three attributes. He employs the cluster of activities as a substitute for defined covariates (hour of the day, day of the week, and day of participation in the ESM) that strongly affect the response rate, because the complete cross-classification of 18 hours of the day, 7 days of the week, and 7 days of participation in the ESM yields 882 time slots, for some of which there are no observations, and, therefore, the ratio of the expected versus the observed number of responses (or beeps) – which would have been used in determining the weights – is incalculable.*

*However, the use of the cluster of activities for adjustment has a limitation. Unlike the time budget survey, where hours of activities are recorded in their entirety, the ESM provides data on the activity only at the time of the beep. Unless the activity data are MCAR, the estimate for the number of hours of each activity in a week based on observed data will be biased. Furthermore, even when such bias does not exist, the precision of the estimates for the number of hours of activities based on the ESM data is not high because it does not obtain data on the duration of activities. Hence, weight estimates based on the estimates for the number of hours of activities by attributes (race, gender, and education) are likely to be crude or inaccurate.*

*If variables that affect the response rate are hour of the day, day of the week, and day of participation in the ESM, rather than activities, we should construct weights that adjust for the distributions of these covariates, because the expected distributions of these defined covariates that would be obtained if there were no missing responses are fixed by the ESM design and, therefore, are subject neither to bias nor sampling variability; their use would thus yield much more accurate weight estimates than the use of expected hours of activities. A question, then, is how to handle the issue of zero observations for cross-classification of the three defined covariates. Suppose that only the main effects of hour of the day, day of the week, and day of participation in the ESM affect the response rate as indicated by Jeong's table A.2. Then, we only need to adjust for the marginal distributions of the three defined variables and this can be done as follows.*

*Let $\{f_{hdp}\}$ be the set of 18x7x7 observed response frequencies for the cross-classification of hour of the day (h), day of the week (d), and day of participation (p) in the sample, and let $\{F_{hdp}\}$ be the set of corresponding expected* *frequencies obtained, using Stephen-Deming iterative proportional fitting, by adjusting the three one-way marginal frequencies of $f_{hdp}$ to be equal to those that would be obtained if there were no missing responses. $F_{hdp}$ can be obtained even when many $f_{hdp}$ are zero if the marginal distributions of $f_{hdp}$ do not include zero observations. The weight $W_{hdp}$ for observation at $(h,d,p)$, which makes the total weighted and unweighted numbers of observations equal, is then given as:*

$$W_{hdp} = (F_{hdp}/f_{hdp})(n/N) \text{ when } f_{hdp} \neq 0$$
$$= c \text{ (an arbitrary constant) when } f_{hdp} = 0 \quad \text{(Equation 1)}$$
$$\text{Where } n = \Sigma_h \Sigma_d \Sigma_p \text{ and } N = \Sigma_h \Sigma_d \Sigma_p F_{hdp}.$$

*Suppose further that we wish to adjust, as Jeong did, the distributions of observations by hour of day (H), day of week (D), and day of participation (P) for groups classified by race (R), gender (G), and education (E). Then we can calculate for each of the $F_{hdp}$ 12 combined states of these time-constant covariates if the marginal distributions of $f_{hdp}$ do not include zero observations for each of these states. If there are zero observations for any of these states, then we may apply the iterative proportional fitting for a set of marginal distributions (RH)(RD)(RP)(GH)(GD)(GP) (EH)(ED)(EP)(RGE) instead of (RGEH)(RGED)(RGEP), so that expected frequencies retain the marginal distributions that are identical to those which would be attained if there were no missing responses for the two-way marginal distribution of each of the three time-constant covariates and each of the three defined covariates, and for the three-way marginal distribution of the time-constant covariates. Using the expected frequencies obtained by this marginal adjustment by the Stephen-Deming method, we can obtain the weight by using the extension of Equation 1 for the six-way table of RxGxExHxDxP.*

*Let me now discuss whether the weighting method is the best method, given the assumption that the MAR condition is satisfied. Unlike the use of sampling weights for data from non-equal-probability sampling, the use of weights for adjustment for non-response can eliminate bias in parameter estimates but generates bias in the standard errors of parameter estimates because standard errors depend on unweighted observation counts. Although it is easy to base parameter estimates on weighted counts and standard errors on unweighted counts in the loglinear analysis of cross-classified frequency data (Clogg and Eliason 1987), or to make an adjustment for $\sqrt{n_i}$ for the standard errors of means and proportions by group i, such an adjustment for standard errors is more difficult for general regression models with individual data. Given the assumption that the MAR condition is met and that we can identify the set of covariates that affect the response rate, we should simply use unweighted data in multivariate regression models including the sets of variables that affect the response rate* as control variables, while we may use weights for estimating means and proportions.

An alternative strategy is the method of imputation. Given that several variables affect the response rate, it seems desirable for the ESM data that Jeong analyzes to employ regression imputation rather than conditional mean imputation. The multiple imputation method that preserves the variance of responses rather than the single imputation method is preferable because the rate of nonresponse is fairly high. Regression-based multiple imputation methods still have a variety of options regarding which I cannot make a specific recommendation without some analysis. However, when a psychological variable is the dependent variable, we may effectively employ the time-constant measurements of psychological states that Jeong employs in his and the interactions of these measurements with time as auxiliary variables in the imputation regression. In addition to the authoritative textbook by Little and Rubin (2002), a recent book by Allison (2002) is helpful for the applications of imputation methods. Statistical packages such as the SPSS Missing Value Analysis module and SAS PROC MI (multiple imputation) are also available.

My final topic of discussion is whether Jeong provides good evidence that the MAR condition is satisfied for the ESM data he analyzes. The major evidence that he presents are the results from his analysis in table A.2. The analysis of partial correlations assumes population heterogeneity and time homogeneity, and shows that time-constant psychological states, measured at one time point independently of responses at beeps, are largely uncorrelated with the response rate. Since the ESM is concerned with the time dependence of psychological states, this analysis provides only weak evidence for establishing MAR. On the other hand, the analysis in table A.2 attempts to show that time-varying psychological states and activity states are uncorrelated with the response rate, controlling for day of the week, day of participation, and hour of the day. Since the data for psychological states and activity states are not available for time slots with non-response, Jeong characterizes time-varying psychological states and activity states as a function of the average observed tendency for each of the 882 time slots assuming population homogeneity. However, this method of characterizing psychological states and activity states as a function of time has limitations in assessing their effects on the response rate. First, since variables for psychological states and activity states are functions of the 882 time slots, they can be highly collinear with the combination of the three defined covariates whose combined states generate the 882 time slots, and therefore, it is by definition very likely that the effects of the psychological-state and activity-state variables on the response rate become non-significant once the effects of the defined covariates are adequately taken into account. Hence, the absence of the unique effects of the former variables shown in table A.2 may be artifacts. Second, if the response rate depends on $Y$, the mean of observed $Y$ in the sample at each time point *is biased and, therefore, the effect of the time-specific mean of Y on the rate of non-response may be biased. Although we can assess the effect of psychological variables on the response rate better if we impute Y for non-response, and test whether Y affects the rate of response using data for observed and imputed Ys, the imputation itself may not be very effective if NMAR holds. Hence, it seems that we cannot definitively establish whether the MAR condition is met without some auxiliary information for non-response. However, an adequate adjustment for non-response will still be beneficial even if NMAR rather than MAR holds (Muthén, Kaplan, and Hollis 1987). Therefore, adjusting for missing data by assuming the MAR condition, as Jeong does, is valuable in general, although some limitations for the particular weighting method he proposes exist, as noted above.*

# Appendix B
## Estimating and imputing incomes for middle-class families

*Yona Rubinstein and Casey B. Mulligan*

The 500 Family Study contains a wealth of information about behavior in working families, including detailed data about certain types of behavior such as time use. The study also includes questions about demographics and income, although this information is less detailed. Adults in the study were asked about their annual earnings in their job, not as an exact number, but as it falls into six categories: $0–$20,000; $20,001–$35,000; $35,001–$50,000; $50,001–$75,000; $75,001–$100,000; and $100,001+. This type of income question is asked on a variety of national surveys. By themselves, these categories permit analysts to categorize families by their incomes but do not permit analyses of more detailed income information. For example, does a man from the second category earn three times as much as a man from the first? Or five times as much?

In the absence of experimental data, the "what if" statement is one of the most challenging questions in social sciences research. Many, perhaps most, innovations in econometric techniques are motivated by questions such as: What would have been the observed wages of . . . if they were working? At the beginning of the twenty-first century, almost four decades after microdata became more common in research on social science issues, the vast majority of studies on missing data in sample surveys focus on techniques employed when using "bad" data, rather than on ways to improve it. This practice was noted by Griliches (1986), who provided an economic explanation: "since it is the 'badness' of the data that provides us with our living, perhaps it is not at all surprising that we have shown little interest in improving it." Addressing Griliches's observation, this chapter provides a simple way to "improve" the 500 Family Study data rather than focusing on the econometric/statistical technique.

It is important to properly measure income because it is likely to affect behavior. Without an accurate measure of income, it is likely that statistical models of behavior will understate the contribution of income

491

and overstate the contribution of other factors that are positively correlated with income. This is reason enough to try to enhance the quality of
income measures in the 500 Family Study.

In this appendix, a method of income imputation is developed. While
this method is applied using data from the 500 Family Study, it has implications for other studies. Missing data are imputed by estimating, non-
parametrically, the earnings within income categories using the March
Current Population Survey (CPS), a survey administered to a national
probability sample of housing units. CPS data for the years 1999 through
2001 are used for three reasons. First, the CPS is the largest national
probability sample of household units that includes detailed labor market outcomes as well as diverse personal information. Second, using the
CPS, husband–wife data sets can be reconstructed, replicating some of
the detailed information available in the 500 Family Study data. Third,
the income of individuals who are classified in the top-coded income category in the 500 Family Study data set can be inferred from the income
of similar individuals in the CPS data set.

The CPS March supplements for the years 1999 through 2001 are used
to construct a subsample that replicates the sociodemographic characteristics of the 500 Family Study parent sample. This subsample is divided
into the same six earnings categories as those in the 500 Family Study
data set. Mean wages within wage categories are projected using a set
of personal, spouse, and family characteristics available also in the 500
Family Study parent survey. In other words, a non-parametric approach
is used – looking at the incomes of several CPS persons or households that
are "identical" according to the kinds of demographic and income variables reported in the 500 Family Study. This approach requires a large
CPS sample so that each 500 Family Study person has several apparently
identical CPS persons. This requirement is met by combining three CPS
data sets, which include almost 80,000 households. The non-parametric
approach has the advantage of not imposing a particular statistical model,
thereby allowing the resulting income imputations to be used in a richer
set of behavioral models, as explained below.

An alternative to this approach would be to make an income guess
based on the income categories provided in the 500 Family Study parent
survey. One such guess might be the mid-range – the midpoint between
the bottom of the interval and the top of the interval. For example, an
income of $10,000 might be assumed for a person who reports their
income in the $0–$20,000 category. The mid-range strategy does not help
with persons who report incomes of $100,001+ and, as shown below,
produces estimates that are substantially different from non-parametric
estimates. The estimates described in this chapter are even different from

the CPS unconditional means (i.e., if $9,000 were the average income of all CPS persons with incomes in the $0–$20,000 range, then the unconditional mean strategy would impute incomes of $9,000 to all 500 Family Study persons in that range). Analyses indicate that spouse and family characteristics, as well as personal data, play an important role in explaining personal wages within wage categories. This is especially relevant for the top category of $100,001+. For instance, white married men with children and with incomes in the top category earn $25,000 more than black married men with children in that same income category. Similarly, top-income-category married men with children and a wife who is not employed earn $23,000 more than top-income-category married men with children and a wife who is employed. These calculations do not imply that race or wife's employment have (or do not have) a causal effect on a man's income, but do imply that a man's income can be accurately estimated by using his demographic and family information in addition to the income category reported in the 500 Family Study. A non-parametric approach (to the extent the data allow) does exactly that.

## The Current Population Survey (CPS) – a brief review

The CPS is the primary source of information on the labor force characteristics of the US population. The sample is scientifically selected to represent the civilian non-institutional population (i.e., all persons except active duty military personnel and inmates of prisons, mental hospitals, or other institutions). Respondents are interviewed to obtain information about the employment status of each member of a household 15 years of age and older.[1]

The March CPS supplement provides information on more than fifty different sources of income for the prior year, including earnings ("How much did . . . earn in wages and salaries in 19..?"), income ("How much income from all sources did . . . receive in 19..?"), and non-cash income sources. Information is also provided on the employment status, occupation, and industry of persons 15 years old and over.

Whether for the privacy of the interviewees or for other reasons, the amount earned of a particular type of income is top-coded if it is especially high. In other words, a representative number (known as the "top-code") rather than an exact income number is reported for CPS respondents with especially high incomes. Since 1996, records that were top-coded have a value representing the mean earnings for top-coded individuals with similar characteristics.[2] A type of income is "especially high" if the amount earned for the year exceeds, for instance, $150,000 from main job, or $25,000 from self-employment earnings in the interview years 1999 to

2001. Roughly speaking, high incomes in the CPS are coded like high incomes in the 500 Family Study, because both are top-coded. However, the 500 Family Study top-code ($100,001+) is lower than the CPS top-codes – for example, a person with $120,000 earnings would have his exact income recorded in the CPS, but only "$100,001+" recorded in the 500 Family Study. Because the CPS top-code occurs for particular types of incomes, and then the types are added to get total income, an exact income number is often available for persons with incomes in excess of $150,000 (e.g., a person with $145,000 main job earnings and $23,000 self-employment earnings would have his exact total earnings of $178,000 reported in the CPS). Furthermore, while $100,001+ is the only 500 Family Study number we have for a person with top-coded income, the CPS top-coding procedure replaces all top-coded values with the average amount for all CPS records in the same year requiring top coding. The March CPS also includes some of the same spousal and demographic information as the 500 Family Study. Therefore, in order to numerically impute income for an adult in the 500 Family Study, conditional on her or his annual earnings, individuals in the CPS with similar characteristics, and similar spousal characteristics, are examined.

## Method

### Data

The data used in this appendix come from three consecutive annual March CPS Supplements from 1999 through 2001. The annual data from the CPS demographic supplement cover the period 1998 to 2000. Table B.1 shows the number of observations in each of these years. The data come from 394,855 individuals 0 to 99 years of age, living in 130,800 different households. The CPS classifies households into three types: (1) husband–wife; (2) other male head; and (3) other female head. Only husband–wife households are analyzed in this chapter, which leaves 79,925 households. Using these data, three data sets were constructed: (1) family data; (2) husband personal data; and (3) wife personal data.

Family data include information such as family size, number of children, region, state, and city of residence. Personal data provide information such as age, race, educational attainment, employment status, annual worked weeks, weekly work hours, occupation, industry, and earnings. Table B.2 presents the distribution of annual earnings for husbands and wives in the CPS sample. These data allow persons' average wages within wage categories to be projected using spouse's data in addition to personal and family data.

Table B.1 *Current Population Survey Data: 1999 through 2001*

| Data | 1999 | 2000 | 2001 | All |
|---|---|---|---|---|
| Observations | | | | |
| All | 132,324 | 133,710 | 128,821 | 394,855 |
| Males | 63,870 | 64,791 | 62,625 | 191,286 |
| Females | 68,454 | 68,919 | 66,196 | 203,569 |
| Households | | | | |
| All | 43,759 | 44,028 | 43,013 | 130,800 |
| Husband–wife family[a] | 26,869 | 27,052 | 26,004 | 79,925 |
| Husband–wife family with children less than 18 | 12,459 | 12,488 | 11,931 | 36,878 |

[a] Excludes households where either the head or spouse do not live at home.

Table B.2 *Distribution of annual earnings: married men and women, 16 through 65 years of age*[a]

| | Gender | |
|---|---|---|
| Annual wages and salary | Male | Female |
| No wages | 11.6 | 30.5 |
| 0 to 19,999[b] | 14.7 | 34.3 |
| 20,000 to 34,999 | 22.8 | 19.9 |
| 35,000 to 49,999 | 19.7 | 8.8 |
| 50,000 to 74,999 | 18.6 | 4.7 |
| 75,000 to 99,999 | 5.9 | 1.0 |
| 100,000 + | 6.7 | 0.8 |

Based on the Current Population Survey, March supplements for the years 1999 to 2001.

*Note:* Sample includes: married males and females, 16 to 65 years of age who have (at least) one offspring.

[a] $ of 2000

[b] Positive wages ($>0$)

*Mean wages within wage categories for the CPS sample*

Analyses of the CPS result in two findings: (1) the mid-range is a biased estimate of the mean wages within categories; and (2) personal, family, and spouse characteristics are important in predicting the mean wages at the low end and especially in the top-coded category (analyses available on request). The mid-range is not the best predictor. There is a substantial difference between the mean wages within wage categories and the mid-wage range. For instance, the mid-range in the $35,000 to $49,999 category is $42,500. The average wages of male workers 16 to 65 years of age in this specific wage category is approximately $41,500 (standard deviation: $50). In this particular example, the mid-range wages overstate the mean wages of male workers who earn $35,000 to $49,999.

Moreover, note that the "bias" is not in the same direction for all wage categories. For instance, while the mid-wages of the $35,000 to $49,999 wage category overstate the mean wages of male workers at this wage category, the mid-wages of those who earn $1 to $19,000 understate the mean wages of male workers within this wage category.[3]

Characteristics such as race, age, annual worked hours, and region of residence are relevant in predicting mean wages within wage categories. For instance, the mean wages of black married male workers whose wages are top-coded is approximately $20,000 less than the mean wages of their white counterparts. This is also true for spouse's data – there is a significant difference in the mean wages of married males within the top-coded category according to their wives' annual salary. Spouses' characteristics may play an important role in explaining individuals' wages within wage categories.

In projecting wages within wage categories, it may be desirable to use more than one factor. This is true even for the extreme case of no correlation between the explanatory variables. To minimize the variance of the predicted wages, all the relevant information in the statistical model should be incorporated. A set of univariate distributions might be easy to interpret, but it will not provide an efficient predictor. For this reason, wages are projected using a simple regression model. A non-parametric relationship between observable characteristics and the wages within categories is allowed by using dummy variables.

### The statistical model

The parameter of interest is the wages of person $i$ at period $t$. The information available is a subset of (observed) characteristics which determine person $i$'s wages, as well as person $i$'s wage bounds (hereafter: wage category). The "best" predictor of person $i$'s wages – that is, the minimum variance unbiased estimator – equals the expected wages conditional on all the information available at $t$. Imposing the classical assumption, the best predictor is:

$$\hat{W}_{i,t} = E(W_{i,t} \mid X = x_{i,t}, WC_i = wc_i, M) \qquad \text{(Equation 1)}$$

where $X$ is a vector of observed characteristics (with $k$ elements), $WC_i$ is a vector of dummy variables indicating person $i$'s wage category and $M$ stands for the "economic model" – that is, the underlying process that determines the relationship between $X$ and $W$. Since there is no prior "guess" with respect to the "true" model within wage categories, the non-parametric estimator is the "best" estimator.[4] Therefore, the conditional mean wages within cells are estimated. This is done by estimating, for each wage category, the following specification:

$$W_{iwc,t} = \beta_{0,wc} + \beta_1 Dx_1 + \beta_2 Dx_2 + ... \beta_k Dx_k + U_{i,wc,t}$$

(Equation 2)

where $D_{X_i}$ is a vector of dummy variables with $j - 1$ elements – one for each possible value of $X_1$. For example, let $X_1$ denote years of schooling completed, and assume that years of schooling completed varies between 0 and 16. In this case, the vector $D_{X_i}$ contains $17 - 1$ dummy variables. $\beta_1 = \{b_{1,1}, b_{1,2}, ... b_{1,17}\}$. Thus, the expected mean wages of persons with twelve years of schooling whose wage category is $WC_i = wc_i$ (ignoring other variables) equals:

$$E(W_{i,wc,t} \mid WC_i = wc_i, X_1 = 12) = \beta_{0,wc} + \beta_{1,12} \quad \text{(Equation 3)}$$

### The use of top-coded wage data

38 percent of married males and approximately 7 percent of married females in the 500 Family Study report total annual wages of $100,001 ($ value in year 2000) or more. In comparison, only 6.7 percent of all married males in the CPS report annual earnings higher than $100,000 (see table B.2). Despite the small fraction of persons with annual earnings over $100,000, the size of the CPS data set ensures that there are thousands of observations for persons who report earnings higher than $100,000. Moreover, as already mentioned, the CPS top-code threshold for 1999 to 2001 was $150,000, which means that actual wages are observed for approximately 60 percent of husbands whose wages exceeded $100,000. As for those who were classified as top coded according to the CPS definition, the CPS provides the mean wages conditional on a set of *personal* characteristics.

Let $W_i^0$ stand for the CPS wages of persons whose wages exceed the top-coded wage category according to the 500 Family Study:

$$W_i^0 = \left\{ \begin{array}{l} W_i \text{ if } W_i < \min{(W \mid top\ coded = 1)} \\ E(W_i \mid top\ coded = 1, Z) \quad \text{else} \end{array} \right\} \quad \text{(Equation 4)}$$

where $Z$ is a vector of explanatory variables used by the CPS. Since it does not include spouse's characteristics, it is only a partial set of the explanatory variables used $- Z \in X$. For those classified in the top-coded category according to the CPS definition, the best estimator might be less precise and perhaps biased:

$$bias = E(W_{i,t} \mid X = x_{i,t}, WC_i = top\ coded) - < E(W_{i,t} \mid \hat{X}(Z)$$
$$= \hat{x}_{i,t}(z_{i,t}), WC_i = top\ coded)$$

$$\mathrm{var}\,(E(W_{i,t} \mid X = x_{i,t}, WC_i = top\ coded)) < \mathrm{var} - (E(W_{i,t} \mid \hat{X}(Z)$$
$$= \hat{x}_{i,t}(Z_{i,t}), WC_i = top\ coded)) \qquad \text{(Equation 5)}$$

Yet, given the available data it is still the best predictor.

## Results: imputing wages within wage categories

### Predicted annual wages

Analyses were conducted to identify the mean wages by wage categories, conditional on personal characteristics, family variables, and spouse's characteristics. Overall, fifty-seven dummy variables were used to project the mean wages within wage categories. The benchmark group is (1) white men who are married to white women; (2) parents of one child under 18 years of age; (3) both the husband and wife are 31 to 35 years of age; (4) both are residents of a large city (over 1 million but less than 2.5 million) in the Northeast; (5) both are high school graduates with twelve years of schooling; (6) both work between 49 and 52 weeks (out of 52), usually 40 hours per week; (7) the wife earns an annual salary between $20,000 and $35,000 (analyses available on request).

The mean wages within wage categories vary with personal, family, and spouse characteristics, especially for the top-coded category. For instance, conditional on all observed characteristics, black workers whose annual earnings exceed the $100,000 threshold earn on average approximately $33,000 less than their white counterparts. Note that this gap is almost *two times larger* than the difference between the mean earnings within this wage category when other variables are not controlled for. Other personal characteristics, such as education and age, are also important in projecting wages within wage categories. Note that although many personal and family characteristics are controlled for, spouse's wages still play an important role in predicting their partners' wages *within* wage categories. For instance, among top-coded working males, those whose wives are not working earn approximately $10,000 more than those whose wives do work.[5]

### Imputing wages for different wage categories

The constant term in each regression that was conducted equals the mean wages of persons in the benchmark group. As long as the focus is on the wages of the benchmark group, these constants can be used. As for the wages of other subgroups, terms should be added according to the characteristics of the group of interest. This subsection provides two examples.

*Examples*   The mean wage of married white men who belong to the benchmark category whose annual salary is between $1 and $19,999 (in $ of 2,000) is $13,901. This is the constant for males in the benchmark category for this wage category. For married white men who earn $100,000 or more and are (a) white men who are married to white women; (b) parents of one child under 18 years of age; (c) 31 to 35 years of age, as are their wives (like the benchmark group); (d) live in a large city in the northeast part of the country (like the benchmark group); (e) high school graduates with twelve years of schooling, as are their wives (like the benchmark category); (f) working between 49 and 52 weeks (out of 52), and usually 40 hours per week (like the benchmark group); and (g) whose wife earns an annual salary between $20,000 and $35,000 (like the benchmark group) the mean annual wages are $146,703.

Note that (a), (b), (c), (d), (e), (f), and (g) are *not different* than the characteristics of the benchmark group. Therefore, their mean wage equals the constant term. For married white males who earn $100,000 or more, and are (a) white men who are married to white women; (b) parents of one child under 7 years of age (younger than the child in the benchmark group); (c) 36 to 40 years of age, as are their wives (both older than the benchmark group); (d) residents of a metropolitan area (not a large city as in the benchmark group) in the West (not in the Northeast); (e) college graduates with 16 years of schooling, as are their wives (unlike the benchmark category); (f) work between 49 and 52 weeks (out of 52), usually 40 hours per week (like the benchmark group); and (g) whose wives earn an annual salary between $75,000 and $99,999 (more than wives' annual salary in the benchmark group) the mean annual wages are $135,308.

In this particular example, (b), (c), (d), (e) and (g) are different than the characteristics of the benchmark group. Note that this is not true for (f). Thus, the focus should be on mean differences in earnings. The mean wages of this subgroup equals $135,308 as shown in table B.3.

## Using the imputations to model income effects on behavior

### *Statistical implications*

The non-parametric approach makes it possible to use the projected wages as an explanatory variable with almost no restrictions. For instance,

Table B.3 *Imputing wages*

| Variables | In $ |
|---|---|
| Constant | 146,703 |
| Family characteristics (different than the benchmark group) | |
|    One child under 7 years of age | +623 |
|    Living in the West | +1,340 |
|    Living in a metropolitan area | +5,648 |
| Husband's characteristics (different than the benchmark group) | |
|    Aged 36 to 40 | +7,234 |
|    College graduate | −8,919 |
|    Worked between 49 and 52 weeks | +0 |
|    Worked 40 hours per week | +0 |
| Wife's characteristics (different than the benchmark group) | |
|    Aged 36 to 40 | +2,219 |
|    College graduate | +6,651 |
|    Worked between 49 and 52 weeks | +0 |
|    Worked 40 hours per week | +0 |
|    Wife's total earnings between $75,000 to $99,999 | −26,191 |
| Imputed wage | 135,308 |

both imputed wages, as well as their explanatory variables, can be used as "right-hand side variables."[6] Consider the following example. Suppose one is interested in estimating the effect of parents' education and parents' earnings on the educational attainment of their offspring. For the sake of simplicity, assume that parents' education is the only variable used to impute wages and that offsprings' educational outcome ($Y_i$) is a linear function of parents' education ($X$) and parents' earnings ($W$):

$$Y_i = \gamma_0 + \gamma_1 X_i + \gamma_2 \hat{W}_i + \varepsilon_i \qquad \text{(Equation 6)}$$

where $\hat{W}_i$ stands for parents' imputed wages and $\varepsilon_i$ is the error term.

Yet, since parents' earnings were imputed using the information available on parents' education, Equation 6 should be rewritten as:

$$Y_i = \gamma_0 + \gamma_1 X_i + \gamma_2 \hat{W}(X_i) + \varepsilon_i \qquad \text{(Equation 7)}$$

As Equation 7 makes clear, the "crucial" identifying assumption is that $W(X_i)$ is not a linear function. If this condition does not hold, there is perfect multicollinearity between $X_i$ and $\hat{W}_i$. To illustrate this point, assume that $\hat{W}(X_i) = \delta X_i$. By substituting this term into Equation 7, the expectation of $Y_i$ condition on $X_i$ becomes:

$$E(Y_i \mid X = X_i) = \gamma_0 + \gamma_1 X_i + \gamma_2 \delta X_i = \gamma_0 + (\gamma_1 + \gamma_2 \delta) X_i$$

(Equation 8)

As Equation 8 shows, $\gamma_1$ *and* $\gamma_2$ cannot be identified. In other words, it is not possible to distinguish between the direct effect of parents' education on offspring's educational attainment and the effect of parents' income on offsprings' educational attainment, since parents' education is perfectly correlated with the imputed wages. In general, the effect of $X_i$ on $Y_i$ must exhibit different functional form than the "effect" of $X_i$ on $W_i$. Using a non-parametric approach alleviates this type of problem, at least to the degree that the direct effect of parental education on offspring's outcomes is linear (as in this particular example) and the effect of parents' education on child's own wages is not (and in general – as long as the effects of Z [parents' education in this case] on X and the outcomes Y do not exhibit the same functional form). Stepping outside this example, variables other than education are used to impute incomes. It is then possible to identify an income effect separate from direct effects of various characteristics as long as there are some characteristics predicting income without direct effects, or the direct effects are linear.

### Permanent income theory

Why does income matter for behavior? One reason is that many categories of behavior require expenditures of money and, aside from gifts received, income is by definition the amount of money available to the household. However, income does not limit expenditure on a yearly basis because a household can spend more or less than it earns during the year by borrowing or saving. For this reason, Friedman (1957) and many economists since have suggested that the best quantitative model of consumer expenditure should include "permanent" or lifetime average income, even though most surveys ask only about the income for a particular calendar year. Because each year has its idiosyncrasies with regard to a person's income – perhaps because of the timing of promotions or fluctuations in the labor market – income is imputed based on the average income of several similar persons. Imputed income may thus be a more accurate measure of a person's permanent income than actual yearly income. Although imputed income undoubtedly includes some of the respondent's transitory income (e.g., to the extent that transitory income determines the respondent's income bracket), it is expected that imputed income may well proxy permanent income better than would actual income (if it were available) and thus in many situations better predict behavior.

## Summary

Using data from the CPS March supplement for the years 1999 to 2001, the mean annual wages for individuals were imputed based on (1) a persons' wage category; and (2) observed personal, family, and spouse characteristics. As in many other studies (and the CPS data set), personal characteristics are used to calculate the mean wages within wage categories. Unlike other studies, family characteristics, and especially spouse's characteristics, are used to project mean wages *within* wage categories.

Estimates make clear that the mid-range approximation is a biased estimator of the mean wages within wage categories conditional on observed characteristics. Additionally, as for the top-coded group, where the mid-range procedure cannot be applied, substantial differences are found between the mean wages of workers with different personal characteristics. For instance, black workers earn on average less than white workers, conditional on reporting total annual wages of $100,000 or more. Additionally, spouse's characteristics and especially spouse's labor market outcomes, such as annual wages, play an important role in predicting mean wages within the top-coded wage category.

The findings presented in this appendix suggest that families should not be viewed as an arbitrary group of individuals, not even when measuring individuals' labor market outcomes. The earnings of husbands and wives are correlated, and even in the absence of earnings data from one spouse, family income can be estimated based on the income of the available spouse. This is in agreement with the methods applied by the 500 Family Study in focusing on the characteristics of working families.

NOTES

1. For a detailed description of the Current Population Survey data, see *Current Population Survey, Technical Paper 63RV, Design and Methodology*, Bureau of Labor Statistics and US Census Bureau, 2003.
2. Aggregate income totals from the public use file should therefore match the data published by the Census Bureau. For further details, see: http://www.bls.census.gov/cps/cpsmain.htm.
3. To see why the biases might go in these directions, suppose that the distribution of earnings were single peaked. If one is to the left of the peak, the probability that the individual is near the top of the category is higher than the probability that he or she is near the bottom of the category. Similarly, in categories to the right of the peak, individuals are more likely to be near the bottom of

the interval. Thus to the left of the peak, the interval endpoint strategy yields estimates that are too low. To the right of the peak, the method yields estimates that are too high.

4. As long as there are enough degrees of freedom within each cell.

5. This holds for all subgroups, except females who are top-coded (.5 percent of all females).

6. As long as the variables used to "explain" wages do not explain the outcome of interest in exactly the same way.

# Commentary

## Lars Lefgren

*The Sloan 500 Family Study is a valuable data source for a broad range of researchers. Despite its detail in many areas, however, income is reported only in fairly broad categories. Rubinstein and Mulligan take advantage of information in the Current Population Survey (CPS) to provide a useful method to impute incomes. Using CPS data, they regress the actual earnings of individuals within an earnings category on a set of indicator variables also available in the 500 Family Study. The coefficients from these regressions are then used to impute incomes in the 500 Family Study. The authors show that taking advantage of demographic information yields imputed incomes that differ systematically from more simple alternatives.*

*The authors' method of imputation is both straightforward and sensible. Nevertheless, I would like to make a couple of comments regarding the assumptions implicit in their method of imputation. I then provide additional comparisons between the authors' method and some very simple alternatives.*

*The authors discuss using a non-parametric method of imputing incomes. This method imputes incomes using the mean income of all the individuals within a cell defined by the categorical variables. For example, suppose that there were three binary variables that described an individual (1) black or white; (2) old or young; and (3) high school graduate or dropout. The possible combinations of these three dummy variables generate eight cells (e.g., one cell would be old black high school graduates). It is easy to see that the number of cells increases exponentially with the number of available variables. Because of this, a completely non-parametric approach is unlikely to be feasible with more than a small number of variables. The authors overcome this problem by assuming that income is an additively separable function of the different variables. Thus the effect of being a high school graduate is the same regardless of race or age. Going back to my simple example, the non-parametric method involves a regression with seven (one category is omitted) independent variables. The authors' method requires regressing income on only the three indicator variables. Implicitly, the authors discard the information available from interacting variables rendering their approach slightly less general than is suggested in the chapter. Nevertheless, the authors' method seems appropriate given the large number of variables available for imputing income.*

*My next point concerns the authors' discussion of identification toward the end of the chapter. The authors rightfully point out that when income is imputed using only a set of variables X, it may be impossible to identify the separate effects of X and income due to the collinearity induced by the imputation procedure. This is not a problem for the authors' estimates, however. The authors take advantage of both X as well as the income category of the individual. The information on income category induces variation in imputed income that is independent of X. Thus imputed income will never be collinear with the other covariates that one might want to use.*

*Both of the above points are relatively minor and do not address the following questions of primary interest. First, how close is the imputed income measure to actual income? Second, how well does the measure of imputed income perform in research applications relative to actual income? Third, do simpler imputation methods do appreciably worse than the authors' method? To address these questions, I will use data from the 1999 March CPS to execute an imputation method similar to the authors' – I refer to this as the preferred method. I will also perform the imputation using two simpler methods. (1) I will calculate the mean income of all individuals within a given income category (the average income method); and (2) I will take the average of the interval endpoints (the midpoint method).[1]*

*Before going into the detail regarding the performance of each of these income measures, it is worthwhile to describe in a bit more detail my preferred imputation method. In particular, I examine all married men with positive earnings between the ages of 26 and 55. Earnings are the sum of wage and salary, self-employment, and farm income. I impute income in a manner almost identical to that of Rubinstein and Mulligan. My covariates are slightly different, however. In particular, for each income category I regress actual income on race, age, education, region of residence, location relative to Metropolitan Statistical Area (MSA) central city, spouse race, spouse education, and spouse income indicator variables.[2] Though the sample period and specification differ from Rubinstein and Mulligan's, the approach is sufficiently similar to provide insight into the usefulness of their approach. In order to more effectively investigate the performance of each imputation method, I use only half of the data for imputation and use the other half to perform out-of-sample evaluation.*

*Having briefly outlined my imputation methods, it is now worthwhile to examine how close imputed income is to actual income. The following table shows the average values of imputed and actual income measures. It also shows the mean absolute and mean squared difference between the imputed and actual income measures.*

| Income Measure | Mean | Mean absolute error | Mean squared error |
|---|---|---|---|
| Actual income | 47,086 | – | – |
| Imputed income – preferred method | 46,813 | 9,336 | $5.95^*10^8$ |
| Imputed income – average income method | 46,737 | 9,719 | $6.47^*10^8$ |
| Imputed income – midpoint method | 46,022 | 9,574 | $7.24^*10^8$ |

*This table suggests that the typical differences between imputation methods are not enormous.*[3] *Note that because I am performing out-of-sample evaluation, the means of the first two imputation methods are not equal to that of measured income by construction. The means of all imputed income measures, however, are quite close to that of actual income – the largest difference is just over 2 percent. While the preferred method yields imputed incomes that have lower absolute and mean squared error, the differences are again not large. In particular, the preferred method is associated with a mean squared error that is just 8 percent less than that of the average income method. The difference in mean absolute error is even smaller.*

*The table above presents evidence that simple imputation methods have similar properties in terms of the mean absolute and mean squared error to the preferred method. Nevertheless, the most important measure of performance is how well it does in actual research applications. To investigate this question, I will look at two simple applications. First, I will regress log income measures on a set of education and race indicator variables. I will then examine how the estimated education and race coefficients vary by the measure of income used. Second, I will regress an indicator variable showing whether an individual receives stock dividend income on the log of actual or imputed income along with the same education and race controls. For this case, I will focus on how the income coefficient depends on the measure of income used. For both sets of regressions, I use the half of the sample that was not used to impute income. It is important to note that the estimated coefficients cannot be interpreted as causal effects. Nevertheless, seeing how the coefficients vary with the choice of income measure is likely to shed light on how sensitive empirical findings are to the choice of imputation method.*

*The table below shows results from regressing the log of different measures of income on education and race variables. The omitted categories are white race and high school dropouts. Robust standard errors are in parentheses.*

| Independent variable | Actual income | Imputed Income | | |
|---|---|---|---|---|
| | | Preferred method | Average income method | Midpoint method |
| High school graduate | 0.346 | 0.293 | 0.306 | 0.355 |
| | (0.040) | (0.021) | (0.022) | (0.025) |
| Some college | 0.524 | 0.453 | 0.465 | 0.528 |
| | (0.041) | (0.022) | (0.023) | (0.026) |
| College graduate | 0.891 | 0.816 | 0.807 | 0.869 |
| | (0.044) | (0.025) | (0.026) | (0.028) |
| More than college | 1.202 | 1.078 | 1.060 | 1.100 |
| | (0.047) | (0.031) | (0.031) | (0.032) |
| Black | −0.201 | −0.212 | −0.203 | −0.217 |
| | (0.039) | (0.023) | (0.025) | (0.029) |
| Other | −0.294 | −0.212 | −0.174 | −0.192 |
| | (0.075) | (0.038) | (0.039) | (0.041) |
| Hispanic | −0.182 | −0.219 | −0.222 | −0.252 |
| | (0.032) | (0.020) | (0.020) | (0.022) |
| R-Squared | 0.127 | 0.247 | 0.241 | 0.234 |
| Observations | 8,461 | 8,461 | 8,461 | 8,461 |

Note that the R-squared values should not be taken at face value as the imputation procedure itself eliminates much of the variation in income. Comparing the coefficients does not suggest that one imputation method is clearly better than another. In particular, the preferred and average income methods yield coefficients that are somewhat too small for the education variables – this is less apparent for the racial dummies. The midpoint method yields education coefficients quite similar to those computed using actual income but the coefficients on race are worse than those computed using alternative imputation methods. Overall, this table suggests that no method of imputation clearly dominates the others.

Other applications are likely to include income as an independent variable. For this reason, I include the following table. I regress whether or not an individual receives dividend income on a measure of log income as well as education and race controls. Again, robust standard errors are in parentheses.

| Independent variable | Actual income | Imputed Income | | |
|---|---|---|---|---|
| | | Preferred method | Average income method | Midpoint method |
| Log of income measure | 0.074 | 0.154 | 0.153 | 0.139 |
| | (0.005) | (0.007) | (0.007) | (0.006) |
| High school graduate | 0.065 | 0.045 | 0.043 | 0.041 |
| | (0.011) | (0.011) | (0.011) | (0.011) |

*(cont.)*

| | | Imputed Income | | |
| Independent variable | Actual income | Preferred method | Average income method | Midpoint method |
| --- | --- | --- | --- | --- |
| Some college | 0.142 | 0.111 | 0.110 | 0.107 |
| | (0.013) | (0.013) | (0.013) | (0.013) |
| College graduate | 0.304 | 0.245 | 0.247 | 0.249 |
| | (0.016) | (0.016) | (0.016) | (0.016) |
| More than college | 0.366 | 0.289 | 0.293 | 0.301 |
| | (0.019) | (0.020) | (0.020) | (0.020) |
| Black | −0.157 | −0.139 | −0.140 | −0.141 |
| | (0.016) | (0.016) | (0.016) | (0.016) |
| Other | −0.102 | −0.091 | −0.097 | −0.097 |
| | (0.024) | (0.024) | (0.024) | (0.024) |
| Hispanic | −0.135 | −0.114 | −0.114 | −0.113 |
| | (0.011) | (0.011) | (0.011) | (0.011) |
| R-Squared | 0.173 | 0.190 | 0.190 | 0.188 |
| Observations | 8,461 | 8,461 | 8,461 | 8,461 |

*These results are somewhat surprising. The estimated effect of log income on the probability an individual receives dividends is actually higher when income is imputed than when actual income is used. Furthermore, the R-squared statistics are also higher. This is the opposite of what one would expect given that imputed income is a noisy measure of actual income. Rubinstein and Mulligan point out, however, that if imputed income better measures permanent income than does actual income, one might expect the observed difference.[4] The various measures of imputed income yield very similar coefficient estimates and R-squared values – again suggesting that method of imputation is not of critical importance.*

*In conclusion, Rubinstein and Mulligan provide a useful method for imputing incomes for the Sloan 500 Family Study. This method takes advantage of reported income category as well as a number of individual and spouse covariates. Due to the information implicit in the reported income category, the imputed measure of income will not be collinear with other covariates – even those used in the imputation procedure. Using a method similar to that of Rubinstein and Mulligan, I have shown that income measures imputed using many available covariates have lower mean absolute and mean squared errors than incomes imputed using the average income and midpoint methods. These differences are fairly modest, however. When I examine two simple applications using the imputed measures of incomes, the results do not appear excessively sensitive to the exact imputation method. Overall, this brief analysis suggests that Rubinstein and Mulligan's method of imputation is appropriate and at least as good as two simpler alternatives. On the other hand, the performance difference between the suggested method and the simple alternatives is likely* to be quite small. Finally, my results suggest that using imputed income as a dependent variable is likely to lead to higher R-squared values (and lower standard errors) than would be the case using actual incomes. The actual coefficient estimates appear fairly similar, however. On the other hand, imputed income may behave quite differently from actual income when used as an independent variable. Researchers may want to consider these findings when performing analyses using data from the 500 Family Study.

## Ross M. Stolzenberg

It seems so simple to measure money income: just ask people how much money they take in. But it's not that easy. Among survey researchers, and I include myself in that group, conventional wisdom holds that few poor people welcome inquiries about their income, and most rich people find these questions repugnant. After lots of trials and many errors, survey researchers have learned to overcome a lot of the resistance to income questions by artful use of the same linguistic strategy that manners manuals recommend for public discussion of bathroom activities: they speak in euphemisms; encourage vagueness; allow imprecise answers; and do not require respondents to state precisely what it is that they are talking about. For these reasons, and for others too, survey researchers who ask questions about money income usually do so by showing respondents a list of income categories. The categories divide the numbers from zero ad infinitum into a set of ordered non-overlapping intervals. The top category starts high and goes to infinity, just in case Bill Gates and Oprah Winfrey are in the sample and they decide to cooperate. Each interval is labeled with a letter from the alphabet (never a number), and respondents are asked which letter corresponds to the category that corresponds to their income. Respondents never have to use the words "money" or "dollars" or anything like that.

This methodology yields an adequate rate of respondent compliance, so it brings joy to people who make their living by convincing survey respondents to answer questions. But the income categories are necessarily broad, and so they make the data imprecise. Thus is sadness and frustration visited upon people who make their living by analyzing the answers to those questions. However, it is a complex and uneven sadness. On the bright side, there is a lot of information in the imprecise, categorized answers. The information is mixed with random error, but big samples accommodate a lot of random error. On the dark side, imprecision is unevenly distributed. For respondents whose income is below the top category, the primary negative consequence of this imprecision is a loss of efficiency. This problem is a lot like the problems caused by rounding everybody's income to the nearest $10,000. We still learn a lot by knowing whose income *is between twenty and thirty thousand dollars, and whose is between sixty and seventy thousand dollars. For many purposes, we can obtain unbiased effect estimates by simply assuming that everyone in an income category has an income equal to the mean of the upper and lower bounds of the category. This assumption has some costs, of course. For example, it understates the variance of earnings, and so understates the error variance in regression analyses of earnings, which can cause problems that include overestimation of standardized (beta) regression coefficients. And additional complexity arises when some income categories are broader than others.*

*For respondents in the ultimate income category, the open-ended, top income category, the problem is more serious, more like rounding income to the nearest $100,000 or more. Actually, it's worse than that: respondents are usually bunched up at the bottom of the income distribution in the top category, rather than spread out evenly (because, for example, millionaires are more common than billionaires). But we do not know for sure how bunched up they are. In a small or even moderate-sized sample, the rarity of high incomes combined with the randomness of sampling can lead to peculiar and unpredictable distributions. Even in extremely large samples, such as the decennial US Census of Population, we not only lack precise measures of the incomes of individuals in that group, but we lack a suitable estimate of the mean of the group as a whole. Reasonable scholars of high intelligence, admirable prudence, and selfless good-will can and do differ widely in their estimates of that mean. Consequently, analytical results differ, sometimes by a lot, depending on the assumptions made when the mean is estimated. This is an old problem, and it can lead to great uncertainty about the extent to which data are consistent or inconsistent with a particular hypothesis or theory. But there are other problems too: even if we had a good estimate of mean income of persons in the top income category, that mean would be a poor measure of the income of the richest people in the top group. So it seems likely that errors in measuring income are larger, on average, for respondents in the highest income category than for respondents in other categories. In regression analysis, this variation in error variance is the problem of heteroskedasticity.*

*When regression analysis is applied to analyze income data, the greater inaccuracy of income data for incumbents of the top income category raises other problems. If income is an independent variable in these analyses, then the location of these respondents at the extreme end of the income distribution gives their cases high leverage. That is, they exert more than their fair share of influence on our estimates of independent variable coefficients, leaving us with an analysis in which the least accurate data has the greatest influence over the results. High leverage is a solvable problem, or at least an addressable problem, but available solutions always involve analytical decisions and assumptions. Too many decisions and assumptions promote fears that a particular analysis tells more about the analyst than about the data that have been analyzed. In scientific and policy research, these fears are the stuff of high anxiety that one might be wasting one's time, wasting tax dollars, and missing important opportunities to know more about the world and to make it a better place. These are valid and important concerns, and so it is very clear that Rubinstein and Mulligan address a very important topic. In short, they are writing about a technical matter, but they are neither splitting hairs nor obsessing about technicalities with trivial consequences.*

*To the best of my knowledge, Rubinstein and Mulligan propose a method that is new, but seems to rely on a strategy that is closely related to some cruder strategies advanced in the 1960s, and maybe before, for performing cohort analyses with cross-sectional data. Essentially, they use a supplementary data set to estimate covariance between variables for which they have data and variables for which they do not have data. Methods of this sort can be powerful if the main and supplemental data sets are comparable. But that kind of comparability is difficult to assure, even if samples are large and drawn from the same population.*

*Rubinstein and Mulligan are not the first to recognize the many problems caused by open-ended income response categories. Survey research on money income is well established in sociology, demography, political science, psychology, medicine, epidemiology, and other disciplines besides economics. The problem that Rubinstein and Mulligan address is well known in all of these disciplines and has consumed considerable past effort. In sociology, Parker and Fenwick (1983) surveyed the sociological literature on the open-ended income category problem about twenty years ago, with a strong focus on use of the Pareto distribution to estimate the mean of the open-ended category. Some twenty years before that, Herman Miller (1964) addressed the topic briefly in a Census monograph on income. Brief as it was, Miller's consideration of the issue was the standard reference for Census Bureau data users for decades. In the meantime, lots has happened in statistics.*

*In the decades since Miller's (1964) book was published, many statistical methods that were then exotic, difficult, or even un-invented have become commonplace and easy to use. In particular, the following techniques are suitable for the analysis of continuous variables, including income, that have been measured as ordered categorical variables with open-ended top categories:*

- *Ordered Probit and Logit Analysis. If a categorized income or earnings measure is the dependent variable, one might use ordered probit or ordered logit analysis. These regression-like methods provide estimates of the effect of independent variables on the probability that a respondent is located in a particular category of an ordered dependent variable, and the probability that a respondent's income is located in a particular category or higher. In addition to solving problems with the open-ended top income category, these methods avoid difficulties with the lowest income category, which includes people with no income, and those with negative income (i.e., financial loss in the reporting year). Probability measures from an ordered probit or ordered logit analysis may lack intuitive appeal to economists who wish to calculate conditional expectations or rates of return, but ordered logit and ordered probit analysis produce a lot of useful information. Further, some mathematical fiddling and a few assumptions about the distribution of earnings can produce meaningful comparisons with regression analyses of earnings, and even rates of return. In passing, it is worthwhile to note that there is a large literature on methods for analysis of ordinal data.*

- *Multiple Imputation. Rubinstein and Mulligan use the CPS data to impute values for survey respondents who do not provide adequate information about their income. These imputations are probabilistic, so a range of different imputed income values are possible for each respondent. Substantial research and theory provide evidence that analytic results can be made substantially more accurate if several different sets of imputations are made, data from each set are analyzed separately, and results of these separate analyses are averaged (Little and Rubin 1987; Meng 1995; Rubin 1987, 1996; Schafer 1997).*

- *Tobit Methods. Tobin's Tobit regression method was developed to analyze the price that consumers are willing to pay to purchase a good for which there is a minimum price. For such data, expenditure data are unavailable for consumers who are unwilling to pay at least the minimum price. As a topic for statistical analysis, expenditure data for goods with a minimum price is remarkably similar to income data for which there is no income value for those with income above a specified value. So Tobit analysis could be used to estimate the parameters of an income determination function for data like those described by Rubinstein and Mulligan, in which income data are available only for respondents whose income is below a specified maximum. Tobit methods are closely related to sample selection bias correction methods and endogenous switching regression methods. All of these methods are known to require careful use and to sometimes produce misleading results (Stolzenberg and Relles 1997). But there are situations in which all of these techniques are useful.*

- *Latent factor methods. Rubenstein and Mulligan present a measurement model for income and recommend that the output from this model be used in structural models involving income. Latent factor methods integrate the construction of measurement and structural models, permit the use of multiple indicators for cause and effect factors, and allow the incorporation of information from external sources, like the CPS data used by Rubinstein and Mulligan. These methods have proved useful in past research (Muthén 2001; Muthén et al. 1993).*

*Past experience suggests that efforts to correct measurement problems in survey data are most likely to be productive if analysts apply several different correction methods and maintain a skeptical view of them all. Rubinstein and Mulligan's efforts to develop new methods for this purpose is certainly a welcome addition to existing correction techniques.*

## NOTES

1. For the top category, I simply multiplied the top-code value by 1.5.
2. Space constraints prevent me from going into great detail regarding the data and imputation method. A more detailed description of the procedure is available from the author upon request. The regression coefficients are also available from the author.
3. Rubinstein and Mulligan report specific instances in which using their imputation method yields substantially different estimates than simpler methods.
4. Measures of income imputed using observable covariates may be thought to reflect permanent income because an individual's characteristics provide information regarding long-run earnings prospects. On the other hand, I can think of no reason that the midpoint of an individual's income category would be a better predictor of permanent income than actual current income.

# References

Achenbach, T. 1991. *Manual for the child behavior checklist 4–18 and 1991 profile.* Burlington: University of Vermont Department of Psychiatry.

Adam, E., and M. Gunnar. 2001. Relationship functioning and home and work demands predict individual differences in diurnal cortisol patterns in women. *Psychoneuroendocrinology* 26: 189–208.

Adams, G., L. King, and D. King. 1996. Relationships of job and family involvement, family social support, and work-family conflict with job and life satisfaction. *Journal of Applied Psychology* 81: 411–20.

Adorno, T. 1953. How to look at television. *Quarterly of Film, Radio, and Television* 8: 213–35.

——— 1975. Culture industry reconsidered. *New German Critique* 6: 12–19.

Aldenderfer, S., and R. Blashfield. 1984. Cluster analysis. Beverly Hills, CA: Sage Publications.

Alexander, A. 1993. Exploring media in everyday life. *Communication Monographs* 60: 55–61.

Alexander, K., C. Riordan, J. Fennessey, and A. Pallas. 1982. Social background, academic resources and college graduation: Recent evidence from the National Longitudinal Study. *American Journal of Education* 90: 315–33.

Alliger, G., and K. Williams. 1993. Using signal-contingent experience sampling methodology to study work in the field: a discussion and illustration examining task perceptions and mood. *Personnel Psychology* 46: 525–49.

Allison, P. 2002. Missing data. Pp. 7–136 in *Sage university paper series on quantitative applications in the social sciences.* Thousand Oaks, CA: Sage Publications.

Almeida, D., and R. Kessler. 1998. Everyday stressors and gender differences in daily distress. *Journal of Personality and Social Psychology* 75: 670–80.

Almeida, D., E. Wethington, and R. Kessler. 2002. The daily inventory of stressful events (DISE): an investigator-based approach for measuring daily stressors. *Assessment* 9: 41–55.

Amato, P., and A. Booth. 1997. *A generation at risk: growing up in an era of family upheaval.* Cambridge, MA: Harvard University Press.

Amato, P., and B. Keith. 1991. Parental divorce and the well-being of children: a meta-analysis. *Psychological Bulletin* 110: 26–46.

American Association of University Women Educational Foundation (AAUW). 1992. *How schools shortchange girls.* Washington, DC: American Association of University Women.

Ammerman, N. 1997. *Congregation and community.* New Brunswick, NJ: Rutgers University Press.

Ammerman, N., and W. Roof. 1995. Introduction: old patterns, new trends, fragile experiments. In *Work, family, and religion in contemporary society,* eds. N. Ammerman and W. Roof. New York: Routledge.

Anderson, B. 2000. *Doing the dirty work?: The global politics of domestic labour.* London, New York: Zed Books; New York: distributed in the USA by St. Martin's Press.

Arat-Koc, S. 1989. In the privacy of our home: foreign domestic workers as a solution to the crisis in the domestic sphere in Canada. *Studies in Political Economy* 28: 33–58.

Armsden, G., and M. Greenberg. 1987. The inventory of parent and peer attachment: individual differences and their relationship to psychological well-being in adolescence. *Journal of Youth and Adolescence* 16: 427–53.

Axinn, W., and A. Thornton. 2000. The transformation in the meaning of marriage. Pp. 147–65 in *The ties that bind: perspectives on marriage and cohabitation,* eds. L. J. Waite and A. de Gruyter. New York: Aldine de Gruyter.

Ball, S., and C. Vincent. 1998. I heard it on the grapevine: "hot" knowledge and school choice. *British Journal of Sociology of Education* 19: 377–400.

Barnett, R., and G. Baruch. 1987. Determinants of fathers' participation in family work. *Journal of Marriage and the Family* 49: 29–40.

Barnett, R., and K. Gareis. 2004. Parental after-school stress, psychological distress, and job performance. Paper presented at the annual meeting of the American Psychological Association, Honolulu, HI.

Barnett, R., and C. Rivers. 1996. *She works, he works: How two-income families are happier and better off.* San Francisco, CA: Haper San Francisco.

Bartkowski, J., and X. Xu. 2000. Distant patriarchs or expressive dads? The discourse and practice of fathering in conservative Protestant families. *The Sociological Quarterly* 41: 465–85.

Baumrind, D. 1987. A developmental perspective on adolescent risk taking behavior in contemporary America. In *Adolescent social behavior and health,* ed. C. Irwin. San Francisco, CA: Jossey-Bass.

Beach, S., and F. Fincham. 2003. Spontaneous remission of marital discord: a simmering debate with profound implications for family psychology. *The Family Psychologist* 19: 11–13.

Bechtel, R., C. Achelpohl, and R. Akers. 1972. Correlates between observed behavior and questionnaire responses on television viewing. Pp. 274–344 in *Television and social behavior,* eds. E. Rubinstein, G. Comstock, and J. Murray. Rockville, MD: National Institute of Mental Health.

Becker, G. 1991. *A treatise on the family.* Cambridge, MA: Harvard University Press.

Becker, H., and J. Carper. 1962. The elements of identification with an occupation. Pp. 287–300 in *The sociology of science,* ed. B. Hirsch. Glencoe, IL: Free Press of Glencoe.

Becker, P., and H. Hofmeister. 2001. Work, family, and religious involvement for men and women. *Journal for the Scientific Study of Religion* 40: 707–22.

Becker, P., and P. Moen. 1999. Scaling back: dual-career couples' work–family strategies. *Journal of Marriage and the Family* 61: 995–1007.

Bem, S. 1994. *The lenses of gender: transforming the debate on sexual inequality.* New Haven, CT: Yale University Press.

Berk, S. 1985. *The gender factory: the apportionment of work in American households.* New York: Plenum Press.

Bernard, R., P. Kilworth, D. Kreonenfeld, and L. Sailer. 1984. On the validity of retrospective data: the problem of informant accuracy. *Annual Review of Anthropology* 13: 495–517.

Berscheid, E., and H. Ammazzalorso. 2001. Emotional experience in close relationships. Pp. 308–30 in *Blackwell handbook of social psychology*, eds. M. Hewstone and M. Brewer. Oxford: Blackwell.

Bethlehem, G. 2001. Weighting nonresponse adjustments based on auxiliary information. Pp. 275–87 in *Survey nonresponse*, eds. R. Groves, D. Dillman, J. Eltinge, and R. Little. New York: John Wiley and Sons.

Bezilla, R. 1993. *America's youth in the 1990s.* Princeton, NJ: George H. Gallup International Institute.

Bianchi, S. 1995. Changing economic roles of women and men. Pp. 107–54 in *State of the union: America in the 1990s*, ed. R. Farley. New York: Russell Sage Foundation.

1999. New realities of working families: overview. Paper presented at the Economic Policy Institute.

Bianchi, S., and J. Robinson. 1997. What did you do today? Children's use of time, family composition, and the acquisition of social capital. *Journal of Marriage and the Family* 59: 332–44.

Bianchi, S., M. Milkie, L. Sayer, and J. Robinson. 2000. Is anyone doing the housework? Trends in the gender division of household labor. *Social Forces* 79: 191–228.

Bird, C. 1999. Gender, household labor, and psychological distress: the impact of the amount and division of housework. *Journal of Health and Social Behavior* 40: 32–45.

Bittman, M., G. Matheson, and G. Meagher. 1999. The changing boundary between home and market: Australian trends in outsourcing domestic labour. *Work, Employment, and Society* 13: 249–73.

Blau, P., and O. Duncan. 1967. *The American occupational structure.* New York: Free Press.

Bohannon, J., and P. Blanton. 1999. Gender role attitudes of American mothers and daughters over time. *The Journal of Social Psychology* 139: 173–79.

Bokemeier, J., and W. Lacy. 1986. Job values, rewards, and work conditions as factors in job satisfaction among men and women. *The Sociological Quarterly* 28: 189–204.

Bolger, N., A. Zuckerman, and R. Kessler. 2000. Invisible support and adjustment to stress. *Journal of Personality and Social Psychology* 79: 953–61.

Bond, J., E. Galinsky, and J. Swanberg. 1998. *The 1997 National Study of the Changing Workforce.* New York: Families and Work Institute.

Booth, A., and P. Amato. 1994. Parental gender role: non-traditionalism and offspring outcomes. *Journal of Marriage and the Family* 56: 865–77.

Booth, A., K. Carver, and D. Granger. 2000. Biosocial perspectives on the family. *Journal of Marriage and the Family* 62: 1018–34.

Bourdieu, P. 1977. Cultural reproduction and social reproduction. Pp. 487–511 in *Power and ideology in education*, eds. J. Karabel and A. Halsey. New York: Oxford University Press.

1984. *Distinction, a social critique of the judgment of taste*. Cambridge, MA: Harvard University Press.

1986. The forms of capital. Pp. 241–60 in *Handbook of theory and research for the sociology of education*, ed. J. Richardson. New York: Greenwood Press.

2000. *Pascalian mediations*. Stanford, CA: Stanford University Press.

Bradburn, N., and D. Caplovitz. 1965. *Reports on happiness: a pilot study of behavior related to mental health*. Chicago: Aldine.

Bradbury, T., F. Fincham, and S. Beach. 2000. Research on the nature and determinants of marital satisfaction: a decade in review. *Journal of Marriage and the Family* 62: 964–80.

Brewster, K., and I. Padavic. 2000. Change in gender ideology, 1977–1996: the contributions of intracohort change and population turnover. *Journal of Marriage and the Family* 62: 477–87.

Brief, A., and H. Weiss. 2002. Organizational behavior: affect in the workplace. *Annual Review of Psychology* 53: 279–307.

Brown, D., and T. Hayes. 2001. Family attitudes toward television. Pp. 111–35 in *Television and the American family*, 2nd edn., eds. J. Bryant and J. A. Bryant. Mahwah, NJ: Erlbaum.

Browning, D., B. McLemore, P. Couture, B. Lyon, R. Franklin. 2000. *From culture wars to common ground: religion and the American family debate*. Louisville, KY: Westminster Knox Press.

Bruck, C., T. Allen, and P. Spector. 2002. The relation between work–family conflict and job satisfaction: a finer-grained analysis. *Journal of Vocational Behavior* 3: 336–53.

Bryant, W., and C. Zick. 1996. An examination of parent–child shared time. *Journal of Marriage and the Family* 58: 227–37.

Bryk, A., and S. Raudenbush. 1992. *Hierarchical linear models: applications and data analysis method*. Newbury Park, CA: Sage Publications.

Buchmueller, T., and R. Valetta. 1996. The effects of employer-provided health insurance on worker mobility. *Industrial and Labor Relations Review* 49: 439–55.

1998. The effects of health insurance on married female labor supply. *The Journal of Human Resources* 34: 42–70.

Bureau of Labor Statistics and US Census Bureau. 2003. *Current population survey, technical paper 63RV, design and methodology*. Washington, DC: US Government Printing Office.

Burleson, B., and W. Denton. 1997. The relationship between communication skill and marital satisfaction: some moderating effects. *Journal of Marriage and Family* 59: 884–902.

Cacioppo, J., G. Bernston, J. Sheridan, and M. McClintock. 2000. Multi-level integrative analyses of human behavior: social neuroscience and the complementing nature of social and biological approaches. *Psychological Bulletin* 126: 829–43.

Cain, M. 1973. *Society and the policeman's role.* London: Routledge and Kegan Paul.

Cappelli, P. 1993. Are skill requirements rising? Evidence from production and clerical jobs. *Industrial and Labor Relations Review* 46: 515–30.

Carnoy, M. 2000. *Sustaining the new economy: work, family, and community in the information age.* Cambridge, MA: Harvard University Press.

Casper, L., and S. Bianchi. 2001. *Continuity and change in the American family.* Thousand Oaks, CA: Sage Publications.

Castellino, D., J. Lerner, R. Lerner, and A. von Eye. 1998. Maternal employment and education: predictors of young adolescent career trajectories. *Applied Developmental Science* 2: 114–26.

Carstensen, L., J. Gottman, and R. Levenson. 1995. Emotional behavior in long-term marriage. *Psychology and Aging* 10: 140–49.

Cherlin, A. 1992. *Marriage, divorce, remarriage.* Revised edn. Cambridge, MA: Harvard University Press.

Chin, T. 2000. Sixth grade madness: parental emotion work in the private high school application process. *Journal of Contemporary Ethnography* 29: 124–63.

Christensen, K., and R. Gomory. 1999. "Three jobs – two people." *The Washington Post*, Wednesday, June 2, 1999.

Chrousos, G., and P. Gold. 1992. The concepts of stress and stress system disorders: overview of physical and behavioral homeostasis. *Journal of the American Medical Association* 267: 1244–52.

Clements, A., and R. Parker. 1998. The relationship between salivary cortisol concentrations in frozen versus mailed samples. *Psychoneuroendocrinology* 23: 613–16.

Clogg, C., and S. Eliason, S. 1987. Some common problems in loglinear analysis. *Sociological Methods and Research* 16: 8–44.

Cochran, J., and L. Beeghley. 1991. The influence of religion on attitudes toward nonmarital sexuality: a preliminary assessment of reference group theory. *Journal for the Scientific Study of Religion* 30: 45–62.

Cohen, J. 1988. *Statistical power analysis for the behavioral sciences.* 2nd edn. New York: Academic Press.

Cohen, P. 1998. Replacing housework in the service economy: gender, class, and race-ethnicity in service spending. *Gender and Society* 12: 219–31.

Cohen, S., and G. Williamson. 1988. Perceived stress in a probability sample of the United States. Pp. 31–67 in *The social psychology of health: Claremont symposium on applied social psychology 1987*, eds. S. Spacapan and S. Oskamp. Newbury Park, CA: Sage Publications.

Coleman, J. 1987. Families and schools. *Educational Researcher* 16: 32–38.

Coleman, M. 1988. The division of household labor: Suggestions for future empirical consideration and theoretical development. *Journal of Family Issues* 9: 132–48.

Coltrane, S. 1989. Household labor and the routine production of gender. *Social Problems* 36: 473–90.

1996. *Family man: fatherhood, housework, and gender equity.* New York: Oxford University Press.

2000. Research on household labor: modeling and measuring the social embeddedness of routine family work. *Journal of Marriage and the Family* 62: 1208–33.

Coltrane, S., and M. Adams. 2001. Men's family work: child-centered fathering and the sharing of domestic labor. Pp. 72–99 in *Working families: the transformation of the American home*, eds. R. Hertz and N. Marshall. Berkeley, CA: University of California Press.

Crnic, K., and M. Greenberg. 1990. Minor parenting stresses with young children. *Child Development* 61: 1628–37.

Crouter, A., M. Bumpass, M. Head, and S. McHale. 2001. Implications of overwork and overload for the quality of men's family relationships. *Journal of Marriage and the Family* 63: 404–16.

Crouter, A., H. Helms-Erikson, K. Updegraff, and S. McHale. 1999. Conditions underlying parents' knowledge about children's daily lives in middle childhood: between- and within-family comparisons. *Child Development* 70: 246–59.

Csikszentmihalyi, M. 1990. *Flow: the psychology of optimal experience.* New York: Harper and Row.

1997. *Finding flow: the psychology of engagement with everyday life.* New York: Basic Books.

2000. *Beyond boredom and anxiety.* New York: Basic Books.

Csikszentmihalyi, M., and R. Larson. 1984. *Being adolescent: conflict and growth in the teenage years.* New York: Basic Books.

1987. Validity and reliability of the Experience Sampling Method. *Journal of Nervous and Mental Disease* 175: 526–36.

Csikszentmihalyi, M., and K. Rathunde. 1993. The measurement of flow in everyday life: toward a theory of emergent motivation. In *Nebraska Symposium on Motivation: developmental perspectives on motivation*, eds. J. Jacobs and R. Ryan. Lincoln: University of Nebraska Press.

Csikszentmihalyi, M., and B. Schneider. 2000. *Becoming adult: how teenagers prepare for the world of work.* New York: Basic Books.

Csikszentmihalyi, M., K. Rathunde, and S. Whalen. 1993. *Talented teenagers: the roots of success and failure.* New York: Cambridge University Press.

Cunningham, M. 2001a. The influence of parental attitudes and behaviors on children's attitudes toward gender and household labor in early adulthood. *Journal of Marriage and the Family* 63: 111–22.

2001b. Parental influences on the gendered division of housework. *American Sociological Review* 66: 184–203.

Curtner-Smith, M., T. Bennett, and M. O'Rear. 1995. Fathers' occupational conditions, values of self-direction and conformity, and perceptions of nurturant and restrictive parenting in relation to young children's depression and aggression. *Family Relations* 44: 299–305.

Daniels, A. 1987. Invisible work. *Social Problems* 34: 403–15.

Darr, A. 2002. The technicalization of sales work: an ethnographic study in the US electronics industry. *Work, Employment, and Society* 16: 47–65.

Deci, E., and R. Ryan. 1985. *Intrinsic motivation and self-determination in human behavior*. New York: Plenum.

Dehle, C., and R. Weiss. 1998. Sex differences in prospective associations between marital quality and depressed mood. *Journal of Marriage and Family Therapy* 60: 1002–11.

de Kloet, E. 1991. Brain corticosteroid receptor balance and homeostatic control. *Frontiers in Neuroendocrinology* 12: 95–164.

Demo, D., and A. Acock. 1993. Family diversity and the division of domestic labor: how much have things really changed? *Family Relations* 42: 323–31.

Dennehy, K., and J. Mortimer. 1993. Work and family orientations of contemporary adolescent boys and girls. Pp. 87–107 in *Men, work and family*, ed. J. C. Hood. Newbury Park, CA: Sage Publications.

Deschamps, A. 2002. Law, language, and incomplete institutionalization: how does parental involvement differ within two-parent, lesbian headed families? Working Paper: University of Chicago, Alfred P. Sloan Center on Parents, Children, and Work.

DeMaris, A. 1992. *Logit modeling: practical applications*. Newbury Park, CA: Sage Publications.

DeVault, M. 1987. Doing housework: feeding and family life. Pp. 178–91 in *Families and work*, eds. N. Gerstel and H. Gross. Philadelphia: Temple University Press.

——— 1991. *Feeding the family: the social organization of caring as gendered work*. Chicago: University of Chicago Press.

——— 1999. Comfort and struggle: emotion work in family life. *The Annals of the American Academy of Political and Social Science* 561: 52–63.

Di Leonardo, M. 1987. The female world of cards and holidays: women, families, and the work of kinship. *Signs: Journal of Women in Culture and Society* 12: 440–53.

Dobson, J., and G. Bauer. 1990. *Children at risk*. Dallas, TX: Word.

Doherty, W. 2001. *Take back your marriage: sticking together in a world that pulls us apart*. New York: Guilford Press.

Donahue, M., and P. Benson. 1995. Religion and the well-being of adolescents. *Journal of Social Issues* 51: 145–60.

Duncan, O., D. Featherman, and B. Duncan. 1972. *Socioeconomic background and achievement*. New York: Seminar Press.

Dunn, L. 1959. *Peabody picture vocabulary test*. Circle Pines, MN: American Guidance Service.

Dunn, L., and L. Dunn. 1997. *Peabody picture vocabulary test–III. Examiners' manual*. Circle Pines, MN: American Guidance Service.

Dwyer, C., and L. Johnson. 1997. Grades, accomplishments, and correlates. Pp. 127–56 in *Gender and fair assessment*, eds. W. Willingham and N. Cole. Mahwah, NJ: Erlbaum.

Eagle, B., E. Miles, and M. Icenogle. 1997. Inter-role conflict and the permeability of work and family domains: are there gender differences? *Journal of Vocational Behavior* 50: 168–84.

Eccles, J. 1993. School and family effects on the ontogeny of children's interests, self-perceptions and activity choices. Pp. 145–208 in *Nebraska Symposium on*

*Motivation, 1992: developmental perspectives on motivation*, eds. J. Jacobs and R. Ryan. Lincoln: University of Nebraska Press.

Eggebeen, D. 1992. Family structure and intergenerational exchanges. *Research in Aging* 14: 427–47.

Elder, G. 1998. The life course as developmental theory. *Child Development* 69: 1–12.

Ellison, C. 1991. Religious involvement and subjective well-being. *Journal of Health and Social Behavior* 32: 80–99.

Ellison, C., and J. Bartkowski. 2002. Conservative Protestantism and the division of household labor among married couples. *Journal of Family Issues* 23: 950–85.

Ellison, C., and D. Sherkat. 1993. Conservative Protestantism and support for corporal punishment. *American Sociological Review* 58: 131–44.

Ellison, C., D. Gay, and T. Glass. 1989. Does religious commitment contribute to individual life satisfaction? *Social Forces* 68: 100–23.

England, K., ed. 1996. *Who will mind the baby?* New York: Routledge.

Erickson, R. 1993. Reconceptualizing family work: the effect of emotion work on perceptions of marital quality. *Journal of Marriage and Family* 55: 888–900.

Erikson, E. 1959. *Identity and the life cycle.* New York: Norton.

    1964. Memorandum on identity and Negro youth. *Journal of Social Issues* 20: 29–42.

    1968. *Identity, youth, and crisis.* New York: W. W. Norton.

European Foundation for the Improvement of Living and Working Conditions. 2003. Part-time work in Europe.
    http://www.eurofound.eu.int/working/reports/ES0403TR01/ES0403TR01.pdf

Ex, C., and J. Janssens. 1998. Maternal influences on daughter's gender role attitudes. *Sex Roles* 38: 171–86.

Faust, K., and J. McKibben. 1999. Marital dissolution: divorce, separation, annulment, and widowhood. In *Handbook of marriage and the family*, eds. S. K. Steinmetz, M. B. Sussmann, and G. W. Peterson. New York: Plenum Press.

Family and Medical Leave Act. 1993.
    http://www.dol.gov/esa/regs/statutes/whd/fmla.htm

Feldberg, R., and E. Glenn. 1982. Male and female: job versus gender models in sociology of work. Pp. 65–80 in *Women and work: problems and perspectives*, eds. R. Kahn-Hut, A. Daniels, and R. Colvard. Oxford: Oxford University Press.

Filer, R. 1989. Occupational segregation, compensating differentials, and comparable worth. In *Pay equity: empirical inquiries*, eds. R. Michael, H. Hartmann, and B. O'Farrell. Washington, DC: Urban Institute.

Fincham, F., and K. Linfield. 1997. A new look at marital quality: can spouses feel positive and negative about their marriage? *Journal of Family Psychology* 11: 489–502.

Finn, J., and D. Rock. 1997. Academic success among students at risk for school failure. *Journal of Applied Psychology* 82: 221–34.

Fisher, C. 2000. Mood and emotions while working: missing pieces of job satisfaction? *Journal of Organizational Behavior* 21: 185–202.

Fisher, C., and N. Ashkanasy. 2000. The emerging role of emotions in work life: an introduction. *Journal of Organizational Behavior* 21: 123–29.

Folk, K., and Y. Yi. 1994. Piecing together child care with multiple arrangements: crazy quilt or preferred pattern for employed parents of preschool children. *Journal of Marriage and the Family* 56: 669–80.

Folkman, S., and J. Moskowitz. 2000. Positive affect and the other side of coping. *American Psychologist* 55: 647–54.

Fowers, B. 2000. *Beyond the myth of marital happiness*. San Francisco, CA: Jossey-Bass.

Fowers, B., and D. Olson. 1989. ENRICH: Marital inventory: a discriminant validity and cross-validation assessment. *Journal of Marital and Family Therapy* 15: 65–79.

1993. ENRICH marital satisfaction scale: a brief research and clinical tool. *Journal of Family Psychology* 7: 176–85.

Frankenhauser, M. 1979. Psychoendocrine approaches to the study of emotion as related to stress and coping. Pp. 123–61 in *Nebraska Symposium on Motivation 1978*, eds. H. How and R. Dienstbier. Lincoln: University of Nebraska Press.

Fried, Y., and G. Ferris. 1987. The validity of the job characteristics model: a review and a meta-analysis. *Personnel Psychology* 40: 287–322.

Friedman, M. 1957. *A theory of the consumption function*. Princeton, NJ: Princeton University Press.

Friedman, S., and J. Greenhaus. 2000. *Work and family – allies or enemies? What happens when business professionals confront life choices*. Oxford: Oxford University Press.

Frijda, Nico. 2000. The psychologists' point of view. Pp. 59–74 in *Handbook of emotion*, eds. M. Lewis and J. Haviland-Jones, New York: Guilford Press.

Gager, C., and L. Sanchez. 2003. Two as one? Spouses' personal time together, marital quality and the risk of divorce. *Journal of Family Issues*.

Galambos, N. 2004. Gender and gender role development in adolescence. Pp. 233–62 in *Handbook of adolescent psychology*, 2nd edn., eds. R. Lerner and L. Steinberg. New York: John Wiley and Sons.

Galambos, N., and H. Sears. 1998. Adolescents' perceptions of parents' work and adolescents' work values in two-earner families. *Journal of Early Adolescence* 18: 397–420.

Galambos, N., H. Sears, D. Almeida, and G. Kolaric. 1995. Parents' work overload and problem behavior in young adolescents. *Journal of Research on Adolescence* 5: 201–23.

Galinsky, E. 1999. *Ask the children: what America's children really think about working parents*. New York: William Morrow and Company, Inc.

Gallup Poll. 1995. *Religion in America: 1995 supplement*. Princeton, NJ: Princeton Religion Research Center.

Gelman, A., and J. Carlin. 2001. Poststratification and weighting adjustments. Pp. 275–87 in *Survey nonresponse*, eds. R. Groves, D. Dillman, J. Eltinge, and R. Little. New York: John Wiley and Sons.

Gelman, A., J. Carlin, H. Stern, and D. Rubin. 1995. *Bayesian data analysis*, eds. C. Chatfield and J. Zidek. New York: Chapman and Hall.

General Social Survey. 2000. [computer file] Chicage: National Opinion Research Center [producer and distributor]. See http://webapp.icpsr.umich.edu/GSS/ for information on the GSS. Link last verified September 1, 2004.

Gershuny, J., and J. Robinson. 1988. Historical changes in the household division of labor. *Demography* 25: 537–52.

Gershuny, J., I. Miles, S. Jones, C. Mullings, G. Thomas, and S. Wyatt. 1986. Time Budgets: preliminary analyses of a national survey. *Quarterly Journal of Social Affairs* 2: 13–39.

Gerson, K. 1985. *Hard choices: how women decide about work, career, and motherhood*. Berkeley, CA: University of California Press.

Glass, J. 2000. Toward a kinder, gentler workplace: envisioning the integration of family and work. *Contemporary Sociology* 29: 129–43.

Glass, J., and V. Camarigg. 1992. Gender, parenthood, and job–family compatibility. *American Journal of Sociology* 98: 131–51.

Glass, J., and T. Fujimoto. 1994. Housework, paid work, and depression among husbands and wives. *Journal of Health and Social Behavior* 35: 179–91.

Glass, J., V. Bengtson, and C. Dunham. 1986. Attitude similarity in three-generation families: socialization, status inheritance, or reciprocal influence? *American Sociological Review* 51: 685–98.

Glenn, N. 1996. Values, attitudes, and the state of American marriage. In *Promises to keep: decline and renewal of marriage in America*, eds. D. Popenoe, J. Elshtain, and D. Blankenhorn. Lanham, MD: Rowman and Littlefield.

    1998. The course of marital success and failure in five American 10 year marriage cohorts. *Journal of Marriage and the Family* 60: 569–76.

Goldin, C. 1997. Career and family: college women look to the past. In *Gender and family issues in the workplace*, eds. F. Blau and R. Ebrenberg. New York: Russell Sage Foundation.

Goldscheider, F., and L. Waite. 1991. *New families, no families? The transformation of the American home*. Berkeley, CA: University of California Press.

Goldstein, J., and C. Kenney. 2001. Marriage delayed or marriage forgone? New cohort forecasts of first marriage for US women. *Journal of Marriage and the Family* 66: 506–19.

Goodman, W. 1996. The software and engineering industries: threatened by technological change? *Monthly Labor Review* 11: 37–45.

Gottfried, A. E., A. W. Gottfried, and K. Bathurst. 1995. Maternal and dual-earner employment status and parenting. In *Handbook of parenting: vol. 2: Biology and ecology of parenting*, ed. M. Bornstein. Hillsdale, NJ: Lawrence Erlbaum Associates.

Gottlieb, G. 1992. *Individual development and evolution: the genesis of novel behavior*. New York: Oxford University Press.

Gottman, J. 1993. A theory of marital dissolution and stability. *Journal of Family Psychology* 7: 57–75.

    1994a. *What predicts divorce? The relationship between marital processes and marital outcomes*. Hillsdale, NJ: Lawrence Erlbaum Associates.

1994b. *Why marriages succeed or fail and how you can make yours last.* New York: Simon and Schuster.

2001. What the study of relationships has to say about emotion research. *Social Science Information* 40: 79–94.

Gottman, J., and C. Notarius. 2000. Decade review: observing marital interaction. *Journal of Marriage and the Family* 62: 927–47.

Granger, D., and K. Kivlighan. 2003. Integrating biological, behavioral, and social levels of analysis in early child development: progress, problems, and prospects. *Child Development* 74: 1058–64.

Granger, D., E. Schwartz, A. Booth, M. Curran, and D. Zakaria. 1999. Assessing dehydroepiandrosterone in saliva: a simple radioimmunoassay for use in studies of children, adolescents and adults. *Psychoneuroendocrinology* 24: 567–79.

Granger, D., J. Weisz, J. McCracken, S. Lkeda, and P. Douglas. 1996. Reciprocal influences among adrenocortical activation, psychosocial processes, and the behavioral adjustment of clinic-referred children. *Child Development* 67: 3250–62.

Granovetter, M. 1973. The strength of weak ties. *American Journal of Sociology* 78: 1360–80.

Greenberger, E., R. O'Neil, and S. Nagel. 1994. Linking workplace and homeplace: relations between the nature of adults' work and their parenting behaviors. *Developmental Psychology* 30: 990–1002.

Greene, A., and S. Wheatley. 1992. "I've got a lot to do and I don't think I'll have the time": gender differences in late adolescents' narratives of the future. *Journal of Youth and Adolescence* 21: 667–86.

Greenhaus, J., and N. Beutell. 1985. Sources of conflict between work and family roles. *Academy of Management Review* 10: 76–88.

Griliches, Z. 1986. Economic data issues. In *Handbook of econometrics*, eds. Z. Griliches and M. Intriligator. New York: North-Holland Publishing Co.

Gunnar, M., and D. Vasquez. 2001. Low cortisol and a flattening of the expected daytime rhythm: potential indices of risk in human development. *Development and Psychopathology* 13: 515–38.

Habermas, J. 1975. *Legitimation crisis.* Boston, MA: Beacon Press.

1981. *Theory of communicative action.* Boston, MA: Beacon Press.

Hackman, J., and G. Oldham. 1980. *Work redesign.* Reading, MA: Addisson Wesley.

Hadaway, C., P. Marler, and M. Chaves. 1993. What the polls don't show: a closer look at US church attendance. *American Sociological Review* 58: 741–52.

Hammer, L., E. Allen, and T. Grisby. 1997. Work–family conflict in dual-earner couples: within-individual and crossover effects of work and family. *Journal of Vocational Behavior* 50: 185–203.

Han, S., and P. Moen. 1999. Clocking out: temporal patterning of retirement. *American Journal of Sociology* 105: 191–236.

Han, W.-J., J. Waldfogel, and J. Brooks-Gunn. 2001. The effects of early maternal employment on later cognitive and behavioral outcomes. *Journal of Marriage and the Family* 63: 336–54.

Hart. P. 2003. Imagining the future of work: a strategic research study conducted for the Alfred P. Sloan Center. Washington DC: Peter D. Hart Research Associates.

Harter, S. 1982. The perceived competence scale for children. *Child Development* 53: 87–97.

1999. *The construction of the self: a developmental perspective*. New York: Guilford Press.

Harter, S., and A. Monsour. 1992. Development analysis of conflict caused by opposing attributes in the adolescent self-portrait. *Developmental Psychology* 28: 251–60.

Harter, S., and R. Pike. 1984. The pictorial scale of perceived competence and social acceptance for young children. *Child Development* 55: 1969–82.

Harter, S., S. Bresnick, H. Bouchey, and N. Whitesell. 1997. The development of multiple role-related selves during adolescence. *Development and Psychopathology* 9: 835–53.

Hatfield, E., J. Cacioppo, and R. Rapson. 1994. *Emotional contagion*. Paris: Cambridge University Press.

Hauser, R., and D. Featherman. 1973. Trends in the occupational mobility of US men, 1962–1970. *American Sociological Review* 38: 302–10.

Hauser, S., S. Powers, and G. Noam. 1991. *Adolescents and their families: paths of ego development*. New York: Free Press.

Hays, R., A. Stacy, K. Widaman, M. DiMatteo, and R. Downey. 1986. Multistage path models of adolescent alcohol and drug use: a reanalysis. *Journal of Drug Issues* 16: 357–69.

Hays, S. 1996. *The cultural contradictions of motherhood*. New Haven, CT: Yale University Press.

Hechter, O., A. Grossman, and R. Chatterton, Jr. 1997. Relationship of dehydroepiandrosterone and cortisol in disease. *Medical Hypotheses* 49: 85–91.

Heckman, J. 1976. The common structure of statistical models of truncated, sample selection and limited dependent variables, and a simple estimator of such models. *Annals of Economic and Social Measurement* 5: 475–92.

Hedges, S., L. Janorf, and A. Stone. 1985. Meaning of daily mood assessments. *Journal of Personality and Social Psychology* 48: 428–34.

Heim, C., U. Ehlert, and D. Hellhammer. 2000. The potential role of hypocortisolism in the pathophysiology of stress-related bodily disorders. *Psychoneuroendocrinology* 25: 1–35.

Heinz, W., U. Kelle, A. Witzel, and J. Zinn. 1998. Vocational training and career development in Germany: results for a longitudinal study. *International Journal of Behavioral Development* 22: 77–101.

Heise, D. R. 1988. Affect control theory: concepts and model. In *Analyzing social interaction: advances in affect control theory*, eds. L. Smith-Lovin and D. R. Heise. New York: Gordon and Breach.

Hektner, J., and K. Asakawa. 2000. Learning to like challenges. In *Becoming adult*, eds. M. Csikszentmihalyi and B. Schneider. New York: Basic Books.

Hertz, R., and F. Ferguson. 1996. Childcare choice and constraints in the United States: social class, race and the influence of family values. *Journal of Comparative Family Studies* 27: 248–80.

Hertz, R., and N. L. Marshall. 2001. *Working families: the transformation of the American home*. Berkeley, CA: University of California Press.

Hill, P., and R. Hood. 1999. *Measures of religiosity*. Birmingham, AL: Religious Education Press.

Hochschild, A. 1989. *The second shift: working parents and the revolution at home*. New York: Avon Books.

1997. *The time bind: when work becomes home and home becomes work*. New York: Metropolitan Books.

Hochschild, A., and B. Ehrenreich. 2003. *Global woman: nannies, maids, and sex workers in the new economy*. New York: Metropolitan Books.

Hofferth, S., F. Stafford, W.-J. Yeung, G. Duncan, M. Hill, J. Lepkowski, and J. Morgan. 2002. Panel study of income dynamics, 1968–1999: annual core data [computer file]. ICPSR version. Ann Arbor, MI: University of Michigan, Survey Research Center [producer], 2001. Ann Arbor, MI: Inter-University Consortium for Political and Social Research [distributor].

Hoge, D. 1979. A test of theories of denominational growth and decline. In *Understanding church growth and decline, 1950–1978*, eds. D. Hoge and D. Roozen. New York: Pilgrim Press.

Hoge, D., E. Smit, and J. Crist. 1997. Four family process factors predicting academic achievement in sixth and seventh grade. *Educational Research Quarterly* 21: 27–42.

Hormuth, S. 1986. The sampling of experiences in situ. *Journal of Personality* 54: 262–93.

Hout, M., and A. Greeley. 1987. The center doesn't hold: church attendance in the United States, 1944–1984. *American Sociological Review* 52: 325–45.

Huber, J., and G. Spitze. 1983. *Sex stratification: children, housework, and jobs*. New York: Academic Press.

Hunsberger, B., and L. Brown. 1984. Religious socialization, apostasy, and the impact of family background. *Journal for the Scientific Study of Religion* 23: 239–51.

INSTRAW (International Research and Training Institute for the Advancement of Women). 1995. *Measurement and valuation of unpaid contribution, accounting through time and output*. New York: United Nations Publications.

Isen, A. 1987. Positive affect, cognitive processes, and social behavior. Pp. 203–53 in *Advances in experimental social psychology*, vol. 20, ed. L. Berkowitz. New York: Academic Press.

Ispa, J., M. Gray, and K. Thornburg. 1984. Childrearing attitudes of parents in person-oriented and thing-oriented occupations: a comparison. *The Journal of Psychology* 117: 245–50.

Jacobs, J. 1998. Measuring time at work: are self-reports accurate? *Monthly Labor Review* 121: 42–51.

Jacobs, J., and K. Gerson. 1998. Who are the overworked Americans? *Review of Social Economy* 56: 442–59.

2001. Overworked individuals or overworked families: explaining trends in work, leisure, and family time. *Work and Occupations* 28: 40–64.

2004. *The time divide: work, family, and gender inequality*. Cambridge, MA: Harvard University Press.

Jacobs, L., R. Shapiro, and E. Schulman. 1993. Medical care in the United States: an update. *Public Opinion Quarterly* 57: 394–427.

Johansen, A., A. Liebowitz, and L. Waite. 1996. The importance of child care characteristics to choice of care. *Journal of Marriage and the Family* 58: 759–72.

Johnson, C., S. Stanley, N. Glenn, P. Amato, S. Nock, H. Markman, and M. Dion. 2002. *Marriage in Oklahoma: 2001 baseline statewide survey on marriage and divorce* (S02096 OKDHS). Oklahoma City: Oklahoma Department of Human Services.

Johnson, E., T. Karmilaris, G. Chrousos, and P. Gold. 1992. Mechanisms of stress: a dynamic overview of hormonal and behavioral homeostasis. *Neuroscience and Biobehavioral Reviews* 16: 115–30.

Johnson, J. 1984. A model of social interaction: phase III: tests in varying media situations. *Communication Monographs* 51: 168–84.

Jones, F., and B. Fletcher. 1993. An empirical study of occupational stress transmission in working couples. *Human Relations* 46: 881–901.

Judge, T., A. Erez, J. Bono, and C. Thoresen. 2002. Discriminant and incremental validity of four personality traits: are measures of self-esteem, neuroticism, locus of control, and generalized self-efficacy indicators of a common core construct? *Journal of Personality and Social Psychology* 83: 693–710.

Juster, T., and F. Stafford, eds. 1985. *Time, goods, and well-being*. Ann Arbor, MI: University of Michigan Survey Research Center, Institute for Social Research.

——— 1991. The allocation of time: Empirical findings, behavioral models, and problems of measurement. *Journal of Economic Literature* 29: 471–522.

Kagan, J. 1958. The concept of identification. *Psychological Review* 65: 296–305.

Kahn, R., D. Wolfe, R. Quinn, J. Snoek, and R. Rosenthal. 1964. *Organizational stress: studies in role conflict and ambiguity*. New York: Wiley.

Kalleberg, A. 1977. Work values and job rewards: a theory of job satisfaction. *American Sociological Review* 42: 124–43.

Kamo, Y. 2000. "He said, she said": Assessing discrepancies in husbands' and wives' reports on the division of household labor. *Social Science Research* 29: 459–76.

Kandel, D., M. Davies, and V. Raveis. 1985. The stressfulness of daily social roles for women: marital, occupational, and household roles. *Journal of Health and Social Behavior* 26: 64–78.

Kaplan, E. 1987. I don't do no windows: competition between the domestic worker and the housewife. Pp. 92–105 in *Competition: a feminist taboo?*, eds. V. Miner and H. Longino. New York: Feminist Press.

Karambayya, R., and A. Reilly. 1992. Dual earner couples: attitudes and actions in restructuring work for families. *Journal of Organizational Behavior* 13: 585–601.

Kesic, T., and J. Previsic. 1996. Satisfaction with work and the allocation of professors' time at Zagreb University. *Drustvena Istrazivanja* 5: 147–59.

Kiecolt, K. 2003. Satisfaction with work and family life: no evidence of a cultural reversal. *Journal of Marriage and Family* 65: 23–35.

Kim, J., and P. Moen. 2000. Late midlife work status and transitions. Pp. 487–527 in *Handbook of midlife development*, ed. M. Lachman. New York: John Wiley and Sons.

Kirschbaum, C., and D. Hellhammer. 1989. Salivary cortisol in psycho-biological research: an overview. *Neuropsychobiology* 22: 150–69.

Kirschbaum, C., R. Steyer, M. Eid, U. Patalla, P. Schwenkmezger, and D. Hellhammer. 1990. Cortisol and behavior: 2. Application of a latent state-trait model to salivary cortisol. *Psychoneuroendocrinology* 15: 297–307.

Klute, M., A. Crouter, A. Sayer, and S. McHale. 2001. Occupational self-direction, values, and egalitarian relationships: a study of dual-earner couples. *Journal of Marriage and Family* 64: 139–51.

Kohn, M. 1969. *Class and conformity: a study in values.* Homewood, IL: Dorsey Press.

1990. Unresolved issues in the relationship between work and personality. Pp. 36–70 in *The nature of work: sociological perspectives*, eds. K. Erikson and S. Vallas. New Haven, CT: Yale University Press.

Kohn, M., and C. Schooler. 1969. Class, occupation and orientation. *American Sociological Review* 34: 659–78.

1982. Job conditions and personality: a longitudinal assessment of their reciprocal effects. *American Journal of Sociology* 87: 1257–86.

1983. *Work and personality: an inquiry into the impact of social stratification.* Norwood, NJ: Ablex Publishing Corporation.

Kohn, M., K. Slomczynski, and C. Schoenbach. 1986. Social stratification and the transmission of values in the family: a cross-national assessment. *Sociological Forum* 1: 73–103.

Kousha, M. 1995. African American private household workers and control of the labor process in domestic service. *Sociological Focus* 27: 211–28.

Kubey, R. 1990. Television and family harmony among children, adolescents, and adults: results from the experience sampling method. Pp. 73–88 in *Television and the American family*, ed. J. Bryant. Hillsdale, NJ: Lawrence Erlbaum Associates.

Kubey, R., and M. Csikszentmihalyi. 1990. *Television and the quality of life: How viewing shapes everyday experience.* Hillsdale, NJ: Lawrence Erlbaum Associates.

2002. Television addiction. *Scientific American* 286: 74–81.

Kubey, R., and R. Larson. 1990. The use and experience of the new video media among children and young adolescents. *Communication Research* 17: 107–30.

Kubey, R., R. Larson, and M. Csikszentmihalyi. 1996. Experience sampling method applications to communication research questions. *Journal of Communications* 46: 99–120.

Kurdek, L., and M. Fine. 1993. The relation between family structure and young adolescents' appraisals of family climate and parent behavior. *Journal of Family Issues* 14: 279–90.

Ladurie, E. L. R. 1979. *The territory of the historian.* Chicago, IL: University of Chicago Press.

530    References

Lareau, A. 2000. *Home advantage: social class and parental intervention in elementary education*. Lanham, MD: Rowman and Littlefield.
  2002. Invisible inequality: social class and childrearing in black families and white families. *American Sociological Review* 67: 747–76.
Larson, R., and D. Almeida. 1999. Emotional transmission in the daily lives of families: a new paradigm for studying family process. *Journal of Marriage and the Family* 61: 5–20.
Larson, R., and P. A. Delespaul. 1992. Analyzing experience sampling data: a guidebook for the perplexed. Pp. 55–78 in *The experience of psychopathology: investigation mental disorders in their natural settings*, ed. M. W. De Vries. Cambridge: Cambridge University Press.
Larson, R., and S. Gillman. 1999. Transmission of emotions in the daily interactions of single-mother families. *Journal of Marriage and the Family* 61: 21–37.
Larson, R., and M. Richards. 1994. *Divergent realities: the emotional lives of mothers, fathers, and adolescents*. New York: Basic Books.
Larson, R., M. Csikszentmihalyi, and R. Graef. 1980. Mood variability and the psychosocial adjustment of adolescents. *Journal of Youth and Adolescence* 9: 469–90.
Larson, R., M. Richards, and M. Perry-Jenkins. 1994. Divergent worlds: the daily emotional experience of mothers and fathers in the domestic and public spheres. *Journal of Personality and Social Psychology* 67: 1034–46.
Larson, R., S. Verma, and J. Dworkin. 1999. *Stress and emotion*. New York: Springer Publishing Company.
  2001. Men's work and family lives in India: the daily organization of time and emotion. *Journal of Family Psychology* 15: 206–24.
Lazarus, R. 1999. *Stress and emotion: a new synthesis*. New York: Springer Publishing Company.
Lazarus, R., and S. Folkman. 1984. *Stress, appraisal, and coping*. New York: Springer Publishing Company.
Leichter, H., D. Ahmed, L. Barrios, J. Bryce, E. Larsen, and L. Moe. 1985. Family contexts of television. *Educational Communication and Technology Journal* 33: 26–40.
Lennon, M., and S. Rosenfield. 1994. Relative fairness and the division of housework: the importance of options. *American Journal of Sociology* 100: 506–31.
Lichtenberg, J. 1996. Consuming because others consume. *Social Theory and Practice* 22: 273–97.
Little, R., and D. Rubin. 2002. *Statistical analysis with missing data*. Hoboken, NJ: J. Wiley.
Long, J. 1997. *Regression Models for Categorical and Limited Dependent Variables*. Thousand Oaks, CA: Sage Publications.
Lovallo, W., and T. Thomas. 2000. Stress hormones in psychophysiological research. Pp. 342–67 in *Handbook of psychophysiology*, 2nd edn., eds. J. Cacciopo, L. Tassinary, and G. Bernston. Cambridge: Cambridge University Press.
Lull, J. 1990. *Inside family viewing: ethnographic research on television's audiences*. New York: Routledge.

Lupien, S., and B. McEwen. 1997. The acute affects of corticosteroids on cognition: integration of animal and human model studies. *Brain Research Review* 24: 1–27.

Luster, T., K. Rhoades, and B. Haas. 1989. The relation between parental values and parenting behavior: a test of the Kohn hypothesis. *Journal of Marriage and the Family* 51: 139–47.

MacHale, S., J. Cavanagh, J. Bennie, S. Caroll, G. Goodwin, and S. Lawrie. 1998. Diurnal variation of adrenocortical activity in chronic fatigue syndrome. *Neuropsychobiology* 38: 213–17.

Maier, K. 2000. Applying Bayesian methods to hierarchical measurement models. Chicago, IL: University of Chicago Dissertation.

Majewska, M. 1995. Neuronal actions of dehydroepiandrosterone: possible roles in brain development, aging, memory, and affect. *Annals of the New York Academy of Sciences* 774: 111–20.

Major, B., and E. Konar. 1984. An investigation of sex differences in pay expectations and their possible causes. *Academy of Management Journal* 27: 777–92.

Marchand, J., and E. Hock. 2000. Avoidance and attacking conflict-resolution strategies among married couples: relations to depressive symptoms and marital satisfaction. *Family Relations* 49: 201–06.

Marini, M., and B. Shelton. 1993. Measuring household work: recent experience in the United States. *Social Science Research* 22: 361–82.

Martins, L., K. Eddleston, and J. Veiga. 2002. Moderators of the relationship between work–family conflict and career satisfaction. *Academy of Management Journal* 45: 399–410.

May, R. 1999. Tavern culture and television viewing: the influence of local viewing culture on patrons' reception of television programs. *Journal of Contemporary Ethnography* 28: 69–99.

McCain, G., and K. Tilbe. 1989. Diurnal hormone variation in fibromyalgia syndrome: a comparison with rheumatoid arthritis. *Journal of Rheumatology* 19: 154–57.

McEwen, B. S. 1998. Stress, adaptation and disease: allostasis and allostatic load. *Annals of the New York Academy of Sciences* 840: 33–44.

McEwen, B. S., and M. M. Sapolsky. 1995. Stress and cognitive function. *Current Opinion in Neurobiology* 5: 205–16.

McLanahan, S., and G. Sandefur. 1994. *Growing up with a single parent.* Cambridge, MA: Harvard University Press.

McLuhan, M. 1964. *Understanding media: the extension of man.* New York: McGraw-Hill.

Mederer, H. 1993. Division of labor in two-earner homes: task accomplishment versus household management as critical variables in perceptions about family work. *Journal of Marriage and the Family* 55: 133–45.

Menaghan, E. 1990. Work experiences and family interaction processes: the long reach of the job? *Annual Review of Sociology* 17: 419–44.

Menaghan, E., and T. Parcel. 1990. Parental employment and family life: research in the 1980s. *Journal of Marriage and Family* 52: 1079–98.

    1995. Social sources of change in children's home environment: the effects of parental occupational experiences and family conditions. *Journal of Marriage and the Family* 57: 69–84.

Meng, X. 1995 Multiple-imputation inferences with uncongenial sources of input (with discussion). *Statistical Science* 10: 538–73.

Merrill, D. 1997. *Caring for elderly parents: juggling work, family and caregivers in middle-class and working-class families.* Westport, CT: Auburn House.

Merton, R. 1973. *The sociology of science: Theoretical and empirical investigations.* Chicago, IL: University of Chicago Press.

Miller, A., and J. Hoffmann. 1995. Risk and religion: an explanation of gender differences in religiosity. *Journal of the Scientific Study of Religion* 34: 63–75.

Miller, G., S. Cohen, and A. Ritchey. 2002. Chronic psychological stress and the regulation of pro-inflammatory cytokines: a glucocorticoid-resistance model. *Health Psychology* 21: 531–41.

Miller, H. 1964. *Rich man, poor man.* New York: Crowell.

Miller, J., C. Schooler, M. Kohn, and K. Miller. 1979. Women and work: the psychological effects of occupational conditions. *American Journal of Sociology* 85: 66–94.

Minow, N., and C. LaMay. 1995. *Abandoned in the wasteland: children, television, and the first amendment.* New York: Hill and Wang.

Moen, P., ed. 2003. *It's about time: couples and careers.* Ithaca, NY: Cornell University Press.

Moen, P., M. Erickson, and D. Dempster-McClain. 1997. Their mother's daughters? The intergenerational transmission of gender attitudes in a world of changing roles. *Journal of Marriage and the Family* 59: 281–93.

Moen, P., J. Kim, and H. Hofmeister. 2001. Couples' work/retirement transitions, gender, and marital quality. *Social Psychology Quarterly* 64: 55–71.

Moen, P., and P. Roehling. 2005. *The Career Mystique: Cracks in the American Dream.* Boulder, CO: Rowman and Littlefield.

Moneta, G., and M. Csikszentmihalyi. 1996. The effect of perceived challenges and skills on the quality of subjective experience. *Journal of Personality* 64: 275–310.

Morris, R., and R. Murphy. 1959. The situs dimension in occupational structure. *American Sociological Review* 24: 231–39.

Morse, N. 1953. *Satisfactions in the white-collar job.* Ann Arbor, MI: University of Michigan.

Mortimer, J. 1974. Patterns of intergenerational occupational movement: a smallest-space analysis. *American Journal of Sociology* 79: 1278–99.

1975. Occupational value socialization in business and professional families. *Sociology of Work and Occupations* 2: 29–53.

1976. Social class, work, and the family: some implications of the father's occupation for familial relations and sons' career decisions. *Journal of Marriage and the Family* 38: 241–56.

Mortimer, J., and D. Kumka. 1982. A further examination of the "Occupational Linkage Hypothesis." *The Sociological Quarterly* 23: 3–16.

Mulligan, C., B. Schneider, and R. Wolfe. 2003. Non-response and population representation in studies of time use. Working Paper: University of Chicago, Alfred P. Sloan Center on Parents, Children, and Work.

Muthén, B. 2001. Second-generation structural equation modeling with a combination of categorical and continuous latent variables: new opportunities for latent class/latent growth modeling. Pp. 291–322 in *New methods for the analysis of change*, eds. L. Collins and A. Sayer. Washington, DC: American Psychological Association.

Muthén, B., D. Kaplan, and D. Hollis. 1987. On structural equation modeling with data that are not missing completely at random. *Psychometrika* 43: 431–62.

Muthén, B., T. Tam, L. Muthén, R. Stolzenberg, and M. Hollis. 1993. Latent variable modeling in the LISCOMP framework: measurement of attitudes toward career choice. Pp. 277–90 in *New directions in attitude measurement, festschrift for Karl Schuessler*, eds. D. Krebs and P. Schmidt. Berlin: Walter de Gruyter.

Nakao, K., and J. Treas. 1994. Updating occupational prestige and socioeconomic scores: how the new measures measure up. *Sociological Methodology* 24: 1–72.

Neeck, G., K. Federlin, V. Graef, D. Rusch, and K. Schmidt. 1990. Adrenal secretion of cortisol in patients with rheumatoid arthritis. *The Journal of Rheumatology* 17: 24–29.

Nelson, R. 2000. *An introduction to behavioral endocrinology*. 2nd edn. New York: Sinauer.

Neusner, J. 2001. *Ethics of family life*. Belmont, CA: Wadsworth/Thomson.

Newman, K. 1993. *Declining fortunes*. New York: Basic Books.

Nicolson, N. 1992. Stress, coping and cortisol dynamics in daily life. Pp. 219–32 in *The experience of psychopathology: investigating mental disorders in their natural settings*, ed. M. de Vries. Cambridge: Cambridge University Press.

Nielsen Media Research. 2000. *2000 report on television*. New York: Nielsen Media Research.

Notarius, C., and H. Markman. 1993. *We can work it out: making sense of marital conflict*. New York: Putnam.

Novack, L., and D. Novack. 1996. Being female in the eighties and nineties: conflicts between new opportunities and traditional expectations among white, middle-class, heterosexual college women. *Sex Roles* 35: 57–77.

Ochs, E., and C. Taylor. 1996. The "father knows best" dynamic in dinnertime narratives. Pp. 97–121 in *Gender articulated language and the socially constructed self*, ed. K. Hall. London: Routledge.

Oleckno, W., and M. Blacconiere. 1991. Relationship of religiosity to wellness and other health-related behaviors and outcomes. *Psychological Reports* 68: 819–26.

Olson, D., D. Fournier, and J. Druckman. 1987. *PREPARE/ENRICH counselor's manual*, revised edn. Minneapolis, MN: PREPARE/ENRICH, Inc.

Orden, S., and N. Bradburn. 1968. Dimensions of marriage happiness. *American Journal of Sociology* 73: 715–31.

Oropesa, R. 1993. Using the service economy to relieve the double burden: female labor force participation and service purchases. *Journal of Family Issues* 14: 438–73.

Parasuraman, S., J. Greenhaus, and C. Granrose. 1992. Role stressors, social support, and well-being among two-career couples. *Journal of Organizational Behavior* 13: 339–56.

Parcel, T. 1989. Comparable worth, occupational labor markets, and occupational earnings: results from the 1980 Census. Pp. 134–52 in *Pay equity: empirical inquiries*, eds. R. Michael, H. Hartmann, and B. O'Farrel. Washington, DC: National Academy Press.

Parcel, T., and E. Menaghan. 1994a. Early parental work, family social capital, and early childhood outcomes. *American Journal of Sociology* 99: 972–1009.

1994b. *Parents' jobs and children's lives*. New York: Aldine de Gruyter.

1997. Effects of low-wage employment on family well-being. *The Future of Children* 7: 116–21.

Parker, R., and R. Fenwick. 1983. The pareto curve and its utility for open-ended income distributions in survey research. *Social Forces* 61: 872–85.

Patterson, G., and M. Stouthamer-Loeber. 1984. The correlation of family management practices and delinquency. *Child Development* 55: 1299–307.

Pearce, L., and W. Axinn. 1998. The impact of family religious life on the quality of mother–child relations. *American Sociological Review* 63: 810–28.

Perrewe, P., W. Hochwarter, and C. Kiewitz. 1999. Value attainment: an explanation for the negative effects of work/family conflict on job and life satisfaction. *Journal of Occupational Health Psychology* 4: 318–326.

Perry-Jenkins, M., R. Repetti, and A. Crouter. 2000. Work and family in the 1990s. *Journal of Marriage and the Family* 62: 981–98.

Phelan, J. 1994. The paradox of the contented female worker: an assessment of alternative explanations. *Social Psychology Quarterly* 57: 95–107.

Phelan, J., E. Bromet, J. Schwartz, M. Dew, and E.Curtis. 1993. The work environments of male and female professionals: objective and subjective characteristics. *Work and Occupations* 20: 68–89.

Piotrkowski, C., and M. Katz. 1982. Indirect socialization of children: the effects of mothers' jobs on academic behaviors. *Child Development* 53: 1520–29.

Plutchik, R. 2001. The nature of emotions. *American Scientist* 89: 344–50.

Poloma M., and B. Pendleton. 1989. Exploring types of prayer and quality of life: a research note. *Review of Religious Research* 31: 46–53.

Portes, A. 1998. Social capital: its origins and applications in modern sociology. *Annual Review of Sociology* 24: 1–24.

Press, J., and E. Townsley. 1998. Wives' and husbands' housework reporting: gender, class, and social desirability. *Gender and Society* 12: 188–218.

Presser, H. 1994. Employment schedules among dual-earner spouses and the division of household labor by gender. *American Sociological Review* 59: 348–64.

2003. *Working in a 24/7 economy: challenges for American families*. New York: Russell Sage.

Pruessner, J., O. Wolf, D. Hellhammer, A. Buske-Kirschbaum, K. von Auer, S. Jobst, F. Kaspers, and C. Kirschbaum. 1997. Free cortisol levels after awakening: a reliable biological marker for the assessment of adrenocortical activity. *Life Sciences* 61: 2539–49.

Putnam, R. 2000. *Bowling alone: the collapse and revival of American community*. New York: Simon and Schuster.

Quinn, R., and G. Staines. 2000. Quality of Employment Survey, 1977: CROSS-SECTION [computer file]. Conducted by University of Michigan, Survey

Research Center. ICPSR ed. Ann Arbor, MI: Interuniversity Consortium for Political and Social Research [producer and distributor].

2001. Quality of Employment Survey, 1973–1977: PANEL [computer file]. Conducted by University of Michigan, Survey Research Center. ICPSR ed. Ann Arbor, MI: Interuniversity Consortium for Political and Social Research [producer and distributor].

Radloff, L. 1977. The CES-D scale: a self-report depression scale for research in the general population. *Applied Psychological Measurement* 1: 385–401.

Raine, A. 2002. Biosocial studies of antisocial and violent behavior in children and adults: a review. *Journal of Abnormal Child Psychology* 30: 311–26.

Raskin, P. 2002. The women, work and family project: final report. New York: Alfred P. Sloan Foundation.

Raskin, P., J. Frankel, M. O'Reilly, and K. Sanabria. 2001. Turnover intentions of women with families in a service organization. American Psychological Association, San Francisco, August.

Rathunde, K. 1996. Family context and talented adolescents' optimal experience in school-related activities. *Journal of Research on Adolescence* 6: 605–28.

Rathunde, K., M. Carroll, and M. Huang. 2000. Families and the forming of children's occupational future. Pp. 113–40 in *Becoming adult: how teenagers prepare for the world of work*, eds. M. Csikszentmihalyi and B. Schneider. New York: Basic Books.

Raudenbush, S., A. Bryk, and R. Congdon. 2000. *HLM 5 hierarchical linear and nonlinear modeling* [computer software]. Scientific Software International, Inc.

Reis, H., and S. Gable. 2000. Event-sampling methods. Pp. 190–222 in *Handbook of research methods in social psychology*, eds. H. Reis and C. Judd. New York: Cambridge University Press.

Repetti, R. 1989. Effects of daily workload on subsequent behavior during marital interaction: the roles of social withdrawal and spouse support. *Journal of Personality and Social Psychology* 57: 651–59.

Repetti, R., and J. Wood. 1997. Families accommodating to chronic stress: unintended and unnoticed processes. Pp. 191–220 in *Coping with chronic stress*, ed. B. Gottlieb. New York: Plenum Press.

Riordan, C. 1998. Gender gap trends in public secondary schools: 1972 to 1992. Paper presented at the Annual Meeting of the American Sociological Association, San Francisco, CA.

Risman, B., and D. Johnson-Sumerford. 1998. Doing it fairly: a study of postgender marriages. *Journal of Marriage and the Family* 60: 23–40.

Roberts, L. 2000. Fire and ice in marital communication: hostile and distancing behaviors as predictors of marital distress. *Journal of Marriage and Family Therapy* 62: 693–707.

Roberts, N., and R. Levenson. 2001. Marital stability – the remains of the workday: impact of job stress and exhaustion on marital interaction in police couples. *Journal of Marriage and the Family* 63: 1052–68.

Robinson, J. 1977. *How Americans use time: a social-psychological analysis of everyday behavior*. New York: Praeger.

1985. The validity and reliability of diaries versus alternative time use measures. Pp. 33–62 in *Time, goods, and well-being*, eds. F. Juster and F. Stafford. Ann Arbor, MI: University of Michigan, Survey Research Center, Institute for Social Research.

1999. The time-diary method. Pp. 47–89 in *Time use research in the social sciences*, eds. W. Pentland, A. Harvey, M. Lawton, and M. McColl. New York: Kluwer Academic/Plenum Publishers.

Robinson, J., and G. Godbey. 1997. *Time for life: the surprising ways Americans use their time*. University Park, PA: Pennsylvania State University Press.

Robinson, J., and G. Spitze. 1992. Whistle while you work? The effect of household task performance on women's and men's well-being. *Social Science Quarterly* 73: 844–61.

Robinson, W. 1950. Ecological correlations and the behavior of individuals. *American Sociological Review* 15: 351–57.

Rogoff, N. 1953. *Recent trends in occupational mobility*. New York: Free Press.

Rollins, J. 1985. *Between women: domestics and their employers*. Philadelphia: Temple University Press.

1996. Invisibility, consciousness of the other, and resentment among black domestic workers. Pp. 223–43 in *Working in the service society*, eds. C. MacDonald and C. Sirani. Philadelphia: Temple University Press.

Roof, W., and D. Hoge. 1980. Church involvement in America: social factors affecting membership and participation. *Review of Religious Research* 21: 405–26.

Rosenberg, M. 1979. *Conceiving the self*. New York: Basic Books.

Rosenthal, C. 1985. Kinkeeping in the familial division of labor. *Journal of Marriage and the Family* 47: 965–74.

Ross, C., and J. Mirowsky. 1992. Households, employment, and the sense of control. *Social Psychology Quarterly* 55: 217–35.

1996. Economic and interpersonal work rewards: subjective utilities of men's and women's compensation. *Social Forces* 75: 223–45.

Rubin, D. 1987. *Multiple imputation for nonresponse in surveys*. New York: J. Wiley and Sons.

1996. Multiple imputation after 18+ years. *Journal of the American Statistical Association*, 91: 473–89.

Ruble, D., and C. Martin. 1998. Gender and development. Pp. 933–1016 in *Handbook of child psychology: vol. 3: Social, emotional, and personality development*, eds. W. Damon and N. Eisenberg. New York: John Wiley and Sons, Inc.

Ryu, S., and J. Mortimer. 1996. The "Occupational Linkage Hypothesis" applied to occupation value formation in adolescence. In *Adolescents, work and family: an intergenerational developmental analysis*, eds. J. Mortimer and M. Finch. Newbury Park, CA: Sage Publications.

Sandomirsky, S., and J. Wilson. 1990. Processes of disaffiliation: religious mobility among men and women. *Social Forces* 68: 1211–29.

Sapolsky, R. 1998. Immunity, stress and disease. In *Why zebras don't get ulcers: an updated guide to stress, stress-related diseases, and coping*, ed. R. Sapolsky. New York: W. H. Freeman and Company.

Sapolsky R., L. Krey, and B. McEwen. 1986. The neuroendocrinology of stress and aging: the glucocorticoid cascade hypothesis. *Endocrine Reviews* 7: 284–301.

Sayer, L. 2001. Time use, gender and inequality: differences in men's and women's market, nonmarket, and leisure time. College Park, MD: University of Maryland Dissertation.

Schafer, J. 1997. *Analysis of incomplete multivariate data*. London: Chapman and Hall.

Scherer, K., A. Schorr, and T. Johnstone. 2001. *Appraisal processes in emotion: theory, methods, research*. New York and Oxford: Oxford University Press.

Schneider, B., and J. Coleman. 1993. *Parents, their children, and schools*. Boulder, CO: Westview Press.

Schneider, B., and D. Stevenson. 1999. *The ambitious generation: America's teenagers motivated but directionless*. New Haven, CT: Yale University Press.

Schor, J. 1991. *The overworked American: the unexpected decline of leisure*. New York: Basic Books.

1998. *The overspent American: why we want what we don't need*. New York: Harper Perennial.

Seeman, T., B. Singer, C. Ryff, G. Love, and L. Levy-Storms. 2002. Social relationships, gender, and allostatic load across two age cohorts. *Psychosomatic Medicine* 64: 395–406.

Senécal, C., R. Vallerand, and F. Guay. 2001. Antecedents and outcomes of work–family conflict: toward a motivational model. *Personality and Social Psychology Bulletin* 27: 176–86.

Serido, J., D. Almeida, and E. Wethington. 2004. Chronic stressors and daily hassles: unique and interactive relationships with psychological distress. *Journal of Health and Social Behavior* 45: 17–33.

Sewell, W., A. Haller, and G. Ohlendorf. 1970. The educational and early occupational attainment process: replication and revision. *American Sociological Review* 35: 1014–27.

Sewell, W., and R. Hauser. 1975. *Education, occupation, and earnings: achievement in the early career*. New York: Academic Press.

Sewell, W., R. Hauser, and W. Wolf. 1980. Sex, schooling, and occupational status. *American Journal of Sociology* 86: 551–83.

Seymour, E., and N. Hewitt. 1997. *Talking about leaving: why undergraduates leave the sciences*. Boulder, CO: Westview Press.

Shaw, S. 1988. Gender differences in the definition and perception of household labor. *Family Relations* 37: 333–37.

Shelton, B., and D. John. 1996. The division of household labor. *Annual Review of Sociology* 22: 299–322.

Sherkat, D. and C. Ellison. 1999. Recent developments and current controversies in the sociology of religion. *American Review of Sociology* 25: 363–94.

Shirtcliff, E., D. Granger, A. Booth, and D. Johnson. Forthcoming. A latent-state trait model of salivary cortisol and atypical social behavior in normally developing youth. *Development and Psychopathology*.

Shweder, R. 1998. *Welcome to middle age! (and other cultural fictions)*. Chicago, IL: University of Chicago Press.

Simon, R. 1995. Gender, multiple roles, role meaning and mental health. *Journal of Health and Social Behavior* 36: 182–94.

Smider, N., M. Essex, N. Kalin, K. Buss, M. Klein, R. Davidson, and H. Goldsmith. 2002. Salivary cortisol as a predictor of socioemotional adjustment during kindergarten: a prospective study. *Child Development* 73: 75–92.

Smyth, J., M. Ockenfels, L. Porter, C. Kirschbaum, D. Helhammer, and A. Stone. 1998. Stressors and mood measured on a momentary basis are associated with salivary cortisol secretion. *Psychoneuroendocrinology* 23: 353–70.

Smyth, J., M. Ockenfels, A. Gorin, D. Catley, L. Porter, C. Kirschbaum, D. Helhammer, and A. Stone. 1997. Individual differences in the diurnal cycle of cortisol. *Psychoneuroendocrinology* 22: 89–105.

Somerfield, M., and R. McCrae. 2000. Stress and coping research: methodological challenges, theoretical advances, and clinical applications. *American Psychologist* 55: 620–25.

South, S., and G. Spitze. 1994. Housework in marital and nonmarital households. *American Sociological Review* 59: 327–47.

Spain, D., and S. Bianchi. 1996. *Balancing act: motherhood, marriage, and employment among American women.* New York: Russell Sage Foundation.

Spitze, G. 1991. Women's employment and family relations. Pp. 381–404 in *Contemporary families: looking forward, looking back*, ed. A. Booth. Minneapolis, MN: National Council on Family Relations.

1999. Getting help with housework: household resources and social networks. *Journal of Family Issues* 20: 724–45.

Stanley, S., S. Blumberg, and H. Markman. 1999. Helping couples fight for their marriages: the PREP approach. Pp. 279–303 in *Handbook of preventive approaches in couple therapy*, eds. R. Berger and M. Hannah. New York: Brunner/Mazel.

Stanley, S., H. Markman, and S. Whitton. 2003. Communication, conflict, and commitment: insights on the foundations of relationship success from a national survey. *Family Process* 41: 659–75.

Stephan, C., and J. Corder. 1985. The effects of dual-career families on adolescents' sex-role attitudes, work and family plans, and choices of important others. *Journal of Marriage and the Family* 47: 921–29.

Stinson, L. 1999. Measuring how people spend their time: a time-use survey design. *Monthly Labor Review* 122: 12–19.

Stolzenberg, R., and D. Relles. 1997. Tools for intuition about sample selection bias and its correction. *American Sociological Review* 62: 494–507.

Stolzenberg, R., M. Blair-Loy, and L. Waite. 1995. Religious participation in early adulthood: age and family life cycle effects on church membership. *American Sociological Review* 60: 84–103.

Strauss, A. 1987. *Qualitative analysis for social scientists.* Cambridge, MA: University Press.

Stuenkel, C. 2002. Help wanted: commodification of household services as a strategy for working families. University of Chicago, Department of Sociology Dissertation.

Super, D. 1990. A life-span, life-space approach to career development. Pp. 197–261 in *Career choice and development: applying contemporary theories to practice*, eds. D. Brown and L. Brooks. San Francisco: Jossey-Bass.

Sweet, J., and L. Bumpass. 1996. The National Survey of Families and Households – waves 1 and 2: data description and documentation. Center for Demography and Ecology, University of Wisconsin-Madison. http://www.ssc.wisc.edu/nsfh/home.htm.

Swidler, Ann. 2001. *Talk of love: how culture matters*. Chicago, IL: University of Chicago Press.

Taber, T., and G. Alliger. 1995. A task-level assessment of job satisfaction. *Journal of Organizational Behavior* 16: 101–21.

Taylor, J., and M. Tomasic. 1996. Taylor's measures of dysphoria, anxiety, anger, and self-esteem. In *Handbook of tests and measurements for black populations*, vol. I, ed. R. Jones. Hampton, VA: Cobb and Henry Publishers.

Taylor, R. 1989. Black youth, role models and the social construction of identity. In *Black Adolescents*, ed. R. Jones. Berkeley, CA: Cobb and Henry Publishers.

Taylor, S., L. Klein, B. Lewis, T. Gruenewald, R. Gurung, and J. Updegraff. 2000. Biobehavioral responses to stress in females: tend-and-befriend, not fight-or-flight. *Psychological Review* 107: 411–29.

Terman, L. 1947. *Psychological factors in marital happiness*. New York: McGraw-Hill Book Company, Inc.

Thoits, P. A. 1989. The sociology of emotions. *Annual Review of Sociology* 15: 317–42.

1995. Sociol psychology: the interplay between sociology and psychology. *Social Forces* 73: 1231–43.

Thomson, E., S. McLanahan, and R. Curtin. 1992. Family structure, gender, and parental socialization. *Journal of Marriage and the Family* 54: 368–78.

Thompson, L. 1991. Family work: women's sense of fairness. *Journal of Family Issues* 12: 181–96.

Thornton, A., D. Alwin, and D. Camburn. 1983. Causes and consequences of sex-role attitude change. *American Sociological Review* 48: 211–27.

Tiegs, R., L. Tetrick, and Y. Fried. 1992. Growth need strength and context satisfaction as moderators of the job characteristics model. *Journal of Management* 18: 575–93.

Tolbert, P., and P. Moen. 1998. Men's and women's definitions of "good" jobs. *Work and Occupations* 25: 168–94.

Tuck, B., J. Rolfe, and V. Adair. 1994. Adolescents' attitudes toward gender roles within work and its relationship to gender, personality type, and parental occupation. *Sex Roles* 31: 547–58.

Umberson, D., M. Chen, J. House, K. Hopkins, and E. Slaten. 1996. The effect of social relationships on psychological well-being: are men and women really so different? *American Sociological Review* 61: 837–57.

US Bureau of the Census. 1998. *Statistical abstracts of the United States*. Washington, DC: US Government Printing Office.

2000. Current population survey: annual demographic file, 2000 [computer file]. Washington, DC: US Department of Commerce, Bureau of the Census [producer]. Ann Arbor, MI: Inter-university Consortium for Political and Social Research [distributor].

2001. Married couple family groups, by family income, labor force status of both spouses, and race and Hispanic origin of the reference person. *America's families and living arrangements March 2001: detailed tables for current population report.* Washington, DC: US Government Printing Office.

2002. *Table DP-3: Profile of selected economic characteristics 2000 (by town or city). Census 2000 summary file 3 (SF-3) – sample data.* http:factfinder.census/gov.

US Department of Commerce, Economics and Statistics Administration, Bureau of the Census. 1992. *Classified index of industries and occupations. 1990 CPH-R-4.* Washington, DC: US Government Printing Office.

Vandell, D., and J. Ramanan. 1992. Effects of early and recent maternal employment on children from low-income families. *Child Development* 63: 938–49.

Van Eck, M., H. Berkhof, N. Nicolson, and J. Sulon. 1996. The effects of perceived stress, traits, mood states, and stressful daily events on salivary cortisol. *Psychosomatic Medicine* 58: 447–58.

Ver Ploeg, M., J. Alfonjo, N. Bradburn, J. Da Vanzo, W. Nordouse, and F. Samaniego, eds. 2000. *Time-use measurement and research: report of a workshop.* Washington, DC: National Academy Press.

Waite, L., and M. Gallagher. 2000. *The case for marriage: why married people are happier, healthier, and better off financially.* New York: Doubleday.

Waite, L., and M. Nielsen. 2001. The rise of the dual-earner family: 1963–1997. Pp. 23–41 in *Women and work in the twentieth century,* eds. R. Hertz and N. Marshall. Berkeley, CA: University of California Press.

Waite, L., D. Browning, W. Doherty, M. Gallagher, Y. Lou, and S. Stanley. 2002. *Does divorce make people happy? Findings from a study of unhappy marriages.* New York: Institute for American Values.

Wallis, C. 2004. The case for staying home. *Time.* March 22, 2004.

Walzer, S. 1998. *Thinking about the baby: gender and transitions into parenthood.* Philadelphia: Temple University Press.

Warner, R. 1986. Alternative strategies for measuring household division of labor: a comparison. *Journal of Family Issues* 7: 179–95.

Warr, P., J. Cook, and P. Wall. 1979. Scales for the measurement of some attitudes and aspects of psychological well-being. *Journal of Occupational Psychology* 52: 129–48.

Warren, J., and R. Hauser. 1997. Social stratification across three generations: New evidence from the Wisconsin Longitudinal Study. *American Sociological Review* 62: 561–72.

Watamura, S., B. Donzella, J. Alwin, and M. Gunnar. 2003. Morning to afternoon increases in cortisol concentrations for infants and toddlers at child care: Age differences and behavioral correlates. *Child Development.*

Weagley, R., and P. Norum. 1989. Household demand for market purchased, home producible commodities. *Home Economics Research* 18: 6–18.

Wessman, A., and D. Ricks. 1966. *Mood and personality.* New York: Hold, Rinehart and Winston.

West, C., and D. Zimmerman. 1987. Doing gender. *Gender and Society* 1: 125–51.

Westman, M., D. Etzion, and E. Danon. 2001. Job insecurity and crossover of burnout in married couples. *Journal of Organizational Behavior* 22: 467–81.

Wielers, R. 1997. The wages of trust: the case of child minders. *Rationality and Society* 9: 351–71.

Wilcox, W. 1998. Conservative Protestant childrearing: authoritarian or authoritative? *American Sociological Review* 63: 796–809.

2001 Soft patriarchs and new men: religion, ideology, and male familial involvement. Princeton University Dissertation.

2002. Religion, convention, and paternal involvement. *Journal of Marriage and Family* 64: 780–92.

Wilkie, J. 1993. Changes in US Men's attitudes toward the family provider role, 1972–1989. *Gender and Society* 7: 261–279.

Williams, J. 2000. *Unbending gender: why family and work conflict and what to do about it.* New York: Oxford University Press.

Williams, K., and G. Alliger. 1994. Role stressors, mood spillover, and perceptions of work–family conflict in employed parents. *Academy of Management Journal* 37: 837–68.

Willis, P. 1977. *Learning to labor.* New York: Columbia University Press.

Wilson, W. 1996. *When work disappears: the world of the new urban poor.* New York: Vintage Books.

Winkler, A. 1998. Earnings of husbands and wives in dual-earner families. *Monthly Labor Review* 121: 42–48.

Witte, J. 1997. *From sacrament to contract.* Louisville, KY: Westminster John Knox Press.

Wolf, O., and C. Kirschbaum. 1999. Actions of dehydroepiandrosterone and its sulfate in the central nervous system: Effects on cognition and emotion in animals and humans. *Brain Research Review* 30: 264–88.

Wood, J., and R. Repetti. 2004. What gets dad involved? A longitudinal study of change in parental child caregiving involvement. *Journal of Family Psychology* 18: 237–49.

Woodberry, R. 1998. When surveys lie and people tell the truth: how surveys oversample church attenders. *American Sociological Review* 63: 119–22.

Woodroof, J. 1985. Premarital sexual behavior and religious adolescents. *Journal for the Scientific Study of Religion* 24: 343–66.

Wright, B., and G. Masters. 1982. *Rating scale analysis: Rasch measurement.* Chicago, IL: Mesa Press.

Wrigley, J. 1995. *Other people's children.* New York: Basic Books.

1999. Hiring a nanny: the limits of private solutions to public problems. *The Annals of the American Academy of Political and Social Science* 563: 162–74.

Wuthnow, R. 1998. *After heaven: spirituality in America since the 1950s.* Berkeley: University of California Press.

Wylie, R. 1979. *The self concept: theory and research on selected topics.* Lincoln: University of Nebraska Press.

Yabiku, S., W. Axinn, and A. Thornton. 1999. Family integration and children's self esteem. *American Journal of Sociology* 104: 1494–524.

Yang, S., and F. Magrabi. 1989. Expenditures for services, wife's employment, and other household characteristics. *Home Economics Research* 18: 133–47.

Youniss, J., and J. Smollar. 1985. *Adolescent relations with mothers, fathers, and friends.* Chicago, IL: University of Chicago Press.

# Index